P9-CRK-765

THE WAR

By the same author

HITLERISM (1932)

FROM BISMARCK TO HITLER (1935)

RACE: A HISTORY OF MODERN ETHNIC THEORIES (1939)

A SURVEY OF EUROPEAN CIVILIZATION, 2 vols. (1941-1942)

A TREASURY OF GREAT REPORTING (with R. B. Morris) (1949)

A TREASURY OF BIOGRAPHIES (1950)

GERMAN NATIONALISM: THE TRAGEDY OF A PEOPLE (1952)

HIER HIELT DIE WELT DEN ATEM AN (1953)

THE MEANING OF NATIONALISM (1954)

THE AGE OF REASON (1955)

THE WORLD IN THE TWENTIETH CENTURY (1955)

BASIC HISTORY OF MODERN GERMANY (1957)

DOCUMENTS OF GERMAN HISTORY (1958)

HISTORIC DOCUMENTS OF WORLD WAR I (1959)

THE WAR

A Concise History

1939-1945

by LOUIS L. SNYDER

Foreword by ERIC SEVAREID

SIMON AND SCHUSTER · NEW YORK

Published by Simon and Schuster
A Division of Gulf & Western Corporation
Simon & Schuster Building
Rockefeller Center, 1230 Avenue of the Americas
New York, New York 10020

10 11 12 13 14 15 16 17 18

ISBN 0-671-79652-6
Library of Congress Catalog Card Number: 60-8637
Manufactured in the United States of America

TO IDA MAE—

For those two dozen years and
with thanks for patience and
fortitude beyond the call. . . .

Preface

The devastating man-made holocaust of World War II was fought by the greatest number of men in the history of civilization over the largest area of the world's surface. Nations of diverse beliefs joined forces in a time of desperate trouble to withstand and finally triumph over monstrous tyrannies that would have returned man to the jungle. The cost in human casualties and property damage was astronomical, almost incredible.

As time rolls by and perspective sharpens, the blurred picture of those precarious years from 1939 to 1945 begins to come into focus. It is the purpose of this book to present in concise form the dramatic story from Warsaw to Tokyo Bay of this greatest of all wars, to describe in simple terms the causes of the conflict, the long, bitter, complicated struggle itself, and the results.

Accent is on the essential. From the great mass of material, from the greatest production of printed sources in the history of war, an attempt has been made to extract the most important events, incidents, and trends. The impedimenta but not the tools of the scholar have been deliberately sacrificed. There are no footnotes to heckle the text, but care has been taken to arrive in the vicinity of the truth by attention to the best sources.

Much detail has been eliminated, especially the minutiae of military operations, in favor of a comprehensive picture of broad military movements. Where there are differences of opinion or interpretation, attention is given to both sides. There were victories, defeats, and errors of judgment among all the participants. The goal is economy of narration within a strict sense of history.

I wish to express my deep gratitude to Professor Wilbur G. Gaffney of the University of Nebraska for his invaluable assistance in the research and preparation of this manuscript. Warmest thanks are due to Miss R. E. B. Coombs, Mr. V. Rigby, and Mr. J. F. Golding of the staff of the Imperial War Museum, all of whom helped to make my stay in London during the preparation of this book pleasant and rewarding. And further, a word of thanks to the academic generation of war babies, now college students, whose keen questioning in classes at The City College of New York taught me the value of searching for the essential. Above all, I wish to express my thanks to my wife, who worked with me on this project from beginning to end and whose keen eye for detail rescued me from many pitfalls of grammar and fact.

LOUIS L. SNYDER

Table of Contents

Part IV

PHOENIX: TURN OF THE TIDE

Part V

CRUSADE: SMASHING THE AXIS

APPENDICES

Maps

Introduction

Great war destroys and it builds. It dissolves old ties that bind some peoples together and reinforces the bonds between others. It makes some men bestial and others noble, throws up great leaders while ruining some who professed to be leaders. It breaks bodies and hearts and systems of ethics. It poisons the meaning of existing words and kindles new language to express new concepts and experiences. It speeds up the process of change in the styles and manners of living and gives the world new machines, new clothes, new architecture, new painting; it revolutionizes science, invents new ways to kill a mass of people and to cure fever in a child.

We cannot take its full measure. We had scarcely begun to sift the residue of World War I when its embers burst into the flames of World War II. The second engulfment of human hopes came as less of a surprise than the first. The first taught us that massive butchery through stupidity and military helplessness could happen in our modern age. With the first died many values and assumptions about the inevitability of humanitarian progress that had grown and flowered for a hundred years. But no one intended that. It was in World War II that we learned to question the meaning of a thousand years of belief in the human spirit and shivered in the cold stench of medieval mania loosed from the catacombs of the Dark Ages, for this time men saw in the Germanic insanity mass butchery following from deliberate purpose, down to the last neat medical chart showing the stress-resistance behavior of the lower bowel under hydraulic pressure.

No one book, no shelf of books can take the full measurement of what happened, why it happened and what it did to organized human life upon this earth—not for at least another generation can the written word find the true definitions and terms of reference and so encompass the story in less than fragmentary fashion. It is an immense labor just to assemble the factual record as Professor Snyder has now done, to catalogue the larger events and to indicate their immediate causes and their immediate effects. This he has done with painstaking care; and as one who was personally involved with some of these events, in episodic fashion, I have found that these chapters have clarified portions of my own life for me. He has provided the long thread upon which I can fasten in their proper place the little beads of experience, both bright and bloody, that my own memory has hoarded these fifteen years.

Professor Snyder's facts speak for themselves. Here it is, the whole panorama of men and minds in motion through six fantastic years. The accumulated impact of these facts ought, one would think, to leave the minds of readers who missed the war by time or distance dazed and shaken with the sheer enormity of the effort, the monumental scale of man's vileness and his goodness. But I suppose not. It seemed to me in the war that nature had provided man's imagination with a built-in governor for his own protection. We are so constructed that the nerve ends cannot remember pain or share it out, else the multiplication of pain would have been unendurable. Our emotional system permits only specialization, not generalization, of our suffering. That is why one peasant woman dying in a GI's arms could tear his heart, while the groans of a thousand laid out in a village square could leave him unmoved. Men will chance war not only because death is unthinkable in each private mind but because death cannot be multiplied in the human spirit. A million deaths leave an empty place at only one family table. The reader who missed the war must know this if he is to comprehend how flesh and blood and sanity could survive Stalingrad or Tarawa or Hill 609.

And yet, in the longer meaning of man on earth there are no replaceable faces. In the long meaning war only subtracts—evil along with good, to be sure—but if we believe at all in the human spirit we can only conclude that the net of war is loss, frightful loss. Since a negative cannot be proved, we can only guess at what our common culture lost, for this generation, in those thirty million graves of the last.

The losses we can only assume; it is the changes that we can see even if we cannot yet measure them with finality. We can see that World War II reshuffled the political world of nations. It loosened the ties of the old empires and brought new nationhoods into being with many more on the way. It helped to awaken hundreds of millions of black and yellow people from their long sleep of subservience. It brought the United States of America and all its manifold influences back to the old world to stay. It produced far more nationalism than democracy, although it gave the German people one more chance, perhaps their last, at the democratic effort. It did not produce Communist China because, at least in my own estimation, that would have happened anyway; but it enormously strengthened Russian Communism, not so much by reaffirming its capacities in the great trial of war, but by weakening other societies and by leaving Communist armies astride them.

It taught Europeans, as did World War I, that the fragmentation and ancient animosities of their region of earth must come to an end, but the second war, unlike the first, produced some true and measurable steps in those directions. They are not long steps and they may fall back, but they are the longest steps taken toward the unification of the great European culture and economic complex that have been taken in five hundred years, and this is no slight thing.

Its sorrows crucified many American families and its easy rewards made others rich. It made permanent neurotics and gangsters of some of our young men and serious students of many more, who returned deepened and chastened and hungering for the solid meanings of personal life. It made England a healthier, more just society. It did, after all, put an end to the cruel dictatorships of Germany and Italy and Japan, an end to their imperial dreams and achievements. It cleared a dangerously long path ahead for the Bolshevist's world plan, and the task of containing this will surely prove the identifying mark of this present generation in the history books; but, again, we cannot measure what might have been, and only the reckless will claim that what we now confront is worse than the confrontation a Fascist world victory would have meant.

World War II galvanized the Arabic and Negro worlds into self-consciousness, as well as the Asiatic, and not only because imperial power was weakened. That power had generally been exercised with cool indirection and with very few white bodies. What happened in the consciousness of the ordinary, unlettered Arab and especially the black African, was something different. The wartime physical presence of masses of ordinary white men produced a sea change in hundreds of African communities. For the first time since the coming of the first Portuguese traders and slavers to black Africa the black man saw the white man for what he really was. This winter in Lagos a middle-aged Nigerian politician said to me: "We found out from the GI's what our fathers had never found out from the God-like missionaries and the colonial officers in their white suits. We saw the GI's laughing and weeping and stealing and squabbling and itching for our women, and we began to lose our inferiority complex. White men were no better than we." So did the Chinese find this out, and the Indians and Indonesians and many others. By his hands and his amazing machines, the GI altered the topography of some of these countries; by his unaffected presence, by teaching the "natives" what *he* truly was, he taught them what *they* truly were. If the result shall prove good in the long run, surely this is one of the greatest, if unintended goods that the war spread over the earth.

Black, white or yellow, the war altered the lives and minds of every man, woman and child who directly experienced its impact. I know of people who suffered so much they lost their sanity; I also know of people, mentally ill to the point of insanity, who left their hospitals cured because the war took them out of themselves, directed their spirits toward outward, realistic goals and gave them the inner peace that comes with the knowledge of usefulness to others. I know men, including fellow war correspondents, who were so spoiled by the "glamour" of war that it took them years to accept again the routines of peacetime work; men, including leading professional soldiers, who came truly alive only in the war, literally loved the war and secretly long for its opportunities again. World War II was open sesame for whatever lay in an individual's personal character. If nobility was there it came out; if weakness or bestiality was there, it came out, too. I can remember American privates risking their lives for their comrades and tending them with loving care. I can remember American privates deliberately swerving their truck to smash an Italian peasant and his donkey into the ditch and laughing as they drove on.

War has many faces and endless lessons to teach. It taught governments that traditional notions about industrial capacity and finance were nonsense, in the test. It taught them that free societies can call up a greater discipline than totalitarian societies, that free men can build anything, pay for anything they wish if only they have the will to do so. It taught close observers that there is no such thing as "military science." Running a war or directing a single battle is neither a science nor a business but a kind of rude art in which training and intellect are probably of less consequence than patience, stamina and imagination.

Great war is totally impartial, yet it treats no two men exactly alike. Those on the ground never quite understood those in the air, nor did those in the air understand those on the ground. Twenty miles between those in rear bases and those at the front was as great a spiritual distance as from front to home city, five thousand miles away. All soldiers and sailors and airmen were lonely, even when jammed rib to elbow, farther from home than any map could measure. And most men in the war never quite felt that they were the "ones," the real ones; the whole thought of the wounded and the wounded thought of the dead.

It began, it was somehow endured, it ended; but the shock waves it sent through our societies, our institutions and our nervous systems have not yet died away. It has permanently marked the whole world and all those of the world's inhabitants who knew the war.

Books like this one are not likely to be written after any World War III. Such a war is not likely to consist of a series of episodes with beginning and end, including the classic pattern of defeat or victory and then stalemate, then victory or defeat for one side or the other. Only in the most formal and temporary sense will there be "sides" at all. When it is over there may be men left alive here or there with the spirit to try to piece the story together and write it down, but it will not matter much whether they do or not. History will not matter because history has meaning only as a continuing story, as past implying future. World War II may have been senseless in origin, but its course and consequence had coherence. It added its mementoes to the thousands of statues and monuments and plaques in a thousand cities which attest to the fact that men have always preferred victory to peace. Now, of course, science has news for the sculptors—they won't ever again, at least in the great nations, be designing memorials to national victories or individual heroes. Whether those nations succeed in keeping the peace, or fail.

ERIC SEVAREID

June, 1960

Photographic Highlights of World War II

UPI

CHAMBERLAIN AT BERCHTESGADEN

The Prime Minister of England makes the first of three successive trips by air to Germany in humiliating subserviénce to Hitler. Here the Nazi *Fuehrer* tells Chamberlain that Germany wants the instant inclusion of the Sudeten Germans in the Third Reich, even at the cost of a general war.

UPI

HITLER UNLEASHES A SLASHING ATTACK ON POLAND

September 1, 1939. Motorized German divisions, trained to the teeth, move swiftly on doomed Poland from four different points.

Wide World Photos

HITLER DELIVERS WAR TIRADE

On September 1, 1939, a few hours after his troops had crossed the Polish border, the Nazi *Fuehrer* appears before the German Reichstag in Berlin to deliver a war message without a formal declaration of war.

Imperial War Museum

THE ADMIRAL GRAF SPEE IN FLAMES OFF MONTEVIDEO

On December 17, 1939, at five minutes to eight in the evening, the armored ship *Admiral Graf Spee* is blown up by her crew, after being trapped in the Uruguayan port of Montevideo by British warships. The following morning Captain Langsdorff, commander of the *Spee*, was found dead in his room, a suicide.

Keystone

THE RAPE OF ROTTERDAM

May 14, 1940. Goering's *Luftwaffe* plasters open-city Rotterdam in a thoroughly unnecessary raid. Here a Dutch father, in a state of shock, watches his little daughter who has been killed from the air.

Wide World Photos

TO FIGHT AGAIN ANOTHER DAY: THE MIRACLE OF DUNKIRK

June 7, 1940. The British Expeditionary Force is saved from the Flanders trap. Here a naval petty officer assists a wounded Tommy up the gangway of a destroyer at an unidentified French port. Some 335,000 men were successfully evacuated in this amazing operation.

Wide World Photos

NAZISM TRIUMPHANT
Adolf Hitler and his cohorts realize a dream.

Wide World Photos

THE FACE OF DEFEAT
A Frenchman reacts to the bitterness of subjugation to the Germans.

William Vandivert

DAYLIGHT FIRE BOMB RAID ON LONDON, SEPTEMBER, 1940

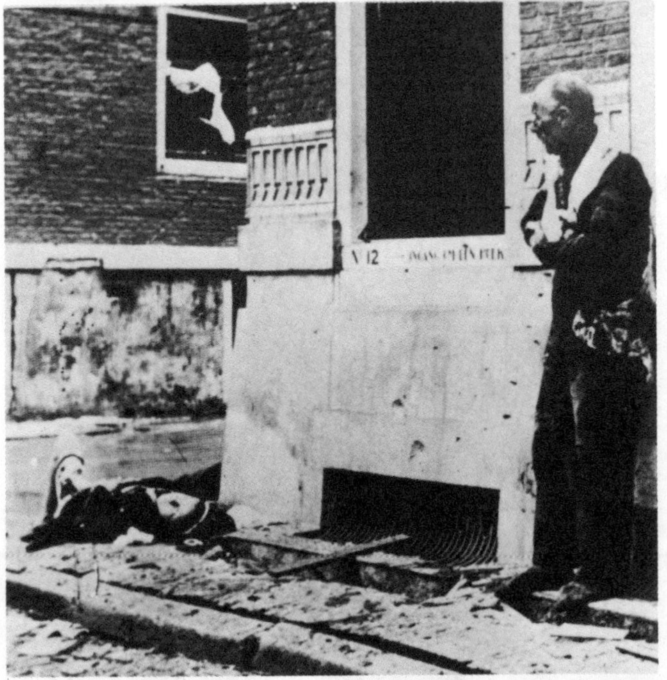

Keystone

THE RAPE OF ROTTERDAM

May 14, 1940. Goering's *Luftwaffe* plasters open-city Rotterdam in a thoroughly unnecessary raid. Here a Dutch father, in a state of shock, watches his little daughter who has been killed from the air.

Wide World Photos

TO FIGHT AGAIN ANOTHER DAY: THE MIRACLE OF DUNKIRK

June 7, 1940. The British Expeditionary Force is saved from the Flanders trap. Here a naval petty officer assists a wounded Tommy up the gangway of a destroyer at an unidentified French port. Some 335,000 men were successfully evacuated in this amazing operation.

NAZISM TRIUMPHANT
Adolf Hitler and his cohorts realize a dream.

Wide World Photos

Wide World Photos

THE FACE OF DEFEAT
A Frenchman reacts to the bitterness of subjugation to the Germans.

William Vandivert
DAYLIGHT FIRE BOMB RAID ON LONDON, SEPTEMBER, 1940

S—
SHEL

SAVE THE ASPIDISTRA

September, 1940. A British family salvages its most prized possessions after a Nazi bombing raid. British morale in the Battle of Britain aroused the admiration of the entire Allied world.

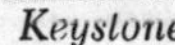

Keystone

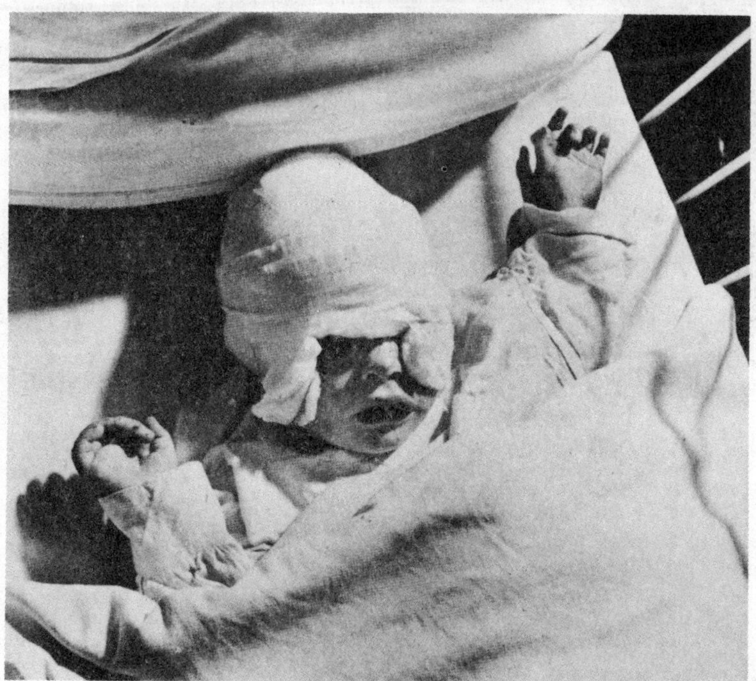

William Vandivert

THE FACE OF WAR

A little British girl suffers a complex brain injury in the Battle of Britain. A team of U.S. Air Force surgeons eventually repaired the damage.

Combine

"'T IS THE EYE OF CHILDHOOD THAT FEARS A PAINTED DEVIL"

September, 1940. Blind British children seek shelter in the Battle of Britain.

Imperial War Museum

COVENTRY FEELS THE NAZI WRATH
The Cathedral of Coventry in November, 1940.

Imperial War Museum

CHEERS FOR BRITAIN'S GOLDEN-TONGUED ARCHITECT OF VICTORY
February 5, 1941. Prime Minister Winston Churchill is cheered by workers in a naval establishment at Plymouth as he makes a tour of inspection of the areas damaged in heavy air raids.

Imperial War Museum

IN THE ELEPHANT AND CASTLE UNDERGROUND STATION
November 11, 1940. The British seek shelter from Goering's *Luftwaffe*.

Wide World Photos

GERMAN TANKS ROLL IN LIBYA

April 14, 1941. Tank units of the German *Afrika Korps* roll along a Libyan highway to occupy Salum on the western Egyptian border.

Imperial War Museum

KAMERAD!

A German tankman faces British steel in the African desert.

Imperial War Museum

HITLER'S INFERNO

No. 23 Queen Victoria Street collapsed during a German air raid, May 11, 1941.

Imperial War Museum

NAZI ICARUS CRASHES IN SCOTLAND

May 13, 1941. The wreckage of the ME-110, in which Rudolf Hess, No. 3 Nazi and deputy to Hitler, made his dramatic flight from Germany to Scotland. Hess was on a self-imposed mission to convince the British that they had lost the war and that they join Hitler in his attack on Soviet Russia.

Wide World Photos

THE ARIZONA IS CRUMPLED BY JAP BOMBS

December 7, 1941. Crippled and toppling, the U.S. battleship *Arizona* pours clouds of smoke into the air. In all probability a bomb passed down the smokestack and exploded the boiler and forward magazine.

Wide World Photos

THIS WAS PEARL HARBOR

The Japanese attack on Pearl Harbor on December 7, 1941 paralyzes U.S. naval and air power in the Hawaiian Islands for the time being.

THE DEATH MARCH OF BATAAN

Defeated American troops, sick, half-starved, begin their "death march" near Mariveles after the surrender on Bataan.

Wide World Photos

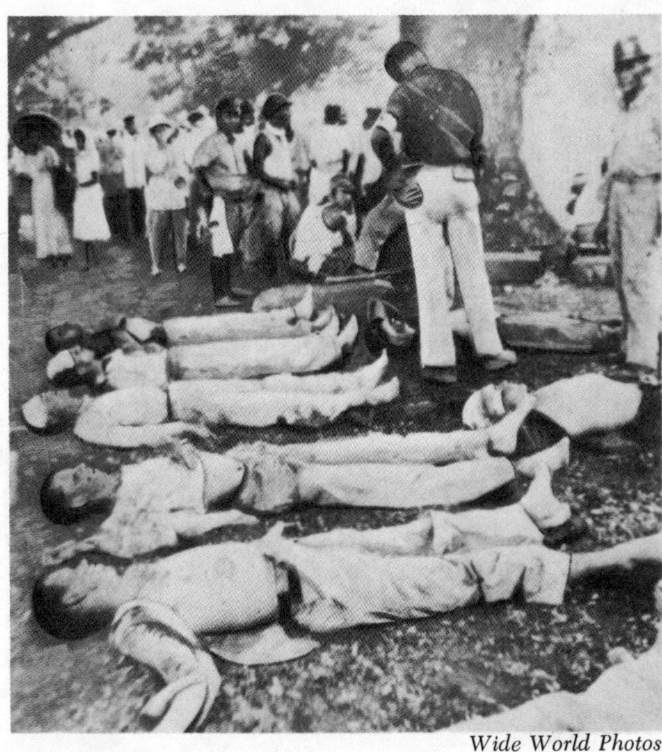

THEY FAILED TO FINISH THE "DEATH MARCH"

Wide World Photos

Wide World Photos

GENERAL DOOLITTLE AND HIS TOKYO RAIDERS PREPARE FOR TAKEOFF

April 18, 1942. Ship and aircraft personnel swarm around the B-25 bombers about to take off from the flight deck of the U.S. aircraft carrier *Hornet* somewhere in the Pacific.

Wide World Photos

U.S. MARINES ADVANCE ON GUADALCANAL

Exhausted, wet from almost continual rains, U.S. Marines tramp into the village of Matankiou on Guadalcanal Island after Japanese troops had been blasted from the area.

Wide World Photos

THE DESERT FOX TWISTS THE LION'S TAIL

Seated in an open car, General Erwin Rommel, famed "Desert Fox" and brain behind the *Afrika Korps*, confers with staff officers.

Imperial War Museum

RETREAT FROM DISASTER

British troops arrive at Newhaven after the unsuccessful raid on Dieppe, August 19, 1942. A smiling Tommy has lost half of his battledress trousers in the encounter.

Special Order of the Day

HEADQUARTERS
18th ARMY GROUP
21st April, 1943

SOLDIERS OF THE ALLIES

1. Two months ago, when the Germans and Italians were attacking us, I told you that if you held firm, final victory was assured.

2. You did your duty and now you are about to reap its full reward.

3. We have reached the last phase of this campaign. We have grouped our victorious Armies and are going to drive the enemy into the sea.

   We have got them just where we want them—with their backs to the wall.

4. This final battle will be fierce, bitter and long, and will demand all the skill, strength and endurance of each one of us.

   But you have proved yourselves the masters of the battlefield, and therefore you will win this last great battle which will give us the whole of North Africa.

5. The eyes of the world are on you—and the hopes of all at home.

FORWARD THEN, TO VICTORY

H. R. Alexander

General,

Commander, 18th Army Group

Imperial War Museum

GENERAL ALEXANDER'S ORDER OF THE DAY CALLING FOR VICTORY IN NORTH AFRICA

HAIL TO THE LIBERATORS
August 13, 1943. Enthusiastic Sicilians surround American GI's as they move toward Palermo in northwestern Sicily. Thirteen Allied divisions conquer Sicily in 39 days.

Wide World Photos

Wide World Photos

AMERICAN AIRPOWER DESTROYS A GERMAN AIRCRAFT FACTORY
Here is a record of the finest example of daylight bombing during the war. The Focke-Wulf-109 factory at Marienburg, East Prussia, lies in ruins after four raids on October 9, 1943 by the 8th Air Force of the U.S. Army. The result was utter devastation.

Wide World Photos

FOUR DAYS OF CONCENTRATED HELL ON TARAWA
For four days, from November 30 to December 4, 1943, the U.S. Marines fought for control of Tarawa, keystone of the Gilbert area. Here the Americans give the occupants of a pillbox (center) a chance to surrender, but the Japanese refused. The Marines moved in and took it. Note how the Marines have a supporting ring of men around the shock troops going into the pillbox.

Imperial War Museum

THE FANTASTIC BURMA ROAD

An American supply column negotiates 21 switchbacks en route to the China front east of Kunming on one of the most extraordinary stretches of road in the world.

Wide World Photos

A JAPANESE PILLBOX ON TARAWA

Japanese emplacements were ingeniously devised to withstand the heaviest kind of attacks.

Wide World Photos

REINFORCEMENTS ARRIVE IN TARAWA

U.S. Marine reinforcements march down the pier toward the palm fringed shore of Tarawa island.

Imperial War Museum

THE GERMANS PREPARE FOR THE EXPECTED ALLIED ASSAULT ON FORTRESS EUROPE

Here German troops are hurrying to erect underwater obstacles on French beaches while the tide is out.

Imperial War Museum

TESTAMENT TO ALLIED PRECISION BOMBING

Amidst the ruins of the city, the spires of Cologne stand out untouched against the sky.

Wide World Photos

"FULL VICTORY—NOTHING ELSE!"

General Dwight D. Eisenhower, Supreme Commander of the Allied forces, gives the order of the day to paratroopers about to take off on the D-Day invasion of Fortress Europe.

Wide World Photos

D-DAY: THE GREATEST INVASION IN HISTORY

American troops wade ashore along the Normandy coast of France. "Submerged tanks and overturned boats and burned trucks and shell-shattered jeeps and sad little personal belongings were strewn all over these bitter sands." (Ernie Pyle.)

Wide World Photos

OPERATION OVERLORD: CONCENTRATED POWER

Overwhelming naval and air support enabled the Allies to land large numbers of men and tremendous supplies to protect the beachheads. Here is a panoramic view of Omaha Beach before Mulberry, the U.S. secret floating harbor, was set up. Barrage balloons hover over the vast assemblage of shipping as the Allies pour in an unending flow of supplies.

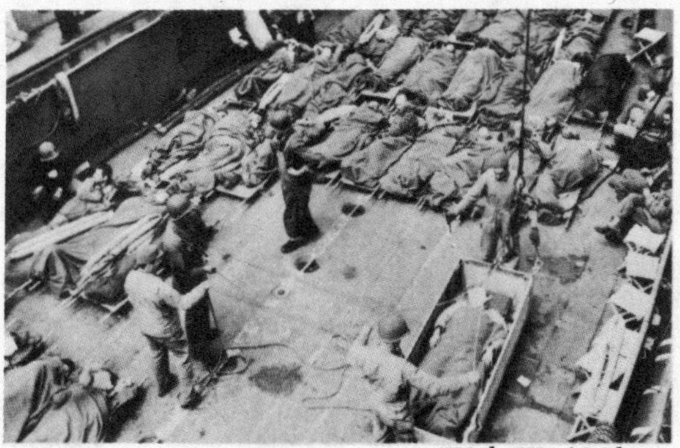

Wide World Photos

THE PRICE OF VICTORY

The Normandy beaches were filled with murderous booby traps, barbed wire, and enfilading fire from machine-gun nests. Here Allied casualties, lying on litters across the deck of a landing craft, await their turn to be hoisted aloft to a hospital ship in the English Channel.

Wide World Photos

PARIS IS LIBERATED

American troops of an infantry division march down the Champs Elysees, Paris, in a victory parade.

Wide World Photos

"I SHALL RETURN!"

October 31, 1944. General Douglas MacArthur wades through the surf as he keeps his promise to return to the Philippines.

Wide World Photos

BLUEPRINT FOR VICTORY: THE CRIMEA CONFERENCE

February 19, 1945. Prime Minister Winston Churchill, President Franklin D. Roosevelt, and Premier Joseph Stalin, meet in the patio of the palace at Yalta. The Big Three completed plans for the final military push against Hitler and made agreements, some open, some secret, on the nature of the postwar world.

Wide World Photos

ON THE SANDS OF IWO JIMA

February 25, 1945. U.S. Marines, pinned down by Japanese fire as they storm ashore, hug the volcanic sands of Iwo Jima beach.

Wide World Photos

TO THE RELIEF OF BASTOGNE

January 6, 1945. A U.S. infantryman crawls under a wire fence as he and his comrades advance over snow-covered terrain toward surrounded U.S. forces in Bastogne in Germany's Luxembourg-Belgium salient.

Wide World Photos

HANDS ACROSS THE DIKES

G.I.'s perform the paternal chore of taking Dutch children for walks through the grounds of the Hoensbrock Castle in Holland. The castle has been converted into a home for 145 children who are cared for by nuns.

Wide World Photos

THE FACE OF WAR

Victorious American troops walk along a debris-filled street in Bonn, Germany, after the capture of that Rhineland city.

Wide World Photos

EPISODE IN MANILA

A wounded G.I. is carried on a litter to a dressing station set up in the wreckage of the Manila City Hall. The bodies are Japanese killed when they attempted to escape from the building as the Americans closed in.

Wide World Photos

THE REMAGEN BRIDGE, KEY TO GERMANY'S HEARTLAND, COLLAPSES ON MARCH 17, 1945

First Army medics stand by to aid men being rescued from the wreckage below. The Remagen bridge, captured accidentally by an American platoon, served as the first span to carry U.S. troops across the Rhine.

Wide World Photos

F.D.R.—CASUALTY OF WAR

A woman is overcome by grief as the Roosevelt funeral cortege passes by in Washington. Millions were shocked by the sudden death of the American President two days earlier on April 12, 1945.

Wide World Photos

HANDS ACROSS THE CHASM

April 25, 1945. GI's of the U.S. First Army extend a welcome to Russian troops on a broken bridge over the Elbe River at Torgau, Germany. Hitler's vanishing Third Reich is thereby cut into two.

Wide World Photos

COMMUNION ON MT. SURIBACHI

A Navy chaplain serves communion to a kneeling Marine on top of Mt. Suribachi on Iwo Jima after capture of the volcano.

Wide World Photos

ROCKET SYMPHONY OFF OKINAWA, APRIL 1, 1945

Rockets streak from an LCI toward the beaches of Okinawa, in the Ryukyus, on the doorstep of the Japanese homeland.

Wide World Photos

A FINISH TO TYRANNY AS TERRIBLE AS ANY IN HISTORY

Bodies of the Sawdust Caesar, Benito Mussolini, and his mistress, Clara Petacci, are hung like sides of beef from the girders of a filling station on the Piazza Loretto in Milan. Infuriated Italians, spitting and cursing, whacked the *Duce's* body with clubs, smashing the skull into hideous disfigurement.

Imperial War Museum

NORDIC SUPERMAN BROUGHT DOWN TO EARTH

Fourteen-year-old members of the *Volksturm* are captured by the Allies. As in World War I, the Germans in the waning days of World War II used older men and callow youths as cannon fodder in the hopeless struggle.

Imperial War Museum

THE GERMAN GOVERNMENT UNDER ARREST

May 23, 1945. Admiral Karl Doenitz, successor to Hitler, Colonel-General Alfred Jodl, and Dr. Albert Speer, arrive at British Military Headquarters.

Wide World Photos

END OF THE NAZI LINE

Reich Marshal Hermann Goering, No. 2 Nazi, stands stripped of medals and diamond baton in a detention camp in Germany.

Imperial War Museum

CAPTORS BECOME CAPTIVES

These SS women, past mistresses of Nazi brutality, had been assigned as guards in the hellhole of Belsen concentration camp. Here they are seen being put to work by the triumphant Allies.

MONUMENT TO NAZI EFFICIENCY

May, 1945. Ghastly scene in a Nazi extermination camp revealed to the world.

Imperial War Museum

Wide World Photos

THRESHOLD OF IGNOMINY

Pierre Laval, Premier of Vichy France, testifies in the treason trial of Marshal Henri Pétain, seated at the right, in the Palais de Justice, Paris, August 3, 1945.

Wide World Photos

HOLOCAUSTAL INCANDESCENCE

August 6, 1945. Hiroshima, Japan, is razed to the ground in a split instant on the explosion of the first atomic bomb in history. The bomb had more power than 20,000 tons of TNT, more than 2,000 times the blast power of the British "Grand Slam," which was the largest bomb ever used hitherto in warfare.

Wide World Photos

NAGASAKI — THE CLINCHER

August 9, 1945. A second atomic bomb was released on Nagasaki, a shipbuilding port and industrial center, with even more disastrous results. It convinced the Japanese that their position was hopeless.

Wide World Photos

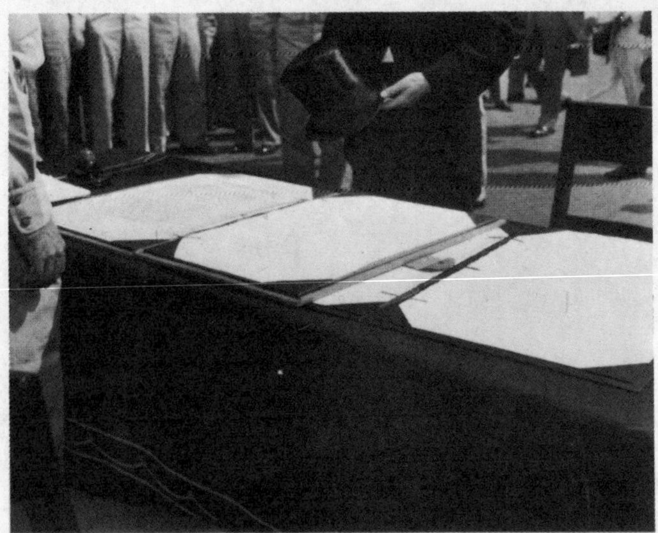

Wide World Photos

THE JAPANESE SURRENDER: END OF WORLD WAR II

September 2, 1945. General Douglas MacArthur, Supreme Commander for the Allied Powers in the Pacific, signs the formal surrender papers on board the battleship *Missouri* in Tokyo Harbor.

Part I

PRELUDE: THE ROAD TO WAR

CHAPTER 1

The Altar of Mars

O judgment! thou art fled to brutish beasts,
And men have lost their reason.

—Shakespeare, *Julius Caesar*,
Act III, Sc. 2.

BLITZKRIEG IN POLAND

Dawn, September 1, 1939.

There was no declaration of war. Across the western borders of Poland poured the first waves of Hitler's mighty war machine. Simultaneously, from East Prussia, Pomerania, Silesia, and Slovakia, nine Nazi columns, rolling at a furious tempo, converged on Warsaw. This was the first major campaign of World War II, a portent of later attacks on the Low Countries, on France, on Crete.

The weather was on the side of the bigger battalions. The clear autumn sunshine was ideal for air operations, the baked Polish plains made to order for the *Panzerwagen*—the German tanks—the rivers at low level for easy crossing.

The German armies moved with inexorable precision. There was something familiar about it. It brought to mind the German invasion of Belgium in 1914, described by Richard Harding Davis: "Like a river of steel [the army] flowed, gray and ghostlike. . . . [It] rumbled by with the mystery of fog and the pertinacity of a steam roller."

But the 1939 version was streamlined. No longer was the main accent on those endless columns of marching soldiers, a few miles a day. Here was the first demonstration of *Blitzkrieg*, lightning war, a stunning revelation of military adaptability in the machine age. The experts were thoroughly confused—"The modern German theory of victory by *Blitzkrieg* is untried and, in the opinion of many experts, unsound" (*Time*, June 12, 1939).

Instead of the static lines of World War I, epitomized at Verdun, where opposing armies dug themselves like moles into the ground and hurled artillery shells at each other, *Blitzkrieg* stressed mobility and fluidity. "The whole battlefield," said one observer, "became an amorphous permeation, like a plague of vermin in a garden." It was a new kind of attack that threw defenders into helpless confusion.

The formula was devastatingly simple. First, prepare the way by fifth-column activity behind enemy lines. Second, in a swift surprise blow, destroy the opposing air force on the ground, thus removing the prime obstacle to land attack. Third, slow up the enemy by bombing from the air all his means of communication and transportation. Fourth, dive-bomb troop concentrations to keep them off balance and prevent them from striking back in strength. Fifth, send light forces—motorcycle infantry, light tanks, motor-drawn artillery—speeding into enemy territory. Sixth, follow these with heavy tanks to carve out mechanized pockets in the rear. Finally, commit the regular infantry, the foot soldier, supported by artillery, to mop up resistance and join up with the advance forces.

The key weapon was the military tank, a track-laying armored car first used by the British in 1916 in World War I. In 1918 it was still no more than a shield for advancing infantry, who fell in behind the moving vehicles. But now the Germans used tanks as a mobile arm of the artillery.

The operations were directed by Germany's most experienced military leaders. In supreme command was General Walther von Brauchitsch, with General Franz Halder as his chief of staff. General Gerd von Rundstedt commanded a group of three armies attacking from the south, and General Fedor von Bock a group of two armies driving from the north. This was superb military leadership.

The attacking Germans far outweighed the Poles. Estimates of German strength vary according to the authority and distinctions made between regular (*Aktiv*), reserve (*Reservetruppen*), and occupation troops (*Besatzungsheer*). There were at least 75 German divisions, including reserve and occupation troops, a total of more than 1,000,000 men. The Germans had a two-to-one superiority in firepower, and 20 times as many tanks as the enemy.

On paper the Poles had an army of 2,000,000 men. But Polish general mobilization did not begin until August 31, 1939, one day before the attack. When the impact came, it was met with 600,000 troops in 30 infantry divisions, 11 cavalry divisions, and one motorized, one mechanized, and one mounted brigade.

Against the mechanized monsters of Hitler's *Panzerdivisionen* the Poles sent their cavalry, booted and spurred. The outcome of the match between horse and internal-combustion engine was not for a moment in doubt.

The first phase of the Nazi *Blitz* came from the air. The *Luftwaffe*, the German air force, had a three-to-one advantage, more than 1,400 first-line aircraft, including dive bombers based on Königsberg and Vienna, against 450 Polish planes. There were virtually no air battles; the Germans concentrated on destroying the enemy planes on the ground. Goering's pilots swooped down on Polish airfields and within two days annihilated almost the entire enemy air force. The mechanized *Wehrmacht* (armed forces) could now move ahead without danger from the skies.

Simultaneously, German dive bombers demolished transportation facilities, bridges, and railroad stations, bombed communications, and trapped the Poles into immobility. There was havoc in the Polish rear, with no possibility for an orderly retreat.

Then *Schrecklichkeit*, the German version of frightfulness, calculated to goad the civilian population into quick submission. The dread dive bombers, *Stukas* (from *Sturzkampfflugzeug*), with terror-provoking whistles in their wings, screamed down to hurl destruction upon Polish cities. Others roared along at treetop level to strafe the refugees cluttering the highways.

Across the Polish border, which, after the rape of Czechoslovakia, had been extended to a length of 1,200 miles, streamed the German armies. The Poles were forced to fall back, fighting a series of desperate delaying actions. Military mystery: Where were the second or third lines of trenches where the Poles might try again to halt the oncoming Germans? The Poles were rapidly pushed back to a natural line formed by the rivers Narew, Bug, Vistula, and San. All they could hope for was to hold out until the rainy season should slow down German operations or until the British and French could relieve them by attacking from the west.

The Polish border had been breached at a dozen points. The Germans moved, not only with infantry, the "queen of battles," but with such trail-blazing motorized units as motorcycles, light tanks, armored cars, motorized artillery, finally with heavy tanks. Racing along, these columns headed for the defenders' nerve centers: road and railway junctions, bridges, telegraph stations, and airfields. As they penetrated deeply into the rear, they were supplied by planes with gasoline, ammunition, and foodstuffs.

There was not only rapidity, but also precalculated method. There were no opposing lines, no head-on clashes, no fronts. Instead, there was a succession of sudden and deep penetrations. Even the German General Command Headquarters was on wheels, able to adapt itself speedily to the situation at hand. It was all most perplexing to the Poles.

The planned confusion was working perfectly. Next, the Germans committed their superbly trained infantry. Pushing ahead according to preconceived plan, the troops raced toward a rendezvous with the extended *Panzer-divisionen.* Together they began to mop up resistance.

It was something like Cannae, where Hannibal won a great victory over the Romans in 216 B.C. Pincers and encirclement, with this innovation—a greater outer encirclement plus an inner one. On the outer rim in the north, one German army cut across the Polish corridor, where it split into two, one section moving still farther northward to reduce the Polish port city of Gdynia, while the other continued on above Warsaw in the direction of Brest-Litovsk. At the southern great semicircle, other spearheads swung wide around Kraków in the direction of Lwów.

Inside the great circle more armies formed a smaller arc around Warsaw. The troops at the northern rim of the smaller circle moved toward Modlin and Kutno across the Vistula to hit Warsaw, while the southern flank drove through Lodz toward the Polish capital. Warsaw was the concentric goal of two powerful enveloping movements.

In a little over a week von Rundstedt was hammering at the outer gates of Warsaw. And within two weeks two armies from the north had trapped 170,000 Poles at Kutno, a hundred miles to the west of the capital.

On September 17, 1939, came further bad news for the Poles. Stalin and Hitler, bedfellows by convenience, now carried out the terms of a secret protocol of the recent Moscow Pact. From the east, again without warning, Russian troops poured into Poland. They were coming, Stalin said blandly, as "liberators" to "protect" Ukrainian and White Russian minorities. There was little resistance as the Red troops methodically occupied the eastern Polish provinces. Within two days they held half of Poland.

The *Fuehrer* had not counted on this swift penetration by the Reds. The Russians had moved so quickly that they had not only cut him off from the rich oil fields of Galicia but also blocked his direct road to the oil of Rumania.

Poland was now trapped between the *Wehrmacht* in the west and the Red Army in the east. There was little she could do. She was crushed like an egg.

Warsaw, capital and largest city of Poland, 389 miles east of Berlin, was completely encircled by German armies. But the Poles, organized under Mayor Stefan Starzynski, "Stefan the Stubborn," still resisted. Polish officers, who had left their surrendering troops outside the city, retreated into Warsaw to form new regiments consisting almost entirely of officers. The civilian population turned out *en masse* to dig trenches and construct fortifications. Tiny dugouts about five yards apart were manned by one or two men with rifles, machine guns, and hand grenades. Trenches zigzagged along streets and backyards in such profusion that it was possible to step from the front doors of apartment houses directly into the trenches.

The Germans first tried the weapons of propaganda. Posters on the outskirts of the city announced in Polish: "Poles! Come to us. We will not hurt you. We will give you bread." Airplanes rained down over the city millions of leaflets demanding surrender, promising enemy troops that they would not be made prisoners of war, and informing the "brave officers" that they would be permitted to keep their swords. The Poles contemptuously refused to take the bait.

Then came an all-out battering, day and night, from the air and from massed artillery. Railroad stations, coalyards, and hotels were gutted and reduced to shambles. The old Saxon palace in Pilsudski Square in the heart of the city was shelled and burned. Thousands of buildings were blown up. Fires spread everywhere. In ten days the great city was reduced to smoking piles of brick, plaster, and debris. There was hardly an undamaged building left.

Food ran low; water supplies and sewers were disrupted. On September 27, 1939, when there was no more ammunition, the defenders capitulated. The next day the garrison at nearby Modlin fortress surrendered unconditionally.

A few isolated units held out in the south and east of Poland until October. A last-ditch effort was made to establish a new base at the Dniester River to await Allied help through Rumania, but in vain. There was some final resistance on October 5, 1939, at Lublin and Lwów, in the southeast.

On September 28, 1939, Foreign Ministers Joachim von Ribbentrop and Vyacheslav Molotov met to divide the spoils of war. A new "Frontier and Friendship Agreement" revised the terms of the original Moscow Pact. Poland, a nation of 150,000 square miles and 35,000,000 people, was split for the fifth time (previous partitions in 1772, 1793, 1795, and 1815), this time roughly along the old Curzon Line, set up in December 1919 by the Allied Supreme Council as the tentative eastern frontier of Poland.

The Germans took under their "protection" 73,000 square miles, including the lion's share of Poland's mining and manufacturing areas, with 22,000,000 people. Once again Hitler had demonstrated to his delighted people that he was the *Mehrer*, the augmenter or aggrandizer, of the Third Reich. To his political laurels was added a great military triumph.

But it was not altogether a cheap victory. The Germans paid for it with 8,082 killed, 27,278 wounded, and 5,029 missing. They lost 217 tanks and 400 aircraft. Small matter to Hitler—his Nazi legions were on the march.

The Russians, outspoken permanent opponents of "capitalistic aggression" and "imperialism," annexed 77,000 square miles of Poland, including its major oil resources, and some 13,000,000 inhabitants.

Before the capitulation, leading Polish officials, including President Ignacy Moscicki, Marshal Edward Smigly-Rydz, and Foreign Minister Colonel Joseph Beck, managed to flee to Rumania, where they were interned. In exile in Rumania, President Moscicki, as was his constitutional right, appointed Wladislaw Rackziewicz, then in Paris, as his successor, and the latter named

THE POLISH PARTITION

General Wladislaw Sikorski to head a new cabinet set up at Anvers in France and later in London. The government-in-exile was promptly recognized by both Britain and France. More than 70,000 Polish troops fled to France and England, and Polish airmen rendered invaluable service in the Battle of Britain.

The agonies of hell now descended upon the hapless Poles, prostrate before the conquerors. Dr. Robert Ley, head of the German Labor Front, forced tens of thousands into slave labor for the Nazi war machine. "Germans," he said, "can never live in the same condition as Poles or Jews." Civil Commissioner Kiessling of Thorn revealed the official German attitude: "The Polish collapse these days has proven anew the inferiority of the Poles. There can be no leniency. In future we cannot work with such people. Poland was German, is German, remains German. What the Poles did not accomplish in twenty years, we shall accomplish in three years. This is our main task."

Some 36,000 square miles of Poland were incorporated into Germany. Another 36,000 square miles were converted into a "Gouvernement General" with Kraków as its capital and the sadistic Hans Frank as Nazi administrator. Nazi Police Chief Heinrich Himmler, one of the most vicious mass murderers of all time, was designated to begin a merciless extermination of Poles and Jews by firing squads and gas chambers.

In a single month Poland had been crushed in one of the speediest campaigns in military history. Thus began the terrible blood bath of World War II.

THE TRAGIC AUDIT OF WORLD WAR I

It had happened before. On November 11, 1918, these banner headlines were emblazoned on the front page of *The New York Times:*

ARMISTICE SIGNED, END OF THE WAR!
BERLIN SEIZED BY REVOLUTIONISTS;
NEW CHANCELLOR BEGS FOR ORDER;
OUSTED KAISER FLEES TO HOLLAND

The guns were silent. For four years and three months, for 1,565 days, the bloodiest and costliest conflict in the history of mankind had been fought by 30 sovereign states including all the so-called Great Powers. A stunned humanity prepared to audit the costs of this abysmal carnage.

The human cost in rough figures: 10,000,000 known dead soldiers; 3,000,000 presumed dead soldiers; 13,000,000 dead civilians; 20,000,000 wounded soldiers; 3,000,000 prisoners; 9,000,000 war orphans; 5,000,000 war widows; 10,000,000 refugees.

Some 65,000,000 men had been mobilized in the deadly struggle. Casualties in one form or another ran to 40 per cent, nearly one-half of the combatants. The generation living through World War I had not comprehended how lethal modern war had become. In sixteenth-century European wars the casualties were approximately one of 20 combatants. In the eighteenth century the ratio narrowed down to one out of seven. Twentieth-century civilization brought the count to one out of two.

The figures in killed alone were enough to stagger the imagination. More than twice as many were killed in World War I as in all major wars from 1790 to 1913, including the Napoleonic campaigns, the three wars of German national unification (against Denmark, 1864; against Austria, 1866; against France, 1870-1871), the Civil War in the United States, the Boer War, the Russo-Japanese War, and the Balkan Wars of 1912-1913.

All the belligerents lost heavily, but two thirds of the men mobilized and two thirds of those killed were on the Allied side. In proportion to its population France suffered the heaviest loss in manpower—1,427,000 killed, 3,044,000 wounded, and 453,500 prisoners or missing. For the United States a comparable tragedy would have meant 5,000,000 killed and 11,000,000 wounded.

Civilian deaths, directly and indirectly attributable to World War I, were even greater than the military losses. In the wake of the conflict came starvation, epidemics, and disease. Aggravated by the war, an influenza epidemic originating in the United States raced around the globe. One of the three most terrible scourges in history, the flu took a heavy toll. More, it is difficult to estimate the serious negative effect of the lowered birthrate of the war years.

How can one reckon the value of human lives in terms of dollars or pounds? What is the gauge to measure lives cut short or the effects upon future generations? After the war sporadic attempts were made to determine the total economic costs. All were based upon elaborate guesswork; exact calculations were impossible because of imperfect records and the reluctance of governments to issue meaningful figures. One thing was tragically clear—twentieth-century war had grown ten times as costly as the nineteenth-century variety. Europe was scraped bare as if by a swarm of locusts.

One historian, E. L. Bogart, estimated in the early 1930's the total immediate economic cost of World War I as $331,600,000,000, including the cost of munitions, machines of war, property losses on land and sea, and production losses. This did not include subsequent billions in interest payments on loans, pensions, and care for veterans.

"Even these incomprehensible and appalling figures," said Professor Bogart, "do not take into account the effect of the war on life, human vitality, economic well-being, ethics, morality, or other phases of human relationships and activities which have been disorganized and injured."

In the four years from 1914 to 1918 British domestic and foreign indebtedness rose from $3,000,000,000 to $25,000,000,000. The average daily cost to all belligerents in the first three years of the war was $123,000,000. By 1918 the struggle was costing $10,000,000 per hour.

Three hundred and thirty-one billion, six hundred million dollars! This amounted to five and a half times as many dollars as the number of seconds that had elapsed since the birth of Christ.

In 1934 the editor of *Scholastic* translated this huge figure into relatively understandable terms. It would have been enough to furnish:

1. Every family in England, France, Belgium, Germany, Russia, the United States, Canada, and Australia with a $2,500 house on a $500 one-acre lot, with $1,000 worth of furniture; AND
2. A $5,000,000 library for every community of 200,000 population in each of the countries; AND
3. A $10,000,000 university for each of these communities; AND
4. A fund that at 5 per cent interest would yield enough to pay indefinitely $1,000 a year to 125,000 teachers and 125,000 nurses, AND
5. Still leave enough funds to purchase every piece of property and all the wealth in Belgium and France at a fair market price.

The carnage and destruction of World War I were truly uneconomic. Before that conflict Norman Angell had pointed out in *The Great Illusion* that war could never pay economically and that destructive forms of production are parasitical and anti-economic. He was dismissed as a pacifist and an impractical idealist.

ECONOMIC TIME-FUSES OF WORLD WAR II

It has been said that war is a series of dramatic incidents between long periods of boredom. But there is precious little drama in the *background* of war.

The effective impulse of twentieth-century war came from clashing of political interests and emotions aroused by these. But underneath were powerful economic and financial factors, forces that had already contributed much to the outbreak of World War I. These interlocking problems were not solved by the peacemakers of Versailles, with the result that, despite some profound changes in economic life, they continued to operate in the background and thus led toward World War II.

The never-simple historical explanation is to be found partly in the economic way of life fashioned in the preceding two centuries. The expansion of Europe was aided by the accelerated pace of economic development—heated competition for markets, for reserves of raw materials, for places to invest excess capital, for the control of land or sea communications. Rivalries and jealousies became increasingly dangerous as nation after nation schemed for a place in the sun.

In a world in which each nation wanted a favorable balance of trade and economic self-sufficiency, each resorted to economic warfare with such weapons as protective tariffs, managed currencies, subsidized trade, and cutthroat competition. There was little sense of common economic welfare. Industrialists looked upon the world as an economic jungle, in which the prize of material success went to the shrewdest and most powerful.

The victorious democracies of World War I failed to achieve economic stability. With the global economic and financial depression of 1929 came panic and havoc. Three dissatisfied nations—Germany, Italy, and Japan—complained loudly that they, the "have-not nations," had not been given their fair share of the earth's surface and its resources.

The democracies, disunited and militarily unprepared, sought to retain their economic dominance in the face of these new challenges. They were willing to make concessions in the hope that appeasement would avert war.

Thus, on the one side came a coördinated effort to break down the old society and substitute for it an Axis-dominated, Axis-serving, "racially pure" Utopia, the end of political man's desire. On the other side, there was a half-hearted attempt to maintain the status quo or something approaching it.

From his Roman balcony Mussolini shouted to the world that an impoverished Italy had been meanly treated. With highly vocal Italian scorn he excoriated the statesmen of Versailles, accusing them of denying Italy the fruits of victory. There were too many people on Italian soil, he charged, and there were too few colonies to house the excess population. How could a new-born, revitalized Italy obtain satisfaction for her needs? Not from the "putrescent corpses" of the fat, bloated democracies, certainly not from that citadel of perfidy—England, nor from that homeland of selfish individualism—France, nor from the prosperity-swollen United States.

Italy, cried the master of Fascism, would attain her rightful place in the hierarchy of nations only by using the millions of bayonets in the hands of her tigerish fighting sons.

Japan, second in time-order of the vocalizing have-not nations, had quickly learned the ways of the West. During World War I, she had played a waiting game, refusing to become deeply involved, but zealously studying and preparing for the big day. Japan developed her own version of *Lebensraum* (living space). The militarists (or *Gumbatsu*), the Elder Statesmen (or *Genro*), and the business interests (or *Zaibatsu*), the latter including the powerful Mitsui and Mitsubishi corporations, all agreed that only more territory for Nippon could solve the problems of a multiplying population and a deficiency of raw materials.

If the tiny isle of England could expand her influence throughout the world, was it not reasonable to expect that the Japanese, chosen people of the Sun God, had the right to similar expansion in the Far East? It was a matter of life or death to obtain raw materials for the insatiable Japanese industrial machine and to acquire colonies for excess population and economic exploitation.

The Japanese would carve out a huge empire in East Asia and make it prosperous by initiative, intelligence, and the *Samurai* sword. Who but the decadent democracies would deny to Japan a better standard of living? And if the United States, whose immigration laws had grossly insulted the great people of Nippon, stood in the way, its navy would receive the same annihilating treatment as had the Russian fleet during the Russo-Japanese War of 1904-1905. Death to the enemy and "*Banzai!*" ("Ten thousand years, forever!") to Japan's glorious future.

From Nazi Germany, the third have-not nation, came repeated and persistent demands for a place in the sun. German economic progress had been phenomenal during the late nineteenth century, when the country was transformed from a predominantly agrarian to a modern industrialized state. Business and banking were concentrated, *laissez faire* was abandoned in favor of protection, the armaments industry promoted, a colonial policy inaugurated. Wilhelm II dismissed Chancellor Bismarck in 1890 and embarked upon a New Course stressing an intensified colonialism and the creation of a major navy to consolidate Germany's position as a world power.

Toward the end of the nineteenth century Britain was the manufacturer, carrier, merchant, and banker of the world. Her colonial empire was first in size, her industry enjoyed a global reputation ("Made in England" was the leading trade-mark of the world's commerce), and her navy ruled the oceans. Some two-thirds of the world's shipping was British.

Germany's economic expansion clashed head-on with the old-established British imperialism. Germans began to challenge Britons in the world's markets. Germany's strategic position in Central Europe made her logically the leader of Continental trade; her great coastal cities of Hamburg and Bremen were leading centers for North European commerce. German economic paternalism, plus efficiency and scientific genius, sparked this upsurge of economic power. Even her late start in industrialization gave Germany the advantage of having her industries equipped at the beginning with the most modern machinery.

Before World War I Germans outstripped Englishmen in many fields, especially in manufacturing, agriculture, commerce, and mining. Statistics on iron-ore production, the key figures in modern economy, reveal the extent of German economic progress in the race with Britain:

Production of Iron Ore

	In Germany—tons	In Great Britain—tons
1880	7,239,000	18,026,000
1890	11,406,000	13,781,000
1900	18,964,000	14,028,000
1909	25,505,000	14,980,000

The figures are enlightening: in 1880 Great Britain produced about two and a half times as much iron ore as Germany, but within less than three decades the Germans had nearly doubled the British rate of production. This, said the Germans, proved that World War I stemmed largely from Britain's jealousy.

The German economy was dealt a hard blow by the defeat of 1918. The Allies appropriated all the German colonies, what was left of the German navy and merchant marine, German working capital, even German domestic animals. The valuable iron-ore deposits of Lorraine went to France. Germany's gold supply evaporated.

The inflation of 1923 hit the German economy with impact, crippling the industrial machine and impoverishing the nation by destroying the value of its money. With its currency, its insurance policies, its savings accounts, and pensions wiped out, the middle class, backbone of the economy, staggered through the economic morass. Had not the Western nations stepped in with the Dawes Plan (1924) and the Young Plan (1929), the German economy might have collapsed altogether. There was a temporary boom as foreign funds streamed into Germany, but the depression of 1929 abruptly halted outside aid.

Then came Hitler's drive for a *Wehrwirtschaft*, or "defense" economy. The *Fuehrer* rigidly controlled the entire system, allocating raw materials, controlling investments, dictating prices and wages, and piling surplus capital into armaments. He deliberately abandoned the Weimar Republic's welfare economy, in which goods were produced for universal consumption, and substituted for it a war economy. The entire Nazi industrial machine, from top to bottom, was geared for war.

This, then, was the new economic challenge. Once again a New Order had appeared in Germany to challenge the democracies. Hitler had two goals in mind: to prevent a repetition of the blockade that smothered Germany in 1918; and to tear up the Treaty of Versailles by the one incontrovertible argument—victory in war.

THE ROLE OF NATIONALISM

In 1848 Karl Marx predicted that a gradual lessening of the sentiment of nationalism and a corresponding growth of internationalism would lead inevitably to the union of the workers of the world. Seldom in the history of thought has any social prophet been more in error.

Marx was fantastically wrong. Far from losing its potency, nationalism in the last century grew more and more intensified until it became the prime generating political force of the twentieth century. Norman Angell penned this memorable sentence: "Political nationalism has become, for the European of our age, the most important thing in the world, more important than civilization, humanity, decency, kindness, pity; more important than life itself."

Errors in judgment about nationalism were responsible in large part for the two World Wars of the twentieth century and for the subsequent peace treaties. The Treaty of Versailles and its parallel treaties after World War I sought to remake the map of Europe on the basis of national self-determination and the will of the victors.

But, instead of settling European antagonisms, nationalism only aggravated them. The boundaries of states still did not coincide with those of population and language. National minorities, which demanded to be freed of foreign domination, continued to protest. Vigorous assertions of national feeling increased in strength and significance.

The mushroom growth of ultranationalism was particularly virulent in Nazi Germany and Fascist Italy, where, by the nature of totalitarian dictatorship, it could be used in the drive to change the map of Europe by force. The dictators did not shrink from appealing to doubtful or illusory principles. The end justified the means. Nothing was more important to the dictators than personal glory, the will to power, and national prestige. The same sentiment gripped the Japanese militarists. Human beings were little more than animals in the global jungle. Hitler, Mussolini, and Tojo would have their people be tigers and lions in a world populated mostly by lambs and sheep.

In the Age of Nationalism, Britain, France, and the United States could live only by expressing the counterirritant of their own nationalism. The blood bath starting in 1939 was in part the logical outcome of increasing antagonism between an order of states established by treaty and other "peaceful" means, and the driving force of the New Order.

The deceptively simple term *nationalism* is in reality a complex historical phenomenon. A knowledge of its meaning is essential but is embarrassingly difficult to establish. Generations of scholars have devoted themselves to clarifying the meaning of nationalism. But there has been no unanimity of definition. One of the reasons is that the meaning of the term shifts with the course of history. Even more, nationalism may mean different things to different people. The word, like *democracy*, is often used to express totally divergent views. We are faced with confusion thrice confounded.

By adding the suffix "-ism" the nation is endowed with new traits that make it more than a mere political or cultural community. Any definition has its weaknesses, but the following may be least objectionable:

> Nationalism, a product of political, economic, social, and intellectual factors at a certain stage in history, is a condition of mind, feeling, or sentiment of a group of people living in a well-defined geographical area, speaking a common language, possessing a literature in which the aspirations of the nation have been expressed, attached to common traditions and common customs, venerating its own heroes, and, in some cases, having a common religion.

Each segment of this definition is open to attack. For example, Switzerland has four languages, but there is a Swiss nationalism; there was no Polish territory from the late eighteenth century until 1919, but Polish nationalism persisted.

Nationalism is first and foremost a state of mind, an act of consciousness, a psychological fact. It is a socially approved symbol used by modern society in its continuing search for security. It is a superimposed, synthetic sentiment. By no means an absolutely necessary way of life, it has been constructed as artificially as was the Panama Canal.

Nationalism, like all historical movements, is deeply rooted in the past. Its first great manifestation was in the French Revolution, which stimulated and spread it. Its composite pattern utilizes some of the oldest and most primitive feelings of man, including love of birthplace and hatred for the foreigner (xenophobia). In the nineteenth century it became a force either for the unification of peoples or for the disruption of old composite states. The idea spread that collectivities of peoples, or nations, would become good and peaceful forces as soon as they were able to break away from multinational states.

In the twentieth century nationalism spread to Central and Eastern Europe and eventually to Asia, the Middle East, and Africa, to countries which, unlike the West, had had no experience with individual liberty. The new form of nationalism in the Age of World Wars subordinated the individual to the state. The accent was on a closed society, instead of on the open society in which a premium is placed upon the freedom of the individual, upon liberty, equality, and fraternity.

"Though national independence brought a great emotional elation to many peoples at the time of its achievement," said the historian Hans Kohn, "the historian will ask himself whether this momentary elation is not too dearly bought. National independence and sovereignty, multiplied and sanctified in the last decades, has not turned out to be a reliable road to a greater individual liberty and more secure international peace."

To nationalism and its effects, then, may be attributed much of the blame for the outbreak of World War II.

INTERNATIONAL ANARCHY

Another basic cause for both World Wars was the lack of effective machinery for regulating relations between nations. In their everyday life human beings found it expedient and necessary to use policemen to prevent asocial conduct. But what about the international scene? Here there was nothing to prevent a nation from going berserk as a result of its frustrating experiences.

In 1926, G. Lowes Dickinson, British essayist, published a significant book titled *International Anarchy, 1904-1913*, in which he recounted the selfish secret intrigues of all the Powers. This international anarchy culminated in World War I. "This much is true," Dickinson wrote, "that until men lay down their arms, and accept the method of peaceable decisions of their disputes, wars can never cease."

Dickinson was not alone in his belief that the only hope for the future lay in international organization. Since the days of Plato, men of wisdom have been saying the same thing. Maximilien de Béthune, Baron de Rosny and Duc de Sully (1560-1641), faithful friend and minister to Henry IV, worked out a "Grand Design" of a vast European federation of 15 states, a "Christian Republic," to be directed by a general council of 60 deputies. But the plan was never carried into effect.

In early modern times, the growth of commerce, the rise of national states, and frequent wars all combined to create the need for a legal code that would operate at a level above the laws of individual national states and restrict their irresponsible actions. Modern international law was systematized and popularized by a Dutchman, Hugo Grotius (1583-1645) in his *Law of War and Peace* (1625). Grotius held that international law embodies rules that each nation is morally required to obey, even if they could not be imposed by a superior force.

Considerable hope was aroused among reasonable men by the two international Peace Conferences organized by Czar Nicholas II of Russia and held at The Hague in 1899 and 1907. But little was done by the delegates to these meetings beyond passing resolutions calling for the promotion of international peace and for humane conduct of war, such as prohibiting poison gas, dum-dum bullets, or the launching of projectiles and explosives from balloons. Note the persistence of the idea of "the laws and customs of war." But the key problem was how to prevent sovereign states from going to war.

World War I made it imperative that a global federation or world-state be formed to promote international accord. But how could international order be achieved on a scene marked by discontent of the defeated powers, disillusionment of the victors, and an America retreating into isolation? The League of Nations, brain-child of Jan Smuts, a South African leader, was offered as a solution.

From the beginning the League of Nations was the special project of President Wilson, who worked himself into the grave on its behalf. "The Covenant we offer," he said, "must be based primarily upon moral sanctions with resort to force only as a final means of action."

Wilson went to the Peace Conference at Versailles in 1919, the first American president to leave the United States during his term of office. The peoples of Europe welcomed him as if he were the Messiah, with cries that seemed to come from the heart of humanity. But the statesmen at Versailles denounced him as an impractical idealist who knew nothing of the realities of diplomacy. Georges Clemenceau, the Tiger of France, annoyed by the Wilsonian Fourteen Points projected as a statement of American war aims, commented: "Wilson has to have Fourteen Points; the Good Lord Himself had only Ten!"

Bitter were the battles among the Big Three—Wilson, Clemenceau, and Lloyd George. The last reportedly complained, in a moment of whimsy: "What am I to do between a man who thinks he is Jesus Christ and another who thinks he is Napoleon?"

Wilson, his nerves shattered by the interminable bickering, was certain that the peoples of the world shared his hatred of war, militarism, and the old secret diplomacy. He did his best to purge the world of war through the instrument of the League of Nations. With great reluctance he even accepted some of the harsher terms of the Treaty of Versailles, the treaty of peace with Germany, in return for support of the League. He was successful in having the full Covenant of the League inserted into the Treaty of Versailles as the first of its 15 parts.

But once home, Wilson found himself embroiled in a battle with isolationist Republican senators who, among other reasons, resented having been left behind on the junket to Versailles. They viciously attacked the League. "The United States must not be trapped in foreign entanglements."

Wilson tirelessly traversed the country by railroad, literally begging the people for support. He warned that if we did not join the League there would certainly be another world war within another generation. After delivering his fortieth speech, at Pueblo, Colorado, he collapsed from nervous and physical exhaustion.

The abstention of the United States was a deadly blow to the League. In *Triumph and Tragedy* (Volume VI of his history of World War II), Winston Churchill states flatly that the League was ruined by the failure of the United States to take an active role. There were other contributing factors, such as the failure to include the defeated powers in the original membership list, the unwillingness of the major powers to disarm, and the survival of power diplomacy. But the League could not survive without American participation.

The League was able to dispose of several dozen minor disputes, most of them legacies of the war. Example—the dispute between Finland and Sweden over the Aaland Islands in the Gulf of Finland.

But observe that these were relatively minor quarrels. After 1931 came the major international disputes. The League failed to halt Japanese aggression in China, to check Italy in Ethiopia, or to handle the problems arising from the Spanish Civil War.

Still, despite its weaknesses, the League of Nations was the most promising institution as yet brought into existence to promote international understanding. A modest beachhead was established in the struggle to establish a world society with a formal constitution. With all its limitations, the first important step had been taken.

The statesmen of the postwar era had learned little. Again they reverted to the futile behavior of the past in the search for security and disarmament. It was the same old story of combinations, treaties, *revanche*.

Germany and the Central Powers, defeated on the battlefields, were united in their desire to repudiate the peace settlements. The Western Powers feared the expansion of Bolshevism, while the Soviet Union was convinced the entire world wanted to destroy her. The French, even though counted among the triumphant Allies, were gripped by a feeling of insecurity. Britain persisted in an attempt to restore the old European balance of power, which would enable her to maintain a dominant position on the Continent. The United States, disgusted with the recurrent European crises, returned to isolation.

This was the soil of an uneasy Europe in which the dragon's teeth for the next war were being planted, soon to spring up as armed hordes. Many men saw it coming. Few could do anything about it.

The more level-headed members of the League, sensing the coming explosion, did their best to forestall it. If there had to be a system of security, the League would do its best to improve it. In September 1923 it unanimously adopted the draft Treaty of Mutual Assistance, calling for member nations to assist one another if attacked. No nation signed the treaty, primarily on the ground that it did not adequately define the terms "aggressor" and "aggression." In October 1924 the League Assembly adopted the Geneva Protocol for the Pacific Settlement of International Disputes, this time clearly defining an aggressor as a "state which resorts to war in violation of the undertakings contained in the Covenant of the present Protocol." Britain opposed the Protocol because it called for global commitments that she was not prepared to make. Again failure for the League.

Meanwhile, the powers reverted to the old system of alliances; this time the combinations were not kept secret. Rival alliances had not prevented

World War I, but the idea persisted. Almost immediately after World War I three systems of alliances were set up—French, Russian, and Italian.

The French, with a virtual fixation upon security, asked for an Anglo-American Treaty of Guarantee to protect them from a future attack by Germany. "We French," they said, "have lived across the Rhine from the Germans for a thousand years. We know them far better than you do. They will attack us again." Neither the British nor the Americans were willing to commit themselves. The French, skeptical of League help, thereupon concluded a series of alliances and alignments with Belgium, Poland, Czechoslovakia, Rumania, Yugoslavia, Soviet Russia, and England. At the same time France encouraged the formation of the Little Entente among Czechoslovakia, Yugoslavia, and Rumania to maintain the Treaty of Trianon, to prevent a restoration of the Hapsburgs, and to oppose any Hungarian irredentist outbreak.

Soviet Russia, fearful of an international combination directed against her, also concluded a chain of nonaggression pacts and commercial treaties with her neighbors. Italy, disappointed by what she considered to be shabby treatment at Versailles, followed suit.

Locarno brought some hope. Gustav Stresemann of Germany, Aristide Briand of France, and Austen Chamberlain of England met at Locarno on October 5-16, 1925, and in an atmosphere of sweetness and light signed a series of seven treaties. Germany finally recognized her western boundaries as set by the Treaty of Versailles, and relinquished her claim to Alsace-Lorraine. France, in return, agreed to halt any efforts to promote a separatist republic in the Rhineland. Evacuation of the Rhineland was promised for an earlier date than had been set at Versailles. Germany was admitted to the League of Nations, as a Great Power. Great Britain, Italy, and Belgium guaranteed the maintenance of the Locarno agreement. Locarno was hailed as the inauguration of a new era of peace and good will.

Nearly three years later, on August 27, 1928, 15 nations signed the Kellogg-Briand Paris Peace Pact, in which they agreed to renounce war as an instrument of national policy and subscribed to the principle of arbitration and conciliation to settle international disputes. By 1933, 63 nations had signed the pact. But added qualifications made its terms equivocal—most signatory powers including the United States reserved the right to take measures judged necessary for self-defense.

It *seemed*, however, that at long last the statesmen of the world would settle their differences around the conference table.

THE RACE TO ARMS

The blind and the foolish never saw the relationship between arms and Armageddon. Adding its weight to the causes of the war was the increasing pace of the armament race. Behind this was the great political force of the 1930's—fear: fear of war, fear of its consequences, fear that one's nation might be unprepared. Decent men who hated war recoiled toward peace, but these same men, living in fear of war's possible outcome, were driven to prepare for it. Nations, keeping jealous watch, came to expect war.

There were attempts to halt the arms race, but they were half-hearted, insincere, incomplete. Statesmen agreed sanctimoniously to reduce arms that had already been outmoded, but they reserved an eagle eye for what each potential enemy was doing in the way of manufacturing deadlier weapons.

The League tried hard. Its Covenant contained several provisions for disarmament, but the nations carefully averted their eyes. Point No. 4 of Wilson's Fourteen Points had mentioned disarmament, but even here there was the inevitable loophole: "Adequate guarantees . . . that national armaments will be reduced to the lowest point consistent with national safety."

The attempt at naval disarmament foundered in rough seas. In 1921-1922 President Harding called the Washington Naval Conference. There was agreement: a ten-year capital-ship holiday, and restriction of remaining ships to a ratio of United States, 5; Great Britain, 5; Japan, 3; France, 1.67; and Italy, 1.67. To meet this ratio the United States destroyed a part of its great fleet. Other nations merely tore up blueprints for projected naval additions.

The Geneva Naval Conference, called in 1927 to limit the construction of small ships, broke up without any accomplishments. The London Naval Conference of 1930 attempted not so much to reduce naval armaments as to limit them. The signatories insisted upon an "escalator clause," permitting each power to exceed the tonnage limits if in its opinion new construction by a non-signatory power threatened its own security.

How could there be any progress in the face of this tongue-in-cheek diplomacy? The London Naval Conference of 1935-1936 was called when Japan suddenly demanded naval equality with the United States and Great Britain. This was too much. The Great Powers terminated the capital-ship holiday and resumed unlimited naval construction.

Equally fruitless was the attempt to limit land armaments. What was the "common yardstick," the fair measure by which disarmament could be achieved without threats to the security of any nation? The League strove vainly for some solution. At the World Disarmament Conference, beginning in Geneva in 1932, President Hoover suggested a one-third reduction of land forces and the total abolition of tanks, bombing planes, and large mobile guns.

But there was a Nazi fly in the ointment. Hitler demanded that Germany be permitted to arm to parity with France. The request was denied. Germany then deserted the Disarmament Conference and in October 1933 resigned from the League. After further meetings, the Conference, hopelessly deadlocked, was permanently adjourned.

Thus the sad story of postwar disarmament. Behind it was a great debate. Proponents argued that the sensible and civilized thing for the nations was to disarm, for without armaments there would be no more wars. In the past, they said, arms races had invariably led directly to war. Once an arms race began, it progressed geometrically, each side seeking to outdo the other. Weapons were quickly outmoded; they were a tricky investment through which the world's wealth was systematically poured down an uneconomic rathole.

On the other side were the advocates of preparedness. The only way to prevent war, they said, was to make oneself so powerful that an aggressor would never risk an attack. Preparedness was the insurance premium against war. Victory would go to the nation which earned it through foresight and readiness. By spending only a fraction of its national income, a people could save itself from the eventual outpouring of money and lives necessary to win. In the final analysis, war was a natural activity of man, to be avoided, if possible, but to be won at all costs once it had begun. It was even charged that disarmament was a dream of Jews, Socialists, and hysterical women.

The debate was settled by the emergence of Hitler. The obvious threat of the Axis led to the abandonment of efforts to limit armaments. In 1933, the year of Hitler's accession to power and the last effective year of the Versailles-League of Nations system, the armies of the world numbered 7,000,000 men, the navies 3,000,000 tons, there were 14,000 military aircraft, and $4,000,000,000 were being spent annually to oil the machinery of war.

In 1938, the year of Munich, the armies of the world increased to 10,000,000 men, naval tonnage to 8,000,000, military planes to some 50,000, and $17,000,000,000 were spent to keep the men and machines of war. These were staggering figures, but they shrank into insignificance once Poland was invaded by the Germans.

The surge to catastrophe was on.

In terms of 1939, the European stop-Hitler coalition (Britain, France, Rumania, Greece, and Poland) seemed to have an edge on the Axis (Germany, Italy, Hungary, and Spain)—282 against 209 divisions. Advantage in sea power went to the Allies (the British Navy alone was strong enough to defeat any combination of two European navies). But the Axis was superior in submarine strength. In the air each coalition had about 6,500 first-line military planes.

But no one could measure the strength of the imponderables—leadership, strategy, tactics, morale, good fortune, role of the neutrals.

THE PSYCHOLOGICAL CLIMATE

Many who lived through the horrors of World War I were emphatic in their first reactions: "Never again!" But they soon forgot, just as men cease remembering the pains of illness and push annoying thoughts deep into the subconscious.

One of the fatal flaws was in the educational process. It was the same depressing story. Impressionable youngsters were nourished on tales of battlefield comradeship, heroism under fire, the glory of victory, the inadmissibility of defeat. Veterans, forgetting the stench and filth of war, boasted to their sons about feats on the battlefield and dropped mysterious hints about that unforgettable leave in Paris.

The process was repeated in the schools. Glamorize the nauseating. Watch the new wars start in the history classrooms.

Why these periodic descents into barbarism? For most people war was a scourge of mankind, inevitable, inexplicable. There was much to learn, but little public interest. A Parliament of Man? Let the bleeding hearts worry about that nonsense! Much more important was the immediate business of making a living, the acquisition of a refrigerator, stock dividends, country-club membership. Material success was the thing! Let the professors worry about past wars.

Dedicated scholars had worked hard to clear up the "mystery" of war. They showed how in the past spiritual limitations on war had been suggested by the teaching of Plato, by the Christian view of nature as corrupt and sinful, and by the application of moral imperatives in education and politics. Further, they revealed how these restraints had gradually broken down under the impact of material progress and the concomitant undermining of morals and ethics. The new science had created an economy of abundance and along with it overwhelmingly destructive weapons.

The thing to do, then, said the scholars, was to devote as much attention to the conquest of the war spirit as to any communicable disease, to relegate war to the status of cannibalism.

The scholars pointed out that man was living in an era of illusion, irrationalism, and aggression. In the democracies, they said, the people, concerned about the maintenance of the status quo, slumbered on the edge of the abyss. And in the have-not nations the masses turned to demagogues who urged them to "think with the blood" and strike for world power. The stage was set for conflict.

There was no easy solution. The scholars had not given a satisfactory response to the key question of 1939: How could the world rid itself of the stench of Hitlerism without the use of force?

CHAPTER 2

From Manchuria to Anschluss: *Stages of Axis Aggression*

The way to gain actual rights in Manchuria and Mongolia is to use the region as a base and under the pretense of trade and commerce to penetrate the rest of China.

—The Tanaka Memorial, 1927

The German State should embrace all Germans, with the task not only of collecting and maintaining its most valuable primitive elements, but also slowly and surely of raising itself to a ruling position.

—Adolf Hitler, 1933

War is to the male what child-bearing is to the female.

—Benito Mussolini, 1936

PROLOGUE I: THE MANCHURIAN CRISIS, 1931

"From the fact of the divine descent of the Japanese people proceeds their immeasurable superiority to the natives of other countries in courage and intelligence."

"Japan must no longer let the impudence of the white man go unpunished."

"It is the duty of Japan to expel Chinese influence from Manchuria and to follow the way of Imperial Destiny."

Thus the challenge from Japanese militarists, hotheads who had rapidly pushed their way to power and who were in a position to lead the nation on dangerous military adventures. No one, they said, could prevent the expansion of an ambitious nation like Japan. The first problem was the acquisition of the Chinese mainland. Then the unconquerable spirit of Japan would spread to the seven seas and the five continents until a *Pax Nipponica* was established all over the world. Anything standing in the way would feel the weight of the *Samurai* sword.

As early as 1914 Japan had violated Chinese neutrality by landing troops in the area around Kiaochow, which Germany had leased from China in 1898. On January 18, 1915, Tokyo presented President Yuan of China with a list of Twenty-One Demands significantly written on War Office stationery watermarked with machine guns and battleships. The aim—to transform China into a Japanese protectorate. Washington vigorously protested the arrogant action, whereupon Japan withdrew most of the demands. The Twenty-One Demands had been only "wishes."

Ogden Nash later caught the spirit in two lines:

How courteous is the Japanese;
He always says "Excuse it, please!"

At the Washington Conference, held after World War I from November 1921 to February 1922, Japan, along with the United States, Great Britain, France, Italy, the Netherlands, Belgium, Portugal, and China, signed the Nine-Power Treaty guaranteeing the territorial integrity and independence of China and establishing the principle of the Open Door, allowing any nation to trade in China. All signatories, including Japan, agreed "not to support any agreements by their respective nationals with each other designed to create spheres of influence or to provide for the enjoyment of mutually exclusive opportunities in designated parts of Chinese territories."

To fiery Japanese militarists any promises, treaties, or agreements were so much dry rot, the impedimenta of decadent Western liberal democracy. As the European situation became increasingly chaotic, Tokyo's war lords saw their golden opportunity. They would take advantage of China's military weakness and embark upon a drive to world power.

The first goal was Manchuria—a half-million square miles of potential wealth. Here could be found adequate supplies to feed the Japanese war machine—iron, coal, copper, lead, manganese, oil shale, even gold. Strategically, Manchuria would provide Japan with a much-needed buffer state vis-à-vis Soviet Russia. Further, surplus Japanese population could be siphoned off to Manchuria.

The foundations for expansion had already been laid. As early as 1919 the *Dai Nippon Kokusuikai* (Greater Japan National Essence Society) had gathered a million members. The *Kokuhonsha* (National Foundation Society) was already at work preaching a xenophobic nationalism.

Along with words went the weapon of political assassination. On November 14, 1930, Prime Minister Yuko Hamaguchi was shot by a young fanatic. In March 1931 the *Sakurakai* (Cherry Society), organized among field-grade officers, attempted a military *coup d'état* under General Kuniaki Koiso, the so-called Tiger of Korea. The plot failed by mere accident when senior officers refused to go along with the conspirators.

In early September 1931 came the first of the China "incidents." Several Chinese bandits exploded a small bomb on the tracks of the Japanese-controlled South Manchurian Railway. The damage was small. A train passed over the spot a few hours later, and subsequent investigation revealed that the destroyed section of track measured exactly 31 inches!

But this was enough for Tokyo's hotheads. This was "banditry" and it would be settled by force. On September 18, 1931, without consulting the legal Reijiro Wakasuki cabinet, Japanese forces struck, and quickly captured Mukden with its barracks of 10,000 Chinese soldiers.

China immediately appealed to the League of Nations. The League responded by organizing the Lytton Commission to investigate the situation on the spot, submit a report, and recommend action.

Meanwhile, the Japanese went ahead with the conquest of all Manchuria, which they completed in January 1932. Then the Nipponese forces turned southward to strike at the heart of the Chinese dragon. Here they were opposed by the Chinese Nineteenth Route Army, which took orders from the radical Leftist government at Canton, not from the Nationalists at Nanking. A five-week battle cost 23,000 lives, 20,000 of them Chinese.

The soil of China was drenched in blood. Infuriated by Chinese resistance, the Japanese destroyed and pillaged the countryside, slaughtered prisoners of war, raped women and killed children. It was an exercise in cruelty that shocked the world. But this was only the beginning.

Tokyo was catapulted into a frenzy of joy. The militarists had been right after all! The most popular tune of the day, "The Song of the Human Bomb," celebrated the feat of three Nipponese soldiers who had blasted a stretch of barbed wire by hurling themselves into it with bombs fastened to their bodies.

Japan transformed Manchuria into the "independent" Republic of Manchukuo (State of Manchu) on March 9, 1932. From his comfortable retirement the last heir of the Manchu emperors, Henry Pu-yi, was imported by Tokyo to become, at first, regent and then, two years later, Emperor Kang Teh. Patriotic Chinese responded by organizing a boycott which cut Japanese exports to China by 94 per cent.

Despairing of receiving any help from the League, the Chinese, on May 31, 1932, accepted an armistice at Tangku. The Japanese were to return north of the Great Wall, while a demilitarized zone would be maintained between the wall and a line drawn roughly from Tientsin to Peiping.

The final Lytton Report, published on October 4, 1932, condemned Japan as an aggressor, but proposed a settlement by which Japan's special interests in Manchuria would be recognized. Shortly afterward Japan withdrew from the League.

During these depressing negotiations, Great Britain, occupied with the economic depression, refused to support sanctions against Japan. Only in Washington was there determined opposition to Japan's bull-in-the-china-shop behavior. On January 7, 1932, Secretary of State Henry L. Stimson proclaimed what was thereafter called the Stimson Doctrine: "[The United States does not] intend to recognize any treaty or agreement... which may impair... the sovereignty, the independence, or the territorial and administrative integrity of the Republic of China... or 'the Open Door policy.'"

Thirty-one inches of track blown up at Mukden had brought Tokyo's militarists the prize of Manchuria. But this was also the first preliminary bout of World War II, the beginning of a chain reaction leading to the explosion over Hiroshima in 1945. The system laboriously built up at Versailles, for which millions of lives had been sacrificed in World War I, had received the first of a series of lethal blows. Others were to follow.

PROLOGUE II: THE CONQUEST OF ETHIOPIA: 1935-1936

From a balcony on the Piazza Venezia in the heart of Rome came another strident denunciation of the status quo, another contribution to the compounding series of aggressions leading to World War II.

With jaw thrust forward, arm waving, eyes flashing, Mussolini hurled his challenge: "We will imitate to the letter those who are lecturing us. They have shown us that when it was a question of creating an empire or of defending it, they never took into account at all the opinion of the world."

The Mediterranean, the *Duce* thundered, was Italy's sea. He would revive the greatness of ancient Imperial Rome and "the glory of Italian arms." He would not be thwarted by the weakling democracies! The world would learn to respect Italian bayonets!

Mussolini's Fascist totalitarian state had met with some success after the March on Rome in October 1922. Enough that Winston Churchill, who should have known better, professed to see some positive aspects in it. The Italian dictator had driven the Communists from the streets of Italy, subjugating them and others with bowel-wrecking doses of castor oil. He had almost eliminated unemployment by the simple expedient of placing the jobless in the army. He had improved industry and agriculture, reclaimed land from the marshes, and inaugurated hydroelectric power stations. He had strengthened the armed forces. And miracle of miracles—it was claimed that he had even made the Italian trains run on time!

But the world depression hit with the impact of a sledge hammer on a country already weakened by economic misfortune and not yet revived—if indeed it could be revived—by the "miracles" of Fascism. Italians began to question their leader's ability to provide for them. Since there was little Mussolini could do to improve the domestic economy, he turned to foreign adventure to keep his Fascist regime in high gear. He had to find some outlet to demonstrate the power of Italian arms.

Sometimes called Abyssinia, Ethiopia, a semicivilized country of 450,000 square miles, was one of the oldest Christian nations in the world. Lying in northeast Africa, it was bounded by Italian Eritrea, French Somaliland, and British Somaliland on the northeast, Italian Somaliland on the southeast, British Kenya on the south, and Anglo-Egyptian Sudan on the west. Its economy was primarily agricultural, but its resources were potentially great, including deposits of gold, silver, manganese, tin, copper, asbestos, potash, sulphur, mica, and some coal and iron. All this was invaluable for the Italian war machine.

There was also an old score to settle. Menelik II, who had ascended the throne in 1889, had brought all Ethiopia under a single rule. Italy wanted Ethiopia even then. Her five-year attempt at conquest culminated on March 1, 1896, in a disastrous massacre of Italians at Adowa. Since then Ethiopia had moved in the orbit of Great Britain and France, both of which had signed a treaty in 1906 guaranteeing its independence.

The fulminating *Duce* demanded that the slate be wiped clean of this humiliation of Italian arms. He would have vengeance for Adowa.

Emperor Haile Selassie, born July 17, 1891, was a well-educated, sensitive, dignified little man, who had served as regent since 1916, as king from 1928 on, and as emperor from 1930 on, after the death of Empress Zauditu. His was a tremendous task—to unify and modernize his backward country despite ethnic and religious differences, the tradition of separatism among local chieftains (*rases*), slavery, and widespread ignorance and superstition. In 1923 Ethiopia was accepted as a member of the League of Nations after Haile Selassie promised to suppress slavery and the slave trade in his kingdom.

For the ambitious Mussolini the still-unresolved issue of slavery was made to order. He would "carry the torch of civilization into Ethiopia," bring an end to the slave trade, acquire riches for his war machine, and turn the attention of grumbling Italians away from their domestic problems. It was certain to be a pushover.

Further—enticing thought—Mussolini would keep pace in the scramble for world power. The *Fuehrer* himself was not at all opposed to the idea of Italian penetration in Africa. The *Duce*'s contemplated adventure would divert him from Europe, area of Hitler's own *Lebensraum.* Furthermore, Mussolini would soon find himself in difficulties with both Britain and France, which had guaranteed Ethiopian independence. Such was the pattern of loyalty among the dictators.

The technique of trumped-up border incidents had already been used effectively by the Japanese at Mukden in 1931. On December 5, 1934, came another in Africa. This time there was a clash between the escort of an Anglo-Ethiopian boundary commission and Italian troops at the Walwal oasis near the border between British and Italian Somaliland. A hundred Ethiopians and 30 Italian troops were killed. Haile Selassie claimed that the oasis was 60 miles inside the Ethiopian frontier and that it had been illegally occupied by the Italians.

The *Duce* thundered wrath. He demanded an apology, an indemnity of 200,000 Ethiopian talers, and punishment for the responsible Ethiopian officers. Haile Selassie refused and brought the matter to the League. Negotiations were slow and painful. Mussolini, with bellicose speeches, began sending reinforcements to Africa. He warned appeasers that he would not be satisfied "by the cession of a couple of deserts, one of salt, one of stone."

The expected assault came on October 3, 1935. Italian forces based in Eritrea streamed across the borders of Ethiopia. Mussolini shouted: "A solemn hour has struck for Italy!"

Its Covenant directly violated, the League acted with unaccustomed speed. At Geneva, a week after the invasion, 50 out of 54 nations in the Assembly (only Italy, Hungary, Austria, and Albania dissented), agreed with the Council that Italy had gone to war in defiance of its obligations. In accordance with Article 16 of the Covenant, League members were instructed not to sell goods to Italy, not to allow the flotation of loans for her, nor to purchase any goods from her (economic sanctions).

There was world-wide outrage at Mussolini's action, and praise for the League's decision as a victory for collective security.

The key issue was oil. But the League had not included oil among its economic sanctions. An embargo on this vital material would have brought Italy to her knees within a few months. Britain and France were reluctant to extend the embargo to oil, from fear that such a vital throttling might force Italy to fight them, literally for survival. The League itself declined to take the crucial step. Furthermore, four nonmembers of the League—the United States, Germany, Japan, and Brazil—were not compelled to honor the sanctions clause. Nor did President Franklin D. Roosevelt's neutrality legislation cover such essential war materials as oil, scrap iron, and steel. Apparently, Mussolini was going to get all the oil, as well as other war matériel, he needed.

At this point appeared two "peacemakers" who managed to worsen an already critical situation. Sir Samuel Hoare, the British foreign secretary, had no doubts that Britain could defeat Italy if necessary, but he was not convinced that Ethiopia was worth a major war. The Fascist-minded French premier, Pierre Laval, sympathetic to Mussolini's drive in Africa as long as it did not disturb French interests there, agreed with Hoare.

The notorious Hoare-Laval Plan was born in December 1935. Italy would be granted outright some 60,000 square miles of Ethiopia along the borders of Italian Somaliland and Eritrea, in return for a corridor of about 3,000 square miles connecting Ethiopia with the port of Assab in Eritrea. In addition, Italy would obtain 160,000 square miles as "a zone of economic expansion and settlement."

In effect, the two generous statesmen would hand over some two thirds of Ethiopian territory as an appeasing gift to the grasping *Duce*.

Hoare and Laval had pledged each other to secrecy. But the wily Frenchman immediately announced the plan to the press. A howl of indignation penetrated England's fog. To give the *Duce* on a silver platter a victory that he had not yet won was more than the sensitive British public, press, and Parliament could stomach.

Astonished by this reception, Hoare resigned, to be succeeded as foreign secretary by Anthony Eden. Laval survived the storm and managed to hold on to his office for another few weeks.

For the Ethiopian campaign Mussolini committed ten divisions, 250,000 troops, plus another 150,000 African natives. Also a huge mass of war matériel, including tanks, motorized units, and planes, all under the competent leadership of Commander in Chief Marshal Pietro Badoglio.

Pitted against this huge force were 35,000 poorly armed Ethiopians and a hastily raised militia of untrained tribesmen bearing old muskets, swords, and spears. They had no tanks, no artillery, no planes. The Ethiopian defense was incompetent and mismanaged. Instead of retiring to the mountains and resorting to guerrilla warfare to tie down the invaders, the rival Ethiopian *rases*, vying among themselves for the honor of first crack at the Italians, hurled masses of men against steel in suicidal frontal attacks.

It was a slaughter.

The war was fought with incredible barbarities on both sides, neither of which paid the slightest attention to the Geneva Conventions. The Ethiopians, overconfident and certain of another Adowa, tortured and beheaded any Italians they could capture. The Italians replied in kind, adding the refinement of mustard gas.

The horrible results as recounted by an eyewitness: "Some were blinded. When others saw the burns spreading upon their arms and legs and felt the increasing pain, whose source and end they could not understand and for whose cure they had no medicine, [they] broke and fled. The Ethiopian forces jerked suddenly backward, horrified, and scattered."

For Mussolini's son, Vittorio, it was "wonderful sport" to bomb Ethiopian cavalry from the safety of a pursuit plane. His reaction was recorded by the press throughout the world: "One group of horsemen gave me the impression of a budding rose unfolding as the bomb fell in their midst and blew them up. It was exceptionally good fun."

The Italians directed two massive spearheads against Ethiopia, one from Eritrea on the north and the other from the Somaliland front. The northern forces began an advance along a huge escarpment, avoiding the ravines on one side and the wastelands on the other, and speedily occupied Adowa.

Contrary to foreign assumptions that the Italians were reluctant fighters, Mussolini's legions moved with dispatch and smoothness. The southern spearhead, under command of Marshal Rodolfo Graziani, moved cautiously, seeking to win over to his side the dissident Ethiopian *rases*.

One Ethiopian stronghold after another fell to the Italians during the opening months of 1936. Haile Selassie himself was defeated at Lake Ashangi in April. On May 2, he escaped from Djibouti in French Somaliland on a British warship and headed for Europe. Addis Ababa, the capital, fell three days later. The campaign ended when Graziani's columns moving up from the south made contact with Badoglio's army in the north.

On May 9, 1936, King Victor Emmanuel III was proclaimed Emperor of Ethiopia. Within a month Mussolini organized Ethiopia, Eritrea, and Somaliland into Italian East Africa, with Marshal Pietro Badoglio as viceroy. In 1937 the *Duce* himself took over the position of Minister for Italian Africa.

The deposed monarch, Haile Selassie, pathetic but still dignified, went to Geneva to plead his case. He stood patiently before the Assembly of the League of Nations, while his efforts to speak were drowned out by shouting Italian newsmen.

It was a prophetic speech:

> I, Haile Selassie I, Emperor of Ethiopia, am here today to claim that justice [which] is due to my people, and the assistance promised to it eight months ago by 52 nations which asserted that an act of aggression had been committed....
>
> It is my duty to inform the governments assembled in Geneva ... of the deadly peril which threatens them....
>
> [It is] a question of the trust placed in states in international treaties [and] of the value of promises made to small states that their integrity and their independence shall be respected and assured. In a word, it is international morality that is at stake....

> Apart from the Kingdom of God, there is not on this earth any nation that is higher than any other. . . .
>
> God and history will remember your judgment.

The League did nothing. Its judgment was indeed remembered by history. On July 16, 1936, after just 241 days of "the first great noble experiment of the coercive powers," the League put an end to sanctions against Italy. Thereby it publicly declared its impotence.

It was another humiliating defeat for the cause of collective security.

In seven months the triumphant Mussolini had won Ethiopia—at the cost of 2,813 Italian troops, 1,593 native soldiers, and 453 Italian workers killed.

Italy remained in the League for another year and a half, and then, following the example of Japan, submitted her resignation. The *Duce* had dealt a body blow not only to the League but also to the entire European theory of international law and the principle of coöperation among nations. Worst of all, he had demonstrated by his assault on Ethiopia that, in the 1930's, might made right. And he had provided Hitler with new ammunition for the unilateral denunciation of treaties.

Another milestone was passed on the road to World War II.

DRESS REHEARSAL: THE SPANISH CIVIL WAR, 1936-1939

From the ulcerous sores of Manchuria and Ethiopia the scene of the developing drama of aggression shifted to the Iberian peninsula. Here the Spanish Civil War, beginning as a local uprising, was soon transformed into a dress rehearsal for World War II.

Twentieth-century Spain was cursed with a politically unstable government, incompetent, corrupt, inefficient. This was a country of men without land. A few thousand grandees owned more than half the land, some one and a half million peasants owned only two per cent, and two million peons owned no land at all. Illiteracy and poverty were widespread in this backward country, a political and cultural anachronism.

World War I brought Spain a measure of prosperity, but after 1919 the country experienced renewed economic distress, political chaos, social unrest, military weakness. In 1921 came military disaster in Spanish Morocco, where a Spanish army of 20,000 men was decimated by guerrilla Riffs under Abd-el-Krim. On September 23, 1923, Captain General Primo de Rivera seized the government and, with the acquiescence of Alfonso XIII, established a military dictatorship under the slogan "Country, Religion, Monarchy." When the world depression hit an already weakened Spain, Rivera resigned on January 28, 1930, and fled to France. Alfonso followed him into exile the following April.

Wild rejoicing greeted the new middle-class Republic, its banner of red, yellow, and purple stripes, and its first president, Niceto Alcalá Zamora. The new government pushed through a series of harsh laws directed against monarchy, army, Church, and aristocracy, all pillars of the Old Regime. Similar steps had been taken in the French Revolution a century and a half earlier. In twentieth-century Spain they were greeted with a riot of dissension —strikes, demonstrations, assassinations. Nearly everyone had a grievance of one kind or another against the new Republic—royalists, Spanish officers, landlords, businessmen, the papacy.

Criticism from the Right was matched by resentment from the Left. When the elections of 1933 showed a victory for the Rightist parties—the revolutionary Left—Anarchists, Syndicalists, and Communists, all of whom believed that the government was too lukewarm in its treatment of the monarchy, aristocracy, Church, and army—was aroused to fury.

When the government, now controlled by the Right, sought to suspend the new land laws and anticlerical legislation, there followed another wave of uprisings, seizure of estates by the peasants, burning of churches, street battles, general strikes, martial law, and political assassinations.

Meanwhile, Fascism was taking firm root. A Fascist group, called the Falange, or Phalanx, was founded by Antonio Primo de Rivera, son of the former dictator. Assistance came at once from Mussolini and Hitler, both interested in fishing in troubled Spanish waters. As early as 1934, Mussolini promised Spanish monarchists that he would send them 20,000 rifles, 20,000 hand grenades, 200 machine guns, and a million and a half pesetas. Spanish generals found sympathetic attention at the German Embassy in Madrid and at German consulates throughout Spain.

The "wave of the future," originating in Rome and Berlin, was beginning to splash its muddy waters over republican Spain.

The reaction to increasing Fascism was the formation of a Popular Front, consisting of middle-class liberals and such Leftists as Radical Republicans, Socialists, Syndicalists, Anarchists, and Communists. Opposed to the Popular Front were monarchists, clericals, Conservative Republicans, and Fascists. In the general elections of 1936 the Popular Front obtained 260 seats in the Cortes, the opposition 213 seats. Once again there was terror from both Right and Left. Orderly government seemed impossible.

What about the army? In this explosive situation the attitude of the military was of critical consequence. "The ambition of every Spanish general," commented the Spanish publicist Salvador de Madariaga, "is to save his country by becoming her ruler."

July 13, 1936. The signal for revolt came when a monarchist leader was murdered. The disgusted generals decided to take matters into their own hands.

Scheduled for the role of generalissimo and dictator was General José Sanjurjo, "Lion of the Riffs," former commander of the Civil Guard. In August 1932, Sanjurjo had led an unsuccessful revolt against the Azaña government. He was captured and sentenced to death, but the judgment had been commuted to life imprisonment. From his exile in Portugal, to which he had escaped, Sanjurjo took a plane from Lisbon to Seville, where he planned to summon the army to overthrow the hated Republic. But the plane crashed and the chosen Man on Horseback was killed.

Second choice for the role was a short, stocky officer who had become a general at the age of 32. Francisco Franco, born December 14, 1892, had organized the Spanish Foreign Legion in Morocco and had worked with French Marshal Henri Pétain to suppress a native revolt led by the ubiquitous Abd-el-Krim. In 1934, Franco was appointed chief of the general staff, a position from which he was dismissed in 1936 when the Popular Front came to power. He was made military governor of the Canary Islands, a post amounting to virtual exile.

Upon the accidental death of Sanjurjo, Franco, disguised as an Arab, flew from the Canary Islands to Morocco in a British plane chartered by some wealthy Spaniards. Here he announced himself as "Commander in Chief of the Fighting Forces in Morocco" and called upon the mainland army to join him. At this time the Spanish army numbered 100,000 men, of whom 15,000 were officers. There was an amazing supply of general officers, a peculiar Spanish custom—195 generals on the active list and another 437 in reserve.

Franco gave the command for revolt on July 17, 1936. Most of the generals and their men immediately fell into line. But the navy and air force remained loyal to the government. Well disciplined and well armed, the Rebels captured Toledo on September 27, 1936.

Thus began three years of sanguinary civil war, with no bounds to the bitterness, the inhumanity, the cruelty. Both sides were guilty of gruesome tortures and atrocities, the worst since the Spanish Inquisition. The Rebel slogan: "Franco, yes! Communism, no!" The Loyalist motto: "*No Pasarán!*" —"They Shall Not Pass!"

The Fascist-minded Rebels, with ten times as many planes, tanks, and heavy artillery pieces as their opponents, speedily conquered the western half of the country. They besieged Madrid in 1937. Steadily advancing against stubborn opposition, Franco was in control of two thirds of Spain by May 1938. He extended his lines to the Mediterranean between Barcelona and Valencia, thus cutting the Loyalist armies in two.

On March 28, 1938, Madrid surrendered, after 32 months of bloody conflict, leaving Franco in control of all Spain.

But this was only half the story. What began as just another Spanish army revolt was soon transformed into an international conflict between the Fascist dictatorships of Italy and Germany on the one side and the Communist dictatorship of Soviet Russia on the other. For both Mussolini and Hitler the Spanish Civil War was a heaven-sent opportunity to extend the range of Fascist power, strike a blow at Communism, and test their troops and weapons under combat conditions.

On July 28, 1936, at the beginning of the conflict, when it appeared that Franco would be unable to transfer his Moors and Foreign Legionnaires from Morocco to the mainland, Hitler had sent 30 Junker transport planes to do the ferrying. This was token aid, to be followed by a flood of munitions, ammunition, guns, and troops, planes, pilots, and mechanics, all sent with the blessings of Hitler and Mussolini.

By 1937, Franco had 30,000 Italian troops and 12,000 Germans under his command; eventually there were at least 100,000 Italian soldiers in Spain. The papacy gave its spiritual support to Franco, "that loyal son of the Church." When Italian troops left for Spain, they received the papal blessing before they left Italian soil.

Soviet Russia, too, was involved. "The liberation of Spain from the yoke of Spanish reaction," Stalin said, "is not the private concern of Spaniards, but the concern of all advanced and progressive humanity." "Advanced and progressive" Russia had sent technicians and matériel into Spain as early as November 1936, and soon began to pour more men and supplies into the country, though not at the same rate as Germany and Italy. Communists trained in Moscow, including Tito of Yugoslavia and Dimitrov of Bulgaria, went to Spain to fight against Fascism.

From all over the world sympathizers with the Spanish Republic enlisted in international brigades to fight in Spain, including an "Abraham Lincoln Brigade" recruited in the United States. Such liberals as George Orwell enlisted in the Loyalist cause in the belief that Franco had to be defeated to halt the march of Fascism. It was rumored that some liberals facing Franco's lines were shot in the back, which, if true, amounts to a curious commentary on the Communist conception of coöperation.

What about France, Great Britain, and the United States?

Although theoretically in sympathy with the Spanish Republic, they sealed its doom by insisting upon strict neutrality. As soon as the civil war began in Spain, a nonintervention agreement was concluded among England, France, Italy, and Germany. The British and French adhered to the agreement; Mussolini and Hitler paid no attention to it. Under international law the legitimate Spanish Republican government had a legal right to purchase arms from the Western democracies, but the latter choked off the desperately needed supplies on the ground that the democracies might become involved in an unwanted war. The *Fuehrer* and the *Duce* had no such compunctions.

Premier Léon Blum, head of the French Popular Front government, studiously avoided arousing Rightist opposition in France by refraining from any visible encouragement of the Spanish Loyalists. Britain supported the international boycott of Republican Spain as a means of staying out of the war. The United States enforced its own neutrality legislation, although this was a civil war to which the American neutrality laws did not apply. President Roosevelt appealed to American citizens not to sell arms to either side. But German and Italian planes that bombed Spanish cities were powered by American gasoline.

Rescued by German and Italian intervention, Franco established a totalitarian dictatorship. He restored the privileges of the Old Regime to army, clergy, and upper classes. He put a halt to the breakup of great estates, returned their land to the grandees, restored sequestered properties to the Church, and reinstituted clerical control over education. He abolished labor unions and forbade strikes. He commenced a reign of terror against all political opponents, arresting somewhere between 500,000 and 2,000,000 political prisoners and subjecting many of them to barbarous punishment. Thousands of refugees escaped to France, where, a serious problem for French authorities, they languished in concentration camps.

On April 7, 1939, Franco announced his adherence to the Anti-Comintern Pact, directed against Communism, implying the addition of Madrid to the Rome-Berlin Axis. (In 1936 Mussolini and Hitler had joined forces in an "Axis," so called because all the European states were supposed to revolve around the two great powers of Germany and Italy, as a wheel revolves around its axle.) On September 27, 1940, Japan formally adhered to the union, now called the Rome-Berlin-Tokyo Axis, or the "Pact of Steel."

After eight years of precarious survival, the Spanish Republic was no more. A million lives had been lost in this fratricidal struggle. Spain was left with a heritage of bitterness, disillusionment, and poverty.

For Hitler and Mussolini it was another great victory against the West, another tightening of the Axis grip on the Mediterranean. For Britain and France it was a grave setback, a blow to their prestige, an omen of worse things to come. For Stalin the events in Spain indicated that possibly his own aggressive interests could be served better by collaborating, at least for the time being, with the Axis rather than with the weak-kneed Western democracies. For the thinning ranks of believers in the League of Nations it was another demonstration of impotence in the face of aggression.

For millions of men it was the harbinger of death to come in a much greater struggle.

THE "CHINA INCIDENT," 1937

Baron General Sadao Araki, Japanese war minister and leader of the war party, called it *Kodo*. The doctrine of *Kodo*, meaning "Way of the Emperor," was a mysterious substance that would expand *Shinto*, the "Way of the Gods," all over the world.

The implication of these doctrines, plus additional behavior codes, was that Japan was the only divine nation with a divine mission to rule the world. The supreme virtue of every Japanese was to fight to victory or death. Surrender was an intolerable dishonor. For example, *Bushido*, the code of chivalry originating in medieval Japan, punished disobedience with death.

"It is a veritable measure of Providence," said Araki in March 1933, "that the Manchurian trouble has arisen. It is an alarm bell for the awakening of the Japanese people. If the nation is rekindled with the same great spirit in which the country was founded, the time will come when all the nations of the world will look up to our *Kodo*. Every impediment to it [must] be brushed aside—even by the sword."

It was clear by now that Manchuria was only the first step. There were explicit warnings. The American ambassador in Tokyo, Joseph C. Grew, reported to Secretary of State Cordell Hull as early as December 1934:

> [The aim of the militarists] is to obtain trade control and eventually predominant influence in China, the Philippines, the Straits Settlements, Siam, and the Dutch East Indies, the Maritime Provinces and Vladivostok... pausing intermittently to consolidate and then continuing as soon as the intervening obstacles can be overcome by diplomacy or force.... We would be reprehensibly somnolent if we were to trust to the security of treaty restraints or international comity to safeguard our own interests, or, indeed, our own property.

Washington began to lend a hand to the hard-pressed Chinese. Through the Reconstruction Finance Corporation the Roosevelt Administration in 1934 extended a $50,000,000 credit to China. American warplanes were sold to the Chinese, and a retired American officer hired to supervise combat pilot training.

This was only token assistance but it aroused deep resentment in the Nipponese war party. Some of the more fanatical hotheads turned to direct action. The first targets of their scorn were at home—the *Zaibatsu*, the businessmen who at this time wanted expansion *without* war, and the *Genro*, or Elder Statesmen, who also wanted expansion but at a moderate pace.

Again the approved weapon was assassination. The killers had no personal animosity against their victims, who, after all, were Japanese. But the fanatics believed that they were ridding the sacred Emperor of nefarious influences and so performing the sacred function of clearing the way for Japan's glorious future. It was too bad, they said, but the procrastinators had to go. The killers would show their personal sorrow by burning incense beside the dead bodies.

In March 1932 a group of army cadets, navy officers, and civilians, members of a secret patriotic society known as the Blood Brotherhood League, assassinated Baron Dan Takuma, chairman of the board of the gigantic Mitsui corporation. On May 15, 1932, the conspirators killed the aged Tsuyoshi Inukai, last of the parliamentary prime ministers. Both the *Zaibatsu* and the *Genro* now became understandingly reluctant to speak out against the saber-rattling militarists.

When, in the elections of February 20, 1936, the Japanese voters returned a majority of liberals to Parliament, the infuriated terrorists decided to strike not only at the moderates but also at members of the Imperial household itself. Six days later, 1,400 young officers and enlisted men seized central Tokyo. Their attempt to assassinate Prime Minister Admiral Keisuke Okada was foiled when his brother-in-law attracted the fire of the killers. They succeeded in slaying Admiral Makoto Saito, the former prime minister who had become Lord Privy Seal to the Emperor; General Watanabe, the inspector-general of military education; and Finance Minister Korekiyo Takahashi.

These were vicious murders. Ambassador Grew revealed some grim details: "Viscountess Saito placed herself in front of her husband [and] said, 'Kill me instead; my husband cannot be spared by the country,' and actually put her hand on the mouth of the machine gun until her wounds forced her aside. . . . Mrs. Watanabe embraced her husband so firmly that the assassins had to force the gun underneath her body."

Meanwhile, Japan was mending her foreign fences. She signed the Anti-Comintern Pact (directed against international communism) with Germany on November 25, 1936. The next June, General Hideki Tojo, then chief of staff of the Kwantung Army, warned Tokyo that Japan must strike at China before Chiang Kai-shek, the Nationalist leader, and the Communists could get together. Another decade and China would be too strong to be conquered.

On July 7, 1937, the curtain was rung up again in China, this time at the Marco Polo bridge near the village of Lukouchiao, 20 miles west of Peiping. The Japanese commander in the area reported that the Chinese had attacked his troops first. "We came to teach the Chinese a lesson. They are getting too bold."

The Japanese war minister agreed: "China must be chastised for her insincerity." The cabinet of Prince Fumimaro Konoye, the Japanese premier, urged caution. But it was too late.

Japanese troops streamed into North China. One after another the leading cities of China were overrun: Nanking (December 1937), the great port of Canton (October 1938), and Hankow (October 1938). The Chinese, led by Chiang Kai-shek, resisted fiercely, but to no avail. By the end of 1938 organized Chinese resistance had virtually ceased.

It was the 1931 incident all over again. Once again came the shocking reports of a Japanese orgy of murder, torture, rape, looting, and pillaging.

The civilian death toll from bombing, famine, and pestilence was appalling. Drunken soldiers bayoneted helpless Chinese. Mothers had to watch their babies beheaded and then submit to raping.

Nevertheless, the Japanese found it impossible to stamp out Chinese nationalism. As they advanced deeper into the interior, they found their thin lines vulnerable to guerrilla attacks. What had started out as a grand conquest degenerated into a stalemate. Japanese manpower and matériel were being drained away. There was life in the dragon. One Chinese general put it this way: "If we can keep this up, China can exterminate the population of Japan while losing 105,000,000 men. We shall have 300,000,000 left."

In the midst of this inconclusive combat came a specific warning to the United States. Japanese planes, on December 12, 1937, bombed and sank the American gunboat *Panay* on the Yangtze River below Nanking as it was escorting three privately owned American tankers. Tokyo, aware that nearly all its scrap iron and steel, as well as two thirds of its oil, came from the United States, quickly apologized for the "carelessness" of its pilots, and paid an indemnity of $2,214,000.

The Japanese did not halt their push in China. In February 1939 they seized the island of Hainan, thereby obtaining a base from which to attack French Indo-China. In May 1939, carefully avoiding a direct attack, they blockaded the British settlement in Tientsin. They knew that any outright assault on Tientsin, Shanghai, or Amoy, port cities in which the Western powers had important concessions, might be regarded as an act of war.

Washington and London sent protesting notes against Tokyo's unilateral repudiation of the Nine-Power Treaty. But the Japanese had no intention of backing down. Once again they had ignored treaties signed by Japan and the Western powers. Recognizing that no European power nor the United States wanted war in the Far East, the Japanese simply went ahead.

Eventually the Japanese-Chinese war was merged into the greater conflict of World War II.

THE FALL OF AUSTRIA, 1938

On the first page of *Mein Kampf*, Adolf Hitler told of his birth at Braunau am Inn, a village in Austria near the German border. "The union [of Germany and Austria] seemed to us youngsters to be the task of a lifetime." And further: "The same blood belongs in a common Reich."

Hitler in 1938 achieved his aim of uniting the two countries. In the process he took a giant step toward World War II.

Austria emerged from World War I reduced from a once-great empire to a small, landlocked republic of 6,500,000 people, one third of whom lived in Vienna. She was bankrupt, her currency worthless, her trade shattered, her people starving. She was rehabilitated to some extent by the League of Nations, which floated a loan for her and stabilized her currency. Politically, she was torn into two opposing camps, the Reds, dominantly Socialists, representing workers and intellectuals, and the Blacks, representing the Fascist, agricultural, and clerical interests. Externally, she was the pawn of a diplomatic game between Germany, Italy, and France.

The Treaty of St. Germain between the victorious Allies and Austria specifically forbade *Anschluss* (union) between Austria and Germany. At first Mussolini opposed the union because he wanted no powerful Germany as his neighbor to create an irredentist movement among the German-speaking inhabitants of South Tyrol. France looked with a jaundiced eye on *Anschluss*, which would weaken the pro-French Little Entente of Czechoslovakia, Yugoslavia, and Rumania.

The rise of the Nazis in Germany was accompanied by a similar movement in Austria. As soon as he came to power in 1933, Hitler began to encourage the Austrian Nazis to attack the regime of Chancellor Engelbert Dollfuss. All the elements of Nazi terror were there—street fights, bombs, shooting of civilians, attacks on officials. Dollfuss, convinced by Mussolini that only a Fascist Austria could withstand Hitler, suspended the republican constitution and established a corporative state with himself as dictator.

This was a highly unsatisfactory state of affairs for the *Fuehrer*. In late July 1934 the Austrian Nazis, with the complicity of their German brethren, struck in an attempted *coup d'état*. Dollfuss was assassinated. Denied medical attention, he was allowed to bleed slowly to death.

There was a burst of official anger in Rome. Mussolini mobilized his army at the Austrian border. Hitler halted, blandly disavowing any aggressive intentions.

Mollified, but still suspicious, Mussolini in January 1935 concluded a pact with France, by which both Italy and France agreed to support an independent Austria. As a *quid pro quo*, France secretly agreed to allow the *Duce* a free hand in Ethiopia. At the Stresa Conference, held in Italy in 1935 to end the bickering among Italy, France, and Britain, Mussolini joined France and Britain in a significant declaration: "The three Powers, the object of whose policy is the collective maintenance of peace within the framework of the League of Nations, find themselves in complete agreement in opposing, by all practicable means, any unilateral repudiation of treaties which may endanger the peace of Europe, and will act in close and cordial collaboration for this purpose."

Even Hitler seemed to be sweetly reasonable. In July 1936 he promised to respect the sovereignty of Austria. But the *Fuehrer* had no intention of allowing the Austrian fish to escape his hook. Elsewhere he was winning one astonishing diplomatic triumph after another. In January 1935, after a plebiscite ordered at Versailles after World War I, the people of the Saar voted 90 per cent for their return to Germany. On this occasion it was an honest vote, supervised by the League of Nations. On March 15, 1935, Hitler created the *Luftwaffe*, the German air force, and the next day repudiated all treaty limitations on armaments and established universal military service. The *Fuehrer* was thumbing his nose at the victors of World War I and getting away with it.

A year later, on March 7, 1936, Hitler ordered his troops into the demilitarized zone of the Rhineland, whose status had been guaranteed by the Treaty of Versailles and the Locarno Pact. There was no reaction from the Western powers. Hitler's generals had been so uncertain of French reaction that they had issued to the advancing troops two sets of orders, one commanding them to retire if the French moved.

The true situation was revealed at the Nuremberg war crimes trial, when Field Marshal Wilhelm Keitel said: "Why, the French could have shoved us out like that, and I would not have been a bit surprised!"

And Paul Schmidt, a Foreign Office interpreter, reported Hitler's worried remarks at the time: "The 48 hours after the march into the Rhineland were the most nerve-racking (*aufregendste*) in my whole life. If the French had marched into the Rhineland, then we should have had to retreat with ignominy, for we had not the military resources at our disposal for even a feeble resistance."

Aggression was in Hitler's mind, but first he needed complete control of the armed forces, many of whose top officers, opposed any adventurous policies. The generals had hoped to dominate the Nazi regime, but they were soon disabused. On August 2, 1934, Hitler had required all his officers to take an oath of personal fealty:

> *I swear before God to give my unconditional obedience to Adolf Hitler,* Fuehrer *of the Reich of the German People, Supreme Commander of the* Wehrmacht, *and I pledge my word as a brave soldier to observe this oath always, even at peril of my life.*

This was the unequivocal oath taken by all the generals and administered by them to their inferiors. It was a psychological weapon destined to lead to moral frustrations at the top level of the military hierarchy.

Even this was not enough for the suspicious *Fuehrer*. To accomplish unchallenged control of the military, he shrewdly turned to his own advantage two scandals in the army, one concerned with prostitution and the other with homosexuality.

On January 11, 1938, the *Fuehrer* graciously attended the wedding ceremony of Field Marshal Werner von Blomberg, his *Reichswehr* minister, and a certain Fräulein Erna Gruhn. It soon developed that the *Reichswehr* minister had taken as wife a lady who had a police record indicating experience in the world's oldest profession. It was scarcely a social status to be equated with the honor of the proud German officers' corps.

The *Fuehrer* went into a rage when he heard the rumors. Believing that he had been deceived deliberately, Hitler denounced von Blomberg, forbade him to wear his uniform, and ordered him not to set foot again in the Chancellery. Von Blomberg, outwardly unconcerned by the scandal and apparently still loyal to his wife, went to Capri on his honeymoon.

Von Blomberg's logical replacement was Colonel General Freiherr Werner von Fritsch, commander in chief of the army. But knifing in the back was common in this gangster milieu. Hermann Goering, who wanted the post of *Reichswehr* minister for himself, submitted to Hitler some "evidence" obtained from Heinrich Himmler indicating that von Fritsch was a notorious homosexual.

Von Fritsch, denying the accusation, demanded an inquiry by a military tribunal. Later he was exonerated but not reinstated. Upon the outbreak of war the crushed general asked for assignment to the Polish front, where, it was said, in obedience to the Prussian military code, he sought a soldier's death on the battlefield. He was killed in action just before the Polish campaign came to an end in the last week of September 1939. According to newspapermen, he had insisted upon serving in front-line observation posts, where few general officers were seen. He was on a major reconnaissance attack when a bullet from a burst of heavy machine-gun fire struck him in the thigh and severed an artery. A young officer with him desperately sought to bind up the wound but the general whispered: "Please do not bother!" In two minutes he was dead.

Scandal or no scandal, Hitler got what he wanted. On February 3, 1938, he announced the retirement of the top echelon of the *Reichswehr* and he himself took over supreme command. He set up a new top military authority, the O.K.W., *Oberkommando der Wehrmacht*, High Command of the Armed Forces. The highest posts went to Colonel General Wilhelm Keitel (promptly labeled by irreverent Germans as "*Lakaitel*"—from the German word *Lakai*—lackey or flunkey, because of his subservience to Hitler), and to the then Colonel General Alfred Jodl. Keitel served as Chief of the High Command, Jodl as Chief of Operations Staff from 1938 to 1945. Both were executed as war criminals at Nuremberg in 1946.

As a reward for his trumped-up charges against von Fritsch, the rotund Goering was given, not as he had hoped, the post of *Reichswehr* minister (Hitler reserved that for himself), but the highly satisfying title of Field Marshal. Goering could now add a jeweled baton to his burgeoning collection of decorations. (That same baton now reposes quietly in a glass case at the military museum at West Point.)

Thus, by taking advantage of two nasty but welcome situations, Hitler at one stroke attained a triple goal: control of the armed forces, dismissal of recalcitrant officers who had opposed him, and the acquisition of a cabal of toadies willing to follow him down the path of aggression. Machiavelli himself could have devised no more effective pattern of conduct.

Meanwhile, the pot was kept boiling inside Austria. Artur von Seyss-Inquart, a traitorous lawyer, leader of the Austrian Nazis, worked zealously on Hitler's behalf. Several days after the purge of the generals, Franz von Papen, the German ambassador in Vienna, visited Chancellor Kurt von Schuschnigg, who had succeeded Dollfuss and intended to continue the policies of his predecessor. Von Papen invited von Schuschnigg to visit Berchtesgaden. The *Fuehrer*, said von Papen, wanted to give him further assurance of his good will and help remove some misunderstandings and frictions that had clouded Austro-German relations.

"You can trust Adolf Hitler's immaculate word of honor," said von Papen. It was a classic piece of mendacity!

The unsuspecting Schuschnigg arrived at Hitler's mountain eyrie unprepared for the kind of reception he got. The *Fuehrer*, putting on the anger act, declined to rise when Schuschnigg entered the room, refused to shake hands with him, and pointedly neglected to address the Austrian chancellor by his title.

It was an agonizing interview. Hitler screamed at his startled visitor: "How have you dared all these years to suppress and to torture *my* people—*my* German people in Austria? Now your hour has come. God has made me *Fuehrer* and ruler of every man and woman of German blood in every country on earth."

Hitler's diatribe was a deliberate blend of piety, boasting, bluff, and menace. He had a historic mission, he said, and he would fulfill that mission because Providence had destined him to do so. "I believe in this mission; it is my life. And I believe in God; I am a religious man. . . . I have achieved everything that I set out to do and have become perhaps the greatest German in history."

Hitler set Schuschnigg straight on the *Duce:* "I know you are thinking of Mussolini. I am filled with admiration for him and his work, and I stand for a far-reaching, firmly based solidarity between Fascism and National Socialism. But the military efficiency of the Italians is quite another question. Don't be under any illusions in that respect. If Mussolini wants to help you, which, incidentally, he certainly will not, then one hundred thousand troops will be sufficient not only to push Italy back from the Brenner Pass but to chase the Italian army as far as Naples."

The *Fuehrer* pointed dramatically to the table. Spread out there were mobilization plans for the invasion of Austria.

Then came the demands: Any Austrian might accept the creed of National Socialism; Austrian Nazis were to be allowed to engage in "legal activity"; all imprisoned Nazis, including the assassins of Dollfuss, were to be released; Seyss-Inquart was to be appointed minister of security; and the Austrian army would immediately accept for duty a hundred officers of the German army.

After ten hours of this browbeating, Schuschnigg agreed to most of the demands. He added that he would have to clear several points with President Wilhelm Miklas. Hitler then promised that he would guarantee Austrian independence in a speech before the Reichstag. But he would keep the German army mobilized on the German frontier pending full acceptance of his demands within three days.

From the German press came glowing reports. The meeting between Hitler and Schuschnigg had been "informal." A "happy peace" had been agreed upon.

Events then moved with startling rapidity. Hitler delivered a three-hour *Reichstag* address denouncing the League of Nations, the democracies in general, Great Britain and Anthony Eden in particular. The 10,000,000 Germans living on the borders of the Third Reich, he thundered, "must no longer be denied the general right of self-determination simply because they are Germans."

Schuschnigg tried to make one last stand. Encouraged by evidence of a new-found popularity among his own people, he announced on March 9, 1938, that he would hold a national plebiscite on the following Sunday on the question of Austrian independence. He was certain that this was the best thing to do under the circumstances.

Hitler was enraged. Here was this pipsqueak of an Austrian using the *Fuehrer*'s own favorite device! From the *Fuehrer* came another ultimatum: Withdraw the contemplated plebiscite or there would be immediate invasion.

Schuschnigg, his nerves shattered, capitulated. He broadcast a farewell message: "President Miklas asks me to tell the people that we have yielded to force, since we are not prepared even in this terrible situation to shed German blood. We have ordered the Austrian army not to resist and to retire. I take leave of the Austrian people with a German farewell and greeting: 'God protect Austria!' " Schuschnigg then collapsed, weeping.

The turncoat Seyss-Inquart was appointed chancellor at midnight on March 11, 1938. The first units of German troops were already across the border. By noon of the next day Vienna was occupied.

In his *Betrayal in Central Europe*, G. E. R. Geyde told how the Nazis took over Vienna:

> The brown flood was sweeping through the streets. It was an indescribable witches' sabbath—storm troopers . . . were marching side by side with police

> turncoats, men and women shrieking or crying hysterically the name of their leader, embracing the police and dragging them along in the swirling stream of humanity, motor-lorries filled with storm troopers clutching their long-concealed weapons... men and women leaping, shouting, and dancing... the air filled with a pandemonium of sound in which intermingled screams of "Down with the Jews! *Heil Hitler! Sieg Heil!* Perish the Jews!... Down with the Catholics! *Ein Volk, ein Reich, ein Fuehrer!*"

Thus came the end of Austrian independence. Hitler had added more than 6,500,000 citizens to his Greater Reich. Now he had access to Austria's iron and timber for his expanding army. Strategically, he had won the key to the Danubian communications system, established geographical contact with Italy, and surrounded Czechoslovakia, the Bohemian bastion. Above all he had demonstrated once again that he could defy with impunity the system of Versailles.

Now Hitler announced to the world that he wanted no more territorial acquisitions in Europe. The claim was to become increasingly monotonous—and mendacious.

There was no serious opposition from abroad. Mussolini bowed to the inevitable. From Hitler he received an ingratiating wire: "Mussolini, I shall never forget you for this! You have my eternal gratitude!"

The *Duce* replied: "My attitude is determined by the friendship between our two countries, which is consecrated in the Axis."

Parisians were bewildered and astonished by the course of events. At this critical moment France was once again in the midst of another cabinet crisis. On March 10, 1938, the day before the Nazi invasion of Austria, Camille Chautemps resigned as premier, to be succeeded by Léon Blum at the head of a watered-down version of the Popular Front.

For the British, too, it was a painful surprise. Lord Halifax could say only: "Horrible! Horrible! I never thought they would do it!" Winston Churchill cast his scorn on his government and called for a Franco-British-Russian Grand Alliance to stop Hitler. When, on March 18, 1938, the Soviet Union called for collective action against an obvious aggression, Prime Minister Neville Chamberlain replied weakly that he did not want to establish "an exclusive group of nations which would be inimical to the prospects of peace in Europe." The union of Germany and Austria, he told the House of Commons, could have been prevented only by resorting to war, and Britain was not ready for war. He intimated that the best way of handling a painful situation was through talks with the dictators.

The shadows of appeasement were already falling on Europe.

Meanwhile, Austria was left to the delicate mercies of the *Gestapo*, the Nazi secret police. President Miklas resigned. Schuschnigg was imprisoned and for 17 months was forced to undergo humiliating indignities. Hitler proclaimed Austria a new *Land* (province) in the Third Reich to be called Ostmark, with Seyss-Inquart as his regent. He ordered plebiscites in both Austria (99.75 per cent "*Ja*") and in Germany (99.08 per cent "*Ja*") to confirm the *Anschluss*.

The shape of things to come in Nazi Austria was revealed by a ceremonial visit of Heinrich Himmler and Rudolf Hess to place wreaths on the grave of Otto Planetta, the assassin of Dollfuss. At least 30,000 arrests were made within a few days. Jews, Socialists, Catholics, anyone merely suspected of anti-Nazi sentiments, all went to the *Gestapo* torture chambers. Jewish homes and shops were plundered. Squads of Nazi ruffians rounded up Jews and made them clean the streets on their hands and knees. Thousands fled to the safety of Switzerland and Czechoslovakia before the borders were shut down. Many Viennese Jews committed suicide.

Thus continued the melancholy chronology of aggression—from Mukden to Walwal to Madrid to Marco Polo Bridge to Vienna. Next on the agenda was Munich and then the plunge to disaster.

CHAPTER 3

The Immediate Causes

A historical revision of unique scope has been entrusted to us by the Creator.

—Adolf Hitler to the *Reichstag*, 1939

Germany is isolating herself and doing it most successfully and completely. Our people were not backward in recognizing some of the mistakes of the Versailles treaty that required remedying, but each time during these last years that there seemed a chance of making progress in understanding, the German government has taken action which has made that progress impossible.

—Lord Halifax, 1939

Disappointed, disillusioned men, uprooted and unbalanced, driven by half-conscious fears and gusts of passion, frantically seek a new rallying point and new attachments. . . . The more pathological the situation the less important is the intrinsic worth of the idol. His feet may be of clay and his face a blank: it is the frenzy of the worshippers which imparts to him meaning and power.

—Sir Lewis Namier, *Vanished Supremacies*, 1958

BOMBASTES FURIOSO: ADOLF HITLER'S WAR GUILT

Allied war propagandists pinned the responsibility for World War I upon Wilhelm II, the German militarists, German industrial magnates, and the Austrian Foreign Minister Leopold von Berchtold. A few arrogant and irresponsible men, it was charged, held such power over the fate of millions that they plunged the world into war. It was said that the Great German General Staff, the ultimate power inside Germany, carefully laid the groundwork over a period of 40 years, firmly advocated aggression, and started the war in August 1914.

This conspiracy theory was quickly repudiated in the postwar era. Most historians concluded that responsibility should be distributed equally among the Great Powers: The war was the end-product of unresolved economic clashes, diplomatic squabbles and intrigues, national rivalries, sword-rattling, and a psychologically unsound conception of security.

David Lloyd George, prime minister of Great Britain from 1916 to 1922, put it in these words: "The more one reads of the memoirs and books written in the various countries of what happened before August 1, 1914, the more one realizes that no one at the head of affairs quite meant war. It was something into which they glided, or rather staggered and stumbled."

Just how much can the will of one man or a small group of men influence the course of history? In the two World Wars a careful distinction must be made between the remote causes—the general overall climate of opinion—and the immediate causes—or the triggering of the explosion. Individuals can have only a limited influence on the remote causes, but their actions can be decisive in the direct background.

As for the immediate origin of World War II, the blame for starting it rests squarely upon Adolf Hitler and Nazi Germany.

Hitler's continued aggressions provided the sparks for the world conflagration. His secret reports captured during the war make it abundantly clear that his aim was to conquer Europe and ultimately control the world. Obsessed with the idea that the superior German "race" was destined to rule mankind, he was ready to smash his way to world power.

"For the good of the German people," Hitler said in his *Secret Conversations*, "we must wish for a war every 15 or 20 years. An army whose sole purpose is to preserve peace leads only to playing at soldiers—compare Sweden and Switzerland." At the same time, Hitler, one of the most consummate liars in history, was informing the world: "I am not crazy enough to want a war. The German people have but one wish—to be happy in their own way and to be left in peace."

Adolf Hitler was the central figure in world history from 1933 to 1945. He was the evil genius who helped bring about a profound transformation in the history of Germany as well as the entire world. What kind of human being was this little man with the Charlie Chaplin mustache?

The character seems to defy all rational analysis. It is becoming increasingly clear that an understanding of the mind of Hitler cannot be achieved without the assistance of the psychologist, the psychiatrist, and the psychoanalyst. The fears, anxieties, hatreds, and hostilities, the neuroses and psychoses of this frenzied man were to affect the lives of all other human beings on earth, from the remotest Hebrides to the South Sea Islands.

H. R. Trevor-Roper, the brilliant Oxford historian, caught the character:

> A terrible phenomenon, imposing indeed in its granitic harshness and yet infinitely squalid in its miscellaneous cumber—like some huge barbarian monolith, the expression of giant strength and savage genius, surrounded by a festering heap of refuse—old tins and dead vermin, ashes and eggshells and ordure—the intellectual *detritus* of centuries.

André François-Poncet, observant French ambassador to Germany until November 1938, described Hitler in his eagle's nest at Berchtesgaden:

> He is changeable, dissembling, full of contradictions, uncertain. The same man with the debonair aspect, with a real fondness for the beauties of nature, who discussed reasonable ideas on European politics round the tea table, is also capable of the worst frenzies, of the wildest exaltations and the most delirious ambitions.

Hitler could melt into maudlin sentimentality in the presence of children or animals or while listening to the music of Richard Wagner, and then within a few moments fly into a rage while ordering his opponents or fancied enemies to be put to death. He was the clinical specimen of the *Teppichfresser*, the man who, when his will is thwarted, reverts to infantilism, foams at the mouth, falls to the floor, and begins to chew the carpet in rage.

The basic character is a familiar one in every German *Bierstube*, although he is not limited to Germany. Self-educated, shrewd, arrogant, he holds forth on every subject under the sun, from food to world politics, from music to military tactics. Pompous and omniscient, he refuses to discuss his ideas but, instead, issues dicta and ukases. He mistakes his intuitions for scientific fact. He knows all the answers to the meaning of history. He lives in a curious dream world and dismisses as insane anyone who disagrees with his judgments and disconnected monologs. He is incapable of understanding moral values, but he is a mass psychologist of diabolical genius. He is, above all, a pathological liar.

Adolf Hitler's unguarded, all-night, off-the-record table talks were taken down in shorthand by his party associates. The quality of mind of this egocentric, hate-laden man may be judged from these typical quotations:

Racial Nonsense: "It's our duty continually to rouse the forces that slumber in our people's blood."

Self-glorification: "There was a time when one could say that there was only one Prussian in Europe and that he lived in Rome.... There was a second Prussian. He lived in Munich, and was myself."

Delusions of Grandeur: "When one enters the Reich Chancellery, one should have the feeling that he is visiting the master of the world."

Psychotic Suspicions: "I never met an Englishman who didn't say that Churchill was off his head."

Hostility: "There's nobody more stupid than the Americans.... I'll never believe the American soldier can fight like a hero."

More clues to the quality of Hitler's mind are found in *Mein Kampf*, his own story of his life and his blueprint for Germany's future. Some of the world's worst literature is paraphrased in the author's gutter style, including Arthur de Gobineau's *Essay on the Inequality of Human Races*, Houston Stewart Chamberlain's *Foundations of the Nineteenth Century*, the spurious *Protocols of the Elders of Zion*, and an ill-digested assortment of interpretations of Nietzsche, Schopenhauer, Haushofer, Frederick the Great, and Carlyle. A hodgepodge of history and fantasy, written in atrocious German, frankly Machiavellian ("Success is the only earthly judge of right and wrong"), *Mein Kampf* became the Bible of the National Socialist movement. After Hitler took power, it was published in gigantic editions, and all party members and civil servants were required to buy it. By 1939 it had sold more than 5,000,000 copies, thereby becoming one of the leading best sellers of all time.

Hitler in power fashioned a totalitarian state. He destroyed all opposing political parties; dissolved the trade unions and confiscated their property and funds; abrogated all individual rights; and coördinated every phase of national life, including Church, press, education, and army. A shocked world witnessed a barbarous campaign "to protect German honor against the Jews." German citizens were imbued with ideas of glorification of the *Fuehrer*, fanatical worship of the Fatherland, intolerant racial prejudice, blind obedience, hatred for all enemies, and zest for war. The economic life of the nation was brought into harmony with the Nazi principle of self-sufficiency.

Hitler could not have implemented his foreign policy without war. His aims were clear: to regain Germany's prestige as a World Power, to bring about a restoration of her former colonies, to promote Pan-Germanism ("One Reich, One People, One *Fuehrer*"), to revive the *Drang nach Osten* (Drive to the East), and to end the "shame of Versailles." The statesmen of the Weimar Republic had done everything in their power to circumvent the Treaty of Versailles, but they drew the line at any attempt to change its territorial provisions. They were sensible enough to know that this could not be done without war, which they were not willing to risk.

Hitler had no such compunctions. Here, too, the record is clear. At a secret meeting held on November 5, 1937, he outlined to his military leaders the practical steps for undertaking aggression against other countries. The minutes of the meeting, as recorded by Hitler's adjutant, a Colonel Hossbach, reveal how the *Fuehrer* planned to wage war two years before the outbreak of hostilities:

> The *Fuehrer* then stated: "The aim of German policy is the security and the preservation of the *Volk* and its propagation. This is consequently a problem of space.... The question for Germany is where the greatest possible conquest can be made at lowest cost.
>
> "German politics must reckon with its two hateful enemies, England and France, to whom a strong German colossus in the center of Europe would be intolerable. Both these states would oppose a further reinforcement of Germany, both in Europe and overseas, and in this opposition they would have the support of all parties. . . ."
>
> If the *Fuehrer* is still living, then it will be his irrevocable decision to solve the German space problem no later than 1943-45. . . . For the improvement of our military political position it must be our first aim, in every case of entanglement by war, to conquer Czechoslovakia and Austria simultaneously, in order to remove any threat from the flanks in case of a possible advance westward. . . . Once Czechoslovakia is conquered—and a mutual frontier of Germany-Hungary is obtained—then a neutral attitude by Poland in a German-French conflict could be more easily relied upon. Our agreements with Poland remain valid only as long as Germany's strength remains unshakable....
>
> The *Fuehrer* believes personally, that in all probability England and perhaps also France, have already silently written off Czechoslovakia.... Without England's support it would also not be necessary to take into consideration a march by France through Holland and Belgium.... Naturally, we should in every case have to secure our frontier during the operation of our attacks against Czechoslovakia and Austria....
>
> Military preparation by Russia must be countered by the speed of our operations; it is a question whether this needs to be taken into consideration at all, in view of Japan's attitude. . . .
>
> Field Marshal von Blomberg and Colonel General von Fritsch, in giving their estimate of the situation, repeatedly pointed out that we should not run the risk that England and France become our enemies....
>
> In view of the information given by the *Fuehrer*, Colonel General Goering considered it imperative to think of a reduction of our military undertaking in Spain....

Even more damning were the confidential remarks made by Hitler to his generals in a conference held on August 22, 1939, a day before the signing of the Moscow Pact and just a week before the invasion of Poland. The *Fuehrer's* words on this occasion were revealed after the war at the Nuremberg trials of the major war criminals:

No one will ever again have the confidence of the whole German people as I have. There will probably never again in the future be a man with more authority. My existence is, therefore, a factor of great value....

Our enemies have men who are below average, no personalities, no masters, no men of action....

For us it is easy to make decisions. We have nothing to lose; we have everything to gain....

All these favorable circumstances will no longer prevail in two or three years....

Therefore conflict is better now. I am afraid that at the last minute some Schweinehund *(pig-dog) will make a proposal for mediation....*

I shall give a propagandist reason for starting the war, no matter whether it is plausible or not. The victor will not be asked, later on, whether he told the truth or not. In starting and waging a war, it is not the Right that matters, but Victory.

No sophistry, no doublespeak, no extenuating circumstances can argue away Hitler's words in this documented passage. This was a barefaced plan of aggression. Adolf Hitler hotly desired war. He worked zealously to bring it about.

It was a tragedy for Germany and the world. This irrational fanatic, this vulgarian vandal, this combination of mediocrity and senseless brutality, could find enough support to become the leader of the Germans and then come within inches of being the master of all Europe. Originally a bit skeptical about this strange Austrian, the German people became more and more convinced of his infallibility as he delivered one crippling blow after another to the system of Versailles. Politically illiterate Germans had little understanding of what was happening to them before the bar of humanity.

In choosing to follow Hitler and his collection of assorted gangsters, the German people must share in the responsibility for the cataclysm of 1939. The contention that Nazism was a bolt out of the heavens, a "catastrophe" that was suddenly visited upon the unsuspecting German people, is as inaccurate as it is untenable. It owed much of its character to a national tradition of discipline and obedience, ground into the Germans by a combination of worship of the State (inspired by the philosopher Georg Wilhelm Friedrich Hegel), Prussian intransigence, and militarism. The Germans who were shocked and amazed by the excesses of Hitlerism never understood that it was the logical outcome of a long and dangerous historical tradition. The mixture of nationalism, romanticism, and historicism (the concept that history is valuable only when used politically) led to a descent into vulgarization and bestiality such as the world has seldom witnessed.

The German officers' corps too, must be blamed in part for the blood bath. Many excuses have been made for the generals, but these cannot wipe out the stains of guilt. The generals were not a coldly efficient camarilla bent on world conquest, but, engulfed in a stodgy professionalism, they failed to check the terrible offenses of Adolf Hitler and in time became his willing collaborators. They were accessories to Hitler's crimes. Their justification was that a soldier honors his oath and carries out his orders.

But where was the boasted sense of Prussian moral discipline? One German officer, General Ludwig Beck, chief of the General Staff from 1935 to 1938, recognized as early as July 1938 that there was still time to repel Nazism and safeguard "the old Prussian virtues": "History will indict the highest leaders of the *Wehrmacht* with blood-guilt if they do not act in accordance with expert and statesmanlike knowledge and assurance. Their duty of soldierly obedience finds its limit when their knowledge, conscience, and responsibility forbid the execution of an order."

These were wise words. But the officers' conscience and sense of responsibility had disappeared in the presence of the almighty *Fuehrer*.

COUP DE THÉÂTRE: MUNICH

The Czechs watched with dismay as the Nazi conqueror submerged Austria in the Third Reich. Now that their southern neighbor was annexed to Germany, it was obvious that they were next in line. And so it was. In his moves against Czechoslovakia the *Fuehrer* proved himself a master of timing; he gave his opponents the least possible opportunity for successful countermoves. It was an amazing demonstration in the political sphere of increasing Nazi strength and the weakness of the democracies.

The Republic of Czechoslovakia, one of the more satisfying products of World War I, had been created in 1919 out of the three former provinces of Bohemia, Moravia, and Austrian Silesia, plus the two former Hungarian provinces of Slovakia and Ruthenia. Capably led by Thomas Masaryk and Eduard Beneš, it became a model of democratic discipline, the most advanced liberal state between the Rhine and Soviet Russia. There were only 30 Communists in the Czech parliament of 300. [In this economically most prosperous of the Succession States were located most of the old Austro-Hungarian industries, including the famed Skoda steel and armaments works.] The vigorous new nation negotiated many fruitful commercial treaties with other countries. It seemed to be destined for a long and prosperous life.

But lying in the Danubian basin, where nationalities were inextricably mixed, Czechoslovakia from the days of its formation was plagued by minority problems. In a population of 14,000,000 there were in addition to Czechs and Slovaks some 3,300,000 Germans, 760,000 Magyars, 480,000 Ruthenians, as well as many Poles and Jews.

The German-speaking residents in former Bohemia, especially the Sudetenland, formed a clamorous minority. Before World War I they regarded themselves as the "superior stock" of the area and looked down upon the

Czechs and all other Slavs as inferiors. After the war, they complained of discrimination against them in administrative positions, pointed out that government funds went mostly to the Czech areas, and insisted that they were in economic distress. There was, indeed, some ground for the latter complaint. The Sudeten Germans had lost heavily by subscribing to Austrian war loans, by speculating in German marks before the 1923 inflation, and by the depression of the early thirties. Among the nearly million unemployed in the little country, over one half were Germans.

Yet, from the beginning, the German minority in Czechoslovakia had been treated more generously and with more consideration than any other minority in the postwar world. The government undertook far-reaching concessions to satisfy them. It honored the Austrian loans to 75 per cent, certainly a generous concession. It proposed a law guaranteeing German-speaking citizens administrative offices in proportion to their numbers in the total population. It gave the Germans full parliamentary representation and equal educational opportunities; actually there were more German secondary schools in Czechoslovakia in proportion to the population than there were schools for the Czechs.

But still the Germans complained. To a rapacious Hitler the situation was made to order. A glance at the map of Central Europe in 1939 will reveal the reasons for Hitler's enthusiasm. Now that Austria had been absorbed into the Third Reich, Germany's appearance on the map gave the impression of a giant wolf's-head, its mouth surrounding western Czechoslovakia, its top canine tooth in Silesia, the bottom tooth in northern Austria. If the wolf closed its mouth, Czechoslovakia would be swallowed.

In 1935 Konrad Henlein, leader of the Sudeten Nazis, and his *Sudetendeutsche Partei*, intransigent and pro-Hitler, captured 60 per cent of the German vote. The party demanded "full liberty for Germans to proclaim their Germanism and their adhesion to the ideology of Germans"—that is, Aryan racialism, hatred of democracy, and blind obedience to a national *Fuehrer*.

In February 1938, Hitler outlined to the German Reichstag, in piteous terms, the "horrible" conditions of his German brethren in Czechoslovakia. The *Trommler* had begun his drum-beating. He announced to the world that the poor Sudeten Germans could rely upon Germany's protection against their Czech oppressors. The controlled Nazi press hysterically denounced Czech "atrocities" against the German minority in Czechoslovakia.

In May 1938, two Germans were killed in a frontier incident. To Hitler these two unfortunate dead Germans were worth their weight in diamonds. Putting on a display of fury, he dispatched troops to the border.

The Czechs, who had the finest army of any of the smaller European countries—180,000 standing, 1,200,000 trained reserves, and first-rate mechanization—were not cowed. They promptly rushed 400,000 troops to the border opposite Germany. France announced that she would honor her obligations to Czechoslovakia, Britain agreed to support France, and Soviet Russia indicated that she would follow suit. Faced with this formidable opposition, Hitler became more reasonable—for the time being—and withdrew his troops.

The incident meant lost prestige for the *Fuehrer*. But he had no intention of being thwarted in Czechoslovakia. At a secret meeting convened at the artillery school of Jüterbog on May 30, 1938, Hitler told his generals: "It is my unalterable will to smash (*zerschlagen*) Czechoslovakia by military action in the near future." He issued a general order fixing October 1, 1938, as the deadline for putting "Operation Green" into effect.

Throughout the summer of 1938 the reptile Nazi press continued to attack the Czechs. Puppet Henlein's followers used the weapons of agitation, terror, threats, and bluffs inside the country. All this was done to allow Hitler "honorably" to rush to the aid of the German minority. As a goal he wanted the Czechs to renounce all their foreign military alliances and to agree to establish a Nazi state inside Czechoslovakia.

Meanwhile, in the Western democracies, there was hardening of the diplomatic arteries. The feeble behavior of Britain and France during these critical months seemed to many to be incredible. The British prime minister, Neville Chamberlain, with the consent of France, sent Lord Runciman to Prague as a kind of unofficial outside arbitrator. Urged on by Runciman, the Czechs offered generous concessions to Henlein. They would agree to a division of Czechoslovakia into cantons on the Swiss model. "All nationalities would share proportionately in all state offices and in state enterprises, monopolies, institutions, and other organizations." At the same time they promised a large grant of money to the Sudeten Germans for economic relief.

On September 12, 1938, in a violent speech, Hitler insisted that he intended to come instantly to the aid of the oppressed Sudeten Germans. And, for the benefit of Britain and France, he announced that the most impregnable defenses ever constructed by man were being rushed to completion on Germany's western frontiers.

The next day there were further prearranged incidents, whereupon President Beneš proclaimed martial law.

At this point, with the crisis precipitated, Chamberlain joined the actors. He flew from London to Berchtesgaden, the first of three humiliating trips by air to appease the Nazi dictator.

Hitler brusquely informed Chamberlain that the Sudeten territory must be included at once in the Third Reich or there would be general war. Hitler would agree only to give Chamberlain time to consult with his ministers. Chamberlain flew back to London where he conferred with his own divided cabinet and with French Premier Édouard Daladier and Foreign Minister Georges Bonnet.

On September 20, 1938, Great Britain and France, without consulting Prague, notified Czechoslovakia that she must "deliver the districts mainly inhabited by the Sudeten Germans" to Hitler in order to prevent a general European war. If she agreed, her future independence would be guaranteed. The Czechoslovak cabinet decided to yield; then it resigned.

Once more Chamberlain flew to Germany, this time to Godesberg, to inform Hitler of the capitulation and to work out the details.

At Godesberg, Chamberlain found Hitler in a towering rage. The *Fuehrer* made more demands, more severe than those he had made at Berchtesgaden. He shouted that the Czechs had until October 1 to meet them or the German army would march. Germany was going to take what belonged to her and no one was going to stop her!

Astonished, Chamberlain could scarcely speak. Hitler gave him a map on which he had indicated what parts of Czechoslovakia he was going to take immediately. Chamberlain took the map, agreed to present it to the Czechs without recommendation, and flew back home.

Again there were British conferences with the French. The Czechs indignantly rejected the Godesberg ultimatum.

At this point Mussolini got into the act. He proposed a four-power conference to discuss the deadlock. Chamberlain, by this time desperate, grasped at the straw.

On September 26, 1938, three days before the scheduled meeting at Munich, Hitler spoke at the Sportpalast in Berlin. He assured Chamberlain and the world that, if the Sudeten problem were solved, Germany would present no more territorial claims in Europe.

"We have now come to the last problem which has to be solved and will be solved," Hitler shouted. "It is the last territorial demand that I have to make in Europe. In 1919, 3,500,000 Germans were torn away from their compatriots by a company of mad statesmen. The Czech state originated in a huge lie and the name of the liar is Beneš."

At this moment, reported *The New York Times*, "Herr Hitler's voice rose to a harsh scream as he pronounced the name of the Czech president. The *Heils* from the audience reached a frantic pitch."

Chamberlain accepted the call to Munich, and for the third time made the trip to Germany. It was an extraordinary spectacle—the head of the British government journeying to Germany, literally to beg for peace. "Even if it should fail," he said, "I should still say it was right to attempt it. For the only alternative is war."

At the Munich talks, to which no Czechs were invited, Chamberlain and Daladier accepted all of Hitler's demands. It was agreed that the German army should move into Czechoslovakia on October 1, 1938, that an international commission should be set up to supervise plebiscites in all the areas in which the German population was not in the majority, and that the four powers—Germany, Italy, France, and Great Britain—would guarantee the borders of Czechoslovakia. The Czechs were required to leave behind in the regions annexed by Hitler all goods and materials, especially munitions. At the same time Great Britain and Germany signed a treaty of friendship.

Thus, Czechoslovakia was sold down the river by the powers that had created her and had been expected to protect her.

Chamberlain, now having Hitler's promise that he would make no further territorial claims in Europe, flew home to receive a wild ovation. "I believe," he said, "it is peace for our time."

Hitler's word was worth exactly nothing. Having acquired a third of the country and nearly a third of its population, he brought forth new demands. First, the Czechs must allow him to construct a military highway across the country. Then he demanded the right to decide on the disposal of Slovakia and Ruthenia, naming himself as arbiter as to how much land was to be ceded to Hungary and Poland.

Emil Hácha, then president of the Czechoslovak Republic, protested. He was summoned to Berlin. There Hitler put on another demonstration of tantrums. The Czech president was browbeaten until he was compelled, on March 15, 1939, to sign a treaty which turned his country into a German protectorate. Hitler proclaimed himself the "Protector of Bohemia and Moravia." He also "accepted" the Protectorate of Slovakia. Simultaneously, the German army entered Prague. Czechoslovakia ceased to exist.

Thus at Munich four men in four hours signed away the peace of Europe. The news at first brought a reaction of tremendous relief throughout the world. Had not a world war been avoided? But then came the sober aftermath: It soon became obvious that appeasing the Nazi *Fuehrer* was as intelligent as surreptitiously handing out funds to a blackmailer.

The central figure in the uproar was Neville Chamberlain. He was depicted as a craven and futile man who had allowed himself to be bluffed by Hitler. John Bull, it was said, had been transformed into a nonresistant Quaker.

Others in Britain hailed Chamberlain as a hero. Recently a British historian, P. K. Kemp, sought to erase the image of two decades ago:

> The prime minister, Mr. Neville Chamberlain, asked for a report from the chiefs of staff on the military implications of an alliance with France and other European states to resist by force any German attempt to attack Czechoslovakia. Their reply was categorical. They stated, without making any qualifications, that the country was not ready for war.

This was, it was said, the true background of Munich. Chamberlain had to avert war at all costs until his rearmament program could begin to bear fruit. He was placed in a position from which there was no escape. He had to gain time—that above all, above national prestige, national honor, the obloquy of future generations. His overriding duty was to gain time.

On the other side, there were some embarrassing questions. Peace at any price? Peace over the prostrate body of Czechoslovakia? Peace without honor? Peace—or just the beginning of a terrific world crisis? Was it reasonable, just, or logical to purchase peace at the expense of others? And how long would the uneasy peace last?

One thing was certain after the fall of Czechoslovakia. If Hitler were not stopped, all eastern Europe would fall quickly to his voracious Third Reich. And then—what about France, and Britain, and the British colonies?

As on so many other occasions, Winston Churchill was among the first to see the consequences. He went straight to the heart of the matter:

> I will begin by saying what everybody would like to ignore or forget but which must nevertheless be stated, namely, that we have sustained a total and unmitigated defeat, and that France has suffered even more than we have.... And do not suppose that this is the end. This is only the beginning of the reckoning. This is only the first sip, the first foretaste of a bitter cup which will be proffered to us year by year unless, by a supreme recovery of moral health and martial vigor, we arise again and take our stand for freedom as in the olden time.

International tensions rose steadily. This was diplomatic frustration at its worst. Hitler had already chosen the road of conquest, while Chamberlain strove desperately to strengthen an alliance system to stop the Nazi *Fuehrer* in both east and west. The British prime minister issued a series of warnings and signed stronger pledges than Britain had ever made in peacetime. Without the coöperation of Moscow—the absent coalition member whose presence could have contained Hitler—it was a hopeless task.

The drift to war had the relentless momentum of Greek tragedy. No one seemed able to do anything to head off the impending catastrophe.

Munich had proved to Hitler's cocksure satisfaction that Britain and France, decadent nations of democratic shopkeepers, would not fight. Next stop,. Warsaw—and "Tomorrow the World."

BARGAIN CYNICAL: THE HITLER-STALIN PACT

The event in 1939 that jolted the world into realization that time had run out was not another Nazi assault on a small, weak nation. It was the news of the signature on August 23 of a nonaggression pact between Hitler's Germany and Stalin's Russia.

The pact provided that the two parties would not resort to war against each other, would not support any third power in the event that it attacked either signatory, would consult on all matters of common interest, and would each refrain from associating with any grouping of powers aimed at the other. A secret protocol (made public in 1948) divided Eastern Europe into eventual German and Russian spheres, and each signatory was given territorial gains in the lands lying between them.

It was astonishing, incredible! But there it was—the political bombshell of the century, the cynical, cold-blooded bargain that made it possible for Hitler to launch his war. For years there had been a war of ideologies between the hostile totalitarian states. Each had heaped fulsome abuse on the other. Hitler had pilloried and excoriated Bolshevism as the archenemy of civilization, and Stalin in turn had denounced the Nazis as Fascist beasts. Now came a surprising end to the war of words.

But from the vantage point of historical hindsight the Hitler-Stalin pact was not at all an astounding phenomenon. This was *Realpolitik*, realistic politics devoid of sentiment for both sides. The Nazi and Soviet dictators entered the partnership for mutual benefits and each intended to maintain the pact only so long as it was to his special benefit.

For Hitler the agreement was an unmixed boon. Above all it had relieved him of the fate of Wilhelm II, who had been caught between two fronts in World War I. The *Fuehrer* did not want to worry about the immediate eastern front in the event that Britain and France really came to Poland's aid. He believed that Britain and France would not fight. True, he had played up the Bolshevik menace as long as England and France had allowed him through appeasement to win victories in Spain, Austria, and Czechoslovakia. Now that he could get no further concessions from the West and now that obstacles were placed in his path, he would turn *temporarily* to Soviet Russia. He would emphatically not forget the menace of Bolshevism; later, after he had smashed the democracies, it would be easy for him to trump up charges against the Kremlin, turn on it, and smash the Bolsheviks.

Similarly, Stalin saw advantages in the pact. For years he had dreaded a combination of Britain, France, and Germany that might be directed against Soviet Russia. The British and French guarantee to fight in case Germany violated Polish independence (March 31, 1939—a courageous departure from a traditional policy and a crucial dividing line in Europe history) marked the end of appeasement and in effect offered Stalin a choice between the Western Allies and Germany. From this point on Stalin played a cat-and-mouse game with both the Allies and Germany, using one against the other. If the anti-Nazi powers would not do business with him, he would do business with Hitler. He would not allow London and Paris to channel Fascist expansion eastward. More, the Soviet Union, weakened by military purges and uncertain of the intentions of Britain and France, needed all the time she could get to complete the military industrialization envisioned by the Third Five-Year Plan.

Both Hitler and Stalin were ready for the pact. They got together and signed.

The sequence of events leading to the pact:

March 10, 1939: Stalin on foreign policy before the 18th Congress of the Bolshevik Party: He had decided "not to allow our country to be drawn into conflicts by warmongers who are accustomed to get others to pull the chestnuts out of the fire for them." There was extraordinary interest in Berlin. Was this a hint at *rapprochement*, reconciliation?

April 4: Hitler issues a top-secret directive, Case White, calling for operations against Poland. Target date—September 1. The fact that he had concluded a ten years' friendship pact with Poland in January 1934 was of small consequence to the *Fuehrer*.

April 28: Straw in the wind—Hitler in a major speech omits his usual denunciations of "Jewish Marxism" and the "subhuman monsters in the Kremlin."

May 3: Straw from Moscow—Maxim Litvinov, the Soviet foreign commissar, distinguished by his anti-German position, is suddenly relieved of his post and is succeeded by Vyacheslav Molotov.

May 20: Molotov asks for better economic and *political* relations with Germany.

May 23: At conference with his military chiefs (Goering, Keitel, Brauchitsch, Raeder, *et al.*) in the Chancellery in Berlin, Hitler said: "Danzig is not a subject of dispute. . . . We are left with the decision to attack Poland at the earliest opportunity. . . . It is not ruled out that Russia might disinterest itself in the destruction of Poland."

August 3: Hitler informs Stalin that Germany is now ready "to remold German-Russian relations."

August 10: Franco-British military commission arrives in Moscow and is treated with every courtesy. But soon it is caught in a run-around of mysterious delays, obstructions, interminable negotiations. For Stalin this is a kind of insurance in case the pact with Hitler did not materialize. More, by keeping alive negotiations with the West, Stalin could thereby force Hitler to pay a higher price for collaboration.

August 12: Stalin replies to Hitler that he is ready to "discuss by degrees" all political questions, including Poland.

August 14: Hitler, who wants no discussion by degrees, requests that Stalin receive Foreign Minister Joachim von Ribbentrop to talk over "joint territorial questions in Eastern Europe" (partition of Poland).

August 15: The German ambassador informs the Kremlin that "ideological contradictions should not prohibit reasonable coöperation of a new and friendly type."

August 16: Hitler informs the Soviet government that Germany is prepared to sign a nonaggression pact.

August 18: Ribbentrop sends wire to Moscow literally begging Stalin to receive him at once.

August 19: Stalin, having played the game long enough, decides to conclude deal with Hitler and so informs the Politburo.

August 20: Meanwhile, Hitler, distraught because there is as yet no word from Moscow, sends a personal message to Stalin asking him to see Ribbentrop at once. "The tension between Germany and Poland has become intolerable."

August 21: Stalin agrees. On receiving the good news, Hitler gives way to a hysterical outburst of joy. According to an eyewitness, Hitler began hammering on the walls with his fists, uttering inarticulate cries, and finally shouted exultantly: "I have the world in my pocket!"

August 23: Pact is signed in Moscow. Stalin proposes toast: "I know how much the German nation owes to its *Fuehrer*. I should like to drink to his health."

August 24: Ribbentrop returns to Berlin. Hitler, overjoyed, comes from Berchtesgaden to greet him as "a second Bismarck."

Apparently, the shrewd Hitler had won still another diplomatic success. Both the German and Soviet peoples, as well as their respective sympathizers abroad, were profoundly shaken by the political somersault. But this made no difference to the elated *Fuehrer*. At the very moment when the Anglo-French military mission was cooling its heels in Moscow, he had gotten the green light from Stalin to smash Poland by promising Russia a share of the spoils. He had eliminated, for the time being, the danger of war with Russia.

One thing was certain—the bottom had fallen out of Franco-British negotiations with Russia. There was consternation in London and Paris at the extent of Hitler's cynicism and Stalin's duplicity. From Neville Chamberlain came saddened but firm words: "Whatever may prove to be the nature of the German-Soviet agreement, it cannot alter Great Britain's obligations."

The Hitler-Stalin Pact achieved what Britain had wished to prevent. It destroyed Poland which had been a protective bulwark for Germany as well as Europe against Russian communist expansion. It brought the Soviet armies westward, a process started by Hitler in 1939 and carried on by him in 1941 in his aggression against Russia. As a consequence the Soviet army came to the Elbe, where it might never have come otherwise.

Part II

FUROR TEUTONICUS: HITLER'S DAYS OF GLORY

CHAPTER 4

The Issues Joined: Hitler Strikes

It has been alleged that, if His Majesty's Government had made their position more clear in 1914, the great catastrophe would have been avoided. Whether or not there is any force in that allegation, His Majesty's Government are resolved that on this occasion there shall be no such tragic misunderstanding.

—Chamberlain to Hitler, August 22, 1939

SOVIET RUSSIA VERSUS THE "GALLANT FINNS"

September 3, 1939. Millions of Britons heard Neville Chamberlain broadcast a weary message from London:

> This morning the British ambassador in Berlin handed to the German government a final note stating that unless we heard from them by 11 o'clock that they were prepared at once to withdraw their troops from Poland, a state of war would exist between us. I have to tell you now that no such undertaking has been received and that consequently this country is at war with Germany....
>
> Now [he concluded] may God bless you all and may He defend the right. For it is evil things that we shall be fighting against—brute force, bad faith, injustice, oppression, and persecution. And against them I am certain that the right will prevail.

That same day reluctant France also declared war. The entire British Commonwealth, with the exception of Eire, rallied to London.

In the United States, President Franklin D. Roosevelt spoke to a people enjoying a warm Labor Day week end:

I have said not once but many times that I have seen war and that I hate war. I say that again and again.

I hope the United States will keep out of this war. I believe that it will. And I give you assurance and reassurance that every effort of your government will be directed to that end.

As long as it remains within my power to prevent it, there will be no blackout of peace in the United States.

Events moved rapidly after the partitioning of Poland. The two partners in aggression, Hitler and Stalin, began new moves on the chessboard of power politics. Both were bound by the ten-year nonaggression pact, but there was little trust between the two dictators. Each went his separate way while keeping a wary eye fixed on the moves of the other.

For Hitler the prognosis was good. With Poland out of the way and Soviet Russia presenting no threat, at least temporarily, the *Fuehrer* could eventually concentrate his strength against the western Allies. For the time being he was relieved of that nightmare of German military history—a *Zweifrontenkrieg*. Everything was going according to the plans blueprinted in *Mein Kampf*. No one would trap the world's foremost military genius, Adolf Hitler, into a two-front war!

It was a time of decision for Stalin. True, he had foiled Anglo-French efforts to involve him in a destructive war with the Third Reich. But the swift Nazi conquest in Poland unnerved him. This was more than he had expected. There was always the possibility, too, that the unpredictable German would turn on him. As a master chess player he must always think several moves ahead of his opponent. He must strengthen his barriers in the north.

The key to the problem was in the Baltic states. In the Moscow Pact of August 23, 1939, Stalin had been careful to insist upon the inclusion of a secret protocol designating the Baltic states as a Soviet sphere of influence. The conquest of Poland now provided him with an opportunity, for which he had long been waiting, to close the doors in the Baltic region. He wanted no Sudeten problem there.

Four Baltic states were involved—Estonia, Latvia, Lithuania, and Finland. On September 29, 1939, the same day on which Molotov and von Ribbentrop signed the agreement partitioning Poland, the Soviet Union, in flat violation of previous pledges, forced Estonia to sign a treaty permitting the U.S.S.R. to establish military garrisons and naval and air bases on Estonian soil.

Shortly afterward came similar treaties with Latvia (October 5) and Lithuania (October 10). As a reward Lithuania was given Vilna and some contiguous territory.

No one doubted that these were but preliminary steps to outright annexation. "We declare," said Molotov, "that all nonsense about Sovietizing the

Baltic countries is only to the interest of our common enemy of anti-Soviet provocateurs." Thus spake Molotov.

There was success, therefore, for the Kremlin in three of the four Baltic republics. An iron belt was being forged around the eastern end of the Baltic.

But what about Finland? Although the farthest north of the Baltic states, Finland was in an important strategic position vis-à-vis the Soviet Union, and if controlled by a hostile power she would be an enormous threat to Russian security. Leningrad, with its population of 3,200,000, was only some 20 miles from the Finnish frontier. And on the Karelian Isthmus, within artillery range of Leningrad, the Finns had constructed the Mannerheim Line, a great belt of fortifications named after their commander in chief, Field Marshal Karl von Mannerheim.

First came the diplomatic byplay of threats: On October 5, 1939, the Soviet government invited Helsinki to send a negotiator to the Kremlin to discuss "certain questions of a concrete political nature." What the Russians wanted soon became clear. The Finns were to surrender a part of the Karelian Isthmus so that Leningrad would be placed outside effective artillery range. More, they were to cede to Russia land in the extreme north. The Soviet-Finnish frontier was to be demilitarized. Further, Finland was to grant the Soviet Union a 30-year lease on the port of Hangö on the Gulf of Finland for the establishment of a Soviet naval base. In return, Moscow would cede to Finland 2,134 square miles of Soviet territory along the east-central border of the republic.

The Finns, realizing their difficult position, intimated that they would be willing to yield on all demands except one. It was incompatible with their national sovereignty as well as with their neutrality to lease or sell a site on their soil for a foreign military base.

Promptly, as if by push-button control, the press in the U.S.S.R. and the Communist parrot-newspapers throughout the world opened a campaign of abuse against the Finns. How could the Finns be so obstinate in the face of reasonable, just, and fair demands? Were not the Finns aware, hinted *Pravda*, the official Soviet organ, that they might meet the fate of Poland? Headlines in the Russian newspapers screamed that the Finns were preparing to attack the Communist motherland. Since Moscow had caught cold, the New York *Daily Worker* promptly sneezed in sympathy.

The next step was predictable: Finns were accused of firing on Soviet border patrols. The Finns refused to withdraw their troops from the frontier unless the Russians did likewise. Negotiations broke down on November 13, 1939. On November 28 the Kremlin denounced the 1932 nonaggression pact with Finland. Two days later Russian planes were bombing Helsinki and Viipuri.

Soviet strategy called for a five-point invasion of Finland at north, center,

RUSSIA VS. FINLAND

and south. One force marched on Petsamo in the north. A second set out to capture the railroad connecting Kemijärvi with Tornea on the Swedish frontier. A third was to strike at Suomussalmi to cut Finland at her waist. A fourth was to strike along the shores of Lake Ladoga to outflank the Mannerheim Line. And the fifth was to hit directly at the Mannerheim Line. If everything went according to plan, Finland would be an easy conquest and the world would again be presented with a *fait accompli* before any forestalling action could be taken.

The League of Nations, however, acted with astonishing speed. Although the Kremlin sent a note to the League with the tidings that it was not at war with Finland, on December 14, 1939, the Soviet Union was ejected from the League for an action of aggression (the only state to be expelled in this manner as unworthy of membership). The Secretariat of the League authorized all member nations to send any assistance they might care to give to the embattled Finns. The rebuke had no effect on the Russians.

Meanwhile, on December 1, 1939, a Finnish "People's Government" was set up near the Soviet border by Otto Kuusinen, a Finn who had lived as an exile, mostly in the Soviet Union, for some 20 years. The Kuusinen "cabinet" proclaimed its loyalty to the U.S.S.R.

But the lionhearted Finns themselves had no sense of loyalty to Moscow. The entire world was astonished by the skill and heroism of their defense. Nothing like it had been expected. It was David against Goliath. More than 100,000 Russians moved into the little country only to be repulsed by a handful of defenders. The amazing Finns destroyed entire divisions and threw others back to the borders where they had started. They fought until further resistance spelled suicidal folly. History has recorded few braver epics than this.

What was behind the setback to the Russians? Mostly, egotism and ignorance. Across the borders streamed the first Red troops loaded down with bundles of propaganda leaflets, pennants, and banners. Others marching behind brass bands believed that they would be welcomed as "liberators from the capitalist oppressors." Seldom has an invading force been so quickly disabused of its beliefs. Inadequately trained, badly briefed, the Russians were unprepared for a long winter campaign, the 65,000 Finnish lakes, or the furious Finnish defense. Unaccountably, the Russian commanders failed to safeguard their supply lines. There was little coördination between the five invading armies which carelessly tried an enveloping maneuver on a grand scale under prohibitive weather conditions.

The Finns, on the other hand, had the advantage of interior lines. They cleverly shifted their counterattack from column to column. Heavily armed Finnish ski patrols, their white uniforms merging into the countryside, crept silently behind the enemy lines. They ambushed the invaders, dug traps for

Russian tanks, and set off dynamite blasts. Many a Russian was knifed in the Arctic dark.

An eyewitness told the story:

> The Russian debacle was ghastly.... For four miles the road and forest were strewn with the bodies of men and horses; with wrecked tanks, field kitchens, trucks, gun-carriages, maps, books, and articles of clothing. The corpses were frozen as hard as petrified wood and the color of the skin was mahogany. Some of the bodies were piled on top of each other like a heap of rubbish, covered only by a merciful blanket of snow; others were sprawled against the trees in grotesque attitudes. All were frozen in the positions in which they had died.

By the end of 1939 the Russian armies had exhausted themselves in the inconclusive fighting. Not one of the five separate Red drives had met with any success.

Stalin had not dreamed of such fierce resistance. And there was a provoking dilemma. How could he deal with these recalcitrant Finns in a "minor engagement" without revealing to the world the latest Soviet devices and weapons?

But Stalin had to take the chance. He placed General Grigori Stern, an energetic commander, in charge of operations. He moved in his best troops, his finest artillery, his most modern equipment. He abandoned the attack through the snowbound northern wilderness and ordered a direct assault on the Mannerheim Line. He would mass superior Russian manpower, artillery, and planes for an attack on the Finns at their strongest point.

World attention was riveted on the unfolding drama in the little Baltic republic. From many countries came foodstuffs, medical supplies, even implements of war for the courageous Finns. The Italians sent planes, which were held up in transit through Germany. Volunteers flocked to the cause. In the United States there was deep sympathy for Finland, which had held American respect because it had paid in full its debts to the United States. President Roosevelt spoke of Finland as a nation "so infinitesimally small it can do no injury to the Soviet Union." Robert E. Sherwood's play, *There Shall Be No Night*, a sympathetic portrayal of the Finns' war with Russia, was awarded a Pulitzer Prize in 1941.

The attitude of Britain and France was of some importance. In February 1940 they were both within an ace of war with the Soviet Union. A Franco-British expeditionary force of 100,000 men was readied to go to Finland's aid, but Norway and Sweden, though sympathetic, were cowed by Russian threats and refused passage to the Allied troops.

The outcome was inevitable. Soviet military power outnumbered the Finns by 50 to 1. In late February 1940, the Soviet artillery rained some 300,000 shells in one 24-hour period on the concrete fortifications of the

Mannerheim Line, the most concentrated bombardment since that of Verdun in 1916.

On March 11, 1940, the Russians invested the port of Viipuri. The next day, while Britain and France were negotiating with Norway and Sweden for passage of their troops to Finland, a Finnish representative went to Moscow to receive Stalin's terms. On that tragic March day many Finns, in stunned anguish, wept uncontrollably.

A week later the peace treaty was signed.

The Soviet Union imposed terms more severe than her earlier demands. Finland was required to cede to Russia the entire Karelian Isthmus together with Viipuri, the second largest city in Finland. In addition, she had to relinquish the western and northern shores of Lake Ladoga with its cities. Lake Ladoga, the largest lake in Europe, was now wholly within the boundaries of the Soviet Union. Finland lost even more territory: the islands in the Gulf of Finland, a triangle of land in the northeast in the Salla region, and enough of the Rybachi peninsula to give Russia control over the Arctic port of Petsamo and the adjacent nickel mines. She had to consent to the leasing of the Hangö peninsula for 30 years. And, finally, Russia was given the right to construct a railroad across Finland to Sweden.

In all, Finland was forced to cede to the Soviet Union 16,000 square miles of territory, with a population of nearly one-half million. The newly acquired land was promptly organized into the Karelian-Finnish Socialist Federated Republic as another constituent republic in the U.S.S.R. But more than 400,000 Finns in the area, refusing to live under Soviet domination, packed their belongings and trekked across the new border back into Finland. Molotov announced that the puppet Kuusinen government had "dissolved itself."

The proud Finns had paid a heavy price, but at least they had the satisfaction of preserving their independence. The Russians had been successful in getting their demands, but they, too, had paid a stiff price. Some 25,000 Finns had been killed, and perhaps as many as 200,000 Russians.

The Russians had been humiliated before world opinion, but the silent chess player in the Kremlin had never been distinguished particularly by any concern for world opinion. He was consoled by the facts that his strategic position was much improved and that he had increased his defensive strength against attack from the West. The Karelian Isthmus was, indeed, "a dagger pointed at Leningrad," and its acquisition was of vital importance later when Hitler tried to take Leningrad.

JUGGERNAUT OVER DENMARK

The triumph in Poland delighted both soldiers and civilians in Hitler's Third Reich. Back from Warsaw came the smiling legions to receive the victor's laurel. Their civilian compatriots were deliriously happy. When Hitler went to war there had been little enthusiasm, no demonstrations, nothing like the spontaneous outburst of enthusiasm in August 1914.

Volte-face! With his lightning war, fought right out of the book, the *Fuehrer* had demonstrated his genius for all the world to see. Surely London and Paris had got the message. All that remained now was to wait for a quick peace.

But there was to be no quick peace.

Hitler knew this better than anyone else. On November 23, 1939, he summoned his generals to a conference in the Reich Chancellery. "My decision is unchangeable," he announced. "I shall attack France and England at the most favorable and earliest moment. . . . No one has ever achieved what I have achieved. My life is of no importance in all this. . . . I have to choose between victory and annihilation. . . . I choose victory. . . . Fate demands no more from us than from the great men of German history. . . . I shall shrink from nothing and shall destroy everyone who opposes me. . . . I shall destroy the enemy. . . . In this struggle I shall stand or fall. I will not survive the defeat of my people. . . . But there will be no defeat. We shall emerge victorious. Our age will merge into the history of our people."

Before attacking France and England, however, there remained some unfinished business.

Foreign correspondents knew during the last week of March 1940 that events of great consequence were in the offing in northern Europe. Correspondent William L. Shirer, stationed in Berlin, said in one of his broadcasts: "Some people here believe [that] the war may spread to Scandinavia yet. It was reported in Berlin today that last week a squadron of at least nine British destroyers was concentrated off the Norwegian coast and that in several instances German freighters carrying iron received warning shots. . . . From here it looks as if the neutrals, especially the Scandinavians, may be drawn into the conflict after all."

Shirer was right. Until this point Hitler's conquests had been swift, and the problem of supplies had not yet become acute. But for a war against the Great Powers of the West, he needed more than one source of supply.

Iron was the magic word. High-grade Swedish ore was carried westward from the mines by railroad to the Norwegian port of Narvik, loaded on German freighters, and then brought down in territorial waters as far as the Skagerrak. The Norwegian navy escorted the vessels on the principle that Norway was obliged to keep her waters "open to all legitimate traffic by ships belonging to the belligerent countries."

Hitler reasoned that London would show respect for the rules of war. However, he thought it best to take no chances. Perhaps Britain might extend her blockade to cut off the supply of iron ore from Sweden through Norwegian territorial waters past Denmark to the Third Reich. Consequently, as early as 1939, he ordered plans to be drawn up for the invasion of Denmark and Norway.

London informed Norway on April 8, 1940, that it had "decided to prevent unhindered passage of vessels carrying contraband of war through Norwegian territorial waters." Notice was given that mines had been laid along the Norwegian coast in such a way as not to interfere with "the free access of Norwegian nationals or ships to their own ports or coastal hamlets." Oslo promptly demanded removal of the mines.

From Berlin came an ominous statement: "Icily cold, Germany watches these developments. Icily cold, Germany watches the unfolding of the drama. Icily cold, Germany reserves her own decisions to meet the situation."

If anything, Hitler was burningly hot. Before he moved there were several verbal and actual feints. Field Marshal Hermann Goering announced on April 8, 1940, that "a decisive blow must be struck in the West," and hinted that German troops were being concentrated on the Western front and along the Swiss border.

The next morning, April 9, 1940, at 5 A.M., the Danish government received a German note saying that Berlin had "indubitable evidence" of Allied plans to use Scandinavia as a battleground. Since the Scandinavian countries could not defend themselves adequately, Hitler would move in to "protect" them. This was the Nazi version of the old chestnut!

In the meantime, the Germans had already cut off all Denmark's communications with the outside world, a preliminary step to the usual Nazi technique of overrunning a country before it could obtain help. The gangster Dillinger had done the same thing in the early 1930's when he had cut off all phone wires in the small towns before blowing up the local bank.

There was no chance for the Danes to reply. Hitler paid no attention to his treaty of nonaggression with Denmark, for which he himself had asked. The Nazi armies rolled across the unfortified frontiers without any formal resistance.

Within a matter of hours the Nazi legions were in Copenhagen. The Royal Guard at the palace offered only token opposition. King Christian X and Premier Thorvald Stauning accepted the situation only under protest. The king issued a proclamation urging his people to recognize an accomplished fact and to maintain "a calm and controlled attitude."

Twenty-four hours—and the scalp of another country was hanging from Hitler's belt.

THE CONQUEST OF NORWAY

At 1:30 A.M. on April 9, 1940, the commander of three warships stationed on the west coast of Oslo Fiord, the great indentation which continues the

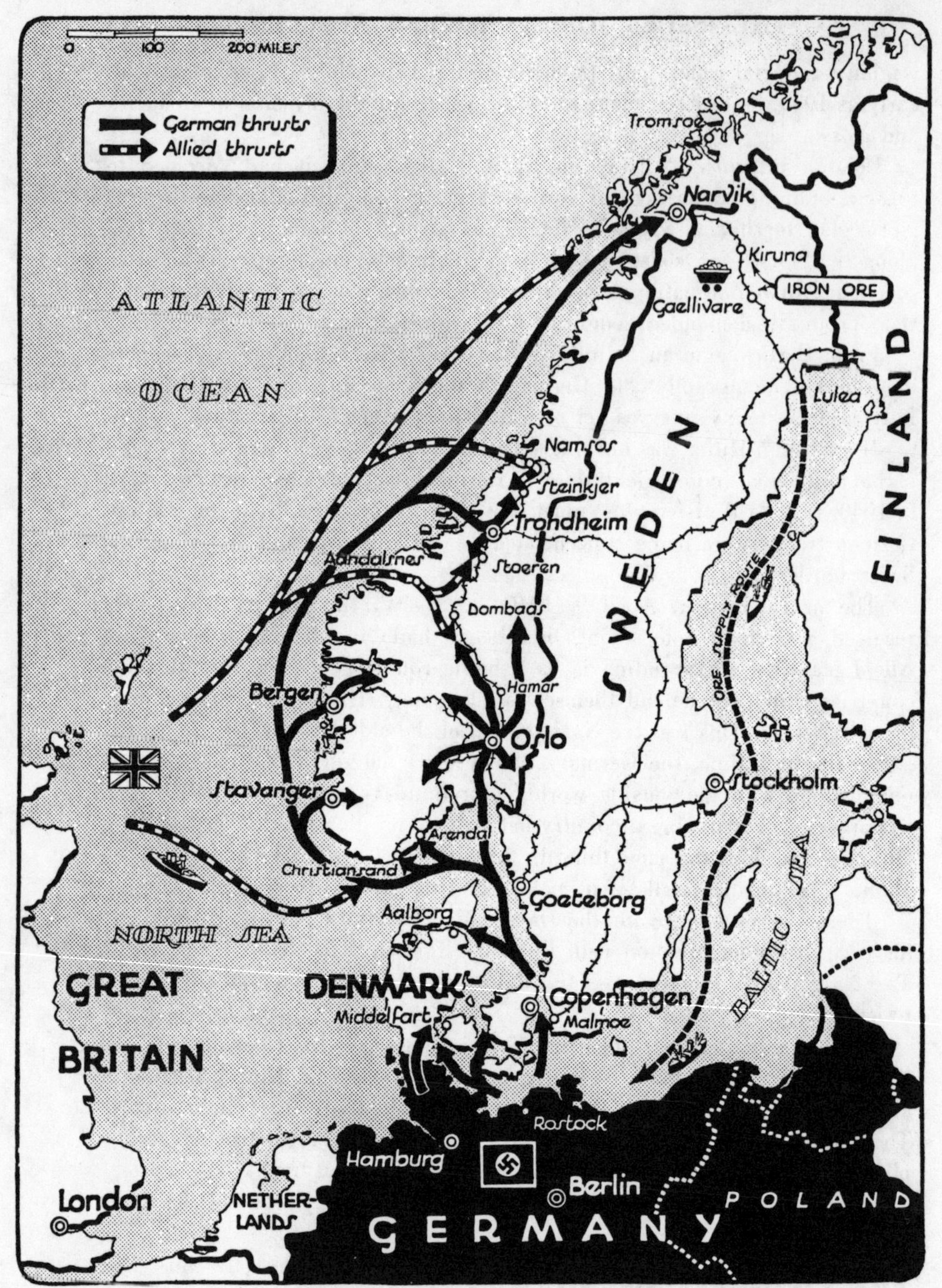

SCANDINAVIA INVADED

inverted "V" of the Skagerrak and the Kattegat, received a telegram supposedly from Dr. Koht, the Norwegian foreign minister. The phony message, in reality sent by the Nazis, ordered him not to fire on German warships which would be coming up the fiord. At first he obeyed without question.

At 5 A.M. the German minister in Oslo handed a note to Dr. Koht demanding the immediate surrender of Norway to German administration on the ground that the Allies were prepared to seize the country. Dr. Koht indignantly refused.

Within a few hours the Germans were attacking throughout Norway. As *Luftwaffe* bombers swooped down on Fornebo Field, Oslo's chief airport, a swarm of transport planes covered the country and dropped parachutists on Oslo, Bergen, Trondheim, Stavanger, and Narvik. Simultaneously, German warships, transport ships, and supply ships steamed into every important port from Oslo in the southeast to Narvik on the northwest and discharged their cargoes of men and machines.

The Norwegians were caught unprepared. There was some resolute fighting, especially in Oslo and around Narvik, but the Norwegian army was no match for the German air force. *Messerschmitt* patrols swarmed over the west coast, while other formations swept out over Helgoland Bight in an acrial blockade of the "protected" nation.

Within a few hours every important harbor, all airfields, and five of the six divisional Norwegian headquarters were in German hands. By 4 P.M. green-clad German troops, after a 35-mile march from Moss, on the coast, were in the streets of Oslo and in command of the government buildings.

This was no fly-by-night maneuver, no sudden whim of the *Fuehrer*. The campaign was perfectly prepared and timed. Germans who, as hungry children, had been taken into Norwegian homes during the famine years after World War I now returned in Nazi uniforms as strutting conquerors. The Nazi *Weltanschauung* had little use for normal canons of ethics and morality.

The conquest on land was decisive, but the Germans paid a stiff price at sea. Into Oslo Fiord Hitler sent his pocket battleship *Deutschland*, the 10,000-ton armored cruiser *Blücher*, the light cruiser *Emden* of 5,600 tons, the *Brummer*, a gunnery-training ship of 2,140 tons, and a screen of mine sweepers, torpedo boats, and motor craft. Against this powerful force the Norwegians had the mine layer *Olav Tryggvason*, moored at a buoy in the roadstead of Horten, several smaller ships lying at the quaysides without steam up, and four submarines. Before the city of Oslo were the Oscarsborg defenses.

At 3:30 A.M. the lookouts at Oscarsborg sighted the German cruiser *Blücher* towering over its escort vessels. The Norwegians then fired the old 11-inch guns of the fortress at point-blank range. Two salvos hit the warship and set it blazing. Then, from the fixed torpedo defenses of the narrows, two torpedoes crashed into the sides of the *Blücher*. The German warship heeled over and sank, with 800 members of the crew and 1,500 men of the landing party, including *Gestapo* units who were to police the new territory.

The training ship *Brummer* was also sunk by the Oscarsborg guns, and the *Deutschland* and *Emden* were hit and damaged. The main German sea thrust on Oslo was broken. It was a heavy loss for the Germany navy, the first of the defeats that were to cripple the German fleet for the remainder of the war.

But this setback was not enough to prevent the conquest of all Norway. The government of Premier Johan Nygaarsvold retreated to the lake hamlet of Hamar, north of Oslo, while half the population of Oslo moved to the north. King Haakon VII fled from place to place; hunted by German planes, he eventually escaped to England where he set up a government-in-exile.

On the afternoon of April 9, 1940, D.N.B., the official German news agency, announced that the Nygaarsvold regime had turned over its powers to a cabinet headed by Major Vidkun Quisling. At 8:30 that evening Quisling issued a radio proclamation ordering the people to cease resistance and avoid "criminal destruction of property," and further demanded that the Norwegian army obey his "National Government."

Quisling's activities contributed to the success of the Nazi invasion. The old idea of a "fifth column" had been used during the Spanish Civil War when General Emilio Mola, Franco supporter, approached Madrid with four columns and said that he had a "fifth Nationalist column in the city." Quisling, while Norwegian minister of war from 1932 to 1933, had appointed some Nazi sympathizers to positions of authority. One of these was the military commander at Narvik, who neglected to issue orders to defend the port when the Nazis attacked it.

The traitor Quisling enriched modern language with a new word—*quisling* came to stand for any fifth-column betrayer of the homeland for foreign countries. "Quisling," commented the London *Times*, "has the supreme merit of beginning with a *q*, which (with one august exception) has long seemed to the British mind to be a crooked, uncertain, and slightly disreputable letter, suggestive of the questionable, the querulous, the quavering of quaking quagmires and quivering quicksands, of quibbles and quarrels, of queasiness, quackery, qualms, and Quilp." The "august exception," as pointed out by H. L. Mencken, was *Queen*.

Backed by a small group of Norwegian Nazis, Quisling coöperated with the German invaders, who installed him as chief executive of Norway. He was scornfully repudiated by the Norwegian government-in-exile at London. When he failed to convert his countrymen to the New Order, he was removed from his office by the German commissioner, Joseph Terboven. But in

September 1940, after a groveling mission to Berlin, Quisling returned to head the *Nasjonal Samling*, the only political party permitted in Nazi Norway. For five years he ruled his country despite resistance from his own people. He died before a Norwegian firing squad after the Hitler regime collapsed in 1945.

In smashing Norway the Nazis utilized not only the services of Quisling and his cohorts but also a whole series of Trojan-horse *ruses de guerre*. On the day of the invasion there appeared at Norwegian ports many innocent-looking coal freighters. At the appointed hour the hatches of these ships were opened to disgorge fully equipped Nazi troops. This took place even at Narvik, a long distance from Germany, indicating the weakness of the German argument that immediate "protection" of Norway from Allied invasion was vital. These freighters had to leave German ports at least a week earlier to be on time for the secret rendezvous.

There were further typical Nazi stratagems. An example—German warships entered the port of Kristiansand ostentatiously flying the French flag and under the protection of false orders issued to the commander of the port.

British Intelligence was caught flatfooted by the suddenness and magnitude of the Nazi operation. Aroused by Hitler's bold stroke from an eight-month trance, British war leaders felt impelled to make a show of strength. On April 14, 1940, they landed a small force of Territorials and other troops at Namsos and Andalsnes, ports flanking Trondheim, the key to central Norway. These troops and their supplies were to be used to frustrate the German invasion of Norway. It was a dangerous maneuver, for the area, 500 miles from bases in Scotland, was well beyond British fighter range, and the Nazis controlled the air.

The result was catastrophic. What happened to these British troops sent in against crack German forces, without air support or artillery, was described by Leland Stowe in a report to the Chicago *Daily News* on April 25, 1940:

> GÄDDEDE, NORWEGIAN-SWEDISH FRONTIER, APRIL 25—Here is the first and only eyewitness report on the opening chapter of the British expeditionary troops' advance in Norway north of Trondheim. It is a bitterly disillusioning and almost unbelievable story.
>
> The British force which was supposed to sweep down from Namsos consisted of one battalion of Territorials and one battalion of the King's Own Royal Light Infantry. These totaled fewer than 1,500 men. They were dumped into Norway's deep snows and quagmires of April slush without a single antiaircraft gun, without one squadron of supporting planes, without a single piece of field artillery.
>
> They were thrown into the snows and mud of 63 degrees north latitude to fight crack German regulars—most of them veterans of the Polish invasion—and to face the most destructive of modern weapons. The great majority of

these young Britishers averaged only a year of military service. They have already paid a heavy price for a major military blunder which was not committed by their immediate command, but in London.

Unless they receive large supplies of antiaircraft guns and adequate reinforcements within a very few days, the remains of these two British battalions will be cut to ribbons.

After only four days of fighting, nearly half of this initial B.E.F. contingent has been knocked out—either killed, wounded, or captured. On Monday, these comparatively inexperienced and incredibly underarmed British troops were decisively defeated. They were driven back in precipitate disorder from Vist, three miles south of the bomb-ravaged town of Steinkjer....

Although almost exhausted from lack of sleep, the British officers maintained remarkable calm. But this was a small military machine with vital cogs missing. Able to bomb at will, the Germans had seriously disrupted the organization of the little British expeditionary vanguard in their first four days at the front.

Forty British fighting planes at present could probably clear the skies over the entire Allied Norwegian fighting zones and all vital sectors of their rear guard north of Trondheim. The British troops are praying that these fighters will arrive soon before it is too late....

Tremendous initiative ... has been handed to the Germans north of Trondheim by one of the costliest and most inexplicable military bungles in modern British history.

It has been handed to them by those high British authorities who thrust 1,500 young Territorials into the snow and mud below Namsos ten days ago without a single antiaircraft gun or a single piece of artillery.

At Narvik, the most northern port, there was some success for the British. The battleship *Warspite* broke into the fiord and sank seven enemy destroyers. The British took Narvik, but soon relinquished it when Hitler's advance in the Low Countries in the early summer made it imperative that all troops be recalled for defense of the home island.

June 8, 1940. Outnumbered, beaten in battle, the British Expeditionary Force withdrew from Norway. British ships sent to cover the evacuation were attacked by heavy German naval units. In the action the British carrier *Glorious* and two destroyers were sunk, while several other ships were damaged.

For London this was shocking news. "Fortune has been cruelly against us," said Winston Churchill, overlooking, perhaps, any responsibility of the British War Office for the disaster. Britain's finest troops, the Scots and Irish Guards, he admitted, had been baffled "by the vigor, enterprise, and training of Hitler's young men.... We, who had command of the sea and could pounce anywhere on an undefended coast, were outpaced by the enemy moving by land across very large distances in the face of every obstacle."

For Hitler the conquest of Norway was highly satisfying. He now had strategically located bases from which his planes could dominate all Scandinavia, imperil British shipping, and strike at Britain itself. With naval and submarine bases in Norway he was no longer worried about attack on his northern flank. More, he had diverted badly needed supplies of dairy products, fish, minerals, metal ores, and timber from the Allies. He confiscated almost all Norway's gold reserves for his own war machine.

"Germany, by its action," said Foreign Minister Joachim von Ribbentrop, "has saved the countries and the peoples of Scandinavia from annihilation, and will now guarantee truc neutrality in the north until the war's end."

"True neutrality," indeed. The war was going well for the master of Berchtesgaden. Hitler held absolute sway over 80,000,000 Germans; some 14,000,000 Poles were under his domination; more than 7,000,000 Czechs took orders from his Reich-Protector Baron Konstantin von Neurath; now his "wartime protection" was extended to 3,000,000 Norwegians and 3,750,000 Danes.

But all was not lost for Britain and the Allies despite the spring disaster. They had learned some valuable lessons the hard way. Norway was the eye-opener showing how badly the Allies had misjudged the war. It should have been clear now even to the most obtuse that Allied naval superiority meant little without adequate air support, a lesson not fully learned even a year and a half later when the British lost the *Repulse* and the *Prince of Wales* off the Malay coast because of inadequate air cover. Moreover, the British learned that *Blitzkrieg*, as demonstrated by the Nazis in Norway, could work even in mountainous and snowy terrain.

Most of the Norwegian merchant fleet, the fourth largest in the world, escaped from the Nazis and joined the Allied pool of ships. These thousand or more ocean-going vessels helped keep Britain supplied with oil and food without which she could not have lasted long in the war. And, lest they be seized by Hitler, the Faroe Islands, Iceland, and Greenland, all formerly tied to Denmark, were occupied by British and Canadian forces.

In recent years new light has been cast on the Scandinavian invasion by the publication of Admiral Raeder's memoirs and by British sources. German historians have long maintained that by invading Norway Hitler was actually beating the British to the punch. The Allies, they say, were definitely planning the invasion of Norway and were awaiting a legal excuse. This was, they say, the essential difference between the Allied and German plans. This point of view has been substantiated to some extent by British official histories. The British and French after Finland's collapse decided to lay mines in Norwegian waters, a move that they expected would result in a German invasion of Norway. If invasion came, the Allies intended to land troops in Narvik to take the port and the railway to Sweden.

THE RAPE OF HOLLAND

Hitler's speech was Napoleonic both in conception and wording:

"The hour has come for the decisive battle for the future of the German nation. For 300 years the rulers of England and France have made it their aim to prevent any real consolidation of Europe and above all to keep Germany weak and helpless. With this your hour has come. The struggle which begins today will decide the fate of the German people for a thousand years. Now do your duty."

Basic in the plan to conquer the West was an assault on the Low Countries—Holland, Belgium, and Luxemburg. Then France would be overrun, and from bases there the Nazis could strike at England. Hitler knew that a frontal attack on the defensive Maginot Line would be too costly, hence he would outflank it by sweeping his mechanized armies irresistibly across the three small countries in an arc directed at Paris. It was a virtual repetition of the famed von Schlieffen plan of 1914 on how to fight a two-front war against France and Russia.

The opposing forces were approximately equal in manpower. For the invasion of the Low Countries, Hitler had 89 divisions (including 10 armored), and a reserve of 47, a total of 136 divisions. These forces were divided into three army groups under Generals Fedor von Bock, Gerd von Rundstedt, and Ritter Wilhelm von Leeb. The French had 106 divisions, the Belgians 20, the British 13, and the Dutch 10, a total of 149 Allied divisions.

But this approximate equality of manpower meant little. The Allies' forces were a coalition of untried national armies, loosely coördinated and without common military experience. The French army, despite its great reputation, was in decline. The *Wehrmacht*, on the other hand, already blooded in the Polish and Scandinavian campaigns, was superior at this time in liaison and command, fully equipped, and superbly trained.

The Dutch field army was relatively modest: 4 army corps each of two divisions, 24 frontier battalions, 24 brigades, 14 regiments of army artillery, less than a dozen squadrons of planes, and a few antiaircraft guns. With this weak defense the Dutch were to bear their share of the German assault.

The German campaign was prepared with traditional thoroughness, efficiency, and skill. Nothing was left to chance. There was some fifth-column activity, though we must be careful in this case as elsewhere not to exaggerate its intensity. German "tourists," "salesmen," and "students," all carefully briefed, ranged through the Dutch countryside preparing the way for invasion. German agents stole the uniforms of Dutch policemen, postmen, railway conductors, and trainmen, and smuggled the clothing across the border. Some help came from the pro-Fascist followers of Anton Mussert and Rost van Tonningen, Dutchmen sympathetic to Fascism. German agents controlled key bridges, waterworks, and canals. But in the final analysis it was the strength of the *Wehrmacht*, not the fifth columnists, which meant a successful invasion.

The Dutch, neutral in World War I and untouched by war for a century, were not blind to the German preparations. Like the Belgians, they tried to avoid giving the Germans an excuse to attack, and refrained from mobilizing their armies. They were aware that they could expect little immediate help from the French, whose forces were dispersed on the Maginot Line and along the Italian frontier, or from the British, who were doggedly seeking to put their military house in order after two decades of unpreparedness and "business as usual." The only thing the Dutch could do was to slow down the advance of the enemy until help came. Where most other countries depended upon artillery and firepower for protection against invasion, the Dutch relied upon their ability to flood extensive areas of their homeland by breaking strategic dikes once the enemy had crossed the border. More, they mined bridges, constructed pillboxes, and set up road blocks. Every man was assigned to his post when the attack came.

There was some warning. On the evening of May 9, 1940, agents of the Dutch Intelligence Service sent a five-word message to their government: "Tomorrow at dawn. Hold tight!"

But the German attack, when it came, was so fast and was delivered with such thunderous impact that the Dutch resistance was hopeless almost from the very beginning. It was *Blitzkrieg* all over again, effective, powerful, ruthless. The earlier lightning war in Poland paled in comparison.

At 4 A.M. on May 10, 1940, again without any advance notice, German parachutists, some dressed in Allied uniforms, equipped with machine guns and radios, and rubber boats to cross canals and flooded areas, hurtled down onto airfields and strategic points all over the tiny country. Jumping from low levels, many were killed or drowned. But on they came, like a swarm of locusts.

Simultaneously, screaming dive bombers attacked bridges, railroad stations, and forts. The small Dutch air force was soon destroyed. Nazi tanks roared along the level terrain, slicing the thin defense lines into segments. Coördinated units set up islands of invasion behind the lines. Then came the swift-charging infantry divisions to join the parachutists to mop up resistance.

Two hours after the invasion began, the German minister at The Hague gave the usual Nazi explanation. There was irrefutable evidence, he said blandly, of an immediate threatened invasion by Britain and France of the Low Countries, prepared long beforehand and with the knowledge of the governments of Holland, Belgium, and Luxemburg. He demanded that the invaded countries submit at once. The alternative was annihilation.

Forced at long last to recognize the end of their neutrality, the Dutch and Belgians accepted the state of war with Germany and asked for British and

French assistance. It was far too late. The Nazi *Blitzkrieg* rolled on like an express train. The Dutch fought desperately. Even women struck back with knives, guns, any weapons they could get their hands on. Infuriated, the Dutch killed any fifth columnist they could identify. But to halt the German war machine was an impossible task.

Crossing the long Dutch frontier, which had no natural obstacles, was easy for the Germans. The main line of defense was the Gelder Valley and the basin of the Eem and the Grift. Beyond this position lay Fortress Holland, its eastern line stretching from Muiden to Utrecht, which could be flooded along its entire length. But within a few days the Germans penetrated both the Valley position and Fortress Holland itself, linking up with the airborne troops who had already immobilized The Hague and Rotterdam.

The Dutch declared Rotterdam to be an open city. The Germans paid no attention. The Dutch commander received a three-hour ultimatum to surrender. Shortly after the deadline, he capitulated. But the Germans, fearing that British help might come soon, had already started the bombers on their way. On May 14, 1940, the great city was subjected to a hideous bombardment. Within seven and a half minutes the *Stukas*, flying low over the metropolis, completed their murderous assault. Between 30,000 and 50,000 civilians were killed and two square miles in the heart of the city reduced to rubble. The 28,000-ton liner *Statendam*, one of the largest ships in the Dutch passenger fleet, lay smoldering in the harbor.

It was a senseless, brutal, unnecessary assault, one of the most inexcusable atrocities of the war. When, later in the war, the German public protested against the "barbarities" of Allied air raids, they were told to "Remember Rotterdam!"

If the sorely tried Dutch could find any comfort in their period of trial it was the fact that the invading Nazis were frustrated in one of their major objectives—to seize Queen Wilhelmina, members of the royal family, and government leaders as hostages to warn other countries which might be tempted to thwart Hitler's will. After being chased across the country by the advancing German troops, the royal family and governmental figures managed to elude their pursuers and flee across the North Sea in a British destroyer. They were bombed on the way by German planes, but they made it to England with literally nothing but the clothes they wore.

Meanwhile, British destroyers also took off a battalion of Irish and Welsh Guards and 200 marines who had been sent to hold the Hook of Holland. A Buckingham Palace retainer described the Dutch queen, stunned after her terrifying experience and escape to England, "sitting there with apparently no interest at all in life, content just to be alive." But Queen Wilhelmina soon recovered her composure and from London she and her ministers were free to command the vast Dutch colonial possessions.

Within five days, by May 15, 1940, it was all over. The slaughter was so great that General Henrik Winkelman, in command of the Dutch forces, ordered a cease fire. The little Dutch army had suffered 100,000 casualties, a quarter of its strength. Organized resistance continued for a few days in Zeeland and then simmered down.

Hitler placed Holland under the rule of Artur von Seyss-Inquart, noted for his Nazi ferocity, who two years earlier had helped hand over his native Austria to the Third Reich. The Dutch, stern and unbending, began a campaign of passive resistance which made them a thorn in the Nazi side. The German occupation authorities complained that the Dutch did not understand "the true spirit of the New Order."

They understood only too well.

THE COLLAPSE OF BELGIUM

On that fateful May 10, 1940, the German hurricane hit the Low Countries all along the western front from the North Sea to Luxemburg. The Dutch capitulated in five days, the Belgians, better prepared than most small countries, lasted for just 18 days.

Like Holland, Belgium had been careful to avoid giving the Germans any excuse for attack. In 1936, two years after his accession, Leopold III, King of the Belgians, announced that his country must pursue a policy "exclusively and entirely Belgian." He would enter into no alliances with the Western Powers which might provoke his giant neighbor to the east. Like Switzerland and Holland, Belgium would remain neutral.

Britain and France were eventually forced to endorse the Belgian stand, releasing her from all obligations under the Locarno treaties. At the end of 1937, Hitler, as a kind of *quid pro quo*, had given his word to respect Belgium's integrity and inviolability, unless she took part in military action against Germany. Leopold was to learn the hard way exactly what Hitler's pledges were worth.

Once again there was the same spectacular pattern—fifth columnists, no ultimatum, then *Blitzkrieg:* slashing air attack, light armor, 2,800 tanks advancing at great speed, infantry. Within hours, half the Belgian air force was destroyed on the ground. One German army smashed at the Maastricht bridgehead and the fort of Eben Emael commanding the Albert Canal, along which the Belgian army was massed. A second spearhead swept through the wooded mountain system of the Ardennes in southeast Belgium, between the Meuse and Moselle, which some Allied military experts had regarded as impassable.

The pivot of the Belgian defense was the giant fort of Eben Emael, perched above the surrounding country near the border and covering the

THE LOW COUNTRIES FALL

bridges of the Meuse and Albert Canal. This was said to be the most fortified single stronghold in the world—if not impregnable, at least powerful enough to sustain an assault until help came from the West. The Germans took the fort within 36 hours.

Throughout the winter of 1939-1940 the Germans had ingeniously prepared the attack. Using accurate reports of espionage agents, they constructed a full-scale model of Eben Emael and made specially trained engineers and parachutists thoroughly familiar with every square inch of the structure. Realistic exercises were held day after day. When the time came, the attackers, acting automatically, carried out the plan to perfection. It was a striking example of German *Gründlichkeit* (thoroughness).

It was still dark on the early morning of May 10, 1940, when twelve *Luftwaffe* gliders, each carrying a dozen troops armed with explosives, guns, and ammunition, landed on the flat roof of the great fort. Like robots the Nazi commandos went to work. Protected by smoke screens, they pushed detonating charges into the barrels of the big guns, dynamited observation posts, exits, and ventilator shafts, and destroyed the ammunition elevators with hand grenades. Small units crawled from cupola to cupola, dropped their explosive charges, and then clambered to safety.

It was an almost uncannily fantastic operation. The garrison of 1,200 Belgians, unprepared for and confused by this novel attack, was soon trapped inside its own fortifications. The commander of the fort appealed for help to the near-by forts of Pontisse and Neuchâteau, which responded by bombarding the superstructure of Eben Emael with shells! This might possibly have had some military justification (indeed, there was nothing unique about it), but one astonished war correspondent could scarcely believe it: "The spectacle of one Belgian fort firing on another was the ultimate satire on immobile defense."

At 12:30 A.M. on May 11, 1940, the garrison of the world's most powerful fort surrendered. Casualties were light—the Belgians lost only 60 dead and 40 wounded, the Germans even fewer.

As soon as the Germans crossed the border, Leopold appealed to the Allies for aid. All British forces on the Continent, plus a portion of the French army, headed for Belgium at top speed. On the same day of the surrender of Eben Emael, the Belgians evacuated their positions along the Albert Canal and retired to a line running roughly from Antwerp to the vicinity of Louvain. The British held the line from Louvain to Wavre, where they were joined by French troops.

Two days later, on May 13, 1940, Lieutenant General Ewald von Kleist disrupted the Allied defense plan. He achieved a memorable breakthrough by crashing through the supposedly impassable Ardennes. The Germans crossed the Meuse barrier and opened a 50-mile breach between Namur and Sedan.

The Belgians, with French and British support, fought to exhaustion. But the situation became even worse. Within seven days German tanks reached the Channel via Abbeville, cutting the Allies in two. The British Expeditionary Force and remnants of the French First, Seventh, and Ninth Armies were pushed to the Channel. When the Germans captured Calais and Boulogne, only the port of Dunkirk was left as a possible escape route.

Meanwhile, several members of the Belgian cabinet visited King Leopold at Castle Wynendael in the midst of the woods south of Bruges. In long and futile discussions they urged him to leave Belgium and set up a government-in-exile. Leopold flatly refused. He complained that the Belgian army was bearing the brunt of the German attack. Under no circumstances would he leave Belgian soil. It was better, he said, to surrender than to fight another battle which would lead to Belgian annihilation without benefit to the Allies. "I shall remain in Belgium and stand by my people."

Leopold issued an Order of the Day to his army: "Whatever may happen, I shall share your fate."

At 5 P.M. on May 27, 1940, Leopold asked the Germans for an armistice. The next day nearly 400,000 weary and dispirited Belgian troops surrendered unconditionally to the Germans. Leopold was placed in protective custody in a castle near Brussels. His cabinet escaped to London.

Leopold's defection set off a violent controversy. From his viewpoint he was acting from motives of integrity and common sense. His army was thoroughly trounced and it was necessary that he, as King of the Belgians, save his people from further slaughter.

But Allied leaders were appalled by Leopold's action, which left them in a serious predicament. British and French troops, sent to help the Belgians, were endangered by Leopold's precipitate action and open to complete annihilation. He should have held on just a bit longer, they argued, just long enough to allow his friends to escape the relentless Germans. In 1914, said the critics, his father, Albert I, had contemptuously defied the Germans to the end, but now the ungrateful son had panicked at the critical moment and had left the Allies in a most precarious position.

Nor did the Belgian people forget. Leopold's surrender (as well as what the public believed to be his general anti-French and pro-German attitude) cost him his throne. In 1951, after a plebiscite revealed his unpopularity, Leopold was forced to abdicate in favor of his son Baudouin.

THE FALL OF LUXEMBURG

The tiny European Grand Duchy of Luxemburg, 999 square miles, 55 miles long and 34 miles wide, was taken in a matter of hours by Hitler's hordes. The neutrality of its 300,000 hard-working people had been guaranteed by the Great Powers. But to Hitler, Luxemburg, bounded by Germany on the east, by Belgium on the north and west, and by France on the south, was strategically important. This was on the route for his main thrust.

The victory over Luxemburg on May 10, 1940, was scarcely an impressive one for Nazi arms. Luxemburgers would have been hard pressed had they taken on the Pontifical Armed Corps of the Vatican or the Palace Guards of Monaco.

Grand Duchess Charlotte fled first to France and then to the United States. Several thousand citizens of the little nation were removed to Germany to join the swelling ranks of slave labor. And Hitler had added another country to his list of conquests.

WHAT PRICE CHURCHILL?

Neville Chamberlain, the man of Munich, had tried appeasement and complacency—with disastrous results. The British people were tired of and disgusted with his tone of aggrieved self-righteousness as well as his extraordinarily wrong pronunciamentos—"Peace for our time!" and "Hitler has missed the bus." He had been responsible for the British conduct of the war, and Britain was doing poorly. There was a grave need for more vigorous and imaginative leadership. Chamberlain had failed.

The House of Commons was in an angry mood. The debate was sharp and bitter. "We are fighting today for our life," said one member of the House, "for our liberty, for our all; we cannot go on being led as we are." He closed with Cromwell's ringing words to the Long Parliament: "You have sat too long here for any good you are doing. Depart, I say, and let us have done with you. In the name of God, go!"

The embattled prime minister tried to get the opposition to join a national coalition, but he failed. On May 8, 1940, his majority in the House of Commons fell to 81 as 130 Conservatives abstained from giving the government a vote of confidence.

After the war, Winston Churchill described the critical moment: "The stroke of catastrophe and the spur of peril were needed to call forth the dormant might of the British nation. The tocsin was about to sound."

On May 10, 1940, just as Hitler struck again without warning against the neutrals—Belgium, Holland, and Luxemburg, a pale, broken man emerged from No. 10 Downing Street. With head bowed he entered an automobile and was driven to Buckingham Palace, where he spent 20 minutes with the king.

The announcement came that night: "The Right Honourable Neville Chamberlain resigned the office of Prime Minister and First Lord of the Treasury this evening, and the Right Honourable Winston Churchill accepted His Majesty's invitation to fill the position. The Prime Minister desires that all Ministers should remain at their posts and discharge their functions with full freedom and responsibility while the necessary arrangements for the formation of a new administration are made."

Chamberlain made his valedictory in a broadcast to the Empire: "You and I must now put all our strength behind the new government.... And we must fight until this savage beast who has sprung out of his lair at us is finally overthrown.... I had no doubt that some new and drastic action must be taken to restore confidence.... It was apparent that some unity could be attained under some other Prime Minister. . . . My duty was plain. I saw His Majesty."

Once again British history was running true to form. Again and again, in moments of grave peril, an energetic and inspired John Bull had appeared to unite the people of Britain in the face of disaster. This time the call for leadership was answered by a man of cherubic countenance and iron heart. He was to infuse fresh energy into the British war effort in a manner without parallel in modern history.

Winston Leonard Spencer Churchill, born November 30, 1874, was the son of Lord Randolph Churchill and an American mother, the former Jennie Jerome of New York. In his long and remarkable career this stormy petrel almost boxed the political compass as he moved from one party to another. He was made First Lord of the Admiralty in 1911, in which position he, together with Lord Fisher, prepared the navy for its great test of World War I.

Churchill's conduct of naval affairs in World War I brought him some unpopularity and strong criticism. One idea dominated his sense of strategy—he wanted to strike at the Central Powers from "the soft underbelly of Europe" (the obsession remained during World War II). The result was the unsuccessful Gallipoli campaign in 1915. Not until nearly half a century later did the Allies learn that they had been within a few inches of victory. Churchill, as on so many other occasions, might well have said "I told you so!"

In 1925 Churchill joined Stanley Baldwin's government as chancellor of the Exchequer, and made the decision that returned England to the gold standard. Soon after Hitler's rise to power, Churchill in a sensational address warned his countrymen of the growing menace of Nazi Germany. The most voluble critic of Chamberlain's appeasement policy, he urged the House of Commons to recognize the danger of Hitlerism to both Europe and the world.

To his political enemies Churchill was a flamboyant troublemaker. In the days immediately preceding the war, London was covered with huge signs bearing the words "What Price Churchill?"

The new prime minister acted swiftly and resolutely. He set up a three-party coalition cabinet, which still included Chamberlain in a minor capacity, several of the latter's outstanding critics such as Anthony Eden and Alfred

Duff-Cooper, Viscount Halifax as foreign secretary, and several Laborites including Clement Attlee and Ernest Bevin.

"I was sure I should not fail," Churchill later confessed. "I slept soundly and had no need for cheering dreams."

Churchill's first move was to set up a ministry of aircraft production under Lord Beaverbrook, the newspaper baron, to speed the production of airplanes. The prime minister urged all Englishmen to forget the old intramural insults: "If we quarrel about yesterday, we shall lose tomorrow."

This was the realistic, pugnacious leadership that Britain needed and for which Britons had waited. Fearless, unconquerable, energetic, gifted with a driving zeal, Churchill turned out to be one of the great war leaders of history. Not the least of his abilities was an inspired gift of oratory. His first speech as prime minister to the House of Commons revealed the caliber and stature of the man:

> In this crisis I hope I may be pardoned if I do not address the House at any length today. I hope that any of my colleagues, or former colleagues, who are affected by the political reconstruction, will make allowance, all allowance, for any lack of ceremony with which it has been necessary to act. I would say to the House, as I said to those who have joined this Government: "I have nothing to offer but blood, toil, tears and sweat."
>
> We have before us an ordeal of the most grievous kind. We have before us many, many long months of struggle and of suffering.
>
> You ask, what is our policy? I will say: It is to wage war, by sea, land, and air, with all our might and with all the strength that God can give us; to wage war against a monstrous tyranny, never surpassed in the dark, lamentable catalogue of human crime. That is our policy.
>
> You ask, what is our aim? I can answer in one word: It is victory, victory at all costs, victory in spite of all the terror; victory, however long and hard the road may be; for without victory, there is no survival. Let that be realized; no survival for the British Empire; no survival for all that the British Empire has stood for, no survival for the urge and impulse of all the ages, that mankind will move forward toward its goal.
>
> But I take up my task with buoyancy and hope. I feel sure that our cause will not be suffered to fail among men. At this time I feel entitled to claim the aid of all, and I say, "Come, then, let us go forward together with our united strength."

Neville Chamberlain, the prime minister who had trusted the word of Adolf Hitler, retired from the Churchill cabinet in October 1940. He died shortly thereafter.

DUNKIRK—MIRACLE OF DELIVERANCE

At 12:30 P.M. on May 27, 1940, Leopold III, King of the Belgians, sent an urgent message to the British command: "The Belgian army is losing heart. It has been fighting without a break for the past four days under a heavy bombardment which the R.A.F. has not been able to prevent. Having heard that the Allied group is surrounded and aware of the great superiority of the enemy, the troops have concluded that the situation is desperate. The time is rapidly approaching when they will be unable to continue the fight. The King will be forced to capitulate to avoid a collapse."

The time rapidly approached within four hours. At 5 P.M. Leopold made his decision to send an envoy to request an armistice. The next day, May 28, 1940, the king ordered his troops to lay down their arms in unconditional surrender.

Leopold's eventual defeat was expected, but his abrupt decision, while, perhaps, saving Belgian lives, placed many British and French troops in acute danger. The left flank of the Allied armies were left open. The German forces had driven with astonishing speed across southeastern Belgium and had then moved toward Abbeville just 15 miles from the French channel coast. Now the whole British Expeditionary Force, plus French (the entire First French Army, parts of the Seventh and Ninth), Poles, and Belgians, were trapped.

Scenting victory, the Germans surged in for the kill. On May 29, 1940, a jubilant German communiqué proclaimed that the fate of the British and French armies was sealed.

The British could hope only to salvage their broken forces. Isolated, they were left only with the single port of Dunkirk as a means of escape. There was no choice—they had to get away from the Continent or they would be annihilated. To delay the enemy they opened the flood sluices around Dunkirk. The French fought rear-guard delaying actions at Lille and Cassel. A small British force held out against the Germans hammering at Calais. While the British and French fought through fire and flood, the bulk of the trapped army fell back on Dunkirk.

The Germans pushed at Dunkirk from all sides. Their artillery pounded until the town was aflame and the water supply shattered. *Luftwaffe* bombers destroyed the docks. The East Mole, a breakwater of planks, just wide enough for three men to walk abreast, and the open beaches were all that remained. A pall of smoke hung over the port.

The British had foreseen a possible disaster. As early as May 14, 1940, a B.B.C. announcer, in the usual calm and well-modulated tone, had told the British radio audience: "The Admiralty have made an order requesting all owners of self-propelled pleasure craft between 30 and 100 feet in length to send all particulars to the Admiralty within 14 days from today." Two weeks later the House of Commons was warned "to prepare for hard and heavy tidings."

From May 26 to June 4, 1940, came Operation Dynamo, called the Nine Days' Wonder by John Masefield and "a miracle of deliverance" by Winston

Churchill. From a huge room carved out of the chalk under Dover Castle, Vice Admiral Bertram Ramsay, with a staff of only 16 men, guided the rescue operations. "There," wrote Edward R. Murrow, "above the port used by Caesar's galleys when they ran the cross-channel ferry, in a room where the words scrawled by prisoners taken from Napoleon's ships are still visible, Ramsay ran the show and demonstrated again the British genius for improvisation."

From England there set out one of history's strangest armadas. In all there were some 887 vessels, civilian craft and naval units. It was a bewildering variety—motorboats, lifeboats, French fishing boats, Dutch schuits, Channel ferries, sloops, mine sweepers, drifters, destroyers. There were merchantmen, passenger steamers, private yachts, even tugs with strings of barges. There were large speedboats, Thames fire-floats, dockyard tugs, coasters, colliers, and paddle steamers. There was a car ferry on its first trip in the open sea. There was the old *Brighton Belle* that had carried holiday crowds in the days before the Boer War and was now being used again, as in World War I, as a mine sweeper. In and around this collection of seagoing oddities sped the fast units of the Royal Navy.

Dunkirk was almost unique in the annals of warfare in that a *civilian* population helped the rescue of a trapped army. This was a British Navy operation, with civilian aid. The closest thing to it in modern times occurred in World War I, when the taxicab drivers of Paris were mobilized to rush last-ditch reinforcements to the front to stop the oncoming Germans.

The strange fleet was manned by every kind of Englishman from Mrs. Miniver's husband to Sea Scouts whose previous experience had been limited to daring voyages on the Thames. There were Cockney taxi drivers spouting a new kind of naval language, longshoremen from the London docks, clerks from the City wearing bowler hats and carrying umbrellas, fishermen and bankers, dentists and butchers, bright-eyed youngsters and myopic oldsters determined to have a lick at the enemy. All were wet, chilled, and hungry. But all sailed superbly on to the pillars of smoke and fire rising from Dunkirk.

Traffic across the Channel was a nightmare. Sleek destroyers dashed in and out among the fleet, their wash nearly capsizing the smaller vessels. There was one collision after another as scores of boats and ships were battered and scraped and stove in. The air was split by oaths, quarrels, shouting.

But the amazing flotilla continued on toward the target—the enormous pall of smoke hanging over Dunkirk. A magical order seemed to form out of the chaos. An outside ring of naval units covered the sky with curtains of antiaircraft fire. Pilots of the Royal Air Force, youngsters weary from lack of sleep, manned every available plane to drive off the German bombers.

The beach at Dunkirk was black with lines of weary and sleepy troops.

They staggered from the dunes to the shallows and fell into the little boats. The foremost ranks were shoulder deep in the water. After these were dragged into the boats, the rear ranks moved up, from ankle-deep to knee-deep to waist-deep to shoulder-deep, until they, too, were pulled into the small craft. The men were then brought to the bigger boats, scrambling up the sides on rope nets or ladders. All the boats, little as well as big, listed drunkenly with the weight of the men. But still they came by the tens of thousands.

For nine days it went on, the impromptu fleet plying back and forth, until 338,226 men, 139,911 French and Belgian, the rest British, were saved. Out of the rescue boats onto the soil of England, staggering with fatigue, stepped an army of dirty, famished troops. Many were blood covered or oil spattered. One reporter noted that they had brought with them half the canine population of Belgium and France. "Some of the dogs were shell-shocked; they whimpered; but the men didn't."

Reporters at the British ports obtained some absorbing eyewitness stories from the survivors:

A sergeant major: "Although we came back wounded, we have given them plenty to remember us by. At times the slaughter was wholesale. Column after column of Germans were mowed down by our Bren guns. The morale of our men was superb. When they were embarking, bombers raided the ships and one gun crew was put out of action. Wounded men went to take a share in feeding the guns."

A trooper: "I never believed anything like the wall of fire our ships put up to screen troops was possible. Shells fell in a mathematically straight line behind our positions, while beyond the line British planes dropped bombs like hail. Jerry never had a chance to get us."

Another trooper: "When we were hit by bombs we swam ashore, but when the ship didn't go down we swam back to her again to take her out of the harbor. Then she turned turtle and we had to swim again. Some of us were in the water for hours before we were picked up by a British warship."

A veteran of World War I: "The British put a barrage a mile long to stem the advance. I fought in the last war, but I have never seen anything like it. The Germans advanced right into it, disregarding danger. Their casualties must have been enormous."

An artilleryman: "It's an inferno over there; a hell made by man. The Germans asked for a truce to bury their dead after a 36-hour barrage had held up their advance. We replied: 'There's no truce!' And we gave them another seven hours of barrage."

All the precious equipment which the British forces had taken to the Continent for the Battle of France was left behind on the beaches. London admitted the loss of 6 British destroyers (*Basilisk, Havant, Keith, Grafton, Grenade,* and *Wakeful*), 7 French destroyers, 3 auxiliary naval craft, and 24 smaller boats. On the evening of June 4, 1940, the Admiralty issued a communiqué:

> The most extensive and difficult combined operation in naval history has been carried out during the past week.
>
> British, French, and Belgian troops have been brought back safely to this country from Belgium and northern France in numbers which, when the full story can be told, will surprise the world.
>
> The withdrawal has been carried out in face of intense and almost continuous air attack and increasing artillery and machine-gun fire.
>
> The success of this operation was only made possible by the close coöperation of the Allies and of the Services, and by never-flagging determination and courage of all concerned.
>
> The rapid assembly of over 600 small craft of all types was carried out by volunteers. These showed magnificent and tireless spirit. [*There were 222 naval vessels and 665 other British ships at Dunkirk.*]
>
> The Admiralty cannot speak too highly of the services of all concerned. They were essential to the success of the operation and the means of saving thousands of lives.
>
> The withdrawal was carried out from Dunkirk and from beaches in the vicinity. The whole operation was screened by naval forces against any attempt by the enemy at interference by sea.
>
> In addition to almost incessant bombing and machine-gun attacks on Dunkirk, the beaches and the vessels operating off them, the port of Dunkirk and the shipping plying to and fro were under frequent shellfire. This was to some extent checked by bombardment of the enemy artillery positions by our naval forces. Naval bombardment also protected the flanks of the withdrawal. Losses have been inflicted upon both these forces.
>
> The operation was rendered more difficult by shallow water, narrow channels, and strong tides. The situation was such that one mistake in the handling of a ship might have blocked a vital channel or that part of the port of Dunkirk which could be used. Nor was the weather entirely in favour of the operation. On two days a fresh northwesterly wind raised a surf which made work at the beaches slow and difficult. Only on one forenoon did ground mist curtail enemy air activity.
>
> A withdrawal of this nature and magnitude, carried out in face of intense and almost continuous air attack, is the most hazardous of all operations. Its success is a triumph of Allied sea and air power in face of the most powerful air forces which the enemy could bring to bear from air bases close at hand.

That same day, June 4, 1940, the Germans claimed Dunkirk with 40,000 prisoners. But they were shocked and perplexed by the successful evacuation. Beforehand they had announced confidently that "the ring around the British, French, and Belgian armies is definitely closed."

Britain still ruled the waves. What had seemed to be a devastating defeat had been turned into a magnificent moral victory. In the words of A. D. Divine, one of the volunteers in the rescue fleet: "It was a brutal, desperate adventure forced upon us by the most dire disaster, carried out under the eyes of an enemy flushed with victory, elated with the certainty of conquest. It was carried out in defiance of time, of circumstance, of death itself."

Churchill soberly reminded the nation that "Wars are not won by evacuations." At the same time he issued an eloquent challenge: "We shall fight on the seas and oceans, we shall fight with growing confidence and growing strength in the air, we shall defend our island, whatever the cost may be, we shall fight on the beaches, we shall fight on the landing-grounds, we shall fight in the fields and in the streets, we shall fight in the hills; we shall never surrender."

CHAPTER 5

From Sitzkrieg *to* Blitzkrieg: *The Collapse of France*

Too few children, too few arms, too few Allies.
—Marshal Henri Pétain, June 1940

THE PHONY WAR

Sitzkrieg, Sit-down War, Bore War, War of Words, Phony War.

In the East, while Poland was being obliterated by Hitler's *Blitzkrieg*, France, her ally in the West, made no move to distract the German legions. During the early days of September 1939, French troops moved cautiously a few miles into German territory, only to retreat promptly when the main German forces were shifted to the West.

In 1914 the French had gone to war in an outburst of patriotic enthusiasm. In 1939 they answered the call to arms like somnambulists, without spirit, unanimous only in rejecting what they believed to be an absurd and monstrous war. Sit it out. Nothing would happen. We French won't be bled again. The mad hope lingered that somehow a real clash might be averted. True, in *Mein Kampf*, Hitler had called France "Germany's irreconcilable and mortal enemy." But that vulgar madman across the Rhine would stop his nonsense sooner or later.

What chance did Hitler have against the mighty French army? With its 800,000 combat troops, its trained reserves of 5,500,000, in a total male population of 20,000,000, it was the strongest fighting machine in Europe. Everyone knew that! Had not General Maurice Gustave Gamelin, the chief of staff, assured his people that his troops would make mincemeat of the

Germans? Admittedly, the French *poilu*—the infantryman—looked sloppy in his uniform, but he was well grounded in the essentials and he was a tough fighter, especially when on the defensive. His ordnance was old, he lacked planes and tanks, but he knew war—he had learned it at Verdun and the Somme in World War I. He was not exactly overjoyed by the necessity of combat, but once he got started he would teach the blasted Huns to stay on their side of the border.

The French military psychology, purely defensive, was strength, built into continuity and permanence. The Maginot Line, Europe's No. 1 fixed frontier, the world's most elaborate fortification system, was drawn in steel and concrete. Planned for some years beforehand, but actually begun in 1929 by War Minister André Maginot, it stretched from Switzerland to Montmédy in a series of gigantic pillboxes connecting France's old fortifications with two great new fortresses, Hackenberg and Hochwald, covering the iron and industrial region of Lorraine.

Into the Maginot Line went half a billion dollars and later an army of 300,000 men. It was an amazing construction—a series of huge underground forts on six levels, quarters for officers and men, ammunition dumps, general stores, water tanks, kitchens, barracks, power stations for ventilation and lighting, telephone exchanges, miniature railroads, elaborate drainage systems, ammunition hoists, hospitals, rest rooms, all invulnerable to shells and bombs. Above ground were the casemates, served by elevators, holding guns pointed only toward the east.

But there was a curious weakness in the Maginot Line. The men who planned it did not intend it to be more than a partial defense, but the French public deemed it a total defense. From the Meuse to the Pas-de-Calais area, the classic route of German invasion in the past, the terrain was open or only slightly protected. It was a shockingly shortsighted defensive credo. The fast-moving, elastic German avalanche of steel would have no trouble outflanking the "impregnable" Maginot Line.

Hitler's response was a gigantic bluff. The Siegfried, or Limes Line, was a lightly-built triple line of fortifications supposed to run from Switzerland to Luxemburg, with its key point at the rebuilt fortress at Listen opposite French Mulhouse. A half million men under Germany's great road-builder, Dr. Fritz Todt, were hastily mobilized to speed up the work and pour concrete to make the Third Reich invasion-proof. But there was nothing like the French effort. Hitler had no intention of fighting a war of fixed defense. Hence, he spread concrete dragon's teeth over the earth to delay an enemy long enough for reserves to be moved to the point of penetration.

In its early days it was a strange war. Gunners in both the Maginot and Siegfried Lines deliberately tried to avoid damaging the other side. They were uncannily accurate in framing an enemy post with a ring of shells, all of which fell directly around but not on the target. The French, apparently anesthetized by Hitler's war of nerves, even demobilized some of their troops and sent them home.

The British, too, were overconfident. The British Expeditionary Force had crossed to France to the strains of:

We'll hang out our washing on the Siegfried Line—
If the Siegfried Line's still there!

THE ASSAULT ON FRANCE

An end to the honeymoon came with the fierce Battle of Flanders, which freed the German troops for a southward swing against France. The French High Command knew that desperate measures had to be taken to halt the German *Blitzkrieg.*

On May 18, 1940, Premier Paul Reynaud reconstructed his cabinet, taking the ministry of defense for himself and appointing Marshal Henri Pétain, the 85-year-old hero of Verdun, as vice premier. The next day he removed General Maurice Gustave Gamelin from supreme command of the army and replaced him with General Maxime Weygand, the 72-year-old former chief of staff to Marshal Ferdinand Foch.

While the fighting at Dunkirk was still in progress, Weygand gave orders to establish a line south of the Somme and Aisne Rivers, from Abbeville to Montmédy, and called for feverish preparations to meet the Nazi onslaught. Thirty-seven divisions were sent to the hastily constructed Weygand Line. It was far too late.

On June 3, 1940, came the first air raid on Paris. Two days later Hitler unleashed 100 divisions in a terrific attack at four points—across the Somme into northern Normandy; south of Amiens in a spearhead directed at Paris; down the Oise River in another arrow toward the French capital; and around the northern flank of the Maginot Line. The assault came with the impact of several thunderbolts.

The *Luftwaffe*, ranging the skies virtually unopposed, hurled destruction on the French troops below. German tanks, in clusters of a hundred or more, raced through the countryside, scattering the disorganized French and destroying everything before them. On June 6 the French reported enemy attacks, with 2,000 tanks, from the sea to Chemin des Dames.

Weygand soon lost control of "Europe's finest army." The German tanks had smashed through his first defenses. He tried to catch them in concealed traps behind the lines, but he could not. He failed because the French army was already beaten, and partly because other commanders had not used this same stratagem of defense in depth earlier in the campaign.

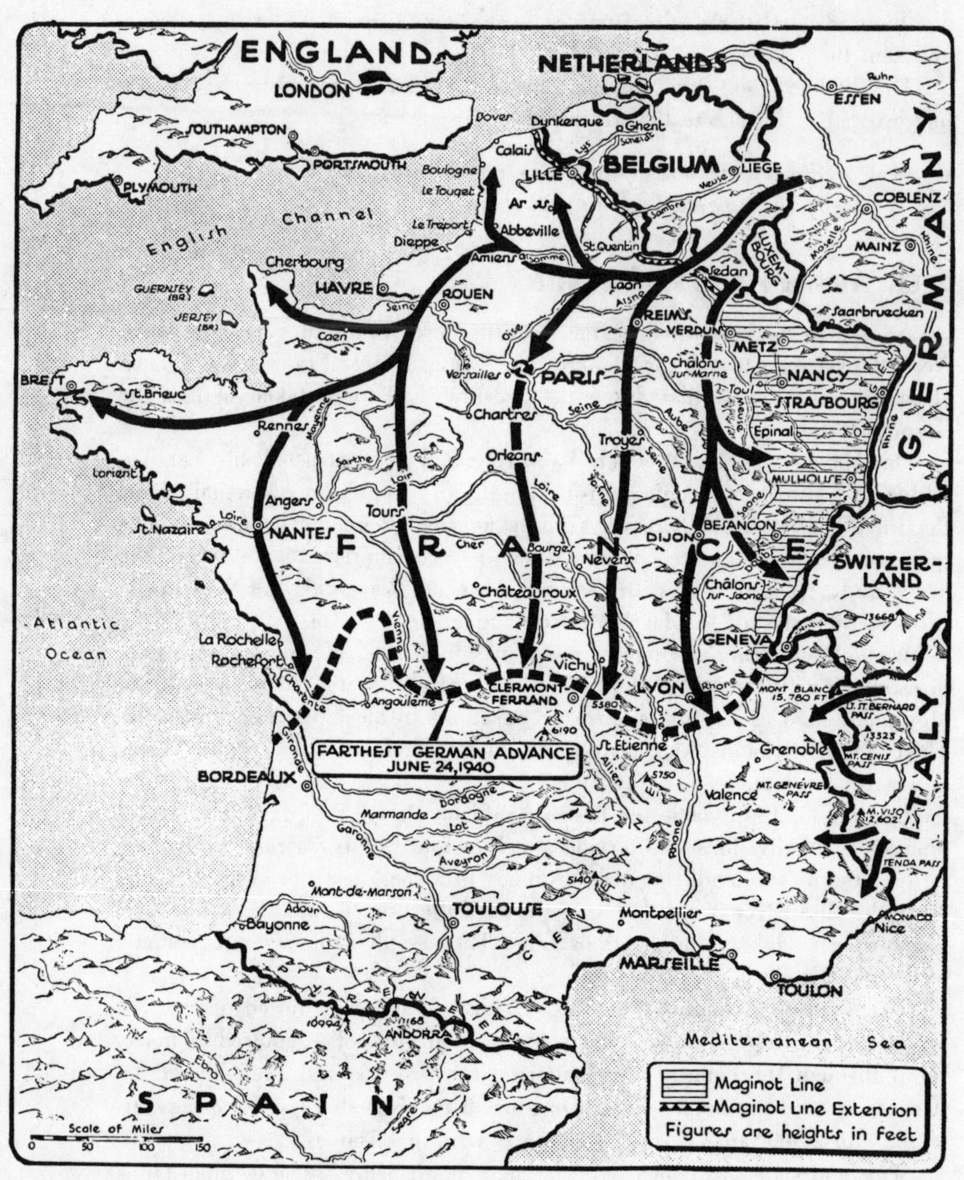

BATTLE OF FRANCE, 1940

The speed of the German drive left no time for effective counterattack. The Germans, moving fast, pierced the makeshift Weygand Line at either extremity above Beauvais and above Reims, while the French army plunged into headlong retreat, reeling southward under massive German blows.

All France degenerated into panic, terror, hysteria, confusion.

There was chaos on the roads. The onrushing Germans, aiming to immobilize the retreating enemy, deliberately induced a mass exodus of the civilian population. Hundreds of thousands of refugees, desperately anxious to escape from Paris, jammed the roads south to Bordeaux for a distance of 400 miles. They used everything that could move—carts, bicycles, taxicabs, trucks, bakery vans, roadsters, even hearses. All these were loaded with human beings, shouting, wailing, cursing.

It seemed to be a field day for Hitler's young supermen. German pilots in speedy *Heinkels* roared up and down at tree level over the roads where civilian refugees were trapped and helpless in the traffic jams. Bombs and bullets burst among the automobiles, carts, farm wagons, and bicycles, catching humans and horses in a deadly mélange of flame and smoke. Lining the roads leading south from Paris were hundreds of bodies spread-eagled in grotesque attitudes of death.

"It was difficult to believe," wrote Virginia Cowles, an eyewitness, "that these were the citizens of Paris, citizens whose forefathers had fought for their freedom like tigers and stormed the Bastille with their bare hands. Try to think of noise and confusion, of the thick smell of petrol, of the scraping of automobile gears, of shouts, wails, curses, tears. Try to think of a hot sun and underneath it an unbroken stream of humanity flowing southwards from Paris, and you have a picture of the gigantic civilian exodus that presaged the German advance."

Quentin Reynolds, the great reporter, covered 50 miles in eight hours. "Thousands of these people had come from the north, many had been on the road for two weeks. They had only one thought: move south. Move away from terror that swooped down from the skies. Move away from the serfdom that would be theirs under German rule. Few had any money. Few knew where they were going. . . . Those on bicycles managed to keep going, winding in and out of the massed traffic. . . . We passed stranded cars every few minutes. Sometimes people pushed their cars, hoping that there would be fuel in the next town. There was no fuel in the next town."

On June 11, 1940, as the French armies were retiring across the Marne, the government, concluding that the defense of Paris was suicidal and fearful lest the city suffer the same fate as Warsaw and Amsterdam, left for Tours.

THE JACKAL STRIKES: MUSSOLINI'S DAGGER IN THE BACK

A day earlier, on June 10, 1940, had come jarring news for Frenchmen already reeling under German blows. With the enemy only 35 miles from Paris, word came that 400,000 Italians had invaded France through the Riviera.

The *Duce* had become more warlike with each successive Nazi triumph. He was pleased by the success of German arms, but at the same time he was concerned lest Italy be left behind in the race for glory and prestige. It was not pleasant to be relegated to an inferior role. He, Mussolini, was seldom consulted on German plans, which "were locked in the impenetrable bosom of the *Fuehrer*." The *Duce* had complained: "Hitler always faces me with a *fait accompli*."

The Italian dictator was adept at the game of double cross. In September 1939 he had let word leak out to the British minister in Rome that, despite the Rome-Berlin Axis, Italy would not enter the war, an assurance that may have encouraged London to challenge Hitler. Now, in 1940, when it appeared that France was finished and the European war virtually won by Germany, Mussolini would throw in his Fascist legions and share the spoils of victory.

The way had already been prepared on March 18, 1940, when Hitler and Mussolini met at the Brenner Pass for a session of mutual admiration and consultation. From this time on the Italian press and radio stepped up its campaign to ease the way for war. There was not much enthusiasm among Italians, but Mussolini had willed his war.

Premier Paul Reynaud, overwhelmed by a thousand pressing problems, sought desperately to ward off the coming Italian blow. He made a last-minute offer of concessions to Italy in North Africa, but Mussolini, intrigued by the possibility of a bloodless victory, was in no mood to accept trifling grants. He had already made his decision for war.

At 4:30 on the afternoon of June 10, 1940, the Italian foreign minister, Count Galeazzo Ciano, Mussolini's son-in-law, called the French ambassador to the Chigi Palace and gave him this brusque message for his government: "His Majesty the King-Emperor declares that Italy considers herself in a state of war against France beginning tomorrow, June 11." A quarter of an hour later an identical communication was handed to the British ambassador. Italian troops were already on the move.

At 5 o'clock that same day a huge crowd appeared in the Piazza Venezia in Rome to hear Mussolini speak. There was nothing spontaneous about the demonstration, which was carefully stage-managed in approved Fascist style. Members of the Roman Fascist Party were ordered to meet at certain areas and proceed to the square. The *Giovani Fascisti* (Young Fascists), youths from 18 to 21, were placed in the center of the crowd to whip up enthusiasm. Shopkeepers were told to close for the day promptly at 5 o'clock. All day loudspeakers throughout the ancient city blared announcements that the *Duce* was going to make a critical pronouncement to the Italian nation. Of such stuff was the dictator's popularity made.

The speech, punctuated by shouts of "*Duce! Duce! Duce!*," was emotional and bellicose, summarizing Italian grievances, beseeching the people to fight on to victory, and warning the Balkan countries and the Mediterranean nations that any breach of neutrality would have dire consequences.

> Fighters of land. sea, and air, Blackshirts of the revolution and of the legions, men and women of Italy, of the Empire and of the Kingdom of Albania, listen!
>
> The hour destined by fate is sounding for us. The hour of irrevocable decision has come. A declaration of war already has been handed to the Ambassadors of Great Britain and France.
>
> We take the field against the plutocratic and reactionary democracies who always have blocked the march and frequently plotted against the existence of the Italian people.
>
> Several decades of recent history may be summarized in these words: Phrases, promises, threats of blackmail, and, finally, crowning that ignoble edifice, the League of Nations of 52 nations.
>
> Our conscience is absolutely clear.
>
> With you, the entire world is witness that the Italy of Fascism has done everything humanly possible to avoid the tempest that envelops Europe, but all in vain. . . .
>
> If today we have decided to take the risks and sacrifices of war, it is because the honor, interests, and future firmly impose it, since a great people is truly such only if it considers its obligations sacred and does not avoid the supreme trials that determine the course of history.

Mussolini went on to explain that Italy was taking up arms, after having solved the problem of her continental frontiers, to clear the issue of her maritime frontiers. Break the territorial and military chains that confined Italy in her sea! A country of 45,000,000 souls was not free if it did not have access to the ocean!

The European conflict, said the *Duce*, was only a phase of the logical development of the Fascist revolution. It was a war of the poor, numerous working people against the bloated plutocratic imperialists who ferociously clung to a monopoly of all the riches on earth. It was a conflict between "fruitful, useful peoples" and "peoples in decline," a conflict between two ages, two ideas.

The *Duce* then reminded his hearers that he was loyal to his Axis partner:

> Italians, in a memorable mass meeting in Berlin, I said that according to the rules of Fascist morals when one has a friend one marches with him to

> the end. This we have done and will continue to do with Germany, her people, and her victorious armed forces.

He closed in grandiose style:

> On this eve of an event of import for centuries, we turn our thoughts to His Majesty, the King and Emperor, who always has understood the thought of the country.
>
> Lastly, we salute the new *Fuehrer*, the chief of great allied Germany.
>
> Proletarian, Fascist Italy has arisen for the third time, strong, proud, compact as never before.
>
> There is only one order. It is categorical and obligatory for every one. It already wins over and enflames hearts from the Alps to the Indian Ocean: Conquer!
>
> And we will conquer in order, finally, to give a new world of peace with justice to Italy, to Europe, and to the universe.
>
> Italian people, rush to arms and show your tenacity, your courage, your valor.

From the Allied world came scorn, derision, and indignation. Churchill contemptuously dismissed Italy's action in one word—"Cowardice." In an address at the University of Virginia, President Roosevelt commented acidly: "On this tenth day of June, 1940, the hand that held the dagger has struck it into the back of its neighbor. On this tenth day of June, 1940, from this university, founded by the great American teacher of democracy, we send forward our prayers and our hopes to those beyond the seas who are maintaining with magnificent valor their battle for freedom."

The entry of Italy into the war brought against the Allies an army of 1,000,000 men, a navy of more than 700,000 tons, and some 4,000 planes. The effect on France was negligible—Hitler had already won his victory there. What it meant was that there would be an inevitable spread of the fighting in the Balkans, the Mediterranean, Suez, and North Africa.

For Mussolini it meant that his miscalculation would cost him an empire.

MAGNIFICENT FIASCO: THE BRITISH OFFER UNION WITH FRANCE

On June 12, 1940, Winston Churchill flew to Tours in a last-minute attempt to persuade the French cabinet to honor its promise not to sue for a separate peace and to carry on the war from North Africa. M. Reynaud agreed, but by this time his colleagues were certain that the situation was hopeless. General Weygand, defeatist, predicted that "England's neck would be wrung like a chicken's."

June 14, 1940. The triumphant Germans, led by an Austrian honor vanguard, entered Paris. They found a deserted, ghostly quiet city. The few remaining Parisians watched in silence as Hitler's rosy-cheeked, immaculate young warriors stomped through the streets. Le Bourget, the great airport, was a shambles. Along the Champs Élysées only one café was open. Hotels were closed, taxicabs had disappeared, the streets were virtually empty. Within hours the swastika was flying from every prominent and historical structure in the city, from the Quai d'Orsay, the Arc de Triomphe, the Eiffel Tower, the Palais de Justice, and the Hôtel Crillon, where the invaders set up military headquarters.

From the Italian press came hoots of derision over the fall of Paris. The *Lavoro Fascista* in huge headlines gloated: "*C'est Paris!* Capitalists, Jews, Masons, and snobs all over the world, are in mourning." The *Tevere* was liberal with advice: "Let that nation of carrion learn once and for all time, in the torture of direst defeat, to respect the honor of other peoples. Let them remain on their knees for centuries. And as for the English, let them remember that their time will come."

The first ceremonial review of the victors was held on the spacious Place de la Concorde, where two German planes, in a mingled gesture of pride and contempt, landed and delivered that morning's newspapers. It was an arrogant expression of German efficiency. The next day the boulevards of Paris were covered with lines of German army vehicles bearing troops and supplies to battle areas outside the city.

"All is lost!" wailed Premier Reynaud. Desperately he appealed to Roosevelt to send "clouds of airplanes." (M. Reynaud's first appeal to President Roosevelt was on June 10; published, June 13; new appeal, 11:30 P.M., June 13; the President's reply, June 15.)

June 16, 1940. The French front was cracking. The Germans, who were breaking through in Champagne, announced that they had pierced the Maginot Line and were pushing the French across the Loire. The situation was deteriorating rapidly.

On that same day Churchill proposed that France and Great Britain combine into a Franco-British union. It was an astonishing proposal—especially in view of Britain's traditional attitude of splendid isolation from the Continent. Such was the gravity with which Churchill regarded the imminent fall of France.

The proposed Declaration of Union called for a constitution providing for joint organs of defense, joint foreign, financial, and economic policies. Every citizen of France would have immediate British citizenship, and every British citizen would become a citizen of France. Both countries would share responsibility for repairing the devastation of war, and the resources of both would be equally applied to that purpose.

As far as the current war was concerned, the British proposal suggested a single war cabinet, with all the forces of Britain and France under its direction. It would govern from wherever it best could. The two parliaments were to be formally associated.

"The Union appeals to the United States to fortify the economic resources of the Allies, and to bring her powerful material aid to the common cause.

"The Union will concentrate its whole energy against the power of the enemy, no matter where the battle may be.

"And thus we shall conquer."

Behind this fine gesture there was political purpose. It was hoped that the proposal would strengthen Premier Reynaud's position in an important meeting of the French cabinet held at 5 P.M. on June 16. Despite the desperate condition of their army, members of Reynaud's cabinet began to search for hidden motives in the British offer. *À quoi sert de le faire?* What good would it do? asked Reynaud's colleagues. France was about to collapse under the impact of Hitler's war machine, and surely Britain would be next. From all sides came calls for surrender, from Pétain, from Laval, even from Reynaud's circle of close friends.

The British offer was rejected. Nothing came of the extraordinary scheme. A few hours later Reynaud resigned. He was succeeded by Marshal Henri Pétain, who promptly led France down the road to Fascism.

Once again Hitler had triumphed.

On June 17, 1940, the Germans announced that Orleans and Metz had been captured and that the Swiss frontier had been reached near Besançon. On this day the aged Marshal Pétain told the people by radio that he had assumed political control. "It is futile to continue the struggle against an enemy superior in numbers and in arms. It is with a heavy heart that I say we must cease the fight. I have applied to our opponent to ask him if he is ready to sign with us, as between soldiers after the fight and in honor, a means to put an end to hostilities."

The old marshal had forgotten that the ancient scruples and conventions concerning combat were no more. Twentieth-century war was far less chivalrous, more bloody and calculating. As if Hitler would talk to him as one soldier to another! Pétain surrendered before he had even asked what were the terms of an armistice.

That same day the German armies were in possession of a quarter of all France. There was wild rejoicing in the streets of Berlin. The incomparable *Fuehrer* had done it again! In ten months the Nazi steam roller had crushed seven countries, including "invincible" France.

Propaganda Minister Joseph Goebbels congratulated the victorious German legions: "You have just one more battle to win, then the bells of peace will ring." That peace, said Goebbels, would be dictated to the Allies in London.

COMPIÈGNE: A MASTERPIECE OF REVENGE

Four miles north of the town of Compiègne and about 45 miles north of Paris stood a rustic clearing. Here, at 5 A.M. on the morning of November 11, 1918, in his private railway car, Marshal Ferdinand Foch had dictated terms of surrender to the Germans at the conclusion of World War I.

The French had carefully preserved the historic car and around it had constructed a memorial. At the end of the avenue there was a monument to Alsace-Lorraine: a large sword representing the Allies penetrated the limp eagle of the German Empire, over the inscription "*To the heroic soldiers of France, defenders of our country and of right, glorious liberators of Alsace-Lorraine.*"

In the center of the clearing was a great granite block inscribed: "*Here on the eleventh of November, 1918, succumbed the criminal pride of the German Empire, vanquished by the free peoples which it tried to enslave.*" A small stone, some 50 yards away, marked the point at which the railroad car of the German plenipotentiary had stood. This stone, set between a pair of rusty railway tracks, bore only three words: "*The German Plenipotentiary.*"

For the Francophobist of Berchtesgaden these were fighting words. When France fell, the *Fuehrer*, intoxicated by the wine of revenge, had danced an exultant jig (carefully photographed for posterity). Now he stage-managed the French surrender with dramatic vindictiveness. He, the lonely corporal of World War I, would grind the French noses into the dirt of Compiègne at the very spot of Germany's 1918 humiliation. Thereby he, the great Hitler, would right a historical wrong.

At 3:15 on the afternoon of June 21, 1940, Hitler alighted from his automobile before the Alsace-Lorraine monument. He was in uniform with the Iron Cross below his left breast pocket. Behind him was bemedaled Field Marshal Hermann Goering, holding his jeweled baton, Colonel General Wilhelm Keitel, chief of the High Command, Colonel General Walther von Brauchitsch, commander in chief of the German army, Erich Raeder, Grand Admiral of the German Fleet, Foreign Minister Joachim von Ribbentrop, and Rudolf Hess, Hitler's deputy. The Germans moved slowly around the clearing, reading the inscriptions.

The armistice railway car had been moved about 75 yards to the shelter of a museum, but German engineers, the day before, had rolled it back to its original site. The Germans now entered the car, Hitler taking the seat once used by Marshal Foch.

A few minutes later the French delegation appeared in the clearing. It was composed of General Charles Huntziger, spokesman for the envoys, General of Aviation Jean Marie Joseph Bergeret, Rear Admiral Maurice Athanase Le Luc, and Léon Noël, former French ambassador to Poland.

The guard of honor snapped to attention but did not present arms. The German and French officers exchanged salutes, but there was no handshaking. The Frenchmen then entered the car.

Hitler and his entourage rose from their seats, a subtle reminder that the French in 1918 had not granted that courtesy. Hitler gave the Nazi salute, the German and French officers exchanged military salutes. At a nod from Hitler, General Keitel began to read the preamble to the armistice terms:

> In reliance on the assurance given to the German Reich by the American President Wilson and confirmed by the Allied Powers, German forces laid down their arms in November 1918.
>
> Therewith was ended a war which the German people and their government had not wanted and in which the enemy, despite tremendous superiority, did not successfully in any way conquer the German army, navy, or German air force.
>
> However, at the moment of the arrival of the German Armistice Commission, violation of the ceremoniously given promise began. On November 11, 1918, in this car there began the time of suffering of the German people.
>
> What dishonor and humiliation, what human and material suffering had its outbreak here! Broken promises and perjury conspired against a people which after more than four years of heroic resistance had only one weakness —belief in the promises of democratic statesmen.
>
> On September 3, 1939—25 years after the outbreak of the World War—England and France again declared war on Germany without any basis.
>
> Now the decision by arms has been reached. France has been conquered. The French government has requested the Reich government to make known to them the German conditions for an armistice.
>
> In the historic Compiègne Forest, designated for the reception of these conditions, this is done in order once and for all to wipe out by this act of redeeming justice the memory which for France was no glorious page in its history, but which the German nation has always felt as the deepest humiliation of all times.
>
> After heroic resistance, France has been defeated and broken down in a sequence of bloody battles.
>
> Germany, therefore, does not intend to give the armistice conditions or armistice negotiations characteristic of aspersions against an enemy so brave.
>
> The purpose of the German demands are:
>
> 1. To prevent a resumption of the fight.
> 2. To offer to Germany all guarantees necessary for continuance of the war against Great Britain, which Britain forces upon Germany, as well as
> 3. To create preconditions for the formation of a new peace whose essential contents will be reparation for the wrong done to the German Reich by force.

This was enough for the beaming *Fuehrer*. He would not waste his precious time by remaining to discuss details. Glancing once more at the stolid Frenchmen opposite him, he abruptly stood up, raised his arm in the Nazi salute, and, followed by his party, left the car. A military band struck up *Deutschland über Alles* and the *Horst Wessel Lied*. The shaken French delegation then left for a near-by tent to begin a telephone conversation with the French government now at Bordeaux.

The entire proceedings took exactly 27 minutes.

Then came 27 hours of armistice discussions. Hitler's terms were hard. All German prisoners were to be released immediately. The French were to disarm and discharge their troops. All French warships were to put in at ports controlled by the Axis. German forces would occupy more than half the area of France including the Atlantic coastline down to the Spanish border. The French would meet the costs of the occupation. Unoccupied France would be administered by a regime friendly to Germany.

At 6:50 P.M. on June 22, 1940, the armistice was formally signed by the German negotiators and by the French envoys, the latter with tears in their eyes. Hitler ordered the historic railway car to be taken to Berlin.

Thus was imposed on France the most humiliating defeat in all her history. No other great power in modern times had ever fallen so far so fast as France in her inept struggle against Hitler. The world was left aghast.

In Berlin, masses broke into the strains of *Wir fahren gegen Engeland* ("We Sail against England"):

Our flag waves as we march along.
It is a symbol of the power of our Reich,
And we can no longer endure
That the Englishman should laugh at it.
So give me thy hand, thy fair white hand,
Ere we sail away to conquer Eng-e-land!

The German press roared acclaim. The *Frankfurter Zeitung* hailed the proceedings at Compiègne as "a shame wiped out" and "a piece of great history." "This time the defeated nation has been struck down by weapons alone in a military catastrophe without parallel, and no friendly help stood at the victor's side. Germany, which was once without belief and without hope, is today stronger than for many centuries. All eyes turn now to the gas-blinded lance corporal of 1918."

Two days after Compiègne, Hitler alighted from his motor car at the Hôtel des Invalides in Paris. Stopping in the central crypt, he looked silently on the fine sarcophagus of red porphyry containing the remains of the great Napoleon.

Outside was the hushed corpse of Paris.

On July 19, 1940, Hitler, in the flush of victory, created a host of new field marshals—von Brauchitsch, von Rundstedt, von Reichenau, von Leeb, von Bock, von Kluge, von Witzleben, Keitel, and the *Luftwaffe* generals Kesselring, Sperrle, and Milch.

The *Fuehrer* was at the peak of his Olympian grandeur. His armies were now triumphantly poised along the greatest front in history. The irresistible Nazi tide had surged westward across Europe: Poland in 26 days; Norway in 28 days; Denmark in 24 hours; Holland in 5 days; Belgium in 18 days; France in 35 days!

The New Europe was being carved out precisely the way Hitler had described it in *Mein Kampf*.

WHY FRANCE FELL

There is no easy explanation for the sudden and shocking fall of France. "The greatest mistake a historian could make," said the historian William L. Langer, "would be to try to construct a neat, logical pattern when in actual fact everything was confusion and contradiction." True enough—there were literally dozens of factors interwoven in a maze of conflicting patterns.

The myth of French military strength, notoriously exaggerated, was shattered by Hitler's fast-moving steel monsters. As it turned out, the Germans were superior in every department of war—in manpower, in leadership, in *esprit de corps*. The French General Staff, mistakenly assuming that the Germans would batter themselves to death against the Maginot Line, were trapped by the sheer audacity of the German onslaught.

A puzzling question: Why did French military leadership neglect to fortify the terrain in the Ardennes region?

The French were beaten in 1940 by a skillful, bold enemy ready to pounce on any weakness. They thought that the central sector of their defense, with the heights of the Ardennes backed by the Meuse River, would be neglected by the Germans; yet this was the precise sector where Hitler made his most effective penetration. Worst of all was the French tendency to underrate the role of air power. In 1937, at a time when Germany was zealously producing at least 1,000 planes a month, French factories turned out just 38 planes per month.

The body of France was prostrate in political chaos, weakened by the traditional dissension of bloc government. Year after year it was the same story—collapsing cabinets, civic disunity, political corruption, eternal intrigues, personal vendettas, an amazing variety of selfish factionalisms. Both Right and Left tore at each other in savage battles. The bureaucracy was ensnared in red tape. There was no effective leadership, neither a Churchill nor a Roosevelt to rally the masses to a crusade against Hitlerism.

Added to this impossible political situation was an economy drained by corruption and the historic French reluctance to pay taxes. The industrial organism was weakened by the sit-down strikes of 1936 and by continuing squabbles between employers and employees.

Psychologically, the French were tired, dejected, demoralized, asking only to be left alone. Gone was the military *élan* of Revolutionary France, Napoleonic France, or the France of World War I. A generation of French writers successfully indoctrinated vast sections of the population with the thesis that pacifism was the only way for a civilized nation. Dunkirk convinced these and many others that resistance to Hitler was plainly stupid. Let others assume the task of trapping the bestial little fanatic beyond the Rhine!

France was betrayed as well as defeated. Before the outbreak of war a subversive fifth column did its work well, carefully preparing the way for Hitler's *Panzer* divisions. Its propaganda was devilishly effective. The British were using Frenchmen as pawns; Britons were ready to fight to the last Frenchman. Nazi agents, disguised as tourists and salesmen, established contact with defeatist French elements. Once the war was on, the agents helped the invaders by giving false information, signaling German planes, issuing false and contradictory orders, encouraging sabotage and desertions. French Fascists and Communists, irreconcilable opponents, united only in undermining the foundations of French survival.

General de Gaulle summed it up this way: "France lost the war for very definite reasons. First, our military system did not develop any mechanized strength in the air and on the ground; second, the panic paralyzed our civilian population when the German mechanized units advanced; third, the tangible effect the fifth column had on the minds of many of our leaders; and fourth, lack of coördination between us and our Allies."

France, home of Napoleonic glory, fountainhead of the Western Enlightenment, fell like a rotted log, ground into the dust under the conqueror's heel.

Such was the harvest planted by ostrich-headed militarists, ambitious and selfish politicians, deserters and traitors, and reaped by a people who forgot that eternal vigilance is necessary for the maintenance of liberty, equality, and fraternity.

To the British, Americans, and later the Russians was left the job of killing the voracious dragon that was Hitlerism.

CHAPTER 6

Their Finest Hour: Britain Stands Alone

Even if, which I do not for a moment believe, this island or a large part of it were subjugated and starving, then, our Empire beyond the seas, armed and guarded by the British fleet, would carry on the struggle, until, in God's good time, the New World, with all its power and might, steps forth to the rescue and the liberation of the Old.

—Winston Churchill, June 4, 1940

We challenge the lion of England,
For the last and decisive cup.
We judge and we say
An Empire breaks up. . . .

Listen to the engine singing—get on to the foe!
Listen, in your ears it's ringing—get on to the foe!
BOMBS, OH BOMBS, OH BOMBS ON ENGLAND!

—German *War Song Against England*, 1940

Napoleon tried. The Dutch were on the way,
A Norman did it—and a Dane or two.
Some sailor-King may follow one fine day;
But not, I think, a low land-rat like you.

—A. P. Herbert, September 1940

THE BATTLE OF BRITAIN

What General Weygand had called the "Battle of France" was over and the Nazis were victorious. The Battle of Britain was about to begin.

What concerned the British most after the fall of France was the disposition of the French fleet. The armistice provided that the fleet should be interned, and Hitler had promised not to use it. But of what earthly value was Hitler's word? Moreover, many high officers in the French navy were strongly anti-British and might be inclined to go along with the *Fuehrer*. In that case, German, Italian, and French fleets combined might cripple British sea power and the war would be lost.

There was no problem about French ships in British ports, all of which were taken over on July 3, 1940, with virtually no bloodshed. The crews either joined the Royal Navy, or organized themselves as Free French units, or returned to France. Other units at Alexandria were demobilized by mutual consent.

But the greater part of the French fleet lay off the French North African port of Oran in Algeria. On that same day, July 3, 1940, three of Britain's largest warships, commanded by Vice Admiral Sir James F. Somerville, steamed into Oran. Somerville sent to the French commander, Vice Admiral Marcel B. Gensoul, an ultimatum offering several alternative courses of action. Gensoul could (1) join forces with the British against the Germans; or (2) sail to a British port, where his crews would be repatriated and the ships or their equivalent restored to France after the war; or (3) sail to the French West Indies, where his ships would either be demilitarized or entrusted to the United States until the end of hostilities.

Unless one of these three alternatives were taken within six hours, Somerville declared, the French fleet would be sunk to prevent it from falling into German or Italian hands.

Gensoul elected to fight. The British reluctantly opened fire, sinking or disabling three French battleships, a seaplane carrier, and two destroyers. One badly hammered battleship, the *Strasbourg*, and several smaller craft managed to escape and eventually reached Toulon. Another French capital ship stationed at Dakar was immobilized by a surprise attack.

The British Admiralty took a few moments to relax following this good news.

From Germany came the strident voice of Adolf Hitler: "I am not the vanquished seeking favors, but the victor speaking in the name of reason." Hitler was giving the British a last chance to surrender before their complete annihilation. In view of the invincibility of German arms he would be willing to arrange "a common-sense peace through negotiations."

The *Fuehrer*, that kindly man, was inclined to be magnanimous. All he wanted was recognition of his conquests, Germany's colonies returned, acknowledgment of his role as the arbiter of Europe, and, above all, Winston Churchill thrown out of office. The British would do well to take his advice. After all, had he not paid tribute to British fighting qualities in *Mein Kampf*, the ultimate compliment? And were not the Anglo-Saxons of the same racial stock as their brother Germans?

"It was, perhaps," said the British historian, J. W. Wheeler-Bennett, "the most outstanding example of the 'Love-hate' complex toward Britain which so many Germans through the ages have shared with Wilhelm II and Adolf Hitler."

Perhaps it would have been good logic and better common sense for the British to accept Hitler's offer and thereby extricate themselves from a disastrous situation. They had seen their allies, one by one, fall victims of Nazi power. Their troops had been driven from Norway and from the Continent. Dunkirk had been a glorious retreat, indeed, but British troops had abandoned all their heavy equipment there, and after that fiasco there were only a hundred tanks in all England. The British were ill prepared to carry on. In 1940 they alone remained at war with Hitler, the conqueror of Europe, just as in 1807 they alone opposed Napoleon, then the master of Europe.

To the *Fuehrer*'s offer Britons replied with a contemptuous silence. Nothing, however, could silence the golden tongue of Winston Churchill, who, with the British people, now stood alone between Hitler and the realization of his grandiloquent ambitions.

From Churchill came the measured words:

> Upon this battle depends the survival of Christian civilization. Upon it depends our British life, and the long continuity of our institutions and our Empire. The whole fury and might of the enemy must very soon be turned on us. Hitler knows that he will have to break us in this island or lose the war. If we can stand up to him, all Europe may be free and the life of the world may move forward into broad, sunlit uplands. But if we fail, then the whole world, including the United States, including all that we have known and cared for, will sink into the abyss of a new Dark Age, made more sinister, and perhaps more protracted, by the lights of perverted science.
>
> Let us therefore brace ourselves to our duties and so bear ourselves that, if the British Empire and its Commonwealth last for a thousand years, men will still say, "This was their finest hour."

All Englishmen, from lord to fishmonger, from lady to servant girl, from Land's End to the Shetlands, rallied to the cause.

Hitler had paused for six weeks after the fall of France. Thus far he had made no preparations for a cross-Channel move and he was caught short by his own success. One reason he hesitated to press in for a kill at Dunkirk was his uncertainty. He feared a French attack to the rear, a British troop-landing elsewhere in France, and the possibility of Russian aggression.

In those six weeks the British began the process of transforming their little island into a mighty fortress. Every man in the country was placed at the disposal of the government, as was every shilling. Any possible fifth column was stopped in its tracks by the arrest and imprisonment of suspects. The Civil Defense Service, fire fighters, repair units, and demolition squads were promptly organized; special efforts were made to protect such essential services as water, sewerage, electricity, gas, and telephone lines; all citizens were required to serve as fire watchers for incendiary bombs; the Home Guard, consisting of older men, appeared spontaneously, eventually totaling more than 1,000,000 men. Factories went on a round-the-clock schedule to turn out planes, guns, and shells.

Meanwhile, from the American stockpiles of World War I came such invaluable stopgap weapons as Springfield rifles, Browning machine guns, and artillery pieces. These would have to do until the assembly lines started rolling.

The British guessed correctly that the burden of defense would fall on the Royal Air Force. They had 1,475 first-line planes to send into combat against the 2,670 aircraft Hitler had set aside for his campaign against England. British engineers and physicists had already developed radar, a miraculous precision instrument with which to counteract the coming air assault. In addition, they perfected counterdevices to jam the directional radio beams from the Netherlands and France which were used to guide high-flying *Luftwaffe* planes.

Nothing was left to chance. Trenches were dug and concrete pillars placed on possible landing fields. Target areas were covered with a maze of balloons flown on steel cables to trap low-flying planes. Watches were set up against parachutists. All guideposts were removed from the roads, and motorcar owners were instructed to disable their cars before locking them up for the night.

The most important weapon of all was British determination to fight to the death.

August 6, 1940. From his country home, Karin Hall, Field Marshal Hermann Goering issued orders for the first great mass attack on England. Several days later the fury of the *Luftwaffe* was unleashed against the coastal towns of southern England, against aircraft factories and fighter fields. In wave after wave, in groups of a hundred or more, an armada of a thousand planes—shrieking *Stuka* dive bombers, fast *Messerschmitts* and *Focke-Wulfs*, heavy *Dorniers*—struck at Britain in an all-out attack.

Young Royal Air Force fighters, prodigies of skill and daring, plus a few score Poles, Czechs, Frenchmen, and Belgians, rose in speedy Spitfires and

Hurricanes to meet Hitler's death birds. It was a battle royal. Incredibly fierce were the dogfights, a vast, wild jamboree of twisting, tangling, flame-spitting planes, a crazy din of spattering machine-gun fire. The sky was thick with mushroom puffs from antiaircraft shells. Swarms of raiders tore viciously at the moored barrage balloons; many got through and dumped their lethal loads on targets below. Again and again the German planes pounced down out of the sun, some crashing in plumes of smoke, others rocketing into the Channel and sending up huge white geysers.

That first day at least 53 Nazi airmen met a flaming death. The score mounted day by day during the next fortnight. In one August week the *Luftwaffe* lost 256 planes to the British 130.

Hitler had failed in his first attempt to drive the R.A.F. from the skies as a step toward invasion.

Churchill paid a magnificent tribute to the handful of intrepid pilots, many of them still in their teens:

> The gratitude of every home in our Island, in our Empire, and indeed throughout the world, except in the abodes of the guilty, goes out to the British airmen who, undaunted by odds, unwearied in their constant challenge and mortal danger, are turning the tide of the World War by their prowess and by their devotion. Never in the field of human conflict was so much owed by so many to so few.

There were new war councils in Germany. Frustrated, Hitler decided to turn to a familiar German nonsecret weapon, *Schrecklichkeit.* He would strike terror into the hearts of this persistent enemy by smashing London as he had smashed Warsaw and Rotterdam. Sporadic attacks on the British capital had already been made, and German airmen were certain that they could wipe the city from the face of the earth. Witness these cocksure words, dated August 18, 1940, from the diary of a German aviator, Gottfried Leske, in *I Was a Nazi Flier* (1941): "Today I flew over the biggest city in the world. I knew with absolute certainty, as though I could foretell the future: This all will be destroyed. It will stand but a few days more. Until the moment the *Fuehrer* pronounces its death sentence. Then there will be nothing left but a heap of ruins."

Death sentence had been pronounced on London by the *Fuehrer*!

The first mass onslaught on London itself came on September 7, 1940, when huge flights of German planes attacked. "This is the historic hour," said Goering, "when our air force for the first time delivered its stroke right into the enemy's heart."

T. H. O'Brien, an official British historian, thus summarized the results of *Luftwaffe* operations against London on September 7 and 8, 1940:

> Between five and six o'clock on the evening of Saturday, 7 September, some 320 German bombers supported by over 600 fighters flew up the Thames

> and proceeded to bomb Woolwich Arsenal, Beckton Gas Works, a large number of docks, West Ham power station, and then the City, Westminster and Kensington. They succeeded in causing a serious fire situation in the docks. An area of about 1½ square miles between North Woolwich Road and the Thames was almost destroyed, and the population of Silvertown was surrounded by fire and had to be evacuated by water.
>
> At 8:10 P.M. some 250 bombers resumed the attack, which was maintained until 4:30 on Sunday morning. They caused 9 conflagrations, 59 large fires and nearly 1,000 lesser fires. Three main-line railway termini were put out of action, and 430 persons killed and some 1.600 seriously injured.
>
> After the fire brigade had spent all day in an effort to deprive the enemy of illumination, some 200 bombers returned at 7:30 in the evening to carry on the assault. During this second night a further 412 persons were killed and 747 seriously injured, and damage included the temporary stoppage of every railway line to the south.

From Churchill came a defiant judgment on Hitler: "This wicked man... this monstrous product of former wrongs and shame, has now resolved to try to break our famous Island race by a process of indiscriminate slaughter and destruction."

For the next 23 consecutive days the planes of the *Luftwaffe* roared in from Calais and up the Thames valley to the great metropolis. They came sometimes in mass formations of 250 craft, sometimes in small flights of a dozen planes, dropping tons of explosives and incendiaries, smashing at docks, houses, churches, factories, railways.

On September 13, 1940, bombs hit near Buckingham Palace, shattering several hundred windows in the royal residence and tearing huge craters in the courtyard. Two days later the *Luftwaffe* made another mass daylight attack on southern England and London. At first the British claimed that losses of German aircraft on that day amounted to 185, but later revised the figure to 56.

Yet the *National Zeitung*, a newspaper controlled by Goering, proclaimed that "at an extraordinarily rapid rate, London drifts toward its fate." D.N.B., the official German news agency, reported this communiqué of the German High Command: "Despite overcast skies the German Air Force continued retaliatory attacks yesterday and last night on military objectives in middle and south England, with especial attention to London. Dock and harbor facilities in the British capital suffered blows. Our fighters were successful in air battles over London."

London was stunned but defiant. The British fought back, their antiaircraft crews functioning with skill and effectiveness and the R.A.F. striking heavily at the invaders. Reporters and foreign correspondents were unanimous in praising the morale of the British under this air *Blitz*. Mollie Panter-Downes, in her weekly "Letter from London," dated September 8, 1940, presented an accurate word-picture in the *New Yorker*:

> The calm behavior of the average individual continues to be amazing. Commuting suburbanites, who up to yesterday had experienced worse bombardments than people living in central London, placidly brag to fellow passengers on the morning trains about the size of bomb craters in their neighborhoods, as in a more peaceful summer they would have bragged about their roses and squash. . . . The courage, humor, and kindliness of ordinary people continue to be astonishing under conditions that possess many of the merry features of a nightmare.

This was truly an amazing display of patience and fortitude. To those who expressed admiration, Londoners replied that "It isn't heroism at all. It's just that we British lack imagination!" Whatever complaints there were were well within the tradition of British understatement and unconscious humor. An elderly retired army officer resident in Great Snoring (sic!) wrote a letter to the editor of a journal in which he stated that too many war bulletins were bad for the nerves. "Let us have instead lectures on our historical and gallant fights for freedom and also a few calming nature talks."

Many Britishers were more upset about the limitations on horse racing than about the frequency of enemy air raids. *The Times* Cricket Correspondent protested mildly against daylight raids: "Interruptions such as occur these days make it quite impossible for a captain to declare his innings closed at a moment even approximate to that which would normally allow a reasonably close finish."

Britons were naturally concerned about their children, many of whom were evacuated from London; and there was almost as much concern about animals. Many worried about the effect of bombing noise on the country's bird population. The London press reported gravely that Monkey Hill at the Zoo had received a direct hit, "but the morale of the monkeys remained unaffected." Despite the food shortage, Englishmen made special efforts to keep their pets alive. Hitler in truth knew little about the fiber of the people he was trying to beat to its knees.

Helen Kirkpatrick reported in the Chicago *Daily News* on September 9, 1940:

> London still stood this morning. . . . But not all London was still there. . . . I walked through areas of rubble and debris in southeastern London this morning that made it seem incredible that anyone could be alive, but they were, and very much so. . . . Near one of many of Sir Christopher Wren's masterpieces, houses were gutted structures with windowpanes hanging out, while panes in a church were broken in a million pieces. . . . It is pretty incredible . . . to find people relatively unshaken after the terrific experience. There is some terror, but nothing on the scale that the Germans may have hoped for and certainly not on a scale to make Britons contemplate for a moment anything but fighting on. Fright becomes so mingled with a deep almost uncontrollable anger that it is hard to know when one stops and the

other begins. And on top of it all London is smiling even in the districts where casualties have been very heavy.

On October 1, 1940, Edward R. Murrow reported over the Columbia Broadcasting System:

> Today, in one of the most famous streets of London, I saw soldiers at work clearing away the wreckage of nearly an entire block. The men were covered with white dust. Some of them wore goggles to protect their eyes. They thought maybe people were still buried in the basement. The sirens sounded, and still they tore at the beams and bricks covering the place where the basements used to be.
>
> They are still working tonight. I saw them after tonight's raid started. They paid no attention to the bursts of antiaircraft fire overhead as they bent their backs and carried away basketfuls of mortar and brick. A few small steam shovels would help them considerably in digging through those ruins. But all the modern instruments seem to be overhead. Down here on the ground people must work with their hands.

The Germans unveiled a new weapon—the delayed-action bomb, which the British promptly dubbed the UXB, or unexploded bomb. The projectile buried itself into the ground and exploded later. For the harried Civil Defense Services there was no effective way to ascertain whether the buried projectile was a UXB or an ordinary bomb that had failed to explode. Officers and men of the Royal Engineers, assigned to the task of rendering the UXB's harmless, showed rare courage in grappling with these infernal machines that might have blown them to bits at any moment.

On September 12, 1940, an eight-foot UXB, weighing a ton, buried itself in the outer foundations of St. Paul's Cathedral near the southwest tower. A bomb-disposal squad, working coolly and silently, dug nearly 30 feet down around the bomb while a gas-main burned furiously in the midst of the excavation. It took nearly three days, but the squad finally extracted the devilish missile and transported it to Hackney Marshes, where it was detonated. The west portico of St. Paul's was saved by this display of raw courage.

Made hesitant by heavy losses, Hitler, in October 1940, shifted from daylight to night bombing, a tacit admission that his air attack had failed. He would now lower the morale of the British by wrecking their sleep, at the same time reducing his own losses. Coming in large formations at 30,000 feet, the German bombers shifted their target area from London to the Midland industrial cities of Birmingham and Manchester. By the end of October 1940 the Nazi air onslaught began to slow down.

The first phase of the Battle of Britain was concluded.

It was by no means all over. The air attacks on England continued well into June 1941, when most of the *Luftwaffe* was transferred to the Russian front. On the night of November 14-15, 1940, German bombers, active from dusk to dawn, smashed the heart out of Coventry in Britain's smoky Midlands, the city through which Lady Godiva had ridden nearly 900 years earlier to end a more local oppression. Whole blocks of buildings were churned by incendiary and high-explosive bombs in the night attack. The famous fourteenth-century brownstone cathedral, except for its 303-foot spire, was left a jumble of stone and mortar. More than a thousand known dead and wounded were left by that scourge, not counting unknown numbers trapped in the pile and stone and smoking timber. It was a night of unmitigated terror.

On the night of December 29-30, 1940, London received its most savage pounding of the war in a huge incendiary raid. More than 1,500 fires were started in the heart of the City, many of them in such historic old landmarks as the Guildhall and eight Wren churches.

In the spring of 1941 the *Luftwaffe* shifted its main attacks to the ports of Hull, Plymouth, and Bristol, but also continued hammering away at Liverpool, Manchester, and Birmingham. Eight successive raids on Plymouth left it a smoldering ruin, blasted more heavily than Coventry. The defenders used every possible trick to confuse the Germans, such as dummy fires to lead the raiders away from important targets.

In the first three months of the raids 12,696 Londoners lost their lives. During the war the Germans dropped an estimated 12,222 tons of bombs on London, killing a total of 29,890 and injuring more than 120,000. The Germans caused enormous material damage, but they never succeeded in halting British industrial production or in stopping the flow of overseas shipping. Any loss in production was more than made up by the importation of planes, ammunition, munitions, and supplies from the United States and Canada.

A major factor in winning the Battle of Britain against the numerically superior *Luftwaffe* was the development by a British team of physicists from Birmingham University of the resonant cavity magnetron, a new and powerful device that became the heart of all radar equipment. James Phinney Baxter, 3d, President of Williams College, later described the vital role of this device: "It sparked the whole development of microwave radar and constituted the most important item in reverse Lend-Lease." Radar helped make possible winning not only the Battle of Britain, but also the Battle of the Atlantic, the landings on the beaches of Normandy, and the pin-point bombing that later reduced German targets to shreds.

The *Luftwaffe* paid dearly for its overconfidence. In *Their Finest Hour* (1949) Churchill listed aircraft losses in the Battle of Britain from July 10 to October 31, 1940, as follows:

British Fighters Lost by R.A.F. (complete write-off or missing) 915
Enemy Aircraft Actually Destroyed (according to German records) 1,733
Enemy Aircraft Claimed by Us (Fighter Command, A.A., Balloons, etc.) 2,698

Hitler lost the Battle of Britain because, by shifting indiscriminately from target to target, he made the elementary mistake of striking with a maximum force at too many scattered points, instead of concentrating on one target at a time. He discovered to his dismay that his *Luftwaffe* could not cope with both the R.A.F. and the unbreakable British spirit, which hardened instead of softening under his massive blows.

The British never faltered. When in December 1940 a motion was made in Parliament to consider peace, it was quickly voted down, 341-4. At long last the *Fuehrer* had come up against a people who would not knuckle down either to his hysterical oratory or to his massive bombs, and who were able and willing to fight back.

OPERATION SEA LION FIZZLES

"There are no more islands," said Adolf Hitler.

Immediately after the signing of the armistice with France on June 22, 1940, the Germans began feverish preparations for what was to be a history-making adventure—the invasion of the British homeland for the first time since the Norman Conquest of 1066. Philip II had attempted it with his Invincible Armada in 1588, only to lose 63 of his 128 sail to a combination of British resistance and catastrophic weather. Napoleon Bonaparte had gazed long and greedily at the cliffs of Dover, but, pleading a tendency toward seasickness, he had the good sense not to risk a repetition of his naval defeat at Trafalgar.

But the master of Berchtesgaden and his astrologers were certain that this time things were different. Nothing—not even Britain's firm resistance—could stand in the way of "the greatest German of all time" and "the greatest genius in the history of warfare." That obstinate nation would be worn down by the U-boat blockade and by devastating attacks from the air upon her ports, cities, and industries. Then they would feel the might of Nazi muscle on their own little precious isle.

Operation Sea Lion it was called.

The preparations were plain for all the world to see. Ports along the French, Belgian, and Dutch shores were crammed with small vessels of every description, and ashore a host of workers were busy 24 hours a day. German troops zealously practiced landing exercises.

The British, of course, had no intention of sitting idly by and allowing the Germans to gather strength for a knockout blow. In daily sorties R.A.F. pilots rained bombs on the enemy ports. There were rumors that the British intended to discourage the invasion fleet by dropping great supplies of gasoline among the concentrated craft and then firing a blazing inferno. Whatever happened, one thing was clear—the British would retaliate with every possible resource.

Directive No. 16, Adolf Hitler to the Supreme Command of the Armed Forces, 16 July 1940:

> *As England, in spite of the hopelessness of her military position, has so far shown herself unwilling to come to any compromise, I have therefore decided to begin to prepare for, and if necessary to carry out, an invasion of England. This operation is dictated by the necessity of eliminating Great Britain as a base from which the war against Germany can be fought, and if necessary the island will be occupied. I therefore issue the following orders. . . .*

Hitler's directive made it clear that preparations for the entire undertaking must be completed by the middle of August.

There were doubts among the professionals of the German army and navy about the feasibility of the project. Those who dared triggering another Hitler tantrum pointed out that the Royal Navy was very much alive. The U-boat campaign, they ventured to suggest, had not yet destroyed Britain's capital ships. Moreover, the *Luftwaffe* did not possess the heavy armor-piercing bombs necessary to cripple the giant battleships. Goering, for all his blustering promises, was not producing enough air power to provide an umbrella for the projected invasion. The British navy and air power might well annihilate the invasion flotilla.

On August 10, 1940, Hitler changed the date of Sea Lion to late September. On September 4 he declared in a speech: "If the people of England are puzzled and ask 'Why doesn't he come?' I shall put your minds at rest. He is coming!"

September 15, 1940, was a black day for Goering and his *Luftwaffe*. The R.A.F. on that day shot down 56 Nazi planes. Something was radically wrong with the softening-up process. Two days later Hitler again postponed the date for Sea Lion.

On October 21, 1940, Hitler grudgingly set aside all plans for Sea Lion for the rest of the year. The next date was set for the spring of 1941. It was a critically important decision, vital for the outcome of the war. It meant that Britain had won the first round, and, as it turned out, a decisive one.

Then, on June 22, 1941, Hitler suddenly turned on Soviet Russia; Sea Lion was totally forgotten in the *Fuehrer*'s zeal to bring Operation Barbarossa against the Kremlin to a successful conclusion. The *Fuehrer* would have further victories, but on him lay the curse of ultimate defeat.

After the war Field Marshal Erich von Manstein in *Verlorene Siege* (Lost Victories) (Bonn, 1955) revealed the importance attached by German military brains to Sea Lion:

> The conquest of Britain by Germany would have deprived the other side of the very base that was indispensable—in those days at any rate—for a seaborne assault on the continent of Europe. To launch an invasion from over the Atlantic without being able to use the island as a springboard was beyond the realm of possibility in those days.

But Sea Lion could not be carried out—with a good proportion of the *Luftwaffe* lying smashed on the fields of England. A *Punch* cartoon, dated September 4, 1940, showed a farmer giving directions to an inquiring hiker: "Eglantine Cottage? Go down the lane past the *Messerschmitt*, bear left and keep on past the two *Dorniers*, then turn sharp right and it's just past the first *Junkers*."

CHAPTER **7**

Lifeline Neptune: War on the Seas

> ***Sea power, when properly understood, is a wonderful thing.***
>
> **—Winston Churchill, *Their Finest Hour***

> ***All that which concerns the sea is profound and final.***
>
> **—Hillaire Belloc, *The Cruise of the* Nona**

THE SINKING OF THE *ATHENIA*

September 3, 1939. It was just 12 hours after the British declaration of war. *Oberleutnant* Fritz-Julius Lemp, commanding the U-30, a small 650-ton Nazi submarine, was at this moment just 250 miles off the northwest coast of Ireland. With luck he would have the glory of striking the first blow against Britain.

Through his periscope Lemp sighted a ship in a bearing favorable for attack. Establishing its British identity, he ordered four torpedoes to be sent into the side of the oncoming vessel. He gave no warning. One of the torpedoes hurtling toward the liner struck it and exploded in the ship's vitals. It was the 13,500-ton S.S. *Athenia* of the Donaldson Atlantic Line, Captain James Cook in command.

In the late summer days of 1939, at a moment when the Nazis were poised at the Polish border, thousands of travelers in both England and Europe frantically sought passage home to the United States and Canada. The *Athenia* was one of the ships used for this purpose. It hurriedly took on passengers, first at Glasgow, then at Belfast, and finally, by lighter, at Liverpool, and sailed on September 2, 1939, for Quebec and Montreal.

Aboard were 1,102 passengers, men, women, and children, a majority of whom were Canadian and American citizens, and a crew of 315. The passengers on the small, single-stacked liner were uneasy but unwilling to believe that the Germans would be so foolish as to attack an unarmed passenger ship.

They were mistaken. On the following evening—a Sunday and the day Britain entered the war—the *Athenia* was sent to the bottom of the Atlantic. Thanks to timely rescue operations (other vessels promptly reached the scene and took survivors to Glasgow, Belfast, and Halifax) and to the fact that the *Athenia* was properly equipped with lifeboats and rafts, only 112 lives of the 1,417 aboard were lost. Of these 69 were women and 16 children.

U-boat commander Lemp later claimed that he had mistaken the *Athenia* for an armed merchantman, since she was off the normal shipping lanes and zigzagging. Whether this was true or not or whether he was overeager to get on with the war will probably never be determined. It is strongly possible that Lemp was lying. Had he judged the *Athenia* to be a merchantman or cruiser he would probably have notified his home base as soon as it was safe to do so. Instead, he maintained radio silence. Not until September 30, 1939, when he returned to base, did he *verbally* inform Grand Admiral Doenitz, head of the German submarine service, that he had sunk the *Athenia*.

The Nazi government at Berlin, unaccustomed to admitting mistakes of any kind, had no intention of expressing regret for the incident. Doenitz was told to deny all responsibility and to keep the matter secret. He ordered Lemp to remove from the U-30's war diary the page describing the sinking and substitute for it another page omitting the record of the attack. This was to avoid a possible leak when the usual eight copies of the U-boat war diaries were prepared for training purposes.

Lemp himself lost his life a few years later while he was under counterattack by a convoy escort, and hence was not able to testify after the war on the facts concerning the sinking.

Immediately after the sinking of the *Athenia*, Propaganda Minister Dr. Joseph Goebbels fashioned a Nazi smoke screen. He heatedly denied that a German submarine had attacked the passenger ship. What had happened, he charged, was the explosion of an infernal machine hidden on the ship on orders of Winston Churchill! Churchill's nefarious plan, he said, was to set up a new *Lusitania* incident and thus again snare the United States, this time speedily, into war. It was a typical example of British perfidy, said the little Nazi propaganda expert.

No one, except millions of Hitler-hypnotized Germans, was taken in by Goebbels's stupid invention, of a type outdated since World War I. British and American newspapers promptly denounced the sinking as a renewal of German terror tactics. For the Allied world the incident provided quick proof that German war lords, like the Bourbons, had forgotten nothing and learned nothing.

It was to be a war of frightfulness all over again, as the ruthless corsairs of *Lusitania* infamy ranged the seas again.

BLOCKADE AND COUNTERBLOCKADE

The Treaty of Versailles had been designed to discourage Germany from making any further attempts to seek a place in the sun. Its drastic naval provisions permitted her to retain only 6 battleships, 6 light cruisers, and 12 torpedo boats. She was not allowed to have any submarines. She could build no warships except for replacement. Her naval personnel was limited to 15,000 men including at the most 1,500 officers.

During the era of the postwar Weimar Republic, the Germans amazed the naval experts of the world by constructing three "pocket battleships," the *Deutschland*, *Admiral Scheer*, and *Admiral Graf Spee*. These marvels of construction were the size of cruisers but packed the punch of battleships. The Germans were able to save weight by using welding instead of riveting, light armor, and guns of a new, light-weight type.

On June 18, 1935, Hitler signed a naval agreement with Great Britain, calling for a new German navy constructed to 35 per cent of the strength of the Royal Navy. The Germans were permitted to build U-boats up to 45 per cent of, and after 1938 to 100 per cent of parity with British submarine tonnage. Hitler promptly built his first three U-boats of the postwar period and then gave orders to construct the undersea craft as fast as possible.

The British public had forgotten the gravity of Germany's U-boat campaign in World War I, but the Admiralty had a long memory. Britain's wartime existence depended upon imports of food, raw materials, and munitions. There were tens of thousands of miles of sea lanes to be guarded. Moreover, there was a serious problem closer to home. Ireland had been helpful in World War I, but it was certain that the new Irish Free State would not permit England to use Irish ports in any future war.

Winston Churchill, who knew something of naval warfare, warned of the need to remain strong on the seas. In an address to the House of Commons on March 16, 1939, he expressed his "horror" on learning that it had been proposed to scrap the five 15-inch-gun battleships of the *Royal Sovereign* class, one in 1942, one in 1943, and the rest in 1944.

"In other days," said Churchill, "I used to say that when the ace is out the king is the best card. These old ships can play their part.... We shall certainly be forced in any war that may occur in the next few years to reinstitute the convoy system. [The five *Royal Sovereigns*] are the very ships which would be the surest escorts of your ocean convoys. . . . Why . . . should we lead out to the slaughter-yards these great vessels? . . . I was very glad to hear Lord Chatfield yesterday lay down the sound doctrine that it is the duty of the Royal Navy to 'seek out and destroy the enemy's fleet.' "

There was, of course, no indiscriminate naval disarmament. When the war broke out in 1939, the Allied naval resources were overwhelming:

	Great Britain	*France*	*Germany*
Battleships	12	5	3
Battle cruisers	3	2	2
Cruisers	62	19	4
Aircraft carriers	7	2	—
Destroyers	178	69	21
Submarines	56	75	57

In combined tonnage the British fleet alone was nine times that of Germany, some 2,000,000 tons against 235,000 tons.

Hitler knew it would be suicidal to challenge British supremacy on the surface of the seas, to say nothing of the combined naval strength of Great Britain and France. Both sides were aware that they would have to revert to the strategy of 1914—blockade and counterblockade—each side seeking to strangle the enemy and starve it out of the war. Again it was to be a war of supply.

In the opening months the marine pattern of 1914 was repeated. Within a few days the Royal Navy drove all German merchant ships either into their home ports or into neutral harbors where they were interned for the duration. The British Admiralty immediately placed all British merchant shipping under its orders. Both belligerents quickly published extensive contraband lists of goods subject to seizure, and, as was to be expected, the British were far more successful in denying such goods to the enemy.

On November 27, 1939, the British extended the blockade by prohibiting the importation of German goods into neutral countries and by introducing the navicert system, controlled by British authorities in neutral harbors. (Navicerts were certificates granted by British consuls at ports, certifying to the unobjectionable character of a ship's cargo.) In the first months of the war the British allowed some freighters to enter the ports of the neutral countries, even though they were aware that many cargoes eventually made their way to Germany. Merchantmen were also permitted to proceed to Italy (the British hoped to keep Italy neutral by this and other concessions).

Churchill regarded Germany's free use of Norway's territorial waters as the greatest obstacle to an effective blockade of Hitler's Reich. "This legal covered way," he said, "has been the greatest advantage which Germany

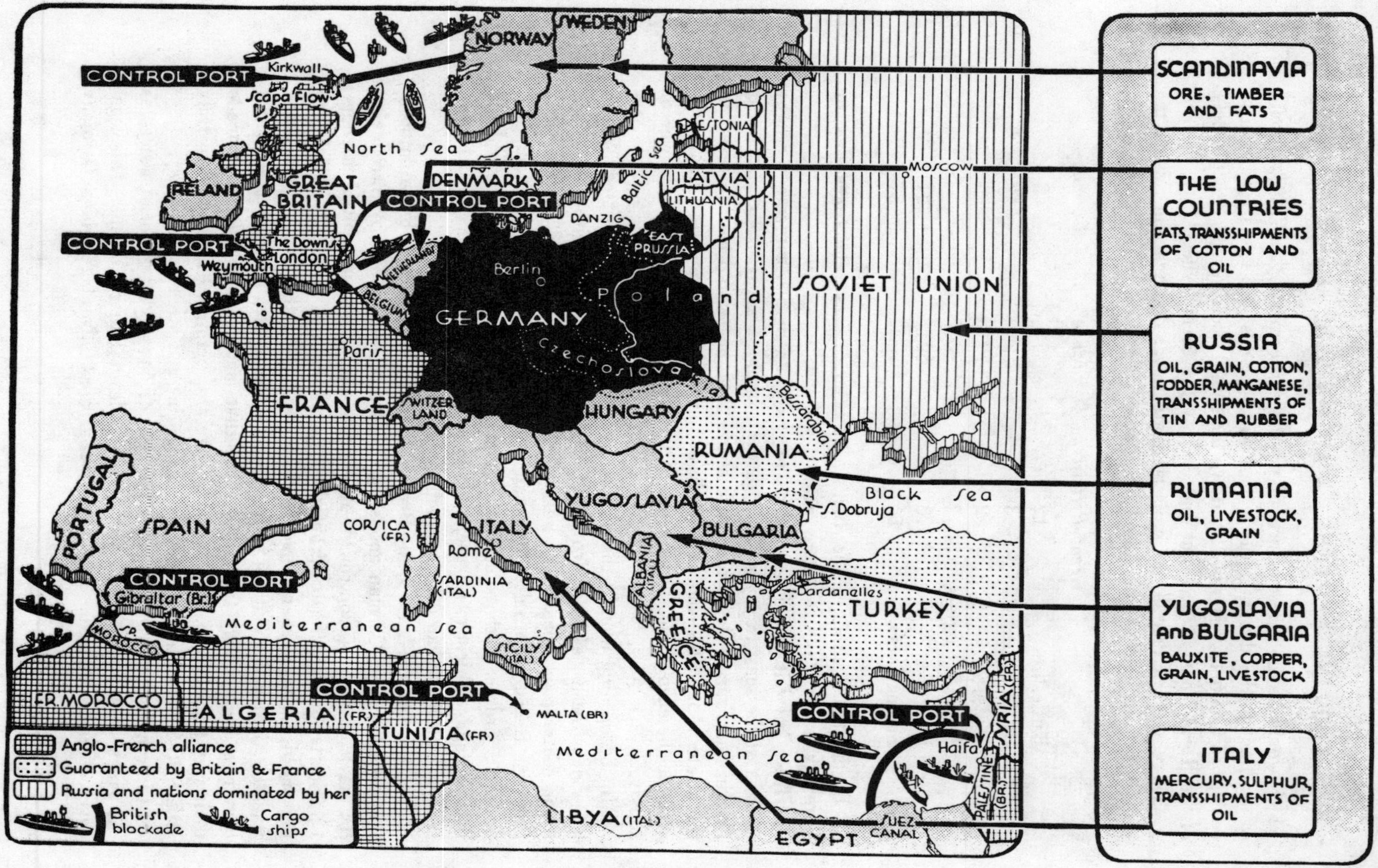

SCANDINAVIA
ORE, TIMBER AND FATS

THE LOW COUNTRIES
FATS, TRANSSHIPMENTS OF COTTON AND OIL

RUSSIA
OIL, GRAIN, COTTON, FODDER, MANGANESE, TRANSSHIPMENTS OF TIN AND RUBBER

RUMANIA
OIL, LIVESTOCK, GRAIN

YUGOSLAVIA AND BULGARIA
BAUXITE, COPPER, GRAIN, LIVESTOCK

ITALY
MERCURY, SULPHUR, TRANSSHIPMENTS OF OIL

CONTROL PORT
Kirkwall
Scapa Flow
North Sea
NORWAY
SWEDEN
ESTONIA
LATVIA
LITHUANIA
Baltic Sea
Moscow
IRELAND
GREAT BRITAIN
DENMARK
CONTROL PORT
CONTROL PORT
The Downs
London
Weymouth
NETHERLANDS
BELGIUM
DANZIG
EAST PRUSSIA
Berlin
GERMANY
Poland
SOVIET UNION
Czechoslovakia
Paris
FRANCE
SWITZERLAND
HUNGARY
Bessarabia
RUMANIA
Black Sea
S. Dobruja
PORTUGAL
SPAIN
YUGOSLAVIA
BULGARIA
CORSICA (FR)
ITALY
Rome
SARDINIA (ITAL)
ALBANIA (ITAL)
GREECE
Dardanelles
TURKEY
CONTROL PORT
Gibraltar (Br.)
SP. MOROCCO
Mediterranean Sea
SICILY (ITAL)
FR. MOROCCO
ALGERIA (FR)
CONTROL PORT
MALTA (BR)
TUNISIA (FR)
CONTROL PORT
Haifa
SYRIA (FR)
PALESTINE (BR.)
Mediterranean Sea
LIBYA (ITAL)
EGYPT
SUEZ CANAL

Anglo-French alliance
Guaranteed by Britain & France
Russia and nations dominated by her
British blockade
Cargo ships

THE ALLIED BLOCKADE

possessed in her efforts to frustrate the blockade." German freighters, returning from the outer seas, used this 800-mile route in safety. And, in addition, ships carrying high-grade Swedish ore followed Norwegian territorial waters down to the Skagerrak, where they were protected by German air power and mine fields.

In World War I the Allies had convinced the Norwegians to sow mines in their own territorial waters, but now the Norwegians, undoubtedly worried about Hitler's reactions, refused to take similar action. Oslo even instructed its navy to provide escorts for the iron-carrying freighters, on the ground that Norwegian waters were open to all legitimate traffic of all belligerent countries. The Norwegians obviously had some faith in British respect for international law. But the Germans?

Added to the surface and undersea war was blockade by mines. As in World War I, the British planted mines from Scotland to Norway and across the English Channel, all designed to bottle up enemy warships and merchant vessels. The Germans countered by strewing magnetic mines (exploded by the proximity of any large mass of iron, as the hull of a ship) off the approaches to British harbors. Many British ships caught by magnetic mines went to the bottom before British naval experts discovered the "degaussing" belt to neutralize the ships' magnetic fields.

For the Germans, who had good reason to remember the slow but deadly blockade of World War I, there was only one possible answer—U-boats and more U-boats to break the stranglehold.

THE U-BOAT CAMPAIGN

German Admiral Erich Raeder wanted no arguments that had disturbed the war lords of 1914-1918. There was to be an all-out unrestricted submarine warfare—immediately—to sever Britain's lifelines.

The German surface fleet was admittedly inferior to that of the British. Therefore Germany was compelled to attack from below the surface or from the air. U-boats, already posted at their stations in the Atlantic, must strike at once, strike hard, and continue to strike hard. Then Britain, with her imports cut down, her factories closing, and her population starving, would yield to the Third Reich.

But the facts of U-boat life were something else again. At the outbreak of World War II Germany had only 57 U-boats, of which only 22 were equipped for Atlantic operations—Type VII of 600 to 1,000 tons displacement, surface speed 16-17 knots and submerged speed 8 knots, and Type IX of 740 tons, surface speed 18 knots and submerged speed 7.3-7.4 knots. The remainder were mostly Type II, so-called "Dugouts" averaging 250 tons, surface speed 13 knots and submerged speed 6.9 knots, intended for coastal duty or for training rather than operational use.

With this modest fleet of undersea craft the Germans were going to challenge the might of the Allied navies and merchant marines. But, on Hitler's orders, frantic efforts were being made to bolster the U-boat fleet.

From the point of view of Allied seamen the German U-boats were treacherous monsters of the deep that lay in wait for their prey and then without warning belched their torpedoes. But to Germans the U-boat crews were heroic sons of the Fatherland who risked life and limb in the most dangerous kind of warfare. It was impossible, they said, for U-boat commanders to give warning to their victims—that had been tried in World War I with disastrous results. With their thin hulls the U-boats could be rammed to death by even a small freighter. They must hit and run.

Further, said the Germans, life aboard the U-boat was no picnic. The crew, averaging 46 men, had to sleep in shifts. They were hemmed in for months in close quarters, every inch of space being used for machinery, torpedoes, and supplies. The air was heavy with the odors of the bilges, Diesel oil, and unwashed humanity. At sea the frail craft rolled and pitched and heeled over. And always there lurked the possibility of sudden death from depth charges, bombing attacks from the air, or the sharp prow of a speeding destroyer.

The opening attacks were deadly. During the first week of the war, at least a dozen British merchant ships were sent to the bottom. Some 67 Allied ships were destroyed by U-boats during the first two months of the war. But these cost the Germans 20 of their original seagoing submarine fleet.

The Allies soon adopted the convoy system that had been so successful in 1917-1918. A large number of merchant ships set sail in a pattern carefully planned beforehand, guarded near shore by aircraft and in the open sea by escorts of destroyers and heavier warships. The destroyers constantly circled the convoy and on detection of a U-boat went to the attack while the members of the convoy dispersed to meet at a new rendezvous.

To meet this strategy Grand Admiral Karl Doenitz, in June 1941, when the number of U-boats at sea had risen to 32, devised the so-called wolfpack tactics. As soon as a U-boat commander made contact with a convoy, he would report its size, position, speed, and course to all German submarines in the vicinity. Upon this signal all would close in to attack. To facilitate the work of the wolfpacks, special fleet supply ships were kept at sea for refueling and repairs.

In 1942 the Germans introduced a refinement in the wolfpack technique. With more U-boats available, they distributed the packs in echelon across the path of a convoy over hundreds of miles. In this way they could keep the convoy under attack for days and nights on end, and reduce the crews of both freighters and warships to exhaustion.

The situation was more favorable for U-boat commanders than it had been in World War I. Then their home bases were limited to a narrow North Sea frontage. But after the fall of France in 1940, German submarine bases were established along the mainland coasts all the way from Norway to Spain.

During the first six months of 1942, Germany's U-boat strength was built up to 101 submarines, of which an average of only 19 were able to be on station. In this period the Germans sank 585 ships, totaling over three million tons. The undersea craft reached their deadly worst in early 1943 when they sank 96 ships in a space of 20 days. But the collapse of the U-boat war came in May 1943 following the prodigious antisubmarine effort of the Allies, who pitted thousands of ships, hundreds of thousands of fighting men, and billions of dollars in equipment against the U-boat wolfpacks.

Doenitz admitted Allied superiority as early as December 14, 1943: "The enemy has rendered the U-boat war ineffective. He has achieved his object not through superior tactics or strategy but through superiority in the field of science; this finds its expression in the modern battle weapon: detection. By this means he has torn our sole offensive weapon in this war against the Anglo-Saxons from our hands."

The advantage slowly went to the Allies when the Germans eventually found it impossible to keep submarine construction up with their losses. This, plus their lack of success in countering the new detection devices of the Allies, meant defeat in the U-boat war.

In the six years of the war the Germans, by their own figures, counted 2,700 British, Allied, and neutral ships destroyed on the Mediterranean Sea and the Atlantic and Indian Oceans. For this they paid with the loss of 783 U-boats and 32,000 men. Doenitz ordered that U-boats continue operations regardless of the fantastic cost in casualties. In his *Memoirs: Ten Years and Twenty Days* (1959) he proudly told how his crews unflinchingly met their self-immolation. Among those lost were his own two sons and his son-in-law.

Although they were the losers in this gigantic game of oceanic hide-and-seek, the Germans caused the British Admiralty many sleepless months. Churchill himself noted that: "The only thing that ever really frightened me during the war was the U-boat peril. [It] was our worst evil."

Because of the limited range of their U-boats the Germans revived the raider activities that had taken a great toll of Allied shipping in World War I. The raider *Emden* sent some 74,000 tons of Allied shipping to the bottom. The raider *Altmark*, with 300 British prisoners aboard, was finally detected by British planes in February 1940 as she headed along the Norwegian coast to seek shelter. When she entered an ice-filled Norwegian fiord, the British cruiser *Cossack* went in after her. The captain of the *Altmark* tried in vain to ram the British warship. In an action reminiscent of Elizabethan days, sailors from the *Cossack* leaped to the deck of the German raider, overcame the enemy in hand-to-hand fighting, and rescued their comrades.

The Nazi government heatedly protested through neutrals against "this gross violation of Norwegian waters." The officials of the British Foreign Office, with tongue in cheek, made no audible comment.

LEUTNANT PRIEN SINKS THE *ROYAL OAK*

The sinking of the passenger liner *Athenia* had reflected no glory on German U-boat commanders. They were out after bigger game.

On September 16, 1939, came considerably more satisfying news for the Germans. *Kapitänleutnant* Schuhardt caught the 22,500-ton converted aircraft carrier *Courageous* off the coast of Ireland and sent it to the bottom of the Atlantic. A body blow to the British navy, this was what counted in the quickening war at sea.

One month later, on October 14, 1939, came an electrifying German naval exploit. *Leutnant* Prien, later *Kapitänleutnant*, commanding the U-47, succeeded in penetrating the harbor defenses of Scapa Flow, the great naval base at the southern Orkneys, Scotland, and sank the 29,150-ton battleship *Royal Oak*, one of Britain's 12 capital ships.

The British had set up two kinds of defenses to protect the landlocked anchorage at Scapa Flow. The outer rim of seven entrances or sounds was guarded by round-the-clock patrols. Inside the various sounds there was a maze of nets, booms, and sunken blockships. The possibility of a U-boat's piercing these defenses was small indeed. Twice at the end of World War I German submarines had attempted it, with disastrous results to themselves.

The U-47 was a small Type VII craft of 517 tons, with limited speed. *Leutnant* Prien carefully studied Intelligence reports concerning the defenses of Scapa Flow. He concluded that the Achilles heel was in Kirk Sound, one of the smaller entrances, which was protected by two blockships sunk across the channel at its narrowest point. But he had to navigate his slow submarine through the channel with its strong tidal flow up to 10 knots, squeeze past the blockships, get into the Flow, cause as much damage as he could within minutes, and then get out again. It was a tall order.

Prien chose the night of October 13-14, 1939, on the basis of weather forecasts of complete darkness and favorable tides. The night turned out to be brightly lit by Northern Lights. But Prien decided to go in anyway.

Remaining on the surface, he steered the U-47 gingerly through the channel of Kirk Sound at low tide, edging his way around the sunken blockships. Inside the Flow, made brilliant by the Aurora Borealis, he headed for the main anchorage. He was astonished to find it empty. He had no way of knowing that, while he was outside in Pentland Firth awaiting nightfall, at least 15 heavy units of the Royal Navy had put to sea.

But there to the north he recognized the silhouette of the *Royal Oak*. Beautiful prey after all!

Still on the surface, Prien took careful aim and sent his entire load of five torpedoes at his target. Only one hit. He then reloaded his spare five torpedoes in the empty tubes and at short range sent them hissing broadside toward the *Royal Oak*.

This time all five hit. The explosions literally lifted the ship into the air, leaving wreckage, fire, and smoke. More than 800 of the 1,200 men aboard died with their ship. Within minutes the naval base burst into a riot of activity. Destroyers knifed through the Flow searching for the intruder, the long fingers of searchlight beams probed sky and sea, the staccato of machine-gun fire reverberated across the water.

Prien now faced the most trying part of his adventure—how to get out of Scapa Flow. Shrewdly, he kept the U-47 close to the shore so that its silhouette would be difficult to recognize against the dark background of the surrounding hills. Avoiding detection several times by the narrowest of margins, he headed for Kirk Sound. Here, especially at the narrows of the channel, he had to buck the fast incoming tidal stream. He ordered maximum speed, but even then the tide nearly swept his craft back into the Flow. Slowly, ever so slowly, with the care of a blind man, he skirted the blockships and reached the safety of the open sea. Mission accomplished!

It was a skillful and daring feat, grudgingly applauded even by the British. Prien's exploit was facilitated by an accident of good fortune. The British Admiralty had long been dissatisfied with the two blockships in Kirk Sound, and on the very evening when the U-47 made its sortie a third overage vessel was being towed on its way from London to be added to the obstacles there.

For the Germans it was sweet revenge. Scapa Flow had been the scene of the internment of the German fleet after World War I, a humiliation that still rankled among German seamen. To unforgetful Germans Prien's achievement was the first step in revenge for the Battle of Jutland (1916).

Prien himself was destined to enjoy only a brief time of glory. On March 17, 1941, while attacking a convoy, he went to his death under the waters of the Atlantic.

THE SCUTTLING OF THE *GRAF SPEE*

For the Allies there was exciting news from Montevideo.

The German *Panzerschiff Admiral Graf Spee* was the pride of Nazism and the symbol of Hitler's rising naval power. Launched at Wilhelmshaven in

1934, she was the third and last of Germany's pocket battleships, cleverly designed by German naval technicians to circumvent the Treaty of Versailles. She was a miracle of naval construction—a fast, light, heavily armored warship unsurpassed for its size in firepower and speed.

The *Graf Spee* was as long as three New York city blocks and as wide as a four-lane superhighway. She had a complete belt of armor as well as two protective decks. Among her armament were six 11-inch guns, eight 6-inch rifles, and eight 19.7 torpedo tubes. She could cruise at 26 knots. It was said that she could outrun anything that she could not outshoot.

At the British Coronation Naval Review in 1937, Hanson W. Baldwin, military and naval correspondent for *The New York Times*, described the *Graf Spee*: "She was a sight to stir a seaman's heart—the lean strength of her fine, flowing lines and her unbroken main deck sweeping to abaft the after turret."

A sight, indeed, to peacetime mariners, but to British sailors she was a vicious engine of destruction and a terror in battle. When war broke out, the *Graf Spee*, under the command of *Kapitän* Hans Langsdorff and with a crew of 1,107, dashed for the southern seas to prey on Allied commerce. The nations of the Western Hemisphere had drawn a 300-mile safety belt around themselves inside which no belligerent warships were to penetrate. The Nazis, of course, paid no attention. For two months the *Graf Spee* cruised the South Atlantic, sending at least nine craft to the bottom.

For the British Admiralty this was serious business. In early December it advised Brazilian authorities to permit the sale of British fuel to Nazi freighters which stopped at Brazilian ports. There was no altruism here, nor any stupidity. The British suspected correctly that these fuel-laden freighters were on missions to refuel Nazi raiders at sea. The idea was to follow them to the rendezvous point.

On the morning of December 13, 1939, the graceful *Graf Spee*, slicing the waters of the Atlantic like a giant knife, appeared across the horizon off the coast of Uruguay. But this time, instead of finding a weak, isolated opponent, she came smack up against three British cruisers that had been sent to find her, the fast 8,390-ton *Exeter*, the 7,030-ton *Achilles*, and the 6,985-ton *Ajax*.

This was more than *Kapitän* Langsdorff had expected, but he rushed to the attack. In the early dawn he at first sighted only the *Ajax* but then found himself surrounded by three British men-of-war.

All three British ships sent volley after volley against the *Graf Spee*. The latter, finding the guns of the *Exeter* especially damaging, turned her batteries to the *Exeter*. In four hours the heaviest of the British cruisers was put out of action.

Below decks, locked in the *Graf Spee*'s hold, 60 British seamen, taken from the merchant ships sunk by the *Spee*, sang and cheered wildly as the German ship shuddered from the blows of British shells.

The running sea fight went on for 14 hours. Although she seemed to be giving a good account of herself, the *Graf Spee*, still pounded by shells from the *Achilles* and the *Ajax*, put on forced draft and headed southwest in search of a haven.

The British warships followed her until she came to Montevideo harbor, where she sought refuge in neutral waters. More than 30 of her crew had been killed and some 60 wounded.

The latter stage of the battle was within sight of the Uruguayan shore. Crowds heard the thunderous booming of the big guns and saw the mountains of smoke rising from the fray.

In Montevideo the crew of the *Graf Spee* buried 36 of their comrades and hospitalized the wounded. Damage-control crews hurried to repair the battered ship. Though *Kapitän* Langsdorff requested at least 15 days to complete repairs, he was told by the Uruguayan government on December 15 to leave the harbor within two days or be interned with his crew. Protesting the decision, Langsdorff ordered that supplies be taken on from the German freighter *Tacoma*, also in the harbor.

Meanwhile, the British cruisers, keeping a deathwatch outside the harbor, cruised along, waiting. British naval reinforcements, though days away, sped at forced draft toward Montevideo. The British, acting as usual under such circumstances with shrewd foresight, were careful to fill the radio waves with false reports of overwhelming naval forces already close to the scene of action. Langsdorff must have concluded that the entire Royal Navy was closing in on his sleek warship.

For five days there was great uncertainty. What would become of the *Graf Spee* and her crew? By this time the entire world was awaiting the outcome of the sensational drama. Would the *Graf Spee* head out to sea to challenge British naval might?

The answer came at 6 P.M. on Sunday, December 17, 1939. The *Graf Spee* weighed anchor and maneuvered uncertainly along the Rio de la Plata, watched by some 300,000 persons on shore. In the fading daylight everyone expected a sea battle.

The German battleship suddenly slowed and finally stopped. The tugboats alongside moved away. Then a pillar of black smoke shot skyward amidships. There were bursts of flame. The sound of explosions rumbled across the waters. As the flames spread, the ship seemed to shake and listed. Within three minutes her hull was on the bottom.

Kapitän Langsdorff and all the members of his crew reached safety aboard other boats. Before abandoning his ship, the last man to leave, Langsdorff sent a bitter wireless message ashore. He protested that the refusal to allow the *Spee* to remain in the harbor "makes it necessary for me to sink my ship near the coast and save my crew." He and his crew were interned.

Early on the morning of December 20, 1939, Kapitän Langsdorff, veteran of Jutland, sat in his room at the Naval Arsenal in Buenos Aires. He wrapped the flag of the old Imperial German Navy around him (thus by implication rejecting the Nazi Navy), and put a bullet into his head. He had made the initial mistake of seeking shelter within the River Plata. And then, instead of fighting it out, he had subjected himself and his ship to a politician's decision.

Hitler himself had given the order to scuttle the marine masterpiece rather than see her humiliated in defeat, and, more probably to keep from compromising the warship's no doubt secret construction and weapons. The *Fuehrer* had gone into one of his notorious rages upon hearing the news from Montevideo. Sink the ship—this was his way of saving face in the first naval battle of the war.

It was a theatrical finish to a brief but destructive career. Naval experts as well as armchair strategists the world over found harsh words for Hitler's order to destroy his ship. The *Graf Spee*, they said, had entered the port of Montevideo at high speed, her turrets still intact. Had she headed out to challenge British sea power, she might well have been sunk, but she would have died gloriously.

For the Allied nations the end of the *Graf Spee* was a hopeful note in a time of increasingly bad news from the battlefronts.

THE SINKING OF THE *BISMARCK*

German surface raiders took a heavy toll of British shipping. But at the end of May 1941 the Germans suffered a serious loss in one of the war's biggest naval engagements. The superdreadnought *Bismarck*, the pride of the German navy, together with the *Prinz Eugen* and several smaller warships, left their hiding place in a fiord near Bergen to prey on British convoys.

British reconnaissance planes detailed for this specific duty recognized the huge enemy ships almost immediately, and units of the British fleet were dispatched to find them. H.M.S. *Hood*, a giant battle-cruiser, was in the vicinity on Atlantic convoy duty. She was ordered to engage the raiders.

The great warships met off the coast of Greenland on the morning of May 24, 1941. Soon after the battle began, the *Hood* received a direct hit and went to the bottom.

J. R. N. Nixon, a Reuter's correspondent, witnessed the engagement:

> Standing on the bridge of one of His Majesty's ships, I saw the *Hood* go down only 200 or 300 yards away with her guns still firing. The end of the mighty *Hood* was an almost unbelievable nightmare. Shortly after the engagement began shells hit the 21-year-old battle cruiser. There was a bright

sheet of flame and she blew up, apparently blasted by an unlucky hit in her thinly armored magazine loaded with powder. Parts of her hull were thrown hundreds of feet into the air and in a few minutes all that remained was a patch of smoke on the water and some small bits of wreckage. The battleship *Prince of Wales* was hit soon afterward by a 15-inch naval shell, but the damage was slight.

The *Prince of Wales*, together with the cruisers *Suffolk* and *Norfolk* and accompanying destroyers, continued to pour shells on the *Bismarck*, which in turn damaged the *Prince of Wales*.

Taking advantage of the snow, mist, and squalls of the Arctic waters, the *Bismarck* and the other German warships slipped away and eluded the British units.

Then began an amazing chase of 1,750 miles. The *Bismarck*, lost for 31 hours, was probably headed for the safety of a French port, probably either St. Nazaire or Brest.

In London there was restrained excitement. From the British Admiralty, which had been following the sea battle via radio, went orders to points as far away as Newfoundland and Gibraltar for every available warship of the British fleet to converge on the area to hunt for the *Bismarck*. Meanwhile, the German battlewagon, its radio silent, knifed like a ghost ship through the ice floes.

Two days later the crew of an American-built Catalina plane spotted the fleeing *Bismarck*. That plane wrote the death warrant for the pride of Hitler's fleet. Planes, destroyers, and heavy fleet units closed in.

For the pilots on the British aircraft carrier *Ark Royal* the news was almost too good to be true. Again and again the Nazi press had reported the sinking of the *Ark Royal*; now its crew had a heaven-sent opportunity to prove that rumors of the death of their ship were greatly exaggerated.

May 26, 1941. Torpedo-carrying planes from the *Ark Royal* were sent out to harass the *Bismarck* until the British ships could close in on her. The planes dropped their cargoes of death. One American-made torpedo hit the *Bismarck* amidships, and a second crashed into her stern. This second torpedo crippled the steering gear and caused the giant warship to wander around and around in uncontrollable circles. The German warship also lost much of its speed as it attempted in vain to evade its attackers.

At this time the *Bismarck* was just 400 miles off the French coast. During the night small British naval units, destroyers led by the *Cossack*, caught up with the floundering monster and rained shells on her from every direction.

The next morning the powerful *King George V* and the *Rodney* appeared on the scene. An eyewitness told how salvos from 14- and 16-inch guns "bored their way through the Krupp armor like cheese." The *Bismarck* wallowed in the seas like a punch-drunk fighter unable to protect herself.

Her decks were littered with wreckage. Dense clouds of yellow cordite smoke enveloped the dying ship.

By the morning of May 27, 1941, the *Bismarck* was a battered wreck, her superstructure mangled, her giant guns pointed crazily in all directions. From the jagged shell holes in her sides came blazing sheets of fire. Panicky crew members, preferring a watery death to being burned to a crisp, leaped into the Atlantic.

The *Dorsetshire*, last British ship with any torpedoes left, closed in. Three more torpedoes crashed into the mortally wounded battleship. With her colors still flying, the *Bismarck* slowly heeled over to port, turned upside down, and sank beneath the waves. It was exactly 10:40 P.M.

The *Dorsetshire* and *Maori*, assigned to pick up survivors, found the waters too rough to lower boats. Instead, lines were thrown out to the swimmers and jumping ladders let down the sides. A hundred men were rescued. The two British ships hurried away when reports came in that a submarine was in the vicinity.

The destruction of the great German warship came at precisely the right psychological moment for the British public, just when British troops were being evacuated from Crete. Even better, the loss of the *Hood* had been avenged. The total British casualties in the action (apart from H.M.S. *Hood*) were 25 killed and 13 wounded.

The British Admiralty, the British public, and the entire world now became aware of what air power meant, even in naval warfare.

THE RACE FOR NEW WEAPONS

The Germans began to use the magnetic mine, their first secret weapon, immediately after the outbreak of World War II. In the first few weeks there were several unexplained sinkings with no evidence of submarines in the vicinity. Apparently the Germans were using a mysterious new weapon against which the paravanes of the old mine sweepers were ineffective. There was great concern in London. Every vessel in British waters was in danger. The sinkings were increasing alarmingly.

From a prisoner of war the British learned that the Germans had perfected a new type of magnetic mine. Small coastal type U-boats of 250 tons, each carrying a half-dozen mines instead of the usual torpedoes, laid some such mines. Similar ones were dropped by parachute. Cylindrical in shape, about seven feet long, constructed of aluminum alloy, they weighed over 1,000 pounds and were charged with 660 pounds of T.N.T. The mines lay on the bottom, with no cables, and thus avoided the paravanes designed to explode them. They were exploded when a passing iron hull completed an electric circuit in the body of the weapon. These devilish weapons were strewn in the shipping lanes, particularly in the North Channel, St. George's Channel, the approaches to the English Channel, and in the Thames Estuary.

Unless something drastic could be done about these magnetic mines, the traffic to and from England would surely be paralyzed. Almost incredible was the story of how the British solved the problem. First it was necessary to recover and study an intact specimen. On November 23, 1941, news came to the Admiralty that night-sentries on the Thames Estuary had seen a German plane drop a mysterious object near the beach. A second one was discovered the next morning. Hurriedly summoned naval mine experts cautiously examined the two mines, photographed them from every angle, and then, flirting with instant death, carefully removed the detonators.

From Winston Churchill came the order: "Find the answer. Work night and day, but find the answer!"

The response was little short of phenomenal. Scientists stripped the precious mines down to their smallest parts, and within 12 hours gave the Admiralty not only the secret of the mine but also a sure means of counteracting it. With some irony and some glee they appropriated the principle of magnetic flux devised originally by a German scientist, Karl Friedrich Gauss (1777-1855), and used it to counter the new weapon. They would simply reduce a ship's magnetic field by "degaussing," that is, discharging a powerful current at periodic intervals through a cable fastened around the hull of the ship at the upper deck level.

Soon miles of degaussing cable flowed from factories to ports, where they were installed on warships and merchantmen. Thus, in record time, Allied ships were immunized against Germany's first great secret weapon.

The battle of detection was on.

The Germans used a variation of the magnetic mine in the acoustical torpedo, which "heard" the sound of a ship's engines and then headed in the direction of the sound. As a countermeasure the Allies devised "noisemakers" to be towed behind the ships to confuse the rigid mechanical brain of the torpedo.

The locating of U-boats was a matter of high priority. Allied scientists invented instruments so delicate that they could even hear the voices of the crews in submerged submarines. Sonar (*S*ound *N*avigation *a*nd *R*anging), also called ASDIC by the British (*A*nti-*S*ubmarine *D*etection *I*nvestigating *C*ommittee), developed shortly after World War I, was now considerably improved. This instrument, together with hydrophones, revealed submerged U-boats or underwater mines by means of inaudible high-frequency vibrations reflected from the objects. The Germans countered by sheathing their submarines with a thin rubber skin to insulate the sounds.

Most important of all was the race to improve radar (*ra*dio *d*etection *a*nd *r*anging). Scientists in all countries knew its principles and worked feverishly to perfect it. Radar was an ingenious apparatus that emitted and focused a scanning beam of ultra-high-frequency radio waves, and, through the reception and timing of reflected waves, fixed the distance and direction of any object in the path of the beam. This eye could see through darkness, clouds, water, or fog. Shore installations, ships of the fleet, and merchantmen were already equipped with the huge, cumbersome apparatus with its large aerial screens. As early as the spring of 1939 the British had set up 18 radar stations from Dundee to Portsmouth, at which a round-the-clock watch was kept uninterrupted for six years. These stations, with their huge spanning arcs—the watchdogs of the air-raid warning service—served Britain well in her air war.

But could radar play a role in the vital battle with the U-boats?

Here the German scientists were due for some unpleasant surprises. In their radar research they were handicapped by being under the orders of Hitler, who impatiently decreed that no scientific research be pursued which could not produce a conclusive result within a year. Moreover, the German scientists made the mistake of concentrating on *decimeter* wave-lengths in developing their radar sets, while their Allied counterparts took the opposite path by perfecting short waves in *centimeters.* The difference turned out to be crucial.

Until June 1942, German U-boat commanders regarded it as safe to surface during the night to recharge batteries or attack a convoy. But now they were mystified when Allied aircraft had no difficulty in spotting them, playing searchlights on them, and then attacking them. In July a dozen U-boats were sunk, in August another 15, most by sudden air attacks. The Germans soon established that the attacking planes were emitting pulses while searching for their targets. Obviously, they were using radar, but how in the world did they find room on the planes for those huge sets and screen aerials?

The Germans countered by installing small receiver sets called "metox" after the firm which made them, together with small cross-shaped aerials known as "Biscay crosses." This device worked acoustically. As soon as the U-boat surfaced, the aerial was rotated in all directions, while below an observer sat at a metox set waiting for the hum of approaching aircraft. The submarine would crash-dive as soon as the telltale pulses were heard. For a time it seemed to work well.

Then came what the Germans sadly called the Black May of 1943. During that month 43 U-boats were sunk. Even with metox the boats were being found and destroyed. Perhaps enemy aircraft were intercepting the metox oscillations and following them to their target. Orders went out from Kiel to abandon all metox sets.

But the destruction continued. German scientists, engineers, and technicians finally found the answer by reassembling what appeared to be a small insignificant instrument salvaged from a half-destroyed British plane. It was a mechanical marvel, a miniature radar set working on the incredible wave-length of nine centimeters.

So that was it! *A radar set geared in centimeters instead of decimeters!* More irony: the scanning tube was a version of the Braun tube invented by a German scientist. With this ingenious device the British had broken the back of the German U-boat campaign.

Now that the fangs of their most effective weapon were drawn, the desperate Germans sought to construct more and better submarines. They built larger streamlined versions, the conning-tower superstructure severely limited, the antiaircraft guns more powerful, the radar search receivers more effective. Most impressive of all was the new *Schnorkel* (a dialect word for *nose*), an air mast which protruded out of the water. Consisting of two tubes, one for air induction, and the second for carrying away the exhaust gases from the engines, the new device enabled the U-boat to recharge its batteries and renew its air without surfacing for weeks on end.

But it was too late. The Allies had already won the battle of the seas.

ESCAPE OF THE *SCHARNHORST* AND *GNEISENAU*

The destruction of the *Bismarck* convinced the Germans that there was no sense in committing their remaining capital ships in the Battle of the Atlantic. British air and sea power were far too strong. The assault on Britain's lifeline would have to be made by U-boats.

The *Scharnhorst* and *Gneisenau* were at anchor in Brest harbor on the French coast, where they were joined by the *Prinz Eugen*, which had escaped in the *Bismarck* fiasco. Here the giant battlewagons were uncomfortably exposed for eight months to British air attack. Why keep them there? The *Fuehrer*, haunted by the fear that the Allies intended to land in northern Norway and threaten his flank, decided that it would be best to transfer his capital ships to a Norwegian fiord. From this vantage point they could protect his northern flank and at the same time be used to harry the Allied convoy route to North Russia.

The problem of moving the warships was not an easy one. The northern route around Scotland was far too dangerous, exposed as it was to British air power and the Royal Navy. The only other way was to make a dash for it directly through the English Channel.

During the month of January 1942 a flotilla of German mine sweepers, ingeniously camouflaged, cleared the mines on the road from Brest along the French, Belgian, and Dutch coasts as far as Helgoland Bight. It was a highly secret maneuver, executed with efficiency and thoroughness.

Early on the morning of February 12, 1942, the *Scharnhorst*, *Gneisenau*, and *Prinz Eugen*, surrounded by a screen of destroyers and torpedo boats, moved out of Brest at high speed and headed eastward through the Channel. In preparation, the Germans had jammed the entire British radar system, leading the British to expect and prepare for a giant air raid. The flotilla slid easily past British ports, shore batteries, and airfields, passing the narrowest part of the Channel without hearing a shot.

When the alarm was finally sounded on the British shore, the German fleet was already off the Belgian coast. Six Swordfish, British torpedo planes, swooping in to attack, were shot down by *Focke-Wulf* and *Messerschmitt* fighters detailed for exactly this purpose. The zigzagging German warships successfully eluded British destroyers and torpedo planes. The *Scharnhorst* struck a mine and was slowed down for several hours, but she survived and went on, reaching home port safely. In the air action the British lost 20 bombers and 16 fighters, the Germans 15 fighters.

The unbelievable had happened. There was great excitement in Berlin. The Germans had humiliated the Admiralty by running a gantlet of British sea power in British home waters.

But even Hitler knew that wars were not won by running away from the enemy.

TRAPPING THE *SCHARNHORST*

In 1942 Hitler completed the task of shifting his main naval strength to Norway. The plan was to cut the Allied convoy route to Russia. In the Norwegian fiords were assembled the *Scharnhorst, Gneisenau, Prinz Eugen, Tirpitz, Lützow, Scheer, Hipper, Köln, Nürnberg*—the cream of German naval strength, all ready to spread havoc in the North Atlantic. All that was left of the German fleet, it was still a formidable threat.

Between January and March 1943, under cover of round-the-clock darkness, two convoys totaling 48 British and American merchant ships, made the dangerous voyage to Murmansk. Forty arrived safely. But it was a hard task for the Royal Navy to protect such convoys. Each time a convoy made its way laboriously to Russia, destroyers and other warships had to be transferred from the critical Atlantic theatre, where the U-boat campaign was in high gear.

With the return of daylight weather, the Admiralty decided to suspend operations on the Murmansk run until autumn. For Stalin, hard pressed on the Eastern Front, this was almost equivalent to desertion by his allies. By late September 1943 he was insisting angrily upon resumption of the flow of supplies from the West.

On October 1, 1943, Churchill promised a series of four convoys in November, December, January, and February, each of some 35 British and

American ships. But first he asked the Kremlin to satisfy a list of grievances—such as allowing the reinforcing of naval personnel in North Russia, visas for the additional men, and lifting such restrictions as censorship of private mail. He added that this was no contract or bargain, "but rather a declaration of our solemn and earnest resolve."

Stalin replied testily that supplies to Russia were very much an "obligation" in the common struggle against Hitlerite Germany, but grudgingly met the conditions, provided Russia could have "reciprocity." After further difficult discussions it was agreed to resume the convoys in November 1943.

This exchange indicated the extreme difficulty of working with the Russians in a war against a common enemy. In the queer topsy-turvy scheme of things created by Communism, Stalin was fighting a war within a war. His alliance with the West was only temporary, for, according to Marxist-Leninist theory, there could be no peace until the capitalist class had been liquidated. He would accept help from the West, but he would do his best one day to cut the throats of his benefactors.

Each time a convoy set out for Russia a naval force went along. In addition, to set a trap for German raiders, a task force of heavier units of the Royal Navy tagged along on a course parallel to but well away from the convoy. The December 1943 convoy was to bring good fortune to the British. It left port protected by a strong escort of three cruisers, *Belfast*, *Norfolk*, and *Sheffield*, 14 destroyers, and a ring of corvettes and small craft. Some distance away to the southeast were the battleship *Duke of York*, the cruiser *Jamaica*, and four destroyers, all headed by Admiral Sir Bruce Fraser, commander of the Home Fleet.

German agents flashed word to Kiel about the sailing of the convoy. Grand Admiral Karl Doenitz promptly fell into the trap. Late on the afternoon of Christmas Day 1943, he sent the *Scharnhorst* with a screen of five destroyers out from Alten Fiord for what seemed to be a perfect duck shoot—a prize of a half million tons of shipping. He had confidence in the *Scharnhorst*, a 26,000-ton battle cruiser, fitted with nine 11-inch guns. With its speed of 29 knots it was faster than any British battleship. There would be good news to report to the *Fuehrer*!

The opposing fleets sighted each other simultaneously about 150 miles north of North Cape. By prearranged signal the lumbering ships in the convoy turned about while the British cruisers flung themselves on the *Scharnhorst*, ignoring the fact that the German ship could throw more metal in one salvo than all three cruisers together.

In the rapid exchange of fire both the *Scharnhorst* and the *Norfolk* were hit. A hurried message went to the main British fleet to join the battle.

Suddenly, the *Scharnhorst* broke off and vanished into the twilight, headed south through heavy seas. Behind her sped the bulldog cruisers with radar eyes glued on their prey. Meanwhile, Admiral Fraser's powerful force hurried north at full speed.

At 4:17 P.M. the *Duke of York's* radar detected the *Scharnhorst* just 20 miles away. Fraser broke radio silence and ordered the *Belfast* to "illuminate the enemy with a star-shell." As the star-shell burst high up at 4:50 P.M., there in dead center was the inviting silhouette of the Nazi warship!

Behind the display of teamwork that followed were centuries of British naval tradition. The *Duke of York* opened fire at 12,000 yards, her five 14-inch guns sending more than three tons of hot steel charging through the air, in the words of one observer "like a maddened express train." At the same time, the British destroyers closed in for the kill.

This was more than the Germans had expected. The *Scharnhorst* turned east and with her guns still belching fire used her speed to draw away from her tormenters. But the Nazi warship was mortally wounded. At 7 P.M. she began to slow down. Now all the British ships raced in to pound the *Scharnhorst* to pieces at close range. Daring destroyer commanders brought their speedy vessels in to 2,000 yards and sent torpedo after torpedo into the sides of the dying monster, already a mass of flames.

Finally, the *Scharnhorst* turned wearily on her side, coughing flame and smoke, and went under.

British destroyers hurried in to pick up survivors. They could rescue only 36 of the complement of 1,970 officers and men.

THE DEATH OF THE *TIRPITZ*

The mighty *Tirpitz*, 42,000 ton goliath, capable of a speed of 31 knots, with eight 15-inch guns and a host of smaller batteries and a crew of 2,200 men, was the only surviving German battleship. Her sister ship, the *Bismarck*, had been caught and sunk by the British in May 1941. In early 1942 she was one of the remaining capital ships sent to Norwegian waters. She was another thorn in the flesh of the British lion.

On March 6, 1942, the *Tirpitz* dashed out of her Norwegian anchorage for the first time to attack a convoy bound for Murmansk. She failed to find it. Three days later, she was spotted by British planes. The British pilots sent at least 20 torpedoes toward the fast German warship, but all of them missed. From her four-barreled pom-poms the *Tirpitz* sent up a wall of fire that brought down a dozen of the attackers. She then slipped away at 28 knots and disappeared in the direction of Narvik.

British Intelligence soon learned that the *Tirpitz* was at her moorings in the Alten Fiord and undamaged. In September 1943, escorted by the battle cruiser *Scharnhorst* and ten destroyers, the *Tirpitz* took part in a damaging raid on Allied installations at Spitzbergen.

On the night of September 23, 1943, two of six British midget submarines pulled off a highly successful coup. Slipping through a triple-screened net barrage in Alten Fiord unobserved, they attached a heavy limpet mine to the keel of the *Tirpitz.* First the thud of a heavy explosion under water, then the great hull of the battleship rose and fell back. The turbines were lifted out of their bearings and the engines rendered useless.

It took six months for the Germans to repair the *Tirpitz* well enough so that she might be removed to a Baltic dockyard for refitting.

Then began a deadly cat-and-mouse game. While the Germans worked frantically to make the great ship seaworthy, British reconnaissance pilots kept eagle eyes focused. The British avoided further attacks until the repairs were almost completed.

Then, on April 3, 1944, when there were signs that the warship was ready to be moved, British Barracuda bombers from aircraft carriers and others from a base at Archangel swooped down on the *Tirpitz* like a swarm of hornets. They scored 15 hits in 11 minutes and left 168 German dead and 320 wounded on the battered decks.

The Germans were getting thoroughly tired of this frustrating game. This time they towed the crippled battleship into the Sandesund in Tromsö Fiord, primarily because the German front was being drawn back from the north of Norway. It was a sure invitation to disaster, since the *Tirpitz's* new position was some 200 miles closer to Britain.

Great expectations in London! The British stepped up their attacks, in July, in August, again in September and October 1944. Further hits destroyed the forward top deck of the warship. Not a single fighter plane appeared during these months to help the *Tirpitz.* Goering's *Luftwaffe* apparently had more pressing business at home.

November 12, 1944. This time nearly 60 British Lancasters, half of them loaded with six-ton bombs, flew all the way from Scotland to Tromsö Fiord. The Germans detailed a squadron of veteran *Messerschmitt* fighter pilots to intercept the raiders.

The British then executed a shrewd maneuver which completely fooled the enemy. Near the target, half the British force—those *without* bombs—veered off sharply toward Bardufoss, a German airfield. The *Messerschmitts* obediently followed.

But the other 29 bombers, loaded to the hilt with destructive power, headed toward Tromsö Fiord. At their ease the Lancasters dropped their cargo of bombs on the *Tirpitz.*

Mortally wounded, the great battlewagon heeled over on her starboard side. Some 1,400 officers and seamen were killed or drowned, 397 were saved; 400 of the complement, on leave, lived to tell the terrible story.

The British Admiralty, understandably satisfied, could now move its capital ships to the Far East. They were desperately needed there.

CHAPTER 8

The Struggle for the Mediterranean

England will be beaten. Inexorably beaten. This is a truth which you should get into your head.

—Benito Mussolini to Count Galeazzo Ciano, 1939

I need a few thousand dead to justify my presence at the peace table.

—Benito Mussolini to Marshal Rodolfo Graziani, June 17, 1940

EXTENSION OF THE WAR

The Mediterranean basin was an obscure and quiet theatre during the first year of the war. It scarcely merited the attention of news-gathering agencies. But all belligerents were aware of the vital importance of North and East Africa, the Balkans, the Middle East, the Mediterranean itself.

For the British, with responsibilities all over the globe, the Mediterranean—and its great strategic arc of Gibraltar-Malta-Suez—was a lifeline to India and the Far East. In 1939 their defenses were pitifully weak—small garrisons at Gibraltar and Suez, several divisions in Egypt with some 250 antiquated planes, and two fleets, one at Alexandria and one at Malta. Before long the Mediterranean was closed to British merchant shipping, forcing a long journey around the southern tip of Africa. The fall of France placed the British in an even more precarious position. French troops were withdrawn from the Middle East, leaving the precious oil fields open to Axis assault. With French naval bases in the Mediterranean denied to British warships,

THE STRATEGIC MEDITERRANEAN

with Malta isolated and incessantly bombed, the British had to husband their strength until reinforcements could be sent to the area.

General Sir Archibald Wavell, commander of British forces in the area, had 36,000 men in Egypt, 27,000 in Palestine, 9,000 in the Sudan, 8,500 in Kenya, and 1,500 in British Somaliland, all without heavy equipment and weak on antitank armament. With these pitifully small forces Wavell could hold on only by combining bluff with aggressive action at a few points chosen by himself.

In the critical autumn of 1940, when the British were hard pressed in the homeland, Churchill searched his military cupboards and sent reinforcements to Wavell from England, India, Australia, and New Zealand. Along with them went a valuable supply of Matilda tanks to build up the Army of the Nile.

The entire picture in the Mediterranean changed abruptly when Italy entered the war against France. Hungry for conquest, Mussolini, Generalissimo of the Italian Armies of Land, Sea, and Air, resolved to liberate Italy from her imprisonment in the Mediterranean and carve out for himself an African empire at the expense of Britain. Like Napoleon, he would seek to humiliate Britain by throwing a block across her lifeline, overthrowing Egypt and the Anglo-Egyptian Sudan, and then go on to restore the glory of ancient Rome.

For this the *Duce* had half a million troops in Africa, a fleet of 10 battleships and supporting warships operating from strategic bases, and air squadrons based on Libya. Unlike the British, his lines of communication were short.

The prognosis seemed good. The British would have to withdraw the bulk of their fleet from the Mediterranean and send it home to fight the Battle of Britain and the Battle of the Atlantic. Mussolini talked a good war: He would then launch a desert *Blitzkrieg* against Egypt and the Suez Canal. Next, he would send one army under Marshal Rodolfo Graziani to invade Egypt from the west, and another under the Duke of Aosta to strike northward from East Africa; between them they would crush the decadent British and force them out of Africa altogether.

From a balcony in Rome, it seemed easy.

BATTLE FOR AFRICA: ROUND I

In Eritrea and Italian Somaliland, in East Africa, the Duke of Aosta, a member of the Italian royal family, had 200,000 Italian and native troops under his command, ready to advance upon the Anglo-Egyptian Sudan and Egypt from the south. Many of them were veterans of the earlier Ethiopian campaign.

Against this massive force the British in Italian Somaliland had only a garrison of 1,500 British and native troops.

On August 4, 1940, Italian armies in three spearheads moved against both British and French Somaliland at the entrance to the Red Sea. The next day they captured Zeila and Hargeisa and a day later Oodweina. On August 11 they attacked the main British positions at Tug Argan on the Hargeisa-Berbera road in Somaliland. During the night of August 15–16 the British, outnumbered, outgunned, caught from both north and south, withdrew. A day later they began to embark at Berbera and completed the evacuation of Somaliland on the night of August 19.

From Rome came trumpeting announcements of a "magnificent victory" in East Africa.

For Mussolini this was superb news. The fall of France had secured the rear of his armies in Tunisia, and the British were fighting for life in their own homeland. An August 20, 1940, the emboldened *Duce* announced the "total blockade" of British possessions in the Mediterranean and Africa.

Next stop—Egypt.

On September 14, 1940, a second army of 250,000 Italians under Marshal Rodolfo Graziani moved from Bardia and Fort Capuzzo in Libya and across the Egyptian border. Soon the invaders were 60 miles inside Egypt. Fearing the desert, the Italians hugged the coast, where they were subjected to shelling by the Royal Navy, and finally halted at Sidi Barrani to await reinforcements and supplies for a drive on Alexandria.

The British retired to Mersa Matruh, railhead of the line of Alexandria.

Meanwhile, the British fleet, far from retiring to home waters as Mussolini had predicted and expected, ranged the Mediterranean, shattering Graziani's supply lines and spoiling for a fight to the finish with the Italian navy. The *Duce*, to prevent invasion of Italy's coastline, kept the major part of his fleet in home waters at Taranto, his naval base on the heel of the Italian boot. The offensive-minded British seadogs decided not to wait.

The attack came on the evening of November 11, 1940. A British task force steamed to a position off Taranto Bay.

From the deck of the aircraft carrier *Illustrious*, nine Swordfish, the oldest operative aircraft still in service, rose in two waves. Skimming the water, the planes launched their torpedoes into the midst of the Italian fleet. It was one of the first aerial torpedo attacks of the war, and one of the most successful. Within minutes Taranto Harbor was a bowl of flames.

Three of six Italian battleships, two cruisers, and two auxiliaries were smashed in the daring assault. The cost to the British—two planes lost, one officer killed, and three men taken prisoner.

The rest of the Italian fleet scurried for safer waters, leaving the British in complete naval control of the Mediterranean.

"A crippling blow," Churchill said the next day.

THE BALKANS: ROUND I

Axis eyes now turned to the Balkans, the seething cauldron of Europe—source of oil, grain, butter, hogs. The Balkans under Axis control meant the severance of important Allied lines of communication along the land bridge to the Middle East.

The Balkans had long been cut through by a host of conflicting interests and rivalries. Greece, alienated by Mussolini's bombardment of Corfu in 1923 and forewarned by his annexation of Albania in 1939, naturally was pro-Ally.

Yugoslavia, too, favored the Allied cause, since she had never forgotten the unwillingness of the Italians to help the Serbians in World War I nor was she disposed to overlook Mussolini's pretensions in the Adriatic.

Rumania, desiring above all else to be left alone, was suspicious of all her neighbors—of Hungary, which wanted Transylvania; of Bulgaria, from which she had taken some territory in the Dobruja in the Second Balkan War in 1913; and of the Soviet Union, which had its eyes on Bessarabia, a Russian possession in 1914.

Hungary was too close to Germany to be safe from aggression.

Turkey, though anti-German and anti-Italian, underwent a series of elaborate contortions to maintain her neutrality. In October 1939 the Turks had made an agreement with the Allied powers, but insisted that the treaty include a clause exempting them from war against the Soviet Union.

It was confusion thrice confounded.

Both Mussolini and Hitler, as a preliminary step to Axis expansion, wanted an end to the interminable Balkan quarrels. At first both attempted diplomatic offensives designed to assure control without the use of force. The tested formula—propaganda, threats, use of economic pressure. The challenge—coöperation or destruction.

On August 30, 1940, Hitler and Mussolini "negotiated" the so-called Vienna Award, an agreement signed among Germany, Italy, Hungary, and Rumania. The purpose was to remove sources of friction in the Balkan countries and keep them in line. Rumania was forced to cede 3,000 square miles of southern Dobruja to Bulgaria and 16,000 square miles of the northern half of Transylvania to Hungary.

King Carol II of Rumania yielded to avoid any further encroachments by the Soviet Union, which had already taken the Rumanian province of Bessarabia. Infuriated, the Rumanians accused their king of cowardice in the face of threats and forced his abdication on September 3, 1940. Carol turned his throne over to his son Michael, who was obliged to entrust what was left of his country to a Fascist dictatorship under strong man General

Ion Antonescu. The constitution was suspended and Parliament dissolved on September 5.

On October 7, 1940, German troops entered Rumania to reorganize the Rumanian army, to be followed by the Italians on October 14, both "by invitation." The country was brought into the new Axis order.

The Axis diplomatic offensive was making headway. Hungary, under threat of annihilation, joined the Axis several days before Antonescu signed at Berlin. On November 24, 1940, Slovakia, a German protectorate since March 1939, was also brought into the Axis. In the interim, diplomatic pressure was exerted on Yugoslavia and Bulgaria to join the Axis camp.

Only the Greeks remained adamantly opposed to Axis pretensions in the Balkans.

ITALIAN FIASCO IN GREECE

October 15, 1940.

A war council was called in Rome. Three Italian destroyers had been sunk in Mediterranean operations, the British Admiralty announced that day. But at the Rome war council one after another of *Duce's* generals arose to boast of their readiness for combat. The troops, one said, "were excessively eager to fight and advance." Another asserted that "enthusiasm is at its highest point." General Quirino Armellini later revealed: "They spoke of seizing Greece or Yugoslavia in the same offhand way they would decide to order a cup of coffee!"

It was an exhibit of criminal stupidity. What the obtuse generals failed to tell Mussolini would have been enough to chill his grandiose ambitions. In reality, the Italian troops had no stomach for war. They were ill prepared. They were badly led. Thousands of them were destined to freeze to death in the mountains of Albania and Greece as a sacrifice to the *Duce's* ambitions.

For Mussolini the tinseled edifice of Fascism demanded a cheap victory. The thundering successes of Nazi arms had been satisfying—up to a point. Hitler's legions had gone from one impressive victory to another, while Italian prestige was fast fading into the background. It was all too embarrassing. The *Duce* must present the world with new evidence of Fascist might, preferably a quick victory on the European mainland to supplement the African campaign.

The strutting Fascist gamecock turned his eyes on Greece. There it was! There was really nothing to it—43,000,000 Italians with a modernized, mechanized army would smash 9,000,000 ill-armed Greeks overnight. Fascist glory would be perpetuated in a blood sacrifice. And then Italy would raise a score of new triumphal arches.

The groundwork was laid in familiar Axis style. In mid-August 1940,

Mussolini began negotiations with Greece. He demanded that Greece renounce the guarantee of her independence made by Britain in 1939. King George II and Premier Joannes Metaxas indignantly refused. Thereupon the *Duce* blasted Greece as an "unneutral" country which secretly helped Britain and indulged in terror tactics on the Albanian frontier. He began massing Italian troops, and hastily found the usual border incident.

At 3 A.M. on October 28, 1940, the Italian minister at Athens presented a three-hour ultimatum, listing Italian grievances and demanding permission for Italian occupation of several strategic Greek areas for the duration of the war. Before the Greeks had a chance to reply (they rejected the ultimatum), 200,000 Fascist troops moved across the border of Albania.

The Italians bombed Patras. The British promised help. Two days later the Admiralty announced the mining of Greek waters. On November 6, 1940, Churchill and Lord Halifax announced a British loan of £5,000,000 for Greece. British troops were already landing on Greek soil.

For the Italians this was supposed to be one of the easiest pushovers of the war. The Greeks had only a few hundred antiquated planes, no mechanized equipment, and few heavy arms. There was an additional handicap in that the Greek defensive Metaxas Line faced Bulgaria and not Albania—the wrong direction.

For several days happy Italian troops, singing *Giovinezza*, the Fascist hymn, and enjoying the wine of victory, raced down the valleys of northern Greece. But Mussolini's judgment had been faulty: He had ordered his troops to advance through mountainous regions at the wrong time of the year.

The Greek *Evzones*, selected infantrymen recruited from the mountain regions, had no intention of fraternizing with the enemy. In their stiff white kilts they took to the hills and mountains. General Metaxas, brilliant tactician, waited until the Italian columns were extended in the narrow valleys and away from their supply bases. Then he struck. His seasoned mountain warriors lobbed artillery shells down onto the massed Italians. It was a slaughter. One by one the Italian columns were cut to pieces.

The infuriated Greeks now closed ranks for a smashing counterattack. The Italians, demoralized, hampered by poor roads and heavy rains, without stomach for this kind of fighting, plunged into wild retreat.

For Rome the news was all bad:

November 8-10: 3rd Alpini division trapped in Pindus gorges; 5,000 prisoners.

November 19: Greeks announce Italians driven back across the Kalamas.

November 21: Greeks enter Koritza, the most important Italian supply base in Albania, where they take many Italian prisoners and much prized Italian military equipment.

December 1: Greeks capture Pogradets.

December 6: Greeks occupy Santi Quaranta.
December 8: Greeks occupy Argyrokastro and Delvino.
December 23: Greeks occupy Himarra.

By the end of the year a quarter of Albania was in possession of the small Greek army.

For the Italian people, fed for years on a diet of Fascist invincibility, this was a stunning blow. Mussolini, characteristically, tried to brazen it out. "We'll break the backs of the Greeks," he shouted, "and we don't need any help!" But he was to get help, whether he wanted it or not.

The *Duce's* reaction brings to mind the passage in *John Brown's Body* about the little peddler who had taken to spying as he passed freely through the lines of both armies. When he was finally caught, he stood up in his wagon, looked around him, and reflected that they were all nice boys; he knew them all. "They couldn't be going to hang him. But they were!"

THE BRITISH STRIKE IN AFRICA

There was to be more bad news for the Italians.

The Italian army which had invaded Egypt in September 1940 stood poised at Sidi Barrani waiting to build up strength for an assault on Alexandria. It got no farther. Opposite it was General Sir Archibald Wavell, who had reinforced his small Army of the Nile with picked Australian, New Zealand, Indian, Polish, and Free French troops. Wavell, who had learned about desert warfare under the famed Lord Allenby of Meggido in World War I, managed despite difficulties to build up a striking force of 40,000 men. All were superbly trained in coördinated desert warfare.

On December 9, 1940, Wavell moved his tanks out of Mersa Matruh in what was to be a "raid in force." It turned out to be something far more significant. Hitting at the Italians with surprise and with terrific power, Wavell captured Sidi Barrani within two days and took prisoner its entire garrison of white and native troops.

The British offensive gathered momentum. By the middle of December the bewildered Italians were driven out of Egypt altogether. On December 23 London announced that 35,949 Italian prisoners were counted in the African campaign. On January 5, 1941, Bardia, the Italian stronghold in Libya, together with 30,000 troops, fell. The next stop was Tobruk, which capitulated to the Australians on January 22 after a ferocious attack from sea, air, and land. Here the bag of prisoners amounted to 25,000, and 50 tanks were captured.

Wavell now raced his mobile army westward. On January 30 he struck at Derna, where the Imperial Forces won the prize of an important water supply. A week later, on February 6, the rampaging Australians stormed

Benghazi by the coastal road, and took the town, after Tripoli the most important city in Libya. To London went the signal from the Australians: "Benghazi is in our hands!" Six senior Italian generals surrendered with the city.

Meanwhile, from deep in the desert southwest of Derna, a column of 25 British tanks and motorized infantry cut across 150 miles of unmapped desert and trapped the Italians retreating from Benghazi.

It was a scintillating campaign. In two months the Army of the Nile had conquered the entire northern coast of Africa from Sidi Barrani to Benghazi, and in the process had captured 113,000 prisoners (more men than were in the entire attacking force), 1,300 guns, and vast supplies of war matériel. In this lightning campaign the British put at least 10 Italian divisions out of commission, at the cost of 1,774 casualties, of whom 438 were killed.

This was the first great British land victory of World War II. The pressure was now lifted from Suez. This was highly satisfying news for a British public grown accustomed to reports of defeat after defeat on the far-flung battlefields.

There were more surprises for Mussolini in East Africa. The Italians had won the opening battles there, but they were not long to enjoy their triumph.

In January 1941 a British spearhead advanced southeastward from Khartoum in the Sudan and headed toward the Italian armies. In Eritrea, the pick of the Italian troops entrenched themselves on mountaintops and held out for several weeks, only to succumb to relentless British pressure.

Another British column moved eastward from Nairobi in Kenya and on January 29, 1941, entered Italian Somaliland. The invaders were helped considerably by natives, who rose against the Italians, harried their lines of communication, and in general made life miserable for Mussolini's warriors. The British swung northward toward Addis Ababa, in the heart of Ethiopia.

The Italians evacuated the capital on April 5, 1941. In the final battle two British forces combined to overwhelm the Duke of Aosta, who capitulated at Amba Alagi on May 16, 1941. Ethiopia, first of Mussolini's conquests, was liberated.

Gone was Axis control of the Red Sea coast. Now American Lend-Lease supplies could reach Egypt. The picture in Africa began to look brighter for the Allies.

Meanwhile, the Royal Navy continued both its assault on Italy and its whittling down of the Italian fleet. On February 9, 1941, in broad daylight, a British task force bombarded Genoa, destroying power plants, railroad stations, and stores accumulated on the docks. That same day Churchill broadcast a message to the United States: "Give us the tools and we shall finish the job."

On March 27, 1941, an Italian naval force rashly tried to intercept a

British convoy carrying troops and supplies to Greece. Mussolini's seamen were asking for trouble and they got it. British reconnaissance planes discovered the Italians off Cape Matapan, ancient Toenarum, the precipitous southernmost point of Greece. Elements of the Royal Navy set out for the kill.

Using radar-directed guns in the darkness, the British sank the Italian cruisers *Fiume, Pola,* and *Zara,* and three destroyers, severely damaged a new battleship, and inflicted heavy damage on other enemy vessels. British aircraft based in Greece took part in the battle. The only British loss was two aircraft.

British seamen who boarded the Italian cruiser *Pola* before it sank found a scene of incredible confusion. The decks were littered with bottles and packages of clothing prepared by seamen abandoning the ship. Some Italians who had not jumped overboard were in a drunken stupor. The *Pola* had not fired a gun.

With his battle-shy fleet paralyzed at Cape Matapan, his armies defeated in Libya, East Africa, and Greece, Mussolini was fast approaching the point of no return.

Enraged and disgusted, Hitler decided that he would have to step into the Mediterranean picture. To North Africa he sent General Erwin Rommel, his most efficient student of mechanized warfare, to take charge of the Axis forces there.

Rommel, appearing on the scene with a mechanized division and a force of fighter and bomber planes, opened his offensive on April 3, 1941. The balance in Libya was immediately altered in favor of the Axis. Within a few days he took Bardia and was storming Tobruk.

Wavell quickly retired to his Egyptian bases, leaving at Tobruk a strong garrison of Australians who were to undergo a ferocious siege. In a display of raw courage, the "Rats of Tobruk," supplied by the Royal Navy and the R.A.F., held out for eight months until relieved.

On April 11, 1941, the British announced the loss of 2,000 prisoners, including three generals, in the Libyan withdrawal. In a lightning ten-day thrust Rommel had recovered most of North Africa. Once again the Axis was poised on the threshold of Suez. But Rommel, too, had to pause to await reinforcements. Then the German invasion of Russia, beginning on June 22, 1941, resulted in a halt of war matériel he needed to continue his attack.

The opening struggle for Egypt had ended in a draw.

THE BALKANS: ROUND II

Before attacking the Soviet Union, Hitler wanted assurance that no hostile power would endanger him from the Balkans. It was all-important to secure his southern flank. He would not only continue his diplomatic offensive there, but he would also punish the recalcitrants by invading them. He would rescue the *Duce* in Greece (a thankless task, but it had to be done), and then he would go on to tie up with French Vichy forces in Syria and the pro-Axis elements in Iran and Iraq.

Natürlich (naturally), he would carry on the war of nerves. Rumania and Hungary were already satellite states under Axis domination. One by one the other Balkan countries were supposed to capitulate. On March 1, 1941, Bulgaria signed a formal alliance with the Axis (approved by the Sobranje, the Bulgarian unicameral national assembly, by a vote of 150 to 20), and the next day German troops were in Sofia and Varna.

Only Yugoslavia and Greece remained unintimidated.

Yugoslavia was the largest Balkan state, 95,576 square miles in area (three-quarters the size of Italy), with a population of 14,000,000. To bring Yugoslavia into line, Hitler used his troops in Bulgaria and Hungary as a threat. On March 25, 1941, Yugoslavia was forced to sign the Tripartite Pact by which she became the newest member of Hitler's New Order. Germany agreed to respect Yugoslav sovereignty and territorial integrity and not to demand passage for German troops.

The Yugoslav people reacted with consternation and boiling anger. Two days later, on March 27, 1941, came a 2 A.M. revolution. A cabal of army officers under General Dušan Simovic, in a *coup d'état*, arrested the leading members of the government, forced the regent Prince Paul from the throne, proclaimed 18-year-old Prince Peter as king, and organized a coalition government including all parties except those who had subscribed to the agreement with Germany.

Hitler could not tolerate this rebuff. The controlled German press promptly shouted that the Soviet Union was behind the anti-German demonstrations in Yugoslavia and that Yugoslavs were beating German residents and burning their homes. It was the familiar Nazi campaign preliminary to invasion.

The invasion came, mercilessly swift, at 5:15 A.M., April 6, 1941. A thousand Nazi planes plus 20 divisions of nearly 650,000 troops, in a new *Blitzkrieg*, struck at airfields, bridges, communications, vital services. In a matter of hours Yugoslavia was without electricity, telephones, radio.

It was a remarkable campaign—the Germans pushed across mountainous terrain hitherto regarded as *blitz*proof. From Rome came news that the Italian government had decided to act, with all its forces, in close collaboration with Germany. Pushing through the mountain passes in southeastern Bulgaria, one German spearhead turned southward toward Greece, while others drove across Yugoslavia to meet the Italians at the Albanian border. Another column advanced from Hungary toward Zagreb, still others moved southward from Rumania, and entered Belgrade, the Yugoslav capital.

In 11 days it was all over. The country was cut to pieces. The position of the Yugoslavs was so hopeless that they had to surrender. On April 17, 1940, the Germans announced the capitulation of the entire Yugoslav army. That same day an R.A.F. Sunderland evacuated King Peter from Kotor.

Yugoslavia was then carved into slices, portions going to Germany, Italy, Hungary, and Bulgaria, while the rest was frozen into a satellite state.

But to occupy Yugoslavia was not to conquer it. Guerrillas took to the hills, and continued resistance in the mountains, forests, and villages. They harried the invaders, immobilized their convoys, hit them pitilessly, especially the Italians. From then until the end of the war Hitler's troops in Yugoslavia found themselves in a hornet's nest.

DUNKIRK II: GREECE

On April 6, 1941, the same day that he invaded Yugoslavia, Hitler sent several columns racing into Greece from both north and east. One spearhead, after a bloody battle at Rupel Pass, moved down the spacious valley of the Vardar, outflanked the Metaxas Line (designed to protect Greece from attack through Bulgaria), isolated three Greek divisions, and captured Salonika, where the Vardar flows into the sea. It took just two days.

The sudden smash-in of the German *Panzers* was a staggering blow to the Greeks. Twelve divisions of the best Greek fighters were poised on the other side of the country along a crescent-shaped line in Albania to contain the Italians.

Harried Greek commanders tore up their battle plans on the news that the Germans had attacked from the rear. "We'll throw them into the sea—the Baltic Sea!" Had not President Roosevelt declared that Yugoslavia and Greece would get all possible help? The Greeks had courage—but the Germans had mobile armor and knew how to use it.

The British had to intervene, more for political than for military reasons. They detached 56,657 veteran troops, mostly Anzacs, from Libya, and sent them to Greece to engage an army of half a million Germans. It was a futile gesture. In addition, it so weakened the British Imperials in Libya that they were forced to retreat there.

Hitler's plan was to overrun the British forces in the east while the Italians counterattacked from the west. It worked, despite fierce resistance. Nazi armor pushed south through the Monastir Gap toward Florina, splitting the Greek and British forces. The Anzacs retreated slowly across the flat Thessalonican plain, their columns strafed and cut up by the *Luftwaffe*. There was little air support from the R.A.F. as one forward airfield after another was relinquished to the advancing Germans.

At Thermopylae (where a famous battle had been fought in 480 B.C. by Leonidas and the Greeks against Xerxes and the Persians) the Adolf Hitler

BLITZ IN THE BALKANS

S.S. Motorized Division was held up for three days by a small force of Anzacs, Britons, and Greeks—just long enough to permit the Allies to fall back on Athens. But the Germans turned westward and trapped a Greek army at Yanina.

It was obvious now that the British had to get out of Greece at once. The Greek government was frank in its message to the British: "You have done your best to save us. We are finished. But the war is not yet lost. Save as much as you can of your army to help win elsewhere."

The evacuation would be a difficult one; there was no air support as at Dunkirk. The *Luftwaffe* roamed the skies unopposed and German *Panzertruppen* were racing southward in both east and west. Leaving tough units to guard their retreat, the British finally reached the southern beaches on April 23, 1941. On that day King George of the Hellenes and the Greek government escaped to Crete in an R.A.F. Sunderland.

The next few nights, fortunately for the British, were moonless. On the beaches they smashed their big guns or destroyed them with grenades, rolled their tanks into the sea, and set fire to stores of gasoline. Whole battalions of men lay concealed during the day to escape the eyes of the *Luftwaffe*. At night the troops were transferred to waiting ships.

Some 43,000 men, including Britons, Australians, and New Zealanders, were evacuated, about half to Crete and half to Egypt, with the loss of four transports and two destroyers. The last men were taken off from the Kalamata area on the night of April 30–May 1, 1941. In the Greek ports and along the southern shores of Greece the Germans found only a mass of twisted wreckage. But at least 15,000 Imperial troops were lost in the Greek debacle.

This meant a heartbreaking tragedy for the Greeks. German intervention had robbed them of independence despite their magnificent victory over the Italian invaders. For the British it was another setback in the effort to keep the Germans away from Suez. Washington promptly announced that Greek cash and credits in the United States, estimated at $45 million, would be frozen.

For Hitler it was a triumph. Briefly he maintained the fiction of Italian control by allowing Mussolini to occupy portions of Greece. But that was just a gesture. He soon extended German administration completely over the hapless country.

DUNKIRK III: CRETE

The fiasco in Greece, a harsh blow for the Allies, was to be followed by more bad news. Nazi power, full weight, was to fall on the island of Crete in the first large-scale airborne attack in history. Nothing like it had ever been seen before.

Crete, called Candia by the Italians, Khandah by the Arabs, and Kirid Adasi by the Turks, is the main island in the chain which divides the Greek archipelago from the eastern basin of the Mediterranean. It is about 160 miles long, its width varying from 35 down to 7½ miles. The rugged southern coast is difficult of access, but the northern coast has long stretches of beach.

Beginning systematic explorations in 1894, archaeologists uncovered the "hundred-city" island and the famed palace at Knossus. Legend has it that Zeus, the supreme deity of the Greeks, was born on Crete. Here Icarus, son of Daedalus, was said to have flown with his father on wings made of wax and feathers, until the sun melted the wax and Icarus fell into the sea.

For the modern British, Crete was much more important than merely an archaeological paradise or the home of the best mules in the world and the sure-footed agrimi, wild mountain goats. It was a vital point on the lifeline to India, it protected both Palestine and Egypt, it threatened Italian communications with the Dodecanese Islands, and its great natural harbor at Suda Bay sheltered elements of the Royal Navy.

The garrison on Crete consisted only of three infantry battalions, armed with several heavy and light antiaircraft batteries, coast-defense artillery, and searchlights. The 27,000 British, Australian, and New Zealand troops evacuated from Greece brought with them only 9 infantry tanks and about 35 random planes.

In command was Major General Bernard C. Freyberg, a swashbuckling New Zealander, winner of the Victoria Cross for gallantry in action in World War I. To Winston Churchill, who had never quite overcome the enthusiastic hero worship of his youth, this New Zealander was the ideal warrior for a difficult assignment.

"One day in the 1920's," Churchill wrote later, "when I was staying at a country house with Bernard Freyberg, I asked him to show me his wounds. He stripped himself, and I counted 27 separate scars and gashes. To these he was to add in the Second World War another three. But, of course, as he explained, 'You nearly always get two wounds for every bullet or splinter, because mostly they have to go out as well as go in.' " Churchill, the romantic, was impressed by all this.

But neither Freyberg's courage nor a spirited defense could prevent a smashing German victory in Crete.

Sensing the coming onslaught, the British attempted to reinforce the island. But it was too late. In the first two weeks of May 1941 they could land only a few thousand tons of supplies in the face of *Luftwaffe* attacks.

Then it came—at 8 A.M., May 20, 1941—the first time in history that airborne troops with few heavy weapons overcame superior land forces.

First, German aircraft bombed and machine-gunned everything they found moving on the roads and airfields. Almost at once they put antiaircraft batteries out of action.

Then, in a sensational display of teamwork, with clockwork precision, shock troops parachuted from transport planes at heights varying from 300 to 600 feet. They came by the hundreds, including Max Schmeling, former heavyweight champion of the world. Many were disguised in uniforms that blended into foliage, others wore New Zealand battle dress, still others were dummy parachutists designed to draw enemy fire while live Nazis landed elsewhere. It was a brilliantly coördinated assault.

General Henry H. Arnold, chief of the U.S. Army Air Forces, described the fantastic scene:

> They came in gliders carrying from 12 to 30 soldiers. They were towed by lumbering old transports unsuited for aerial combat, but ideal for this new purpose, with as many as 10 or 11 gliders strung out behind each plane. In an incredibly short time the Germans, by air transport and gliders, landed 15,000 troops on the island, together with their rifles, light machine guns, heavy machine guns, and field pieces. They even brought medical supplies and radio equipment.

At first it was a duck shoot for the British, New Zealand, and Greek defenders, who spotted the parachutists one by one before they hit the ground. Most of the initial 3,500 German shock troops dropped by parachute were killed. Many fell into the sea, where, caught in the shrouds of their parachutes, they were drowned. Others, dangling helplessly from trees, were picked off by sharpshooters. Cretans, armed with rusty knives, slaughtered Germans in the ravines or on the beaches.

But on they came, with no regard for casualties. Once the Germans seized the airfields, nothing could stop their glider trains and troop-carrying planes. The aircraft came in at the rate of 20 per hour, crash-landing on the airstrips surrounded by wrecked planes.

With uncontested control of the air (the R.A.F. planes in Africa, 350 miles to the south, were too far away to help), the Germans drove across Crete from the west, while the Italians pushed from the east in the textbook pincers movement.

Simultaneously with the airborne invasion, a convoy of German and Italian troop-carriers, torpedo boats, and small Greek caïques set out from Greek ports for Crete.

Warned by British Intelligence, Admiral Sir Andrew Browne Cunningham dispatched a light naval force to intercept the convoy. The British caught the invasion fleet at 11:30 P.M. on May 21, 1941, just 18 miles north of Canea, on the northwestern coast of Crete. Three British cruisers and four destroyers knifed through the overloaded transport fleet and sent some 400 troops to the bottom. Another 5,000 troops in a second convoy escaped.

But in the next two days the Royal Navy took a fierce pounding from hundreds of enemy land-based bombers and torpedo planes. The British lost the cruisers *Gloucester* and *Fiji*, and three destroyers, including the *Kelly*, whose commander, Lord Louis Mountbatten, was rescued from the sea. The British East Mediterranean Fleet withdrew from Cretan waters for the time being.

By the end of May all hope of holding the island was gone. The remainder of the defensive forces, covered by rearguard troops, withdrew from Maleme, Canea, and Suda Bay across the island to Skafia, a small fishing village at the foot of a 500-foot high cliff on the southern coast. Once again the British demonstrated that they never abandoned an expeditionary force. The trapped troops, hiding by day in caves, were taken at night aboard destroyers, which brought them over 350 miles to Egypt through a hail of enemy bombs. Half the British garrison was saved. At least a thousand more were rescued later by commando raiders.

It was another defeat for the British. In addition to losing their troops on Crete, they had nearly 2,000 naval casualties, and lost a total of 3 cruisers, 6 destroyers, and 29 smaller craft. More, one battleship, 4 cruisers, and 7 destroyers were damaged.

These were severe losses. It was a shake-up for British prestige. If Crete could not be held against air assault from Greece, a hundred miles away, what would happen if Hitler mounted an attack on England from Calais, only 20 miles away?

The Germans, too, paid a stiff price. They suffered 17,000 casualties to win Crete, and lost 170 troop-carrying aircraft. Goering's crack Seventh Air Division was so mauled that it could not be used again for further campaigns in the Middle East. This was to be the last such large-scale operation attempted by the German High Command.

But with Crete in his hands, Hitler could protect Greece, hamper the Royal Navy in the Mediterranean, and once again threaten Egypt, Suez, and the Middle East from the air.

WAR IN THE MIDDLE EAST

The war in the Middle East was a sideshow, but an important one. Hitler was attracted by its oil fields and by its strategic value for an attack on Suez. Since the Arabs were supposed to respect force, they would be shown enough of it to convince them that their future lay with Nazi Germany.

The Allies, too, needed the Middle East not only for its oil but also as a land bridge for supplies to the Soviet Union after she was attacked by Germany. As early as the spring of 1941 the Allies took several swift steps to erect a line of friendly buffer states in the region. Even if Hitler were successful in seizing Constantinople and the Straits, he would still be barred from the Red Sea and the Persian Gulf by territory under Allied control.

When the British were ordered to evacuate Iraq by Rashid Ali Beg Gailani, its pro-Nazi ruler, they replied, in April 1941, by throwing him out and establishing a pro-Allied regime. In early May 1941 Nazi agents stimulated disorders that endangered the pipeline to Haifa and the oil wells of Mosul and Kirkuk, all vital for the British Mediterranean fleet. General Sir Archibald Wavell rushed a force of armored cars 400 miles across the desert and crushed the revolt on June 1. On that day British troops entered Baghdad. The critical oil supply was protected.

Immediately after the fall of France, pro-Vichy French officers under German domination plotted to hand over the French-mandated states of Syria and Lebanon, key positions vis-à-vis Egypt and the Suez Canal, to the Axis. On June 8, 1941, British Imperial and Free French forces entered Syria and Lebanon from Palestine and Iraq with the R.A.F. and the Royal Navy coöperating. There was no resistance in Syria until the line Chameh-Merj-Ayoun-Mount Hermon was reached.

On June 21 Damascus fell to the Free French loyal to General de Gaulle; three weeks later the Vichy French sued for an armistice. The British ousted pro-Axis administrations from both countries and established friendly regimes, thereby securing one flank in the Middle East.

The Allies now turned to Iran (Persia), whose ruler, Riza Shah Pahlevi, was sympathetic to the Axis cause.

In August 1941, after Hitler's invasion of the Soviet Union, British and Soviet troops moved jointly into Iran to keep it from falling into German hands. In January 1942 the British and Russians signed a treaty guaranteeing "to respect the territorial integrity, sovereignty and political independence of Iran," and promising that both countries would evacuate their troops from Iran no later than six months after the end of hostilities. The United States subsequently agreed to this arrangement at the Teheran Conference in December 1943.

In this series of swift, unorthodox maneuvers, carried out under the noses of the Germans, the back door to Eastern Europe was slammed against the Axis. It was perhaps one of Hitler's great mistakes after the conquest of Crete not to throw all his power into the Middle East, instead of turning against Russia.

Turkey remained a thorny problem for the Allies. Warily declining to abandon neutrality, the Turks indiscriminately sold supplies to both sides. Impressed by Hitler's advance in the Balkans, the Turks, on June 18, 1941, signed a treaty of "mutual trust and sincere friendship" with Germany and permitted armed Axis ships to pass through the Dardanelles.

CHAPTER 9

Fissure: Germany Attacks Russia

> ***The German army in fighting Russia is like an elephant attacking a host of ants. The elephant will kill thousands, perhaps even millions, but in the end their numbers will overcome him, and he will be eaten to the bone.***
>
> **—Colonel Berndt von Kleist, 1941**

FANTASTIC ICARUS: RUDOLF HESS

On May 10, 1941, came a profound sensation, minor in the tumbling march of events, but betraying weaknesses in the Nazi hierarchy. Rudolf Hess, No. 3 Nazi after Field Marshal Hermann Goering, made an extraordinary flight to Scotland on a one-man, self-inspired mission of peace.

Hess held a glamorous array of titles: Deputy *Fuehrer*, Leader of the Nazi Party, Member of the Secret Cabinet Council for Germany, Reich Minister without Portfolio, Member of the Ministerial Council for the Defense of the Reich. Born in Egypt in 1894, he had met Hitler on a French battlefield in 1918. He was with Hitler at the unsuccessful Beer Hall Putsch of 1923 in Munich. Imprisoned with Hitler at Landsberg, he transcribed *Mein Kampf*, and was probably responsible for many ideas expressed in what by common consent is one of the crudest books ever written. It was Hess who taught Hitler the theories of Karl Haushofer, the high priest of German geopolitics.

Hess's star rose with Hitler's. The Nazi leader was fond of the tall, dark-eyed, beetle-browed Hess, whom he made successively a moderator for Nazi party squabbles, a member of his personal staff, and eventually one of the six members of the Nazi war cabinet.

In turn, Hess had a doglike devotion for his *Fuehrer*. His specialty was leading audiences in hysterical *Heils!* to the Leader. "*Mein Fuehrer*," he would shout hoarsely, "our trust in you is unlimited! God protect our *Fuehrer*!"

After the outbreak of war, Hitler's time was largely monopolized by a succession of such important people as generals, admirals, and statesmen. The puppylike, modest, sensitive Hess found himself being pushed farther and farther into the background and away from Hitler's intimate circle.

Would it not be wonderful if he, Hess, could win back his beloved *Fuehrer* by a magnificent act of immolation in which he would sacrifice himself for the good of the Fatherland? He, Hess, meant nothing, but the *Fuehrer* was the destiny of Germany.

It was a terrible tragedy, Hess thought, for Germans and British—ancient Teutonic relatives, after all—to fight one another. Here was a God-given time for a supreme act of devotion. He would fly alone to England, make peace, destroy the two-front war, and thus pave the way for his master to smash Bolshevism for all time.

Hess was certain that he would find help in England. At the Olympic Games in Berlin in 1936 he had met a British aristocrat who later became the Duke of Hamilton, with whom he had struck up a friendship. When war came, he wrote to the duke, presenting a peace feeler, but the latter, on advice of government officials, did not reply. Nevertheless, Hess reasoned, if he could once get to England, the duke, as Lord Steward, would surely have access to the king and assist him on his mission of peace. He expected aid and comfort from the duke, whom he regarded as pro-Nazi.

Hess at this time was both physically and psychically ill. Not only was he suffering from tuberculosis, but there were also indications of mental troubles. He prepared for his flight with traditional Teutonic thoroughness. Hitler had barred him from flying, but by some fast talking he convinced Willi Messerschmitt, the aircraft designer, to give him facilities for long-distance flying training inside Germany. He concentrated on learning air navigation, and apparently was an apt student.

On May 10, 1941, Hess took off from Augsburg in an unarmed *Messerschmitt* plane. He had no gas for a return trip. Dressed as a flight lieutenant of the *Luftwaffe*, he carried a map on which he had penciled his course. He brought along photographs to establish his identity.

It was an 800-mile flight, and Hess did a remarkable job of navigation. He had intended to land his plane, but, unable to find a suitable spot, he stalled for a crash and bailed out. He floated down on a Scottish farm, fewer than a dozen miles from Dungavel, his objective, and fractured an ankle. He made no resistance when a pitchfork-bearing farmer captured him. Authorities moved him to a military hospital in Glasgow.

The naïve Nazi talked volubly to his captors. Germany, with her combination of air and submarine power, with a determined people in complete unity, was certain to win the war. Now that France was beaten, Britain could not possibly survive. Hitler was in full sympathy with the British people and was deeply pained by the necessity of waging war against them. If only the good British people knew the kindness and thoughtfulness of the *Fuehrer*!

There was a way out, said Hess. If the British would call off hostilities, they could join the Germans in a crusade against Bolshevism, a long-time bogey of the British "ruling classes." Britain would have a free hand in her own Empire, while Hitler would be given control of Europe. Of course, there were some minor conditions: Germany's colonies must be returned, Iraq must be evacuated, and there must be an armistice with Italy. This was but a small price to pay for peace. But Hitler, Hess added stoutly, would not negotiate with the present British government. Churchill was just too much for the *Fuehrer* to take. Would the British mind throwing him out?

From Berlin there came an outburst of Nazi-patented fury. The news of Hess's flight enraged Hitler, who immediately called a meeting of his intimates and prepared a press release:

> It seemed that Party Member Hess lived in a state of hallucination, as a result of which he felt he would bring about an understanding between England and Germany. . . . The National Socialist Party regrets this idealist fell a victim to his hallucination. This, however, will have no effect on the continuance of the war which has been forced on Germany.

British public reaction varied from astonishment to ridicule. The incident was another example of that long-standing failure of the Germans to understand the psychology of the British people. The Nazi entourage of Hitler knew only the insignificant pro-Fascist elements in England—they had no idea of what the British *people* were like. It was ludicrous, even a little sad.

The British authorities ordered that Hess be treated with dignity, as if he were an important general who had fallen into their hands. He did not get to see the people for whom he had so "important" a message. He was removed by various stages to the Tower of London, where he was imprisoned until October 6, 1945, when he was transferred to a cell at Nuremberg.

"Whatever may be the moral guilt of a German who stood near to Hitler," commented Churchill later, "Hess had, in my view, atoned for this by his completely devoted and frantic deed of lunatic benevolence. He came to us of his own free will, and, though without authority, had something of the quality of an envoy. He was a medical and not a criminal case, and should be so regarded."

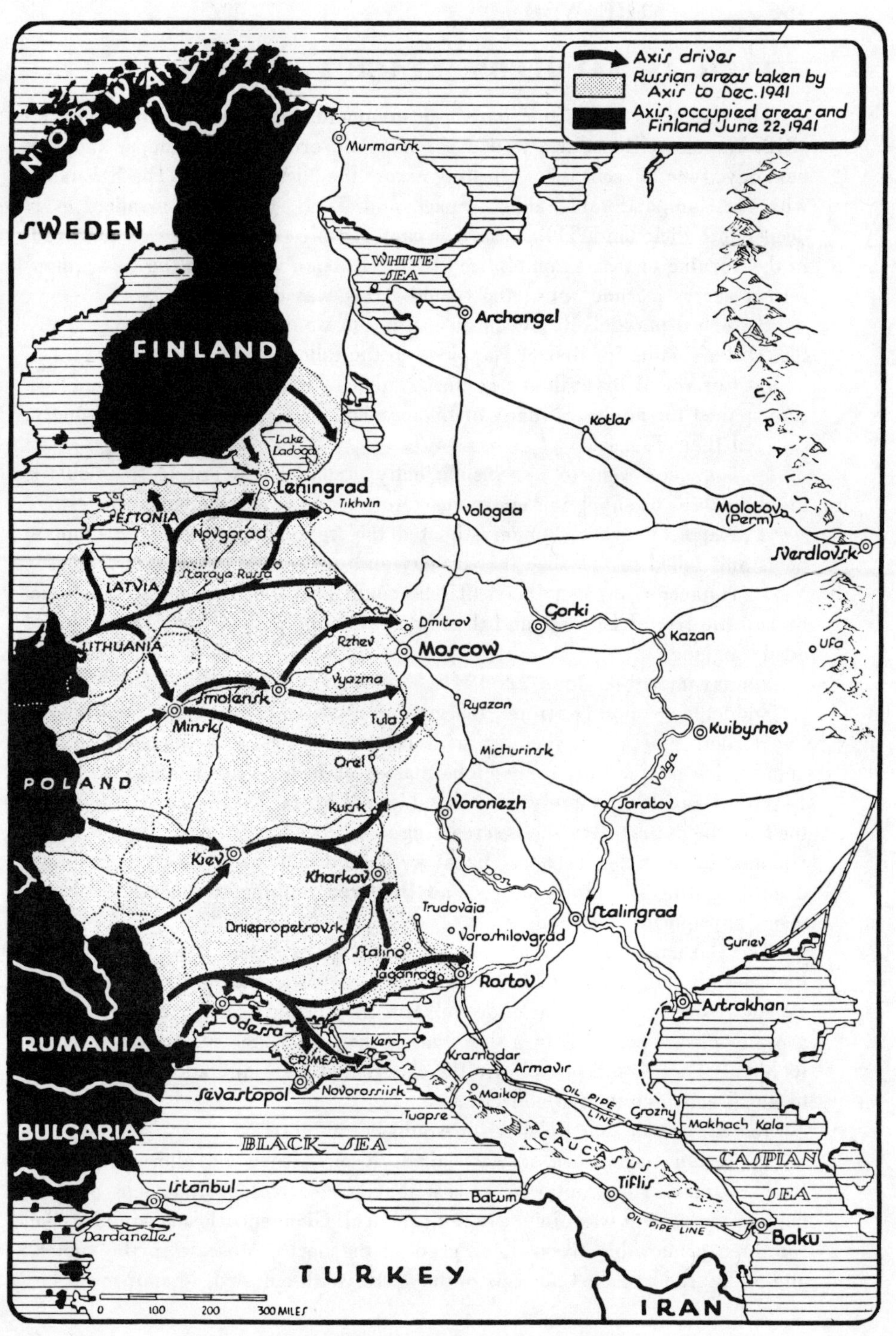

THE NAZI ATTACK ON RUSSIA

HITLER AS NAPOLEON: STAGE I—ATTACK

The countries of Europe had been conquered one by one. On June 21, 1812, Napoleon Bonaparte issued a bombastic order to his troops, and the next day, June 22, sent them crashing across the Niemen River. The Russians, with their imponderable allies—Space and Time—lured the invaders ever deeper into their land. The conqueror captured Moscow, but he was ensnared in the burning city and immobilized by the Russian winter. In the subsequent retreat across ice and snow, the Grand Army was destroyed.

Historical parallels do not mean much, but we can toy with them. Substitute Hitler's name for that of Napoleon in the following items:

... Certain of his military genius, Napoleon went on the Russian adventure against the advice of many of his marshals and generals and persistently rejected their counsel.

... Napoleon went to war insufficiently prepared and failing to calculate the difficulties of supplying enormous forces along overextended lines.

... Napoleon gravely underestimated the fighting qualities of his opponents and failed to visualize the strategy and tactics they were bound to use.

... Napoleon was convinced that he could beat the Russians as easily as he had the rest of Europe, and then he could simply await the fall of blockaded England.

Sunday morning, June 22, 1941.

Suddenly, without warning, the gigantic Nazi war machine surged across the borders and began the war with Russia—the most savage duel in the annals of warfare. Two tremendous masses of men collided head-on. Along 1,800 miles of front there was a veritable hell on earth—planes roaring over the battlefields; artillery shells screaming in a cacophony of death; giant tanks ripping vicious holes in enemy lines; swift fluid maneuvers on open ground; deadly fighting in ruined streets and shattered buildings; pincers, encirclement, entrapment, attrition.

The Germans had a plan, and, as was to be expected, it was brilliant in both design and execution. Using the *Blitzkrieg* so spectacularly employed in Poland, Norway, France, and the Balkans, they would speedily cut the Soviet army to pieces, enfold it in a thousand pockets, and then methodically drain its blood. They would immobilize the clay-footed giant and add the Red scalp to an already impressive collection.

Just six weeks, and Bolshevism would be no more.

Operation Barbarossa it was called. It envisioned no alternative to a frontal attack. The front was so vast that any sort of encirclement or outflanking movement was obviously not practical. Giant spearheads would strike for three prime objectives—Leningrad in the north, Moscow in the center, and Stalingrad and the Caucasus in the south. With one sledge-hammer stroke, the Third Reich would obtain the granary of the Ukraine, the industrial Donetz basin, and the Caucasian oil fields.

Stalin had used every effort to avert an attack by Hitler. His deliveries of food and raw materials to Germany under an agreement of January 1941 were faithfully maintained during the weeks preceding the attack. Timewise, the offensive hit him with stunning surprise, but he had guessed that sooner or later he would have to face the Nazi hordes. His total manpower available, active and reserve, was 12,000,000, consisting of 160 infantry and 30 cavalry divisions, and 35 motorized and armored brigades. But it was futile to risk even these huge forces against past masters in mechanized warfare.

The Russians would rely in the long run primarily on their ancient allies —Space, Time, and Winter. They knew about the tactics of Quintus Fabius Maximus, surnamed *Cunctator* ("the delayer"), who in 217 B.C. had cut off Hannibal's supplies, harassed him incessantly, and had done everything except fight. "Defense in depth" the Russians called it—allow the enemy to cross the frontier, hit his communications, strike hard at his flanks, above all remain patient in defeat. These tactics had worked wonders for the Russians against the Swedes in the eighteenth century and against Napoleon in the nineteenth.

The Russians were oriented psychologically for this kind of war—once the initial shock was over. Living close to nature, they had a great capacity for enduring hardship, and had no fear of their endless forests or of the biting cold. They had a great equanimity about life and death. They would fight—not only men, but women and children—burn their own homes and factories, blow up bridges, dynamite their dams, destroy everything in the invader's path. When hopelessly surrounded they would resist all the harder. The Germans were due for some surprises.

True, the Russians had made a poor showing against tiny Finland. But that was only a minor police action compared to the struggle against Hitler.

From the beginning of the Russian campaign, Hitler's legions operated under handicaps, most not visible on the surface. Contemptuous of Russian stamina and sure of their own invincibility, the Germans overextended themselves instead of concentrating their power on a few vital points. Furthermore, this time there had been no treacherous internal fifth column to smooth the way for invasion. There had been no preliminary softening psychological warfare as there had been in Norway, Holland, and France, no stirring up of domestic quarrels, no Trojan-horse tactics. Instead of the usual long triumphal march, the invaders eventually found themselves up against phantom retreats, scorched earth, fluid resistance, guerrilla tactics. It was a very unsatisfactory kind of war for Nazi warriors.

Worst of all, despite the early victories, the Germans were handicapped by weak leadership. True, the German armies of some 135 divisions were commanded by the finest professional military brains on earth—von Brauchitsch, Halder, von Rundstedt, von Bock, Guderian, von Kleist, Kesselring, von Leeb, Hoepner, Strauss, Blumentritt, and a host of others. But the top voice of command was that of an essentially illiterate World War I corporal. Hitler's prescription for any military situation—hold fast and never retreat. German generals, for all their brilliance, were helpless in the long run against this square-headed, infantile conception of how to fight wars. To the other troubles of the generals was added the hopeless task of fighting the *Fuehrer*'s monomania of no retreat.

Within a few weeks the *Luftwaffe* (as usual) had air supremacy over Russia, after destroying a large part of the Soviet air force on the ground. German motorized units sliced through the frontier defenses, and by July 2, 1941, boasted of an astounding haul—150,000 prisoners, 1,200 tanks, and 600 big guns. Minsk was taken in short order, and the armies now headed for the Dnieper and Dvina. Here the defensive Stalin Line was pierced and the way into Russia opened.

Russian resistance stiffened here, but not enough to recapture the Stalin Line. On July 10, 1941, Smolensk, only 200 miles from Moscow, was under assault by German infantry. In just 18 days the onrushing Nazi legions had pushed two-thirds of the distance to the Russian capital. They had fought one successful battle after another and had advanced over poor roads in all weathers from the borders to the neighborhood of Moscow.

"Russia is broken!" Hitler shouted to all the world. "She will never rise again."

Into Berlin from the Russian front came news of smashing, glorious victories. "In seven short days," proclaimed the Propaganda Ministry, "the *Fuehrer*'s offensive has smashed the Red army to splinters, the decision is reached, and the eastern continent lies, like a limp virgin, in the mighty arms of the German Mars."

Germans beamed with joy. The magnificent *Fuehrer* was right again. And almost 200,000,000 units of slave labor were soon to be added to Germany's mighty war machine to make the implements of war. Soon the *Wehrmacht* would be free to turn west and smash England, that recalcitrant island.

From that island had come the voice of Churchill on the very day Hitler turned on Russia. "Any man or state who fights against Nazism," said Churchill in a broadcast, "will have our aid. . . . It follows therefore that we shall give whatever help we can to Russia."

The Russians, of course, wanted help. On July 8, 1941, Maxim Litvinov broadcast in English from Moscow: "Great Britain and the U.S.S.R. must strike together now, without respite, untiringly." Litvinov had been dismissed as Soviet Foreign Commissar in May 1939 just before the Hitler-Stalin Pact. Now he was back in Stalin's good graces.

In the south, the independent-minded Ukrainians, long alienated by Stalin's iron-fisted dictatorship, greeted the German invaders with cries of joy. Hundreds of thousands surrendered in the belief that Hitler had come as a liberator. And here the Nazi *Fuehrer* made one of the most colossal errors of his career. Instead of assuring an alliance with the Ukrainians by the simple expedient of fair treatment, he put many of them to death and enslaved the rest. Shocked and humiliated, the Ukrainians could only rally to the defense of their own soil.

HITLER EXPLAINS HIS RUSSIAN INTERLUDE

Why did Hitler suddenly turn on the Soviet Union and attempt to destroy her before beginning his final assault on Great Britain? In the archives of the German Foreign Office is an extraordinary letter which Hitler sent to Mussolini giving the reasons for his *volte-face*. We can assume that it gives at least some elements of truth as the *Fuehrer* saw it. More, it summarizes the German position on the war at this time. The letter, dated June 21, 1941:

> *Duce!*
>
> I am writing this letter to you at a moment when months of anxious deliberation and continuous nerve-racking waiting are ending in the hardest decision of my life. I believe—after seeing the latest Russian situation map and after appraisal of numerous other reports—that I cannot take the responsibility for waiting longer, and above all, I believe that there is no other way of obviating this danger—unless it be further waiting, which, however, would necessarily lead to disaster in this or the next year at the latest.
>
> The situation: England has lost this war. With the right of the drowning person, she grasps at every straw which, in her imagination might serve as a sheet anchor. Nevertheless, some of her hopes are naturally not without a certain logic. England has thus far always conducted her wars with help from the Continent. The destruction of France—in fact, the elimination of all west-European positions—is directing the glances of the British warmongers continually to the place from which they tried to start the war: to Soviet Russia.
>
> Both countries, Soviet Russia and England, are equally interested in a Europe fallen into ruin, rendered prostrate by a long war. Behind these two countries stands the North American Union goading them on and watchfully waiting. Since the liquidation of Poland, there is evident in Soviet Russia a consistent trend, which, even if cleverly and cautiously, is nevertheless reverting firmly to the old Bolshevist tendency to expansion of the Soviet State. The prolongation of the war necessary for this purpose is to be achieved by tying up German forces in the East, so that—particularly in the air—the German Command can no longer vouch for a large-scale attack in the West. I declared to you only recently, *Duce*, that it was precisely the success of the experiment in Crete that demonstrated how necessary it is to make use of every single airplane in the much greater project against England. It may

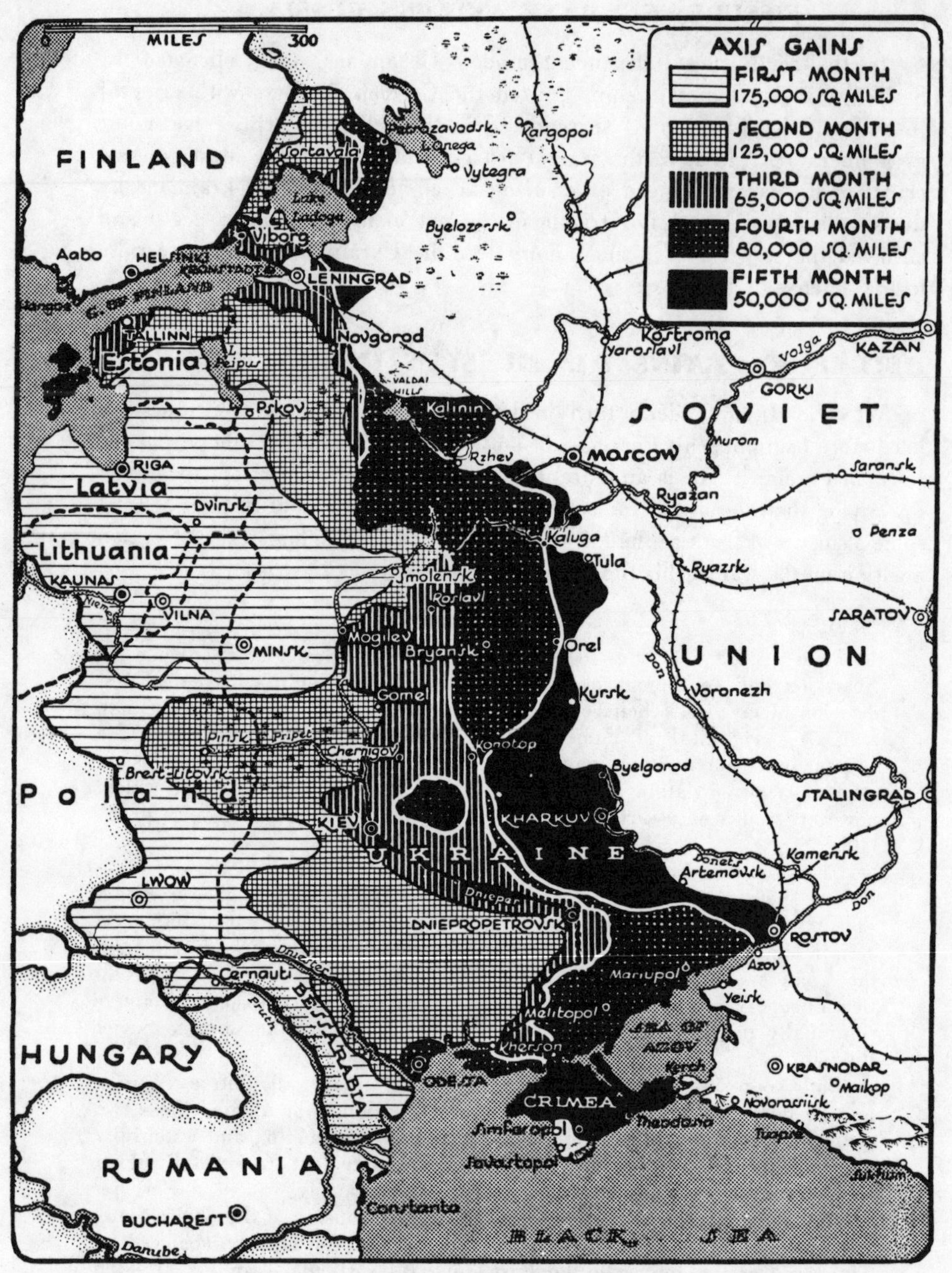

FIVE MONTHS OF RUSSIAN WAR

well happen that in this decisive battle we would win with a superiority of only a few squadrons. I shall not hesitate a moment to undertake such a responsibility if, aside from all other conditions, I at least possess the one certainty that I will not then suddenly be attacked or even threatened from the East. The concentration of Russian forces . . . is tremendous. Really, all available Russian forces are at our border. Moreover, since the approach of warm weather, work has been proceeding on numerous defenses. If circumstances should give me cause to employ the German air force against England, there is danger that Russia will then begin its strategy of extortion in the South and North, to which I would have to yield in silence, simply from a feeling of air inferiority. It would, above all, not then be possible for me, without adequate support from an air force, to attack the Russian fortifications with the divisions stationed in the East. If I do not wish to expose myself to this danger, then perhaps the whole year of 1941 will go by without any change in the general situation. On the contrary, England will be all the less ready for peace for it will be able to pin its hopes on the Russian partner. Indeed, this hope must naturally even grow with the progress in preparedness of the Russian armed forces. And behind this is the mass delivery of war material from America which they hope to get in 1942.

Aside from this, *Duce*, it is not even certain whether we shall have this time, for with so gigantic a concentration of forces on both sides—for I also, was compelled to place more and more armored units on the eastern border, and also to call Finland's and Rumania's attention to the danger—there is the possibility that the shooting will start spontaneously at any moment. A withdrawal on my part would, however, entail a serious loss of prestige for us. This would be particularly unpleasant in its possible effect on Japan. I have, therefore, after constantly racking my brains, finally reached the decision to cut the noose before it can be drawn tight. I believe, *Duce*, that I am hereby rendering probably the best possible service to our joint conduct of the war this year. . . .

Any desires, suggestions, and assistance of which you, *Duce*, wish to inform me in the contingency before us, I would request that you either communicate to me personally or have them agreed upon directly by our military authorities.

In conclusion, let me say one more thing, *Duce*. Since I struggled through to this decision, I again feel spiritually free. The partnership with the Soviet Union, in spite of the complete sincerity of the efforts to bring about a final conciliation, was nevertheless often very irksome to me, for in some way or other it seemed to me to be a break with my whole origin, my concepts, and my former obligations. I am happy now to be relieved of these mental agonies.

With hearty and comradely greetings,

Your

[*Adolf Hitler*].

MOUSETRAP AT MOSCOW

"Today begins the last great decisive battle of the year!"

Thus, on October 2, 1941, Hitler spoke to his legions poised for another assault on Russia. His initial thrust had penetrated 400 miles into Soviet territory. Now his destination was just 200 miles ahead—Moscow, central point of the Soviet communications system and symbol of Bolshevik power. Nothing would stop him, neither rain, snow, nor sleet, hell nor high floods.

Hitler's generals—General Walther von Brauchitsch, General Franz Halder, and General Fedor von Bock—favored a concentrated drive on Moscow with every ounce of German power on Russian soil. But Hitler wanted to work by the book. He would achieve a super-Cannae, a vast encircling movement, which, taking Leningrad in the north and the Ukraine in the south, would turn inward and converge upon Moscow.

There were heated objections from the *O.K.W.* (*Oberkommando der Wehrmacht*, High Command of the Armed Forces). Hitler had his way. Field Marshal Wilhelm von Leeb would continue his attack on Leningrad in the north, Field Marshal Gerd von Rundstedt would strike at Odessa and Kiev in the south. At the center von Bock would lead his 17 infantry divisions, 2 motorized infantry divisions, 1,000 tanks, and 900 aircraft to breach the enemy lines and drive on Moscow. Von Bock would work out a series of encirclements within the greater arc. One spearhead would drive northeast from Smolensk toward Kalinin, outflanking Moscow from the north; another would hit Orel and Tula, outflanking Moscow from the south; and a third would push directly east through Vyazma and make a direct frontal assault on Moscow.

It was a key decision—and a mistaken one. Von Bock's powerful mobile forces were split in such a way that the better part of their strength was sent to the Leningrad and Kiev fronts in north and south, leaving him with mostly infantry to make his frontal attack on Moscow. Clausewitz, the great Prussian philosopher of war, would have corrected Hitler.

Initially all went according to plan. In three weeks von Bock's armored columns reduced the distance to Moscow from 200 to less than 70 miles. The Russian defenders, their bodies forming a tragic roadway, were crushed by the seemingly irresistible Nazi military machine.

Everywhere there was the smell of death in the earth. The Russian soil was scarred by craters, pitted by shell bursts, chewed by tank threads. By the end of October von Bock's troops on the Moscow front were at Vyazma in the center sector, Kalinin in the north, and Tula on the south. By sheer weight of numbers the Germans had cracked the enemy front lines. Moscow was almost encircled. Meanwhile, von Rundstedt's forces overran the Crimea, with the exception of besieged Sevastopol.

The Soviet capital seemed about to fall. As the Germans straightened their lines in the great bulge around the city, the Soviet government and the diplomatic corps fled to Kuibyshev, some 500 miles to the east. Stalin remained behind the red-towered walls of the Kremlin. The Russian strategy was to concentrate reserves before Moscow and outside the ring of encirclement, and then launch a powerful counterattack.

November 1941. "Napoleon weather!" proclaimed the Moscow radio.

The German offensive ground to a halt. For Hitler it was a moment of decision. Should the winter campaign be called off and preparations made for a gigantic spring assault? "No!" said the *Fuehrer*. The offensive must be resumed. Both sides were exhausted, he argued, and the one with the most will power would win. A last mighty drive and Moscow would be his.

Again there were objections from the generals. But the *Fuehrer*'s will was German military law. On November 15, 1941, the Germans pushed off on their second great offensive against Moscow. Hitler's strategy was to bypass the capital on the north and take the railway junctions behind it.

Four days later, the full fury of winter, Russia's most potent ally, fell on the Germans. Despite snow, fog, and rain the Germans fought their way mile by mile closer to the capital. Dimitrou—40 miles away, Gorki—29 miles, Kabushki—22 miles. By December 2, 1941, advance elements of von Bock's forces penetrated to the suburbs of the city.

There they were—the gilded towers of the Kremlin against the leaden sky!

So near but yet so far. The thermometer dropped below zero. The whole countryside withdrew into white blankness, surprising to the Germans, used to a much more temperate climate. In this weather Hitler's supply could not keep up with his armor, which created the critical gap. Water froze inside the boilers of German locomotives. Lubricants hardened in artillery pieces, machine guns, and rifles. The Germans had to keep fires burning underneath their tanks, lest the engines freeze and burst. For all their famous engineering skill, the Germans had never perfected the oil-cooled engine. Without rations, the famished troops began to eat their horses, frozen to death.

Worse, Hitler's legions were inadequately clad against the Russian weather. At first few were worried about it. Had not the *Fuehrer* promised that the Kremlin would be German before cold weather set in? But—horrifying predicament—here were the Germans dressed in light uniforms and trapped in the snow and cold before Moscow. Ironically enough, the efficient German military mind had issued each German soldier one pair of shoes to his *exact* measurement, allowing the wearing of no more than one pair of socks. This was dangerous policy in Russian weather. Hitler was waging, in some ways, a cheapskate sort of war. Or there had been negligence somewhere. The result was many thousands of frozen German feet.

There were hurried appeals back to Berlin. Propaganda Minister Dr. Joseph Goebbels called for a massive collection of overcoats and furs to be dispatched to the Russian front. German civilians responded patriotically. But it was months before warm clothing could reach all the troops.

The Russians, on the other hand, clad in fur jackets, padded felt boots, woolen underclothes, and fur caps with large earpieces, stolidly went about the task of striking back at the frostbitten, miserable German invaders. Ivan knew how to serve under General Winter.

Inside and outside the besieged Holy City of the Revolution there was constant movement. Reserves marched west to enter the front lines. To the east, away from the danger zone, women, children, and the aged moved in straggling lines to escape the German danger.

Henry C. Cassidy, a foreign correspondent, recounted the story:

> Thousands of women, mobilized by their house committees and still wearing their city clothes, went by train, bus, and truck into the mud, slush, and cold west of Moscow, there to dig tremendous ditches and anti-tank ditches, running like scars across the countryside. The fortifications extended back into the city itself, where steel, sandbags, and earthwork barricades were raised. The Palace of the Soviets, a naked skeleton of steel girders, which was to have risen as the world's highest building, started to come down as raw material for defense. The Moscow Metro, most modern subway system in the world, was given over to movements of troops and supplies.
>
> In all small shops which were not evacuated, work was turned entirely to war orders. One, which had been making pots and pans, started turning out hand grenades. Another, which usually made cash registers and adding machines, began producing automatic rifles.

Berlin was still confident. On December 2, 1941, the Propaganda Ministry advised all newspaper editors to leave space on their front pages to announce the fall of Moscow. The news never came through.

Four days later, the day before Pearl Harbor, Marshal Georgi Zhukov, who had used his reserves sparingly, sent them all into action in a blazing counterattack against the half-frozen German tank formations. The offensive hit both north and south of Moscow, catching the German tanks stalled in the ice and snow with their treads down.

Hurried calls came from field commanders to Hitler asking permission for a planned withdrawal. The *Fuehrer* snarled like a tiger: "No withdrawal! Not a single yard of retreat!" He threatened public degradation and death for all commanders who failed to follow his orders.

Nevertheless, on December 8, 1941, Berlin announced that the Eastern offensive was being suspended because of the "weather." The excuse was that winter had fallen three weeks earlier than anticipated. It was an admission of defeat. In six months, by official German figures, the *Wehrmacht* had lost 162,314 killed, 577,767 wounded, and 33,334 missing. The Germans had come within sight of the towers of the Kremlin only to find their whole front being pushed back for distances varying up to 200 miles. Russian stubbornness plus Russian winter had prevailed. Never again would Hitler be able to attack Russia upon more than one sector at a time.

History was repeating itself in its ironic, haphazard way. Twenty-five years earlier during the course of World War I Field Marshal Paul von Hindenburg had declined to make a deep penetration of Russia. That country, he said, had no heart against which a mortal blow could be struck.

Hitler learned this the hard way.

LEVÉE EN MASSE AT LENINGRAD

At the head of the Gulf of Finland and at the mouth of the Neva River, northwest of Moscow, lies Leningrad, one of the largest and most important cities of Europe. Shortly after the outbreak of World War I, the name of St. Petersburg, because of its German origin, was changed to Petrograd. In March 1924 it became Leningrad in honor of Nikolai Lenin, father of the Bolshevik Revolution of 1917.

Leningrad and Stalingrad! City of the founder and city of the top Red disciple. To these names the superstitious *Fuehrer* attached an almost mystical significance. Once the twin cities of revolutionary Russia were invested, the Soviet regime would tumble like a house of cards and he, the conqueror, would outshine Napoleon on the pages of history.

For Hitler there were strategic as well as psychological considerations. In German hands Leningrad could be linked around the eastern shores of the Gulf of Finland with Finland, now on the Axis side. Leningrad would be the northern pivot of a gigantic pincers movement to crush Bolshevism.

Immediately upon the invasion of Soviet Russia, while other *Panzer* forces struck on the central and southern fronts, powerful Nazi forces swept north toward Leningrad. The left wing crashed through Estonia and trapped all the Russians there. The right wing surged around in the direction of Leningrad, which it reached by the end of August 1941.

Again came the familiar *Blitzkrieg* pattern—pulverization from the air, light forces driving ahead, swiftly-moving armor followed by artillery and infantrymen. This time the Germans were helped by Field Marshal Karl von Mannerheim and the Finns, who had ample reason to resent their treatment at Russian hands. During September and October 1941, the invaders all but completed the encirclement of the city.

All but, but not quite. Despite desperate efforts, the Germans could not take Leningrad. On November 1, 1941, began a siege of 16 months, one of the most extraordinary in history. Again the Germans made a key error—they had failed to prepare a siege artillery, since they were under the impression that they would not need it.

Hitler's strategy was to choke the city of three million people to death. German troops cut off one by one nearly all means of access to the city—three highways, 12 railroads, the canal system, and the port itself. The Russians doggedly held onto the remaining water route across Lake Ladoga.

Across the frozen lake went a truck highway, and over this single road through the long nights poured supplies of munitions, ammunition, and food.

All Leningrad dug in to meet the assault. Workmen dropped their tools, took up rifles, and went into the trenches; their places in the factories were taken by women and children. There was no fuel for cooking. Water had to be brought from the river, wells, and canals. The food supply diminished to the vanishing point.

Hitler had not counted on this unconquerable spirit. In the spring of 1942 more than 400,000 weak and weary Russians appeared with shovels on the streets to clean up the city. During the winter the sewers and drains had been put out of action by German shells and there was danger of epidemics. In a few days these desperately tired people, old and young, dumped into the rivers and canals the accumulation of snow and filth that might have poisoned Leningrad.

With the thaw in April 1942, the Germans renewed the siege in full force. Nothing seemed to work against this rock of intransigence. The *Luftwaffe* cut the railroads to both Moscow and Murmansk. Day and night German artillery blasted the city block by block.

But the people of Leningrad refused to give in. Under bombing and shellfire they continued working at their jobs, and afterward, despite gnawing hunger, pitched in to help repair the fortifications ringing the city. They planted truck gardens in every available inch of space, and, after work, crawled to them on hands and knees to avoid the flying steel fragments.

The tide of German assault turned back on itself. There was to be no German occupation of Leningrad, either then or later.

CHAPTER **10**

The United States: Arsenal of Democracy

> ***And not by eastern windows only,***
> ***When daylight comes, comes in the light;***
> ***In front the sun climbs slow, how slowly!***
> ***But westward, look, the land is bright.***
>
> **—Winston Churchill, 1941, quoting Arthur Hugh Clough (1819-1861)**

> ***The forward march of Hitlerism can be stopped —and it will be stopped. Very simply and very bluntly—we are pledged to pull our own oar in the destruction of Hitlerism.***
>
> **—Franklin D. Roosevelt, Navy Day Address, October 27, 1941**

PRELUDE: THE GREAT DEBATE

The outbreak of World War I in 1914 hit the American people with the impact of a thunderbolt. At first there was no overwhelming public majority for one side or the other; if anything, much American opinion was anti-British and pro-German. But a combination of circumstances eventually brought the United States into the conflict, and the weight of American arms and production turned the scale in favor of the Allies.

After 1918 came a feeling, amounting almost to a national neurosis, that the United States had been tricked into the war. The sentiment was carefully nourished by a revisionist campaign. The country retreated into isolation lasting throughout the era of the Long Armistice from 1918 to 1939. The European Continent, it was said, was a hellhole of sore spots, of irreconcilable hatreds, of interminable quarrels. If the Europeans wanted to destroy one another, let them fight within their own borders. As for Americans, let us remain safe behind the Atlantic moat and heed the advice of George Washington to avoid entanglements in European affairs. Enough of the stupid bloodletting!

But there were complicating factors. The steady disintegration of peace in Europe following the rise of Hitler forced the American people, much against their will, to think deeply about what they would do in the event another war broke out. Many believed that the only sensible course was true neutrality, no matter what happened. This sentiment was bolstered to some extent by the findings of a Senate committee headed by Senator Gerald P. Nye of North Dakota, which in 1934 began to examine the record of the munitions industry during World War I.

On the one side isolationists began to demand that Congress enact neutrality laws so strict as to render impossible American involvement in another European war. On the other side believers in "collective security" insisted that the world was now too small for a nation as large and powerful as the United States to remain aloof from any war on a large scale. If war came, it might overwhelm the United States regardless of either neutrality legislation or the will of the people. The only intelligent course was to throw the weight of the United States on the side of the peace-loving nations to curb aggressors. Neutrality was not enough. It was essential to work actively to prevent war.

From the beginning of his presidency in 1933 Roosevelt made it clear that he was an advocate of collective security. While Hitler blustered his way along the road to war, Roosevelt demonstrated again and again that he had not changed his mind about collective security. On October 5, 1937, he delivered his famous "quarantine of aggressors" speech in Chicago:

> It seems to be unfortunately true that the epidemic of world lawlessness is spreading. When an epidemic of world disease starts to spread, the community approves and joins in a quarantine of the patients in order to protect the health of the community against the spread of the disease. . . . War is a contagion, whether it be declared or undeclared. It can engulf states and peoples remote from the original scene of hostilities. We are determined to keep out of war, yet we cannot insure ourselves against the disastrous effects of war and the dangers of involvement. . . . There must be positive endeavors to preserve peace. America hates war. America hopes for peace. Therefore, America actively engages in the search for peace.

If in 1914 Americans were astonished by the sudden surge to war, in 1939 they were amazed that the conflict had been so long deferred. This time a better-informed public, having no illusions about responsibility for aggression, was distinctly anti-Hitler from the very beginning. Except for a small and negligible company of the uninformed, the bigots, and the crackpots, most Americans detested the Nazi *Fuehrer* and all he represented—his berserk fanaticism, his bestial inhumanity, his itch for aggression and world power.

Americans found themselves in an uncomfortable dilemma. Most were determined this time to avoid a shooting war, but at the same time they realized that a German victory would mean incalculable harm to the American way of life, perhaps an end to it. The questions were immediate and vital: Should the United States retreat into isolation and pray for an Allied victory? Should she give all aid "short of war" to the Allies? Should she prepare immediately for eventual participation in the conflict?

On September 5, 1939, a few days after the invasion of Poland, President Franklin D. Roosevelt issued a proclamation of neutrality restating the terms of the Neutrality Act of 1937. The proclamation placed an immediate embargo on shipping of arms and munitions to all belligerents. From a practical point of view the British were hit hardest of all. Controlling the seas, they could prevent the Germans from access to American goods, but at the same time they themselves were denied desperately needed war matériel. American neutrality legislation, they charged, was equivalent to presenting the Germans with an Atlantic fleet.

As in World War I, the British, in order to prevent war cargoes from reaching the enemy, introduced the navicert system requiring the search of merchant ships in American ports before they sailed for Europe. This practice, in addition to stoppage and search of American vessels on the high seas, resulted, again as in World War I, in a sharp exchange of notes between Washington and London.

President Roosevelt, alienated by Axis aggression, was from the very beginning sympathetic to the Allied cause. On September 3, 1939, two days after the opening of the war, he declared: "This nation will remain a neutral nation, but I cannot ask that every American citizen remain neutral in thought as well." On September 8, 1939, he proclaimed a limited national emergency.

Convinced that there were flaws in the 1937 neutrality legislation, Roosevelt called on Congress to revise it along more reasonable lines. Congress responded on November 4, 1939, with a repeal of the arms embargo and an authorization for "cash-and-carry" export of arms and munitions to belligerent powers. The bill passed the Senate (October 27, 1939) by a vote of 63-30, and the House (November 2, 1939) by a vote of 243-181. The President was required to name the belligerent states and United States shipping was forbidden to carry passengers or freight to any state identified as a belligerent. American citizens were denied travel on belligerent vessels, obviously an attempt to forestall another *Lusitania* (or *Athenia*) episode. Cash-and-carry enabled Britain and her allies to buy supplies without exposing the United States to the risk of having its citizens aroused by German submarine sinkings. At the same time the administration asked for a "moral embargo" against Japan because of her bombing of open cities.

The sudden fall of France in June 1940 and the desperate plight of Britain aroused deep fears in the United States. At this time, as from 1914 to 1917 when the United States intervened in World War I, Americans regarded the Royal Navy as indestructible. They felt that no matter what happened on the European Continent, control of the Atlantic Ocean, that great defensive moat, would remain in friendly British hands. But now, with Hitler rampaging through Western Europe, Americans had to face the possibility of a complete German victory.

Suppose Germany's noisy *Fuehrer* did manage to invade England and bring it into his New Order. Would he be content to stay in Europe on his side of the Atlantic? How about Latin America, at which he had already directed streams of Nazi propaganda? Would Hitler show any more respect for the Monroe Doctrine than he had for other "scraps of paper"? Even if Hitler decided not to send his brown hordes to the Western Hemisphere, how would the United States function in a world dominated by fire-eating dictators? And how about the possibility that the United States might eventually be forced to fight these dictators alone? These were all disturbing questions and all of them reflected the anxieties and fears of the American people.

Meanwhile, in the halls of Congress, in the press, on the air, on street corners, and in the stores of the smallest villages raged the Great Debate between interventionists and isolationists. The two positions were diametrically opposed.

The interventionists regarded the war as a struggle to the death between the authoritarian and democratic ways of life. The Axis, they charged, was obviously bent on world domination. Once Europe was gone and the Royal Navy defeated, Latin America would be next. Sooner or later the United States, whether it liked it or not, would have to meet the Axis threat. In the meantime it would be best to keep Britain alive. Scandalized by the conduct of both the Nazi gangsters and the Japanese war lords, the interventionists called for support for the crusade to defend civilization and free institutions all over the world.

Actually, among the interventionists there were very few Americans who wanted military intervention in the war at this time. By intervention they meant all possible aid for the Allies "short of war." It was their way of expressing their contempt for Hitler and all his works. The interventionist movement hoped to keep the war on the other side of the Atlantic. The ace card of the interventionists was the support of their position by the President of the United States.

On the other side of the coin were the isolationists. A surprisingly large number of Americans were willing to take their chances on a Nazi victory. They wanted only one thing—the United States must keep out of the war. The arguments of the interventionists, they said, could be dismissed as impractical do-goodism and hogwash. Keep out of those cynical European quarrels! Had not World War I demonstrated the futility of mixing in the business of others? True, we might lose money as long as the war lasted, but financial losses as a neutral would be small compared to the astronomical costs certain to come if we took part in the war.

To the isolationist side streamed pacifists, pro-Germans, "professional Irishmen," many others who bore grudges against Britain for one reason or another.

Chief among the advocates of a die-hard isolationism were Senator Burton K. Wheeler, of Montana; Senator Gerald P. Nye, of North Dakota; the two LaFollette brothers, of Wisconsin; Representative Hamilton Fish, of New York; William Randolph Hearst and his newspaper chain; and Colonel Robert R. McCormick of the *Chicago Tribune*. They were joined by Norman Thomas, the Socialist leader and pacifist. Behind the movement was a strong and well-financed organization called the "America First Committee," which initiated a vigorous campaign to discredit the interventionists or anyone who showed any partiality for the embattled British.

One of the apostles of isolationist and appeasement sentiment was Public Hero No. 1—Charles A. Lindbergh, Jr. In 1927 young Lindbergh had winged his way across the Atlantic in a small, single-engined plane "into the brilliant light of history and unimagined fame." He was far less successful in enduring the storms of public adulation. Alienated by the constant invasions of his privacy, this shy, stalwart young man adopted a reticent attitude toward press and public.

After being entertained royally by Field Marshal Hermann Goering in Berlin, Lindbergh came away with the firm conviction that Nazi air power was unbeatable. It was a highly unpopular position for the majority of Americans. The aviator who had received the greatest and most frenzied ovation in the nation's history saw his popularity diminish.

On April 30, 1941, Lindbergh presented the isolationist arguments in a speech in New York City on behalf of the America First Committee.

> It is not only our right, [Lindbergh said] but it is our obligation as American citizens to look at the war objectively and to weigh our chances for success if we should enter it. I have attempted to do this, especially from the standpoint of aviation; and I have been forced to the conclusion that we

cannot win this war for England, regardless of how much assistance we extend.

I ask you to look at the map of Europe today and see if you can suggest any way in which we could win this war if we entered it. Suppose we had a large army in America, trained and equipped. Where would we send it to fight? The campaigns of the war show only too clearly how difficult it is to force a landing, or to maintain an army, on a hostile coast.

Suppose we took our Navy from the Pacific, and used it to convoy British shipping. That would not win the war for England. It would, at best, permit her to exist under the constant bombing of the German air fleet. Suppose we had an air force that we could send to Europe. Where would it operate? Some of our squadrons might be based in the British Isles; but it is physically impossible to base enough aircraft in the British Isles alone to equal in strength the aircraft that can be based on the Continent of Europe. . . .

There is no better way to give comfort to an enemy than to divide the people of a nation over the issue of foreign war. There is no shorter road to defeat than by entering a war with inadequate preparation. Every nation that has adopted the interventionist policy of depending on someone else for its own defense has met with nothing but defeat and failure. . . .

War is not inevitable for this country. Such a claim is defeatism in the true sense. No one can make us fight abroad unless we ourselves are willing to do so. No one will attempt to fight us here if we arm ourselves as a great nation should be armed. Over a hundred million people in this nation are opposed to entering the war. If the principles of democracy mean anything at all, this is reason enough for us to stay out. If we are forced into a war against the wishes of an overwhelming majority of our people, we will have proved democracy such a failure at home that there will be little use for fighting for it abroad. . . .

A week later, on April 30, 1941, *The New York Times* printed an editorial, "Let Us Face the Truth," which in effect replied to Lindbergh and the isolationists. It read in part:

. . . There is no isolation. There are only lines of defense. Distance is vanishing. Strategy is everything. And strategy in this year of grace has become the art and science of survival. . . .

Those who tell us now that the sea is still our certain bulwark, and that the tremendous forces sweeping the Old World threaten no danger to the New, give the lie to their own words in the precautions they would have us take. . . .

There are moral and spiritual dangers for this country as well as physical dangers in a Hitler victory. There are dangers to the mind and heart as well as to the body and the land.

Victorious in Europe, dominating Africa and Asia through his Axis partners, Hitler could not afford to permit the United States to live an untroubled and successful life, even if he wished to. We are the arch-enemy of all he stands for: the very citadel of that "pluto-democracy" which he hates and scorns. As long as liberty and freedom prevailed in the United States there would be a constant risk for Hitler that our ideas and our example might infect the conquered countries which he was bending to his will. In his own interest he would be forced to harry us at every turn. . . .

There is no escape in isolation. We have only two alternatives. We can surrender or we can do our part in holding the line. We can defend, with all the means in our power, the rights that are morally and legally ours. If we decide for the American tradition, for the preservation of all that we hold dear in the years that lie ahead, we shall take our place in the line and play our part in the defense of freedom.

F.D.R.'S POINT NO 1: INCREASED U.S. DEFENSES

By the end of June 1940 Hitler had chalked up a succession of victories—the invasion of Denmark and Norway, the conquest of the Low Countries, and the fall of France. The swift march of events, especially the fall of France, shocked the United States into action. "We are in the presence not of local or regional wars," said Secretary of State Cordell Hull on October 26, 1940, "but of an organized and determined movement for steadily expanding conquest. Against this drive for power no nation and no region is secure save as its inhabitants create for themselves means of defense so formidable that even the would-be conquerors will not dare to raise against them the hand of attack."

Already, in his annual budget message on January 3, 1940, President Roosevelt had requested $1,800,000,000 for national defense and new appropriations of $1,182,000,000. On May 16, 1940, he sent a message to Congress asking for a production program of 50,000 planes a year.

There was immediate intense interest inside Germany. Fifty thousand planes a year? *Unglaublich!* Unbelievable! From aviation expert Field Marshal Hermann Goering came a roar of ridicule. From propaganda expert Dr. Joseph Goebbels came denunciations of "President Roosevelt's bluffing." From Adolf Hitler came a medical opinion: "There's no doubt about it, Roosevelt is a sick brain!" Fifty thousand planes a year! It was just not possible. (Yet, from early 1940 to the end of the war American plants produced 296,601 warplanes, an average of nearly 60,000 a year.)

On May 31, 1940, with the fall of France imminent, Roosevelt requested an additional $1,277,741,170 for the acceleration and development of military and naval requirements. By this time the outlines of Roosevelt's four-point program were becoming clear—increased defenses, domestic preparations, hemisphere solidarity, and Lend-Lease.

The expenditure of funds soon skyrocketed. On July 20, 1940, Roosevelt approved a bill authorizing a two-ocean navy and providing for the construction of 200 warships, including seven battleships of 55,000 tons each. This was to be the greatest naval expansion in history, designed eventually to give the United States a navy equally powerful in both Atlantic and Pacific. The entire defense program provided for an expenditure of at least $28,000,000,-000, just $12,000,000,000 less than the entire national debt.

On August 18, 1940, President Roosevelt and Prime Minister W. L. Mackenzie King of Canada met at Ogdensburg, New York, and agreed to establish a Permanent Joint Board on Defense. Canada was already a training ground for airmen and troops.

Money was important for defense, but manpower even more so. On August 27, 1940, Congress authorized induction of the National Guard into Federal service, and initial units were called out four days later. Then came conscription. On September 16, 1940, the Selective Service Training and Service Act, known as the Burke-Wadsworth Bill, was approved by Congress. The first law in American history providing for compulsory military service in time of peace, it called for the registration of all men between the ages of 21 and 36, and for the training over a one-year period of 1,200,000 troops and 800,000 reserves. Isolationism was dying hard. The act confined the service of selcctees to the Western hemisphere, American territorial possessions, and the Philippines.

In the first registration, held on October 16, 1940, 16,400,000 men were listed, and two weeks later, on October 29, the first draft numbers were chosen by lot in Washington. On August 18, 1941, some four months before Pearl Harbor, the term of service was increased from one year to 30 months, the House voting 203-202 on the extension.

On September 3, 1940, Roosevelt negotiated a defense deal with Britain that left no doubt as to where his sympathies lay. The British were desperately in need of destroyers. They had lost 10 at Dunkirk, 75 more were damaged, and fully half their destroyer fleet was out of action. The agreement provided for the transfer of 50 four-stacked, flush-decked, overage American destroyers to the British, in exchange for a 99-year rent-free lease of naval and air bases in Newfoundland, Bermuda, the Bahamas, Jamaica, St. Lucia, Trinidad, Antigua, and British Guiana. The destroyers were promptly handed over to the British, and the United States just as speedily began to fortify and garrison the new bases. The President's executive action, without consulting Congress, was a bold and unprecedented move made at considerable risk, but it was invaluable to British defense in the raging Battle of the Atlantic as well as an important boost to British morale.

Both Roosevelt and Churchill feared German seizure of Greenland after the Nazi occupation of Denmark in 1940. On April 9, 1941, American naval forces took over Greenland after an agreement with the Danish government-in-exile pledging the United States to defend Greenland against invasion and in return giving the United States the right to operate air, naval, radio, and other defense installations there. A similar agreement was made with Iceland on July 7, 1941. From these areas as well as from continental America, the

United States air forces could patrol the western half of the Atlantic while the British concentrated on the eastern half.

POINT NO. 2: DOMESTIC PREPARATIONS

At the same time domestic preparations went ahead at top speed. The Federal Bureau of Investigation moved against fifth columnists with such celerity that their activities were reduced to a minimum. The Alien Registration Act of June 28, 1940, commonly called the Smith Act, strengthened existing laws governing the admission and deportation of aliens.

Since the emergency situation called for bipartisanship in government, President Roosevelt took into his cabinet two Republican leaders, both of whom strongly supported aid to Britain. Former Secretary of State Henry L. Stimson became Secretary of War, and Colonel Frank Knox, publisher of the *Chicago Daily News*, Secretary of the Navy. Under the chairmanship of Dr. Vannevar Bush arose the National Defense Research Committee, later superseded by the more comprehensive Office of Scientific Research and Development. On June 22, 1940, Congress adopted national-defense tax measures designed to yield nearly $1,000,000,000 annually, and the national debt limit was raised from $45,000,00,000 to $49,000,000,000.

In the presidential election of November 5, 1940, Roosevelt was voted an unprecedented third term, defeating the Republican candidate, Wendell L. Willkie, by an electoral vote of 449 (38 states) to 82 (10 states). With this victory Roosevelt succeeded in shattering one of the most deeply embedded taboos in American history. In his campaign Roosevelt assured American parents that "your boys are not going to be sent into any foreign wars." Roosevelt interpreted his victory as national approval of his vigorous foreign policy.

The next month, on December 20, 1940, Roosevelt established the Office of Production Management with industrial leader William S. Knudsen as director; members included Sidney Hillman as representative of labor, and Secretaries Stimson and Knox as delegates of the administration. The committee was assigned the tasks of coördinating defense production and speeding aid "short of war" to the anti-Axis nations. In a fireside chat (Roosevelt liked to deliver "homey" talks over the radio) on December 29, 1940, the President spoke of the Axis threat to American security, and called for a national production effort that would make the United States the world's "arsenal of democracy."

There was fierce opposition from the isolationists. But most Americans were not neutral. They hated Hitler and all his works and they wanted the democracies to win. A typical reaction was the organization by William Allen White, a famous mid-Western journalist, of a nation-wide Citizen's

Committee to Defend America by Aiding the Allies. Many Americans took a realistic view of the critical situation: If Hitler were to win in Europe the United States would not be safe from his ambitions. It was as simple as that.

POINT NO. 3: HEMISPHERE SOLIDARITY

The third point of the Roosevelt program, dedicated to the "good neighbor" policy, was designed to weld the nations of the Western Hemisphere into a united front against the Axis. The trend was prefigured as early as a month after the outbreak of war when, on October 3, 1939, the Inter-American Conference, by the Declaration of Panama, proclaimed sea safety zones south of Canada. All belligerent nations were warned to desist from any naval action within these zones.

The Pittman Resolution, of June 16, 1940, called for a strengthening of the military defenses of the Latin-American republics and authorized the sale of munitions to the governments of the Western Hemisphere. Several days later Secretary of State Cordell Hull served notice on Italy and Germany that the United States would not recognize any transfer of title from one non-American power to another of any region of the Western Hemisphere.

This vital new interpretation of the Monroe Doctrine was endorsed by the delegates of 21 republics at the Pan-American Conference in Havana on July 30, 1940. All agreed that, collectively or individually, the American republics in their common interest might take over and administer any European possession in the New World endangered by aggression. They took measures to counteract fifth-column activities in the Americas and agreed upon closer economic relations. These firm decisions put a stop to Hitler's attempt to extend the Brown Network of Nazism among the nations of Latin America.

POINT NO. 4: LEND-LEASE

Without the United States, Britain would have been doomed at the beginning of the war. London at once placed huge orders with American firms. From September 1939 to August 1940 the British Commonwealth ordered 95 per cent of all American exports of airplanes and airplane parts, and 90 per cent of its firearms, munitions, and explosives. Between September 1939 and the end of 1940 the United States sold 132 merchant ships to Britain, 43 to Canada.

In response to Churchill's appeal after much British war matériel was lost at Dunkirk, the War Department released to Great Britain such surplus or outdated stocks as 600,000 rifles, 80,000 machine guns, 316 trench mortars, and 900 field guns. More than $43,000,000 worth of equipment was sent in the one month of June 1940. American guns, tanks, shells, and planes were rushed across the Atlantic to a Britain which desperately needed them.

But the voracious maw of war consumed ammunition, munitions, machines, tools, instruments, fuel, all the matériel of modern war, almost as rapidly as they reached the fronts. In addition, after a year of fighting, the British saw their financial reserves approaching the vanishing point. Lacking gold to purchase goods, they were helpless under the prevailing cash-and-carry American legislation. Meanwhile, the anvils of Hitler's foundries and factories were ringing around the clock from Norway to Spain. Only the industrial might of the United States could prevent British collapse.

In this precarious situation startling news came from the New World. President Roosevelt, in his annual message to Congress on January 6, 1941, enunciated the famous "Four Freedoms"—freedom of speech and expression, freedom of worship, freedom from want, and freedom from fear. It was a double-barreled weapon in the war of words. Not only did it express the ideals of the American way, but it also by implication roundly damned Hitler, Mussolini, Tojo, and the whole Axis ideology.

These were golden words, but something else was in the air. A few weeks earlier Roosevelt in a fireside chat had commented that in case of fire one would naturally lend his garden hose to a neighbor, with the understanding that it be returned, but would not first try to sell the hose. To Congress the President spoke bluntly: "Let us say to the democracies: 'We Americans are vitally concerned in your defense of freedom. We are putting forth our energies, our resources and our organizing powers to give you the strength to regain and maintain a free world. We shall send you in ever-increasing numbers, ships, planes, tanks, guns. That is our purpose and our pledge.' "

For two months Congress hotly debated the issue. Gradually, the point of view prevailed that Roosevelt was right: The United States must balance its own defense against the cash value of weapons and supplies for the Allies.

The result was "H.R. 1776," the Lend-Lease measure, which passed the Senate (March 8, 1941) and the House (March 11, 1941). The law empowered the President to manufacture, sell, lend, transfer, lease, or exchange any war matériel to "the government of any country whose defense the President deems vital for the defense of the United States." The President was given complete discretion, even to the extent of not requiring any repayment if he did not wish it. Two weeks later Congress authorized an initial appropriation of $7,000,000,000 for Lend-Lease.

The isolationists screamed to high heaven that this was tyranny. During the Lend-Lease debate bands of isolationist "mothers" prayed on the pavements before the White House. Democratic Senator Burton K. Wheeler of

Montana asserted that Lend-Lease would "plow under every fourth American boy." Public opinion, however, was won to Roosevelt's position.

To Winston Churchill Lend-Lease was "an inspiring act of faith," "a monument of generous and far-reaching statesmanship," and "the most unsordid act in history." The British prime minister had good reason for his generous praise. Lend-Lease was probably the most important single innovation of the war with the possible exception of the atomic bomb. The flow of American guns, tanks, shells, and planes to the Allies became heavy enough to turn the scales against the Axis.

It was a measure of Hitler's provincial ignorance that he had no idea of the extent or the potentialities of the American production machine. Apparently he preferred the mysticism of his astrologers to the sober figures of economists about American industrial capacity. Had he been taken on a guided tour of Pittsburgh and Detroit in 1939, in all probability he would have moved heaven and earth to stay out of trouble with the United States. Wars, said an anonymous sage, are not won by contempt.

THE ATLANTIC CHARTER

On July 25, 1941, Former Naval Person (code name for Winston Churchill) cabled President Roosevelt that he was sailing from England on August 4 for a secret rendezvous. Behind him "to mind the shop" Churchill left Major General Sir Hastings Ismay, chief of staff to the minister of defence, and Air Chief Marshal Sir Charles Portal. The British party left on the *Prince of Wales* with an escort of destroyers. Radio silence was maintained all across the Atlantic lest the Germans become aware of a super-choice target for their U-boats.

Meanwhile, to insure secrecy, President Roosevelt, who was supposed to be on a holiday cruise, was transferred at sea to the cruiser *Augusta*. He left his yacht behind him as a blind. The two parties arrived at their rendezvous in Placentia Bay, Newfoundland, on August 9, 1941.

While military advisers and economic experts conferred on matters of mutual interest, the two chiefs of state drew up "a rough and ready wartime declaration" of the principles on which the war was being waged. Most of the joint statement was written by Churchill, but Roosevelt weighed every word and made suggestions for changes and additions. The Atlantic Charter, dated August 12, 1941, was to play a significant part in completing the pattern of the war. Its text:

> The President of the United States of America and the Prime Minister, Mr. Churchill, representing His Majesty's Government in the United Kingdom, being met together, deem it right to make known certain common

principles in the national policies of their respective countries on which they base their hopes for a better future for the world.

First. Their countries seek no aggrandizement, territorial or other.

Second. They desire to see no territorial changes that do not accord with the freely expressed wishes of the peoples concerned.

Third. They respect the right of all peoples to choose the form of government under which they will live; and they wish to see sovereign rights and self-government restored to those who have been forcibly deprived of them.

Fourth. They will endeavor, with due respect for their existing obligations, to further the enjoyment by all States, great or small, victor or vanquished, of access, on equal terms, to the trade and to the raw materials of the world which are needed for their economic prosperity.

Fifth. They desire to bring about the fullest collaboration between all nations in the economic field, with the object of securing for all improved labor standards, economic advancement, and social security.

Sixth. After the final destruction of the Nazi tyranny they hope to see established a peace which will afford to all nations the means of dwelling in safety within their own boundaries, and which will afford assurance that all the men in all the lands may live out their lives in freedom from fear and want.

Seventh. Such a peace should enable all men to traverse the high seas and oceans without hindrance.

Eighth. They believe that all the nations of the world, for realistic as well as spiritual reasons, must come to the abandonment of the use of force. Since no future peace can be maintained if land, sea, or air armaments continue to be employed by nations which threaten, or may threaten, aggression outside of their frontiers, they believe, pending the establishment of a wider and permanent system of general security, that the disarmament of such nations is essential. They will likewise aid and encourage all other practicable measures which will lighten for peace-loving peoples the crushing burden of armaments.

The Atlantic Charter was not an alliance, nor was it binding; it merely stated the ideal toward which the two great democracies intended to strive. In many ways it was reminiscent of President Wilson's Fourteen Points issued on January 8, 1918, during the last year of World War I. This earlier statement, however, had been an expression of *American* war aims. The Atlantic Charter, on the other hand, was a declaration by *two* Great Powers. "The fact alone," wrote Churchill later, "of the United States, still technically neutral, joining with a belligerent Power in making such a declaration was astonishing." In the last paragraph there was a clear intimation that the United States after the war would join with Great Britain in policing the world until the establishment of a world community of nations.

Both Roosevelt and Churchill were practical politicians who understood that the immediate chance of the United States Senate's ratifying an alliance with Great Britain was very small. The next best thing in the way of important imponderables was a dramatic statement devoted to "the final destruction of the Nazi tyranny" and the hope for a better world. Deeply concerned by Nazi propaganda for a New Order in Europe, they wanted to provide an alternative more acceptable to Europeans steeped in the traditions of the Enlightenment. No one knew how the war would end, but to the troubled peoples of Europe the Atlantic Charter was the ideal for which they had sacrificed their property and the lives of their sons.

The meeting off Newfoundland was not only to draw up the Atlantic Charter but also to make provision for the survival of Russia under the Hitler attack, then more than a month old. The arrangements made by Roosevelt and Churchill were to cost both the United States and Britain many ships and hundreds of lives of merchant seamen on the famous Murmansk run around the north of Norway.

The Soviet Union, unwilling to be left out in the cold, soon endorsed the Atlantic Charter, including its provision for "a peace which will afford to all nations the means of dwelling in safety within their own boundaries, and which will afford assurance that all the men in all the lands may live out their lives in freedom from fear and want." This provision penetrated to all corners of the world—even to Budapest in Hungary. Nine governments-in-exile joined the Soviet Union in assenting to the high-minded principles of the Atlantic Charter.

TOWARD THE PRECIPICE

On July 7, 1941, President Roosevelt announced that units of the American Navy had reached Iceland to supplement, and ultimately to replace, the British forces already there. The Battle of the Atlantic was approaching a crisis. Many freighters being sunk by German U-boats carried Lend-Lease materials. But Roosevelt, sensing that the American public and Congress were reluctant to start a shooting war, ordered that American warships and aircraft merely "patrol" the western Atlantic and inform the British of the whereabouts of any submarines.

The effectiveness of these patrols aroused the anger of Germany's U-boat commanders, who struck back fiercely. On September 4, 1941, the American destroyer *Greer* was attacked off Iceland by a German submarine, but escaped. President Roosevelt within a week ordered all U.S. destroyers to attack any submarines on sight, even though the German Government blamed the *Greer* for the incident. On October 17, the U.S. destroyer *Kearny* was torpedoed, but not sunk, off Iceland with 11 casualties in the crew. On October 30, another destroyer, the *Reuben James*, was sunk by torpedo off Iceland, with 99 of her crew reported missing.

In Congress there were heated denunciations of these attacks. The Senate by a vote of 50-37 now approved repeal of the restrictive sections of the 1939 Neutrality Act and the House followed by a vote of 212-94. The measure, which became law on November 17, 1941, authorized the arming of American merchant ships and allowed them to carry cargoes inside combat zones to belligerent ports.

The United States was on the verge of complete participation in the war.

Part III

PALADIN:
THE ALLIES ON THE DEFENSIVE

CHAPTER 11

The Rising Sun of Japan

Japan is steeped in German ideas and regards war as an industry because from war she has secured all the extensions of her Empire. . . . She means to exploit China and build herself up until she becomes a power formidable to all the world. . . . [She will] *threaten the safety of the world. . . . But the country that she would menace most would be our own, and unless we carefully maintain a very superior navy in the Pacific, the day will come when the United States will take the place of France in another great war to preserve civilization.*

—Senator Henry Cabot Lodge, 1919

The violence, fury, skill, and might of Japan exceeded anything we had been led to expect.

—Winston Churchill

HOLOCAUST AT PEARL HARBOR

It was 8:10 A.M., Hawaiian time, 1:40 P.M Eastern Standard time, Sunday, December 7, 1941.

A young boy was scooting along on his bike from Honolulu to Pearl Harbor, the chief U.S. naval base in the North Pacific. He was carrying an urgent communication from Washington. General George C. Marshall, U.S. Chief of Staff, recognizing that negotiations with Japan had broken down, had sent an alert to Pearl Harbor. An attempt to send the message by Army radio having failed because of bad static, it was forwarded through commercial channels to Honolulu. The Honolulu office gave it to the boy with instructions to get it to Pearl Harbor as quickly as possible. He was on his way when the first bombs fell. He dived for a roadside ditch and stayed there for several hours while bombs hurtled from the skies.

Shortly before this there had been indications that something was radically wrong. But by a combination of unfortunate circumstances the attacking Japanese were able to achieve complete surprise.

At 6:45 A.M. the American destroyer *Ward*, on routine patrol duty off the naval base, identified and sank a Japanese midget submarine. No one on the destroyer dreamed that it might have been part of a large task force.

During the first two weeks of September 1941 Japan's senior naval officers met in conclave at the Naval War College in Tokyo to discuss the strategy of an attack on Hawaii. A month later, on October 5, a selected group of pilots was briefed on the plan. On November 5, came Combined Fleet Top Secret Operational Order No. 1, to be followed within two days by Order No. 2 calling specifically for an attack on Pearl Harbor.

The task force of 72 warships, under the command of Vice-Admiral Chuichi Nagumo, included the battleships *Hiei* and *Kirishima*, the heavy cruisers *Chikuma* and *Tone*, the light cruiser *Abukuma*, the carriers *Shokaku*, *Zuikaku*, *Akagi*, *Kaga*, *Soryu*, and *Hiryu*, 25 submarines, and an assortment of 16 destroyers and many auxiliary vessels. This powerful force sailed from Tankan Bay in the Kurile Islands on November 25, 1941, under complete radio silence and with instructions to sink any vessels encountered. The warships refueled at sea on December 3 and set their course southeast toward Pearl Harbor.

On that same day, December 3, came the code message "East winds, raining," the signal for all Japanese diplomatic and consular agents in the United States to destroy all their papers. The rendezvous point, 1,460 miles northwest of Pearl Harbor, was reached on December 4. The next day, December 5, came the radio message "Climb Mount Niitaka" to the Japanese task force at sea. It was the irrevocable, fateful order to attack Pearl Harbor.

The task force began its run to Pearl Harbor at top speed. Out went reconnaissance planes, submarines to block any American ships that might break out of the harbor, and midget subs.

Meanwhile, 13 American B-17's, which had taken off on December 6 from Hamilton Field, California, were roaring in about 200 miles to the northeast of Hawaii. At the same time, from the northwest the Japanese carriers began flying off the first of their 260 planes.

Shortly after 7:00 A.M., two U.S. privates, Joseph L. Lockard and George E. Elliott, were watching their mobile radar set on the northern slope of Oahu. An oscilloscope signal began to blip wildly. The screen showed what seemed to be a swarm of aircraft approaching at a distance of 137 miles. One of the privates immediately phoned Lieutenant Kermit Tyler at the Information Center. Tyler's answer was disastrous for many men then still alive at Pearl Harbor. The gist—"Forget it!" The lieutenant assumed that these were the friendly B-17's expected from the mainland. It was a human mistake, but a costly one.

A half hour later through the fleecy clouds over towering Diamond Head came the roar of 189 Japanese bombers.

Behind this astonishing attack was a story of steadily deteriorating relations between the United States and Japan. Japan had been the first of the have-not nations to embark upon a program of expansion. When she invaded Manchuria in 1931 she had set in motion the pattern of aggression that led to World War II. On November 25, 1936, she signed the Anti-Comintern Pact with Germany and Italy, and the following summer began large-scale military operations in China. Although successful in investing several large Chinese cities, Japan was caught in the Chinese quagmire and failed to subjugate the entire country. It was necessary to find some honorable way out of the undeclared war.

The outbreak of war in Europe in 1939 provided Japan with a golden opportunity not only to wind up the "China Incident" without interference from foreign meddling but also to expand to the south. There were two major prizes waiting to be taken—French Indo-China with its rice, coal, tin, and zinc, and the Dutch East Indies with their rubber, oil, and tin. Great Britain, traditional policeman of the Far East, had its hands full attempting to stave off the Nazi *Fuehrer*; the Dutch and French, both of whom had fallen quickly to Nazi domination, could do little to protect their interests in Asia; and the United States appeared to be concerned mainly with European affairs. It seemed an auspicious time for Japanese militarists to launch their "Greater East Asia Co-Prosperity Sphere."

The aggressive designs of Japanese militarists had been indicated as far back as 1927 when an important conference, attended by all leading military and civil officials, was held in Tokyo by Prime Minister Giichi Tanaka. The Tanaka Memorial, first published in 1929 by the Chinese, may well have been (as charged by Japanese) a clever forgery, but it did sum up the opinions current in Japan in the late 1920's, which were to dominate in the 1930's. The Tanaka Memorial read in part:

> In Japan her food supply and raw materials decrease in proportion to her population. If we merely hope to develop trade, we shall eventually be defeated by England and America, who possess unsurpassable capitalistic power. In the end, we shall get nothing. . . . Our best policy lies in the direction of taking positive steps to secure rights and privileges in Manchuria and Mongolia. . . .
>
> Having China's entire resources at our disposal we shall proceed to conquer India, the Archipelago, Asia Minor, Central Asia, and even Europe.

There was, indeed, widespread economic distress inside Japan. The strain of the war in China and the needs of an expanding population could be solved, said the militarists, only by taking advantage of the world situation and embarking upon a program of expansion.

The United States took a dim view of this program, since she had committed herself to maintain the Open Door principle in China and by the Nine-Power Treaty of 1922 had promised "to uphold the sovereignty, independence, and territorial and administrative integrity of China." Moreover, she resented the growth of Nipponese sea and air power and detested the brutal war against China.

The economic war between the United States and Japan gradually increased in tempo and irritation. In 1938, as the result of pressure placed on manufacturers by the State Department, the sale of American aircraft to Japan was halted. In July 1939 Washington abrogated the American-Japanese commercial treaty of 1911 and placed trade on a day-to-day basis. On July 26, 1940, President Roosevelt froze all Japanese assets in the United States, and the nations of the British Commonwealth of Nations immediately did the same thing. An Export Control Act authorized President Roosevelt to regulate or interdict the export to Japan of machine tools, chemicals, and strategic materials. A blockade established by the ABCD powers (America, Britain, China, and the Dutch East Indies) soon cut off some 75 per cent of imports into Japan.

From the Japanese militarists came shrill cries of anger. Feverish war preparations began. All political parties were merged into a single monolithic Imperial Rule Assistance Association. The premier, Prince Konoye, who had been seeking to arrive at some sort of settlement with the United States, was warned by his minister of war, General Hideki Tojo: "To carry on negotiations, for which there is no possibility of fruition, and in the end to let slip the time for fighting would be a matter of the greatest consequence."

The man who engineered the attack on Pearl Harbor was Admiral Isoroku Yamamoto, commander in chief of the Imperial Japanese Navy. Yamamoto had an intense hatred for America and the West. It was said that he imbibed this resentment from his father, who told him bedtime stories of "the barbarians who came in their black ships, broke down the doors of Japan, threatened the Son of Heaven, and trampled on the ancient customs." In the belief that "the fiercest serpent can be overcome by a swarm of rats," he carefully amassed an armada of aircraft carriers long before December 7, 1941, and supervised the training of a force designed to obliterate American power in the Pacific. For his triumph at Pearl Harbor, Yamamoto received the personal congratulations of Emperor Hirohito.

In September 1941 Tokyo tried without success to induce President Roosevelt to attend the meeting somewhere in the Pacific for an airing of

Japanese-American difficulties. Romantics project the interesting theory that, since the Japanese militarists were in control at this time (and in light of what later happened at Pearl Harbor), it was not at all improbable that this was an elaborate scheme to capture the president of the United States.

In mid-October 1941 Prince Konoye gave up the struggle for moderation and resigned. He was succeeded by General Hideki Tojo, the "Razor Brain," whose new cabinet of army and navy officers "smelled of gunpowder." The anti-American campaign went into high gear.

On November 10, 1941, Winston Churchill in a Mansion House speech promised that "should the United States become involved in war with Japan a British declaration would follow within the hour." He also revealed that powerful British naval forces could now be sent to the Far East.

The next day Frank Knox, U.S. Secretary of the Navy, warned that danger threatened not only in the Atlantic but that the United States "likewise faced grim possibilities on the other side of the world—on the far side of the Pacific." From Tokyo came word from the U.S. ambassador, Joseph C. Grew, that Washington must be vigilant against a sudden Japanese attack on areas not immediately involved in the Sino-Japanese war.

Then came an elaborate piece of play-acting by the Japanese militarists, planned so that Japanese naval units could have time to reach Pearl Harbor for the surprise attack. On November 14, 1941, Tojo's special envoy, Saburo Kurusu, arrived in San Francisco on his way to Washington to assist the Japanese ambassador, Admiral Kichisaburo Nomura, in a last-ditch effort to "maintain the peace." Kurusu announced to the press that he had come "to make a touchdown." It is highly probable that neither he nor Admiral Nomura was aware that they were being used as decoys in a fixed game.

At the preliminary negotiations on November 17, 1941, with Secretary of State Cordell Hull, the Japanese representatives presented a list of "minimum demands": an end to the American financial and economic embargo; cessation of military and economic aid to China; a hands-off policy in China; recognition of Manchukuo; full access to the Dutch East Indies for Japan; and acknowledgment of Japan's Greater East Asia Co-Prosperity Sphere. The envoys requested Hull to bring the demands to the attention of President Roosevelt, since they could not be held responsible for the conduct of their government if an answer were delayed.

The response came on November 25, 1941, in a strongly worded note presenting these counterdemands by Washington: withdrawal of Japanese forces from China and Indo-China; a joint guarantee of the territorial integrity of China; Japanese recognition of the Chinese Nationalist government of Chiang Kai-shek; a nonaggression pact between the Pacific powers; future adherence of Japan to the rules of law and order in her relations with other countries; and Japanese withdrawal from her association with the Axis powers. In effect, the Japanese were being asked to make a complete about-face.

Meanwhile, Magic, the U.S. Army and Navy cryptanalytic division, which had broken the Japanese radio code, was intercepting messages which made it clear that Tokyo had little confidence in the Washington peace negotiations. One important communication was missed by the Americans: On November 5, 1941, the Combined Fleet Top Secret Operational Order No. 1 was issued.

On November 25 the Japanese task force under Admiral Yamamoto sailed toward Hawaii. Simultaneously, the Japanese foreign minister instructed Nomura in Washington to avoid giving the impression that Japan wished to break off negotiations.

On November 27 Secretary of War Henry L. Stimson warned General Douglas MacArthur, the Philippine-based commander of the U.S. armed forces in the Far East, that the negotiations seemed "for all practical purposes" to be ended.

In Tokyo on December 1, 1941, an Imperial Conference made a formal decision to strike. A fleet of warships and transports was sent to the Gulf of Siam in a successful effort to confuse U.S. Army and Naval Intelligence, which believed that Japan would strike at the East Indies or possibly Singapore. Washington sent an inquiry to Tokyo regarding Japanese intentions. As if Tokyo would reveal such intentions!

On December 6, 1941, Japanese troops poured into Indo-China. Simultaneously, Magic intercepted Tokyo's answer to Secretary Hull's counterdemands of November 25. It was a flat rejection.

That same day, as General Marshall prepared a hurried alert to Pearl Harbor, President Roosevelt dispatched a personal appeal to Emperor Hirohito:

> I address myself to Your Majesty at this moment in the fervent hope that Your Majesty may, as I am doing, give thought in this definite emergency to ways of dispelling the dark clouds. I am confident that both of us, for the sake of the peoples not only of our great countries but for the sake of humanity in neighboring territories, have a sacred duty to restore traditional amity and prevent further death and destruction in the world.

On the next Sunday, December 7, 1941, there was no reply from Tokyo. At one o'clock that afternoon, Washington time, the Japanese emissaries, Kurusu and Nomura, asked for an audience with Secretary Hull, who agreed to meet them at 1:45 P.M. They arrived at 2:05, just 20 minutes late. Hull kept them waiting another 17 minutes in an outer room of his office.

Richard L. Turner, an Associated Press newsman, reported:

> Gone was the blithe breezy aplomb that had characterized their numerous previous visits to the Department. There was a tight-lipped, almost embarrassed smile for newsmen, and an absolute refusal to answer questions.

> Kurusu paced the diplomatic reception room. Nomura sat stolidly upon a leather divan; only a frequently tapping foot betrayed his perturbation.

At this moment Hull received the flash that the Japanese had attacked Pearl Harbor. The envoys were admitted to his office. Nomura handed him the final Japanese reply to the American formula for peace in the Pacific. Hull gravely read the farrago of insults and misstatements, charging among other things that the United States was guilty of scheming for an extension of the war. Then the Secretary of State turned to the Japanese ambassador and responded with a verbal blasting without precedent in the history of American diplomacy.

In a voice choking with anger Hull said (this passage is stripped of some accompanying Tennessee expletives): "I must say that in all my conversations with you during the last nine months I have never uttered one word of untruth. This is borne out absolutely by the record. In all my 50 years of public service I have never seen a document that was more crowded with infamous falsehoods and distortions—infamous falsehoods and distortions on a scale so huge that I never imagined that any government on this planet was capable of uttering them."

Wordlessly the Japanese left.

Pearl Harbor, 3,500 nautical miles from Japan, the major American outpost in the Pacific on the southern shore of the island of Oahu, was studded with protective guns, powered with the most modern weapons. Its harbor could accommodate the entire United States fleet. The Army and Navy commanders at Pearl Harbor were concerned mostly about local sabotage. They knew that Japanese military intelligence had agents in Hawaii sending home reports on topography and on the number and type of naval units there. On the fateful morning of December 7 the commanders at Pearl Harbor were interested mostly in a U.S. expedition to Wake and Midway, which, fortunately, had taken two carriers and seven heavy cruisers into the relative safety of the open sea.

The battleships moored at piers along Ford Island were in Condition 3—the antiaircraft battery partly manned, and about one-third of the ships' crews off on shore leave. The men handling the recently installed radar apparatus were still in the early stages of their training. There was no special air reconnaissance out of Pearl Harbor. And most of the ship and aircraft crews were either sleeping late or off on leave.

> In fine homes on the heights above the city, [wrote a newsman] in beach shacks near Waikiki, in the congested district around the Punchbowl, assorted Japanese, Chinese, Portuguese, Filipinos, Hawaiians, and *kamaainas* (long-settled whites) were taking their ease. In the shallow waters lapping Fort De Russy, where sentries walked post along a retaining wall, a few Japanese and Hawaiians waded about, looking for fish to spear. In Army posts all

over Oahu, soldiers were dawdling into a typical idle Sunday. Aboard the ships of the fleet at Pearl Harbor, life was going on at a saunter. Downtown nothing stirred save an occasional bus.

Then from the southeast across Diamond Head came the first wave of 189 planes with the insignia of the Rising Sun emblazoned in red on their wings. There were big four-motored jobs, dive bombers, torpedo-carrying planes, some pursuits. Appearing out of the morning haze, they swept in low from the sea. Directly in their path was a tiny private plane, flown by a surprised young lawyer out for a Sunday-morning ride. Soon he found himself in the midst of all hell. His craft riddled with machine-gun bullets, he succeeded in making a safe landing. By this time Pearl Harbor was being plastered with bombs.

The Japanese pilots, familiar by good briefing with every inch of their concentrated target, were devastatingly accurate. Torpedoes launched from bombers tore at the moored battleships. Dive bombers swooped down on Hickam and Wheeler Fields, immobilizing the grounded aircraft. Tons of explosives were dropped as towering flames leaped up and coils of thick black smoke clouded the sky.

Seventy combat ships, including eight battleships, were at Pearl Harbor that beautiful Sunday morning. Moored in single file like huge wallowing sitting ducks in the middle of the harbor were the *Arizona*, *Nevada*, *Maryland*, *Tennessee*, and *California*. The *Oklahoma* was berthed alongside the *Maryland*, the *West Virginia* beside the *Tennessee*. Among the additional targets were the *Pennsylvania* in drydock at the Navy Yard and the old *Utah*, used by the Americans themselves as a target ship.

The Japanese struck again and again through the fleecy clouds, first with aerial torpedoes, then with heavy bombers and dive bombers. The attacking pilots swooped up and down the line of battlewagons and mercilessly strafed them with machine-gun bullets.

The alarm of "General Quarters" came within a few minutes. The surprised Americans, fighting as well as they could in the unequal battle, sent up volleys from pom-poms and machine guns. The staccato of fire was accompanied by wild curses directed against "the slant-eyed sons of bitches."

A bomb went straight down the funnel of the *Arizona* and exploded with devastating effect in her forward magazine. The entire fore section from bow to foremast burst into flames and broke away from the aft portion as the warship began to settle. Great fingers of oily smoke reached into the sky. Despite heat and fire, crewmen jumped overboard and tried to swim ashore through the batches of searing oil. More than a thousand men, including Rear Admiral Isaac C. Kidd, died in the flaming hulk. The *Arizona* continued to burn for two days.

The *West Virginia*, hit by torpedoes, her superstructure a mass of flames, began to settle by her bow. Among the casualties was her commander, Captain Mervyn S. Bennion, killed when a bomb fragment penetrated the bridge of his ship. The *Oklahoma*, her side split wide open, heeled over and sank within ten minutes, her bottom showing grotesquely above the surface. Hundreds of American seamen were entombed in the giant warship. The *California* listed heavily to her port side. The *Maryland*, *Pennsylvania*, and *Tennessee*, all hit by huge bombs that left gaping holes, were surrounded by blazing oil. The *Nevada*, sinking, headed for shore.

The decks of the stricken ships were covered with shattered, burned, and bleeding men, some silent in shock, some screaming in agony. Swimmers strove desperately to avoid the inferno of flaming oil. Worst of all, 2,343 American officers and enlisted men were dead, and 1,272 wounded. Nearly a thousand men were missing.

For this shockingly successful attack the Japanese paid with the loss of only 29 aircraft, 5 midget two-man submarines, and one fleet submarine.

"The U.S. Navy," reported one newspaper, "was caught with its pants down."

In fact, within an hour the United States suffered greater naval losses than in the whole of World War I. Between April 6, 1917, and November 11, 1918, the United States had lost one armored cruiser, two destroyers, one submarine, three armed yachts, one Coast Guard cutter, and two revenue cutters—but not a single capital ship. At Pearl Harbor half the entire U.S. Navy was crippled and American striking power in the Pacific was virtually paralyzed.

The reaction in Japan was ecstatic. In blazing headlines the *Japan Times and Advertiser*, mouthpiece of the Foreign Office, claimed: "U.S. PACIFIC FLEET IS WIPED OUT!" The paper asserted that Japan had reduced the United States to a third-class power overnight, as witness direct accounts and photographs from forces which carried out the attacks.

The Secretary of the Navy, Frank Knox, flew immediately to Honolulu to survey the damage and report back to the American people. It was depressing news. "The air attack," he said, "simply took us by surprise. We weren't on air alert." This admission astonished the entire nation, which had believed that its men were at battle stations from Manila to Pearl Harbor.

On that early Sunday afternoon the American people were doing what they usually did—reading newspapers, or lounging with their coffee, or listening to the radio. The flash "PEARL HARBOR BOMBED BY JAPANESE" came at 2:22 P.M., Eastern Standard Time. The news was met at first with incredulity and then with a blast of outrage.

Thousands of the 132,000,000 Americans reacted in precisely the same way: "Why, the yellow bastards!" Others exploded with variations of "We'll stamp their buck teeth in!"

As the extent of the disaster seeped through the curtain of censorship, there followed an even greater nationwide outburst of anger. The prevailing mood was best expressed by Senator Burton K. Wheeler, who had led the Senate bloc opposing President Roosevelt's foreign policy: "The only thing to do now is to lick hell out of them!"

Only a few hours after Pearl Harbor, Emperor Hirohito issued a formal declaration of war, couched in terms of medieval grandiloquence: "We, by grace of Heaven, Emperor of Japan, seated on the throne of a line unbroken for ages eternal, enjoin upon you, our loyal and brave subjects: We hereby declare war on the United States of America and the British Empire."

Twenty minutes after the declaration of war was read over the Tokyo radio, a Japanese university professor went on the air to read a broadcast titled: "Good Morals."

On the evening of December 7, 1941, President Roosevelt called a cabinet meeting and later conferred with Congressional leaders. The two houses of Congress met in joint session the following day at 12:30 P.M. The President opened his address with the memorable words: "Yesterday, December 7, 1941—a date which will live in infamy...."

There was no debate such as had taken place when President Wilson had asked for a declaration of war in April 1917. Without a single speech and without a wasted word, the Senate voted unanimously for war against Japan, while the House passed the formal declaration with only one dissenting vote. The first woman ever to sit in the House of Representatives, Republican pacifist Jeanette Rankin of Montana, was at least consistent—she had voted against war with Germany in 1917. Wan, tight-lipped Representative Rankin stated her reason for her lone dissenting vote—she said that *somebody* should go on record to indicate that a "good democracy" does not always vote unanimously for war.

Winston Churchill, who had not forgotten his pledge of November 10, 1941, acted with typical speed. His cabinet authorized an immediate declaration of war on Japan. Because of the time difference in England and the United States the British declaration came even before that of the American Congress.

Churchill told a cheering Parliament:

> Now that the issue is joined and in the most direct manner, it only remains for the two great democracies to face their task with whatever strength God may give them. We may hold ourselves very fortunate, and I think we may rate our affairs not wholly ill-guided, that we were not attacked alone by Japan in our period of weakness after Dunkirk. . . . It is of the highest importance that there should be no underrating of the gravity of the new dangers we have to meet, either here or in the United States. . . .
>
> We have at least four-fifths of the population of the globe upon our side. We are responsible for their safety and for their future. In the past we have

> had a light which flickered, in the present we have a light which flames, and in the future there will be a light which shines over all the land and sea.

Other nations quickly followed the lead of Britain—New Zealand, Canada, China, the exiled governments of Greece, Yugoslavia, and the Free French. Soviet Russia, busily holding off Hitler, stayed out of the war against Japan until August 1945.

On the evening of December 9, 1941, President Roosevelt spoke to the nation. After reviewing the events that led up to Pearl Harbor, he reminded his fellow Americans that this was a war not only for their survival but for the survival of all those spiritual values which Americans had long nourished and defended.

> The true goal we seek, [he said] is far above and beyond the ugly field of battle. When we resort to force, as now we must, we are determined that this force shall be directed toward ultimate good as well as against immediate evil. We Americans are not destroyers—we are builders.
>
> We are now in the midst of a war, not for conquest, not for vengeance, but for a world in which this nation, and all that this nation represents, will be safe for our children. We expect to eliminate the danger from Japan, but it would serve us ill if we accomplished that and found that the rest of the world was dominated by Hitler and Mussolini.
>
> We are going to win the war and we are going to win the peace that follows.
>
> And in the difficult hours of this day—through dark days that may be yet to come—we will know that the vast majority of the members of the human race are on our side. Many of them are fighting with us. All of them are praying for us. For in representing our cause, we represent theirs as well —our hope and their hope for liberty under God.

Adolf Hitler went into one of his rare moments of euphoria when he heard the news from Pearl Harbor. This was language he understood and approved. Once again the Japanese had proved to his satisfaction that they deserved the *Fuehrer*-bestowed title of honorary Aryans. The exiled German Kaiser, Wilhelm II, who had warned about the "Yellow Peril" and who had died in Holland on June 4, 1941, must have turned uncomfortably in his new grave.

To the Reichstag Hitler proclaimed: "A historical revision of unique scope has been entrusted to us by the Creator." He went on to denounce "the unholy trinity of capitalism, Bolshevism, and Jewry." The United States, he thundered, was seeking "to take over the British Empire." Now in firm alliance with God, Hitler and Mussolini announced that their countries were joining Japan. The satellite states of the Axis—Rumania, Hungary, and Bulgaria—followed suit.

Congress agreed that "a state of war has been thrust upon the United States" and declared that a state of war existed with Germany and Italy.

Within a week some 35 nations, representing one-half the world's population, were at war. The conflict was now of global proportions, and almost all peoples of the world were directly or indirectly involved.

The attitude of Latin America was vital for the United States. In the summer of 1941, in the midst of the debate on neutrality, President Roosevelt revealed that he had documentary evidence to show that Hitler planned to carve South America into five vassal states and to replace all existing religions by a Nazi cult in which *Mein Kampf* was to serve as the Bible. Latin Americans were already concerned by Axis trade invasions of their countries.

The Japanese attack on Pearl Harbor awakened all Latin America to its grave danger. Within five days nine Caribbean countries (Costa Rica, the Dominican Republic, Haiti, Honduras, Nicaragua, El Salvador, Cuba, Guatemala, and Panama) declared war on Japan, Germany, and Italy. Most other American nations broke off diplomatic relations with the Axis within a few weeks, but Chile and Argentina held back until 1943 (Argentina finally declared war in March 1945). Brazil's declaration of war against Germany and Italy on August 22, 1942, had a profound effect all over South America and the Caribbean. The Brown Network in South America, into which Hitler and the Nazis had poured funds and tremendous effort, was quickly shattered.

Latin Americans had some reservations about their giant North American neighbor, but they were realistic enough to prefer American faults to those of the Nazis. Resentment disappeared in the crucible of a common effort. The Central American republics later offered Washington bases to defend the Panama Canal. Brazil, especially, critically important from a geographical point of view, was to give extraordinary aid to U.S. naval and air power. And Colombia was to offer the United States bases anywhere within her borders, an extraordinary concession on the part of any sovereign power.

On the morning after Pearl Harbor was attacked, recruiting stations all over the United States were jammed with eager volunteers. The American people, Democrats and Republicans alike, interventionists and isolationists, labor and capital, closed ranks in an unprecedented display of national unity. Herbert Hoover put it this way: "American soil has been treacherously attacked by Japan. We must fight with everything we have."

Even Charles A. Lindbergh, Jr., apostle of isolationism, announced: "Now it has come, and we must meet it as united Americans regardless of our attitude in the past toward the policy our government has followed. . . . We must now turn every effort to building the greatest and most efficient Army, Navy, and Air Force in the world."

The impact on Americans had been stunning, but recovery was not long in coming. Shock quickly gave way to a strengthening of resolve.

The sneak attack on Pearl Harbor brought the Japanese great unpopularity throughout the non-Axis world. Nor was their cause helped by indiscriminate gloating after the event. In Mexico City, Japanese Ambassador Yoshiaka Murua announced that he was confident that his country would defeat the United States "because Japan has never lost a war." After her declaration of war on Japan, Nicaragua jailed the country's entire Japanese population—Gusidi Yakata and Juan Hissi. The Chinese vice-consul at New Orleans said (according to a copywriter on *Time* magazine): "As far as Japan is concerned, their goose is overheated."

Angry crowds in metropolitan American cities watched while Japanese consuls burned their books and papers. There were calls to intern the Japanese-American population.

Pearl Harbor, to put it mildly, was a disaster for the United States. But it was not, as the Japanese had hoped, the end of American striking power. An important part of the fleet escaped the holocaust. Within a year all the ships sunk or damaged, except the ruined *Arizona*, were repaired and put back into action. "The essential fact is," said Secretary of the Navy Frank Knox, "that the Japanese purpose was to knock out the United States before the war began. In this purpose the Japanese failed."

Four days after the attack on Pearl Harbor, Italy and Germany declared war on the United States. The prospect of a war with America came as a blow to the German people. For years Dr. Joseph Goebbels, the Nazi propaganda chief, had hammered away at the idea that Germany since 1933 had been protecting itself from evil "International Jewry" gathered around "President Rosenfeldt." He had described the United States as "an automobile, radio, jazz-band, five-and-ten-store, Jewish plutocratic civilization." Despite this type of propaganda most Germans regarded America as a nation of magnificent accomplishments and enormous strength, certainly not a country to fight. Many had not forgotten the lessons of World War I, when American strength thrown into the balance meant the end of Imperial Germany.

One further aspect of the Pearl Harbor tragedy remains to be noted. As soon as the war was over a great debate began to rage concerning the circumstances surrounding Pearl Harbor and the coming of the war.

Shortly after the end of the war, a Joint Congressional Committee investigated the Pearl Harbor attack. Thirty-nine volumes of testimony and exhibits were published, from which historians have drawn varying conclusions. The Committee issued Majority and Minority statements, both of which summarized the conflicting viewpoints.

The main conclusions of the Majority Report:

> 1. The December 7, 1941, attack on Pearl Harbor was an unprovoked act of aggression by the Empire of Japan. . . .
>
> 3. The diplomatic policies and actions of the United States provided no justifiable provocation whatever for the attack by Japan on this nation. . . .
>
> 4. The Committee has found no evidence to support the charges, made be-

fore and during the hearings, that the President, the Secretary of State, the Secretary of War, or the Secretary of the Navy tricked, provoked, incited, cajoled, or coerced Japan into attacking this Nation in order that a declaration of war might be more easily obtained from Congress. On the contrary, all evidence conclusively points to the fact that they discharged their responsibilities with distinction, ability, and foresight and in keeping with the highest traditions of our fundamental foreign policy.

5. The President, the Secretary of State, and high Government officials made every possible effort, without sacrificing our national honor and endangering our security, to avert war with Japan.

6. The disaster at Pearl Harbor was the failure . . . of the Army and the Navy to institute measures designed to detect an approaching hostile force, to effect a state of readiness commensurate with the realization that war was at hand, and to employ every facility at their command in repelling the Japanese. . . .

9. The errors made by the Hawaiian commands were errors of judgment and not derelictions of duty.

The Minority Report expressed an opposing viewpoint:

The failure of Pearl Harbor to be fully alerted and prepared for defense rested upon the proper discharge of two sets of *interdependent* responsibilities: (1) the responsibilities of high authorities in Washington, and (2) the responsibilities of the commanders in the field in charge of the fleet and of the naval base.

The evidence clearly shows that these two areas of responsibilities were inseparately essential to each other in the defense of Hawaii. The commanders in the field could not have been prepared or been ready successfully to meet hostile attack at Hawaii without indispensable information, matériel, trained manpower and clear orders from Washington. Washington could not be certain that Hawaii was in readiness without the alert and active cooperation of the commanders on the spot.

The failure to perform the responsibilities indispensably essential to the defense of Pearl Harbor rests upon the following civil and military authorities: FRANKLIN D. ROOSEVELT—President of the United States and Commander in Chief of the Army and Navy. HENRY L. STIMSON—Secretary of War. FRANK KNOX—Secretary of the Navy. GEORGE C. MARSHALL —General, Chief of Staff of the Army. HAROLD R. STARK—Admiral, Chief of Naval Operations. LEONARD T. GEROW—Major General, Assistant Chief of Staff of War Plans Division.

The failure to perform the responsibilities in Hawaii rests upon the military commanders: WALTER C. SHORT—Major General, Commanding General, Hawaiian Department. HUSBAND E. KIMMEL—Rear Admiral, Commander in Chief of the Pacific Fleet.

Secretary of State, CORDELL HULL, who was at the center of the Japanese-American negotiations bears a grave responsibility for the diplomatic conditions leading up to the eventuality of Pearl Harbor but he had no duties as a relevant link in the military chain of responsibility stemming from the Commander in Chief to the commanders at Hawaii for the defense at Pearl

Harbor. For this reason and because the diplomatic phase was not completely explored we offer no conclusions in his case.

The debate was now on in full fury.

Roosevelt's detractors, the revisionists, made the serious allegation that the President and his advisers had led the country into war while professing peace and that this was done behind the backs and without the knowledge of the elected representatives of the American people. They charged that, when Roosevelt found isolationist opposition too strong, he maneuvered Japan into striking at Pearl Harbor. "He lied the American people into war because he could not lead them into it," was the judgment of one Roosevelt opponent.

William Henry Chamberlin, author, lecturer, and editorial writer for the *Wall Street Journal*, wrote: "Like the Roman God Janus, Roosevelt in the prewar period had two faces. For the American people, for the public record, there was the face of bland assurance that his first concern was to keep the country out of war. But in more intimate surroundings the Chief Executive often assumed that America was already involved in war."

The historian, George Morgenstern, concluded: "No amount of excuses will palliate the conduct of President Roosevelt and his advisers. The offense of which they stand convicted is not failure to discharge their responsibilities, but calculated refusal to do so. They failed—with calculation—to keep the United States out of war and to avoid a clash with Japan."

Another group of revisionists, including historian and sociologist Harry Elmer Barnes, publicist John T. Flynn, and historian Charles C. Tansill, charged that Roosevelt had turned to war to cover up his failures in domestic policies. He wanted to assure his own reëlection, they asserted, and furthermore he had grandiloquent ideas of world leadership. Barnes stated flatly: "Roosevelt and Hull knew from the cracked Japanese code that the Japanese peace offers were sincere and reasonable, but, neverthless, rebuffed them and provoked the Japanese attack on Pearl Harbor."

Furious counterattacks came from defenders of the wartime President. Historians Basil Rauch, Dexter Perkins, and William L. Langer maintained that Roosevelt did everything he possibly could to keep America out of war short of abandoning American principles and exposing the nation to extreme danger. Instead of being subjected to this shameful revisionist criticism, they said, Roosevelt should be credited with gaining time for preparedness at a critical era in the nation's history.

Joseph W. Ballantine, a State Department expert on the Far East, put it this way: "The Japanese were not offering to negotiate a reasonable settlement by processes of agreement: they were presenting demands, to be accepted or rejected. The United States had only two choices: either to yield to the Japanese demands and sacrifice principles and security, or to decline to yield and take the consequences."

A second group of Roosevelt defenders, notably historians Thomas A. Bailey and Arthur M. Schlesinger, Jr., and Robert E. Sherwood, playwright and speech-writer for Roosevelt, admitted the charges of the revisionists that Roosevelt had committed America to the cause of the anti-Axis powers. But they found justification in the opposition of the isolationists who were ready to throw a roadblock in the way of actions necessary for the security of the nation.

"Because the masses are notoriously short-sighted," wrote Bailey, "and generally cannot see the danger until it is at their throats, our statesmen are forced to deceive them into an awareness of their own long-run interests. This is clearly what Roosevelt had to do, and who shall say that posterity will not thank him for it?"

THE OCTOPUS REACHES OUT

The crippling blow dealt by the Japanese at Pearl Harbor was only one of a series of strikes throughout the Far East.

The Nipponese offensive, like an exploding skyrocket, went off in every direction. Almost simultaneous with the attack on Pearl Harbor, the Japanese air and naval forces hit at Kota Bharu in British Malaya, Singora in Thailand, Singapore, Hong Kong, Guam, Midway, Wake Island, and the Philippines. It was an extraordinary display of far-flung, coördinated military, naval, and air power.

Behind it was a strategy long prepared. From newly-acquired bases the Japanese swarmed against the enemy, usually appearing with overwhelming strength at critical fighting points. The way for conquest was smoothed by treacherous fifth columns in each of the areas selected for infiltration or assault.

Nipponese fighting men understood the tactics of infiltration and dispersal. They were conditioned to prefer death to surrender. Trained to survive on rations of hard rice, they could live on the land if necessary. Camouflaged to look like leaves, uttering animal cries as signals. they were experts at blending into the jungle and avoiding detection. Strapped in trees, they could remain motionless for hours and then snipe at or drop grenades on their opponents. Wearing rubber sneakers, they could infiltrate behind enemy lines, appear at the most unlikely spots, and throw unwary troops into confusion.

Both the British and Americans at first underestimated the fighting quality of Japanese shock troops. They had been misled by the apparent failure of Japan to subdue China in short order. Untrained in jungle combat, British Imperials and American G.I.'s at first found themselves at a grave disadvantage. But they soon learned that, despite the use of eccentric tactics, Japanese operations were in the long run stereotyped and that the pattern was always

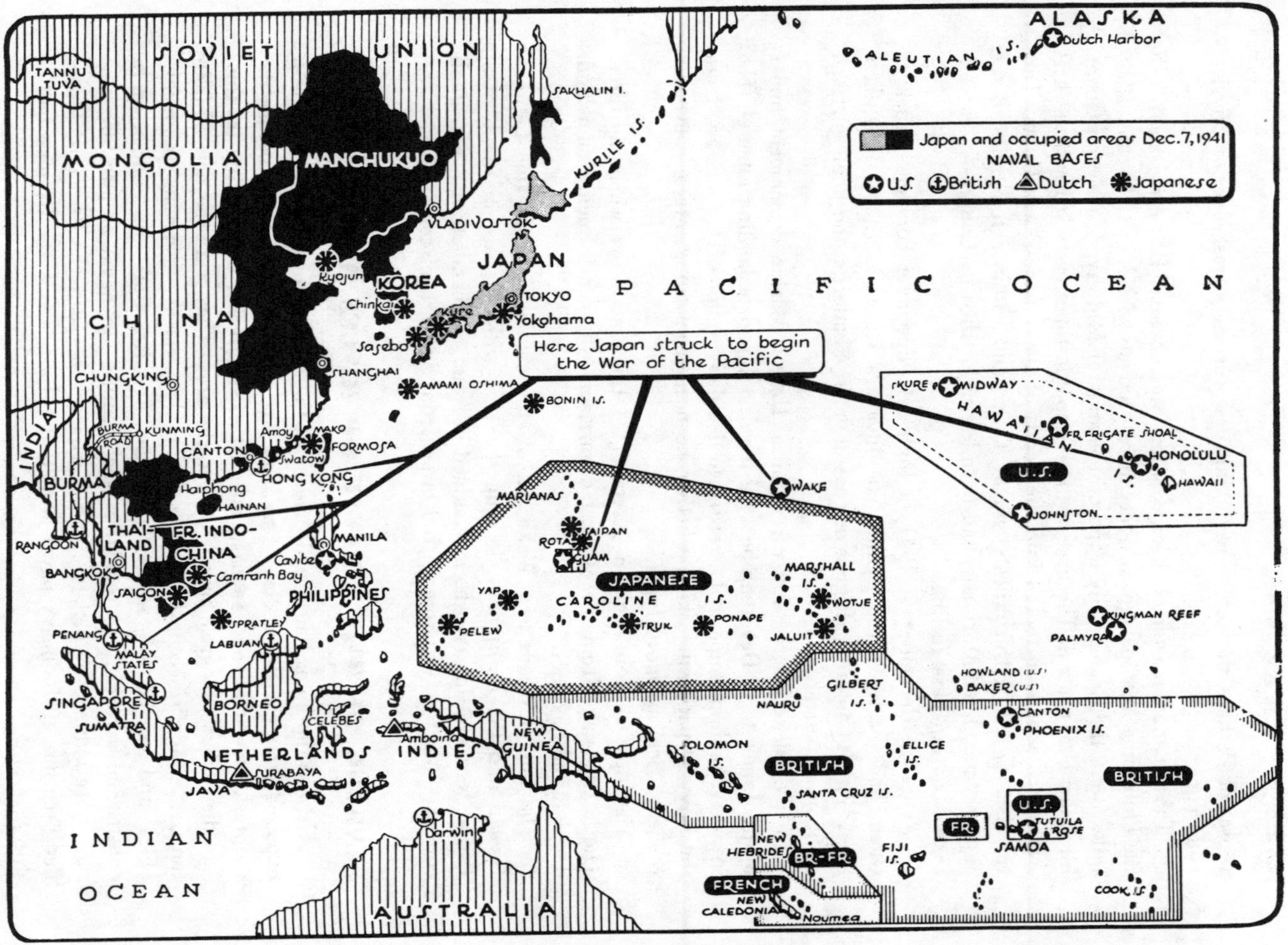

THE PACIFIC A WAR ZONE

repeated. Perhaps the key to early Japanese successes was superior physical endurance.

The Japanese master plan for conquest was obvious. Between Hawaii and the Philippine Archipelago, at intervals respectively of 1,304, 1,185, and 1,508 miles, were the strategically important islands of Midway, Wake, and Guam, all under U.S. control. The first of these steppingstones eastward and the first American possession to fall into the hands of the Japanese was Guam. This tiny island, only 1,155 miles south of Tokyo and within a few miles of the Japanese-mandated Marianas, had been left unfortified by Congress as a concession to Japanese feelings.

At dawn, December 7, 1941, a flight of Nipponese bombers struck at Guam and plastered the island. The invaders stormed ashore three days later. Without antiaircraft guns or coastal defense batteries, the small garrison of 555 men surrendered.

Wake Island offered stiffer resistance. Here a Marine detachment under Major James P. S. Devereux beat off the first Japanese landing attempt. The invaders, held up temporarily, retired to lick their wounds. To a message from the Navy Department asking whether he needed anything, Major Devereux replied: "Send us more Japs!"

The Japanese were back on December 23, this time in overwhelming force. The last message from the exhausted garrison—"Urgent! Enemy on island. The issue is in doubt."

The fall of Guam and Wake cut off the communications line between Hawaii and the Philippines, leaving the U.S. with no base in the Central Pacific west of Midway, which remained in American hands. But it was small comfort—Midway was some 3,700 miles from San Francisco.

SINKING OF THE *PRINCE OF WALES* AND *REPULSE*

Help in the immediate naval defense of the southwestern Pacific had been expected from the Royal Navy based on Singapore. Some months before the outbreak of war in the Far East, the British Admiralty, anticipating trouble, had dispatched two great men-of-war to the area. They were the new 35,000-ton battleship *Prince of Wales* (pronounced by naval experts to be unsinkable) and the 32,000-ton battle cruiser *Repulse*. Both, of course, were constructed according to the latest specifications in naval architecture and both were manned by picked crews. Earlier in the year, the *Prince of Wales* had been one of the heavy naval units that helped to sink the German battleship *Bismarck*.

On December 8, 1941, soon after he had received news of the Japanese landings in Malaya, Vice Admiral Sir Tom Phillips, commander of the British Far East Fleet, a courageous but inexperienced officer, put to sea with the

Prince of Wales, the *Repulse*, and the destroyers *Electra, Express, Vampire*, and *Tenedos*. His mission was to smash the Japanese transports and landing craft before they could disembark their troops.

It turned out to be a gross error of judgment. In taking his fleet into enemy waters without looking to the skies, Admiral Phillips was violating a basic tenet of up-to-date naval strategy—*never risk capital ships in the vicinity of enemy air power without an adequate air screen.*

Churchill's later explanation to the House of Commons was embarrassingly weak:

> These ships had reached the right point at the right moment, and were in every respect suited to the task assigned them. In moving to attack the Japanese transports and landing craft which were disembarking the invaders of Siam and Malaya at the Kra Isthmus or thereabouts, Admiral Phillips was undertaking a thoroughly sound, well-considered offensive operation, not indeed free from risk, but not different in principle from many similar operations in the North Sea and in the Mediterranean.

But the *outcome* was quite different. The British fleet steamed northward. When only 50 miles off the coast of Malaya and only 150 miles from Singapore, it was spotted by Japanese reconnaissance planes.

A Japanese war correspondent, Yukio Waku, reported the grim drama:

> Our planes continued a reconnaissance flight over the seas off the eastern coast of the Anambas Islands. Columns of black smoke were sighted far on the horizon. Careful reconnaissance told us that the smoke columns were those from the enemy fleet, which included the *Prince of Wales* and the *Repulse*. A wireless operator began to send out information to our bombing base on the location of the enemy fleet. Imperial Air Force bombers, on receipt of the wireless message, took off in a big formation, with torpedoes loaded, in defiance of the bad weather. Our bombers caught sight of the British Far Eastern Fleet, which seemed to have noticed our attempt and started fleeing in zigzag at full speed of 30 knots under cover of the dark clouds. In the gathering twilight which prevented our further search for the enemy fleet, we were obliged to head for our base, with inexpressible regret.

Next morning the Japanese bombers were out in force. They approached at 10,000 feet strung in a line in the brilliant sunlit sky. From 11:15 A.M. on, for an hour and a quarter, the Japanese pilots carried their assault home with consummate skill and determination in both high-level bombing and torpedo attacks. Two high-level attacks both scored hits, and then three waves of torpedo aircraft, nine in each wave, sent their torpedoes roaring into the flanks of the British battlewagons. It was much like a pack of dogs tearing viciously at two wounded bucks.

Cecil Brown, then correspondent for C.B.S., today Far East Bureau Chief, N.B.C., was on the *Repulse*. His account, one of the great journalistic reports of the war, ended as follows:

That the *Repulse* was doomed was immediately apparent. The communication system announced: "Prepare to abandon ship. May God be with you!" Without undue rush we all started streaming down ladders, hurrying but not pushing. It was most difficult to realize [that] I must leave the ship. It seemed so incredible that the *Repulse* could or should go down. But the *Repulse* was fast keeling over to port and walking ceased to be a mode of locomotion. I was forced to clamber and scramble in order to reach the side. Men were lying dead around the guns. Some were half hidden by empty shell cases. There was considerable damage all around the ship. Some of the men had been machine-gunned. That had been unquestioned fact.

All around me men were stripping off their clothes and their shoes and tossing aside their steel helmets. Some are running alongside the three-quarter-exposed hull of the ship to reach a spot where they can slide down the side without injuring themselves in the jagged hole in the ship's side. Others are running to reach a point where they have a shorter dive to the water. . . .

As I go over the side, the *Prince of Wales* half a mile away seems to be afire, but her guns are still firing the heaviest. It's most obvious she's stopped dead and out of control due to her previous damage. . . .

Later the ship was under water. Phillips and Leech [Admiral Tom Phillips and Captain Leech, skipper of the *Prince of Wales*] were the last from the *Wales* to go over the side, and they slid into the water together. It's probably their reluctance to leave the ship until all possible men had left meant their death, since it's most likely they were drawn down by the suction when the *Wales* was on her side and then settled at her stern with her bow rising in the air.

Swimming about a mile away, lying on top of a small stool, I saw the bow of the *Wales*. . . . When the *Wales* sank, the suction was so great it ripped off the life belt of one officer more than 50 feet away. . . .

Since the tide was strong and there was an extremely powerful suction from both ships, it was extremely difficult to make any progress away from the ship in the thick oil. The gentle, quiet manner in which these shell-belching dreadnoughts went to their last resting place without exploding was a tribute of gratitude from two fine ships for their fine sailors.

Neither the *Prince of Wales* nor the *Repulse* blew up despite direct hits by aerial torpedoes. This probably accounted for the survival of more than 2,000 of the almost 3,000 men on board the ships. (The *Prince of Wales* carried 1,700, the *Repulse* 1,250). The behavior of the British crews was admirable, recalling the judgment of an anonymous observer: "Believe me, I shall never more take my hat off for anything less than a British seaman."

There were alarming headlines in London:

H.M.S. *PRINCE OF WALES* AND H.M.S. *REPULSE* SUNK
By Japanese air attack in operations off Malayan coast;
2,330 saved from both ships;
c.600 missing, including Admiral Sir Tom Phillips and
Captain Leech, commanding the *Prince of Wales*

It was a catastrophe almost as shocking as that of Pearl Harbor. Before the war the value of battleships had been questioned by experts who deemed them too vulnerable in the air age. Now there were grave further doubts. The sinking of the two giant dreadnaughts brought quick revision of the notion that victory over Japan would be quick and easy. Singapore was doomed.

Winston Churchill spoke to a solemn House of Commons:

> In my whole experience I do not remember any naval blow so heavy or so painful as the sinking of the *Prince of Wales* and the *Repulse* on Monday last. These two vast, powerful ships constituted an essential feature in our plans for meeting the new Japanese danger as it loomed against us in the last few months. . . . The continued waves of attacks achieved their purpose, and both ships capsized and sank, having destroyed seven of the attacking aircraft. . . .
>
> Naturally, I should not be prepared to discuss the resulting situation in the Far East and in the Pacific or the measures which must be taken to restore it. It may well be that we shall have to suffer considerable punishment, but we shall defend ourselves everywhere with the utmost vigor in close coöperation with the United States and the Netherlands. The naval power of Great Britain and the United States was very greatly superior—and is still largely superior—to the combined forces of the three Axis Powers. But no one must undertake the gravity of the loss which has been inflicted in Malaya and Hawaii, or the power of the new antagonist who has fallen upon us, or the length of time it will take to create, marshal, and mount the great force in the Far East which will be necessary to achieve absolute victory.

The incident in the South China Sea changed the whole picture in the Far East. A stunning blow, though not an irreparable one, it nevertheless gave the Allies serious food for thought.

STRANGLING THE PHILIPPINES

Tokyo was certain that America's mid-Pacific outposts were canceled permanently out of the war. The Yamamoto-Tojo war plan now called for an amphibious offensive against the Philippines. For the Japanese, possession of the Philippines, especially the port of Manila, one of the finest natural harbors in the Far East, was essential as the key to control of China, French Indo-China, Burma, Malaya, and the Dutch East Indies. The Philippine Archipelago, consisting of some 7,083 known islands and islets, 500 miles off the southeast Asiatic mainland, extends about 1,150 miles north and south from Formosa to Borneo. It lies directly on the trade routes from Japan to the rich oil deposits and minerals of the Dutch East Indies. The largest islands are Luzon (40,814 square miles) in the north and Mindanao (36,537 square miles) in the south. Here was the strategic heartland of the Far East.

The United States had annexed the Philippines during the Spanish-American War after Admiral George Dewey's victory over the Spanish fleet in

Manila Bay in May 1898. At one strike the U.S. had extended its frontiers some 7,000 miles across the Pacific Ocean. To meet the increasing demand for Philippine independence, Congress on March 24, 1934, passed the Tydings-McDuffie Act, approved by the Philippine legislature, which provided for Philippine independence after a ten-year transitional period. In the meantime the U.S. would be permitted to keep military forces in the islands.

The day after the attack on Pearl Harbor, Japanese planes struck at Clark Field near Manila and the next day at the naval base at Cavite, thus depriving the Americans of the bulk of their Philippine air and naval support. Within three weeks the Japanese, under command of Lieutenant General Masaharu Homma, completed a major amphibious assault and some seven minor landing operations on the north and south shores of Luzon. Almost unopposed, columns of hardened shock troops drove on to Manila.

The weight and diversity of the Japanese attacks took the defenders by surprise. General Douglas MacArthur, in command of the American-Filipino forces in the islands, reported to Washington on December 27, 1941: "Enemy penetration in the Philippines resulted from our weakness on the sea and in the air. Surface elements of the Asiatic Fleet were withdrawn and the effect of submarines has been negligible. Lack of airfields for modern planes prevented defensive dispersion and lack of pursuit planes permitted unhindered day bombardment. The enemy has had utter freedom of naval and air movements."

With Cavite immobilized, Admiral Thomas C. Hart, U.S. Asiatic Fleet commander, ordered the feeble remnants of his vessels southward to a line from Surabaya in Java to Darwin in Australia, 1,500 miles from Manila. His destroyers managed to convoy 200,000 tons of merchant shipping to safe Australian waters. This U.S. naval retreat was highly satisfying to the Japanese war planners—they had cut the lines between the Philippines and Australia and had got the American fleet out of the way.

Next came the expected assault on Manila, outpost of American power in the Orient. The Philippine capital was militarily indefensible. The day after Christmas 1941 there appeared across the front of the City Hall in Manila two huge banners bearing the words: OPEN CITY and NO SHOOTING. To prevent a wholesale slaughter of the populace, the remaining American forces were ordered to evacuate the city. Roads were cluttered with terrorized people trying to reach safety in the hills; trains were jammed with refugees. The Manila radio repeatedly broadcast the declaration of "Open City," acknowledged by the Tokyo radio the same day.

On December 27, 1941, and continuing on the next day, successive waves of aircraft rained destruction on the undefended metropolis. The port installations were bombed to smithereens, the entire city plunged into an inferno of flame and smoke.

Throughout the night of January 2, 1942, Japanese troops poured into the stricken city. They found the neighboring naval base at Cavite leveled by their own bombs and by demolition squads of defenders. The quartermaster corps had opened the warehouses and allowed the public to take what it wanted before the rest of the supplies were destroyed.

The Japanese issued warnings to the remaining civilians. The code of *Bushido* accorded no rights to the vanquished and threatened disobedience with death: "Anyone who inflicts, or attempts to inflict, an injury upon Japanese soldiers, shall be shot to death. If the assailant, or attempted assailant, cannot be found, we will hold ten influential people who are in or about the streets of municipal cities where the event happened." The New Order in Asia had come to Manila.

In the entire Philippines at this time General MacArthur had only 60,000 lightly trained native troops, 11,000 expert Filipino scouts, and about 19,000 Americans representing the various armed forces. Unable to meet the Japanese attack head-on, he ordered a retreat to the Bataan Peninsula, which offered good prospects for a stand until help could come.

Just 25 miles long and 20 miles wide across its base, Bataan juts out from Luzon like a great finger pointed at the Cavite naval base a dozen miles away. Bataan was protected from sea attack by heavy guns at the near-by island of Corregidor. Dominated by two extinct volcanoes, crisscrossed by ravines and mountain streams, dotted with hills and jungles, Bataan was ideal country for a spirited defense. Its only two roads adequate for a mobile army were covered with tank traps and barbed-wire entanglements.

During the first week of January 1942, American-Filipino troops retreated from both ends of Luzon, joined at San Fernando, and began the last stage of their journey into Bataan, fighting delaying actions all the way. It was a costly maneuver. Major General Jonathan M. Wainwright's North Luzon Force was reduced from 28,000 to 16,000, largely by desertion of Filipinos, who simply went home. Brigadier General Albert M. Jones's South Luzon Force was more fortunate: of the 15,000 men he commanded when the march was started, some 14,000 reached Bataan.

Exhausted and hungry, the defenders streamed into prepared positions on Bataan. Here the oncoming Japanese subjected them to every kind of attack including frontal onslaughts, flank actions, concentrated artillery bombardment, and sea-borne infiltrations.

The Japanese commander, Lieutenant General Homma, sent General MacArthur a message: "Your prestige and honor have been upheld. However, in order to avoid needless bloodshed and save your . . . troops you are advised to surrender. . . . Failing that, our offensive will be continued with inexorable force." The only answer from the Americans was increased artillery fire.

Efforts to relieve the garrison were fruitless. The Japanese sank most of the supply ships sent to Luzon.

The troops sang a desperate song:

We're the battling Bastards of Bataan;
No mama, no papa, no Uncle Sam;
No aunts, no uncles, no cousins, no nieces;
No pills, no planes, no artillery pieces.
. . . And nobody gives a damn!

There was ample justification for the lament. Rations were cut in half during the first week in January, and within a few weeks the supply of food almost disappeared. The men ate the meat of dogs, iguanas, monkeys, mules, carabao, and snakes, and whatever berries and roots they could find in the jungle. They ransacked the peninsula for all edible vegetation.

As the supply of drugs dwindled, the troops were stricken by such dread diseases as malaria, dengue, scurvy, beriberi, and amoebic dysentery. Thousands, rendered immobile, were placed in makeshift hospitals. The tattered uniforms of those who could walk gave no protection against jungle thorns and miserable nights. Gaunt, undernourished, and disease-ridden, the garrison fought on against hopeless odds.

What to do about MacArthur? Should the brilliant general surrender with his men or should he be saved for the future Allied war effort? It was a most difficult decision for Washington. Only after weeks of negotiation was MacArthur persuaded to leave his men to the mercy of the Japanese. "Your services there," General George C. Marshall informed him, "might well be less pressing than at other points in the Far East."

On February 22, 1942, President Roosevelt gave a direct order to MacArthur to leave Luzon, go to Mindanao for a week, and then be transferred to Australia to assume command of the over-all counterattack. The news reports stated that the transference was made at the request of the Australian government. Churchill later asserted that he had suggested to Roosevelt the idea of MacArthur's escape in much the same way that he, as prime minister, had ordered Lord Gort to leave Dunkirk before the forced evacuation.

The evacuation of MacArthur, his family, and his staff through enemy-controlled territory was a remarkable feat. On March 12, 1942, the party of 21 was taken by P.T. boat through cleared mine fields to Mindanao, from which, after four days, it was flown to Darwin. To General Wainwright, who was left in command of the garrison, MacArthur gave orders to "defend Bataan in as great depth as you can," and, if it were necessary for him to surrender, "to destroy as much as you can so that it cannot be used against an American effort to recapture the Philippines."

On his arrival in Australia, MacArthur announced: "The President of the

United States ordered me to break through the Japanese lines and proceed from Corregidor to Australia for the purpose, as I understand it, of organizing the American offensive against Japan, a primary purpose of which is the relief of the Philippines. I came through and I shall return."

During the first week of April, the defending American garrison disintegrated, finally surrendering on April 9, 1942. Eight days later, the U.S. War Department announced the surrender, giving the number of men at 35,000, and stating that General Wainwright and the remnants of his force had escaped to Corregidor. By this time it had become obvious to all the world that the Americans were taking a severe beating from the Japanese in the Philippines.

Tragic was the climax of the story of Bataan.

Thousands of American and Filipino soldiers of all grades and ranks made a series of death marches starting on April 10, 1942. The route of 85 miles went eastward across the southern tip of Bataan, then northward to Orani, next northeastward to San Fernando, a rail junction in Pampagna Province, where the prisoners were to board a train for internment in a concentration camp.

One march turned out to be a special kind of Japanese hell. Formed by their captors into columns of fours, the prisoners staggered forward under the blinding sun, over the hot earth, through the grayish white dust. All were filthy, dazed, nearly mad with thirst and starvation. The sadism and stupidity of the Japanese guards were almost incredible. They beat to death any unlucky prisoners who were caught with Japanese money or articles in their possession, on the assumption that such trifles must surely have been stolen from the bodies of Nipponese dead. They slugged the helpless marchers, robbed them of their money, watches, and fountain pens, jabbed them with bayonets, cursed and taunted them with food and water which they threw away.

Behind the main contingent a mop-up squad murdered those who dropped out because of exhaustion, illness, or abuse. Filipino natives who tried to help the prisoners were driven off by the frenzied guards.

On the sixth day the captives, numb with shock, were herded into a barbed-wire compound at San Fernando. Many died of malaria, dysentery, and dengue fever. The survivors were then packed and locked into antique box cars without room to move. The only ventilation came from slits. Overcome by the foul air and the stench of vomit, many fainted, their faces buried in filth on the floor boards. After a three-hour ride and another seven-mile hike, the remaining prisoners were finally interned at O'Donnell prison camp in the jungles of Arlac Province.

Both the American fighting man and the American public found it difficult to equate the bestial guards of Bataan with stereotypes of Japanese courtesy, cherry blossoms, Geisha girls, and poetry competitions. Many who were appalled by the death march resolved that the Japanese must pay for this deliberate humiliation of American troops.

The fall of Bataan ended formal resistance on Luzon, but as long as Corregidor and her sister forts across the bay remained in American hands the Japanese would be denied the use of Manila Bay. In the elaborate tunnel system of Corregidor, protected from both air and artillery attack, were housed the American command, the Philippine headquarters, a thousand-bed hospital, and a vast quantity of supplies. Here American and Filipino officials, officers, men, nurses, workers, convalescents, all rubbed elbows in a molelike existence.

All hope of holding or regaining Bataan was gone. During April and the first days of May 1942, the Japanese covered Corregidor with tons of shells and bombs. Flesh and blood could not long endure this merciless pounding, nor could the concrete and steel on the rock stand up forever. One by one the gun emplacements and the pillboxes were knocked out.

The besieged garrison went about the grim business of destroying everything that might be of value to the invaders. At Mariveles Bay the Dewey floating dock, which had served the U.S. Asiatic Fleet for many years, was blown up, and near-by ships were scuttled. The garrison smashed its arms and burned code books and other papers.

The end came on May 6, 1942. Corregidor was surrendered, after five months' resistance.

The loss of the Philippines plunged the Allied world into profound gloom. True, resistance at Bataan and Corregidor had upset the timetable of the Japanese, forcing them to commit more men and supplies than they had intended and delaying their plans by some six months. But it was a complete and devastating defeat for the Allies.

The Japanese had put an army of nearly a hundred thousand out of action and had driven American sea and air power back to the Malay barrier. They now had one of the best harbors in the Orient, from which they could supply bases to the south and southeast and drive on to the wealth of the Dutch East Indies. Equally important, they now presented a formidable obstacle to any Allied thrust to cut the line between Tokyo and the oil and tin of the East Indies.

MALAYA AND SINGAPORE

Manila in the Philippine Islands, and Hong Kong and Singapore on the mainland, had formed a triangle of Anglo-American power in the Far East. Japanese occupation of Canton in 1940 made this triangle indefensible. The first of the three great outposts to fall was Hong Kong. On Pearl Harbor day and for two weeks more, Japanese aircraft relentlessly bombed the city. The defenders refused a demand to surrender, whereupon Japanese landings were made under cover of darkness, the invaders heading straight for the reservoirs. With the city's water supply cut off, the British garrison, some 10,947 troops, surrendered on Christmas Day, 1941, after a 17-day siege.

In the clubs of Singapore, at the foot of the Malay Peninsula, officers of famous regiments appeared in immaculate uniforms, imbibed the drinks of the tropics, and lived on complacently in the spirit of Rudyard Kipling's nineteenth century.

On this island the British had constructed what was widely regarded as the strongest naval base in the world—the Gibraltar of the Pacific. Singapore was supposedly impregnable. It might well have been unconquerable from the sea, but it was vulnerable from the Malay mainland, upon which it depended for its water. Further, the British could not count on native support, for they had not given the Malayan people Commonwealth citizenship nor did they have any armed Malayan force comparable even with the Filipino scouts.

Most important of all, the British troops at Singapore and in Malaya had not been trained for jungle fighting, an inexplicable oversight of a military command supposed to be prepared for all eventualities.

Naval strength, gin-and-tonic, cricket and golf, and hollow squares! But the observant Japanese had their eyes trained on the entire Malay Peninsula. Here was the greatest source of natural rubber in the world as well as a huge supply of tin. Jutting into the South China Sea, the peninsula stemmed from the 30-mile wide Isthmus of Kra, the southern offshoot of Thailand (Siam), to its foot at Singapore. Its east side was covered with jungle and swamps; the west, separated from the east by a huge mountain ridge, had north and south roads and a railway.

The Japanese had an army of 200,000 specially trained jungle fighters poised in Thailand and Indo-China. They intended to send these troops straight down the peninsula and take Singapore through its back door. On the morning of Pearl Harbor day the Japanese bombarded Kota Bharu on the northeast coast of the Malay Peninsula and then landed on the beaches. That same day the main force of General Tomoyuki Yamashita's 25th Army secured the beachhead. There were further landings to the north at Singora, from which the troops marched down the east coast of the Isthmus of Kra, while another division crossed the Thailand-Malaya border and moved down the west coast. For the next three weeks these columns pushed steadily south.

The jungles were supposed to be impregnable, but the Japanese knifed through them in a masterpiece of infiltration. Moving in forced marches through rice fields, swamps, rubber forests, and jungles, using collapsible boats for the jungle streams, the invaders defeated the British in skirmish after skirmish. Again and again Japanese troops appeared deep in the rear of the enemy. The British sent out tanks of 1918 vintage to meet opponents minutely trained in the intricacies of jungle fighting.

In the middle of January 1942 the British, outwitted, baffled, demoralized, staggered back the length of the peninsula, crossed the causeway to Singapore, blew up the bridge, and settled down to await either help or a final assault from the enemy. At Singapore there were neither underground caverns as at Malta nor any man-made tunnels as at Corregidor, nor any possibility of an evacuation such as that at Dunkirk. The British rushed in some reinforcements, which arrived just in time to share the defeat with the garrison.

For a month the Japanese assaulted the island from both ground and air. On February 11, 1942, Yamashita called on the garrison to surrender. There was no reply. Three days later the attackers captured the reservoirs. On February 15, 1942, Lieutenant General Sir Arthur Ernest Percival surrendered with between 55,000 and 60,000 troops.

Again there were gloomy headlines in London:

> SINGAPORE FALLS
> Surrender signed 7 P.M. local time, 12:30 P.M. British time;
> General Percival states cause was shortage of water, food, petrol, ammunition;
> Estimated 55,000-60,000 British and Imperial troops captured

It was one of the most humiliating defeats ever suffered by British arms. Winston Churchill was saddened but defiant: "I speak to you," he told the House of Commons, "under the shadow of a heavy and far-reaching military defeat. It is a British and Imperial defeat. Singapore has fallen. All the Malay Peninsula has been overrun. . . . This . . . is one of those moments when the British race and nation can show their quality and their genius. . . . We must remember that we are no longer alone. We are in the midst of a great company. Three-quarters of the human race are now moving with us. The whole future of mankind may depend upon our action and upon our conduct. So far we have not failed. We shall not fail now. Let us move forward steadfastly together into the storm and through the storm."

RETREAT IN BURMA

Next on the Japanese timetable was British Burma, land of Buddhist temples, tinkling bells, coolie labor, and precious stones.

For hundreds of years a petty battleground of minor princes, Burma in World War II became world-important largely because of the 800-mile

Burma Road, vital supply line to China. This famed road had circumvented the areas held by Japan and, in effect, meant the opening of a back door into China.

Burma is slightly larger than Texas. Stretching along the eastern side of the Bay of Bengal, it is a hilly jungle country broken up on three sides by mountain ranges. A neglected ward of the British Empire, Burma had no land communications with India because of the opposition of monopolistic shipping interests. The main port of Rangoon, celebrated in Kipling's "Mandalay," was at the mercy of the dominant sea power in the vicinity. Burmese natives had little faith in either the British or the British slogan, "Keep cool and trust us." Inside Burma a pro-Japanese fifth column industriously prepared for invasion.

The Japanese assault on Burma was synchronized with that on Malaya, but it was to take somewhat longer because the country was larger. Two days after Pearl Harbor, advance Japanese units penetrated the Burmese border at the Isthmus of Kra. The main strike came on January 15, 1942, when a powerful force of shock troops infiltrated through the jungles and in two weeks captured Moulmein, opposite Rangoon on the Gulf of Martaban.

Meanwhile, a second Japanese force pushed through North Burma from the Shan States against Moulmein and Rangoon, then subsequently north on Lashio, the terminus of the Burma Road. Once again Japanese mobility and proficiency in jungle fighting paid big dividends.

Crossing the broad Salween River, the Japanese circled around to the north of Rangoon, while other units slipped across the Gulf of Martaban to hit the city from the south and west. On March 6, 1942, the British evacuated the great port. All essential demolitions were completed before the Japanese entered Rangoon the next day.

Through the next two months there was a desperate game of hide-and-seek. The persistent Nipponese advanced along the Irrawaddy, Sittang, and Salween rivers, pushing the British toward the borders of India and China and the Himalayan foothills. Two divisions of British and Indian troops, preceded by a horde of refugees, escaped along obscure jungle trails to Bengal. Hampered by mechanized armor unsuitable for jungle fighting, outmaneuvered, outfought, and exhausted, the British Imperials were no match for the Japanese. It was Malaya all over again.

Meanwhile, help came from Lieutenant General Joseph W. ("Vinegar Joe") Stilwell, Chiang Kai-shek's newly appointed (March 10, 1942) chief of staff, who came down from the north to take command of the 5th and 6th Chinese armies in Burma. Stilwell made the mistake of staying too long in South Burma, where he was cut off from the Burma Road by the Japanese force entering Burma from Thailand. His problem now was to press northward faster than the Japanese could outflank him.

In May 1942 came the epic 21-day retreat. Hampered by the all but impenetrable jungle, lashed by torrential rains, attacked by king cobras and vipers, sloshing through rivers and streams, pushing up and down steep mountains, Stilwell's ragged force managed to escape into Assam. Many died on the way. It was one of the most bitter retreats of modern times, ranking with the Long March of the Chinese Communists in physical hardship and sustained effort. When General Stilwell burst out of the jungle with his ragged followers he made a frank appraisal: "The Japs ran us out of Burma. We took a hell of a beating!"

By mid-May 1942 most of Burma was under Japanese control. Some four-fifths of the British Imperials were safely evacuated, their heavy equipment left behind. Worse, the Burma Road was now sealed off. In August 1942 the Japanese set up a puppet government in Burma.

With the Burma Road closed the problem of how to send supplies to Chiang Kai-shek became critical. One solution was a spectacular airlift over the forbidding Himalayan barrier between India and China to Kunming, from which the supplies could be transported by land to the Chinese at Chungking. The trick was to veer north to evade Japanese Zeros based in Burma. Hardy American pilots in unarmed C-47 transport planes, pioneer covered wagons of the air, made the dangerous five-hour journey over the "Hump," Himalayan peaks rising to 24,000 feet. In May 1942 only 80 tons of supplies were delivered in this fashion; by February 1943 some 3,200 tons were brought across the Hump. It was far too little.

The disappointed Allied world could take some consolation from the performance of Allied airmen. This at least gave some indication of what was coming in the future.

In 1937, in the early days of the fighting against Japan, Chiang Kai-shek had engaged as China's civilian adviser for air training a slightly deaf, outspoken, hard-bitten American officer, Claire L. Chennault, who had just been retired from the Army at the age of 47 for medical reasons. His job was to whip the Chinese hodgepodge of an air force into battle trim. He had some rather unorthodox ideas about air fighting that had embroiled him in bitter disputes with conservative military leaders in Washington.

In 1941 Chennault came home to recruit American volunteers to fight for China. He raised and trained a group of pilots officially known as the American Volunteer Group. But to the delighted Chinese these flamboyant, devil-may-care pilots became known as Flying Tigers, and the name persisted. Chennault himself became "Old Leatherface" to his Chinese friends.

Chennault set up headquarters 150 miles from Rangoon. He never had more than 49 obsolete combat planes in action at any one time nor more than 70 trained pilots under his command (they were paid $600 a month and $500 a kill). The Flying Tigers proved to be a thorn in the side of the Japanese.

For 65 precious days they operated in two-plane teams, and tenaciously held the Burma Road while tons of supplies were rushed to China.

This tiny but scrappy air force exploded the myth of Japanese aerial invincibility. In the seven months after Pearl Harbor, from December 19, 1941, to July 4, 1942, by official count, the Flying Tigers destroyed 297 Japanese planes, racked up 300 probables, and killed 1,500 Japanese. Equally important, they kept the jittery Nipponese off balance and upset Tokyo's timetable for the subjugation of China.

Eventually, the Flying Tigers were incorporated into the U.S. Fourteenth Air Force under Chennault. In this capacity Chennault became responsible to Lieutenant General Joseph W. Stilwell, commander for a time of the whole China-Burma-India theatre of war. At once there were snarling conflicts between the two, which finally ended in Chennault's retirement. Vinegar Joe, a great infantry soldier, regarded the airplane as merely another means of transportation. ("Think, man," Stilwell shouted at Chennault, "it's the ground soldier slogging through the mud and fighting in the trenches who will win the war." "But goddammit, Stilwell," Chennault shot back, "there aren't any men in the trenches!")

When he was trapped in Burma, Stilwell refused to be flown out: "The Air Force didn't bring me here and it doesn't have to fly me out. I'll walk." Stilwell then embarked on his epic retreat through the jungle, that heroic but miserable journey which the Air Force regarded as altogether unnecessary.

JAVA AND AUSTRALIA

The Japanese octopus now spread its tentacles toward Australia and its 7,000,000 inhabitants. But first it had to grasp the island of Java, lying between the Java Sea on the north and the Indian Ocean on the south. The most important island and the most populous of the Dutch East Indies, Java was rich in rice, quinine, oil, and manganese. It was defended by a not-altogether reliable native force of 100,000, plus some obsolete planes, several Dutch destroyers and submarines, remnants of the American fleet that had escaped from the Philippines, and several British and Australian warships. An American attempt to strengthen the defense of Java turned into a major loss when the U.S. tender *Langley*, carrying fighter planes for Java, was sunk by Japanese bombers.

The Nipponese proceeded warily. On December 24, 1941, a small force landed at Luching and a week later another army stormed ashore at Brunei, both in British North Borneo, and captured the oil fields there. At the same time, because of British resistance at Singapore, the Japanese turned farther east, driving in to the northern coastline of New Guinea and landing troops at Rabaul in New Britain.

The first Japanese strike at Java came through the Macassar Straits. There, on January 23-28, 1942, four American destroyers, assisted by units of the Dutch navy, inflicted serious losses on an enemy convoy. The damage was stated as 15 transports sunk, 22 damaged.

But the victory was only momentary. At the end of February 1942 a motley Allied fleet, consisting of five cruisers and nine destroyers, all under command of Dutch Admiral Helfrich, set out to challenge two Japanese flotillas, both of which were superior in numbers and firepower. The Battle of the Java Sea, the last Allied effort to save Java, was a catastrophe for the Allies. This entire fleet fell to the overpowering Japanese. The battle began on February 27 in the late afternoon and lasted for three days until the whole Allied force was wiped out.

An Admiralty communiqué issued on March 14, 1942, gave the losses as follows: 5 cruisers, H.M.S. *Exeter*, H.M.A.S. *Perth*, U.S. *Houston*, Dutch *Java* and *de Ruyter*; 6 destroyers, H.M.S. *Electra*, *Jupiter*, *Encounter*, *Stronghold*, U.S. *Pope*, Dutch *Kortenaer*; 1 sloop, H.M.A.S. *Yarra*. Japanese losses were not known.

A day after the Battle of the Java Sea the Japanese landed in three places in Java: at Bantam near Batavia, at Indramayu (mid-Java), and at Rembang (110 miles from Surabaya), the last big oil center in the Netherlands East Indies. There was nothing now to stop the conquest of all Java.

Soon after the fall of Singapore, the Japanese completed the subjugation of Sumatra, thus shutting Java off from the west. Then came the conquest of Java. Once again, as at Bataan, Singapore, and Rangoon, the Japanese invaders pushed inexorably ahead. This time they were served by many well-paved roads over which they rushed in record time. By March 9, 1942, all the Netherlands East Indies surrendered, relinquishing 98,000 prisoners to the triumphant Japanese. Dr. Van Mook, Lieutenant Governor General of the Netherlands East Indies, escaped to Australia, where he informed the press: "We are here to collect all the forces we can. . . . There should be an end to destroying and retreating."

Australia was an attractive plum for the Japanese. Possession of this great island-continent, 2,974,581 square miles, would round out the Japanese New Order in the Pacific. As early as February 1942 the Nipponese bombed Port Darwin, the only major naval base in North Australia. During the next two months, the Japanese methodically tried to isolate the great continent from the north, occupying New Britain, New Ireland, the Admiralty Islands, the Gilbert Islands, and parts of New Guinea.

Australia alone could not stem the tide of Japanese conquest. General MacArthur, who arrived there on March 17, 1942, immediately began to set up a defense system. Heavy military and naval reinforcements began to flow in from the United States.

Meanwhile, some Japanese strategists called for abandonment of the attempt to invade North Australia and for striking instead against Sydney and Melbourne on the southeastern coast. Holding these great cities, they would await at their leisure the fall of the rest of the continent. Next would come the cutting of the American-Australian lifeline at New Caledonia and New Zealand.

For six months thc triumphant Japanese had pushed pell-mell through Allied defenses in the Pacific. Enough was enough. Both British and Americans were sick to death of the long series of ignominious retreats.

In the first week of May 1942, American observation planes discovered a heavy concentration of enemy shipping in the Coral Sea separating Australia from the Solomon Islands. The naval and air battle had already begun off the Solomon Islands when part of the Japanese invasion fleet was intercepted by U.S. naval and air forces. The battle was resumed on May 7-8 in the Coral Sea.

The great Battle of the Coral Sea was the first naval engagement in history in which surface ships did not exchange a shot. On May 9 the Japanese fleet withdrew northward, presumably to join the main concentration of Nipponese shipping power. But not before American planes from the *Lexington* and *Yorktown* had sunk seven major enemy warships: the Japanese carrier *Ryukyu*, four cruisers, and two destroyers, while heavily damaging another carrier, three cruisers, and three destroyers.

American losses, too, were heavy, including the carrier *Lexington*, one destroyer, and one tanker. Although both forces withdrew simultaneously, the U.S. had begun to cork up Japanese expansion.

JAPAN AT FLOOD CREST

The Battle of the Coral Sea was the Japanese high-water mark.

For the time being the war lords of Tokyo had to be content to digest their glutting gains. They had chalked up a remarkable score—in six months they had acquired control of a huge empire over 3,000 miles of ocean, with millions of square miles of land and millions of people, a vast area running west to east between India and Hawaii and north to south from Siberia to Australia. More, in a bold jump they had occupied Attu and Kiska, the westernmost isles of the Aleutian Archipelago, from which they could threaten Alaska and even mainland North America.

The master plan seemed to be working to perfection. Time after time the Japanese had appeared at critical points with overwhelming superiority, operating from bases reckoned only hundreds of miles from Tokyo, while the Americans had to move their forces in terms of thousands of miles. It was truly a phenomenal expansion—and no one could predict its end.

The fall of the Philippines, Malaya, Burma, and the Dutch East Indies brought the red sun of Japan into dangerous proximity to India. Already the Andaman Islands in the Bay of Bengal were in Japanese hands.

What about India? London was concerned about the deterioration in Anglo-Indian relations and the possibility that India might be next on the Japanese timetable. The Indian army and Indian industry had been contributing to the British war effort, but at the same time there was a widespread sentiment of defeatism and disillusion throughout the counry. Agitators claimed that the British were using the war as an excuse to postpone indefinitely any progress toward Indian independence. In London there was resentment when it was reported that Indians had given substantial aid to the Japanese in Burma.

In March 1942 the British government sent Sir Stafford Cripps to Delhi to mend British fences in India. He was authorized to suggest to Indian leaders that immediately after the war there would be created a self-governing Indian Union, with Dominion status, the right to secede from the Commonwealth, and a constitution to be drafted by the Indians themselves. But Cripps made it clear that, as long as the war lasted, the British government of India, the Viceroy and his assistants, must and would retain responsibility for Indian defense.

The discussions were long and exhaustive. Mohammed Ali Jinnah and the Moslem League at first seemed favorably disposed toward the offer. But the Hindu Indian Nationalists, or Congress Party, flatly demanded independence "here and now." Mahatma Gandhi, long-time thorn in the paw of the British lion, dismissed the offer as "a postdated check on a bank that is obviously crashing," and called for a revived campaign of noncoöperation with Britain and nonresistance to Japan. There were wild riots, which subsided only after Gandhi and other Indian leaders were arrested and clapped into jail.

The Cripps mission failed to focus Indian public opinion against Japan. India continued to fight on the Allied side without much enthusiasm but with the belief that after the war the victorious Allies might be inclined to support her demand for independence.

CHAPTER 12

The United States at War

> ***. . . Sail on, O Ship of State!***
> ***Sail on, O Union, strong and great!***
> ***Humanity with all its fears,***
> ***With all the hopes of future years,***
> ***Is hanging breathless on thy fate!***
>
> **—Henry Wadsworth Longfellow,**
> **"The Building of the Ship"**

BEHEMOTH: FORGING THE TOOLS OF VICTORY

Pearl Harbor brought the United States into the war as a totally involved participant. Until this point the defense program had been limited to the continental United States and strategic parts of the Western Hemisphere. In May 1940 the United States had only a small regular army, a one-ocean navy, and a modest air force. Now, with war on a dozen global fronts, it became necessary to revamp civilian peacetime economy. President Roosevelt's four-point program—increased defenses, domestic preparations, hemisphere solidarity, and Lend-Lease—went into high gear.

Swift steps were taken to provide the necessary men. Manpower resources were placed by executive order in the hands of a nine-man War Manpower Commission (W.M.C.), established in April 1942. The draft age was lowered to 18, and all males between 18 and 38 were subjected to selective service, with deferments limited to war industries, agriculture, the clergy, and hardship cases. An army of 12,000,000 men (and 200,000 women) was organized, equipped, and trained. Equally phenomenal was the expansion of naval construction and air power. The United States emerged as a Great Power equipped to maintain parity with any nation, on land, sea, or air.

The first and immediate concern was control of the seas. "It is only by shipping," said Churchill in a secret session of the British Parliament in 1942, "that the United States or indeed we ourselves can intervene either in the eastern or the western theatre." Almost overnight appeared a tremendous bridge of ships, without which the Allies could neither have continued the struggle nor survived. The United States became the leading shipbuilding nation of the world, producing 28,000,000 gross tons from January 1, 1942, to the end of the war, thereby easily replacing the 21,000,000 tons lost to enemy action. By 1945 the United States and Britain, despite losses, had more merchant shipping than had existed in the entire world in 1939. The Americans, reducing the period of construction from 30 to seven weeks, produced Liberty ships in sections, put them together like automobiles on assembly lines.

Over this bridge of ships millions of tons of war materials were ferried to Britain. The convoy system was so successful that of 17,000 vessels sailing under American naval protection only 17 were sunk by U-boats. Giant liners, the *Queen Elizabeth*, the *Queen Mary*, and others, transported more than 200,000 troops in five years without sighting a submarine.

The home front was protected by rigid security measures. There was little trouble from the dissident political groups. During the period of neutrality American Communists had been violently antiwar. But when Hitler invaded Russia, they became zealous supporters of the Allied cause and consistently supported the government in its war measures.

The problem of the A.J.A.'s (Americans of Japanese Ancestry) in both Hawaii and California was handled unwisely and clumsily, especially on the mainland. The A.J.A.'s were divided into the *Issei*, born in Japan and ineligible for American citizenship, and the *Nisei*, the second generation, American-born and American citizens by virtue of the Fourteenth Amendment. In addition, there were some of the third generation, or *Sansei*.

In Hawaii the A.J.A.'s numbered fully a third of the population. Grave fears were expressed as to what they would do in the event of a Japanese invasion. There were demands that all be interned or be sent to the mainland, but they were needed for the labor supply and were allowed to remain in their homes. As it turned out, the Hawaiian Japanese soon revealed their intention of remaining loyally at work. They participated in every type of defense activity and worked hard to prove their patriotism.

In California the Americans of Japanese descent constituted only a small part of the population, under two per cent. But here, in response to a public outcry about espionage and sabotage, all the Japanese in California, aliens and citizens alike, were removed from the immediate vicinity of the West Coast. Under military orders they were sent to "relocation camps," hastily constructed in the interior. Here they lived under far from satisfactory conditions. The entire move was ill-advised, unreasonable, unfair, unnecessary. The Japanese evacuees, with few exceptions, conducted themselves in a dignified manner. Those A.J.A.'s who fought in the American army compiled a superb record, despite what amounted to petty persecution of their families.

In June 1942 the Federal Bureau of Investigation arrested eight Nazi saboteurs who had been landed by U-boat on the Long Island and Florida coasts. All eight were convicted by secret military tribunal; six were electrocuted and the other two were given long prison terms. On July 23, 1942, 28 individuals, including among others William Dudley Pelley and Gerald Winrod, were indicted as seditionists (the indictments were dismissed in 1946 and the Department of Justice was rebuked by the court for "lack of diligence" in prosecution). But so effective was the work against saboteurs and fifth columnists that the United States, unlike other countries, had virtually no difficulties with internal enemies.

The industrial economy was strengthened by special attention to rationing and price controls. Rationing was begun on December 27, 1941, first with automobile tires, and then extended to sugar, coffee, gasoline, meat, fats and oils, butter, cheese, processed foods, and shoes. The Office of Price Administration (O.P.A.), established on January 30, 1942, fixed price ceilings on all commodities with the exception of farm products and set up rent controls in defense areas.

To meet the labor shortage, President Roosevelt, on February 9, 1943, decreed a minimum work week of 48 hours, with time-and-a-half for the extra eight hours. On April 8, 1942, the War Manpower Commission froze 27,000,000 workers in their jobs, and the President issued a hold-the-line order freezing prices, wages, and salaries. The Smith-Connally Anti-Strike Act, June 25, 1943, made strikes illegal in plants seized by the government, and unions were held liable for damage suits for failure to give 30 days' notice of intention to strike in war industries.

Top priority was given to the business of strangling the enemy's industries. A series of specially appointed agencies went to work on a classified system of specific allocations of all strategic war materials. The Anglo-American Blockade Committee systematically starved the German economy by cutting off key commodities. The Germans desperately offered a hundred times the peacetime prices for such irreplaceable industrial items as diamonds for cutting tools, tungsten, platinum, and ball bearings. By preclusive purchasing, buying regardless of price, the Allies prevented the enemy from obtaining these critical industrial materials. Spain, Portugal, Turkey, Switzerland, and Sweden, which might have furnished such materials, were discouraged by the threat of blacklisting.

Astronomical was the multiplication of American production. It was said to be one of the wonders of the modern world, but this "miracle of production" could be traced to three bedrock elements that went into it: higher prices; more people at work; longer hours of work. On January 13, 1942, President Roosevelt appointed Donald M. Nelson as chairman of the War Production Board (W.P.B.) to mobilize the nation's resources for the total war effort. From tens of thousands of factories working around the clock came finished tools of war, more war materiel than produced by the rest of the world combined. It was an awesome example of audacious planning, mass activity, prodigious energy. Industrial leaders and millions of workers labored in harmony in the most gigantic production program in the history of mankind. There could be no slowdowns with the sons of both rich and poor at the battlefronts.

The days of business as usual were past. Within a year after Pearl Harbor the United States was equaling the entire Axis war production though the latter had a decade's head start. By 1943 the Americans were far ahead. By the end of the war the United States had produced 296,601 planes, 87,000 tanks, 2,434,553 trucks, 17,400,000 rifles, 315,000 pieces of field artillery, and 4,200,000 tons of artillery shells. Those were the figures that meant destruction of the Axis.

It was a costly process, placing a tremendous burden upon American credit. By the end of the war the national debt had risen from $50,000,000,000 to over $250,000,000,000, and the annual budget from $10,000,000,000 to $100,000,000,000. Before the United States went to war, 90 per cent of the national revenue had been allocated to civilian needs; by the end of the war, with a budget increased tenfold, the figures were reversed and 90 per cent of the enormous American production was being devoted to war needs. Tax rates spiraled to meet these huge costs; the American people borrowed against future income to pay for the war.

Further steps were taken to strengthen hemisphere solidarity. At the Rio de Janeiro Conference, January 15–28, 1942, the representatives of 21 American republics voted to recommend to their respective governments a break in diplomatic relations with the Axis. There was one discordant note—on August 16, 1944, the United States froze Argentina's gold assets in the United States because of that nation's refusal to coöperate fully against the Axis. In March 1942 air bases were established in Guatemala to defend the Panama Canal Zone. There were friendly greetings between President Roosevelt and President Getulio Vargas of Brazil (January 28, 1942), and between President Roosevelt and President Avila Camacho of Mexico (April 21, 1942).

Lend-Lease mounted steadily. The record was astounding. By April 1944 some $30,000,000,000 had been spent, of which $20,000,000,000 went to the British, $4,000,000,000 to Soviet Russia, $2,000,000,000 to Latin America, and $500,000,000 to China. At this time, of every dollar the United States was spending to fight the Axis, 14 cents went to Lend-Lease. At the end of the war the total of Lend-Lease amounted to the astronomical figure of $50,226,845,387.

To Britain went over 25,000,000 tons of construction supplies, $1,000,-000,000 worth of ordnance, the same amount in tanks and military vehicles, 5,750,000 tons of steel, 500,000 tons of other metals, several hundred thousand tons of high explosives.

To Soviet Russia, over dangerous sea and land routes, went a total of $4,750,000,000 in war matériel. Without this stream of supplies Soviet Russia might not have survived Hitler's blows.

The effects of Lend-Lease were felt on every battlefield on the globe--in Soviet Russia, the Middle East, China, India, the South Pacific. The Axis was literally engulfed under a sea of American war production. Equally important were the tremendous supplies of foodstuffs sent to the Allies. In the spring of 1941, when there were only a few weeks of reserve rations in England, the first Lend-Lease ship carrying cheese, evaporated milk, and eggs appeared in British waters at precisely the critical moment.

Lend-Lease was not entirely a one-way affair. The process in reverse increased steadily as the war went on. The Allies on their part supplied the United States with goods and services valued at nearly $8,000,000,000. By the middle of 1944 the British had repaid more than $2,000,000,000 in supplies given our troops abroad. The Russians repaid by silently pointing to the mounds of Nazi corpses on Soviet soil.

CHAPTER **13**

New World of the Triumphant Axis

This hand, to tyrants ever sworn the foe,
For Freedom only deals the deadly blow;
Then sheathes in calm repose the vengeful blade,
For gentle peace in Freedom's hallowed shade.

—John Quincy Adams, *Written in an Album*, 1842

France has lost a battle, she has not lost the war.

—General Charles de Gaulle, from London, June 18, 1940

HITLER'S NEW ORDER IN EUROPE

For the Allies 1942 was a year of dismay. Hitler was on the way to enclosing the entire Mediterranean and the Near East in a huge vise. Then, moving eastward, he would establish contact with the Japanese, who had themselves already carved out a huge Pacific empire.

Few people then knew, wrote General George C. Marshall later, "how close Germany and Japan were to complete domination of the world" and "how thin the spread of Allied survival has been stretched."

There was a glimmering hope. By 1942, 28 nations, representing Europe, Asia, and both Americas, had joined the Western-Soviet war against the Axis. All were pledged to fight to the end against the Axis and under no circumstances to sign a separate peace. To this great combination President Roosevelt gave the name United Nations. Before the end of the war another 21 nations joined the coalition against the Axis.

Germany was still powerful. In April 1942 the *Wehrmacht* had between 260 and 300 divisions (25 armored or tank divisions, 35 motorized divisions, at least 200 infantry divisions, from 4–8 airborne divisions), altogether between 7,000,000 and 10,000,000 troops. In the German Navy there were a half-dozen battleships, at least a dozen cruisers, two carriers, 30 to 40 destroyers, and from 125 to 175 submarines. In the *Luftwaffe* there were from five to seven air fleets with well over 5,000 tactical planes. And best of all from Hitler's viewpoint these men were thoroughly trained, efficient, and in high morale. The incredible dream of Hitler's *Mein Kampf*, once dismissed as the ravings of a megalomaniac, seemed to be on the way to realization. In the fall of 1942, as the war swung into its fourth year, the little man of Berchtesgaden was even more satisfied with the way things were going.

With great glee the *Fuehrer* harangued his cronies on the status of the New Order of the Greater German Reich. He intimated that he himself, the greatest German of all time, was well on the way to becoming the undisputed master of Europe, of a self-sufficient, self-sustaining continent, unconquerable from the outside, secure under the tyranny inside, an impregnable fortress that would last a thousand years. And in the future there was the delectable prospect of world power. The Germans would no longer be a *Volk ohne Raum* (a people without space).

In sole command would be the self-confident Teutonic *Herrenvolk*, a monolithic ruling class, lords of the earth. They alone would control continental industry, the huge estates, the great fortresses, the new *Autobahnen*, superhighways spreading like the key lines of a spider web from one end of Europe to another.

Beneath the Germanic Aryan-Nordic masters would be two-score occupied nations, all organized like medieval fiefs for the benefit of the master race. The lowly *Hilfsvolk*, "the helping people," 250,000,000 serfs, would do the dirty work for their lords and masters. Starved and submissive, these inferior human beings would be given just enough education to read directions. Denied medical attention, they would eventually die off, and good riddance.

To Nazi Germany flowed a huge supply of labor, materials, and money—workers from France and Belgium, foodstuffs from Denmark, oil from Rumania, grain and coal from Poland. Europeans watched helplessly as their young men, machinery, horses, cattle, and grain were systematically expropriated, piled into endless trains, and sent to the heartland of the Teutonic "master race." In one year alone the German confiscation of property by seizure, fines, and reparations reached a total of $36,000,000,000. It was plundering on an unprecedented scale. Those historic loot-players, the Huns, the Vandals, the Goths, were, in comparison, mere pin-money operators.

There were many favorable signs for the *Fuehrer*'s personal astrologer. It seemed that Hitler had suppressed the resistance movement and had driven it underground. He had so heavily fortified the whole Atlantic coastline from Norway to the Pyrenees that any attempt to storm it was almost certain to meet disaster. His sea-sharks were devouring enemy shipping at a highly satisfactory rate. He saw no prospect of a second Allied front in the west. He had inflicted one reverse after another on his enemies. In North Africa his desert troops were only a few miles from Alexandria, and the conquest of Egypt seemed inevitable.

True, Hitler had failed to take Leningrad and Moscow in the east. That was regrettable. But he had one foot in Stalingrad and he would soon sweep up the Volga to drive on Moscow from the east. Any sensible person could see that it was only a matter of time! His armies were already deep in the oil-rich Caucasus; he had won the Maikop oil fields; he would cut the American supply route in the Middle East to Soviet Russia; and then he would make a juncture with honorable, honorary Aryan allies, the Japanese.

No liberating reforms, like those of the French Revolution and Napoleon, followed in the wake of German conquest. *Divide et impera!* Hitler knew how to divide the occupied nations and rule them by force.

The *Fuehrer* revived the national differences between Czechs and Slovaks, between Flemings and Walloons, between Serbs and Croats, and played one against the other. He treated each nation according to its value for his war machine, its "racial" character, and the degree of resistance it had shown to him in the past. He gave those peoples who produced food and war materiel for Germany a strict but orderly administration. Thus, the Danes, who rated as good Nordics, were granted what amounted to German citizenship and were honored by being taken into the Anti-Comintern Pact. But those who incurred his wrath he treated with unparalleled brutality.

Hitler split his New Order into several categories of variedly governed areas. First were the territories annexed and incorporated into the Third Reich. Subjected to Nazi *Gleichschaltung* (coördination) were Austria, the Sudetenland, Alsace-Lorraine, Memel, Danzig, Teschen, Eupen, Malmédy, Luxemburg, parts of Slovenia, and areas of East and West Prussia.

Next were the two territories, Czechoslovakia and Poland, neither incorporated into Germany but regarded as parts of a Greater Germany. Hitler had only contempt for the Czechs, whose country he had dismembered before the war. The central portion of Czechoslovakia became an autonomous area known as the Protectorate of Bohemia-Moravia, administered by a Reich Protector, and designed for future colonization.

In Czechoslovakia the *Gestapo* began a policy of terror against civilians, a campaign that rose to a horrible climax. In 1941 Hitler replaced Baron Konstantin von Neurath with Reinhard Heydrich as Reich Protector of Bohemia and Moravia. Heydrich, in his late thirties, had originally been a naval officer but had been expelled from the officer corps for "conduct unbecoming to an officer and a gentleman" in connection with a young girl. A vicious sadist, he went to extremes in his assignment to frighten the Czechs into submission.

Driven to desperation, Czech patriots on May 27, 1942, attempted to assassinate Heydrich. The assailants escaped and the Germans decreed a state of emergency in the Protectorate. On June 4 Heydrich died of his wounds. Six days later, the German authorities, suspecting that Lidice harbored the killers, wiped out the entire village. Every male adult was murdered and the women and children were dispersed throughout central Europe.

The Nazis admitted the massacre, one of the most ruthless reprisals in history. They were never allowed to forget it.

Hitler reserved his most brutal treatment for the Poles. They were, he said, a subspecies of mankind, the scum of the earth, fit only for the conqueror's boot. He incorporated the western parts of Poland into Greater Germany and set up the central provinces as the Government General of Poland under the whiplash administration of Hans Frank. He saw to it that Poland's political and intellectual leaders were systematically slaughtered.

To the next group of countries, considered of strategic importance, Hitler sent his personal satraps. Occupied France and the British Channel Islands (occupied by the Germans on June 30–July 1, 1940) he placed under the administration of General Otto von Stuelpnagel (1940–1942) and then of General Karl Friedrich von Stuelpnagel (1944–1945). General *Freiherr* Alexander von Falkenhausen was sent to govern Belgium and a section of northern France.

Another category included those countries under semicivilian, supposedly autonomous, rule. Norway was placed under Reich Commissioner Joseph Terboven, assisted by the oily collaborationist Vidkun Quisling; Holland under Reich Commissioner Artur von Seyss-Inquart.

To the Ostland and the Ukraine were sent German commissioners responsible to Alfred Rosenberg, Nazi philosopher and special Reich Minister for Eastern Occupied Territories. Denmark was allowed to retain her own monarch and parliament.

The pattern of Nazi occupation was repeated in the Balkans. A rigid pro-Nazi regime was established in 1941 in Yugoslavia, after large portions of the country were awarded to neighboring Italy, Hungary, and Bulgaria. Hungary was given half of Transylvania; Bulgaria was awarded parts of Serbia, Thrace, and the Dobruja; and Rumania was given Transnistria. An Italian vice-regent was sent to administer Albania.

Throughout this patchwork of annexed, occupied, and controlled satellite states, Hitler sent Nazi raiding squads to replenish labor for the German war effort. Invading homes, appearing suddenly at street corners and railroad station, the S.S. (*Schutz-Staffeln* squads, the "élite," disciplined, black-shirted Nazi bodyguards assigned to special missions) indiscriminately rounded up thousands, herded them to assembly points, and then shipped them like cattle, in freight cars without elementary sanitation, back to the Reich.

Inside Germany, under the whip of their masters, the captives were forced to make munitions, repair roads, mine coal, work in the fields. Nearly 5,000,000 unfortunates, of whom about 1,000,000 were Poles, were imported into Germany, where they were housed in primitive camps, fed just enough to maintain life, and forced to undergo unspeakable tortures. Regularly flogged, the slave laborers endured all the insults their sadistic guards could invent.

For the Jews of Europe the New Order was literally hell on earth. As conqueror of Europe, Hitler translated his psychopathic hatred of the Jews into a vast and terrible pogrom. To him, as to his intellectual and emotional master, the great composer, Richard Wagner, the Jews were "the plastic demons of the decline of mankind." First in Poland and later in Germany the Jews were subjected to a campaign of vilification, torture, and annihilation without parallel in the story of civilization. More than 400,000 Jews died of blows, bullets, disease, or hunger in and around Warsaw during the Nazi occupation. From February 1940 to June 1942 the entire Jewish community was systematically humiliated and eventually exterminated.

In a diary kept by one of the victims appeared this entry: "An eight-year old child went mad. Screamed, 'I want to steal, I want to rob, I want to eat, I want to become a German!'" In the piercing cry of this child, in this horrible perversion of the will-to-survive, was epitomized the grotesqueness, the moral atrophy, the vileness of Hitler's New Order. This was human existence at its nadir.

The policy of genocide, the attempted destruction of whole ethnic groups, was one of the cardinal Nazi sins against mankind. A generation reared to question the too-often fabricated atrocity tales of World War I became only slowly aware of the real German horrors of World War II. Not until after the war was the whole rotten story of mass extermination told.

RASCALS AND MOUNTEBANKS: THE COLLABORATORS

Ambitious men, intoxicated by the success of Nazi arms, flocked to the standard of the crooked cross.

It was a variegated lot of scoundrels and adventurers. In Holland there were Anton Adrian Mussert, leader of the Dutch Fascists, and Rost van Tonningen; in Belgium it was Léon Degrelle, founder of the Rexist Party, Fascists; in Denmark the chief of the Nazi fifth column was Fritz Clausen; in Finland there were the pro-Nazi president, Rysto Ryti, and a temporary resident, the Norwegian Knut Hamsun, world-famous novelist known for his portrayals of life among farmers and laborers.

To patriots the most contemptible recreant of all was Major Vidkun Quisling, who contributed his name to similar traitors and fifth columnists. Head of the Norwegian Nazis, Quisling had been minister of war for a brief period in 1932–1933. In this position he had appointed a number of pro-Nazi garrison commanders who promptly surrendered their charges to the Germans when Hitler invaded Norway in April 1940. Hitler rewarded him by making him puppet ruler of Norway. As totalitarian proconsul, Quisling ruled Norway for more than four years, only to be executed after the war by his countrymen.

Who can say what were the motives of the band of quislings, who, unlike the majority of their countrymen, accepted the perverted ideology of Nazism? There were probably many reasons. Some turncoats were convinced Fascists, who decided it was wise to ride the wave of the future. Others were power-mad men who believed that Hitler was invincible and that it would be both advisable and profitable to mount the Nazi bandwagon. Some concluded that the best way for their country to ride out the tornado of Hitlerism was to compromise with the invaders and accept a subservient status until help could come from the West. Still others saw in collaboration the most effective way to combat Bolshevism. Finally, there were the confused and bewildered who against their will were impressed into service by their Nazi masters.

Vichy France was the classic home of large-scale collaboration. On June 14, 1940, the cabinet of Paul Reynaud resigned under the onus of military defeat, whereupon the collaborators assumed control. Marshal Henri Pétain, venerated hero of Verdun, the great battle of World War I, became premier, with Pierre Laval as foreign secretary, and Admiral Jean François Darlan as minister of marine. The government sued for an armistice with Germany, signed on June 22, 1940, which split France into a northern section occupied by the Germans and a southern area under French administration with its capital at Vichy.

On July 10, 1940, the Chamber of Deputies and the Senate, in joint session as the National Assembly, awarded unlimited power to Marshal Pétain by a vote of 569–80. As Chief of the State, Pétain abolished the presidency, sent the Chamber and Senate home indefinitely (he could not eliminate them altogether), and set up Vichy France as a corporative state.

Marshal Pétain's "national revolution" rejected the old watchwords of "Liberty, Equality, Fraternity" in favor of the new totalitarian ideology of "Work, Family, Fatherland." Vichy France, taking the path of collaboration with Nazi Germany, became an undisguised police state with the usual secret police, imprisonments without trial, deportations, and executions. There was the familiar pattern of coördination: the press was gagged; censorship and controls were instituted; strikes and lockouts were made illegal; youth organizations were set up under state control, as in Germany and Austria; laws were promulgated against the Jews.

Hard on the heels of the conquering Germans came experts of the "Economic Mobile Units," ordered to strip French industry for the benefit of the Third Reich. Nazi thinking ran along these lines—since France was slated to be an agricultural storehouse in Hitler's New Order, she would not need any machinery to make luxury items for export throughout the world. The Germans left intact those factories which they could use for their own ends.

"France," proclaimed one of Hitler's economic experts, "must remain agricultural. We shall move her industry to the Ruhr, leaving her unburdened by mechanical things. The New Order cannot tolerate misfits."

How was it possible for France, home of the Enlightenment, of democracy, liberalism, egalitarianism, constitutionalism, tolerance, and decency, to descend to this lowly status as Hitler's lackey? The defeat of their armies had left Frenchmen confused, bewildered, stupefied. Many turned to Vichy because the situation seemed to provide for no alternative. Hitler held some 2,000,000 French prisoners of war, whom he used to blackmail the French people into acquiescence. Frenchmen wanted to save these men, as well as Paris and other French cities, from German vengeance.

There is another explanation, perhaps a bit more subtle. There had always been a strong minority of Frenchmen who continued to believe in those principles of authority (veneration of the strong man) and discipline (obedience to the strong man) they associated with the Old Regime and the Napoleonic legend. The liberal-democratic ideology of 1789, 1848, and 1875 had clashed repeatedly with the authoritarian tradition of Napoleon Bonaparte and Louis Napoleon. In Pétain and Vichy these minority Frenchmen saw an answer to their hopes. France would not forever remain under German control, they reasoned, but would eventually seek its own way along authoritarian lines. Hence, they would support Vichy until the current unpleasantness was over and Frenchmen could get out from under the German heel. They would accept the transitory situation and look hopefully to a better future.

To the enraged resistance fighters of the underground this was the way of treason. They would have none of it.

RESISTANCE: OCCUPIED EUROPE HITS BACK

With the European Continent in his hands, Hitler was offered an opportunity such as had been accorded few men in the past.

But the German *Fuehrer* made a fundamental mistake. Had he offered the defeated nations a dignified role in a reorganized Europe, he might well have been able to consolidate his conquests. He might even have received strong and valuable support for his war against the Soviet Union. But instead, with squareheaded lack of foresight, he pronounced his New Order to be the rule of the master German Race over inferior peoples. He would use local traitors in the process of consolidating his iron control over the occupied countries.

Unfortunately for Hitler, the collaborators never formed more than a small malignancy on the body of Occupied Europe. Once the shock of occupation wore off, resistance increased everywhere. Hitler had hoped to turn his victims into submissive slaves. Instead, he was faced with obstreperous, recalcitrant bands of vengeance-minded foes—in France the *Maquis* (after the French for underbrush), in Poland the guerrillas, in Yugoslavia the *Chetniks* and Partisans, in Greece the *Andartes*. These resistance groups made life miserable for the "master race" from one end of the continent to the other.

The pattern was European-wide. Armed bands sniped at Germans from the hills and at night sneaked down to derail trains, blow up bridges, clear roadblocks, and explode ammunition dumps. Guerrillas fell on isolated sentinels and cut their throats; they knifed or garroted German officers in the dark and dumped their bodies into canals and rivers. In the factories, humming with war production, members of the underground gave go-slow signals, threw sand or powdered glass into the gears of their machines, manufactured dud shells, or surreptitiously dropped poison into food being canned for the German army. All this was done at the risk of torture or death, but despite vicious reprisals it never ceased.

The underground was well informed. It received information on what was happening in the war from the B.B.C., the British radio, and duly spread it to the people. In return the underground supplied London with a fantastic amount of information. Underground railroads (similar to those secret routes used in the United States before and during the Civil War to facilitate the escape of slaves) helped hundreds of Allied airmen and prisoners of war escape from the enemy. Underground newspapers appeared regularly, some mimeographed, some printed, all issuing warnings on the activities of collaborators and in general keeping alive the urge for liberation.

In time the resistance movement took on the character of a military campaign. Saboteurs trained in England were dropped by parachute on the occupied countries to join up with local patriots. In Norway, Holland, and France the resistance groups were carefully coördinated, but in Yugoslavia and Greece the various movements fought each other with almost as much ferocity as they exhibited against the Germans.

For the Germans the task of tracking down this burgeoning resistance was as frustrating as placing a thumb on quicksilver. They tried every trick in the handbook of war to discourage the assassinations and the sabotage. They executed thousands—to no avail. There were always others ready to take the places of those tortured and beaten to death by *Gestapo* agents.

All this mystified Hitler. Knowing little about what went on beyond the borders of Germany and Austria, he assumed that other peoples would react in the same way as his docile, disciplined, and obedient Germans. He never understood the power engendered by hatred of the tyrant, by love of country, by the urge of freedom. Nor did his phony crusade against Bolshevism attract much support.

The tough fighters of the resistance wanted no Teutonic crusaders on their soil, for whatever reasons. Hence the heroism, the sacrifice, the war within war, the sullen refusal to collaborate.

From the fiords of Norway and the canals of Amsterdam to the beaches of Nice it was much the same—silent death to the invader—or, at the least, hamper him and frustrate him. Denmark was supposed to be a happy and contented satellite state, the showplace of Nazism. But the Danes did not respond as Hitler had hoped. Although outwardly conforming, from king to peasant, they treated the Germans with silent contempt. More than 10,000 Danes escaped to join the British army. Some 40,000 others, calling themselves "moles," joined the underground.

When orders came to transport Danish Jews to Germany for execution in gas chambers, the compassionate Danes, receiving advance information, sent thousands of the unfortunates on their way to Sweden. To Hitler's orders that increasing supplies of foodstuffs be expropriated in their country, the Danes responded by eating themselves to exhaustion so that as little food as possible reached the bellies of the hated Germans. The *Gestapo* worked overtime, sending many thousands to concentration camps and executing more than a thousand Danes. But the flames of resistance in the small country never dimmed.

It was the same in Norway, systematically plundered of its merchant marine, its machinery, its movable goods. The Nazi proconsul, Major Vidkun Quisling, tried hard to serve his German masters, but the 3,000,000 Norwegians never capitulated. More than 50,000 escaped, some to Sweden, most to Britain and Canada, where they served in the Allied armed forces and in the merchant marine.

During the occupation the Norwegian underground secretly transported an average of 20 persons a day to Sweden. Led by Paul Berg and Bishop Eivind Berggrav, many teachers, ministers, workers, and peasants scorned Quisling, treated the Germans with contempt, and struck back at the invaders. The extent of the sabotage in Norway was so great that Hitler was forced to maintain an army of 300,000 men there, troops he could have used elsewhere. The *Gestapo*, moving with customary sadism, put at least 50,000 Norwegians through the torture chambers.

The Belgians, old hands at resistance, harried the Germans to distraction. Almost immediately after the surrender of the Belgian army, German officers found on their doorsteps copies of the world's oldest underground newspaper, *Free Belgium*, "Volume 1, New War Series." The first editorial: "Never forget that the Germans are criminals, barbarians, murderers! Don't swallow their lies!" This was infuriating to the Germans, who could never track the paper down. It was assembled and printed at great risk; copy was passed along in hollow canes, umbrellas, and false-bottomed satchels. The paper never missed a deadline, though hundreds of German agents tried to find its printing plants.

In Holland, Artur von Seyss-Inquart, the Reich Commissioner, could muster only five per cent of the population as active collaborators. The Dutch used their canals as a convenient repository for enemy troops whose throats were cut in the dark. Some 180,000 Hollanders passed through German concentration camps, and more than 10,000 of Holland's Jewish population were transported to Germany and to death in the gas chambers.

Amsterdam was the scene of one of the most poignant episodes of the war. In early August 1944, after spending two years of terror hiding in the secret rooms above a spice factory, a 15-year-old girl, Anne Frank, her sister, her parents, and four others, were discovered and arrested by the Nazis. Anne herself, apparently guilty only of the crime of being Jewish, died in the concentration camp at Bergen-Belsen.

At the beginning of her ordeal, Anne began keeping a diary, which had been given to her on her birthday. Several weeks before the end she made this entry: "In spite of everything I believe that people are really good at heart. I simply cannot build up my hopes on a foundation consisting of confusion, misery, and death."

Other entries: "Surely the time will come when we are people again, and not just Jews." "I don't think I shall easily bow down to the blows that inevitably come to everyone."

Anne Frank's diary was found and published in Holland in 1947. Eventually it found its way, translated into 21 languages, around the world. The play, "The Diary of Anne Frank," has been performed on the stages of 30 countries, including West Germany, where audiences wept silently as the story of the doomed adolescent was unfolded on the boards.

The sensitive little Jewish girl of Amsterdam who, despite her nightmarish existence, believed that people were still basically good, became for some people a legendary figure, like the martyred Joan of Arc. Certainly this unflinching child became the final victor over the evil that was Adolf Hitler.

The Nazi terror reached monstrous proportions in Poland, where the resistance matched the ferocity of the invader. Poland never had a Quisling or a fifth column. Poles by the thousands escaped to form one of the largest fugitive units among the Allies and to fight on a score of fronts. In Poland the agents of the *Gestapo* met with an espionage system as subtle as their own.

The Poles were caught between Nazis and Russians. In April 1943 the Germans announced the discovery of the bodies of 10,000 Polish officers buried in a common grave in the Katyn forest near Smolensk, and promptly accused the Russians of "this inhuman bestiality." The Polish government-in-exile asked for an investigation by the International Red Cross, a request denounced by the Russians. The Katyn incident was never fully clarified. It is known only that the cream of the Polish officer corps was wiped out in one of the most barbaric massacres of all time—either by the Germans or the Russians.

Although the French were shocked into a coma by the suddenness of their national disaster, their spirit of resistance soon hardened. Most Frenchmen rejected Pétain, Laval, and the despised Vichy government. More than 100,000 escaped to Britain, where they joined the Allies and fought against the Axis. To Laval's intensive propaganda campaign to induce volunteers to serve with the Germans, young Frenchmen replied by slipping through the enemy lines to join de Gaulle.

Resistance was multiplied when Hitler persisted in the task of draining France of all available manpower. German agents, in one of the biggest manhunts in history, began to search for 40,000 Frenchmen to construct the fortifications of Hitler's Fortress Europe. Available Frenchmen disappeared, hiding out in the cities or fleeing the countryside to join the *Maquis*.

The pace of French resistance quickened in 1941. Old *poilus*, civilians, workmen, students, clerks, and women were organized into commando, intelligence, and sabotage units. There were fourscore resistance newspapers, including *Combat*, *Franc-Tireur*, and *Libération*. At first these papers were mimeographed and later printed, reaching a circulation of half a million daily. Assembly lines in the factories mysteriously broke down; trains were derailed; bridges blown up; automobiles set afire; communications lines cut. Unwary Germans were killed with knives, hand grenades, and bombs.

The German authorities began to shoot hostages, as many as 50 Frenchmen for every German killed, in a modern, more brutal version of the old Frankish *Wergeld*. But it was to no avail. By the time the Allies stormed the Normandy beaches, the French underground had developed into an army of half a million, an indispensable arm of the invaders. The spirit was unconquerable. During the closing months of the war, the *Maquis* began to place posters reading: "Get your Hun now; there won't be enough to go around."

At the head of the French resistance was the tall, unbending figure of General Charles de Gaulle. Tactless, undiplomatic, sharp-tongued, but bold and courageous, De Gaulle epitomized the French mood for resistance. He had been undersecretary of defense when Paris fell. He escaped to London, whence he summoned his countrymen to join him in resistance. He sought to constitute around himself the unity of lacerated France.

De Gaulle's Free French (later Fighting French) movement soon reached vast proportions. Simultaneously, another resistance group, the Imperial Council, under General Henri Giraud, was forged in Algiers. The two movements consolidated in 1943. French Equatorial Africa, the French Cameroons, French India, French Oceania, and New Caledonia in the Pacific rallied to the Fighting French.

Without the consent of the British and American governments the French resistance took possession of the French mandates in Syria and Lebanon and also seized the islands of St. Pierre and Miquelon. Though alienated by de Gaulle's haughty demeanor, Churchill and Roosevelt eventually recognized him as leader of the French resistance (Roosevelt not until October 1944).

There was fierce opposition to the Germans in Yugoslavia and Greece, but in both these countries the resistance forces became embroiled in internecine struggles which reduced the nations to chaos.

In Greece the E.A.M. (National Liberation Movement), with the toughest and best-organized fighters, was more pro-Communist than anti-Nazi. Some 30,000 strong, the E.A.M. waged ferocious war against the E.D.E.S. (Greek Democratic Liberation Army). The latter group was supported both by the Greek government-in-exile and by the British. In October 1944 the British sent 3,000 troops to defend the Greek government against elements aiming at its overthrow. Eventually, the E.A.M. was driven to the hills. After the war, in the elections of March 1946 the royal family was brought back.

Similarly, there was war-within-war in Yugoslavia. The Chetniks, mostly Serbians, serving under General Draja Mihailovich, sympathetic to the monarchy, fought indiscriminately against Germans, hostile Croats, and Communists. A new leader in the Yugoslav resistance movement appeared in Josip Broz, later known as Tito, a Croat by birth and a Communist agitator by profession. Tito's 100,000 followers were so successful in their guerrilla warfare against the Germans that by the end of 1943 they were holding some 20 Nazi divisions at bay in Yugoslavia. Six offensives against Tito by Germans and Italians failed to collapse his movement. Tito's slogan: "Death to Fascism, Freedom to the People!"

Meanwhile, Tito commenced open warfare against his rival, Mihailovich. In late 1943, Churchill intervened in this quarrel by throwing the weight of Anglo-American aid to Soviet-sponsored Tito, partly because of Tito's superior strength and partly in vexation over what he believed to be Mihailovich's inactivity. Churchill's unexpected move brought him sharp criticism after the war.

Efficiently consolidating his power, Tito executed his rival in 1946 for "treasonable Fascist activities." For a time Tito became the darling among

Soviet puppets, but the Russians found that the marriage was unfortunate. The honeymoon lasted until 1948, when Tito was denounced by the Kremlin for "deviations from the party line" and as "a traitor to Communist solidarity."

Tito, asserting that he was only seeking for Yugoslavia what Stalin had done for Russia, successfully maintained Yugoslavia's independence. From Moscow came surly anathema. Titoism was pronounced a dirty word—along with Trotskyism.

STRANDS OF HOPE: GOVERNMENTS-IN-EXILE

One after another, governments-in-exile were established to maintain a framework of organization that would help establish the old authority once Hitler was defeated. Most set up headquarters in London, and all were recognized as members of the United Nations coalition. They took over control of fighting contingents and merchant seamen and pooled them with Allied units. They broadcast propaganda to their peoples at home and kept alive the hope that one day they would be liberated. They remained in communication with homeland resistance forces, to whom they sent espionage agents, commandos, and supplies.

As early as 1941, governments-in-exile working in London included Belgium, Holland, Luxemburg, Norway, Czechoslovakia, and Poland. Most functioned smoothly through the worst days of the occupation, but those in Eastern Europe became embroiled in struggles between "liberal" (revolutionary) and reactionary forces. In Denmark King Christian X governed as he had before the occupation, but a Danish Council organized in London in late 1940 coöperated fully with the Allies.

King Leopold III of the Belgians refused to escape with his ministers. For the remainder of the conflict he lived in Belgium and in Germany as a virtual prisoner of war. In his absence his brother Charles was elected regent, holding that post until Leopold was restored to his throne in July 1950. But his disappointed and disgruntled people forced him to abdicate within a month in favor of his 19-year-old son, who became Baudouin I.

Queen Wilhelmina of the Netherlands, her family, and her ministers reached London after a dramatic escape. She returned after the liberation to receive a tumultuous welcome.

Grand Duchess Charlotte of Luxemburg had a similar experience, as did King Haakon VII of Norway.

Soon after the opening of hostilities, Eduard Beneš, former president of Czechoslovakia, and Jan Masaryk, son of the country's founder, Thomas Masaryk, organized a Czechoslovak Committee in London, which was recognized by the United States, Britain, and the Soviet Union (by the latter only after the German invasion of Russia) as the legal government of Czechoslovakia.

The governments-in-exile of Greece, Poland, and Yugoslavia functioned from London but with compounding difficulties, primarily because they were already authoritarian to a greater or lesser degree and because of domestic difficulties on the issue of Communism.

After Greece fell in April 1941, King George II and his ministers fled from Athens to Crete, thence to Cairo, and finally to London. In Greece itself clashes between rightist and leftist forces produced a bitter civil war lasting from December 4, 1944, to January 11, 1945. The liberal forces eventually won out.

King Peter of Yugoslavia and his government went through a similar trial. At home the fratricidal clashes between the monarchist General Draja Mihailovich and the Communist-oriented Marshal Tito culminated with the triumph of Tito and his "National Communist" movement.

Most complicated of all was the historical tragedy of Poland, subjected in late 1939 to its fourth partition. A Polish government-in-exile was set up, first in Paris and then in London under General Wladislaw Sikorski. From 1940 to 1942 the Sikorski government functioned smoothly, as Polish troops, pilots, and seamen fought on all the major battle fronts. Then came a gradual deterioration of relations between the exile government and the Soviet Union, whose armies were approaching the former Polish frontier and had no intention of stopping there. Following the discovery in 1943 of the Katyn massacre, relations between the two governments were broken off. At the height of the crisis General Sikorski was killed in a plane crash, to be succeeded by Stanislaw Mikolajczyk, head of the Peasant Party, Poland's strongest popular group.

The rift between the Soviet Union and Poland brought serious concern to both Britain and the United States, both of whom found it impossible to heal the growing estrangement. Here was the first sign of rupture between East and West, later to emerge as the cold war.

Moscow, without consulting its Western Allies, supported the Communist partisans of the Lublin administration. At the Teheran Conference in November 1943, Stalin induced Roosevelt and Churchill to concede the Soviet claim of an eastern Polish frontier corresponding to the previous Curzon Line.

Encouraged by the Soviet Union, the Polish underground in Warsaw under General Tadeusz Bor-Komorowski rose against their German captors, whereupon they were massacred while near-by Russians neglected to come to their aid. In London Poles were infuriated by what they called a shameless betrayal.

In December 1944 the Lublin Poles proclaimed themselves the provisional government of Poland. They were promptly recognized by Moscow, but not by Washington or London until the Yalta Conference of February 1945.

By this time it was clear that the Soviet Union was determined to impress its own political pattern not only on Poland but also on the whole of Intermediate Europe. Stalin, with his troops already ensconced in the area, had jumped the gun in the race for power in the postwar era.

THE NEUTRALS

To only a few nations of Europe went the blessings and profits of neutrality. These had either a favorable geographical location, or a persistent desire not to be drawn into the war, or, as in the case of Franco Spain, the ability shrewdly to play one side against the other.

Switzerland, classic home of neutrality, prosperous, snug in its protective mountain fortress, stayed out of both World Wars. The Swiss kept an army of a half-million men in permanent mobilization. They mined roads and tunnels on all the invasion routes. Even Hitler was discouraged by the prospect of assaulting the small mountain bastion. Furthermore, it was not necessary, for the Swiss went on a 24-hour schedule to manufacture precision instruments, ammunition, fuses, textiles, and shoes for the rapacious German war machine.

Swiss sympathies lay on the other side. It was said that the Swiss worked for the Nazis six days a week and prayed for the Allies on the seventh. To this little island in a sea of Nazism came several hundred thousand refugees as well as a wave of flight capital. Swiss banks indiscriminately guarded the money of both sides.

In Ireland all parties insisted upon strict neutrality, a departure from the precedent of World War I. London complained that Ireland was a hotbed of Axis espionage, that the Irish granted Axis ministers in Dublin far greater liberties than ordinarily extended to ambassadors of belligerent nations, and that German *Luftwaffe* pilots used lighted Irish cities as check points when attacking England. The Irish replied that, even though they were not at war, they were contributing tens of thousands of their sons to fight in British units and to work in British factories. It was small consolation for an embattled Britain.

Sweden, on the northern periphery of Hitler's Fortress Europe, made herself indispensable to both sides, thereby maintaining her record of never having gone to war in more than a century. Immediately after the outbreak of hostilities, the Swedes warned the world in general and Hitler in particular that upon the first violation of their frontiers they would destroy every factory, mine, and train in their land including steel plants and ball-bearing factories. This was language Hitler understood. He exempted Sweden from attack.

At the same time the Swedes favored the Western powers as against either

Germany or Soviet Russia. They contributed generously to send food to the Dutch, Poles, Norwegians, Danes, and Czechs; they took foreign children into their homes; they granted asylum to several hundred thousand refugees; and they passed on to the Allies information on German activities.

The two other Scandinavian countries, Denmark and Norway, bitterly resented Swedish neutrality. But under the circumstances there was nothing they could do to convince the Swedes to accept their own subservient status.

Turkey, in an exposed position on the southern flank of the Nazi-Soviet struggle, was in the touchy spot of favoring the Allies but simultaneously resisting the threats of the Axis powers. Despite pressure from both sides, she maintained her neutrality until February 23, 1945, when she declared war on Germany and Japan. There was method in the decision: Ankara was undoubtedly stimulated by the Allied decision not to invite to the coming San Francisco Conference to organize the United Nations any country that had not entered the war against the Axis by March 1, 1945.

Portugal, under the dictatorship of Antonio de Oliveira Salazar, dean of European autocrats and "gentleman Fascist," sat out the war as a neutral. Though traditionally friendly to Britain, she sold to both sides her precious supplies of tin and wolframite (a source of tungsten, which is used for alloying steel). Along with Switzerland, she was a favored repository of flight capital from all the belligerents. Portugal emerged from the war with a capital surplus, a hard currency, and a proportionately low public debt.

Spain, too, stayed out of the war. During the six years of World War II, dictator Francisco Franco put on the most dazzling virtuoso performance since the Frenchman Blondin walked across Niagara Falls on a tight rope just a century earlier. Franco signed the Anti-Comintern Pact in 1939, but when the war broke out he shied away from becoming a belligerent. Sensing the advantage of neutrality for his land devastated by the civil war, he adopted a policy of "nonbelligerency" during the first three years of the conflict. Pro-Axis in sympathy, he helped Germany and Italy in various ways, sheltering their fleets, servicing their planes, providing them such strategic materials as wolframite, and allowing Axis espionage systems to function on Spanish soil. He even dispatched the Spanish "Blue Division" of 18,000 men to help fight the Russians.

During this period the Allies were forced to keep a sizable army across from Gibraltar to prevent a possible Axis assault on that bastion.

When in 1943 the growing strength of the Allies became evident, Franco shifted his position from nonbelligerency to benevolent neutrality. To him this meant a process of bargaining with one side or the other, or both. He made no attempt to interfere with the Allied landings in North Africa. He now permitted Allied espionage agents to operate in Spain, allowed interned Allied aviators to leave the country, and eventually halted the export of wolframite to Germany. He emerged from the war with a firm dictatorial grip on his country.

SYKEWAR: THE BATTLE OF WORDS

Dr. Joseph Goebbels, fanatical little propagandist, apostle of violence, successfully sold the Nazi philosophy to the German people. Hitler rose to power on a barrel of Goebbelsian slogans:

> "The Germans are a super-race destined to rule the world!"
> "Adolf Hitler is the greatest German of all time!"
> "The highest reward is to die for the *Fuehrer*!"
> "Down with the Versailles *Diktat*!"
> "Today Germany, tomorrow the world!"

In the greater task of psychological warfare—sykewar—Goebbels was a dismal failure. History repeated itself. In World War I awkward German propaganda experts suffered ignominious defeat in the battle of words. It was to happen again in World War II.

Goebbels planned his psychological sabotage as carefully as a military campaign. From his headquarters at No. 58 Lehrterstrasse, Berlin, he sent out streams of Nazi propaganda to all corners of the world. His object was to disrupt and disunite the peoples by stirring up racial and religious hatreds and by undermining their confidence in their own governments. He hammered away at the point that the Germans were fighting in the interests of European culture. After Nazi Germany attacked Russia, Goebbels began to present the British and Americans as dupes of Stalin and claimed that Germany alone was bearing the brunt of the crusade against Slavic Bolshevism.

Goebbels began by treating the war as another election campaign. He allowed the masses at home to share vicariously in the exploits of the German armies. At first he published extremely low casualty figures. But when he saw Nazi triumphs vanishing, the loot disappearing, and lightning war degenerating into a war of attrition, he had to use different methods. Now he embarked upon a campaign of pessimism and public mourning. He warned that, unless Germany fought to the end, there would be famine, dismemberment of the Third Reich, slavery under the Jew. Again it was the Jew "who has built up a terroristic military power in Bolshevism" and who "camouflages himself as plutocracy and capitalism in Britain and America." The goal was to stimulate the German people to further effort and sacrifice.

On the foreign scene priority No. 1 for Goebbels was South America. Millions of Germans had emigrated to that area and millions of German marks had been invested there.

Goebbels also spent great sums to undermine the war effort of the United States, seeking with the assistance of Bundists and phony front organizations to create confusion and discord and drive the country into two huge hating camps. In this he was singularly unsuccessful. The German Library of Information in New York turned out reams of documents in colloquial English, with little effect on the public. To Américans and most other peoples Hitler, instead of a Teutonic knight in shining armor, was regarded either as a comic figure or a bloodthirsty maniac. His camarilla of toadies, far from meriting respect outside of Germany, was dismissed as a gang of selfish midgets in the seats of the mighty. Words could not erase the widspread impression that Germany had gone mad.

In contrast, British propaganda was based on hope, on new, vigorous action, on struggle for the attainable ideal. Churchill's famous speeches of May, June, and July 1940 served the purpose of clarification, enlightening the people, pointing the way for their conduct in the future, stirring them into a surge of activity. Clarification was death for Nazism.

Every conceivable propaganda device was used by both sides, including radio, leaflets, photographs, special publications, and mobile public-address systems. German radio propaganda divided events of the day into black and white. Hitler, the most important speaker and featured performer, made no fireside chats, as did Roosevelt. Instead the German *Fuehrer* customarily harangued the masses. He was imitated by a chorus of flunkies, among them Axis Sally and the traitors Lord Haw Haw, Jane Anderson, Fred Kaltenbach, and Otto Koischwitz.

Over the airwaves *ad nauseam* came the essentials of the Nazi myth: Hitler, the god of light, was opposed to the Jews, the power of darkness; Germany, a state of thinkers and activists, was a Wagnerian paradise ("No one," thundered Goebbels, "has a greater right to possess a world empire!"); the hierarchy of the Nazi Party reflected the greatness of the *Fuehrer*; the enemies were the hypocritical Englishman, the bluffing American, the bestial Russian; the nations of Western Europe were deadly but honorable enemies, but Jews, Russians, and Poles were subhuman vermin destined to extermination.

Most effective of all were the "paper bullets," leaflets to spread demoralization, at first fired at the enemy in artillery shells and later dropped by the millions from planes over enemy lines. German leaflets, in easily understood G.I. language, gave specific instructions on how to feign at least a dozen illnesses: how to contract malaria or venereal disease ("Recommended: 'Naples gonorrhea,' because it does not respond easily to standard treatment"). The most successful of all German leaflets was one in the form of a green leaf thrown over France in huge quantities: "If you fight England's battles, your soldiers will fall like autumn leaves."

Few German propaganda leaflets were as effective as the green leaves. Members of Hitler's entourage could not resist the urge to get into the act. Heinrich Himmler, *Gestapo* chief, projected a scheme to drop propaganda leaflets in South Africa by attaching them to the legs of migrating storks. A German stork expert called in for consultation put an end to the scheme. The storks, he said, would be killed by the explosion releasing the leaflets. Therefore, he explained, the idea was certain to backfire because the Boers of South Africa, while they did not love the British, did, with their Dutch heritage, love storks. Disgruntled, Himmler went back to his specialty of garroting Jews and Poles in the black dungeons of the *Gestapo*.

A typical German leaflet was illustrated with a picture of a wild party of draft dodgers embracing scantily clad women and a second picture showing an American G.I. on the battlefield with his bleeding intestines torn out. The legend:

> THE DRAFT DODGERS ON THE HOME FRONT EXPECT EVERY JOE TO DO HIS DUTY.
>
> G.I.'S, HAVE YOU EVER FIGURED IT OUT?
>
> 70 American men out of a hundred are enjoying peace in civil life; 22 are training and stationed back home;
>
> 8 are doing their bit overseas;
>
> FOUR MEN OUT OF A HUNDRED ARE ENGAGED IN ACTUAL FIGHTING.
>
> Some 60 divisions have reached the fronts, combat troops as well as service units, totaling more than 2,155,000 officers and men, who accompanied these divisions abroad.
>
> Adding the million men of the Air Forces, there is a TOTAL OF 3,055,000 G.I.'s on the world's battle fronts. (*Stars and Stripes*, September 20, page 4.)
>
> And only about half of these are doing the grim, nasty job of actual fighting.
>
> Almost every day you front-line men read of people at home leaving war jobs for something more secure which will carry them through the postwar period.
>
> For you the advice of these people is: KEEP SOLDIERS IN THE ARMY AFTER THE WAR UNTIL JOBS CAN BE SECURED FOR THEM.
>
> THE DRAFT DODGERS AT HOME EXPECT EVERY JOE TO DO HIS DUTY!

Another German leaflet dropped over American lines was illustrated with a figure of Death grasping a G.I. The message:

> YOUR FIRST WINTER IN EUROPE.
>
> EASY GOING HAS STOPPED!
>
> Perhaps you've already noticed it—the nearer the German border, the heavier your losses.
>
> Naturally. They're defending their own homes.
>
> Winter is just around the corner—hence diminishing A.F. activity.

More burden on the shoulders of the infantry, therefore heavier casualties. WHO IS CASHING IN ON THE HUGE WAR PROFITS AT HOME, WHILE AMERICANS SHED THEIR BLOOD OVER HERE?

Anglo-American experts operated on the principle that propaganda to be effective had to be not only factually true but credible. They found that the ultimate weapon in the war of words was simply to tell the truth. One of the most successful Allied propaganda enterprises was *Frontpost*, "A Newspaper for German Troops," a weekly paper produced by the Twelfth Army Group and distributed by medium bombers of the U.S. Ninth Air Force. The Germans learned that its columns invariably reported the exact military situation, and they depended upon it rather than their own press. Captured German troops often asked for back issues so that they could be brought up-to-date on the news.

American leaflets gave advance warning to civilians about to be bombed: "You are specifically advised that from now on, no shelter or refuge within the above named districts can be considered safe. Your life depends upon the immediate execution of these orders. Act now! Out of the battle areas! Out of the war!"

Most effective of all were the Allied *Passierscheine* (safe-conduct passes), which induced tens of thousands to surrender:

> The German soldier who carries this safe conduct is using it as a sign of his genuine wish to give himself up. He is to be disarmed, to be well looked after, to receive food and medical attention as required, and to be removed from the danger zone as soon as possible.
>
> [Signed]: DWIGHT D. EISENHOWER
> Supreme Commander
> Allied Expeditionary Force

In North Africa, Arab boys retrieved these *Passierscheine* and sold them to German and Italian troops for fancy prices. When their sons were conscripted for dangerous service in North Africa, Italian parents bought safe-conduct passes on the black market and gave them as going-away presents with the advice to use them as soon as possible. Later in the war the passes were made even more attractive by embellishing them to give the appearance of gilt-edge bonds or university diplomas.

Allied propagandists dropped pencils, bars of soap, seeds, matches, and needles and thread, all inscribed with slogans, by the millions on enemy lines. Soap and matches, especially, were received as rare gifts from heaven.

Japanese propaganda for their troops stressed the idea that the highest reward on earth was to die for the Emperor-God. *Hakki Ichiu*, philosophy of predestination, would bring "the eight corners of the world under one roof." "Smash the red-haired barbarians of the West!" "To us," said the Nipponese sykewar experts, "facts are of no importance. What is important is intuition!" On the Japanese radio for home consumption came repeated stories of fantastic conquests and débâcles for the enemy.

Japanese propaganda for enemy troops was as clumsy as the German. Tokyo Rose, with a silken bedroom voice, played popular tunes interspersed with a line of sexy chatter which convulsed American G.I.'s: "But the girl back home is drinking with some 4-F who's rolling in easy money. Maybe they'll have supper, too. Mm-m-m-m-m, wouldn't a nice thick steak taste good right now, in some café? But you won't get any of that out here for a long time. And now another song...."

Japanese leaflets followed the same line. A typical one showed an attractive girl and the copy: "*Don't wait to die.* Before the bombs fall, let me take your hand and kiss your gentle cheeks and murmur. Before the terror comes, let me walk beside you in garden deep in petaled sleep. Let me, while there is still a time and place. Feel soft against me and rest... rest your warm hand on my breast...."

THE GREATER EAST ASIA CO-PROSPERITY SPHERE

By mid-1942, while Hitler was coördinating a hostile Europe, the Japanese had made astonishing strides in the Far East. Slashing through supposedly impassable jungles, storming ashore on one island after another, Nipponese warriors had carved out a huge Western Pacific empire between India and Hawaii, between Siberia and Australia, acquiring 3,000,000 square miles. Even more important from the military point of view, they had won control of 95 per cent of the world's natural rubber and 70 per cent of its tin, vital materials in both war and peace.

How to organize and administer this huge empire? The master-minds of Tokyo divided it into an Outer and an Inner Zone. The Outer Zone, consisting of the Dutch East Indies, Thailand, Burma, Indo-China, Borneo, and the Philippines, was to be held as long as possible while being exploited for raw materials and vital supplies for the defense of the Inner Zone. The Inner Zone, made up of Japan proper, Manchukuo, Korea, and Formosa, was to be maintained at all costs, even if the surrounding zone was pierced by the enemy. The Outer Zone was expendable if necessary; the Inner Zone was to be defended to the death.

In November 1943, when the American counteroffensive was getting under way in the Pacific, the Greater East Asia Conference assembled in Tokyo to consolidate power for the coming critical days. To this meeting came all the puppets, collaborators, and the renegade Subhas Chandra Bose, head of the "Provisional Government of Free India." After long discussion, the delegates reaffirmed the central doctrine of "Asia for the Asiatics" and proclaimed war against Western imperialism. They also suggested an extensive series of political concessions to all members to maintain their loyalty and coöperation. To win the loyalty of China, Burma, Indonesia, the Philippines, there were promises of equality, independence, self-government.

It was a simple matter to find collaborators throughout the vast reaches of Asia. The weakling Henry Pu-yi, heir to the Manchu dynasty that had lost power in 1911, was already installed in Manchukuo. The renegade Wang Ching-wei, deserter from the Chinese Nationalist government in 1938, was made puppet ruler of Occupied China, in which position he meekly took orders from the Japanese ambassador, General Nobuyuki Abe. Other pliable minions appeared like mushrooms—Ba Maw in Burma, Emilio Aguinaldo in the Philippines, Luang Pibul Songgram in Thailand, Achmed Soekarno in Indonesia.

Japanese military governors were sent everywhere to "advise and assist." Agents for Japanese industrial organizations revised the currencies of the conquered lands, established the Yen Bloc controlled by the Bank of Japan, and arranged "cultural pacts" designed to absorb the new countries into the Japanese way of life. It was a gigantic task, one that would have taxed the ability and imagination of nations more experienced in imperial expansion. It turned out to be too much for the Tokyo militarists.

At first the Japanese conquerors maintained the fiction that they had come as friendly fellow-Asiatics, as equals, allies, and liberators, who would bring prosperity and stability to those laboring under the Western yoke. They would grind into dust all relics of Kipling's "White Man's Burden." They would eliminate the influences of the decadent and alien West and restore the purity of Asiatic civilization. Tokyo would remain the hub, the center of the huge wheel of Greater Asia.

But then came a rising spirit of resistance. Only a brief experience of Japanese rule was enough to convince the peoples of Asia that Japanese imperialism was if anything more grasping than that of the West. Along with Japanese promises came barbaric administrators, bloodsucking economic agents, an increased opium traffic, and rising food shortages. Were these the fruits of common Asiatic citizenship?

In Malaya, Indo-China, Burma, Thailand, and the Philippines, resistance fighters, impelled by varying motives, began to strike back. It was the same story as in Occupied Europe—smashed lines of communication, harried garrisons, local coöperation with the Allies. The Japanese retaliated with increasing brutality, only to find the resistance matching atrocity for atrocity, savagery for savagery. For white civilians and prisoners of war the Japanese reserved barbaric and senseless cruelties—carefully noted for postwar justice.

Part IV

PHOENIX: TURN OF THE TIDE

CHAPTER 14

The United States Halts Japan

> ***I tell you naught for your comfort,***
> ***Yea, naught for your desire,***
> ***Save that the sky grows darker yet***
> ***And the sea rises higher.***
>
> **—G. K. Chesterton, "The Ballad of the White Horse"**

REVANCHE—INSTALLMENT NO. 1: THE DOOLITTLE RAID

Except for the fall of Wake Island, the Central Pacific remained quiet for months after Pearl Harbor. Then came electrifying news—an American bombing-raid on Tokyo! There was something attractively mystifying about it—the Japanese capital was thousands of miles away from any American air base. True, the spectacular feat had little practical effect on the over-all course of the war. It was on a tiny scale, nothing like the enemy attack on Pearl Harbor, but it was "real American stuff," a portent of things to come. It provoked the all-time understatement of the whole war—the wonderfully ironic lead of an American reporter's story, beginning, "The Doolittle raid, although hardly decisive. . . ."

First reports came from a Tokyo broadcast:

> Enemy bombers appeared over Tokyo for the first time in the present war. inflicting damage on schools and hospitals. The raid took place shortly past noon on Saturday [Tokyo time, April 18, 1942]. Invading planes failed to cause any damage on military establishments, although casualties in the schools and hospitals are as yet unknown. This inhuman attack is causing widespread indignation among the populace.

For unadulterated double-standardism this broadcast deserved the award of a bitter rice-cake. Nipponese airmen had mercilessly bombed Pearl Harbor as well as a host of other targets from Korea down to Burma. Now, with the shoe on the other honorable foot, air raids had suddenly become "inhuman." Not only that, the raid, far from attacking "schools and hospitals," had been restricted to armament plants, dockyards, railroad yards, plane factories, and the nearby Yokosuka naval base—a case of hitting only planned objectives. The raiders could easily have blasted the Imperial Palace, but they scrupulously followed orders not to strike at that inviting target.

The planning had begun only a few weeks after Pearl Harbor. Lieutenant Colonel James H. Doolittle, a 45-year-old peacetime stunt flyer and barnstormer, suggested to his superior officers that he be allowed to lead a bombing attack on Tokyo. At first the idea was dismissed as crazy. But the fast-talking aviator was deadly serious.

Given the green light, Doolittle prepared for the raid with the utmost secrecy and thoroughness. His call for volunteers for an unnamed secret mission brought many times the number of pilots and crewmen who could be taken. The plane he chose was the B-25, a North American medium bomber of excellent speed, gas consumption, bomb capacity, and ability to take rough handling.

Three months were spent in painstaking preparation. Guided by white lines on the ground, the flyers made hundreds of practice take-offs in the shortest possible distance. Crewmen studied maps, pictures, and silhouettes for instant recognition of their course and objectives. The top-secret Norden bombsight was replaced with a simple 20-cent sight which would be no loss if captured.

Flyers and planes were loaded on the aircraft carrier *Hornet*, commanded by Admiral William F. ("Bull") Halsey, Jr. Training continued aboard the flattop. There were lectures on navigation, meteorology, and the topography of Japan; the gunners practiced shooting at kites flown above the *Hornet*.

The original plan was to proceed to a point within 400 miles of Tokyo, launch the planes just before dark, make the strike at night, and then arrive at Chinese airfields in the early morning. But 800 miles from Tokyo the carrier ran across and sank a small Japanese ship. It was feared that the crew had used its radio to warn Tokyo (the fear later proved to be groundless). The take-off time was moved up ten hours, thereby adding considerably to the hazards of the mission.

At 8:20 A.M. on April 18, 1942, in rough weather, the B-25's took off from a bobbing and slanting deck. With Doolittle piloting the lead plane, all 16 got away and headed for Japan, wave-hopping to escape enemy radar.

The Japanese, taken entirely by surprise, did not spot the raiders until they had almost reached their objectives. Roaring in at treetop level, the attackers hit their planned targets with almost every bomb. Japanese planes from a near-by training field rose to intercept the invaders, but they had no success. Antiaircraft fire was furious but ineffectual; the Japanese brought down one of their own barrage balloons.

Doolittle described the raid:

> We approached our objectives just over the housetops, but bombed at 1,500 feet. The target for one plane was a portion of the navy yard south of Tokyo, in reaching which we passed over what apparently was a flying school, as there were a number of planes in the air. One salvo made a direct hit on a new cruiser or battleship under construction. They left it in flames.
>
> After releasing our bombs we dived again to the treetops and went to the coast at that altitude to avoid antiaircraft fire. Along the coastline we observed several squadrons of destroyers and some cruisers and battleships. About 25 or 30 miles to sea the rear gunners reported seeing columns of smoke rising thousands of feet into the air.
>
> One of our bombardiers strewed bombs along a quarter of a mile of aircraft factory near Nagoya. Another illuminated a tank farm. However, flying at such low altitudes made it very difficult to observe the result following the impact of the bombs. We could see the strike, but our field of vision was greatly restricted by the speed of the plane and the low altitude at which we were flying. Even so, one of our party observed a ball game in progress. The players and spectators did not start their run for cover until just as the field passed out of sight.
>
> Pilots, bombardiers, and all members of the crew performed their duties with great calmness and remarkable precision. It appeared to us that practically every bomb reached the target for which it was intended. We would like to have tarried and watched the later developments of fire and explosion, but even so we were fortunate to receive a fairly detailed report from the excited Japanese broadcasts. It took them several hours to calm down to deception and accusation.

The most hazardous part of the venture was getting away from Japan. All the planes escaped safely, but as they scattered they ran into a storm. With gasoline reserves drained, bucking head winds, in darkness above strange territory, most of the men bailed out.

Eight who landed in Japanese-occupied areas were taken prisoner. The rest came down in China and made their way with the help of Chinese to Chungking. Of the 80 airmen, 71 eventually arrived home.

The people of Tokyo were stunned and shaken by this thrust into Japan's supposedly impregnable defenses. Without the protection of air-raid shelters mobs gave way to panic, running in all directions, pushing, shouting, screaming. High Japanese officials went to an audience with the Emperor to apologize for their negligence. The army officer in charge of Tokyo's antiaircraft defenses committed suicide. A mass burial of Japanese marines killed at Yokosuka was held three days later.

Most mystifying of all to the Japanese—how did the raiders get to Tokyo?

The inability to figure out where the raiders were based was almost as disconcerting as the raid itself. Was it from the Hawaiian Islands, 3,850 miles away? Or from the Aleutians, 2,850 miles; or the Philippines, 2,300 miles; or the China coast, 1,350 miles; or Vladivostok, 50 miles?

Washington, of course, supplied no clues. Two days later the War Department issued a communiqué describing the scope of the raid but not disclosing its base. In a press conference, President Roosevelt facetiously remarked that the airmen had taken off from Shangri-La, the fictional Tibetan retreat of James Hilton's novel, *Lost Horizon.* The Japanese took the joke seriously. And the Berlin radio reported: "Doolittle carried out his air attack from the air base Shangri-La which was not otherwise described by Roosevelt."

The Nipponese were in a bitter mood. Immediately after the War Department's delayed communiqué, the Tokyo radio announced in an English-language broadcast the execution of "some of Doolittle's companions," and added: "This same policy will be continued in the future. And by the way, don't forget, America, make sure that every flyer that comes here has a special pass to hell, and rest assured it's strictly a one-way ticket."

Not until March 12, 1943 was the fate of the captured Doolittle raiders learned. President Roosevelt commented: "It is with a feeling of deepest horror, which I know will be shared by all civilized peoples, that I have to announce the barbarous execution by the Japanese government of some of the members of this country's armed forces who fell into Japanese hands as an incident of warfare."

Tokyo refused to give the names of the men executed or those spared.

BLOODY NOSE AT MIDWAY

"Japan loses pants trying to save face!"

Thus the reaction of one seaman to the Battle of Midway, the turning point of the naval war in the Pacific. For the first time in more than three centuries the Japanese navy tasted defeat. For the United States it meant recovery of the balance of naval power lost at Pearl Harbor. From this time on the defenses of the Japanese Empire were penetrated in a series of successive strikes that eventually brought the American navy into Tokyo Bay.

It was obvious to all who knew Japanese strategy that the Nipponese would move to avenge the humiliation of Doolittle's raid on Tokyo. From the Manchurian Incident to early January 1942 Japan's war lords had experienced a rapid succession of great victories. Their initial objectives were attained. Now began the Great Debate in Tokyo. Should a victorious Japan go on the defensive and hold what she had won, or should she resume the attack and break the back of the enemy?

The choice—attack! The direction? There were three alternatives—

toward Australia, toward India, or toward Hawaii. Admiral Isoroku Yamamoto, Commander in Chief Combined Fleet, demanded that it be Midway.

Midway Island, only 1,135 miles west northwest of Pearl Harbor, was the farthest outpost of the Hawaiian chain, with the exception of small Kure Atoll, 60 miles beyond. The entire atoll of Midway was but six miles in diameter, and only a small part of it was dry land. But as the sentry for Hawaii, Midway was a key point in a new outer defense perimeter of Japan —Kiska-Midway-Wake-Marshalls-Gilberts-Guadalcanal-Port Moresby.

At the same time, Yamamoto argued, Midway would provide Japan with an advance base for amphibious operations. Most important of all, it would draw out the U.S. fleet to be destroyed in decisive battle and bring a speedy end to the war. The scrappy Yamamoto had his way. But his Combined Fleet crowd and the Naval General Staff began to quarrel violently over details of the projected Midway operation. The Doolittle raid put a quick end to the debate. Now it was a matter of face. There must be no delay.

On May 5, 1942, Imperial Headquarters issued the order: "Commander in Chief Combined Fleet, in coöperation with the Army, will invade and occupy strategic points in the Western Aleutians and Midway Island." The date was set for June 7, 1942.

The assault on Midway was to be the most gigantic operation in the history of the Japanese navy. For it there were assembled more than 200 ships, including 11 battleships, 8 carriers, 22 cruisers, 65 destroyers, and 21 submarines, together with more than 700 planes. This massive strength was divided into five major tactical forces (Advance Expeditionary Force; Carrier Striking Force; Midway Occupation Force; Main Body; and Northern Area Force), all under command of Admiral Yamamoto.

The Sunday punch would be delivered by the First Carrier Striking Force under Vice Admiral Chuichi Nagumo, with four great carriers supported by two battleships, two heavy cruisers, a light cruiser, and a dozen submarines. Nagumo would soften up Midway with his planes, deliver the first blow at the U.S. Pacific fleet if it challenged, and the Main Body with its big battlewagons would then move in to finish the blow. Then the loaded transports would bring in 5,000 ground troops, take Midway, and convert it into a huge air base.

The plan seemed perfect, the possibility of success excellent. But there was one vital defect: The Japanese depended on the Americans doing exactly what was expected of them. The overconfident Nipponese assumed that they would achieve tactical surprise and that U.S. fleet reaction would not get under way until the assault on Midway had begun. That was a serious miscalculation.

U.S. Intelligence had broken the main Japanese diplomatic code, and Washington knew of the Midway project almost as soon as it was decided upon. Admiral Chester W. Nimitz, Commander in Chief U.S. Pacific Fleet, recalled Task Force 16, commanded by Rear Admiral Raymond A. Spruance, and Task Force 17, under Rear Admiral Frank J. Fletcher, from the South Pacific and deployed them to the northeast of Midway. Here they could, if necessary, make surprise flank attacks on the enemy and "inflict maximum damage by employing strong attrition tactics" (Navy talk for air strikes). The Americans had three carriers, seven heavy cruisers, a light cruiser, 14 destroyers, and about two dozen submarines.

Nimitz correctly gauged the enemy drives in the Java Sea and at Dutch Harbor to be diversionary thrusts designed to conceal the real point of the attack in the center at Midway. His plan was that of an alert football quarterback: Refusing to be diverted by enemy right-end or left-end runs, he concentrated his power against attack at his center.

On the afternoon of June 3, 1942, a Catalina patrol plane sighted a large enemy force approaching Midway Island from the southwest. It turned out to be part of an armada converging on Midway from several different directions. The next morning a hundred Japanese bombers and fighters bounced off their carriers northwest of Midway and headed for the island.

The American fleet, still several hundred miles to the east, could not provide fighter protection, but from Midway 26 Army, Navy, and Marine torpedo planes and dive bombers rose to meet the invaders.

Coming in horizontal formations for the initial strike, the Japanese, according to plan, dropped their bomb loads on both Eastern and Sand Islands, peeled off, and continued the dive-bombing. Then they flew at a low altitude to a rendezvous in the southwest for a start back to their carriers. At least 40 Japanese planes never got there.

The American airmen from Midway reported direct hits on a battleship and a carrier. The attack was made through so heavy a curtain of antiaircraft fire that only nine of the original 26 American planes returned to Midway.

Thus far the Japanese seemed to have the best of it. One more attack and Midway would be theirs. But fate was unkind to Nippon—there were to be no more strikes on Midway. The startled Japanese ran into a hail of fire, death, and destruction. As at the Coral Sea, this was a battle in which planes did all the fighting. The big warships did not exchange a shot.

The American attack was thunderous and highly successful. Bombs and machine-gun bullets splashed over the superstructure of zigzagging ships; raging fires seared the Japanese vessels; great pillows of smoke churned upward; internal explosions sent new gushes of smoke and fire belching from the warships. Overhead, Japanese planes circled desperately, their frustrated pilots unable to land on battered mother ships. Japanese destroyers sped around in frantic efforts to remove survivors from capital ships.

From the *Hornet, Yorktown,* and *Enterprise* torpedo planes, followed by dive bombers, scored hits on enemy carriers, battleships, and cruisers. Nagumo was caught with his planes down. On the second day of the battle, Flying Fortresses from Hawaii joined the naval airmen and those from Midway to plaster the Japanese fleet.

Aboard the battleship *Yamato*, Admiral Yamamoto had lost his appetite. Informed that his four carriers were sunk, he canceled the invasion plans and sent out orders for a retreat westward. To protect his withdrawing fleet from attack by American land-based planes, he ordered four heavy cruisers to move in and shell the Midway airstrips. American submarines were waiting for them.

What had started out to be a Japanese offensive became within a matter of hours a race for life. Caught in a trap, the enemy fleet, harried and crippled, followed Yamamoto's orders, took advantage of the thick weather, broke off the engagement, split up, and, abandoning blazing ships, desperately sought to make its way homeward.

The entire American surface fleet in the vicinity chased the beaten enemy westward until shortage of fuel forced an end to the action. There was another compelling reason for the Americans to break off—it was wiser, perhaps, under the circumstances, to steer clear of Yamamoto's heavy battlewagons.

In four days the Japanese armada that had sailed so confidently for Midway lost at least 5,000 men. Four aircraft carriers (*Akagi, Kaga, Soryu*, and *Hiryu*) and a heavy cruiser (*Mikuma*) were either twisted wrecks or sunken hulks; the heavy cruiser *Mogami* was severely damaged; two destroyers were battered; there was slight damage to another destroyer, an oiler, and the battleship *Haruna*. There were 322 planes lost (280 on carriers when they sank).

The Americans, too, paid a heavy price. They lost the carrier *Yorktown*, abandoned and sunk by an enemy submarine, the destroyer *Hammann*, and a total of 147 aircraft (109 carrier-borne and 38 shore-based). The *Enterprise* alone lost 14 out of 37 dive-bombers, 10 out of 14 torpedo bombers, and one Wildcat.

But Midway remained in American hands. The far stronger Japanese fleet was outsmarted and outfought. Responsible for the victory above all was the success of American Intelligence, which knew when and where the attack would come and which made it possible to strike the enemy with a devastating blow at precisely the right moment. "Had we lacked early information of the Japanese movements," said Admiral Nimitz, "and had we been caught with carrier forces dispersed, the Battle of Midway would have ended differently."

Secondly, while the Americans fought from a concentration of maximum strength, the Japanese made the fatal mistake of dividing their huge force into groups placed too far apart for effective action (Yamamoto's Main Body was 300 miles back; Nagumo's carriers were northwest of Midway; Kindo's Main Occupation Force was further to the south; and Kurita's support group with invasion transports was stacked at the southwest).

Worst of all for the Japanese was the infection of "Victory Disease," a naïve and arrogant overconfidence, a belief in their invincibility, and the mistaken notion that the Americans would not come out and fight. Quite the opposite, the U.S. fleet was spoiling for an opportunity to come to grips with the Japanese. The Nipponese were to learn to their dismay that there was a vast difference between attacking sitting ducks at Pearl Harbor and attempting to strike an enemy ready and willing to do battle.

American hopes had been fulfilled—the Japanese had chosen a battleground for a major naval engagement in American waters. It was something like Tsushima (the great naval battle of May 27–28, 1905, in which the Japanese defeated the Russians) in that one force had traveled an immense distance before being brought to engagement. But there was a difference—Tsushima had been fought in Japanese waters and it was the Russians who had done the traveling. Midway was fought in American waters; when it was over the surviving Japanese ships had to go a long way to get home.

A shocked and bewildered Yamamoto headed back to Tokyo to report catastrophe to his emperor and to his ancestors. "I felt bitter," commented Nagumo's chief of staff, "I felt like swearing."

Midway was the first decisive defeat inflicted upon the Japanese navy in modern times. American strength had forced Yamamoto to abandon his mission despite his carefully laid plans and superior gun power. The blow forced the Japanese planners back on their heels in an unaccustomed role of the defensive. The grandiloquent plan to conquer Fiji, New Caledonia, and New Zealand was now canceled.

For the Americans it was a brilliant victory, a gallant fight, a satisfying triumph. It firmly ended all threats to Hawaii and the West Coast. From this point on the Japanese were to be confined to their home waters or to the South Pacific, except for a brief stay in the Aleutians.

Midway also marked an end to the old strategy of surface warships as operational units. From now on both sides were to operate in task forces built around one or more carriers.

"Pearl Harbor has been partially avenged," commented Admiral Nimitz.

ACTION IN THE ALEUTIANS

On the northern flank came a Japanese attack on Dutch Harbor, the American naval base in the Aleutian Archipelago, some 2,000 miles north of Hawaii. This desolate chain of islands, like a giant causeway, stretched a thousand miles across the North Pacific from the Alaskan mainland westward almost to the Kamchatka Peninsula in Soviet Siberia. It was enveloped in fog, ice, and mud.

In 1930 the United States had renewed its pledges, originally made in the Washington Naval Treaty of 1922, not to construct or expand naval fortifications on Guam or the Aleutian Islands. Pearl Harbor changed all that. Primary air bases at Fairbanks and Anchorage in Alaska were already set up, and plans were being rushed for constructing a chain of bases along the Aleutians. Dutch Harbor, toward the east end of the Archipelago, was not yet completely fortified; it was defended only by a modest force.

On June 3, 1942, on the same day that another enemy force was discovered off Midway, a Japanese task force, consisting of two carriers, two cruisers, and three destroyers, converged on Dutch Harbor. The invaders expected little or no resistance. Suddenly, out of the fog, from the west, of all places, appeared a force of American planes, which tangled with the Nipponese aircraft and swooped down on the invading ships. The Japanese, thoroughly confused and suspecting that they had fallen into a trap, broke formation and fled.

They were unaware that earlier the Americans had built two secret air bases, with landing fields made from portable steel mats, at Cold Harbor, east of Dutch Harbor, and on Umnak Island, almost 100 miles farther west.

It was not a complete American victory, because the enemy paused long enough in his retreat to occupy Kiska, Attu, and Agattu, about 850 miles west of Dutch Harbor. The Japanese were now on American soil, even if it consisted of far-flung island outposts.

The occupation brought several advantages to the Japanese: The islands were steppingstones to the North American mainland; they could now intercept shipping between the United States and Soviet Russia; and they could now expect the air over their home islands to be free of American bombers in force.

Late in August 1942 an American task force brought army troops to the Andreanof Islands, 125 miles west of Kiska. From this new base American planes bombarded the Japanese positions on the Aleutians and took a heavy toll of ships.

In October 1942 the Japanese retired from Attu and Agattu and began to reinforce their installations on Kiska.

RECOIL IN THE PACIFIC: GUADALCANAL

There was no conventional front in the vast ocean spaces. The whole Western Pacific, from Alaska to Australia, embraced a series of zones in which Japanese and American forces overlapped and permeated each other. Nipponese expansion reached southward from the home islands, feeling in every direction for the weaknesses of the enemy. Most of the key Pacific islands were now in Japanese hands, their garrisons trained and prepared to fight to the last man.

The setbacks in the Coral Sea and at Midway in May and June of 1942 impelled the Imperial Japanese Navy to revise its overall strategy. The Battle of the Coral Sea foiled the first Japanese thrust at Australia through Port Moresby in southeastern New Guinea. The Battle of Midway was a resounding victory in the Central Pacific and put a block on further Japanese expansion eastward.

Japanese planners thereupon decided that it would be best to keep away from the Central Pacific, where the claws of the American eagle were being sharpened at Pearl Harbor. The strategy was to turn once more to the southwest, where two separate blows could be directed at Australia. The first thrust would be a drive across the Owen Stanley Mountains to take all of New Guinea. The second would be a simultaneous seizure of the Solomon Islands. The two striking forces would be based, one on Port Moresby at the southeastern tip of New Guinea and the other on Guadalcanal at the southeastern end of the Solomons. The Japanese already had a powerful air base at Rabaul on New Britain, between New Guinea and the Solomons, as well as the small island of Tulagi in the Solomons. From these points an all-out offensive could be mounted against Australia.

Vital to the new Japanese strategy were the Solomon Islands, a volcanic archipelago, 17,000 square miles, 700 miles in length from northwest to southeast. The native population of some 200,000 Papuans and Polynesians had been under Australian administration since World War I. The climate was hot and humid, the night mists filled with effluvia emanating from putrescent matter in the swamps and jungles, the insects pesky and dangerous, the whole area malaria-ridden. Control of Guadalcanal in the Solomons would cut the American lifeline to New Caledonia and Australia.

For the coming great battle for the Pacific the American command was divided between navy and army leaders. Admiral Chester W. Nimitz, from headquarters at Pearl Harbor, commanded the North, Central, and South Pacific forces. General Douglas MacArthur, who had been ordered from the Philippines to Australia in 1942, was placed in command of forces in the Southwest Pacific from the China coast eastward to the Solomon Islands.

The American strategy, like that of Japan, was based on attack, though some military historians regard the attack on Guadalcanal as essentially a defensive maneuver to protect American supply lines. The loss of Singapore had closed the direct route from the United States to the Indian Ocean. From the Allied point of view it was necessary to cut off the tentacles of the Nipponese octopus one by one until an offensive could be mounted on the main body. There would have to be a long, costly build-up, during which time the

Americans had no choice but to leave the Japanese dominant in the Pacific. Combat losses since Pearl Harbor had reduced American first-line aircraft carriers from seven to three. And little could be accomplished without the help of the big flattops, as demonstrated at the Coral Sea and Midway.

American production met the challenge. Within two years some 50 carriers of all sizes, some new, some reconverted warships, appeared in the Pacific. Naval aircraft increased tenfold. American strength gathered for the big assault.

The advance would be made by leapfrog tactics, a kind of naval version of the land *Blitzkrieg*. A task force of tremendous strength would be sent to take a key island. Battered by the big guns of battleships and by dive bombers, the island would be invaded, conquered, and an air base immediately constructed. Then repeat the maneuver at another island closer to the enemy homeland. It was not necessary to take every Japanese-held island. Many would be bypassed, leaving the enemy garrison isolated. Then, with the tentacles of the octopus either cut off or paralyzed, drive irresistibly on to the home islands of Japan.

On July 4, 1942, a reconnaissance pilot reported the ominous news that the Japanese were in the process of making an airstrip on Guadalcanal. This was it! A hurried decision was made to strike as soon as possible.

On August 7, 1942, a powerful American task force, commanded by Vice-Admiral Robert L. Ghormley, appeared off the southern Solomons. The pre-landing bombardment to soften up the defenses was short, lasting only three hours. Then from transports the First Marine Division and elements of the 2nd Marine Division, which had been stationed in New Zealand, stormed ashore on Guadalcanal and its satellite islands—Florida, Tulagi, and Gavatu.

Opposition was violent in the three adjacent islands. On Gavatu the Marines ran into a hornet's nest—the Japanese, fighting desperately from caves, died to a man. The landing itself on Guadalcanal was unopposed on the ground. The Marines captured the unfinished airfield and renamed it Henderson Field.

Then began a battle which lasted for six months, with the most terrible kind of fighting on land and a series of six encounters at sea.

At dawn on August 9, 1942, just two days after the landings, a Japanese task force of cruisers and destroyers, covered by aircraft from Rabaul, rushed down to strike at the Allied naval forces guarding the beaches of Guadalcanal. Helped by the rainy weather, the Japanese within an hour sank three heavy American cruisers and the Australian cruiser *Canberra*, with little damage to their own warships. Near-by to the east—like so many sitting ducks—were loaded American transports waiting to disembark their troops. But for some unaccountable reason, to be repeated many times in the Pacific war, the

Japanese suddenly broke off the engagement and retired. With them disappeared a golden opportunity to smash the transports.

The fighting on Guadalcanal, a horrible nightmare, gave the U.S. Marines their first taste of jungle warfare, a special type of fighting that was to take place on scores of Pacific islands. The jungle was a formidable obstacle. Huge hardwood trees, buttressed by giant roots, spread their heavy branches toward the sky. Connecting them was a lush tangle of vines and brush forming an almost impenetrable carpet. From the moist ground came the stench of decaying vegetation, decomposition, and putrefaction. Everything was coated with a cloak of dampness and humidity.

Through this hot, humid terrain the Marines hacked their way, wading through swamps, gingerly boating across the rivers. Eyes and rifles were always on the alert for Japanese snipers, who either hid in the underbrush or strapped themselves in the tops of palm trees. The Japanese proved to be masters in the art of merging into the jungle background. Added to the clever enemy were millions of insects, including malaria-ridden mosquitoes, as well as a variety of rats, scorpions, and boa constrictors. At night the Americans found it impossible to distinguish between animal cries and the oral signals of the Japanese.

Samuel Eliot Morison, an eyewitness, described it: "Guadalcanal is not a name but an emotion, recalling desperate fights in the air, furious night naval battles, frantic work at supply and construction, savage fighting in the sodden jungles, nights broken by screaming bombs and deafening explosions of naval shells."

Through August and September 1942, 17,000 Marines, without air cover and exposed to land attack, held a narrow strip seven miles long and four miles wide on the shores of Guadalcanal. Their orders were to hold—especially that vital airstrip—until reinforcements could be brought in.

Both sides sent in more men and supplies. Gradually, the Marines, now assisted by infantrymen, began to fan out through the island. They huddled in foxholes, sloshed through the jungle, hunted the Japanese defenders concealed in caves and dugouts, killed snipers lashed to the branches of trees.

Lieutenant General Alexander A. Vandegrift later told of the fierce fighting (*The New York Times*, August 5, 1945):

> In mid-October, after some planes joined us, our aviation reserves fell desperately low. Ammunition became pure gold. Food problems forced us to settle for two meals a day. Just before a major enemy attack broke, heroic efforts by naval supply brought sufficient relief to see us through.
>
> The ability of the Japanese to bring in reinforcements and to pound our position at the airfield from both air and sea resulted in recurring crises ashore. During the first four months fighting rose each month to a climactic struggle in which a fresh and determined enemy force strove to push our ground troops into the sea. Slashed and repulsed, the enemy withdrew each

time to gird for another try with replenished manpower and supplies.

Meanwhile, we were unable to undertake a full-scale offensive of our own because we lacked sufficient combat troops to drive inland in strength and hold positions guarding the airfield at the same time.

The American naval defeat of August 9, 1942, was followed in the next several months by a series of heavy naval encounters in the waters between Guadalcanal and the adjacent islands, the "Slot," as it came to be known. American forces were assigned the duty of intercepting the "Tokyo Express," which brought reinforcements from Bougainville, the largest island in the Solomons, to Guadalcanal. At the end of October planes from the *Enterprise* and *Hornet* destroyed two Japanese destroyers and heavily damaged two battleships, two carriers, and several cruisers off Santa Cruz Island.

On the night of November 13–14, 1942, came the decisive Fifth Battle of the Solomons, which took place off Guadalcanal. Admiral Ernest J. King, chief of U.S. naval operations, called it "one of the most furious sea battles ever fought."

A Japanese task force, the heaviest surface force yet committed in the war, including at least one battleship of the *Kongo* class, appeared off Guadalcanal to screen a new landing. The Nipponese fleet was gathered in a huge circle to protect the operation.

An American task force, consisting of eight destroyers, two heavy cruisers, and three light cruisers went to the attack. It was David against Goliath, lightweight against heavyweight. Discretion dictated a quick American withdrawal. Instead, the American fleet steamed ahead in a straight line of 3,000 yards directly at the enemy, speeding into the circle, which opened at one end like a mouth gaping with surprise.

The light American warships dodged and lurched and plunged from one enemy warship to another inside the circle. The Japanese, startled by these tactics, which bore some similarity to the unorthodox moves made by Admiral Nelson at the battle of Trafalgar in 1805, began firing across empty space at their own ships. The action, short but deadly, took place in the dark, illuminated by weaving searchlights, flashes from the big guns, streams of tracer bullets, and tremendous orange bursts from exploding ships.

It took only half an hour for the Americans to complete their avalanche of fire from within the circle. It was breathtakingly effective. Had the Japanese fleet remained out of range, its giant guns could have broken the lighter American warships like matches. But the Nipponese were unable to depress their big guns enough to fire on the small but speedy American ships. By boldly charging in at close range, the Americans had found the enemy's weak spot.

The next morning the Japanese were back. An eyewitness, correspondent Ira Wolfert, reported the enemy "still flowing toward us monstrously, like some amputated torso gushing blood from almost every inch, making a last desperate effort to take Guadalcanal."

This time the American fleet was waiting with considerably greater advantage in firepower. The Americans craftily allowed the Japanese to proceed around the north side of Savo Island, and then, speeding up from the southern side, caught them in the classic "crossing the T" maneuver. Again there was a half hour of concentrated hell. Nearly a dozen Japanese ships were left burning and exploding. The remaining Nipponese ships crawled westward away from disaster.

The Japanese Imperial Navy had taken a fearful beating. Its losses were 2 battleships, 1 cruiser, 3 destroyers, and 10 troops transports sunk; 3 cruisers, 6 destroyers, and 2 transports damaged. Several thousand Japanese were killed or drowned. The task force had not been able to hurl a single shell onto Guadalcanal, although, under cover of the battle, it was able to send in a small number of landing boats with reinforcements.

The Americans lost the cruisers *Atlanta* and *Juneau* and 4 destroyers. Two cruisers and 2 destroyers were damaged.

The sixth and final naval battle took place at Tassafaronga on November 30, 1942. A Japanese convoy of troops transports escorted by combatant units to reinforce Guadalcanal was engaged by a U.S. task force. The Japanese lost a destroyer, the U.S. the cruiser *Northampton*. The Japanese retired although the Americans had the worst of it in this engagement.

But the Mikado's navy had taken a severe pounding. Organized resistance on Guadalcanal itself and the satellite islands ceased by early February 1943. Six months of battle for the key islands came to an end.

Hindsight judgment reveals the weakness of the over-all Japanese strategy. New Guinea and Guadalcanal were some 3,000 miles from Tokyo. Over this extended line the Japanese had tried to take both areas, dividing their forces between the two, and, in the process, losing the chance of conquering either one. It was a grievous error.

The Americans at Guadalcanal gave a brilliant demonstration of courage and skill against odds. Theirs was a triumph of teamwork by sea, air, and land forces in amphibious warfare. Since Pearl Harbor the Americans had planned for the day when they could come to grips with Japanese land and naval power. Guadalcanal turned out to be a trap not only for battle-tested veterans of the Imperial army but also for Japanese warships and air force.

From this time until the battles for Iwo Jima and Okinawa, on the doorsteps of the home islands, the Japanese were wary about committing their full strength against an Allied amphibious operation.

CHAPTER 15

Outwitting the Desert Fox

During this night I and a few of my colleagues had remained on the coast road, near the old battle headquarters. From there I could see the continual muzzle flashes and the shells exploding in the darkness. I heard the thunderous roar of the battle. Again and again formations of British night bombers appeared, dropped their deadly cargo on our troops and lit up the whole battle area with their parachute flares, so that all was bright as day. No one can ever measure the burden of anxiety that weighed upon us at this time. That night I scarcely slept at all, walking up and down wondering how the battle would go and what decisions I should take. It seemed to me doubtful whether we could continue for any length of time to resist attacks of the violence which we were now experiencing and which I knew the British could intensify still further. I was quite convinced that I should not await the decisive breakthrough but should anticipate it by withdrawing westward. In case of retreat we must do our best to extricate as many tanks and guns as possible and move them with us. In no circumstances must we await the complete destruction of the Alamein front. Next morning I decided that in the event of heavy pressure from Montgomery I would not await the culmination of the battle, but would retreat to the Fuka Position, some 50 miles to the west.

—General Erwin Rommel, *Krieg ohne Hass* (*War Without Hate*)

AXIS DISASTER AT EL ALAMEIN

"We hold the gateway to Egypt with full intention to act. We did not go there with the intention of being flung back sooner or later."

Thus spoke General Erwin Rommel in the early days of the battle of El Alamein. The words were for public consumption, but the Desert Fox, intelligent realist, had many reservations in the back of his mind.

The Italian *Duce* and the German *Fuehrer*, on the other hand, were undisturbed by doubts. To them this was the eve of a gigantic victory, the practical certainty of a glorious triumph. The advance of the Axis in North Africa had been strewn with monuments to Allied defeat. In Berlin and Rome the radio blared proclamations of coming victory. The press prepared anticipatory editorials. Medals commemorating the deeds of the *Afrika Korps* and the Sardinian Grenadiers had already been struck. New and crisp occupation money was available for distribution. Mussolini, hungry for glory, was not to be caught napping. Already his famous white charger had been sent to Africa to be ready for the victory parade in Cairo. This was going to be total Axis victory, the beginning of the end for the Allies.

From his *Wolfsschanze* (Wolf's Lair), 2,000 miles away in East Prussia, Hitler gazed at huge blown-up maps on which he was "personally conducting the decisive battle for North Africa." He gave additional intense study to his astrological charts. This was to be the realization of a dream—an enormous pincers movement in which one German spearhead was to push through the Ukraine to the Caucasus, while the other was to drive eastward from the deserts of North Africa to the Suez Canal, the jugular vein of the Allies. The loss of Suez would be more deadly to the Allies than the capture of London itself. Hitler's next steps would be to capture the oil fields of the Middle East, smash the wide-open flank of the Soviet Union, finish the business at hand with the stubborn British, and, finally, together with the Japanese, humble the barbarians from North America.

Then the name of Adolf Hitler, such a man as appeared only once in a thousand years, would be forever inscribed in the annals of warfare, surpassing even Alexander and Napoleon.

Thus the grandiose dream—the dream that turned out instead to be a nightmare. El Alamein was, indeed, a grand climax, a decisive battle—but in favor of the Allies. The Allies won at El Alamein because they had the best combination of air, sea, and land power, the most effective supply, and the imponderables of brilliant leadership and solid troop morale. The course of Western society was decided on these dreary sands of North Africa.

The two rival desert armies were poised at El Alamein just 60 miles west of Alexandria on a line running between Tel el Eisa on the Mediterranean coast and the 600-foot pyramidal hill of Qyaret el Hemeimat near the edge of

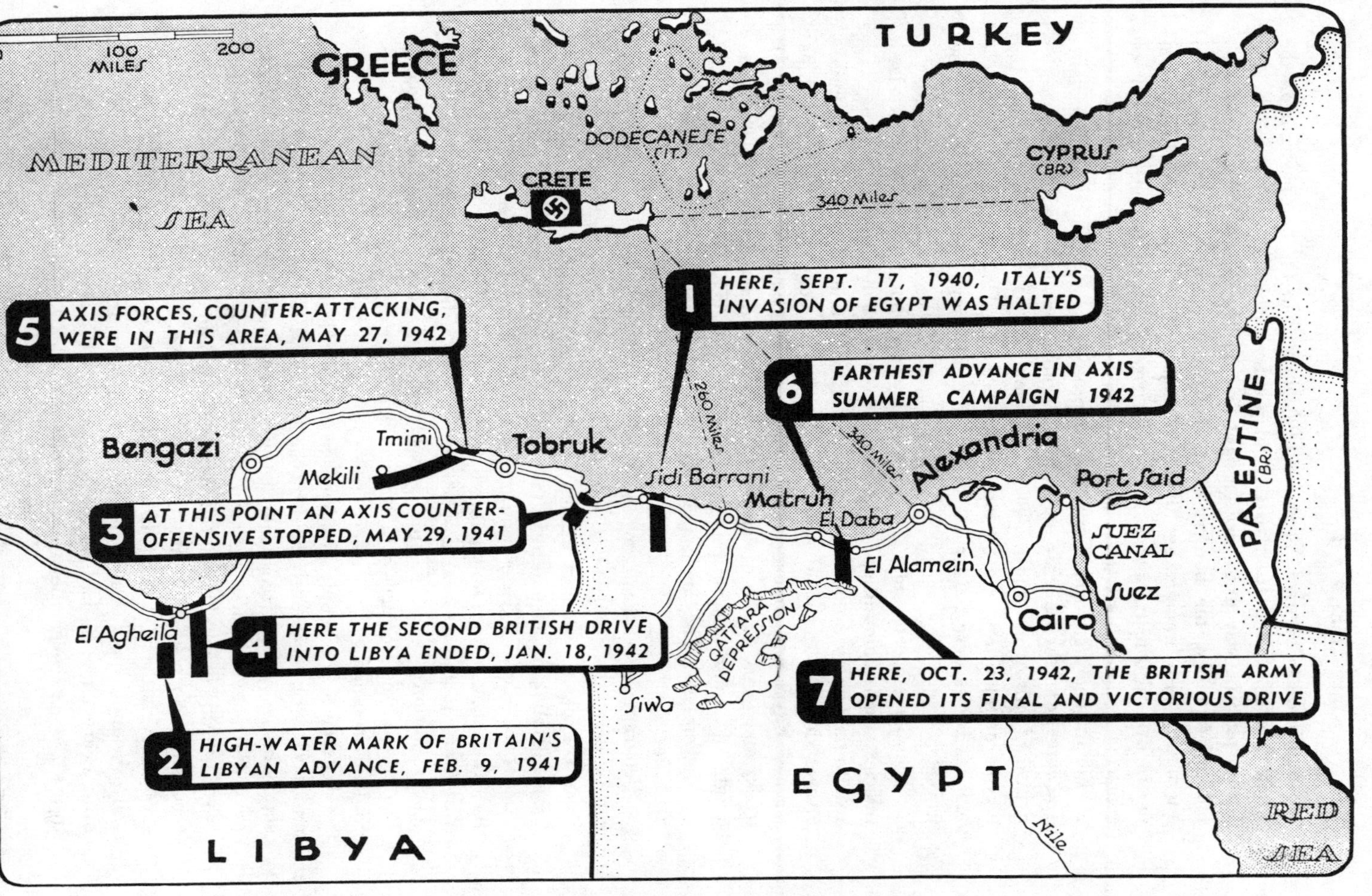

THE BATTLE FOR EGYPT

the impassable Qattara Depression. El Alamein was the one position on the whole North African front that could not be outflanked—the winning side had to push its way to victory straight through the enemy lines. It was forbidding territory, the hardest kind of fighting ground, stretches of sand alternating with innumerable hillocks of dry rock. Unable to dig foxholes in the rocky soil, the troops on both sides were reduced to the extremity of constructing little stone walls as defense spots.

For the coming battle of attrition the problem of supply was all-important. The appetite of the war machines was insatiable. One armored division of the British Eighth Army required *every day* some 70,000 gallons of gasoline, 350 tons of ammunition, and 50 tons of spare parts. The side which could get supplies to its desert warriors would certainly have the advantage in the struggle.

The British were only 200 miles from Suez, but their tanks, motorized vehicles, fuel, ammunition, and munitions had to be brought all the way around the Cape of Good Hope to Port Said, Suez, and Alexandria. The build-up was slow but steady. By early October 1942 a convoy of 18 Allied ships reached Egypt and unloaded new American Sherman tanks, thousands of trucks and jeeps, scores of self-propelled guns, and hundreds of planes. The weight of armor was shifting to the Allied side. The British had another vital advantage: They held the only fresh-water springs in the vicinity of El Alamein.

Geography seemed to favor the Axis in the battle of supply, but geography can be deceptive. The Axis troops at El Alamein were 300 miles eastward from Tobruk, whose port capacity was inadequate; most supplies for the German-Italian forces had to be unloaded at Benghazi, some 600 miles to the west of El Alamein. Three-quarters of the Axis transports setting out from Italy to Benghazi were sunk either by the Royal Air Force or the Royal Navy. Water was another critical problem for the Axis. Since the British had taken the precaution of salting, oiling, or blowing up most of the wells around El Alamein, the Germans and Italians had to bring in every drop of water by land transport.

The key to the supply problem was the island of Malta, the precious air and naval base tenaciously held by the British. Hitler believed that he could supply his troops via Crete while "keeping Malta quiet" through air bombardment. Here again he was mistaken. British warships based on Malta wreaked havoc on Axis supply lines in the Mediterranean, and prevented Rommel from accumulating stocks necessary for the showdown.

Moreover, the R.A.F., controlling the air, harassed the enemy's convoy and overland supply routes and kept the ground troops off balance. Hitler, using every plane he had on the Russian front, could not give his African troops the air cover they so desperately needed. Field Marshal Hermann

Goering, chief of the *Luftwaffe*, characteristically tried to talk his way out of an embarrassing situation. At a conference at Hitler's East Prussia headquarters in early September 1942, Goering ridiculed Rommel's contention that British fighter-bombers had knocked out German tanks with 40-mm. shells sent from America.

"Quite impossible," said Goering, "nothing but latrine rumors. All the Americans can make are razor blades and refrigerators."

Rommel, who had taken the precaution of bringing shell-samples with him, replied, "I only wish, *Herr Reichsmarschall*, that we were issued similar razor blades!"

In August 1942 Churchill, on the occasion of his first conference with Stalin at Moscow, stopped off at Cairo to appraise the situation in North Africa and the Middle East. He took advantage of his visit to reorganize the British command in the face of the crisis engendered by the Axis advance to the gateway of Egypt. He named General Sir Harold Alexander as the new commander in chief of the British Middle East forces. The command of the Eighth Army was a problem. Lieutenant General W. H. E. ("Strafer") Gott, who had been slated for the post, had been killed in a plane crash. After some thought, Churchill chose Lieutenant General Bernard L. Montgomery.

It was a momentous decision. The final battle for North Africa was to be fought by two military geniuses, both able to foresee, outguess, and improvise during the heat of battle. This was truly a battle of Titans.

Bernard Law Montgomery, like Generals Harold Alexander, Alan Brooke (later Lord Alanbrooke), and John Dill, was a North Irishman by descent. Born in London, November 17, 1887, Montgomery attended Sandhurst, the British officers' school, and entered the army in 1908. He served in World War I, during which he was wounded and decorated, and later was assigned to duty in Palestine, Transjordan, and India. At the outbreak of World War II he was an obscure major general who only recently had been pulled out of an officers' pool to command a division in England.

Small, lean but hard as steel, with piercing blue eyes, the 55-year-old Montgomery gave the impression of a hawk. He was a man of extraordinary ego, based not on an Adlerian inferiority complex but upon massive self-confidence. "Give me a fortnight," he said, "and I can resist the German attack. Give me three weeks, and I can defeat the Boche. Give me a month and I can chase him out of Africa." When the battle of El Alamein was going badly, Montgomery announced: "It is now mathematically certain that *I* will eventually destroy Rommel." He looked like a harmless schoolmaster, but his belligerence was built-in: "Tomorrow we shall give the enemy a bloody nose."

Montgomery was overbearing, incalculable, critical of others, even insolent in dealing with both superiors and inferiors. Before he became a general officer, a superior noted on an efficiency report that "Montgomery should attain high rank in the army . . . but to do himself full justice he must cultivate tact, tolerance, and discretion." Exactly. He had a fine capacity for alienating the upper brass, but at the same time, like Rommel, he had an extraordinary ability to arouse a sense of loyalty in the men under his command. To the lowliest private he was always "Monty," distinguishable by his double-badged beret.

Even if it was difficult to get along with Montgomery, he was, nevertheless, one of the most capable officers produced by the British during World War II. Unconventional he was, but he was also a top strategist who had a remarkable knowledge of the nature and problems of mechanized warfare. Witness General Eisenhower's appraisal: "General Montgomery has no superior in two most important characteristics. He quickly develops among British enlisted men an intense devotion and admiration—the greatest personal asset a commander can possess. Montgomery's other outstanding characteristic is his tactical ability in what might be called the 'prepared' battle. . . . He is careful, meticulous, and certain."

Opposed to Montgomery at El Alamein was Field Marshal Erwin Rommel, whose flair for desert warfare had already earned him the nickname of the Desert Fox. Rommel had served as a lieutenant in the Argonne in World War I, and had gradually worked his way to the top of the German officer corps. Energetic, tireless, he was a master of the technical problems of warfare. With keen military imagination and instinctive insight, he seldom followed a preconceived plan, but, instead, able to see a whole field of battle at a glance, he improvised and made adjustments according to the situation. Candid, frank, open, he knew the magnetic art of handling men. His troops idolized him—"The front is where Rommel is!" To the Prussian officer clique he was an upstart. To Hitler, who was envious of his general's popularity, Rommel was, nevertheless, the indispensable combat leader.

Lieutenant General Hans Speidel described Rommel as "a soldier with 'civil courage,' whose love of his country was founded upon truth and rooted in his native soil and timeless nature. Honest with friend and enemy, he was a man who was inwardly free. . . . He was the personification of the good and decent in the German soldier."

Rommel was respected by his enemies. "Throughout the African campaign," wrote Churchill, "Rommel proved himself a master in handling mobile formations, especially in regrouping rapidly after an operation and following up success. He was a splendid military gambler, dominating the problems of supply and scornful of opposition. At first the German High Command, having let him loose, were also astonished by his successes, and were inclined to hold him back. His ardor and daring inflicted grievous disasters upon us. . . . [He was] a great general. He also deserves our respect because, although a loyal soldier, he came to hate Hitler and all his works. . . ."

Rommel's plan of action at El Alamein was primarily directed toward offense, with careful regard for defense. He constructed a maze of barbed-wire entanglements and a series of mine fields laid out in a "ladder defense," a series of rungs behind the front lines. These rungs he called Devil's Gardens, in which the attackers would be surrounded by a murderous defensive fire. But to Rommel this defense plan was only to be used in the event of an emergency. Famous for his fast-moving tactics, he had no intention of fighting a purely defensive battle. With a thousand gallons of gasoline he would be on his way. True, his troops were rocking with weariness, but they were not dispirited. He would keep the enemy off balance, then suddenly strike his line at El Alamein, and break through in a lightning dash to the Suez Canal.

Montgomery's plan was equally careful. The colorful Briton invariably insisted upon the possession of clear superiority in matériel before making a move, a tendency that was to bring him much criticism later in the Battle of the Bulge. "Rommel could do what he liked," Montgomery said later. "I had no intention of launching *our* attack until we were ready. When that time came we would hit Rommel . . . right out of Africa."

As soon as he took command of the Eighth Army, Montgomery made sparks fly. He reorganized the entire army almost overnight. Weeding out incompetent officers, he dismissed generals as well as lieutenants. He visited the front lines, made quick decisions for changes, and talked with his men, instilling into them his own brand of superconfidence. Within a few days every Allied soldier at El Alamein was aware that something new had been added to North African desert warfare—a leader who could match the brilliance of the legendary Desert Fox.

Montgomery scrapped all previous orders and plans for the withdrawal of the Eighth Army to Egypt and the Middle East. He ordered that no longer were dispersed units to be sent against the enemy as in the past to probe for weak points. From this time on, he insisted, every ounce of Allied strength must be committed only in mass formations in overwhelming force. "It seemed to me," he commented later, "that what Rommel liked was to get our armor to attack him. I was determined that would not happen this time. His tanks would come up against our tanks dug in in hull-down positions."

The trick was to outfox the Desert Fox. Montgomery devised a series of ingenious tricks to persuade Rommel that the Allies were going one way when actually they would come by another route. The main attack would come in the north, but Montgomery gave the impression that he was building up for a mass attack from the south.

It was a game of concealment in the northern area of El Alamein. Here Montgomery camouflaged hundreds of his best Sherman tanks, and under cover of darkness he brought up heavy guns. He ordered that tank marks in the sand be carefully covered. He cautioned his troops to give the appearance of as little activity as possible. Here was his strength.

In the southern sector huge dummy fuel depots appeared in profusion. Hundreds of phony tanks and planes were spread over the landscape. Thousands of men seemed to be at work unloading supplies (nonexistent), covering tank tracks, rushing from one place to another. The troops, delighted by their new roles as Thespians, discovered hidden talents in make-believe. It was an expert production of military stagecraft, managed by a master director. The ruse worked: German reconnaissance pilots discovered the tremendous commotion in the south—the swirling dust of movement as before attack, and duly reported a huge concentration of the enemy in the south.

On the last day of August 1942, after assurances from Field Marshal Albert Kesselring and Marshal Ugo Cavallero of Italy that 6,000 tons of fuel were on the way (incidentally, never delivered), Rommel attacked. Launching feints at north and center, he hurled his forces at what he believed to be the enemy's strong point in the south. He would break through along the edge of the Qattara Depression, wheel north for the coast, and then head for Suez.

Allied fighters, including the famed 7th ("Desert Rats") Armored Division, struck back. The Royal Air Force, flying in mass formations without opposition, plastered Rommel's lines.

The Axis tanks headed for the area to the south of Alam el Halfa straight into Montgomery's trap. The wily Briton had arranged for a map to fall into Rommel's hands showing the terrain at Alam el Halfa to be perfect for tank use. When Rommel's mechanical monsters got there, they ground to a halt, hopelessly ensnared in soft sand. Rommel finally caught on. Since he obviously had not taken the enemy by surprise, he broke off the offensive within three days and returned to his original jumping-off position.

Orders came from Hitler: Rommel was to return to Germany, where he would enter a sanatorium in the Semmering Mountains to obtain long-postponed medical treatment. General Georg von Stumme was sent as a replacement during Rommel's absence.

Montgomery waited patiently for nearly seven weeks, carefully winding the spring.

On October 23, 1942, Montgomery spoke to his troops: "*When I assumed command of the Eighth Army I said that the mandate was to destroy Rommel and his Army, and that it would be done as soon as we were ready. We are ready NOW!*"

Late that evening, at 9:40 in bright moonlight, Montgomery began his own offensive, the third and last of the British Libyan campaign, the major Battle of El Alamein.

This was it—all or nothing!

A thousand big guns opened fire on the German positions. First came the lightning-like flashes in the night sky as battery after battery went into action. Then came the ear-splitting crashes of the accompanying thunder. "For twenty minutes," said an eyewitness, "the mighty artillery concentration roared and hammered a deafening chorus. The sound of shells falling on the enemy was like that of a hailstorm in a city of corrugated iron with the rumble of 10,000 drums. It was appalling."

Now the mortars added their sharp sibilants and sparks to the rising tumult. At almost the same instant the machine guns joined in with their shrill chattering. Muzzles burned hot in the night as a hail of fire sped toward the enemy. Rommel's advanced infantry positions were smothered under blast and dust and smoke.

Four hours later the barrage was lifted. For a few minutes there was a strange silence, in almost shocking contrast to the thunderous chorus of the barrage. Then, suddenly, unearthly cries, at first feeble but soon gathering volume, rose out of the desert. It was the weird shout of the charging foot soldier, that inhuman cry heard on a thousand battlefields.

Next came large-scale probing attacks by British light armor. By the following morning two wide corridors, cleared of mines, were driven through the Axis lines.

Montgomery now committed most of his assault divisions in mass—armored units, independent armored brigades, and a good proportion of his tanks, while holding a sufficient number in reserve to be used later if necessary. It was an overwhelming force pitted against 270 German tanks and about 300 almost obsolete Italian tanks (some of the latter fell apart when their guns were fired).

Into action went tested Commonwealth troops—Britons, Highlanders, Australians, New Zealanders, Indians, and South Africans. The fighting was violent, but the edge gradually went to the Allies. General von Stumme, Rommel's replacement, fell dead of a heart attack on the battlefield.

Word of the impending catastrophe, along with appeals for fuel and supplies, was flashed to Hitler at his Wolf's Lair. On the noon of October 24, 1942, the *Fuehrer* phoned Rommel at his sanatorium and asked him if he felt capable of resuming command at El Alamein. Though still unwell, Rommel agreed at once, and flew off via Crete to his headquarters, which he reached on the evening of October 25.

It was too late. British artillery was laying a single rolling barrage along the entire front. The desert was filled with the hulks of burned-out Axis tanks. At hourly intervals the R.A.F. hurtled down to attack Axis tanks already immobilized by lack of fuel. Slow-flying Italian planes, pounced on by speedy British fighters, in desperation unloaded their bombs on their own troops.

The Italians on the ground could not escape because the Germans had taken all their transport.

On October 31, 1942, Rommel led a counterattack, with little effect. He made the mistake of committing his reserves piecemeal, while Montgomery sent his troops in one concentrated blow on a narrow front.

To Rommel from Mussolini came a message of "deep appreciation for the successful counterattack personally led by yourself."

From Hitler came a radio message virtually begging for victory:

> I and the German people are watching the heroic defensive battle being fought in Egypt. We have loyal confidence in your powers of leadership as well as in the courage of the German and Italian troops under your command. In the situation in which you now find yourself, there can be no other consideration than to hold fast, never retreat, hurl every gun and every man into the fray. During the next few days there will be important air reinforcements transferred to the Commander in Chief South. The *Duce* and the *Commando Supremo* will also strain every muscle to see to it that you are supplied with the means to continue the battle. The enemy has numerical superiority, but he, too, will come to the end of his resources. It would not be the first time in history that the stronger will has prevailed against the stronger battalions of the enemy. You can show your troops no other way than that which leads to victory or death.

There it was—advice from the *Fuehrer* to Rommel to use his will power against speeding British armor. But for the Desert Fox it was sour fruit.

Headlines in London, November 4, 1942:

In Egypt Axis Forces Begin Their Retreat Westwards;
Disordered columns on coast road are attacked by air day and night;
260 tanks and 270 guns have been captured or destroyed;
9,000 prisoners have been counted

The Axis forces were now in full retreat and the Allies were pouring through the rear areas. Among the prisoners was General Ritter von Thoma, commander of the *Afrika Korps*, who had denounced Hitler's order to hold fast as "unsurpassed madness." Von Thoma was captured in full uniform with all his decorations. The German general, carrying a canvas bag and dazedly wandering around the battlefield, was picked up by some surprised British troops.

At this point word belatedly came from Hitler to Rommel agreeing to a withdrawal. The Desert Fox and what was left of his proud army, retreating westward, were hotly pursued by the British, and harried by air and naval bombardment as they streamed along the coast road back to Libya. German vehicles became ensnarled in a huge traffic jam. When the Germans reached Mersa Matruh, they were saved from annihilation by a lucky downpour of rain. The Axis had lost 60,000 men, 1,000 guns, and 500 tanks in the rout.

On November 8, 1942, came word of another gigantic pincers movement—this time by the Allies. Operation Torch was under way as Lieutenant General Eisenhower's armies landed at numerous points along the shores of French North Africa. Rommel was now caught between two fires.

For Hitler it was complete and irretrievable disaster, the end of his grandiose dream to conquer Egypt. Eventually, he was to lose all his troops, stores, ammunition dumps, and heavy equipment in North Africa.

For the Allies it was a tremendous success, synchronized as it was with the Soviet victory at Stalingrad and the American triumph at Guadalcanal.

The British public was delighted by the news. Six weeks before El Alamein a British newspaper had conducted a poll on "Who is the best general in the world?" The editors were somewhat embarrassed when Rommel was the winner, hands down. When another poll on the same subject was held after El Alamein the winner this time was Montgomery.

"The Battle of El Alamein," said Churchill, "was the turning point in British military fortunes during the World War. Up to Alamein we survived. After Alamein we conquered."

From this time on, the architect of the desert victory was to be known as Montgomery of Alamein.

OPERATION TORCH: THE U.S. INVADES NORTH AFRICA

In June 1942 President Roosevelt and Prime Minister Churchill met in Washington to consider the next steps in the war against the Axis.

The prognosis was not encouraging. Ships were being lost in American coastal waters at an alarming rate. In North Africa the peripatetic Rommel and his roving tanks were poised at El Alamein for a breakthrough to the Suez Canal. And Marshal Stalin, still suspicious of his allies, was loudly calling for a Second Front, again accusing the British of cowardice, and warning that Russia might not be able to stay in the war unless some pressure were lifted from her armies.

In Washington a high-level decision was made: Operation Overlord (born Roundup), the contemplated mass invasion across the English Channel of Hitler's *Festung Europa*, would have to wait until the summer of 1943, or even later. If, by September 1942, Russia appeared to be on the verge of collapse, then there would be a limited Operation Sledgehammer. Uncle Joe would just have to wait. Overlord could not possibly begin until the build-up was sufficient to forestall another Dunkirk.

Both Roosevelt and Churchill agreed that the European theatre was decisive. Once again Churchill talked "soft underbelly." Roosevelt, who, as early as January 1942, had suggested an American attack on Casablanca in North Africa to be called Operation Gymnast, now revived his earlier plan. Something had to be done, said F.D.R., "to get on Rommel's tail." Churchill agreed.

Operation Torch would be a simultaneous Anglo-American invasion of Northwest Africa to take place not later than October 30, 1942. The objectives:

1. It would trap Rommel in North Africa between the British Eighth Army and the invading forces from the west.

3. It would provide an excellent invasion base for action against southern Europe.

3. It would tighten the anti-Axis blockade and the Western-Soviet alliance.

4. It would give further bases from which the Mediterranean and South Atlantic water routes could be made safe.

5. If successful, it would tend to confirm Spanish neutrality and prevent the wily Franco from entering the war on the side of the Axis.

6. It would forestall any similar action contemplated by the Germans and Italians.

When the news of Torch was communicated to Stalin, he gave his enthusiastic blessing. As a matter of principle he still continued his satirical denunciations of the British for what he called their reluctance to fight the Germans, but he was happy to note that a definite plan was under way to relieve the pressure on his own armies.

The grand strategy for Torch was worked out in London by the Joint Chiefs of Staff. In a surprising move the American Lieutenant General Dwight D. Eisenhower was placed in over-all command. At the outbreak of war Eisenhower was so little known even in his own country that he was identified in a press photograph as "Lt. Col. D. D. Ersenbeing."

Dwight D. Eisenhower was born on October 14, 1890, at Denison, Texas. He was descended from German Mennonites who left the Rhineland for Pennsylvania in the 1730's and later settled in Kansas and then Texas. He was graduated as a 2nd lieutenant from West Point in 1916. In World War I he was assigned to the 19th Infantry at Fort Sam Houston, Texas. In 1918 he was a lieutenant colonel in charge of a tank corps at Camp Colt, Gettysburg, Pennsylvania.

A paper Eisenhower had written about 1930 attracted the attention of General Douglas MacArthur, then chief of staff, who requested that the promising officer be assigned to his office. When MacArthur was sent to the Philippines in 1935 as head of the American Military Mission, he took Eisenhower along with him. Eisenhower remained with MacArthur until 1939. Then followed assignments as chief of staff, 3rd Division, 1940–1941, and of the Third Army, 1941. After the Louisiana war maneuvers he was made chief of the War Plans Division, War Department General Staff, and then became assistant chief of staff, Operations Division, with the rank of lieutenant general. He was made commander of Allied forces landing in North Africa on November 8, 1942, and then commander in chief of Allied Forces in North Africa and full general in February 1943.

Command of the naval forces for the North African invasion was assigned to Admiral Sir Andrew Browne Cunningham, a British naval officer known for his aggressiveness.

Preparations began immediately in both Britain and the United States, where troops were trained in the intricacies of desert and mountain warfare. And the industrial machines of both countries began to grind out the necessary mountains of matériel and supplies.

Every phase of the military planning of Operation Torch had to be worked out in conjunction with an extremely complicated political situation. Both British and American leaders agreed that, as a concession to French sensitiveness, it was necessary to give it the appearance of an American-dominated operation. It was partly for this reason that command of Torch was given to an American general. The French military and civil commanders in North Africa, no matter what they personally thought of the Germans, had given their oaths of loyalty to Marshal Pétain and the government of Vichy France. Only if the Americans appeared in force could these Frenchmen plead "impossible odds" and "overwhelming strength" to the Vichy government and its Nazi captors.

From the American point of view, Torch was a regrettable but absolutely necessary operation. This was the first time in history that the United States had planned what amounted to an unprovoked attack upon a supposedly neutral country. But Vichy had collaborated with Hitler, and as a satellite Axis country in an all-out war it could not expect the safety of neutralism.

Secret diplomatic negotiations were necessary to prepare the way. Robert D. Murphy, the senior State Department officer in North Africa, who had been accredited to Vichy since 1940, was assigned the task of winning the support of the Free French in North Africa. From Murphy to the Allied planners in Washington and London came a stream of valuable reports on the temper of the military and civilian population, the names of officers with pro-Allied sympathies, and the details of French military and naval strength in the area.

This was work of tremendous value. But on one point, as Eisenhower later related, Murphy miscalculated. He was convinced by French Generals Charles Emmanuel Mast, chief of staff in Algeria, and Marie Émile Bethouart, commander of the Casablanca Division, that the French in North Africa were ready to rally behind a leader who would symbolize their desire for freedom. For this they suggested the name of General Henri Giraud, who had escaped from a German prison in World War I and who had duplicated the feat early in 1942. With his record and with his seniority in the French army, said Generals Mast and Bethouart, Giraud would be the ideal figure around whom the French of North Africa would rally and be led into the Allied camp. As later events showed, this advice was erroneous.

To test probable French reception of the invasion, an American military delegation was sent to contact General Mast and others in Algiers. Major General Mark W. Clark and a small staff were conveyed by airplane, British submarine, and runner landing boat to the coast of Algeria. The expedition made its rendezvous, but, when the local police grew suspicious, the French negotiators were forced to get away hurriedly.

General Clark and his little band made a fortunate escape in treacherous waters, in the process losing a substantial bankroll brought to smooth the way. This cloak-and-dagger operation had all the thrills of a Hollywood scenario, including blinking light signals from shore, paddling rubber boats in the darkness, sudden raids by secret police, and dashes for cellar headquarters of the underground.

General Charles de Gaulle, leader of the Free French, was rigidly excluded from the early planning of Torch. Although there was much sympathy for de Gaulle among the French civil population of North Africa, the military chiefs regarded him as a renegade who had been disloyal to his oath. If he were correct in writing off his obligations, then *they* were cowards. From the Allied point of view de Gaulle's assistance could only cause further complications. Moreover, Gaullist units had taken part in the fiasco at Dakar, when attacking Allied forces had retreated in confusion in the face of determined French resistance. British Intelligence assumed that this had been caused by a leak from de Gaulle's London headquarters.

On October 24, 1942, when Montgomery was breaking through the Axis line at El Alamein, a huge convoy under command of swashbuckling Major General George S. ("Blood and Guts") Patton, Jr., and Rear Admiral Henry K. Hewitt sailed from the United States. The next day, October 25, two great Anglo-American forces steamed from British ports. The destination was a rendezvous off North Africa.

At 3 A.M. on November 8, 1942, just 11 months after Pearl Harbor, an armada of 500 warships and 350 transports and cargo ships converged along the North Africa coast and, under air support from Gibraltar, began disembarking troops at Casablanca in Morocco and at Oran and Algiers in Algeria.

Algiers, the center of French military, political, and economic activity in North Africa, and the easternmost of the three major Allied objectives, surrendered on the first day. Here the Eastern Task Force, under the command of Major General Charles W. Ryder, consisted of the U.S. 34th Division,

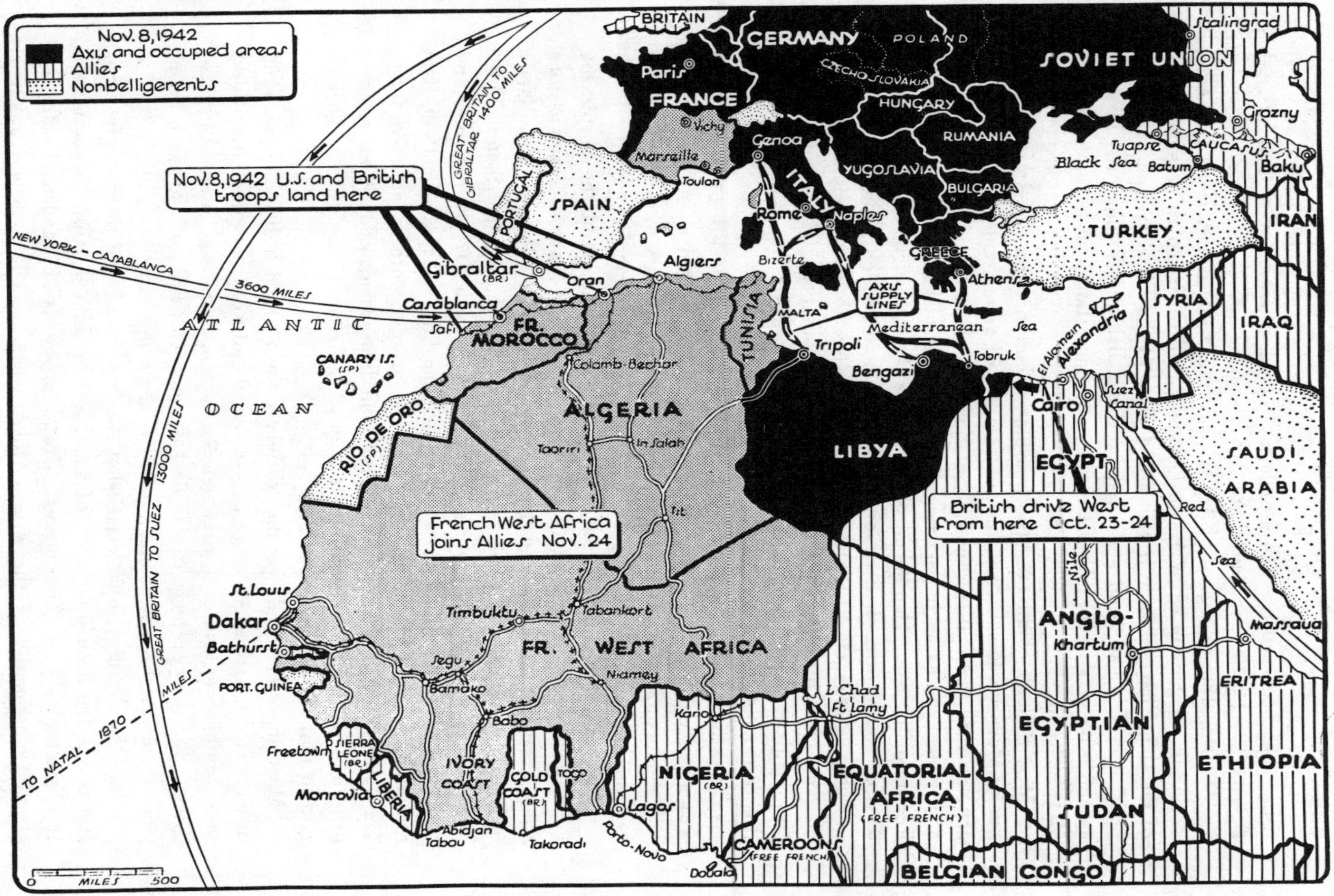

THE NORTH AFRICAN LANDING

which had been stationed in Northern Ireland, a regiment of the U.S. 9th Division, and a Ranger Battalion.

At Oran, 130 miles west of Algiers, resistance was stiffer. Here the Center Task Force, commanded by Major General Lloyd R. Fredenall, was composed of the U.S. First Infantry Division and parts of the First Armored Division, both of which had been stationed in Great Britain. Within two days the assault force was in control of Oran and the important near-by naval base of Mers el Kebir.

Most difficult of all were the Casablanca landings, on the Atlantic coastline of Morocco. Casablanca was the terminus of a long, antique railroad that ran eastward through the foothills of the Atlas Mountains to Oran, Algiers, and Tunis, and as such was essential for the maintenance of a land supply-line to all the troops landed in North Africa. From their coastal batteries in Casablanca the French fired on the assault boats which came ashore. The immobilized French battleship *Jean Bart* hurled 15-inch shells at the fleet offshore until its guns were silenced by dive bombers. The attackers sent tanks both to the east and west of the city to prepare for siege operations. But resistance ceased on November 11, 1942.

Operation Torch, an audacious gamble, took the enemy by surprise. It was a phenomenal tactical and strategic success. Within three weeks some 185,000 men, 20,000 vehicles, and 200,000 tons of supplies were safely ashore at Casablanca, Oran, and Algiers. Further build-up began at once.

This was a triumph of the first order—but what about the perplexing political situation? Fortunately for the Allies, there were no repercussions from Franco Spain. As had been expected, Marshal Pétain immediately ordered resistance and broke off relations with the United States. More important was the attitude of the French in the North African region. Many had been confused in their loyalties since the fall of France in 1940. The reception was mixed—some welcomed the invaders, others opposed them. The local administrators, businessmen, and landowners, almost all entirely pro-Vichy, deplored the landings, but quickly fell into line when it became evident that the invasion was a success.

Most important of all was the attitude of the 14 French divisions scattered through North Africa. Although poorly armed and weak in morale, they could cause untold confusion if they reacted adversely to the Anglo-American assault. The next problem was to deal directly with French leaders and convince them that French troops must be ordered not to resist.

Here the invaders introduced what they believed to be their trump card. Just before the invasion, General Giraud was brought to Allied headquarters at Gibraltar to meet Eisenhower. Giraud brusquely demanded that he be placed in command of the entire Allied expedition. Though not a single

Frenchman was in the Allied command at this time and though the enemy was French, Giraud still insisted that he be granted full command!

Eisenhower disabused him quickly. When, on November 9, 1942, Giraud was flown to Algiers to evolve an agreement with the French authorities there, he was completely ignored. The value of the trump card was exactly nothing.

There was some welcome news in the offing. Admiral Jean François Darlan was in Algiers. Back in February 1941 the anti-British Darlan had been designated as successor to Pétain in the event of the latter's incapacity—and Pétain was an old man. By a quirk of fate Darlan had returned to Algiers, just as the invasion began, to visit his sick son, to whom he was intensely devoted. It was a heaven-sent opportunity. The somewhat mysterious admiral was just the man to win over the dissident pro-Vichy elements. True, any dealings with him would create much public revulsion both in Britain and the United States. Eisenhower knew this, but also, as the responsible field officer, he reasoned that he was in Africa to win an ally, not to kill Frenchmen, but to keep his own casualties to a minimum.

Churchill, too, wanted Darlan's coöperation. "If I could meet Darlan," Churchill remarked to Eisenhower, "much as I hate him, I would cheerfully crawl on my hands and knees for a mile if by so doing I could get him to bring that fleet of his into the circle of Allied forces."

Darlan allowed himself to be convinced. When he was told that the Germans had swiftly occupied all of France as a countermeasure to the North African invasion, he announced that Hitler had violated the armistice of 1940, and that he, Darlan, was now ready to work with the Americans.

This was a vital decision. On November 10, 1942, Darlan ordered all French commanders to cease resistance at once. The French officers, who now had a valid order from a superior, obeyed to the letter. The French governors of Morocco, Algeria, and Dakar offered immediate coöperation.

Eisenhower set up Darlan as the French political chief in all of North Africa and designated Giraud as military chief. Throughout these developments Darlan insisted that he was acting in conformance with the wishes of his chief, Pétain, now helpless in German custody. In acceding to Eisenhower's request, he said, he was carrying out the innermost desires of Pétain.

But a few weeks later, on Christmas Eve, Darlan was assassinated in his office in Algiers by a young anti-Vichy patriot, a terrible end for an unhappy man. The Allies promptly designated Giraud as his successor. Arguments still rage in France as to whether Darlan was a great patriot or a collaborationist turncoat. In either case he was caught in the tragedy of history.

In four days a vast territory running 1,500 miles across North Africa had been added to the Allied cause at the expense of some 860 killed or missing and 1,050 wounded. The western jaw of the vise forged to trap Rommel was ready. More, North Africa was added to the British Isles as a base from which to launch the final assault on Hitler's *Festung Europa*.

"This is not the end," announced Churchill. "It is not the beginning of the end. It is perhaps the end of the beginning."

BLUEPRINT AT CASABLANCA: "UNCONDITIONAL SURRENDER"

The time was now ripe for the master plan to crush the Axis. The Soviet defense of Stalingrad had revealed serious weaknesses in the mighty German war machine. What was needed was a meeting of Allied heads at the summit to survey the entire field, theatre by theatre, of the war throughout the world and to outline future strategy.

In early December 1942 President Roosevelt declined Prime Minister Churchill's suggestion for a rendezvous in Iceland, but agreed to meet the British leader and his advisers at some carefully guarded spot in the recently liberated French empire. On December 22, 1942, it was decided to assemble at Casablanca in Morocco, North Africa. Stalin was invited but declined to leave Moscow because of the great Russian offensive which he himself, as commander in chief, was directing.

From January 14 to 24, 1943, Roosevelt, Churchill, and their chiefs of staff conferred at the Anfa Hotel, some five miles from Casablanca, on a knoll overlooking the sea. The wide verandas of the hotel offered a magnificent view of shimmering blue water, red soil spotted with green palms, and shining white buildings in Casablanca.

Present in these beautiful surroundings was the big brass of the American and British armed forces. Among the Americans were General George C. Marshall, Lieutenant General Dwight D. Eisenhower, Admiral William D. Leahy, Admiral Ernest J. King, Lieutenant General Henry H. ("Hap") Arnold, Lieutenant General Brehon B. Somervell, and two advisers to President Roosevelt—Harry Hopkins and W. Averell Harriman.

The British contingent included Admiral of the Fleet Sir Dudley Pound, Field Marshal Sir John Dill, General Sir Alan Brooke, Air Chief Marshal Sir Charles Portal, Vice-Admiral Lord Louis Mountbatten, and Major General Sir Hastings Ismay.

The British sent to the conference on a 6,000-ton liner an elaborate staff, cipher, and planning organization which had already worked out plans and statistics to the last detail. The British planned it this way: In the course of the summer of 1943, after the remaining Axis forces in North Africa had been destroyed and the Mediterranean opened to Allied shipping, the combined British and American land, sea, and air forces would strike from their

African springboard at the most vulnerable point of Hitler's Europe—from the south.

The proposed attack, continued the British plan, would shatter Italian morale, already crumbling, would throw the Balkans into a ferment, and in all probability would be followed by Turkey's entry into the war. All possible help would be sent to Soviet Russia to keep the Germans busy warding off blows in the East. Meanwhile, Germany would be bombed mercilessly from the air. Gradually, there would be built up in England a huge Anglo-American army and air force for a 1944 cross-Channel invasion. In the Far East, efforts would be made to reopen the Burma Road into China, while the Japanese army would be contained with a minimum of force.

The officers of the Plans Division of the War Department in Washington, on the other hand, came to the conference without the sort of precise plans the British had drawn up. The Americans apparently preferred to improvise as the meeting proceeded. They were skeptical about the logistical possibility of a large-scale cross-Channel operation in the near future.

While the two summit leaders, Roosevelt and Churchill, who liked and respected one another, worked in close harmony in making the final decisions, the technical experts of Britain and the United States who were laying the groundwork had protracted, sometimes bitter, arguments. Field Marshal Lord Alanbrooke (General Sir Alan Brooke), chief of the British Imperial General Staff, in *The Turn of the Tide* (1957) commented on the involved task of reaching common ground at Casablanca:

> When an operation has finally been completed it all looks so easy, but so few people ever realize the infinite difficulties of maintaining an object or a plan and refusing to be driven off it by other people for thousands of good reasons. A good plan pressed through is better than many ideal ones which are continually changing. Advice without responsibility is easy to give. This is the most exhausting job, trying to keep the ship of war on a straight course in spite of all the contrary winds that blow.

One bone of contention was the British insistence upon priority for the European Theatre. Admiral King, an alert, confident sea-dog (Roosevelt liked to say that King was so tough he shaved with a blowtorch), testily called for all-out war against Japan instead of the British-recommended holding operations. King proposed that 30 per cent of the war effort be devoted to the Pacific and 70 per cent to the rest.

British tempers, ordinarily restrained, boiled over at this suggestion. Hardly a scientific way of approaching war strategy, they argued. First things first. Mussolini had to be taken care of, then Hitler, then Tojo. The British believed that to Admiral King the European war was "just a great nuisance that kept him from waging his Pacific war undisturbed." British Air Chief Marshal Sir Charles Portal concluded that it was impossible to convince the hardheaded Admiral King: "We are in the position of a testator who wishes to leave the bulk of his fortune to his mistress. He must, however, leave something to his wife, and his problem is to decide how little he can in decency set apart for her."

Another argument—should Italy be attacked through Sicily or Sardinia? Here the differences did not run altogether on national lines, but were mainly between the Chiefs of Staff and the Joint Planners. The former wanted Sicily as the next step; the latter recommended instead an attack on Sardinia because they thought it could be done three months earlier. Both Churchill and Roosevelt interceded for Sicily, and Sicily it was.

These were tough brotherly battles, but all understood the necessity for agreement. The differences were slowly ironed out.

On January 20, 1943, the conferees made a happy and successful decision on the organization of the Higher Command in North Africa. It was clear that a centralized leadership was needed to coördinate the activities of British, American, and French forces. For this responsible position the command was handed over to General Dwight D. Eisenhower, who had impressed both Roosevelt and Churchill by his remarkable ability to reconcile British and American officers of differing opinions. General Sir Harold Alexander, a senior and experienced British commander, was brought over from the Middle East to act as deputy to Eisenhower, who thus far had had little war experience. These appointments seemed to the Americans a highly complimentary and pleasing gesture, despite their probably political undertones.

On January 22, 1943, General Charles de Gaulle, leader of the Fighting French, arrived at Casablanca in a stormy mood. Already present was General Henri Giraud, who had been appointed to succeed Admiral Darlan, after the latter's assassination, as Supreme French Commander in North Africa. Between the two—de Gaulle and Giraud—there was an intense rivalry. The de Gaullist forces in London and central Africa fiercely attacked every French military and civil official in Africa, and the latter replied in equally harsh terms. This public name-calling embarrassed the Allied cause. It was necessary to reconcile the two emotional Frenchmen and have some French nucleus, solid and united, with which to work.

"My job," said President Roosevelt, "was to produce the bride in the person of General Giraud while Churchill was to bring in General de Gaulle to play the role of bridegroom in a shotgun wedding."

Both Churchill and Roosevelt found it difficult to work with the temperamental, touchy, intransigent de Gaulle. Churchill assumed that the French leader owed his current status to the British and should have been more gracious, grateful, and compliant: "Here he was—a refugee, an exile from his own country under sentence of death, in a position entirely dependent upon the good will of the British government, and also now of the United

States. The Germans had conquered his country. He had no real foothold anywhere. Never mind; he defied all."

"You claim to be France!" Churchill thundered in one of the stormy encounters between the two. "I do not recognize you as France..."

"Then why," de Gaulle interrupted, "and with what rights are you dealing with me concerning her world-wide interests?"

To Roosevelt, de Gaulle was an egoist who regarded himself as a living representative of Joan of Arc, "with whom it is said one of his ancestors served as a faithful adherent." "Yes," Churchill is said to have rejoined, "but my bishops won't let me burn him!"

Feelings were high during those tense days. In the calm of the postwar era de Gaulle explained his position:

> I was starting from scratch. In France, no following and no reputation. Abroad, neither credit nor standing. But this very destitution showed me my line of conduct. It was by adopting without compromise the cause of the national recovery that I could acquire authority. At this moment, the worst in her history, it was for me to assume the burden of France. This was the attitude that was to dictate my bearing and to impose upon my personality a point of view I could never change.

Roosevelt and Churchill could not resist injecting a light note into the highly charged atmosphere at Casablanca. On the morning of January 24, 1943, when the final press conference took place, the two top Allied war leaders, like mischievous schoolboys, contrived to make de Gaulle and Giraud sit in a row of chairs alternating with themselves.

"We forced them," reported Churchill later in high glee, "to shake hands in public before all the reporters and photographers. They did so, and the pictures of this event cannot be viewed even in the setting of these tragic times without a laugh."

But there was more serious business at hand. The conferences wound up with an agreement which in its essentials followed the carefully worked-out plans which the British experts had brought to Casablanca. This promised to:

1. Take offensive action in the Mediterranean by launching an attack on Sicily in the course of the summer. This would help secure the Mediterranean lines of communication, divert German pressure from the Russian front, and start the campaign to knock Italy out of the war. Success here would in all probability bring Turkey into the war as an active ally.

2. Assemble in England the strongest possible force to invade the Continent across the English Channel as soon as German resistance was weakened to the required extent.

3. Continue the heaviest possible air offensive against Germany in preparation for the invasion.

4. Intensify the antisubmarine campaign as "a first charge on the resources of the United Nations."

5. Continue to sustain the Soviet Union by the greatest possible volume of supplies.

6. Maintain operations against Japan but keep them within limits that would not jeopardize the capacity of the Allies to take advantage of any favorable opportunity for the decisive defeat of Germany. Launch a full-scale offensive against Japan as soon as Germany was defeated.

7. Make plans for the recapture of Burma and for operations against the Carolines and Marshalls.

There was a surprising development at the final press conference. President Roosevelt spoke frankly: "Another point, I think we have all had it in our hearts and heads before, but I don't think it has ever been put down on paper by the Prime Minister and myself, and that is the determination that peace can come to the world only by the total elimination of German and Japanese war power.

"Some of you Britishers know the old story—we had a general called U. S. Grant.... In my, and the Prime Minister's, early days he was called 'Unconditional Surrender' Grant. The elimination of German, Japanese, and Italian war power means the unconditional surrender by Germany, Italy, and Japan. That means a reasonable assurance of future world peace. It does not mean the destruction of the population of Germany, Italy, and Japan, but it does mean the destruction of the philosophies in those countries which are based on conquest and the subjugation of other people."

This was the first official reference to the ultimate Allied objective in the war. Unconditional surrender! The phrase ruled out any negotiations with Germany, Italy, or Japan through channels of diplomatic negotiation. The term had not been agreed upon at the conference, and apparently, it was used on the spur of the moment by the American President. Although taken by surprise, Churchill immediately assented on the ground, as he later said, that any divergence stated publicly would have been damaging to the Allied war effort.

Critics immediately pounced upon the term "unconditional surrender" and denounced it as one of the greatest mistakes of Allied policy during the war. The phrase, they charged, convinced the German people that they were to be blotted out from amongst the nations of Europe, and that, as a result, the Germans became determined to fight to the end. Thus, said the critics, the war was lengthened by Roosevelt's action and tens of thousands of Allied lives were sacrificed by a political blunder of the first magnitude. From the viewpoint of the critics, another less harsh phrase, such as "honorable capitulation," might have encouraged the Germans to surrender long before they did.

Roosevelt undoubtedly wanted to prevent a recurrence of the situation after World War I, when the Germans claimed that they had surrendered on the basis of Wilson's Fourteen Points. He did not mean that the German people were to be enslaved or destroyed. But he wanted to make it clear that there were to be no bargains with the Nazis.

It was, indeed, an unfortunate slip, though made in good faith. There were so many facets and implications to a judgment of this kind that it should have been thoroughly discussed before the final press conference. What had happened, Roosevelt later explained to Harry Hopkins: "We had so much trouble getting those two French generals together that I thought to myself that this was as difficult as arranging the meeting of Grant and Lee—and then suddenly the Press Conference was on, and Winston and I had had no time to prepare for it, and the thought popped into my mind that they had called Grant 'Old Unconditional Surrender,' and the next thing I knew I had said it."

For defenders of Roosevelt this frank acknowledgment was enough. Besides, they said, the formula was really the kind of language the Germans understood. But for the legion of critics it was an unpardonable *faux pas*, further evidence of what they called the Rooseveltian capacity for floundering and bungling.

AXIS ROUT IN TUNISIA

Operation Torch brought to the Allies not only Morocco and Algeria but also the whole coast of French West Africa. Here the special prize was the port of Dakar, which had been used by the Axis as a base against Allied Atlantic shipping. Hitler countered by ordering the occupation of all Vichy France. The 60 French warships at Toulon escaped him when the French officers scuttled their own ships.

Hitler acted speedily to contain the Anglo-American thrust in North Africa. He was determined to hold the Tunisian ports of Bizerte and Tunis at all costs. German troops were ferried across the Mediterranean by ship and plane from southern France, Italy, and Sicily. Within a few days these reinforcements were pouring into Tunisia at the rate of 1,500 men a day, and eventually some four divisions became the nucleus of the Fifth *Panzer* Army. From the two first-class, easily defended ports, together with near-by all-weather airfields, Hitler counted on holding the Anglo-American forces until Rommel could build up strength for a massive counterattack.

Although Torch had been an unqualified success, difficulties began to mount for the invaders. Most African harbors, especially that of Algiers, had to be cleared of the detritus of war before they could be put to effective use. The supply problem remained acute. There were but a few good roads and it was necessary to repair the rickety little coastal railroad running some

650 miles eastward from Algiers to Tunis and to guard it against sabotage.

Airborne landings were made by the Allies at several points east of Algiers in the next few days after the initial invasion—on November 11, 1942, at Bougie, on November 12 at Bône, and on November 13 at Djidjelli. A small British force of three brigades of infantry and a brigade of obsolescent tanks, under the command of Lieutenant General Sir Kenneth A. N. S. Anderson, set out on the coastal roads toward the Tunisian border. Within a week Anderson was only 60 miles from Tunis, and by November 28 he was within 12 miles, at a point from which he could look down upon the city.

But it was heavy going, even for a commander of Anderson's special combat qualities. Eisenhower later described it: "The mud deepened daily, confining all operations to the roads, long stretches of which practically disintegrated. Winter cold was already descending upon the Tunisian highlands. The bringing up of supplies and ammunition was a Herculean task."

The Germans counterattacked stubbornly. Eisenhower ordered Anderson to stabilize his line at a point running from Medjez el Bab to the Mediterranean.

Then began the piecemeal process of reinforcement for a final showdown around Christmas. The Germans, too, increased their build-up, pouring in troops and supplies from their bases in Sicily. The arrival of Rommel and his tired, beaten troops in Libya brought the opposing forces there to near equalization. At this time Rommel flew unannounced back to Germany and attempted to convince Hitler that it would be best for the Germans to evacuate North Africa altogether. But the *Fuehrer* angrily ordered him back to his command.

From January 12–24, 1943, came the high-level conference at Casablanca. Rommel, aware that time was with the Allies in the battle of supply, decided that he would have to strike before the enemy could build up overwhelming superiority.

Again there came a powerful but this time desperate thrust by Nazi armor against the Allied lines westward from Faid Pass toward Sbeitla. Caught by surprise, the Americans fought a series of delaying actions on the way back to the Kasserine Pass. Here Rommel's surging army pushed on through hastily constructed defenses in the Pass, and turned northward toward Tebessa and Thala, threatening to cut the Allied armies in two.

Again the amazing Rommel had wrought consternation in the Allied camp. American losses in the ten days from February 14–23, 1943, were 192 killed, 2,624 wounded, and 2,459 prisoners and missing. A group of Flying Fortresses took off in cloudy weather to bomb the Kasserine Pass, but instead dropped their bombs on Souk el Arba, 100 miles away within the Allied lines, killing and wounding a number of Arabs. Eisenhower attributed the difficulties at Kasserine to several factors: to the failure to capture Tunis in the original invasion; faulty work in intelligence; failure to comprehend clearly the capabilities of the enemy; and greenness among the insufficiently trained American troops. But the Kasserine Pass made veterans of the Americans.

To plug the gap at Kasserine, two American divisions raced eastward from Oran in a forced march. The arrival of thousands of trucks from the United States was an important factor in the turning tide of battle. Meanwhile, Allied planes flew thousands of sorties against the Axis lines, helping to slow down the enemy and bringing his clanking tanks to a halt.

The struggle for control of the Kasserine Pass was but one phase of the over-all Tunisian campaign. While the American Patton and the Briton Anderson closed in from the northwest, Montgomery and his Eighth Army surged ahead in the southeast. Here, just to the southeast of Gabès on the coast, the Germans had constructed the Mareth Line, a line of defense which they believed to be impenetrable.

Montgomery's Eighth Army was an extraordinary aggregation of Englishmen, Highlanders, Anzacs, South Africans, Indian Gurkhas, Poles, Czechs, and Fighting French. From October 1942, when it took part in the Battle of El Alamein, until January 23, 1943, when it captured Tripoli, this cosmopolitan army had chased Rommel's *Afrika Korps* for some 1,400 miles, on some days advancing as many as 40 miles. Bypassing the railheads, the army was serviced by a fleet of more than 100,000 trucks.

The Eighth Army reached the Mareth Line at the end of January 1943. Montgomery waited until March 21, and then sent a part of his army on a frontal attack against the Mareth Line and another part on a wide-sweeping movement around its southern flank. The troops surged steadily ahead through the *khamsin*, the searing African wind that filled the air with swirling sand. It was a brilliantly successful maneuver, forcing Rommel to retreat to the Cape Bon peninsula.

The campaign was not yet over. There was still bitter fighting from one mountain range to another. While Montgomery closed in from the south, the Americans and the British to the north collided head-on with fiercely defended Axis positions. For the U.S. 2nd Corps it was Hill 609 dominating Mateur in the Bizerte sector. For the British First Army it was bloody Longstop, which changed hands repeatedly. But Hill 609 and Longstop were the doors to victory.

May 7, 1943. The end came with decisive speed. That day Anderson's First Army crashed through to Tunis, cutting the Axis forces in two. It was exactly 3:40 P.M.

At 4:15 P.M. that same day the American 2nd Corps, joined by several French detachments, broke through to Bizerte.

Rommel escaped the final collapse. The German army and Italian contingents, far from following Hitler's order to fight to the last man, threw away their arms and surrendered. A quarter of a million hard-bitten desert veterans were corralled in prison cages, including all that was left of the famed *Afrika Korps* and Mussolini's vaunted legions.

"From a purely military point of view [Montgomery later wrote in his *Memoirs*], the holding out in North Africa once the Mareth Line had been broken through could never be justified. I supposed Hitler ordered it for political reasons. It is dangerous to undertake tasks which are militarily quite unsound just for political reasons; it may sometimes be necessary, but they will generally end in disaster."

It was, indeed, a disaster for Hitler. For Mussolini it was the end of his vision of a new Roman Empire. There was historical irony in the fact that the *Duce*'s last African troops surrendered near the site of ancient Carthage, which had been destroyed by the Romans in 146 B.C. In less than three years the Italians had lost all their colonies in Africa, an area ten times the size of Italy and with a population of 15,000,000. Worse, more than 250,000 Germans and Italians had been captured in Tunisia.

Total Allied casualties in the Tunisian campaign were fewer than 70,000, of which 20,000 were American. On May 20, 1943, a gigantic victory parade was held in the streets of Tunis.

At long last the Allies were on the march. Now they had bases for the coming assaults on Italy and the Balkans. The Mediterranean could henceforth be used along its entire length for Allied shipping instead of the long sea route around the Cape of Good Hope.

Anglo-American coöperation had received its battlefield test. It worked. "The troops that come out of this campaign," said Eisenhower, "are going to be battle-wise and tactically efficient."

CHAPTER 16

The Pendulum Swings in Russia

I'm not leaving the Volga! When fighting against the Russians there can be no question of surrender.

—Adolf Hitler, January 1943

The drive to free the Soviet Union has begun.

—Joseph Stalin, February 1943

HITLER AS NAPOLEON: STAGE II: *TÊTE DE COCHON*

The German people were not happy. Gone was the great exaltation. Gone was the assurance that this was to be a quick and simple war. Goebbels's captive press spoke repeatedly of magnificent successes on the Russian front, but a different story came home in letters from the troops in the fighting lines. The war was still spreading throughout the globe and control of events seemed to have passed from the hands of the *Fuehrer*.

Some of the more outspoken Germans put it this way: "*Wir siegen uns zu Tode!*" ("We are being destroyed by our victories!")

The initial Nazi *Blitz* during the summer and fall of 1941 had slowed down to a crawl on the Russian steppes. Through that winter, through the most bitter weather in half a century, the *Wehrmacht* had to go on the defensive.

Hitler tried to explain it away. "The Russians," he thundered, "are a cruel, bestial, and animal opponent." He even admitted an error in calculating the strength of the Red forces: "We made a mistake about one thing: We did not know how gigantic the preparations of this opponent against Germany had been, and how tremendous had been the danger which aimed at the destruction not only of Germany but of Europe."

Forbidden by the *Fuehrer* to leave the scorched earth to the Russians, harried by incessant Soviet counterattacks and guerrilla warfare, the stalled German armies had to do something while awaiting warmer weather. Necessity was the mother of improvisation. The troops formed hundreds of defense boxes, generally at communications junctions, into which they could retire in relative security. From these shelters—the Germans called them "*Igels*" or hedgehogs—those in advanced positions in hostile territory could either defend themselves or branch out on offensive forays. Since their communications lines to the homeland were cut, they depended on airlifts for supplies, flown in on *Junkers-52* transport planes—"*Frau Ju*" to the grateful troops.

Conversely, the Reds probed, gnawed away, and struck at the hedgehogs, trying ceaselessly to lure the enemy from the makeshift fortresses. It was a murderous game. While the Germans played for time, the Russians busily went about the task of making the surrounding countryside untenable. Systematically, they blew up roads and railway bridges, anything that could be of use to the enemy. They placed tens of thousands of booby traps at any place where a wire could be attached, on telephones, electric-power lines, water pipes, in stoves, closets, beds. They even perfected teleignition bombs, attached to radio-receiving sets, set to a prearranged wave length, and then exploded from a distance by signal broadcast. Red guerrillas swooped down in sudden forays, destroyed ammunition dumps, derailed trains, and burned tanks. Thousands of Nazis met death at the hands of these hit-and-run guerrillas. The Germans were mystified by this type of organized resistance, foreign to their military handbooks. Above all they feared the cold steel of Red bayonets.

There was another unwelcome surprise for the invaders. The German High Command had expected that, once the Soviet industrial areas were overrun, production would dwindle and the Russian economy would grind to a halt. But instead of being paralyzed, Russian production seemed to increase.

The Russians had performed, in fact, an unprecedented miracle of industrial retreat. As soon as the Nazi legions swarmed across the borders, the Russians transferred whole factories from the west to the Urals, Siberia, and Central Asia. Here, far from the battle lines, masses of men built enormous new war plants—artillery, tank, and shell factories at Omsk and Sverdlovsk; brick plants at Omsk; steel plants at Magnitogorsk. Aircraft factories were constructed within months. The workers suffered in the sharp, cold climate, but they enthusiastically toiled away under most primitive conditions. They had one goal only—help expel the hated German invaders.

Gone was Russian inferiority in tank production. From the faraway factories came new 52-ton tanks, called "white mammoths" by the Germans.

Reckless Red tankmen drove these monsters through giant snowbanks and across frozen rivers and lakes. Russian engineers placed timbers on the ice, covered them with water that quickly froze, and presented the tankmen with a highly satisfactory frozen bridge. Time and again the giant Russian tanks appeared behind the German lines to wreak sudden havoc on the startled enemy.

The Germans, ensconced in their prickly hedgehogs, suffered horribly. But with food supplied by air, they managed to survive the hard winter of 1941–1942. They were still in a position to strike hard at the Russians. True, they had underestimated the enemy, but they would not make the same mistakes again. They would avoid overextending the fighting lines. Instead, they would hurl concentrated force on a limited target in the south.

SEVASTOPOL—VORONEZH—ROSTOV

In the last six months of 1941 Hitler had failed to take either Leningrad on the northern front or Moscow in the center. Before the winter stalemate he instructed the High Command on the nature of a new drive to be started as soon as weather permitted.

This time his objective was limited, but the prize was rich. He would concentrate massive forces in the south. His attack would spring from the Ukraine, where his troops had won spectacular victories in the summer of 1941. From the rich oil fields of the Caucasus he would get the gasoline necessary for planes, tanks, and trucks. At the same time he would cut off the Reds from this precious fuel supply.

There were more advantages. Hitler's drive to the Volga beyond Stalingrad, along with the attack on the Caucasus, would split the northern from the southern Red armies and simultaneously deprive the Kremlin of a vital industrial basin. And with control of the Black Sea he would be in a position to surge on to Egypt around the eastern end of the Mediterranean.

There were several pivotal points in this selected southern battleground: Sevastopol in the extreme southern sector, Voronezh in the north, and Rostov in the center. Once these three cities were taken, then would come the mass attack on Stalingrad to the east. This was the Grand Design to convert disaster into victory. On paper and on the *Fuehrer*'s battle maps it seemed to be the perfect strategy.

The siege of Sevastopol began in December 1941. For the next six months the Russians in that Crimean seaport and naval base held out against frenzied German assaults. It was Leningrad all over again—bombs; shellfire; air attacks; an inferno of fire and smoke; fighting in cellars, quarries, dugouts; starvation; disease.

The struggle reached its roaring crescendo in June 1942, when the Germans hurled every ounce of their power on the burning city. The defenders finally capitulated on July 3, after some had blown themselves up with their last munitions. Everything of military use to the enemy was destroyed.

The next act shifted to the northern wing. Here, poised to the east of the Don River, was a massive Germany army of 60 divisions, 1,000 tanks, and 3,000 first-line planes. Its immediate target was Voronezh, an industrial town of 325,000 inhabitants.

The offensive began with a fierce *Luftwaffe* bombardment of Kursk to the east. By July 7, 1942, powerful *Panzer* spearheads had raced a hundred miles to the Don, crossed the river, and converged on Voronezh.

The Russian counterattack pressed the Germans back across the Don at several points. So furious was the Red pressure that the Germans decided to bypass Voronezh and strike instead against Stalingrad to the southeast. Once again a German plan of action had misfired.

There was better news for Hitler on the central sector. Assisted by reinforcements, including several Rumanian divisions transferred after the fall of Sevastopol, the Germans began to exert terrific strength on Rostov.

At this point the Reds sent into action their giant new 52-ton tanks called KV's, after Marshal Klementi Voroshilov. Heavily armored, bearing three-inch cannon as well as machine guns, the KV's were effective against the smaller German tanks. But there were not enough of them. On July 27, 1942, the Russians evacuated Rostov.

Hitler now divided his triumphant Rostov forces into two major parts. One he sent to the Black Sea coast and the Caucasus with the aim of clearing the area and driving on to the Baku oil fields. This spearhead captured the port of Novorossisk to the east of Sevastopol on September 10, 1942, although the capture was claimed five days earlier. Then the spearhead branched off southeastward toward the Caucasus range and the oil fields. It won Maikop but fell short of the considerably larger oil fields at Grozny, and never reached Baku on the Caspian Sea.

The second major force turned toward Stalingrad and the Volga.

THE EPIC OF STALINGRAD

In September 1918 the Ukrainian town of Tsaritzin had been the scene of an important victory by a Red army under the command of Stalin over General Denikin's White forces. The town was renamed Stalingrad to commemorate the event.

Stalingrad was the outlet of the lower Volga region. Unlike Sevastopol, it had no natural defenses, but instead sprawled along the west bank of the mile-wide Volga, Russia's greatest river. Home of great tractor and armaments plants, it was a proud symbol of the Russian economy. Between this typical Russian boom-town and the oncoming Germans there was open steppe country broken only by a few low-lying hills.

Hitler desperately wanted Stalingrad. Its capture would deal a shattering psychological blow to the Russians and at the same time place the German armies in a strong strategic position. With the key city of the Volga in his hands, Hitler would not only isolate Moscow and Leningrad, but would also cut the last important oil supply from the Caspian Sea route to the Soviet Union. He would make the Volga the easternmost boundary of his Third Reich. To this task the *Fuehrer* assigned General Friedrich Paulus and 330,000 of Germany's best troops.

True, the Germans poised before Stalingrad faced a difficult operation. Although the *Wehrmacht* had suffered severe setbacks at Moscow, Leningrad, and Voronezh, it still had plenty of power left. Hitler had already conquered a third of Russia's vast population and had acquired a third of its chemical industries and a third of its coal and electric power. He had unquestioned superiority in planes, tanks, and guns. One more mighty effort and the gigantic Bolshevik state would topple over. So certain was Hitler that his lucky star would guide him to victory at Stalingrad within a matter of weeks that he moved his Supreme Headquarters and Army High Command from East Prussia to quarters in and around Vinnitsa in the Ukraine.

The epic struggle for Stalingrad began on August 22, 1942. "We are attacking Stalingrad," Hitler announced in the Sportpalast, "and we shall take it."

The initial German bombardment, one of the most concentrated ever made, flattened three-quarters of the city in a single day. But when the Germans penetrated the city, they found that the defenders had no intention of surrendering.

For the next two months, during September and October 1942, there continued one of the most amazing battles of World War II or any war. The German assault reduced Stalingrad to a graveyard of shattered buildings, crumbling walls, and rotting corpses. But, ironically, this enormous destruction helped the Red defense by making the streets impassable. German tanks, stalled in the mountains of rubble and debris, were destroyed by the Russians. Red troops, armed with machine guns, bayonets, and knives, crawled through the smashed apartment houses, factories, alleys, and courtyards, and fell on the Germans from flanks and rear. Some of the most appalling hand-to-hand fighting in history took place in the rubble of Stalingrad. There were bitter struggles not only for every building but for every room. Gains were measured in yards. The Germans, by desperate effort, would clear an entire block, only to relinquish it within hours.

It was unadulterated slaughter. Thousands died each day. It became impossible to bury the dead or even to count them. Russian General Georgi

Zhukov described it perfectly: "I would not have believed such an inferno could open up on this earth. Men died, but they did not retreat."

For the nervous *Fuehrer*, awaiting news from Stalingrad, it was once again shocking and disappointing news. In early November 1942 he made a political speech:

> I wanted to come to the Volga, to a definite place, to a definite city. That city happens to bear the name of Stalin himself. . . . I wished to take the city. We do not make exaggerated claims—now I can tell you that we have captured it. Only a few small sectors are not yet in our hands. People may well ask: "Why does the army not advance faster?" The answer to that is that I do not desire to see a second Verdun. I prefer to reach my objectives by means of limited attacks. Time is of no importance.

The trouble was, said Hitler, that the Russians refused to fight like troops who had been trained according to the normal principles of strategy and tactics. They fought like "swamp animals." And who could guess what a swamp animal would do on his next foray? This brings to mind General Braddock's complaint—he wanted the Indians to "come out of the woods and fight like Englishmen!"

Curious, indeed, was Hitler's combination of facts, excuses, and lies! The fact was simple: The Nazi battering ram against the gates of the Volga had broken down. Once more it was essential that Hitler retreat and regroup his battered forces, withdraw the Sixth Army, secure its new rear, and await a better opportunity. His field generals literally begged him either to reinforce their troops or assent to a withdrawal of several hundred miles, perhaps to Rostov, or even farther to the west. Either this, or once again, as in 1941, they would be trapped by the Russian winter.

From the *Fuehrer* came another outburst of rage: "Stay and fight! *I am not leaving the Volga!*" Again it was a Hitlerian display of military lunacy.

On November 19, 1942, the Russians under Zhukov launched a counterattack in two spearheads, one from the north and northeast and the other from the southeast from the bare Kalmuck plains, both driving westward and toward each other in a pincers movement. The Red *Blitz* relied heavily on cold bayonet steel, always a terrifying weapon to the machine-minded Germans.

Within four days the Russians had captured Kalach on the east bank of the Don, and many other places. In the area of Serafimovitch on a front of 20 miles and 15 miles south of Stalingrad the penetration of German positions was carried to a depth of 40 to 50 miles. Soon the Russian ring closed around 14 divisions of Paulus's Sixth Army.

The timing was perfect. Along with the constricting circle came the dreary Russian winter, trapping the Germans in one of the worst weather areas on earth. Stalingrad lies at the crossroads of two differing and converging climates. From the steppes of the north descend the icy Siberian winds; from the south come the warm currents of the Caspian; cold and warm winds clash convulsively over the area. From late October to early May there are pelting rains, deep snowfalls, violent storms. Once again it was the Russian freeze—and Nazi air power was grounded, armored vehicles put out of action, manpower decimated.

Caught in the Stalingrad pocket, 25 miles wide from east to west, and 12 miles deep from north to south, were most of 20 German and two Rumanian divisions, as well as such varied elements as engineers, Paulus's Sixth Army headquarters, and artillery and *Luftwaffe* ground staffs—in all, between 225,000 and 300,000 men. Under Russian pressure this great force was steadily compressed into a smaller and smaller area. With supply lines cut off, munitions and ammunition dwindled to the vanishing point. When their rations began to shrink, the troops ate horses, dogs, and cats.

Again there were frantic appeals to the *Fuehrer*. Hitler would not move an inch. "I have considered the situation carefully. My conclusions remain unaltered. The Sixth Army will not be withdrawn. . . . The Sixth Army will stay where it is. Goering has said that he can keep the army supplied by air. *I am not leaving the Volga!*"

There was hysteria in Hitler's reactions to the news from Stalingrad. "Send for the corps commander. Tear off his epaulets. Throw him into jail. It's all his fault." He made Paulus a field marshal. He issued a new order: "The forces of the Sixth Army encircled at Stalingrad will henceforth be known as the troops of Fortress Stalingrad."

Thus, by self-delusion, the Stalingrad encirclement became a "fortress."

The weary German troops would hold fast in the fiction that they were inside an impregnable fortress that would be relieved by Hitler's genius. "Stalingrad is the garrison of a fortress, and the duty of fortress troops is to withstand sieges. If necessary they will hold out all winter, and I shall relieve them by a spring offensive."

Where was the *Luftwaffe*? It was the same old desperate cry. Goering's flyers failed to relieve Fortress Stalingrad, especially after the Russians captured the remaining airfields in the Stalingrad pocket.

On December 12, 1942, a fresh *Panzer* division tried to relieve the Sixth Army by piercing the ring at the railroad station of Katelnikovo, only 50 miles from Stalingrad. Red troops under General Rodion Malinovsky hit this relief army and promptly destroyed half its armor. The rest retreated. On January 8, 1943, the Russians presented General Paulus with an ultimatum demanding surrender in 48 hours. Obeying Hitler, Paulus refused.

A week later the Stalingrad pocket was reduced to some 15 miles long and 9 miles deep, and the German garrison was cut to less than 80,000.

January 19, 1943. A typical day's report from the Russian front:

> On Voronezh front Russians capture Valuiki and Urazavo and the railway station of Belaya-Kalitva and Ortsogosk. Total number of prisoners taken in Voronezh offensive 52,000 of which 2,500 are Germans, remainder Italian and Hungarian. Petrovskoie on Caucasian front is captured.

The Sixth Army was in desperate shape. General Kurt Zeitzler reported the story from the German side:

> For the ordinary soldier fighting [at Stalingrad], each day simply brought a renewed dose of hunger, need, privation, hardship of every sort, bitter cold, loneliness of soul, hopelessness, fear of freezing or starving to death, fear of suffering wounds which in such circumstances could not be tended. . . . It was a nightmare without end. . . .
>
> Supplies to the fighting troops had ceased almost completely. The soldiers lacked food, ammunition, fuel, equipment of every sort. . . . Whole formations melted away. The Sixth Army was consumed as by a fire until all that was left was slag.

This went on day after day, the situation growing worse all the time. Only one question remained: How much longer could the battle continue?

By the end of January 1943 Hitler's great Sixth Army, the same army that had smashed through Holland and Belgium in the summer of 1940, was cut to pieces. In the last 20 days of January 1943 more than 100,000 German officers and men had been annihilated in or near Stalingrad in a ring of death. From cellars and caves streamed the last 12,000 ragged, hungry, and frostbitten German troops. Paulus and his staff surrendered in the basement of a department store to a 27-year-old Russian lieutenant. Taken with him were 15 generals, including two Rumanians.

"The road to German shame!" commented one tired German officer.

Stalin described it later: "The Battle of Stalingrad ended in the encirclement of a German army 300,000 strong, its capture and the rout of what remained of it. . . . 146,700 dead Germans were picked up on the field and burned."

Hitler's magical "No retreat!" formula had failed. He was furious with Paulus. That Paulus had surrendered without even the gesture of suicide was inconceivable. *Unvergleichliche Unverschämtheit!* Unparalleled shamelessness! "I have no respect for a man who is afraid of suicide and instead accepts captivity." As for the other generals: "This is the last field marshal I shall appoint in this war." And the troops of the Sixth Army? Hitler insisted that they should have closed ranks and shot themselves with their last bullets.

The Nazi ruffians dissolved in hysteria. All recalled Goering's words at the outbreak of the war: "*Wenn wir diesen Krieg verlieren, dann möge uns der Himmel gnädig sein!*" ("If we lose this war, then Heaven help us!")

For the Germans it was the most devastating defeat of World War II, the graveyard of Hitler's pretensions. "It was," said British historian J. W. Wheeler-Bennett, "perhaps the most monumental isolated example in military history of deliberate and wasteful sacrifice of human life."

Never before in Germany's history had so great a body of troops come to so humiliating an end. Hitler had not wanted a second Verdun, but in many ways Stalingrad had the same elemental fury, the same blind conflict of wills as that earlier blood bath. A wave of German flesh and blood had smashed against a wall of Russian steel, only to be shattered and thrust back, leaving the soil of Russia covered with bodies, still and grotesque in death, of the flower of the *Wehrmacht.* It was as terrible a collapse as that of Napoleon's *Grande Armée* in 1812.

The Russians, too, paid for their triumph with tremendous casualties. They lost more men at Stalingrad than the United States lost in combat in all theatres of the entire war.

Stalingrad was one of the great turning points not only of the war but of world history. From now on Hitler was on the defensive in Eastern Europe. He ordered four days of mourning for his lost legions.

DIVERSION: THE RAID ON DIEPPE

Meanwhile, from Soviet Russia came calls for help. The Russians desperately wanted a Second Front in the West to relieve the pressure on their own troops.

Stalin became more and more demanding. It was grievous military judgment, he said, only to attack German industrial targets from the air. Wars had to be fought and won on the ground. Russia was doing more than her share. He taunted Churchill about British "reluctance" to fight the Germans. Vociferous were the echoes from Communist party-liners in Hyde Park and Union Square.

On August 19, 1942, just three days after Stalin's sarcastic denunciation, the West moved to placate the Kremlin. A strong contingent of British and Canadian troops struck at Dieppe on the French coast. The German defenses were even more formidable than had been expected. For several hours the commandos held a toehold on the shore, only to be thrown back. More than half the invaders were killed or wounded, the others managed to reach the rescue vessels offshore.

Festung Europa, Fortress Europe, was strong. Churchill hurriedly flew to Moscow to explain to Stalin in person that a Second Front in 1942 was impossible without frightful loss of life. Dieppe, he said, had been a costly experiment, but valuable lessons had been learned for the future. He promised that Britain and the United States would in due time strike with overwhelming force, but declared that neither he nor Roosevelt would risk Allied lives in a foolhardy, premature assault. Have patience, he urged.

From Stalin came grunts of disbelief. Again he protested that the fighting men of the Soviet Union were bearing the brunt of the war. Not until the Normandy invasion of 1944 was under way did he grant that Churchill and Roosevelt were as determined as he to annihilate the monstrosity that was Hitlerism.

FROM DEFENSE TO OFFENSE

Moscow, Leningrad, Stalingrad—tombstones in the graveyard of Nazi aspirations.

There was more punishment to come, equally offensive to German sensibilities. How were the Russians able to withstand the onslaught of Hitler's legions and then inexorably push them all the way back to Berlin?

There were no secrets behind this performance. It was plain for all the world to see.

First, the inexhaustible supply of manpower. The Russian population was almost double that of the enemy. Hundreds of thousands died in the struggle, but from all over the vast country, from Leningrad to the Crimea, from Siberia and Asiatic areas, come replacements to fill the ranks.

The German High Command could not match this supply of reserves. By 1943 it could scarcely maintain its divisions at proper strength. Into the declining ranks of the *Wehrmacht* went foreign recruits, "ideological volunteers" pledged to fight against Bolshevism, many of them reluctant fighters, as well as lower-caliber German personnel. As in World War I, even green youngsters were impressed into service to face seasoned veterans.

More vital for the eventual outcome was the quality of Ivan, the Russian soldier. Tough, aggressive, fearless, he was a formidable opponent. No matter what the odds against him, he chose to attack. Alert and industrious, he was talented in improvisation: He would take an empty vodka bottle, fill it with gasoline siphoned from a stalled vehicle, tear cotton batting from his uniform to make a fuse, and then hurl this Molotov cocktail into the treads of Nazi tanks.

The Russian snow, dreaded by the *Wehrmacht*, was Ivan's ally. Camouflaged in white, wrapping his weapon in white cloth, carefully smoothing his tracks, he could sink at night into the snowy background and then suddenly emerge to wreak havoc on the enemy's flanks and rear.

To the perplexed Germans, outfoxed in a thousand subtle ways, Ivan was not even a human being, but a kind of animal insensitive to freezing weather and oblivious to pain and suffering. German military manuals gave fair warning:

> The Russian takes full advantage of this extraordinary sense of orientation, his mastery of camouflage, his willingness to engage in close combat. He never surrenders, even when the woods are surrounded and he is under heavy fire. He often leaves behind observers cleverly installed in trees, to direct artillery fire by radio, even when they themselves are endangered by that fire.

Similarly, the Russians eventually outstripped the Germans at the officer level. Red leadership was superb in strategy, tactics, and flexibility. Where the German generals had to function under the handicap, as Churchill put it, of "Corporal Hitler's intuition," the Soviet marshals and generals were granted wide battlefield discretion by Generalissimo Stalin. Young Red officers who performed well in combat were rapidly promoted, some becoming generals while still in their mid-thirties.

To the explanation of Russia's mounting strength must be added the factors of British aid and American Lend-Lease. As soon as Hitler invaded the Soviet Union, the hard-pressed British began to send token aid; after Pearl Harbor the convoying of American supplies gradually reached the proportions of a flood.

There were three principal routes to Soviet Russia: the most important from British ports to Murmansk and Archangel in North Russia; around Africa to the Persian Gulf and then to the Caspian Sea; and across the Pacific to Siberia. The Murmansk run was a dangerous trip of some 1,500 miles, during which Allied merchantmen, convoyed by the Royal Navy, had to fight off attacks by enemy planes, submarines, and warships operating off the coast of Norway. The freezing weather was almost as bad a menace as the enemy. Many British and American sailors lost their lives on this suicide run.

Less perilous was the long route to Iran (called Persia before 1935), some 12,000 miles from New York. Large numbers of locomotives and freight cars were sent to the repaired Trans-Iranian Railroad, which ran from the Persian Gulf to the Caspian. The supply route to Siberia in the Far East was less effective than the two main routes.

Hitler grossly underestimated American productive capacity. American sources show that by January 1944 the United States had sent to Russia at least 7,800 planes, 4,700 tanks and tank destroyers, 170,000 trucks, and millions of tons of steel and food. The Germans later issued these figures of American help to the Soviet Union: 17,000 planes, 51,000 jeeps, 400,000 trucks, 12,000 armored fighting vehicles, 8,000 antiaircraft guns, 105 submarines, 197 torpedo boats, 50,000 tons of leather, 15,000,00 pairs of boots, 3,700,000 tires, 2,800,000 tons of steel, 800,000 tons of chemicals, 340,000 tons of explosives, 2,600,000 tons of oil products, 4,700,000 tons of food, and 81,000 tons of rubber.

Granted that these figures may have been exaggerated by German Intelligence to explain away the defeat in Russia, still there is ample reason to believe that without massive American and substantial British support Russia scarcely could have taken the offensive in 1943.

Communist party-liners in the United States, obediently echoing Stalin's demand for a Second Front in Western Europe, loudly denied that *any* American aid was going to the hard-pressed Soviet motherland. Soviet Russia, they complained, was being sacrificed deliberately to the barbarous Nazi *Fuehrer*. The promised aid to Russia, they charged, had never materialized. Of such stuff was Communist political blindness made.

The "invincible *Wehrmacht*" was battered all the way from Stalingrad to the old borders of Poland in a series of gigantic blows. Everything about this grueling epic was on a massive scale—armies of millions fighting over great distances, wholesale bloodletting and destruction of property, smashing victory of Red arms, humiliating German retreats.

In the words of historian Walter Phelps Hall:

> The all-conquering Germans . . . were in retreat. From river to river, from city to city they were crushed back toward their Fatherland. The gains of two superhuman years were erased, the brags of Hitler and Goebbels now proved a mockery by German dead, the flower of the *Wehrmacht* scorched beneath the smoldering ruins of a dozen Russian cities, drowned in swamps, strewn carelessly by indifferent death in forests or on wind-swept steppes.

HITLER AS NAPOLEON: STAGE III—IGNOMINIOUS RETREAT

The year 1943, a year of retribution, opened with the Stalingrad triumph, followed by the lifting of the blockade, though not the siege, of Leningrad.

Throughout the remainder of the year, the Russians, shrewdly timing their attacks, working in close coördination, and ingeniously maintaining their supply lines on the few railroads, moved relentlessly westward, regaining some two-thirds of the land they had lost to the invader.

Hitler's scheme for the conquest of Russia was drastically revised downward. In the initial invasion on June 22, 1941, he had struck on a huge, overextended front of some 1,800 miles running from Leningrad in the north down to the Crimea. In 1942 he attacked on a more limited 480-mile sector. The major fighting in 1943 shrank to a 250-mile line in the south running from Orel through Kursk and Byelgorod to Kharkov and down to Rostov.

The *Fuehrer*'s appetite was diminishing perceptibly.

February 1943 was a month of Soviet triumphs. The headlines told the story:

February 3:
RUSSIANS CAPTURE KUPIANSK IN KHARKOV SECTOR; ON VORONEZH SECTOR THEY CUT KURSK-OREL LINE; IN CAUCASUS THEY CAPTURE KUSHCHEVKA

February 4:
RUSSIANS CAPTURE TIM AND SCHIGRY—30–40 MILES FROM KURSK; SOUTH OF ROSTOV THEY CAPTURE MINSKAYA AND KANEVSKAYA

February 8:
RUSSIANS CAPTURE KURSK

February 14:
RUSSIANS CAPTURE ROSTOV, VOROSHILOVGRAD, AND KRASNY SULIN

February 16:
RUSSIANS CAPTURE KHARKOV

February 23:
RUSSIANS CAPTURE SUMI AND LEBEDIN ON KHARKOV FRONT

Rostov was the southernmost key of the entire southern front. Kursk was the main winter bastion of the Germans on the north flank of the southern sector in the Ukraine. Kharkov, in the center, had been held by the Germans for more than a year. Before retreating, both *Wehrmacht* and *Luftwaffe* systematically destroyed Kharkov, leaving it a flaming hulk.

The impetus of the Red drive continued on into March 1943. In the first week of March the Russians, concentrating on the central front, regained Rzhev, 130 miles to the west of Moscow, and a week later (March 12) stormed Vyazma, a vital railway terminus between Moscow and Smolensk. Three days later, on March 15, 1943, the Russians evacuated Kharkov. They had moved too far too fast—it was time to pause and regroup. But thus far the Red winter drive had reconquered 185,000 square miles of Russian soil.

On July 5, 1943, came the expected German offensive—the third since the beginning of the invasion. Some 40 German divisions under Field Marshal Gunther von Kluge struck with enormous power at Kursk. Two mighty war machines collided head-on. The Nazis tried offensives in the Orel, Kursk, Byelgorod sectors. But the days of Nazi *Blitzkrieg* were over—no more fast-moving assaults, no more swarming envelopments. In a matter of days the Germans lost 70,000 men, a half of their armor, a thousand planes.

The Russian counteroffensive came just a week later against the fortified

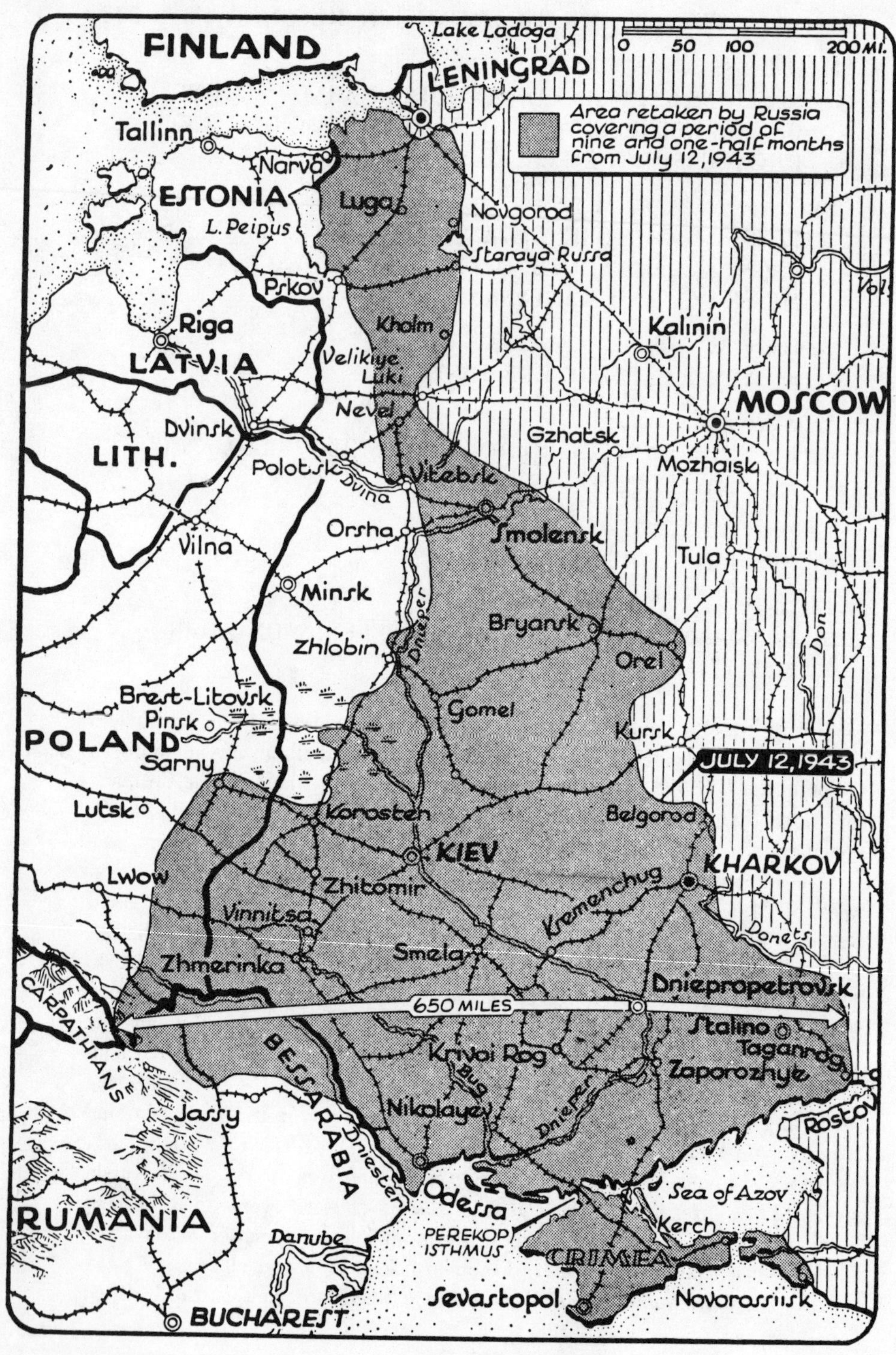

RUSSIAN ADVANCE, 1943-44

German salient at Orel. The Germans, threatened with encirclement, retreated, destroying everything in their path and planting acres of mines as they retired.

On August 4, 1943, Soviet tanks roared into Orel itself. On that same day, Byelgorod fell, 125 miles to the south. The next day Stalin issued a special Order of the Day congratulating the Red troops on the Orel and Byelgorod victories.

Three weeks later the Reds recaptured Kharkov, the fourth time this Russian city had changed hands since 1941. In six weeks the Russians took three vital bases which the Germans had intended to use for another assault on Moscow.

The Red tide swept on irresistibly for the rest of the year. Key points fell to them one after another: Bryansk, a strategic railway junction in the Ukraine; Smolensk, scene of the German Eastern Headquarters in 1941–1942; Dnepropetrovsk, site of Europe's largest dam, which the Russians had partially destroyed in 1941 ("We blew up this dam so as not to allow this first child of the Soviet Five-Year Plans to fall into the hands of Hitler's bandits"); and Kiev on the Dnieper, where the Germans, before retreating from the city, slaughtered the entire Jewish population. After the fall of Kiev in October, the Russians pushed westward to Zhitomir, only 67 miles from the old Polish border.

Entries on the Red tally sheet for 1943:

> 140,000 more square miles recaptured, raising the total retaken to some 325,000 square miles since Stalingrad.
>
> More than 38,000 towns and villages liberated.
>
> A million casualties for "Hitler's beasts."
>
> Total—thus far of German dead and wounded—more than 6,000,000.

Part V

CRUSADE: SMASHING THE AXIS

CHAPTER 17

Coalition: Blueprints for Victory

The power of Germany must be broken on the battlefields of Europe.

—Franklin D. Roosevelt

THE ECONOMIC WAR WITHIN WAR: THE BATTLE FOR OIL

Lured by headlines, people all over the world were fascinated by dramatic reports of struggles to the death on battlefields, ships disappearing beneath the seas, planes blasted out of the skies. But few were aware of the silent conflict in the background—the bitter economic war, which had enormous influence on the eventual outcome of World War II. Victory or defeat depended upon solutions of the problems of agriculture, oil, and war financing, on the production of munitions, on shipbuilding, aircraft production, transportation, engineering, on the role of capital and labor.

All the belligerent countries faced economic problems which called for basically similar measures. The business of wartime living was geared to shortages and restrictions. People were taxed to the hilt, a necessary measure in view of the tremendous expenditures. Rationing, particularly of gasoline, meat, and butter, was introduced early, to be followed by restrictions on coal and clothing. Luxuries disappeared; scarce goods emerged on the black markets. The construction of new housing ceased. Transportation suffered under wartime discomforts and interruptions. The problem of obtaining food both for the army and the civilian population became of prime importance. Everywhere there was a return to the soil, which in many areas had been neglected after a century of industrial and commercial expansion. It became not only necessary but fashionable to tend vegetable gardens in urban open spaces and in bombed sites between buildings.

In this economic war within war the advantages were on the side of the Allies, particularly the United States. In 1942 the Allies had the more abundant economic resources. Their war production was 60% of the world's total. They controlled 86% of the world's oil, 69% of its wheat, 67% of its coal, 64% of its iron, 50% of its sugar. One-half of the world's supply of tungsten, essential in hardening steel, was found in Far Eastern regions under Allied control; another 20% came from the New World. All this was vital—the Allies led from economic strength.

The European phase of World War II proved to be a testing ground between Hitlerian and American industrial production. (By Hitlerian production the *Fuehrer* meant not the output of Germany's industry but rather the giant industrial strength of all continental Europe under Nazi control.) Before the war Hitler observed that Nazified Europe would be a far more efficient and prolific producer of war matériel than the United States. Cartelized German industrial might would triumph, he was sure, over American *laissez-faire* capitalism. He was the totalitarian authority, who, acting with dispatch and speed, would snow-under American industry before it had a chance to get going.

Hitlerian economics functioned at two levels. The first was the immediate policy of spoliation—expropriation, looting. As soon as the Nazi armies smothered a country they systematically stripped it not only of military matériel but also of industrial machinery, raw materials, rolling stock, even luxuries, anything that could be removed and sent to Germany. A stream of wealth flowed into the Third Reich. Few Germans wanted to know how the ingenious *Fuehrer* did it.

At the second level Hitler proposed to create a new, mighty economic unit in Europe, with Nazi Germany as the industrial, financial, and administrative center. Vassal states would be transformed into pastoral, agricultural areas destined to provide food and raw materials for Nazi masters. Hitler introduced his own financial techniques in the occupied countries, seizing gold reserves, establishing credit balances in each country to pay for requisitions and occupation costs, placing Nazi underlings in control of the local industrial, commercial, and banking enterprises. Berlin would be the new hub of a great Nazi wheel moving the economic life of Europe. Hitler was sure that American industry could never compete with this gigantic industrial combine.

Hitler was dead wrong in his conception of American industrial capacity. The American economic system demonstrated that it had the space and power to expand as needed. New ideas, new concepts, new methods emerged in the American system—without being trampled upon by autocratic, totalitarian authority. The over-all smooth efficiency of the American economic system was one of the miracles of the war. There were serious labor, social, and financial problems, such as the necessity of stabilizing prices and wages, but they were solved. The American industrial effort, in conjunction with that of its allies, made certain Allied logistic superiority over the Axis.

Moreover, the Allies won the great economic war for the neutrals, through the preclusive buying program, by which America and Britain were able to buy up scarce materials all over the world while at the same time keeping these out of the hands of the enemy.

The Japanese, too, were defeated in the economic war. The sudden sweep from the home islands all the way south to the edge of Australia caught Tokyo unprepared for economic absorption of its gains. The Major Industries Ordinance of 1941 placed raw materials, labor, and capital for the key industries in the hands of the *Zaibatsu*, the small group of families which had attained great wealth through industrial and commercial manipulation. The *Zaibatsu* acted slowly, selfishly, and without vision—they used their new powers for the continued elimination or absorption of small industries. This was no way to fight a major economic war. The result was that Japanese production did not rise to the level necessary to carry on war against an inevitably rising American counteroffensive. Not until March 1943 was Premier Tojo able to obtain control of key industries, and even then he had to accept advisers from among the die-hard *Zaibatsu.*

Equally as unsuccessful was the Japanese attempt to establish a "Greater East Asia Co-Prosperity Sphere." There was no carefully worked-out economic plan for the new Pacific possessions. The tendency was to improvise, and this was just not enough. Not until Hitler began to build his New Europe did the imitative Japanese set up a plan for a centralized workshop in the home islands which was to be nourished from the agricultural, pastoralized occupied islands.

With the exception of Manchukuo there was little expansion of the Japanese economy in the huge cluster of occupied territories. Tokyo was too busy attempting to cope with the Allied counteroffensive. In only one area was there a clear-cut case of planning: The currency of all the occupied countries was officially linked to the Japanese yen, the Yen Block under the strict control of the Bank of Japan. But in practice the Yen Block was never effective outside Manchukuo and northern areas of China. Throughout the rest of the occupied territories there was the usual chaos of currencies typical of the Far East.

In the silent economic war between Allies and Axis, oil turned out to be the lifeblood of all the belligerents. Without oil all armaments were so much scrap. Every phase of the fighting depended upon it—without it no guns fired, no tanks rolled, no ships sailed, no planes flew.

Oil sparked every invasion drive. It heated tents and billets; it powered mobile laundries; it was used to purify water; it was used in medicines and bug killers; in the form of jellied gas it fueled the deadly flame throwers. At least 60,000 gallons of gasoline were needed each day to keep a single armored division fighting.

Without oil a Chinese junk was a better fighting craft than the mightiest battleship. Oil moved shops, powered engines, lubricated turbines, operated hydraulic turrets and ammunition hoists. Diesel oil fueled the deadly submarines.

Oil was equally as indispensable for air fighting. It powered aircraft, it was used in plastic plane blisters, in rayon parachutes, in asphalt to surface landing strips.

Oil also fought on the home fronts. It kept tractors and trucks operating; it was an essential ingredient of tires; it heated and powered homes and factories; it got war workers to their jobs. Oil kept the gigantic war arsenal moving.

Clearly, then, whoever won the battle for oil would win the war. Admiral Chester W. Nimitz at the beginning of the war stated that victory was a matter of "beans, bullets, and oil." By 1945 he had changed the order to "oil, bullets, and beans."

In December 1941, just when the war was becoming global in scope, there were three great oil areas in the world producing 2,149,000,000 barrels annually (1,700,000,000 in North and South America, 320,000,000 in the Caucasus and Middle East, 60,800,000 in the East Indies, 68,000,000 in other areas). The Allies controlled access to 86% of all this oil, and with it a tremendous advantage in the war.

For the Allies the great problem was to move the oil and gas to places where they were critically needed. In the United States the Big Inch pipeline kept streams of oil moving in an ever-increasing daily volume; from the midwest and the southwest oil flowed to loading terminals where it could be picked up by barge, truck, or tank car. Huge supplies of oil drums became an identifying mark on many an invasion beach. Oil tankers ranged the seas to bring the precious fluid to the battlefronts. Many tankers were sunk by prowling U-boats, but American shipyards, using mass-production methods, built new tankers faster than the Nazis could sink them.

The Allies gave high priority to oil pipelines all over the world. American engineers laid a 1,800-mile line across India and Burma into China. A thousand miles of pipeline followed the troops across North Africa, and after the Normandy invasion in 1944 mobile pipelines were constructed at the rate of 50 miles daily on some days to supply Allied troops moving into Germany.

The Axis, in its thirst for oil, depended upon reserves built up in peacetime, upon supplies seized in occupied countries, but most of all upon synthetics. Hitler realized early that the war might be a long one. "To fight it we must be sure of oil for our machine." Hence, to win access to the great oil regions became a matter of life and death. When he turned on Russia in June 1941, one of his main objectives was the Red Army's oil supply in the Caucasus.

Hitler ordered his U-boat captains to roam the shipping lanes and attack tankers carrying oil from Venezuela or Texas to England. The Allies retaliated by striking hard at synthetic oil plants inside Germany as well as the main sources of natural oil. In the spring of 1942 a small detachment of giant American planes took off from Near East bases for a surprise attack on the Ploesti oil fields in Rumania, the most important single source of natural oil available to the Axis. Nothing much was accomplished on this first raid. The Americans struck again on August 1, 1943, this time after considerably greater preparation. The attack, conducted at treetop height, was, according to General Eisenhower, "reasonably successful." It was learned later, however, that the true oil shortage in Nazi Germany was in production and distribution facilities.

The attacks on Germany's synthetic oil plants were devastating. The official report of the U.S. Government Strategic Bombing Survey, completed shortly after Germany's capitulation, told the story: "Attacks by our bombers on the synthetic war plants . . . played a decisive part in Germany's collapse. . . . It was the . . . Nazis' lack of gasoline, not the loss of plane production, that gave us air superiority."

On the other hand, said General George C. Marshall, "No [Allied] plane has failed to fly, no ship has failed to sail, for lack of oil."

POLITICAL DECISIONS: FROM QUEBEC TO TEHERAN

For the combat soldier of World War II the whole world and the issue of life and death revolved around his immediate sector. Surrounded by the blood and filth of the battlefield, his was not to reason why. His destiny was fixed anonymously by decisions made far away.

Over-all Allied strategy was made at the summit by the Big Three, Franklin D. Roosevelt, Winston Churchill, and Joseph Stalin. The alliance was at best a precarious one. The democratic West had joined for survival with totalitarian Russia, but each faction had reason to suspect the other. The Big Three agreed that Germany and Japan had to be beaten on the battlefield, but along with the military were deep political implications which strained the alliance.

Roosevelt and Generals Marshall and Eisenhower believed that first things must come first: The enemy must be forced to unconditional surrender. And the sooner the better. At stake were the lives of millions of Americans. Critics claimed that by accenting military ends the American President allowed himself to be outwitted politically by Stalin. Furthermore, said his critics, Roosevelt had the naïve impression that by the charm of his own personality he could make the Russian dictator listen to reason. Never in the history of alliances, they charged, was so great a statesman so thoroughly bamboozled by so unstable an ally.

To Churchill war was a deadly game of chess, in which the master player must always think several or more moves ahead of his opponent. In World War I he had attempted to strike Germany from Europe's allegedly soft underbelly and so had led Britain into the disastrous Dardanelles campaign of 1915. Again, in World War II, he insisted that the situation called for an attack from the southeast through the Balkans *before* the cross-Channel invasion. Keep the Russians out of the Balkans, for once they were there, he was sure, they would never get out except at gunpoint. To Roosevelt this was placing the political cart before the military horse. Churchill, grateful for American strength, gave in against his better judgment.

Stalin's suspicions of his partners amounted almost to paranoia. From the moment of Hitler's invasion of Soviet Russia, Stalin began to call for a Second Front in the West to draw pressure away from his own troops. Two proposed Anglo-American operations, Sledgehammer in 1942 and Roundup in 1943, both planned to strike at the coast of France, did not materialize. Churchill, unimpressed by Stalin's demands for an immediate attack in the West, recalled that in the spring of 1940 "without premonition of their own future, the Soviet Government watched the destruction of that 'Second Front' in the West for which they soon were to call so vehemently and to wait in agony so long."

At the Casablanca Conference in January 1943, which Stalin declined to attend because of the critical situation on the Russian front, Roosevelt and Churchill soft pedaled the issue of a Second Front, though they recognized its eventual necessity. There was method in their decision, for there was a shortage of Allied shipping, most of which was urgently needed in the Far East. Moreover, both agreed that it was best to send war materials immediately to Russia via Murmansk and Iran rather than have it stockpiled in Britain to await a cross-Channel invasion. In May 1943, when the two leaders met again at Washington in a conference called Trident, they continued the planning for Overlord, scheduled now for late spring 1944.

Meanwhile, cries from Moscow for a Second Front became even more strident and demanding. During the second half of 1943 came a series of high-level conferences to discuss the issues not only of a second front but also of military coördination for the remainder of the war and blueprints for the subsequent peace.

On August 17–23, 1943, Roosevelt, Churchill, and their advisers met at the First Quebec Conference (code name Quadrant), to discuss military strategy for Europe and Asia. Once again Stalin was conspicuously absent, technically because Soviet Russia was not at war with Japan. There were lengthy discussions about Overlord, set for the target date of May 1, 1944. Resources in the Mediterranean would be distributed with the object of insuring success for the cross-Channel invasion. In the Far East Japan would be crushed primarily by American air and naval power. The Americans would drive for the Philippines and isolate the enemy from his island garrisons and main sources of supply.

The Moscow meeting, beginning on October 18, 1943, and lasting for 12 days, was not a conference of the Big Three. It brought together for the first time their immediate aides in foreign affairs: the British Foreign Secretary Anthony Eden, the American Secretary of State Cordell Hull, and the Russian Foreign Minister Vyacheslav Molotov. At the insistence of Secretary Hull, the Chinese ambassador to Soviet Russia was invited to sign the final pact.

"Stalin," reported Eden, "seemed in excellent humor, and at no point in the evening was there any recrimination against the past. . . . It seems . . . that he no longer regards an overseas operation as a simple matter. It is clear, however, that he expects us to make every effort to stage Overlord at the earliest possible moment, and the confidence he is placing in our word is most striking." The meeting ended with one of those luxurious banquets for which the Russians are famous.

The Moscow Pact had four sections. The first dealt with the broad principles of united action in war and into the peace. The three nations agreed that they would act together to bring about the German surrender, disarmament, and control. Soviet Russia not only promised collaboration to destroy Fascism, but she also agreed that until a world organization was established she would consult her allies whenever necessary.

Second, the three powers agreed that all Fascist forces must be unseated in Italy, and that Italy would be aided ultimately to choose by democratic means her own form of government.

Third, it was agreed that the annexation imposed upon Austria by Germany in March 1938 was null and void. The signers declared that they wished to see reëstablished a free and independent Austria, "and thereby to open the way for the Austrian people themselves, as well as those neighboring states which will be faced with similar problems, to find that political and economic security which is the only basis for a lasting peace."

Finally, from Roosevelt, Churchill, and Stalin themselves came a "Declaration on German Atrocities" that was obviously designed to save as many unfortunates as possible from Nazi vengeance:

> The United Kingdom, the United States, and the Soviet Union have received from many quarters evidence of atrocities, massacres, and cold-blooded

> executions which are being perpetrated by the Hitlerite forces. . . . In their desperation the recoiling Hitlerite Huns are redoubling their ruthless cruelties. . . . The three Allied Powers . . . hereby solemnly declare . . . [that the guilty Germans] will be brought back, regardless of expense, to the scene of their crimes and judged on the spot by the peoples they have outraged. Let those who have hitherto not imbrued their hands with innocent blood beware lest they join the ranks of the guilty, for most assuredly the three Allied Powers will pursue them to the uttermost ends of the earth and will deliver them to their accusers in order that justice may be done.

At the Cairo Conference, beginning on November 22, 1943, Roosevelt and Churchill for the first time brought Generalissimo Chiang Kai-shek of China into their planning. The meeting was the worst-kept secret of the war, with rumors printed all over the world that it was to take place. The agenda was confined to the war against Japan, and the carefully worded communiqués for the press left out Soviet Russia, which was still not at war with Japan.

The communiqué from Cairo announced: "The three great Allies are fighting this war to restrain and punish the aggression of Japan." In other words, it reaffirmed that Britain would keep fighting Japan after Germany was defeated, a matter of some concern to many Americans. Further, China, though hard pressed, would maintain guerrilla warfare until she could be given full-scale aid.

Second, the communiqué said that the three Allies "in harmony with those of the United Nations at war with Japan will continue to persevere in the serious and prolonged operations necessary to procure the unconditional surrender of Japan." Again the debatable term. There would be no negotiated peace in the Far East.

It was further agreed at Cairo that Japan would be stripped of all the conquests she had made since 1894. China would be given Manchuria and Formosa and "in due course" Korea would regain her independence. It was intimated that the Soviet Union would obtain the Kurile Island chain and the southern half of Sakhalin, while the United States would acquire the Japanese-mandated islands in the Central Pacific.

The long-awaited meeting between Roosevelt, Churchill, and Stalin, the summit meeting, the climax of the inter-Allied gatherings, took place November 28–December 1, 1943, at Teheran, capital of Iran. Churchill and Roosevelt each brought 60 advisers, a great array of military and diplomatic brains. Stalin came with a much smaller staff, including these two: Foreign Minister Vyacheslav Molotov and his military chief, Marshal Klementi Voroshilov. At last the Western heads of state were to talk face-to-face with the top Soviet leader.

There was great good fellowship as the Big Three drafted the long-range military operations against Germany. To celebrate his sixty-ninth birthday, Churchill invited the entire group of delegates to the British Embassy for dinner. Some 50 toasts were drunk. Stalin made three memorable toasts. One he proposed to "My fighting friend Roosevelt." Another to "My fighting friend Churchill." And then he asked the assemblage to raise their glasses for this toast: "Without American production the United Nations could never have won the war."

There was little new at Teheran to be added to the understandings that had been reached by the foreign ministers at Moscow. The communiqué was couched in general terms: "We shall seek the coöperation and active participation of all nations, large and small, whose peoples in heart and mind are dedicated, as are our own peoples, to the elimination of tyranny and slavery, oppression and intolerance. We will welcome them, as they may choose to come, into the family of Demócratic Nations." Once again the world was informed that the big powers were determined to set up a world organization.

With a straight face Stalin put his signature on the communiqué which also stated: "We look with confidence to the day when all peoples of the world may live free lives, untouched by tyranny, and according to their varying desires and their own consciences."

The closing paragraph read: "We came here with hope and determination. We leave here friends in fact, in spirit, and in purpose."

DUMBARTON OAKS

What was to be the nature of the joint security organization that had been decided upon in principle at Moscow in 1943?

To seek an answer to this vital question representatives of the United States, Great Britain, the Soviet Union, and China—notably Edward R. Stettinius, Jr., Sir Alexander Cadogan and Viscount Halifax, Andrei Gromyko, and Wellington Koo—met at the Dumbarton Oaks mansion in Washington from August 21 to September 29, 1944. They would make "tentative proposals" for a future world organization.

The negotiations were complicated from the very beginning. Since the Soviet Union was not at war with Japan, the Russian and Chinese representatives did not meet together. Sharp differences immediately arose over the voting procedure to be adopted for the projected Security Council.

Out of the deliberations emerged the Dumbarton Oaks proposals:

1. To maintain international peace and security, to take effective collective measures for the prevention and removal of threats to the peace and the suppression of acts of aggression and other breaches of the peace, and to bring about by peaceful means adjustment or settlement of international disputes which may lead to a breach of the peace;

2. To develop friendly relations among nations and to take other appropriate measures to strengthen universal peace;

3. To achieve international coöperation in the solution of international economic, social, and other humanitarian problems; and

4. To afford a center for harmonizing the actions of nations in the achievement of these common ends.

CHAPTER 18

The Sicilian and Italian Campaigns

Down, down, down. Would the fall never come to an end?

—Lewis Carroll, *Alice in Wonderland*

OPERATION HUSKY—THE 39 DAYS IN SICILY

Next stop—Sicily.

A gigantic triangular island of rock, 10,000 square miles, with 600 miles of coastline, Sicily lies southwest of Italy, closely abutting both Africa and Italy. In North Sicily are the Nebrodici and Madonie mountains and in the northeast is the great volcano of Etna, 11,870 feet high. The short rivers are useless for navigation. There are several good ports: Palermo, the capital, on the northern coast, Syracuse, Catania, and Messina on the eastern coast, the latter just two miles from the toe of Italy across the Strait of Messina.

Sicily in enemy hands was an obstacle to both vertical and horizontal Allied routes along the Mediterranean. For its defense the Axis had assigned 13 divisions—9 Italian and 4 German, some 315,000 Italians, 90,000 Germans, a total of 405,000 men, all under the command of Field Marshal Albert Kesselring. The island was covered with a maze of concrete pillboxes, larger fortifications, and barbed-wire entanglements.

For the Allies an attack upon Sicily was the logical next step after Tunisia as well as the first stroke in a great upward drive toward the heart of the Axis. At the Casablanca Conference, Eisenhower made it clear that he would have preferred Sardinia and Corsica as initial objectives if the military design were to invade Italy, since these islands "lie on the flank of the Italian boot, and their seizure would force a much greater dispersion of enemy strength in Italy than would the mere occupation of Sicily." But he agreed that, if the primary purpose were to clear the Mediterranean for Allied shipping, then Sicily was the proper objective. He finally accepted the Sicilian campaign with the understanding that he was avoiding any commitment "to indefinite strategic objectives in that area."

This reflected a difference of opinion among American and British planners that was to continue for the rest of the war. Generals Marshall and Eisenhower believed that tactical considerations must come first—the most important goal was *military* smashing of the Axis. Whatever was done in the Mediterranean, they reasoned, should be subsidiary to the main attack against Fortress Europe across the English Channel. Anything falling outside this prescription was "politics."

There were objections from Churchill and his British advisers. It was, they said, whether in Sicily or elsewhere, a narrow and dangerous attitude. From the long-range point of view, military action without *political* expediency would bring tragic results, obtaining the shadow rather than the substance of victory. The issue became critical in the latter stages of the war, said the British, when the Marshall-Eisenhower rigidity allowed the Russians to occupy large portions of Eastern Europe, a tragic consequence for which Churchill and the British had issued plain warnings.

The assault on Sicily was to be a stupendous operation, the first large-scale amphibious strike on Axis territory. The necessary bomber and fighter planes and landing boats were now rolling off the assembly lines in gratifying numbers. Nearly 3,000 ships of every kind, from warships to small landing craft, assembled on widely dispersed bases in the Mediterranean, in England, and in the United States, were scheduled to reach a rendezvous south of Sicily at a previously agreed time to discharge men and materials. Assigned to the operation were 160,000 trained and equipped troops, 14,000 vehicles, 600 tanks, and 1,800 big guns. The invading force was to be composed of the U.S. Seventh Army with six divisions, including an airborne, and the British Eighth Army, with seven divisions, including Canadian divisions and an airborne division. Washington was to supply 55 per cent of the air power, the British 45 per cent; London was to provide 80 per cent naval cover.

To Supreme Commander Dwight D. Eisenhower was entrusted the task of correlating and synchronizing these varied forces into a smooth fighting machine. Under his command were five separate and distinct fighting entities —the American army, including the Army Air Forces, the American navy, the British army, the Royal Air Force, and the Royal Navy. Under the Fifteenth Army Group, commanded by General Sir Harold Alexander, were the British Eighth Army led by General Bernard L. Montgomery and the American Seventh Army under Lieutenant General George S. Patton, Jr. Air Chief

Marshal Sir Arthur Tedder was placed in command of the Allied air forces, Admiral Sir Andrew Browne Cunningham of the Allied naval forces.

The possibility of success was good. Determined resistance was expected from the large German garrison on Sicily, as well as from Italian troops. A special factor favorable to the Allies was the mood of the Sicilian people, who had only contempt for the Germans ("They eat up all our chickens!") "Once the Americans and British come," said many Sicilian peasants, "our troubles will all be over."

The first goal of Operation Husky was Italy's Helgoland of the central Mediterranean, the small island of Pantelleria, strategically situated near the narrowest crossing between Sicily and Tunisia, 44 miles from the African coast and 60 miles from Sicily. Previously, Italy had paid little attention to this 2,500-foot rock acquired through absorption of the Kingdom of Naples in 1860, but in 1935 Mussolini converted it into a naval and aircraft base. Topographically, the tiny island was almost impregnable, its coastline and terrain so rocky that assault troops could be landed only through the mouth of one small harbor. Its lone airfield was a precious asset for the Axis.

"We believed," said Eisenhower, "that the [island] could be taken at slight cost . . . upon the assumption that most Italians had had a stomachful of fighting and were looking for any good excuse to quit." He was right. In early June 1943, for six days and nights, the Allies dropped 5,000 tons of high explosives on a limited area in the east of the island. Simultaneously came a concentrated naval bombardment. It was a convincing argument.

On June 11, 1943, just as the invading troops were getting ready to enter their assault boats from the larger ships, the garrison on Pantelleria capitulated with a heavy salvo of oral complaints. There were no casualties among the landing troops, with the exception of one unfortunate Allied soldier who was bitten by a mule. About 11,000 prisoners were taken. Churchill, to meet a wager made with Eisenhower, smilingly paid five centimes for each prisoner taken in excess of 3,000.

During the next two days the smaller islands of Lampedusa and Linosa, both to the west of Malta, surrendered, the former (according to G.I. rumor) to a lone aircraft pilot who had been compelled to land because of lack of fuel. There was now no enemy outpost south of Sicily and the whole assault could be aimed at the great island.

To keep the enemy guessing, always an important factor in Allied strategy throughout World War II, the Allies directed preliminary air attacks at both Sicily and Sardinia, while naval movements suggested an expedition to Greece. On Sicily enemy communications were badly mauled; four of the five train-ferries across the Strait of Messina were knocked out. Air supremacy was established as many of the German and Italian planes withdrew to the Italian mainland.

On July 9, 1943, the great armada with its prodigiously varied assemblage of men and equipment converged on time to its rendezvous south of Malta.

Orders for landings the next day had already gone out when the weather turned foul, with unseasonable northwest winds and heavy swells. But better weather was expected soon. During the night the wind eased, leaving moderate swells and surf on the western Sicilian beaches. Though the defending garrison did not expect an attack, it was still a gamble.

"The apparently unfavorable weather factors," said Admiral Cunningham, "actually had the effect of making the weary Italians, who had been alert for many nights, turn thankfully in their beds, saying 'Tonight, at any rate, they cannot come.' BUT THEY CAME!"

During the night, parachutists were dropped inland to disrupt communications and occupy airfields. The next morning, as sunshine poured on the billowing white surf, a bewildering variety of landing craft, pitching, rocking, and bouncing in the breakers and shallow water, headed for the shores. The Americans used new types of landing craft—the DUKW, an amphibious load-carrier, and the LST (a landing ship, tanks), both of which were to be used later in large numbers in the Pacific. There was some bad luck when a third of the gliders of the First British Air Landing Brigade were released too early by towing craft. Many of the glider troops were drowned.

Before the sun was high that morning, Eisenhower reported that "the success of the landings is already assured."

There was little opposition at first. The invaders found many of the beaches undefended, and the pillboxes deserted. The Axis commanders, partly deceived on the point of attack, had concentrated their forces on the western end of the island, closest to the North African ports in Allied hands. But the invasion came on the southern and eastern coasts.

The Sicilians reacted with cries of joy, with fruit and flowers and wine. The Italian troops offered only token resistance, surrendering in droves, while many just donned civilian clothes and vanished. There was some justification for Italian unwillingness to fight. Many were disgusted by the quality of their equipment and the inefficiency all around them. Allied observers were amazed by the pitiful inadequacy of Italian equipment. Italian ration boxes were found with only a thin layer of provisions on top and a supply of gravel underneath. Some of the Italian planes simply would not fly. Ancient tanks burst into flame at a single hit. No wonder that many were fed up with Mussolini's "efficient" Fascism and all its flamboyant trappings.

The German garrison there, however, including the crack Hermann Goering Division, had no intention of capitulating. From the heights of Mount Etna, the Germans could observe Allied movements on the Catanian plain. This was malaria country, and the infection took a huge toll of fighting strength on both sides.

Once ashore the invaders encountered rugged terrain, slashed by stream beds so deep that any tank breakthrough was almost impossible. Movement on the narrow roads was laborious. The fighting quickly degenerated into an interminable series of small engagements, mostly by artillery and infantry.

Montgomery's Eighth Army, including a Canadian corps which landed to his west, speedily overran the eastern beaches and took the port of Syracuse. From here on he had to pass along a precipitous narrow road along the seaward shoulder of Mount Etna toward Messina. Montgomery drove forward but on July 27, 1943, he was forced to halt on the Catanian plain to await reinforcements.

Once again there was bitter criticism of Montgomery from both military experts and armchair strategists. Montgomery was too timid. Montgomery was too cautious. Witness the pace of his campaigns against Rommel in North Africa. Others sprang to the defense of the tough little Briton. When had he ever sustained a major defeat?

Patton's Seventh Army, landing at Gela and Licata on the southern coast, split into two major sections, one tank force heading rapidly west to take the ports of Marsala and Palermo within two weeks, and the other driving straight to the center of the island. By July 31, 1943, the Americans and British linked up their forces and held a line across the island to the south of Mount Etna, to whose security the Germans, fighting a powerful delaying action, had withdrawn their three-and-a-half divisions.

The relentless Allies pressed the Germans from one strategic height to another. The roads were ground to pulverization in a few days. Traffic was slow as a conglomeration of moving vehicles—tanks, lorries, bulldozers, motorcycles, jeeps—lunged forward in a screaming, groaning, pulsating stream. As the Germans retreated they destroyed bridges and culverts on the shelf roads winding like snakes around precipitous crags along the coast. American and British engineers worked miracles in repairing these vital highways. Eisenhower reported that he saw an almost incredible feat of field engineering on the cliffs facing the sea just to the eastward of Mount Etna. The road had been completely blown away through a gap of 200 yards, and there was nothing left but a sheer cliff hundreds of feet high. Across this gap the engineers, like human spiders, built a trestle capable of supporting the heaviest army loads.

The campaign in Sicily ended on August 17, 1943, just 39 days after the initial landings. General George C. Marshall estimated that the enemy had lost 167,000 men, of whom 37,000 were Germans, the Allies 31,158 killed, wounded, and missing.

The beaten Germans succeeded in transporting by plane and small craft some 60,000 men, two-thirds of their strength, including the Hermann Goering Division, across the Strait of Messina in one of the most successful Dunkirks of the war. The retreat was skillfully carried out under cover of darkness. For once Allied air power failed in an important objective. But the Allies captured enormous amounts of undamaged war materials, especially German and Italian tanks. American and British contingents of specially trained civil affairs officers immediately moved in to control the civilian population.

It was, said President Roosevelt, "the beginning of the end."

The conquest of Sicily demonstrated that the Allies could strike with tremendous efficiency and power on any front, a lesson not lost on the observant Japanese. But, at the same time, there was much criticism of both American and British commanders for what was said to be unimaginative leadership. The Allies, it was charged, had a clear-cut superiority in ground, air, and sea power, but they allowed the cream of German troops to escape to the Italian mainland with relatively light losses.

Sicily was the scene of the widely publicized slapping incident, which nearly ended the career of Lieutenant General George S. Patton, Jr. One of the ablest American field commanders in World War II, Patton was universally regarded as a fine combat soldier. The most brilliant tank expert in the U.S. Army, he was a shrewd student of warfare who understood the value of speed to achieve victory with minimized casualties.

But Patton had an eccentric, almost infantile, streak that tended to diminish respect for his astounding exploits. Wherever he went he wore a holster bearing pearl-handled pistols in the approved Western manner, a highly polished helmet, shiny boots, and a full complement of campaign ribbons. He was spit-and-polish personified. Much too often he delivered political and historical judgments on subjects about which he as well as many other generals knew little or nothing. On the floor of Congress a critic recommended that he be subjected to a "general buttoning-up."

Again and again the patient Eisenhower was forced to extricate his emotional general from one *faux pas* after another. "I well knew," explained Eisenhower, "that Patton delighted to startle his hearers with fantastic statements; many men who believed they knew him never penetrated past the shell of showmanship in which he constantly and carefully clothed himself. But he was essentially a shrewd battle leader who invariably gained the devotion of his subordinates."

During the Sicilian campaign, Patton made a round of hospitals to visit the wounded. Meeting an ambulatory patient, an enlisted man, the general asked him why he was in the hospital. The soldier replied: "General, I guess it's my nerves." Patton went into a rage, screaming a torrent of abuse at the startled soldier, accusing him of malingering, of cowardice, as unfit to be in the same hospital with really wounded men. Doctors and nurses, astounded by the tirade, hesitated to intervene.

A few minutes later Patton met another enlisted man. This time the results were even worse. The general lost control of himself altogether and swung at the soldier's head, knocking off his helmet. Outraged doctors and nurses now stepped between the two. Patton stormed out of the hospital uttering loud imprecations about psychoneurotics and cowards.

It was at best a shocking, brutal, crass performance. Doctors later testified that one of the men had been seriously ill with a temperature of 102°.

The story spread with lightning speed through battle units and back to the United States. Resentment was deep and bitter. When, some months later, a news commentator revealed the incident on the radio, a great public clamor rose for Patton's dismissal.

Eisenhower was placed on an unenviable spot. Patton, obviously, was not indispensable, but he was too valuable a combat leader to be tossed aside. Perhaps his erratic behavior had been due to terrific strain and to the sights and suffering he had seen among the wounded in the hospital. Eisenhower reprimanded him sharply and ordered him to apologize in person to the two enlisted men and the hospital personnel present at the incident. More, he was ordered to appear before the officers and representative groups of enlisted men of each division under his (Patton's) command "to assure them that he had given way to impulse and respected their positions as fighting soldiers of a democratic nation."

Now distressed, penitent, humble, Patton obeyed to the letter. To his chief he wrote: "I am at a loss to find words with which to express my chagrin and grief at having given you, a man to whom I owe everything and for whom I would gladly lay down my life, cause to be displeased with me." There was something of the naughty little boy and the father figure about the entire incident.

Thus spared dismissal, Patton went on to lead the U.S. Third Army from the beaches of Normandy across France and Germany into Czechoslovakia in one of the most dashing campaigns of the war. But Patton never quite conquered his disposition for placing his foot into his mouth while uttering explosive pronunciamentos. Again Eisenhower was embarrassed by a Patton speech "about the need for Great Britain and America to combine to run the world after the victory is won." In a postwar talk the ebullient general dismissed the German Nazi Party as "like the Democratic or Republican party at home." Patton was properly remorseful after each incident.

On December 21, 1945, the 60-year-old warrior died in Heidelberg, Germany, 12 days after his neck was broken in a crash involving his automobile and an army truck. He was buried in a United States Army cemetery among the bodies of the men he had led in action. His grave is democratically marked with a plain cross like those of enlisted men.

THE FALL OF MUSSOLINI

On July 17, 1943, Allied aircraft appeared over Rome and other major Italian cities dropping leaflets with a message from the President of the United States and the Prime Minister of Great Britain:

> At this moment the combined armed forces of the United States and Great Britain, under the command of General Eisenhower and his Deputy, General Alexander, are carrying the war deep into the territory of your country. This is the direct consequence of the shameful leadership to which you have been subjected by Mussolini and his Fascist regime.
>
> Mussolini carried you into this war as the satellite of a brutal destroyer of peoples and liberties. Mussolini plunged you into a war which he thought Hitler had already won. In spite of Italy's great vulnerability to attack by air and sea, your Fascist leaders sent your sons, your ships, your air forces, to distant battlefields to aid Germany in her attempt to conquer England, Russia, and the world. . . .
>
> Every moment that you resist the combined forces of the United Nations—every drop of blood that you sacrifice—can serve only one purpose: to give the Fascist and Nazi leaders a little more time to escape the inevitable consequences of their own crimes. All your interests and all your traditions have been betrayed by Germany and your own false and corrupt leaders; it is only by disavowing both that a reconstituted Italy can hope to occupy a respected place in the family of European nations.
>
> The time has now come for you, the Italian people, to consult your own self-respect and your own interests and your own desire for a restoration of national dignity, security, and peace. The time has come for you to decide whether Italians shall die for Mussolini and Hitler—or live for Italy, and for civilization.
>
> ROOSEVELT
> CHURCHILL

Every word of this skillfully written message struck home to the despairing Italian people. Where, indeed, was the glory promised them by their comic-opera dictator? What had happened to the revival of the brilliance and prosperity of the ancient Roman Empire? Instead, the Italians had seen their sons sacrificed on the battlefield, their fleet whittled down to impotence, their cities devastated, their economy wrecked, their colonies torn away. Disillusioned, disgusted, their morale shattered, their already enfeebled liberties curtailed by *Gestapo* agents, they had had enough.

For more than two decades the world had been fed stories about the gigantic accomplishments of Fascist Italy. Mussolini had cleaned up the mess in Italy. He had made the trains run on time. He had chased beggars from the streets. He had grasped a soft and lazy people by the scruff of their necks and had made them disciplined and efficient.

All exaggerations and lies. Better than anyone else in the world, the Italian people knew the nature of the political monstrosity spawned by Mussolini.

Despite its glittering exterior, the tawdry Fascist state was rooted in quicksand. In its rigid corporate structure every man was a slave to his immediate superior and a little dictator to those below him. The result was that every Italian was conditioned to look out for himself to the exclusion of others. There was no sense of national coöperation, no idea of working together as a team for the common welfare. To the successful opportunist went the spoils, to the hindmost no pity and only contempt. The Fascist regime was so shot through with graft, corruption, nepotism, and inefficiency that it was unable even to feed its armies in the field.

Mussolini's Fascism needed a perpetual series of victories to sustain it. The defeats in North Africa and Sicily were more than it could bear. When the end came, it came with the sudden chill of a disease-laden fog. The *Duce*, still clinging to the illusion of a power already gone, was blown off his pinnacle, and his ignoble experiment vanished into air like an exploded bubble.

Vulnerable Italy was being blasted to rubble by Allied air power. Rail traffic was hopelessly disrupted. Demoralization grew as the food situation became worse and worse. Strikes and riots broke out in northern Italian industrial centers.

In February 1943 there was an indication of an approaching political crisis when, just two weeks after the British Eighth Army had captured Tripoli, Mussolini purged his cabinet and dismissed his son-in-law, Count Galeazzo Ciano, from the post of foreign minister and added a stinging rebuke by appointing him to the minor position of Italian envoy to the Holy See. The enraged *Duce* could decipher the handwriting on the Fascist wall. No doubt about it now, not only his weakling son-in-law but also many others in his entourage were guilty of disloyalty and treason. The obsequious lackeys had once shouted his name to the skies as Italy's man of destiny, but now this band of ungrateful rats was ready to desert the ship. Now they were pointing the finger of scorn at him and blaming him for thrusting the country onto the losing side.

Worst of all, there were men who had been propelled into the seats of the mighty by the *Duce* himself. Dino Grandi, top Fascist leader, former foreign minister and ambassador to Britain; Marshal Pietro Badoglio, the victor of Ethiopia; General Vittorio Ambrosio, chief of the Italian General Staff; the Duke of Acquarone, minister of court. All were ingrates, fools, traitors!

The conspirators against Mussolini played a dangerous game. There was always the danger of the double cross, of denunciation, of arrest. The prime question, as Churchill pointed out, was: "Who would bell the cat?"

The *Duce* would make one final attempt to extricate himself. On July 19, 1943, accompanied by the not-yet-suspected General Ambrosio, Mussolini made one last pilgrimage to Hitler, this time at the Feltre Villa, near Rimini. Gone now were the gaudy trappings of Nazi and Fascist splendor, the firm handclasps, the strutting postures, the smiles of victory. Instead, the chilly atmosphere was tinged with a sense of desperate urgency.

Mussolini asked for more help. The *Fuehrer* responded automatically with a ghostlike harangue. "We must make a supreme effort. . . ." "Sicily must be made into a Stalingrad. . . ." "We must hold out until winter, when new secret weapons will be ready for use against England. . . ." As for reinforcements and additional equipment, those were out of the question. Everything Germany had was badly needed on the Russian front.

Into this lecture plummeted grave news. Rome had been bombed for the first time, by 700 Allied aircraft. Panic-stricken crowds had surged to the sanctuary of Vatican City, and the Piazza of St. Peter's was covered by a mass of frightened refugees. Hitler, who had been expected to stay for two days at Feltre, left abruptly.

Discouraged and embittered, the *Duce* flew back to Rome. As his plane made its landing approach, it swept through a huge cloud of smoke from fires in the Littorio railway station.

Five days later a political volcano erupted. There was a meeting of the Fascist Grand Council, its first since 1939. Once more the *Duce* in a weary replay of the same old record, tried to bluff his way to domination. He would tighten the reins. He himself would assume responsibility. He would throw out the scoundrels and traitors. He would turn the screw. He would bring to bear forces not yet engaged. It had worked on countless earlier occasions. But this time the backbones of Mussolini's listeners were stiffened by despair. Dino Grandi introduced a resolution demanding that the *Duce* immediately relinquish his command of the armed forces in favor of the king. Ciano supported Grandi. Efforts to postpone a decision were shouted down.

After ten hours of debate the voting took place at two o'clock in the morning. The result was decisive. Nineteen voted "Yes" to Grandi's motion, seven "No," and two abstained.

"The position of each member of the Grand Council," Mussolini wrote later, "could be discerned even before the voting. There was a group of traitors who had already negotiated with the Crown, a group of accomplices, and a group of innocents who probably did not realize the seriousness of the vote, but they voted just the same."

The next day, Sunday, July 25, 1943, hoping to obtain the monarch's support, the angered *Duce* called on Victor Emmanuel III. It was a painful interview. Mussolini was bluntly told that he was no longer premier.

"It's no longer any use," said the king. "Italy has gone to bits. Army morale is at rock bottom. The soldiers don't want to fight any more. At this moment you are the most hated man in Italy."

As he left the palace, Mussolini was surrounded by *carabinieri*, placed in a motor ambulance, and driven off to internment on the island of Ponza. That same afternoon the king issued a proclamation announcing that Mussolini had resigned, that he—the king—had assumed command of the armed forces, and that Marshal Badoglio would form a new cabinet.

The *Duce* falls!

The news hit the Italian people with the impact of a tornado. Their pent-up emotions released, surrendering to joy, they rushed to the streets in popular demonstrations, shouting curses at the deposed dictator, tearing Fascist symbols from buildings, and smearing with paint the countless images of Big Brother that had so long stared down at them from nearly every street corner.

The Fascist leaders and police who managed to escape arrest scurried into hiding, while many of the rank and file burned their black shirts and melted away in the sun of Italian freedom. The all-but-forgotten democratic leaders emerged from their hiding places to speak freely for the first time in more than two decades.

The Allied High Command, caught flatfooted by the sudden deposition of Mussolini, failed to act promptly and decisively. On July 29, 1943, Eisenhower issued a statement praising the Italians for ridding themselves of their dictator and intimating that he was ready to deal with the new government. But just now the Allied leaders were bogged down in controversy concerning the "unconditional-surrender" terms promulgated by President Roosevelt at Casablanca in January. Had the situation been handled with more skill and dispatch all Italy might have been brought into Allied hands without the ensuing terrible months of fighting on the Italian mainland. Instead, five weeks of surrender negotiations gave the Germans a vitally needed chance to mend their Italian fences.

Badoglio was a complicating factor. He was incapable of a simple, above-board action, preferring the way of tortuous and devious secret channels, even the double cross and the trickiness of the fox. Admittedly, his was a tremendous task. Italy was thoroughly infiltrated by German agents ready to strike at any sign of defection. Badoglio was caught between three fires—between the suspicious Germans, the emotionally supercharged Italian mobs, and the relentless Allies. It was impossible to satisfy all three.

Hiding behind a screen of false names, Badoglio arranged clandestine journeys to Madrid, Lisbon, and Sicily, secretly meeting Allied agents, suggesting fantastic plots, making demands, submitting counterproposals. He wanted frantically to capitulate, but only with the promise that Italy would escape the dread unconditional surrender. More, he wanted Allied assurance that a huge invading force would land on the Italian mainland simultaneously with the surrender. To be certain, he demanded that Eisenhower acquaint him with every detail of the plan for invasion.

It was an incredible drama suffused with comic-opera overtones. At first Eisenhower, trying to meet Badoglio halfway, sent staff officers on a secret mission to Lisbon. He allowed Brigadier General Maxwell D. Taylor and a companion to go on a secret trip to Rome, where their adventures qualified them for membership in the cloak-and-dagger fraternity. When the negotiations threatened to become interminable, Eisenhower put an end to the bizarre game by ordering renewed and heavy air attacks on Rome and other Italian cities.

The effect was instant and salutary. On September 3, 1943, Badoglio capitulated and signed the document of unconditional surrender, announced by Eisenhower a week later.

The details were never divulged. The major terms were apparently harsh, but the unhappy Italians had little to lose. All Italian soldiers throughout the peninsula and in the Balkans were required to lay down their arms. Most of the remaining Italian fleet, merchant marine, and air force was handed over to the Allies. Corsica and all Italian airfields and naval ports on the mainland and the islands were to be relinquished. Italy was to be disarmed, demobilized, and demilitarized. All Fascist institutions were to be eliminated and the Fascist Party outlawed. It was agreed that, until the Allies captured Rome, an anti-Fascist government would look after Italian affairs under Allied supervision.

An official American report described the surrender of the Italian fleet:

> On the afternoon of 9th September [1943] the battleship *Howe* with four cruisers in company, carrying elements of the First British Airborne Division, steamed up the swept channel toward Taranto. Shortly before, the Taranto Division of the Italian Battle Fleet had emerged from the harbor. As the two fleets passed each other, there was a moment of tension. There was no guarantee that the Italian fleet would observe the terms of surrender and would not, at long last, show fight. But the final challenge by Admiral Cunningham, delivered with the same cold nerve that had characterized all the actions of that great sailor, went unanswered. The Italian Fleet passed out of sight on its way to surrender.

That same day the battleship *Roma* was sunk by German bombers north of Sardinia. The next day, September 10, 1943, the Italian fleet, including four battleships, reached Malta.

A week later, on September 16, 1943, Badoglio broadcast a message to the Italian people. He urged them "to fight the Germans in every way, everywhere, and all the time." "To resist," he said, "is to exist." With this virtual declaration of war, Italy assumed the status of a co-belligerent in the war against Hitler. The official Italian declaration of war on Germany came a month later, on October 13, 1943.

"The Fascist Head Devil," said President Roosevelt, "together with his chief partners in crime, are out of the war."

But, seven weeks after his fall, Mussolini was rescued by the Germans in an escapade bearing all the marks of a Hollywood thriller. On July 26, 1943, Mussolini had been interned on the island of Ponza and had been brought back later to La Maddalena, off the Sardinian coast. At the end of August he was again moved, this time to a small mountain resort in Abruzzi, in central Italy. In mid-September 1943, nearly a hundred German paratroopers, led by a daring S.S. colonel, commando Otto Skorzeny, landed there by glider. Encountering little opposition, the raiders carried the former Italian dictator off in a light Italian plane.

Now the complete puppet of the German *Fuehrer*, Mussolini set up a Fascist Republic in North Italy and proclaimed that he would carry the war to a victorious conclusion. Again came the old tub-thumping. The party organization would be reconstituted. The Axis was reëstablished. "I, Mussolini, resume supreme direction of Fascism in Italy."

But the record was almost worn out by now.

SLUGGING MATCH IN ITALY

There was great enthusiasm among the Allies. The pompous *Duce* and his black-shirted rascals had been thrown out by the Italian people, the new Badoglio government had surrendered unconditionally, and Fascism, with its blatancy and brutality, had been dealt a mortal blow. One more show of concentrated force and Italy would fall like a ripe plum.

But the end was not to come too easily, after all. The battle for Italy turned out to be a hard, bloody slugging match, a long-drawn-out affair lasting from September 1943 to May 1945. Not until the collapse of Hitler's Third Reich did German resistance cease in Italy.

The pattern of fighting was different from that on other fronts. There were no masses of troops assaulting the enemy; they did not "pour ahead" or "plunge through," or "sweep around" the enemy lines. The opposing troops seldom saw one another. Small, isolated groups of men, moving methodically from one position to another, pushed their way up and down mountain inclines. "Never," reported war correspondent Eric Sevareid, "were there masses of men in olive drab locked in photogenic combat with masses of men in field gray. It was slow, spasmodic movement from one patch of silence to another."

The Italian people, disillusioned, disgusted, hopeless, welcomed the Allies as liberators. But they were also beaten down and apathetic and at first did little to ease the way of their conquerors. They had had enough of war. Now they were caught between two regimes—between their new government dominated by the Allies and a still-writhing Fascism controlled from Berlin.

"If the Germans ever get here," said Mussolini in 1940, "they will never go home." For once the *Duce* had stated the truth. Immediately after his fall, the Germans rushed reinforcements to Italy, disarmed the Italians, and took over control of the country. Hitler would not abandon Italy as a lost cause; he would stay there and make the enemy fight for every inch of soil (standard operating procedure in the Hitler lexicon). He chose Field Marshal Erwin Rommel to command the Germans in Northern Italy.

When they went into Italy, the American, British, French, Polish, and Brazilian troops moved into a hornet's nest of German resistance. There was no fast-moving mobile campaign here, but, instead, stalemate, assault, retreat, attack. The veteran Germans, jockeying for position, retreated slowly up the peninsula from one prepared line to another, forcing the Allies to pay a heavy toll in blood for every foot of advance.

The Italian terrain was unrivaled for defensive fighting. On the north were the Alps sweeping in a mighty arc from Nice to Trieste. Below them was the great alluvial tract of the fertile Lombardy-Venetia plain, crossed by many rivers fed from Alpine lakes. Stretching along the peninsula was the Apennine range, running like a backbone in successive sections. To the southeast of Spezia was the limestone range of the Apuan Alps, and beyond them the Tuscan highlands. Next the basin of the Tiber, flanked on the east by the Roman Apennines, split into eastern and western chains. Then a volcanic belt, the plains of the classic Campagna, extending from the malarial Pontine marshes southward to Naples. From here the mountain range continued southward to the extremity of the Calabrian peninsula.

It was formidable defensive terrain, and the Germans skillfully used every feature of it. Covering their retreat, they blew up each bridge, culvert, railroad station, and mountain shelf, and left behind them a maze of land mines and booby traps. For the Allied troops it was a nightmare. Sunny Italy, indeed! They fought their way up and down mountain slopes through choking dust, torrential rains, and mud-soaked roads. Worst of all was the plethora of winding streams—the Sangro, Volturno, Garigliano, Rapido, Arno. "Every damned river in this country is named Volturno!" commented one weary G.I. who could not seem to escape the river.

The softening-up process commenced as early as August 19, 1943, when the Allies began a heavy air attack on enemy airfields and communications centers.

On September 3, two divisions of Montgomery's veteran Eighth Army, consisting at that time of battlewise British and Canadian troops, crossed the Strait of Messina, came ashore under cover of heavy artillery and air bombardment, and established beachheads at Reggio di Calabria on the toe of the Italian boot. They began to advance northward toward Calabria against a skillful delaying action. By evening they occupied Reggio, Catona, and San Giovanni. Commandos took Bagnara and Melito.

Six days later, on September 9, 1943, the Americans embarked on Operation Avalanche, an amphibious assault designed eventually to take Naples.

The new U.S. Fifth Army (half-American, half-British), under command of Lieutenant General Mark W. Clark, supported by an air umbrella and by naval bombardment, stormed ashore near Salerno, just 45 miles southeast of the Bay of Naples. From the vast armada onto the beaches swarmed a mass of landing craft—a school of mechanical whales spewing forth fighting men. In the first month the Americans and British landed 135,000 troops, 100,000 tons of supplies, and 30,000 motor vehicles.

Meanwhile, a day after the Salerno landings, the Germans occupied Rome and took over protection of Vatican City. Italian units in North Italy, South France, and the Balkans quickly capitulated, and the Germans occupied Pavia, Parma, Cremona, and Bergamo in North Italy.

For the Allies there was worse news—the Germans were waiting at Salerno. Holding the high ground on north, east, and south, they zeroed a massive artillery barrage onto the crowded beaches. The Americans tried to dig into the pebbly shores and dried mud-flats.

Four days after the landings the Germans counterattacked around Salerno and retook some of the ground occupied by the Fifth Army.

"It is another Dunkirk!" screamed the Berlin radio.

The Allies replied with massive air assaults from bases in Sicily and North Africa, hitting the Germans on the hills outside Salerno and striking at enemy airfields at Foggia in the east. At the same time, Montgomery pushed northward from Reggio di Calabria some 150 miles in a slow march hindered by terrain and German resistance. Though the advance was slow, the Eighth Army's presence prompted the Germans on September 15, 1943, to retire toward Naples.

Meanwhile, on September 9, on the day of the Salerno landings, 6,000 picked men of the First British Airborne Division captured the naval base at Taranto on the inside of the Italian heel to the east. From here they struck northward to Bari, thereby gaining control of the Adriatic.

September 1943 was a good month for the Allies. The lower section of the Italian boot was in their hands. The Germans relinquished Sardinia, and

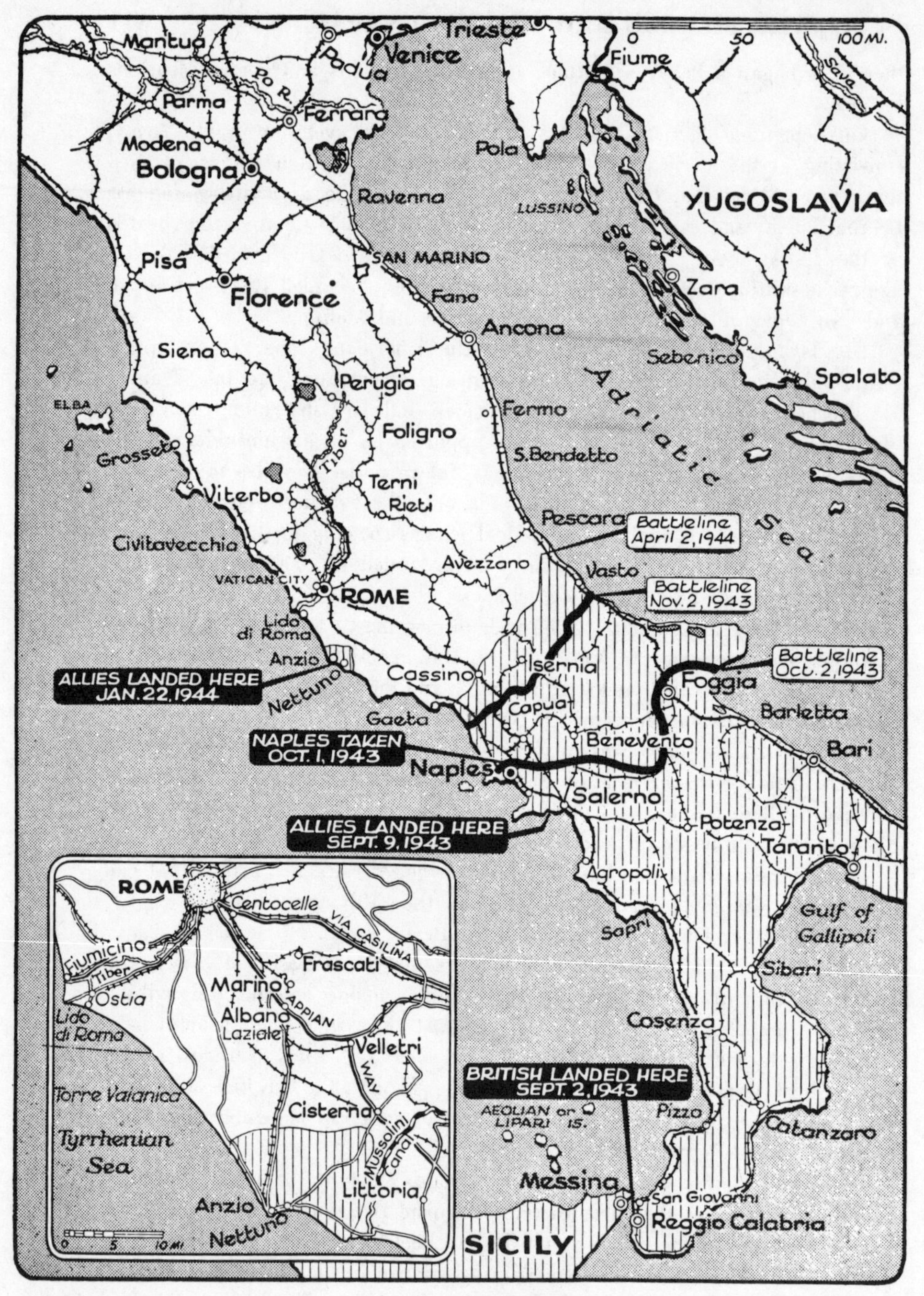

INVASION OF ITALY

Corsica was taken by Fighting French troops helped by local partisans. The greater part of the Italian fleet was now interned at Malta, and Allied naval strength could be released for service in the Pacific.

On October 1, 1943, General Clark and units of his Fifth Army, after driving back the German rear guard around Vesuvius and bypassing the ruins of Pompeii and Herculaneum, entered Naples. They found the city in smoldering ruins, its harbor blocked with wrecks, its people starving and racked by typhus. The withdrawing Germans had taken terrible vengeance on the city. The Allied Military Government, listing 13 categories of atrocities, charged that the Germans:

blew up the main aqueduct in seven places and drained the reservoirs;
smashed pumping facilities and the sewage disposal system;
destroyed generators, transformers, and all essential parts of the electrical system;
ruined the transportation system and carried off all rolling stock from buses to horses to buggies;
crippled the communications system by blowing up the telephone exchange and dynamiting power plants;
razed the major hotels;
blew up tunnels through the hills;
planted time bombs and booby traps which slaughtered the civilian as well as military population;
threw open the doors of 13 prisons and allowed killers and pathological criminals to be released on an already bomb-shattered populace;
demolished the flour mills thus depriving the Neapolitans of their macaroni and bread;
deliberately set on fire with gasoline and hand grenades the University of Naples, the third oldest (founded in 1224 by Emperor Frederick II) and one of the largest institutions of learning in the world, in the worst example of German vandalism since the burning of Louvain Library in World War I;
looted the hospitals of dressings, instruments, and medicines;
carried off many hostages, including the Bishop of Cava Dei Terreni and the Abbot of Badia at Corpo di Cava.

This was planned destruction on a vast scale. German army documents captured by the British Eighth Army revealed that German troops had been ordered to carry out a scorched-earth policy to the limit of their abilities.

The leveling of the University of Naples was senseless sadism. Herbert L. Matthews reported in *The New York Times*:

> The Germans broke into the university after having carefully organized their procedure, with dozens and dozens of five-gallon gasoline tins and sup-

> plies of hand grenades. They went from room to room, thoroughly soaking floors, walls, and furniture, including archives that went back for centuries. Then they threw in hand grenades. There was something apt about it, something symbolic about the whole German attitude. It did not matter to the Germans that they were destroying the accumulated wealth of centuries of scientific and philosophical thinking.

Allied engineers, helped by the people of Naples, worked at top speed to repair the harbor facilities. The Italian navy provided four submarines which supplied electricity for the necessary clean-up job. Within a month, more than 50 wrecks were cleared from the harbor and more than 5,000 tons of supplies a day were pouring into the city. Several airstrips near the city were quickly made operational.

Simultaneously, on the east coast opposite Naples the British Eight Army drove on Foggia and seized the great system of airfields there. Within days Foggia was equipped with new steel-mat runways, pumping plants, pipelines, airdromes, repair shops, and warehouses. And the first of 35,000 Allied airmen began to stream into the area.

Foggia was an all-important conquest. Previously, fighter cover had come from Sicily and could remain over the Salerno beachhead only 15 minutes. Now from Foggia heavier bombers as well as fighters could range far and wide throughout Italy and even strike at Austria and transport centers in the Balkans.

Field Marshal Albert Kesselring, faced by increasing Allied pressure, retired to strong defensive positions on the north bank of the Volturno River, the scene of Garibaldi's triumph over the Neapolitans in 1860.

For the Allies there were only two possible routes to Rome: They might drive along the Via Appia and the coastline, or they might work their way upward along the Via Latina through the interior mountains around the key town of Cassino. Either way it would be tough going for them. For the rest of the year 1943 they tried to push through the mud, dirt, and slush—ever onward. Vehicles broke down and bridges were washed out by the incessant rains. From high ridges of almost solid rock the Germans poured a withering fire down on the Anglo-Americans dug into the chasms, rocks, and half-caves. "They lived like men of prehistoric times," observed one reporter, "and a club would have become them more than a machine gun. How they survived the dreadful winter was beyond us."

The Allied command was reorganized. Eisenhower was called to England to plan Operation Overlord, and took with him Generals Montgomery, Bradley, and Patton. General Sir Harold Alexander was left behind as Allied commander in Italy, with Lieutenant General Mark W. Clark in command of the U.S. Fifth Army and Lieutenant General Sir Oliver Leese heading the British Eighth Army.

The Germans, too, made some important changes. Rommel was transferred to the French front, while Kesselring was assigned command of all German forces in Italy. To defend Rome the Germans, in January 1944, consolidated a defensive position called the Gustav Line with Cassino as its center. "The Gustav Line," said Hitler, "must be held at all costs for the sake of the political consequences which would follow a completely successful defense. The *Fuehrer* expects the bitterest struggle for every yard."

The Allied response, Operation Shingle, was designed to break the winter deadlock.

January 22, 1944. Under an umbrella of bombers the Allies made another spectacular leapfrog jump to the beaches of Anzio, a little town 33 miles south of Rome on the shores of the Tyrrhenian Sea. The aim was to turn the flank of the Gustav Line. The First British Division landed just north of Anzio and the U.S. 3rd Division just south below Nettuno. Within days the Allies landed 70,000 men and 18,000 vehicles.

Though the Germans were caught unprepared, Kesselring soon had three Axis divisions commanding the heights around the beachhead. Exposed Anzio meant terror and death for the Allies. There was no cover on the open, rocky beaches, no place to hide. German 88's, unabated, hurled a mass of steel down on the immobilized troops. The rosy picture of a quick breakthrough faded into the fear that this was another Dunkirk. But the Allies held on. Hitler regarded the failure of his Fourteenth Army to throw the Allies into the sea at Anzio as an unmitigated disaster.

There was little gloating on the Allied side. Eric Sevareid reported the landing as "a stupid mistake." "The story of Anzio," said Churchill, striking his usual cheery note, "was a story of high opportunity and shattered hopes, of skillful inception on our part and swift recovery by the enemy, of valor shared by both." Eisenhower was more optimistic: "In the final outcome the Anzio operation paid off handsomely. . . . The move undoubtedly convinced Hitler that we intended to push the Italian campaign as a major operation."

For the miserable, dirt-streaked troops caught at Anzio, for the Willies and Joes of Bill Mauldin's G.I. cartoons, it was concentrated hell. The fact remained that casualty lists were much too long. It took four months, more than six divisions, and oceans of blood and sweat to break out of Anzio.

Thus blocked on the coastline, the Allies had to turn back to the center of the Gustav Line. About fifty miles southeast of Anzio was the town of Cassino, ancient Casinum, where Marc Anthony, Roman consul in 44 B.C., had once held orgies. On a hill overlooking the town, at an elevation of 1,175 feet was the site of ancient Roman fortifications, on which St. Benedict in 529 A.D. had established the monastery of Monte Cassino. This monastery, sacked by the Lombards in 580–590, rebuilt in 720, destroyed by the Saracens in 884, and again reconstructed in 914, had become the fountainhead of Western monasticism.

Monte Cassino had great ecclesiastical significance, but on the Allied war maps it was merely Hill 516. The enemy had control of the rocky, zigzag roadway twisting up one side to the stone monastery at the top. The structure itself, some 200 yards long, was not occupied by the Germans, but that could not be known by the Allies at the time. From the Allied viewpoint the fortified mountain area and the monastery formed a single military unit from which a deadly fire could be directed on the areas below.

The first attacks on the German positions in and around Cassino came in January in an effort to mask the Anzio landings. After a bloody repulse of American troops at the Rapido River, New Zealand and Indian troops under command of General Bernard C. Freyberg came into the line in February and managed to capture several hills north and northeast of Hill 516, as well as a third of Cassino, but no more.

It was obvious that the chances of taking Monte Cassino by direct assault were remote and equally obvious that it had to be controlled. What to do about the famed shrine of Christendom. Should it be leveled from the air, thereby risking the condemnation of Catholics throughout the world? The Allied command, in a quandary, finally decided that it had to be done.

On February 14, 1944, American planes dropped leaflets addressed to "Italian Friends" and signed "The Fifth Army":

> We have until now been careful to avoid bombarding Monte Cassino. The Germans have taken advantage of this. The battle is now closing in more and more around the sacred precincts. Against our will we are now obliged to direct our weapons against the Monastery itself. We warn you so that you may save yourselves. Leave the Monastery at once. This warning is urgent. It is given for your good.

The Germans near-by paid no attention to the leaflet. In the monastery itself the eighty-year-old Abbot Gregorio Diamare, the monks, lay brothers, and refugees who had sought sanctuary there could do nothing to escape the impending bombardment.

The attack began the next day. In this assault 142 B-17 Flying Fortresses and 112 Mitchell medium bombers dropped 576 tons of bombs on Monte Cassino. The interior of the cathedral and the five cloistered courtyards were reduced to dumps of rubble. "Bright flames," reported a British war correspondent, "such as a giant might have produced by striking titanic matches on the mountain-side, spurted swiftly upwards at half-a-dozen points. Then a pillar of smoke 500 feet high broke upwards into the blue." The monastery was hit hard, but the Germans held on to the high ground.

For the faithful there was an element of wonder—the only two places to escape damage were the cell used by St. Benedict and the tomb in which his remains rested for 1,400 years since his death.

In early March 1944 both sides bogged down in the mud and slime. On March 15, another aerial bombardment was directed at both the town of Cassino and the monastery, this time by 500 planes and 1,400 tons of bombs. Again the damage was heavy, but the Germans still fought in the rubble and ruins. Three-quarters of the town was occupied by the Allies, but their tanks could not penetrate the cratered roads and blocked streets.

There was an ironic twist to the fighting—in this, the most mechanized war in history, machines were of little use. The battle had to be fought between small units of foot soldiers with rifles, hand grenades, and machine guns. Tanks, artillery, planes, and vehicles of all sizes had to give way to the humble mule pack. An Italian mule on the slopes of Monte Cassino was worth a dozen of the giant mechanical monsters.

As expected, the bombing of Monte Cassino aroused heated debate during and after the war. General Mark W. Clark wrote in his memoirs:

> I say that the bombing of the abbey . . . was a mistake, and I say it with full knowledge of the controversy that has raged around this episode. . . . Not only was the bombing of the abbey an unnecessary psychological mistake in the propaganda field but it was also a tactical military mistake of the first magnitude. It only made the job more difficult, more costly in terms of men, machines, and time.

At the same time, General Clark disclaimed responsibility for the bombing and indicated that his subordinate, General Freyberg, was to blame for forcing the action on him. British commentators, angered by Clark's implications, heatedly denounced him for what they regarded as an ungracious attempt to escape responsibility for a necessary act of war.

CHAPTER 19

The Setting Sun of Japan

In the middle of the twentieth century Japan will meet Europe on the plains of Asia and wrest from her mastery of the world.

—Premier Shigenobu Okuma, during World War I

The war keeps increasing in ferocity day by day and we are now being confronted by a situation where the fate of the Greater East Asia sphere and the rise and fall of Imperial Japan will be decided.

—Premier Hideki Tojo after U.S. landings at Kwajalein in the Marshalls, February 1944

STRATEGY IN THE PACIFIC

The reduction of Japanese power in the Pacific was to tax American ingenuity and endurance. In the two years since Pearl Harbor the Nipponese had seized a vast area, together with enormous supplies and natural resources, running all the way from the Aleutians in the north down to the Solomon Islands off Australia. With undisputed control, they had surrounded their military vitals with what they regarded as invulnerable layers of fat.

Throughout this "Greater East Asia Co-Prosperity Sphere," Premier Hideki Tojo had set up national governments, ostensibly independent but actually under Japanese direction. The puppet governments, of course, pledged their support against the Allied powers. Tokyo's aims were to solidify Japanese control and digest the huge territories acquired since Pearl Harbor.

The Allied task of penetrating Japan's concentric ring of defense, calling for long, costly amphibious counterattacks, was to be undertaken by the United States. The Allied nations agreed that the European theatre came first. Yet manpower and supplies had to be sent at the same time to the Far East. For two years the U.S. Pacific Command had to work with limited means to conduct a strategic defense and tactical offensive, attempting gradually to acquire bases. First, American power would penetrate the outer layers of fat and then drive on to the heart of the empire.

The over-all stratcgy was carefully worked out in Washington by the Joint Chiefs of Staff. General Douglas MacArthur was given command of the Southwest Pacific Theatre, consisting of Australia, New Guinea, the Netherlands East Indies, and the Philippines. Admiral Chester W. Nimitz was placed in command of the larger Pacific area, including all the islands from the Solomons in the south to the Aleutians in the north, the Gilberts, the Marshalls, the Carolines, and the Marianas. The China-Burma-India theatre (C.B.I.) on the Asiatic mainland was assigned at first to Lieutenant General Joseph W. Stilwell, and later, in August 1943, established as a separate Southeast Asia Command under Vice-Admiral Louis Mountbatten, with Stilwell as his deputy.

The plan was to approach Japan in a series of leapfrog hops from one island to another by coördinated air, sea, and land attacks. Each successive conquest would yield harbor facilities and airfields from which strikes could be made at the next objective. No attempt would be made to take all the enemy strongholds; many would be left bypassed as the attackers strangled Japanese shipping lanes. Such heavily defended bases as Rabaul or Truk would be bombed frequently from the air, but never assaulted. The objective was to save as many lives as possible by using at certain selected points the constricting power of blockade instead of direct assault.

For this purpose the United States assembled in the Pacific the most powerful and diversified armada in naval history. By 1944 American naval strength was three times that of Great Britain, many times that of Japan. In a little over three years it had increased from 1,076 to 4,167 ships, from 383 to 613 warships, from 1,744 to 18,269 planes, from about half a million up to three million men to man the ships and planes.

Above all, the build-up called for the transfer to the Pacific of aircraft carriers in overwhelming strength. By August 1944 nearly a hundred carriers of all sizes, including at least a dozen giant flattops, were in Pacific waters. Admiral Nimitz thus brought his own bases with him over the vast reaches of the Pacific. Every warship, no matter what its size or type, was attended by a special kind of supply and repair ship, thereby making it unnecessary to send vessels back to faraway bases for repairs or supplies. This armada would clear the sea lanes, send out planes for bombing attacks on specified targets, bring in the assault troops and keep them supplied.

The Americans devised a brand-new type of amphibious warfare. Running through the Pacific were hundreds of atolls, islands consisting of a belt of coral reef surrounding a central lagoon. Enormous numbers of new-type landing craft, 80,000 in all, were manufactured for assault through these shallow waters—the LCRS, landing craft, rubber, small, holding six men; the LCVP, landing craft, vehicles and personnel; the LCM, landing craft, medium, holding 60 men or 30 tons of supplies; the LST, landing ship, tank, carrying 132 men and smaller landing craft; the LCIL, landing craft, infantry, large, holding 200 men; the LCT, landing craft, tank; the LSD, landing ship, dock, a huge dry dock filled with power vehicles; and many others. One of the most effective vehicles was the amphibious tractor, which could be floated beyond the range of shore batteries, deployed in normal landing-boat formations, and driven over the reefs to the beaches.

The procedure was worked out with meticulous care. After air and naval bombardment of the island target, successive waves of landing craft would head ashore to discharge men and matériel, to be followed swiftly by construction battalions of engineers, the Seabees, who would build docks, airfields, roads, and bridges at all possible speed.

The task was by no means an easy one, for Japanese defenses were formidable. The defending garrisons were always concentrated in heavily fortified areas from which they could throw intensive crossfire on the attacking troops. On island after island Nipponese engineers built a maze of pillboxes of stone-hard coconut logs, steel rails, and concrete, all covered with several layers of sand. These incredibly strong defense posts were staggered in such a way that when one was stormed and taken it fell under the fire of several others. Most could be put out of action only by shattering bombardment or by powerful hand-to-hand infantry assault. It was a costly process.

THE STRANGE DEATH OF YAMAMOTO

On April 17, 1943, a top-secret dispatch signed by Frank Knox, Secretary of the Navy, was flashed from Washington to Henderson Field on Guadalcanal. The information was detailed: Admiral Isoroku Yamamoto, Commander in Chief Combined Fleet, was leaving Rabaul, the Japanese stronghold, the following morning on the first leg of an inspection tour of bases in the Southwest Pacific. He would be traveling in a *Mitsubishi* (Betty), a twin-engined bomber, most of his staff would follow in another Betty, and there would be an escort of six Zero fighters. All eight planes were to land at 9:45 A.M. at Kahili, an airport at the southeast end of Bougainville, about 300 miles from Rabaul.

The dispatch ended with the order to exert "maximum effort" to destroy Yamamoto. In plainer words, "Get Yamamoto!"

On Guadalcanal there was great excitement. Here was a very special, ready-made target, one who had earned the contempt and hatred of Americans. Yamamoto had planned the attack on Pearl Harbor as well as the strike on Midway. Furthermore, he was accused, unjustly, of boasting that he would dictate peace in the White House.

The task of intercepting Yamamoto was assigned to a squadron of 18 Army P-38 Lightnings. Because of their limited gas supply, the planes would have to operate close to Kahili. Four Lightnings would act as an attack group and the remaining 14 were to be used as a covering force. The latter were to engage the large number of enemy fighter planes expected to rise from Kahili to welcome the visiting admiral.

At take-off next morning from Henderson Field, one of the attacking Lightnings blew a tire and another turned back because of engine trouble. Two substitute planes were assigned at once to the attacking group, leaving just a dozen for cover. To avoid detection the P-38's flew low and skimmed over the water to Bougainville. A few minutes short of the rendezvous the four attack planes climbed to 10,000 feet and the cover group to 20,000 feet.

Then came one of the most remarkable incidents of the war. The success of the American mission depended entirely upon split-second timing and unwitting Nipponese coöperation. Yamamoto, a stiff martinet and a stickler for promptness, arrived exactly on time, just as American Intelligence had predicted.

The Americans sighted the two Bettys and six Zeroes ten minutes before the scheduled landing. But, strangely, no fighters rose from Kahili to give additional protection. It was all over within minutes. The 24 aircraft tangled in a deadly free-for-all. The bombers carrying Yamamoto and his staff went down for the safety of treetop level. It was too late. The Americans sent both planes crashing in flames into the jungle. Yamamoto was later found dead in his seat, his *Samurai* sword still between his knees.

Appalled by the death of their naval hero, the Japanese attributed it to incredibly bad luck. What they did not know was that U.S. Naval Intelligence had cracked the Japanese naval code. Washington was aware of every detail of the Yamamoto inspection mission.

THE SOUTHWEST PACIFIC: UP THE SOLOMONS-NEW GUINEA LADDER

The key Japanese base in the Southwest Pacific was Rabaul on New Britain Island, shielded by numerous minor bases around the Bismarck Archipelago (northeast of New Guinea), the Solomon Islands, the Admiralty Islands, and New Ireland. The Americans decided to avoid a direct assault on

Rabaul and instead render it impotent by air attack and then outflank it in a two-pronged offensive up the Solomons and New Guinea ladder.

On the Solomons side, American troops, supported by Admiral William F. Halsey's South Pacific Fleet, would push northward from one strategic island to another. On the New Guinea side, American and Australian troops under command of General Douglas MacArthur would move up the east coast. Both prongs would have strong air support from the U.S. Fifth Air Force based on Australia and the Thirteenth Air Force from New Caledonia and Guadalcanal. The troops would hit the enemy at his weakest points and confine the strongest Japanese forces in escape-proof pockets. The airmen would pound Rabaul to bits. Thus isolated, the Japanese garrison would be no further menace. This ambitious program was carried out with imagination and power.

The advance in the Solomons began at Guadalcanal, from which the last Japanese garrison had withdrawn in February 1943. On February 21, strong amphibious forces took the Russell Islands, 60 miles northwest of Guadalcanal, after a fierce struggle. Here they constructed an air base from which enemy airfields at Munda on New Georgia Island and Kolombangara in the mid-Solomons were bombed.

The Japanese were infuriated by this presumptuous move of the white devils. From the great Nipponese air bases in the northern Solomons they sent an armada of planes to choke off the impending invasion of New Georgia. The rival air fleets clashed over Guadalcanal on June 16, 1943. American army, navy, and marine pilots brought down 96 Japanese aircraft, while losing only six American planes. (That same day Washington announced that since July 31, 1942, 1,337 Japanese aircraft had been destroyed in the South Pacific area.)

Two weeks later American troops were on Rendova Island in the New Georgia group of Solomon Islands. Some 121 Japanese planes were shot down during continuous air attacks on the landing forces and shipping. The transport vessel *McCawley* was sunk.

Next, Munda was shelled by shore batteries on Rendova after the occupation was completed. The air fleets clashed again. For six weeks it went on, the Japanese losing another 350 planes, the Americans fewer than 100. Munda was taken. Bypassing Kolombangara, the Americans swarmed ashore on Vella Lavella Island on August 15, 1943.

Meanwhile, there was action at sea. The Japanese first attempted to reinforce New Georgia and Kolombangara, which meant challenging American naval power. At the naval battles of Kula Gulf, July 12 and 13, 1943, and Vella Gulf, August 6, American warships sank an enemy cruiser and three destroyers, but lost a cruiser and a destroyer and suffered damage to three other cruisers. There was no clear-cut victory in these sea actions.

But the Japanese decided that enough was enough and began to evacuate the two islands.

The battle for the northern Solomons centered around Bougainville Island, the last Japanese stronghold in the archipelago, where an American force landed and cleared only a small part of the island. But instead of making a frontal assault, the Americans neutralized it by steady air bombardment and eventually cut its supply line to Rabaul by taking the Green Islands at the northwest extremity of the Solomons. The Japanese still fought on at Bougainville and on smaller islands in the Solomons. But they were no longer effective. Nimitz had his bases on the Pacific highway to Tokyo.

On the opposite side of the ladder, MacArthur's Americans and Anzacs moved northward up New Guinea to outflank and isolate Rabaul from the east. Progress was slow along the coastal swamps and in the rugged mountains, both ideal for Japanese defense. The southernmost Japanese garrisons at Buna and Sananända fell on January 19, 1943. Tokyo reacted precisely the same as in the Solomons: It would send heavy reinforcements to Lae and Salamaua, farther up the eastern coast of New Guinea opposite Port Moresby. Off went a heavily escorted Nipponese convoy carrying more than 20,000 troops.

American airmen sighted the flotilla in the Bismarck Sea on March 1, 1943. For two days Flying Fortresses and Liberators trailed and pounded it. Most of the 22 ships in the convoy, 10 warships and 12 transports, with most of the troops aboard, were lost. The Japanese used about 150 aircraft, of which 102 were put out of action. Allied losses were three fighters and one bomber. The Battle of the Bismarck Sea, said General MacArthur, was one of the most decisive battles of the war. It marked the end of Japanese power in the Southwest Pacific.

But the Japanese still persisted. Angered by the naval catastrophe, they struck back in flights of a hundred or more bombers at Allied bases at Port Moresby in New Guinea and Port Darwin in Australia. The Allies retaliated in the air, on the sea, and on land.

American and Australian troops took Salamaua on September 14, 1943, and captured Lae two days later. Both were immediately converted into forward air and naval bases. Then Finschhafen was taken by the Australians on October 2. Next the Allies consolidated their position on February 12, 1944, by occupying Rooke Island, between the Huon Peninsula and New Britain.

While the Americans fought their way up New Britain toward Rabaul, other units made amphibious jumps from central New Guinea 250 miles north to the Admiralty Islands, thus neutralizing Rabaul by cutting it off from Truk, the key Japanese naval base 800 miles to the north in the Central

Pacific. At least 50,000 enemy troops were left stranded in Rabaul and New Britain.

Excellent progress was being made by the Allies in the war against Nippon. In a little more than a year they had advanced more than 3,000 miles in the Southwest Pacific and had cut off some 135,000 Japanese beyond all hope of rescue.

But this was only the start.

THE NORTHERN FLANK: THE ALEUTIANS

Eyes north!

There had been alarm in California, Oregon, Washington when, in early June 1942, just as the Battle of Midway was about to begin, a Japanese task force bombed Dutch Harbor at the eastern end of the Aleutian Archipelago on the Alaskan approaches to the United States. Turned back, the invaders had occupied Kiska and Attu, westernmost of the small chain of fogbound islands. There had been some gain for Japan in the venture: At least it would be difficult for the United States to set up bases from which to attack Tokyo. The Americans could do nothing for the moment to recapture the compromised Aleutians because every ounce of naval, air, and land power was needed in the South Pacific.

It was nearly a year before the counterattack came in the Aleutians. On May 11, 1943, came a demonstration of rising American power. On that day two U.S. forces, the strongest since Guadalcanal, bypassed the main Japanese base at Kiska and landed on Attu, the westernmost island. One contingent landed to the north at Holtz Bay, the other to the south at Massacre Bay.

The next three weeks saw the heaviest kind of fighting. The terrain was difficult; between the opposing forces were 2,000-foot mountains. Neither side could use its air power in the abominable weather, complicated by deep mud, ice-cold water, wet snow, soggy tundra, and the eternal fog and mist. The defending Japanese were entrenched in the mountainsides and valleys in strong positions covered by tundra grass and snow and protected by land mines and booby traps. Their final defenses could be reached only along a treacherous ridge with a precipitous drop several hundred feet down on both sides. From the heights they directed a withering fire on the Americans. Every foxhole, every trench, every dugout had to be taken by direct assault.

The two American spearheads, pushing through deep ravines and up and down mountain slopes, merged and headed for Chichagof Harbor, the enemy base on Attu. Though suffering heavy casualties, the Americans by June 2, 1943, wiped out most of the Japanese garrison.

The capture of Attu culminated in one of the biggest *Banzai* charges of the war. It was a grotesquely carnal scene. Colonel Yasuyo Yamasaki's frustrated troops, trapped on a ridge between Chichagof Harbor and Sarana Bay, decided to meet their ancestors in a howling, jabbering, last-ditch suicide charge. On they came—a thousand strong—into the American lines. From the wild ranks came shouts of "Japanese drink blood like wine!" The Americans struck back ferociously, whereupon hundreds of Japanese blew their guts out with hand grenades. Others were killed in the mad attack. Only a few snipers escaped to the hills. Eleven prisoners were taken; 2,000 Japanese were buried by the Americans.

The story of the great suicidal charge at Attu hit the headlines in Tokyo, where it was lovingly compared to the Charge of the Light Brigade, when 600 British cavalrymen rode to their death before Sevastopol on October 25, 1854.

American troops, astonished by this wild fanaticism, found many Japanese "final letters," including these entries:

"Is war such a thing as this? Soon after firing ceases, birds are singing and flying around above the quiet and frozen ground."

"Voices of '*Banzai*' would make a wild god weep."

"I will become a deity with a smile in this heavy fog. I am only waiting for the day of death!"

Attu was American, this time permanently. Its capture meant the isolation of Kiska, the main Japanese base 170 miles to the east. In a preliminary softening-up attack, American warships and planes pounded Kiska with tons of bombs and shells.

On August 15, 1943, the strongest American-Canadian force yet committed in the North Pacific invaded Kiska, only to find that the enemy had vanished under cover of the midsummer fog. For the Allies this was a new experience. The invaders found the hills covered with well-provisioned caves and pillboxes from which the Japanese might have made a strong last-ditch stand. It was learned later that the Japanese had evacuated Kiska on July 28, 1943. The withdrawal was a thing of naval beauty, accomplished by Rear Admiral Shofuku Kimura and his 16-ship task force. Evading American scouting planes and a destroyer blockade, Kimura's ships anchored in the fog-enshrouded harbor, and within the incredible time of 55 minutes removed 5,183 officers, enlisted men, and civilians from Kiska. What seemed to be a magic trick was turned by a combination of Japanese daring, American bungling, and the Aleutian fog.

Kiska was the first Japanese conquest to be abandoned without a struggle. With all the Aleutians in American hands, the threat to Alaska and the West Coast was removed. From newly constructed air bases American bombers could now attack the neighboring Kurile Islands, north of Japan.

Now it was the turn of the people of Tokyo, only 2,174 miles from the Aleutians, to watch the skies in alarm. The Japanese Pacific Empire was now surrounded by air power based on the Aleutians, the Solomons, New Guinea, India, and China.

THE CENTRAL PACIFIC: TERRIBLE TARAWA

The success of Allied operations in the Southwest and North Pacific opened the door for attacks in the Central Pacific. Here the offensive was aimed at the outer defenses of the Japanese Empire through the Gilbert, Marshall, Caroline, and Marianas Islands in a combined land, sea, and air operation of tremendous scope.

The first stage was Operation Galvanic, directed tempest of Allied reprisal in the center. The goal was to win back the Gilberts. These 16 small coral islands, sometimes called the Kingsmill Islands, 166 square miles in area, are near the equator, 2,500 miles southwest of Pearl Harbor on the great circle route from Hawaii to Port Moresby in New Guinea. They had been seized by the Japanese in December 1941.

The initial Allied objectives in the Gilberts were Makin and Tarawa. Preceded by carrier strikes on the surrounding islands, Makin in the north of the Gilberts was invaded on November 20, 1943. Its small garrison was overwhelmed within a few days. Its defenders, stupefied with *sake*, a beer made from rice, sought death in a wild *Banzai* charge. It seemed that the Gilberts would fall as easily as the Aleutians.

But not so. In Tokyo the war lords had boasted that a million men could not take Tarawa. It was an exaggerated claim, but Tarawa did turn out to be a devil's furnace. A typical Pacific atoll, it consists of two dozen small islands joined by coral reef and surrounding a lagoon only a few feet deep. The strong point was Betio, three miles long and a mile wide, defended by 3,000 Japanese Imperial Marines. The garrison was dug in under hundreds of pillboxes covered with five feet of concrete, ten-foot-thick outer walls of sand and coral, and roofed with iron rails laid on coconut logs. American planes and warships hurled tons of bombs on these amazingly durable forts. The island was smothered with smoke and flame.

Surely no human being could be left alive in this inferno! But when U.S. Marines stormed ashore on November 21, 1943, over coral reefs at high tide, they were met with a curtain of fire from the very much alive Japanese garrison. Amazingly enough, the tiny island was literally crawling with enemy troops.

It was one of many such attacks on Pacific islands. Successive waves of assault troops jumped into the water up to their necks and waded ashore under withering fire. At night came the heavier landing barges with more men and tanks.

The next morning the Marines were caught in a deadly cross fire. There were calls for more offshore naval support. But once again the dirty work had to be done by that oldest ingredient of war, the foot soldier. The American troops went about the grim task of flushing out the rat-trapped Nipponese. They reduced the bunkers one by one, assaulting them head-on with flame throwers, grenades, and bangalore torpedoes (long iron pipes containing T.N.T., named after Bangalore, a city in India) thrown directly into the eyeslits and gun ports of the Japanese forts. The pattern grew steadily more efficient as flame throwers doggedly seared the Japanese in their defensive positions. It was war at its nastiest, a spectacle of sheer horror.

The Americans stayed with the attack. Colonel David Monroe Shoup, who led the 2nd Marine Regiment, submitted a classic battle report from Tarawa: "Our casualties heavy. Enemy casualties unknown. Situation: we are winning."

Four days of this, and the fanatical defenders were down to their final suicide charge. The exact cost of the capture of Tarawa, one of the bitterest assaults in the history of the U.S. Marines, will probably never be known. It is believed that the Marines lost 984 officers and men dead or missing, and 2,072 wounded. In addition, the Navy lost flyers from the carriers, coxswains of landing craft, and others. The best approximation of total dead was about 1,100.

Some serious errors were made in the amphibious landings at Tarawa. The naval bombardment was too short, too weak, too inaccurate. The air-strike was badly timed. Much of the war matériel used was unsatisfactory or useless. Some war correspondents waxed indignant about "tragic Tarawa," or "bloody Tarawa," or "terrible Tarawa"; others complained that good American blood had been shed for a few acres of worthless coral.

The lessons learned at Tarawa were of priceless value in opening the road to Tokyo. True, a thousand lives were lost, but it is strongly probable that many more were saved by the U.S. assault on the island.

Hard on the heels of the Marines came the Seabees, naval engineers. Tarawa quickly burgeoned into a major base for the coming attack on the Marshall Islands.

ISLAND-HOPPING: THE MARSHALLS AND CAROLINES

The next phase was Operation Flintlock.

Northwest of the Gilberts, athwart the Japanese lifeline between the Gilberts and Tokyo, lay the larger archipelago of the Marshall Islands. Naval historian Samuel Eliot Morison described it in an attractive image: "If you took twenty necklaces of different lengths, composed of beads of different shapes and sizes, threw them into the bottom of a tank and let in just enough water to cover the smaller beads, you would have a fair chart of the Marshalls." Acquired by Germany in 1885, the Marshalls had been administered

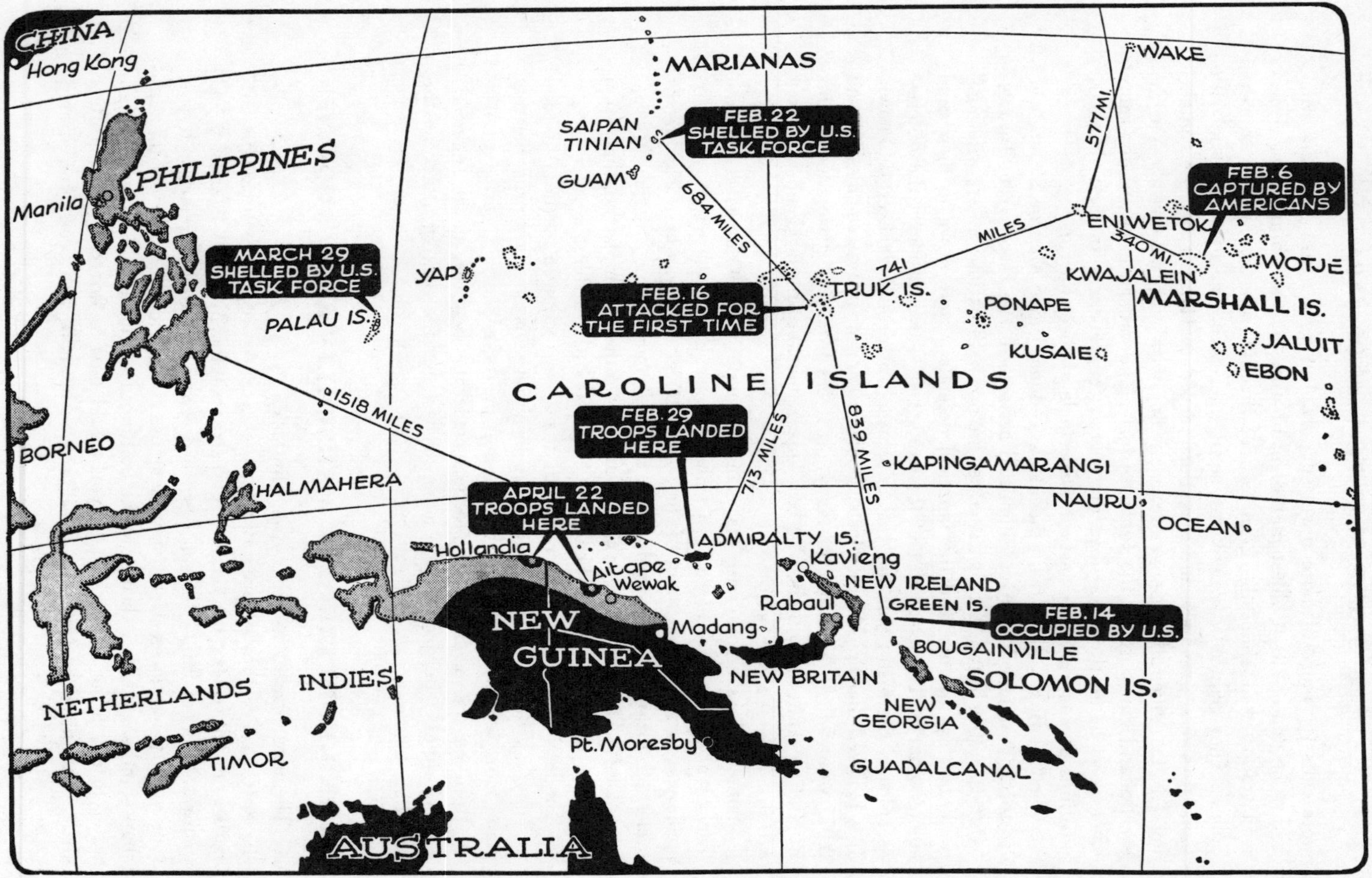

ADVANCE IN THE CENTRAL PACIFIC

since World War I under Japanese mandate. Most of the islands enclosed spacious lagoons. The inhabitants were dominantly Micronesians.

The Americans bypassed the islands of Jaluit and Wotje and headed straight for Kwajalein, the world's largest atoll, 66 miles long and 18 miles wide. American bombers first crippled the airfields. The U.S. Navy had learned at Tarawa that four hours of heavy fire and 3,000 tons of shells and bombs were just not enough to destroy the enemy's coconut-log, steel, and concrete fortifications. The pounding of Kwajalein therefore was begun fully two months before the ground attack. Before the assault troops were to land on Kwajalein and the neighboring islands of Roi and Namur the warships plastered the three islands with an unprecedented 15,000 tons of high explosives, cutting them into a mass of craters.

The troops were the first to set foot on soil that had been Japanese before Pearl Harbor. They were followed by deadly tanks. On Kwajalein there was complete destruction. No building was left standing; the island was a mass of rubble. But—again the now familiar story—from inside the debris and rubble came stiff resistance of machine-guns and rifles handled by very much alive Japanese.

Again, as on Tarawa, came the yard-by-yard advance, the storming of pillbox emplacements with flame throwers, bazookas, and grenades, the slow mopping up, the final enemy suicide charges. An eyewitness reckoned that "No one who was there will ever forget the smell of decaying bodies intermingled with that of burnt coconut wood."

Once again American troops were flabbergasted by the unpredictable actions of the enemy. A Japanese would approach a tank, hold a grenade up against it, and keep it there until it exploded, taking his arm with it but causing no damage to the tank. Japanese officers brandishing swords beat their weapons frantically against the armor plate of tanks, with no effect other than to make themselves perfect targets for the Americans.

Apparently the Americans were learning fast. This time they lost only 356 men while killing 8,122 Japanese. They took the relatively large number of 264 prisoners.

Several weeks later, on February 17–22, 1944, Admiral Chester W. Nimitz sent a task force 340 miles west to take the enemy air base at Engebi in the Eniwetok Atoll. Again there was the same pattern from assault to *Banzai* charges. "We cornered fifty or so," wrote Lieutenant Cord Meyer, "on the end of the island, where they attempted a *Banzai* charge. But we cut them down like overripe wheat, and they lay like tired children with their faces in the sand."

The macabre score this time was 3,434 Japanese, 339 Americans killed.

A thousand miles to the west of Kwajalein was the naval base of Truk, the vaunted Japanese Gibraltar in the midst of the Carolines. This was no ordinary atoll, but a great naval and air base from which the Nipponese sent reinforcements to New Britain, New Guinea, and the Solomons.

On February 16, 1944, Admiral Raymond A. Spruance led a powerful task force to the Carolines. The Japanese, whose fleet had already retired, were caught off guard. From the American flattops roared a huge air force to make a blistering attack on Truk. A few days later Washington announced that 201 Japanese aircraft were destroyed at Truk, and that 2 light cruisers, 2 destroyers, 1 ammunition ship, 1 seaplane tender, 2 oilers, 2 gunboats, and 8 cargo ships were sunk. The U.S. lost 17 aircraft. No attempt was made to storm Truk itself and its garrison of 50,000. It was rendered useless, immobilized, knocked out of the war.

American victories in the Marshalls and Carolines meant that the outer perimeter of the Japanese Empire was pierced. Enemy defenses were either captured, as at Kwajalein, left to starve, as at Jaluit and Wotje, or rendered impotent, as at Truk. With the neutralization of the master base at Truk the U.S. Navy could now roam at will through the Western Pacific.

Part VI

FEU DE JOIE: TRIUMPH OF THE UNITED NATIONS

CHAPTER 20

The Assault on Fortress Europe

> ***Every enemy attempt to break through is to be prevented by tenaciously holding our ground. It is forbidden to shorten the front. It is not permitted to maneuver freely.***
>
> **—Adolf Hitler, July 2, 1944**

PREPARATION: THE COILED SPRING

Directive from the Combined Chiefs of Staff of the U.S. and Britain to Supreme Commander Dwight D. Eisenhower: "You will enter the Continent of Europe and, in conjunction with the other United Nations, undertake operations aimed at the heart of Germany and the destruction of her armed forces."

Southern England was a vast military encampment. Assembled in the ports was the greatest invasion fleet of all time. Battleships, transports, landing craft, destroyers, mine sweepers, every conceivable type of warship and transport vessel stood side by side in the historic harbors. The docks were piled high with war equipment. Everywhere there was intense activity amid an air of expectancy. Tens of thousands of troops were bivouacked on the fields, marching on the roads, practicing landing exercises, firing on the ranges. Overhead the planes roared on preliminary missions to the Continent.

"The mighty host," reported General Eisenhower, "was tense as a coiled spring, and indeed that is exactly what it was—a great human spring, coiled for a moment when its energy should be released and it would vault the English Channel in the greatest amphibious assault ever attempted." After his final inspection of his troops, a satisfied Eisenhower commented: "If their fighting is as good as their training, God help the Nazis!"

The figures alone were astounding. Here were assembled for Operation Overlord 150,000 men, 1,500 tanks, 5,300 ships and craft, and 12,000 planes. The planes were to land three airborne divisions in Normandy, batter the German defenses, cut the routes to Normandy by smashing railroads and bridges, and isolate the beach defenses. Then five divisions—two American, two British, and one Canadian—were to land from the sea on a 60-mile stretch between Caen and the Cherbourg Peninsula. In the first 48 hours 107,000 troops, 14,000 vehicles, and 14,500 tons of supplies were to be landed on the beaches.

Along with these gigantic preparations was played a deadly game of deceit, designed to throw the enemy off balance. In southeast England close to Dover the Allies set up a phantom "First Army Group"—apparently a huge concentration of troops and craft. There was great movement and motion here, even a special radio network busily sending out false orders. This ghostly army was gratifyingly successful—it pinned down 19 Nazi divisions for six weeks after D-Day.

Travel between England and Ireland had already been prohibited to prevent leaks of military information to enemy agents. During the last week of May 1944 the Allied High Command sealed off all exits from England and declared a 10-mile strip in southern England off-limits to all but authorized personnel. Mail from American servicemen to the United States was halted for 10 days.

Only Eisenhower and his staff knew when the code message: "The arrow pierces steel" would go out to the French underground.

There were serious problems. The English Channel was a formidable barrier because of navigational hazards, extreme tidal variations, and changeable weather conditions. The planners were worried about the lack of satisfactory ports along the northern French coastline. But they were certain that once ashore, anywhere from the Lowlands to Spain, there would be freedom of action for the final drive on the German *Herzland*, the heartland of the enemy.

After long study of the German coastal defenses and the disposition of the German divisions, Eisenhower decided to invade a strip of the Calvados coast running from Caen in the east across the Cotentin Peninsula to the great port of Cherbourg. Here the beaches were wide enough to permit the landing of at least five divisions in the initial assault.

Hitler was reeling. His cities were being bombed to smithereens, he had lost North Africa and the chance to take Suez, his troops in Italy had been pushed back to Rome. But he still had 60 divisions in France and the Low Countries, eight of which were assigned to beach defenses and inland garrisons. His Seventh Army defended the Normandy, Cotentin, and Brittany beaches. He correctly guessed Normandy as the probable Allied *Schwerpunkt*, the center of gravity, and here he concentrated strong divisions and armored reserves. This despite the report of German Naval Intelligence that the coast between the Seine and the Cotentin Peninsula was unsuitable for a landing, especially since it was covered by the powerful fortress of Cherbourg. To make certain, Hitler stationed heavier defenses in the Pas de Calais area directly across from Dover.

Hitler's defense plan was rigid, linear. He would simply annihilate the enemy on the beaches and throw him back into the Channel.

Goebbels's propaganda machine had depicted the Atlantic Wall as a fortified coastal line running in a great arc from Holland along the Channel and Biscay coasts to the Pyrenees and extending along the Mediterranean to Toulon. But actually the Germans did not have enough manpower to hold a continuous line of fortifications. Instead, Hitler concentrated heavy forces in each major port and between them set up a system of strong points, many of them miles apart. Frederick the Great would not have approved this strategy: "He who defends all defends nothing."

This German army was not the same as that of the years of triumph, of one smashing victory after another. Losses had been tremendous, and replacements were hard to find. The great *Wehrmacht* was no longer a superb striking force, but instead a polyglot army including Hungarians, Poles, Russians, French, even Negroes and Indians. The divisions manning the Atlantic Wall were composed to some great extent of the very old, the very young, and foreigners impressed into service. But behind them were many seasoned, hardened units.

To meet the expected invasion Hitler called in his most mobile general, Field Marshal Erwin Rommel, whom we remember as the commander of the *Afrika Korps*, and placed him in command of Army Group B, consisting of the Eighty-eighth Corps in Holland, the strong Fifteenth Army strung along the Channel, and the Seventh Army scattered in Normandy and Brittany, a half million men defending 800 miles of coastline.

Far to the rear was Field Marshal Gerd von Rundstedt, Supreme German Commander in France and the Low Countries, with his mobile reserves. The idea was to mass these reserves as soon as the main Allied landing had taken place.

Throughout the spring of 1944, Rommel worked energetically to strengthen the Atlantic Wall. Under his direction masses of laborers and soldiers poured concrete, installed guns, mined the shallow approaches, and covered fields behind the beaches with giant stakes called *Rommelspargel* (Rommel Asparagus) to discourage carrier planes and gliders. The work proceeded slowly because of shortages of steel and concrete. But Rommel made the German defenses on the beaches of Normandy formidable. There were underwater obstacles to break up landing craft. The beaches were heavily mined and covered with barbed wire. The Germans could deliver a withering cross fire from concrete pillboxes and gun emplacements. Roads leading inland were blocked by ditches, antitank walls, and mine fields. Further inland were artillery emplacements from which deadly barrages could be hurled at anything moving on the beaches.

"The war will be won or lost on the beaches," said Rommel. "The first 24 hours will be decisive."

The Germans, like the Allies, played the game of deception. They, too, set up dummy headquarters, moved personnel about, sent columns of tanks on fictitious missions, and issued false radio reports. A shadow army of British and French agents reported every move to London.

Weather was the key factor. The Allied armada was scheduled to move at 4 A.M. on June 5, 1944. But early on the preceding day the weather turned foul. The report was discouraging for the invasion—low clouds, high winds, great waves.

Eisenhower was caught in a dilemma. Air support would be impossible; naval gunfire was certain to be inaccurate; the small landing boats would pile up on the beaches. Weighing all factors, Eisenhower reluctantly gave the order for a 24-hour delay, and recalled the ships already furrowing the Channel white.

At 3:30 the next morning, June 5, 1944, a wind of almost hurricane proportions raged around Eisenhower's command post. The Supreme Commander called for another meteorological conference. Group Captain J. M. Stagg, a Scot, chief of the weather men, made his report: "I think we have found a gleam of hope for you, sir. The mass of weather fronts coming in from the Atlantic is moving faster than we anticipated. We predict there will be rather fair conditions beginning late on June 5 and lasting until the next morning, June 6, with a drop in wind velocity and some break in the clouds."

Brigadier General Walter Bedell Smith recounted the dramatic scene:

> The silence lasted for five full minutes while General Eisenhower sat on a sofa before the bookcase which filled the end of the room. I never realized before the loneliness and isolation of a commander at a time when such a momentous decision has to be taken. . . . He sat there quietly, . . . tense, weighing every consideration. . . . Finally he looked up, and the tension was gone from his face. He said briskly, "Well, we'll go!"

D-DAY: THE FORGE OF VICTORY

Tuesday, June 6, 1944, 3:32 A.M., New York time. From Supreme Headquarters, Allied Expeditionary Forces in Europe, came the radio voice of a public relations officer:

> Under the command of General Eisenhower, Allied naval forces, supported by strong air forces, began landing Allied armies this morning on the northern coast of France.

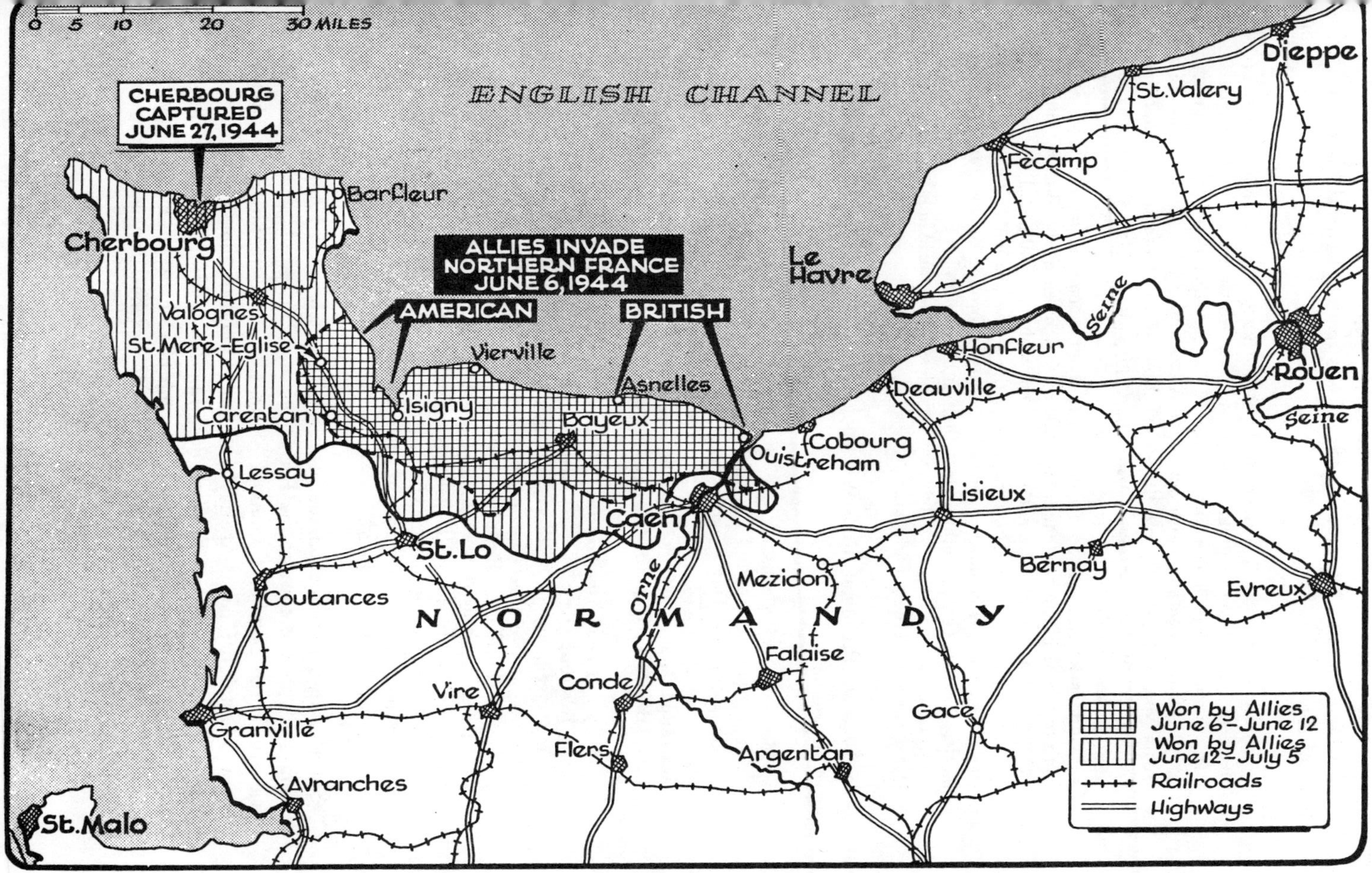

D-DAY AND AFTER

Less than a minute later the announcer was reading General Eisenhower's Order of the Day:

> Soldiers, sailors, and airmen of the Allied Expeditionary Force: You are about to embark on a great crusade, toward which we have striven these many months. The hopes and prayers of liberty-loving people everywhere go with you. In company with our brave Allies and brothers in arms on other fronts you will bring about the destruction of the German war machine, elimination of Nazi tyranny over the oppressed peoples of Europe, and security for ourselves in a free world.
>
> Your task will not be an easy one. Your enemy is well-trained, well-equipped, and battle-hardened. He will fight, fight savagely. But in this year 1944 much has happened since the Nazi triumphs of 1940 and 1941. . . .
>
> The tide has turned. The free men of the world are marching together to victory. I have full confidence in your courage, devotion to duty, and skill in battle. We will accept nothing less than full victory.
>
> Good luck and let us all beseech the blessing of the Almighty God upon this great and noble undertaking.

At 10 A.M. President Roosevelt spoke from the White House to the American people:

> My fellow-Americans.
>
> In this poignant hour I ask you to join with me in prayer:
>
> Almighty God: Our sons, pride of our Nation, this day have set upon a mighty endeavor, a struggle to preserve our Republic, our religion, and our civilization and to set free a suffering humanity. Lead them straight and true; give strength to their arms, stoutness to their hearts, steadfastness in their faith.
>
> They will need Thy blessings. Their road will be long and hard. For the enemy is strong. He may hurl back our forces. Success may not come with rushing speed, but we shall return again and again; and we know that by Thy grace, and by the righteousness of our cause, our sons will triumph. . . .
>
> And, O Lord. . . . Help us to conquer the apostles of greed and racial arrogancies. Lead us to the saving of our country and with our sister nations into a world unity that will spell a sure peace—a peace invulnerable to the schemings of unworthy men. And a peace that will let all men live in freedom, reaping the just rewards of their honest toil.
>
> Thy will be done, Almighty God, Amen.

Shortly after midnight on the eve of D-Day, while the complex fleet of landing ships moved toward the French coast, a thousand bombers of the Royal Air Force Bomber Command began to unload their cargoes on the German coastal defenses. At daylight came another thousand American bombers. From the coast of England deep into the interior of France ranged thousands of planes of all types, a great umbrella of air power covering the landings. Swift fighters strafed the Normandy beaches. It was an awesome demonstration of coördinated air assault.

Outnumbered 50 to 1 (5,000 Allied fighters on the Channel front to a mere 119 for the Germans), the battered *Luftwaffe* had already withdrawn its air bases back to the Paris area. For months Allied aircraft had struck at French and Belgian rail networks, wrecking marshaling yards, destroying locomotives, wiping out enemy air-installations, demolishing all bridges on the Seine and Loire. Unable to move their troops by train, the Germans turned to the highways, only to face further smashing from the air.

Not until D-Day did the Allies single out the Normandy coast for concentrated bombing. It turned out to be a tactical surprise of the first order.

The first troops to land in Normandy were parachutists from troop carriers and gliders of the U.S. Ninth Air Force. Crossing the enemy coast a few minutes after midnight, they landed at Ste. Mère Église beyond the flooded areas behind Utah Beach, which with Omaha Beach, had been assigned to the Americans to secure the west flank.

Many paratroopers dropped into the zone of a German army that had not been alerted to D-Day. But others were not so fortunate. Because of the high winds and fog some men fell as much as 35 miles from their targets. Some were caught in trees, others plunged into swamps, still others were so weighted down by their equipment or the shrouds of their parachutes that they drowned in less than three feet of water.

But despite the shattering chaos at least 13,000 airborne troops were down within four hours. Each American paratrooper was furnished with 10 dollars in newly minted French money, a brass compass, and a small American flag sewn to his right sleeve. For identification he had a dime-store metal cricket such as those used by children: one squeeze (click-clack) to be answered by two (click-clack, click-clack).

Farther to the east the British 6th Airborne Division achieved complete tactical surprise by landing 5,300 paratroopers and airborne infantry nine miles inland near Caen behind Gold, Juno, and Sword Beaches, assigned to the British to secure the east flank.

The American airborne unit quickly captured the flood-control lock north of Carentan on the west flank, while the British to the east landed astride the Orne River. Soon the Allied divisions formed a perimeter around the beaches and isolated the battle area from the rest of France.

Meanwhile, Allied air power paralyzed all German daylight movement from Normandy to Paris. This was coördinated assault with a vengeance.

Just as the sun rose over the French coast the naval bombardment began. It was the greatest duel of sea against shore in all history. Destroyers and cruisers, pushing close inshore, raked the beaches. Farther out the heavies, including six battleships, the British *Rodney*, *Nelson*, and *Warspite* and the American *Nevada*, *Texas*, and *Arkansas*, hurled thunderous volleys into the interior.

Under the hail of air and naval fire the mine sweepers surged in to clear the offshore waters and to mark out channels with buoys for the landing craft. Specially trained volunteers, frogmen dressed in tight-fitting, sea-green rubber suits, leaped into the shallows to destroy the fouling shore obstacles, one line about 50 feet from the shore and the other some 250 yards out.

A hundred miles of French coastline were in the process of being hermetically sealed off by this great push of naval and air power.

To the west, immobilized in the Bay of Biscay, were scores of German U-boats and flotillas of German "E" torpedo boats. As dawn broke three "E" boats out of Le Havre dashed through the smoke screen guarding the Eastern Task Force off the British Gold, Juno, and Sword Beaches and fired 18 torpedoes. They missed the British battleships but sank a Norwegian destroyer. It was the only blow delivered that day by the German navy.

Backed across the Channel, as far as the eye could see, was a jumble of 5,300 ships of every tonnage.

The invaders came ashore on five beaches along a 60-mile line of the Cotentin Peninsula from Montebourg in the west to Caen in the east. From the landing craft through the heavy surf poured a steady stream of men, many weak and miserable from prolonged seasickness. They were greeted by heavy, well-aimed fire. Bullets smashed into the steel landing ramps. Some boatloads of men were wiped out to the last man. As the ramps of the clumsy landing craft were lowered the troops leaped into waist-deep water, some slipping, falling, and drowning, others collapsing with bullets in their vitals. Many others staggered to the sands.

From the Americans came loud Indian war whoops and the amazed reaction: "Goddam, we're on French soil!" On they came, men accompanied by machines, guns, munitions, and trucks, everything from food rations to steel-span bridges to hundreds of thousands of gallons of drinking water. Demolition engineers cleared the lanes. All that day and night the Allies poured reinforcements ashore—36,250 on Utah Beach, 34,250 at Omaha Beach, 83,115 on the British-Canadian sectors.

The first major breakthrough came on the far-right flank on Utah Beach. Here the airborne divisions outfought three German divisions, but suffered 2,500 casualties. And here the U.S. 4th Infantry Division swept ashore, swamping the German defenses at a cost of only 197 casualties.

But on the second American beach at Omaha, and the three British-Canadian beaches named Gold, Juno, and Sword—the four beaches all between the Orne and Vire Rivers—there was concentrated savage fury. The landing sites at Omaha Beach gave little protection. Here the concave strip of sand 50 to 300 yards wide ended in a steeply rising bluff, strongly fortified by the Germans. All the beach exits were mined and heavily defended; the whole area in fact was guarded by mines and barbed wire.

Units of the U.S. 1st and 29th Divisions, about 1,450 men, stormed these fortified bluffs. Men hugged the sands and shrank from the withering gunfire. Others were driven back into the Channel. Still others huddled miserably under the seawall. Here almost every Allied tank was disabled or exploded by German fire even before it could come ashore.

To the east, on Sword, Juno, and Gold Beaches, the British and Canadians sent ashore a powerful armored force consisting of tanks of all kinds to clear mines, blast pillboxes, throw flames. German infantry, quartered in seaside hotels, fought back, inflicting 4,000 casualties. Here, too, it was bloody chaos.

In his reconstruction of *The Longest Day* (1959), Cornelius Ryan recounted some superb stories of the traditional gallantry of the British. Off beachhead Juno a boatload of the Forty-eighth Royal Marine Commandos ran into heavy machine gun fire and men dived for cover behind the superstructure. But the adjutant, Captain Daniel Flunder, merely tucked his swagger stick under his arm and calmly paraded up and down the foredeck. "I thought it was the thing to do," he said later. And in a landing craft heading on to beachhead Sword, Major C. K. King was placidly reading *Henry V*. Amidst the roar of battle, King spoke into the loud-hailer: "And gentlemen in England now abed/ Shall think themselves accurs'd they were not here . . ."

It was hard going in the vast confusion and the price was high: 10,724 casualties, including 2,132 dead. But the Allies were on the Continent to stay.

The Germans had incredibly bad luck. Hitler's Intelligence officers based at Calais were aware of the code message which the Allies would use to alert the European underground for the invasion. It consisted of the first two lines of the poem *Chanson d'Automne*, by the French poet Paul Verlaine. The first radio alert would be:

> "*Les sanglots longs des violons d l'automne*
> (The long sobs of autumn's violins)"

The invasion itself would begin with the second alert and the second line:

> "*Blessent mon coeur d'une langeur monotone*
> (Wounding my heart with monotonous languor)"

The first line was heard on June 1 by a German radio monitoring unit, which flashed the word to Field Marshal Rommel, to Field Marshal Gerd von Rundstedt, over-all commander in the west, and to General Alfred Jodl, Hitler's chief of staff at Berchtesgaden. Then began a bitter comedy of errors as the German command broke down. Jodl, believing that von Rundstedt had alerted his troops, did nothing. Von Rundstedt, assuming that Rommel had given the alert, likewise failed to act.

At this point Rommel made the most critical mistake of his career.

Because the weather was foul (and all previous Allied invasion attempts had been made in fair weather), he decided on June 4 to return by motor to Germany to celebrate his wife's birthday and also to visit Hitler to request reinforcements. When he received word of the invasion, he rushed back to his headquarters, but arrived 24 hours too late to carry out the defensive strategy he had planned.

Besides Rommel a half dozen other German generals were absent from their coastal commands, some, ironically enough, taking part in a *Kriegsspiel*, a war game simulating an Allied landing in France. Two key *Panzer* divisions, which could have mangled the invasion forces in the early stages, could not be committed without Hitler's personal permission.

When the attack came Hitler was asleep, secure in the belief that no invasion force could remain for more than nine hours in France. No one, not even Jodl, dared awaken him from his drugged sleep. Von Rundstedt, amazed by the enormity of Allied power in the invasion, telephoned the *Fuehrer* for orders. Not until two o'clock that afternoon did Hitler call his usual conference. Confident that this was just another Dieppe-style raid, he ordered von Rundstedt to throw the invaders back into the sea.

But it was far too late. The bulk of German troops in the rear, smothered by Allied air attack, did not get into action until D-Day plus one. This time Hitler had really missed the bus.

BEACHHEAD ON HITLER'S *FESTUNG EUROPA*

There was deadly fighting yet to come. The first five days told the story.

On the eastern sector the Canadians penetrated seven miles inland and their patrols cut the Bayeux-Caen highway. The British Second Army, headed for Caen, collided with Rommel's 21st *Panzer* Division, which attempted unsuccessfully to drive the British into the sea. Here the German command made a fundamental error—instead of counterattacking in force it fed troops piecemeal into a defense of Caen. In three days all three British-Canadian beachheads were joined.

The U.S. First Army simultaneously pushed inland from Utah Beach to the west of the Vire and from Omaha Beach to the east of the river. At Omaha Beach the German batteries which had rained a deadly hail on Americans trapped on the beaches were finally wiped out by bombers and by shellfire from the battleships offshore.

Five days and the crust of the German defenses was broken. The British and Americans now held a continuous 80-mile strip of the Normandy coast and had penetrated 20 miles into the interior. Sixteen Allied divisions were ashore.

Lieutenant General Hans Speidel later evaluated those first days:

> The first phase of the invasion ended with an obvious military, political, and psychological success for the Allies. They had overcome the difficulties of the first few critical days without any notable reverses, because of the reliable coöperation of the three services and because of the great effectiveness of their new technical equipment. They had consolidated their position. It had become apparent to us that they could be dislodged or contained in their bridgeheads for any length of time only if strong German air and naval forces could be brought to bear. . . . From June 9 on, the initiative lay with the Allies.

To General Omar N. Bradley the explanation was more simple: "Only by guts, valor, and extreme bravery were we able to make the landing a success."

By D-Day plus 11, exactly 587,653 men and 89,728 vehicles had been put ashore by the Allies.

That same day, June 17, 1944, Hitler called a conference at Margival, north of Soissons, 140 miles to the rear. At the meeting, which lasted from 9 A.M. to 4 P.M., interrupted only for a bolted lunch, the *Fuehrer* brusquely demanded explanations from Field Marshals von Rundstedt and Rommel. Rommel gave a shocking but veracious account of the destructive power of the Allies' weapons and pronounced the German position critical.

Angered, Hitler cut Rommel off: "Don't you worry about the future course of the war. Stick to your own invasion front." He told Rommel to concern himself with military not political matters. The breach between the two was widening to the point of hatred.

D-Day plus 20. A million men were now ashore, opposed by 14 German divisions.

Ingenious Allied engineers found two solutions to the problem of overcoming the lack of port facilities on the hostile shores of *Festung Europa*. First, under the code name Gooseberry, was the construction of an anchorage by sinking old merchant ships in a line, thereby offering an unloading area in relatively sheltered waters. There was little new or novel about this sheltered anchorage—except its scope.

But the Mulberries were something else again, the most fantastic plan of its kind ever used in warfare. Long before D-Day some 19,000 British workers were engaged in building enormous structures of reinforced concrete, something like six-story buildings lying on their sides. They had no idea of what the contraptions were, perhaps floating grain elevators designed to feed the civilian population of the Continent. German agents passed the word to Berlin that the British were constructing huge piers for some special but unknown reason.

Neither British workmen nor the German agents knew that the Mulberries were in fact complete artificial harbors. Three weeks after D-Day the giant sections of the two Mulberries were towed piecemeal across the choppy Channel by dozens of puffing tugs. The great concrete towers were then spliced together, one outside the American beachheads and the other facing the British front.

The Mulberry outside the American beachhead near St. Laurent-sur-Mer was never used. It was wrecked in gale winds which blew for three days, June 19–22, 1944, the worst storm in 40 years. But the second Mulberry near the British beachhead of Arromanches was a thing of mechanical beauty, a miracle of construction, providing an outer roadstead where ocean-going vessels could anchor, and an inner roadstead, where the concrete caissons formed a fixed breakwater. Between the caissons and the shore ran ten miles of steel piers, over which the men and supplies were poured for the build-up. A million troops passed through this amazing man-made harbor or over the beaches before the end of the month. "That Mulberry," said General Speidel, "was of decisive significance."

One of the first major objectives of the Allies was the great port of Cherbourg, to the north of the beachheads.

As the Americans advanced toward the city, the Germans withdrew into its fortifications. They had made it almost impregnable against attack from the sea, but—like the Americans at Manila and the British at Singapore—they had not counted on the possibility of an assault from the land side. Its overland approaches were mildly protected by a semicircle of wooded ridges and underground forts.

"We will capture Cherbourg in ten days if we are lucky," said General Bradley, "in 30 days if we are not." It took just 20 days from D-Day.

Three infantry divisions under Major General J. Lawton ("Lightning Joe") Collins began the direct attack on Cherbourg on June 22, 1944. First came an assault by a thousand bombers and by accurate naval gunfire from the Channel. Under this barrage the infantry advanced, capturing some of the defense works, bypassing others, and rolled into the city under heavy fire.

The German garrison at Cherbourg surrendered four days later, though the last pockets of resistance were not cleaned up until the end of the month. The port of Cherbourg, like Naples, bore mute witness to the Germans' exquisitely methodical destruction. The breakwaters were smashed, the cranes destroyed, the piers covered with a maze of mines and booby traps. American engineers went to work immediately, as on so many previous occasions, to repair the demolished port. But not until August 1944 could the facilities be used extensively. Meanwhile, supplies streamed over the beaches and through the undamaged Mulberry harbor off Arromanches.

INTERLUDE: ROBOT BOMBS

Dr. Joseph Goebbels, never at a loss for words, had excuses for Germany's mounting disasters. Germans! Hold fast! Trust the *Fuehrer*. Had he not promised that the enemy would pay heavily in blood and lives? Soon Hitler, the master warrior, would release his secret *Wunderwaffen*, "wonder weapons" of such terrifying power and hideous destructive capacity that Roosevelt and Churchill would sink to their knees and beg for mercy.

The Allied Supreme Command already had been briefed by secret agents on the German search for the "ultimate weapon." The race for the atomic bomb was on. German scientists knew about harnessing atomic energy, but they were not getting far because of shortages of manpower and war materials, as well as Hitler's lack of faith in long-range projects. Moreover, German nuclear research had suffered a vital setback when in early 1943 Allied commandos had hit German heavy-water installations in Norway.

It was also known that the Germans were at work on other secret weapons, not quite identified. In May 1942, Allied photographic reconnaissance revealed that some kind of long-range-rocket research was going on at Peenemünde on a wooded island in the Baltic and at other experimental plants. Peenemünde was given top priority as a target. In August 1943 a great force of R.A.F. bombers blasted it unmercifully. Thereafter, attacks continued all along the French coast between Calais and Cherbourg against what were believed to be rail-served rocket-launching sites.

On D-Day plus 7, June 13, 1944, the secret exploded on a startled London. Hitler's first *Vergeltungswaffe*, vengeance weapon, the V-1, was a small pilotless jet-propelled plane moving at a speed of 350 miles per hour on a predetermined course and carrying a ton of explosives which detonated on contact. Londoners promptly named it the "buzz bomb" (for its peculiar engine sound) or "doodlebug."

The British immediately took defense measures against the flying robots. They set up an intensified balloon barrage and strengthened antiaircraft units in Kent and Sussex. Many flying bombs were destroyed in mid-passage by R.A.F. pilots, but those that got through to London caused tremendous damage to human flesh, nerves, and property. From June 12–20, 1944, some 8,000 V-1's were sent hurtling toward the British capital, of which about 2,300, or one out of four, reached their target. The cost to London was 5,479 killed, 15,934 wounded, 25,000 buildings destroyed, thousands of others damaged.

Why Hitler did not use the V-1 against the Portsmouth-Southampton area to smash the build-up for Overlord remains one of the great mysteries of the war. Instead, he chose to use it as a terror weapon against civilians.

The British, of course, were concerned about the new weapon. Shortly after the Normandy invasion, Churchill asked Eisenhower to strike at the clusters of launching sites around the Pas de Calais sector as soon as he possibly could. Eisenhower promised to do so.

Ironically, Hitler himself nearly became a victim of his first vengeance weapon. On June 17, 1944, at the Margival conference, he intimated that he intended to visit Cherbourg the next morning. Later that day something in the mechanism of a V-1 aimed at London went astray; the robot turned in the air and headed in the direction of the *Fuehrer*'s command post, near which it exploded. Hitler promptly canceled the Cherbourg visit, boarded a plane, and flew back to Berchtesgaden.

In early August 1944 the *Fuehrer* unveiled the V-2, a rocket bomb which flew at a height of 60-70 miles at a supersonic speed of 3,000 miles per hour. Carrying a ton of explosives, the V-2 descended on its target and buried itself deeply before exploding upward. Unlike the V-1, the V-2 could not be seen, heard, or intercepted in flight; the first warning was the explosion. This merciless weapon took some 8,000 lives, almost as many as the great aerial *Blitz* of 1940. After most of the launching ramps were captured in late August 1944, the Germans that winter aimed their remaining V-1's and V-2's at Antwerp, for its port, and Liége, for its American army installations.

These were terrifying weapons, but again it was the old story of too little and too late. Had they been unleashed earlier in the war, perhaps Allied victory might have been delayed or prevented. As it was, they were the dying gasps of a throttled, beaten *Fuehrer*.

On August 2, 1944, Churchill reviewed the war in the House of Commons: "I no longer feel bound," he said, "to deny that victory may come, perhaps soon."

JULY 20, 1944: THE PLOT TO KILL HITLER

The scene: a wooden *Gästebaracke* (hutment for guests) at Hitler's Wolf's Lair headquarters in East Prussia. The *Fuehrer* had summoned a conference for a progress report on creating new front-line divisions from the Home Guard to halt the Russians, now only 50 miles away.

Lieutenant General Adolf Heusinger, director of the Military Operations Branch and deputy chief of the General Staff, had just reached the final paragraph of his discouraging report: "*Der Russe dreht mit starken Kräften westlich der Duna nach Norden ein. Seine Spitz steht bereits südwestlich Dunaburg. Wenn jetz nicht endlich die Heeresgruppe vom Peipussee züruckgenommen wird, dann werden wir eine Katastrophe. . . .*" ("The Russians are moving with strong power west of the Duna toward Norden. Their forward point is already southwest of Dunaburg. If now finally the army group is not withdrawn from Peipussee, then a catastrophe will. . . .")

At this moment a thunderous roar shook the room.

At 12:37 on that afternoon of July 20, 1944, 37-year-old Colonel Count Claus Schenck von Stauffenberg, chief of staff of the Reserve Army, had entered the conference room. He saluted and apologized for being late as he placed a brief case under the table where the *Fuehrer* sat.

Count von Stauffenberg, of Swabian origin and a descendant of Count August von Gneisenau, one of the founders of the German General Staff, was a young officer of great personal charm. Fifteen months earlier he had been grievously wounded in Tunisia, losing his left eye, his right hand, and two fingers of his left hand, as well as suffering severe leg wounds. During his convalescence, he came to the conclusion that Hitler's lunatic disregard for human decency had so besmirched the name of the German Fatherland that it stank in the nostrils of civilized men everywhere. He would assassinate this madman and bring an end to the senseless war.

In von Stauffenberg's brief case was a bomb of English origin, a slab of plastic high explosive called hexite. Before entering the *Gästebaracke*, he used a little tool to rip the neck of the fuse, a small glass globule containing corrosive acid, which bit into a wire spring. The fuse was set to detonate the bomb in ten minutes.

Muttering an excuse, von Stauffenberg slipped out of the room. Another officer, finding the brief case in the way of his legs, moved it to the far side of the table support, thus placing the support between the bomb and Hitler.

At 12:42 the bomb exploded. The windows of the room were blown out, the roof collapsed, and a hole was blasted in the floor. There were three separate detonations, followed by thick clouds of smoke and yellow flame.

There were shouts of alarm: "*Attentat! Attentat!*" Someone screamed: "*Wo ist der Fuehrer?*" Hitler, miraculously, was still alive.

Four men were killed instantly, 20 others were wounded. Hitler was saved from death by the table top and the oaken support. His right arm was temporarily paralyzed, his right ear permanently deafened, and his legs burned. A falling beam struck his back and pinned him to the floor.

Behind the deed was a conspiracy of officers, including Colonel General Ludwig Beck, 64-year-old former chief of the General Staff; Field Marshal Erwin von Witzleben; Count Helmuth von Moltke, grandnephew of the victor of 1871; and Dr. Karl Goerdeler, former *Oberbürgermeister* of Leipzig. Some months earlier the plotters had gained a powerful adherent in Field Marshal Erwin Rommel, whom most Germans regarded as the *beau idéal* of a Nazi general, but it was never proved that he was aware of the plans for the contemplated assassination.

Hitler hysterically denounced the conspirators as "a small clique of criminally stupid, ambitious officers, devoid of conscience." They were *Schweinehunde*, filthy blue-blooded swine, Prussians who never really understood the nobility of Nazism.

As soon as the news was broadcast that Hitler was alive, the *Gestapo* started its dragnet Operation Thunderstorm, bringing the number of Germans arrested that year to 33,000.

The *Fuehrer's* vengeance was monumental. He had most of the Stauffenberg family killed and distributed the children under false names to strangers. He ordered the other plotters tortured and condemned to death. "It is my wish that they be hanged like cattle."

Hitler's word was still law in the insane Third Reich. Eight of the condemned men were hanged in a small room in the Plötzensee Prison under singularly revolting circumstances. Present were cameramen of the Reich Film Corporation. Eight hooks, as those used in butchers' shops for hanging up sides of meat, were screwed into the ceiling. The prisoners were brought in one by one. First the handcuffs were removed and the victim stripped to the waist. Then a short thin cord was placed around his neck and the other end thrown over a meathook and made fast. He was then lifted. Off came his trousers. Thus he hung naked, twisting in agony as he slowly strangled. The average dying time was five minutes. The cameras worked on without interruption. That evening at the *Reichskanzlei* Hitler had the films run over and over again so that he could enjoy every second of the macabre spectacle. The film was later shown at one of the Cadet Schools in Berlin, obviously to show the perils of disloyalty. But so many of the budding officers became violently nauseated by the barbaric horror that this Nazi training-film was abandoned.

The *Attentat* of July 20, 1944, left Hitler not only sorely wounded but in a state of maniacal self-pity. "The German people," he cried, "are unworthy of my greatness. No one appreciates what I have done for them."

For those wounded at the Wolf's Lair there was a special decoration from the *Fuehrer* bearing the inscription: *"Hitler–20. Juli, 1944."*

GUTS AND BLOOD: THE BATTLE OF NORMANDY

The occupation of Cherbourg blasted Hitler's hopes of driving the Allies into the sea.

The next Allied stage was the conquest of all Normandy. The prospects were excellent. British and American beachheads were secure and reinforcements were steadily flowing to the Continent. Gone now were fears of another Dunkirk.

At the eastern end of the Allied beachhead was the British Second Army, commanded by Lieutenant General Sir Miles C. Dempsey and containing several Canadian divisions. At the western end was the U.S. First Army under Lieutenant General Omar N. Bradley. Together these two armies temporarily made up the Twenty-first Army Group under General Sir Bernard L. Montgomery, the over-all ground forces commander for the invasion. On

July 23 the Canadian First Army was to be created under Lieutenant General H. D. G. Crerar and was to come under Montgomery's army group command. On August 1 the U.S. Third Army under Lieutenant General George S. Patton, Jr., was to become operational and with the First Army was to be grouped under a new U.S. headquarters, the Twelfth Army Group, commanded by General Bradley. The First Army then was to be commanded by Lieutenant General Courtney H. Hodges.

This would be the Allied organization for the remainder of the Normandy fighting.

Because the British on the west faced fairly open country favorable for tanks, the Germans concentrated the bulk of their armored strength around Caen.

On June 25, 1944, even before the fall of Cherbourg, the British moved on Caen from the south, only to meet violent resistance from enemy tank units. The German counterattack was just strong enough to contain the British but not so strong as to inflict a decisive defeat. German reinforcements were slowed because of a continuing campaign by Allied air power against the roads and rails leading into Normandy.

The R.A.F. carpeted Caen with bombs. In early July 1944 the British made another attempt to take the city but succeeded in taking only half the objective. Then on July 18, behind a "carpet bombing" by Allied aircraft, they attacked again. This time they took the rest of the city, but bogged down when heavy rains turned the earth into a sea of mire.

The Allies now shifted their offensive to the American center near St. Lô, farther to the west.

Here, during most of July, the Americans had been fighting for the strategic road center and provincial capital of St. Lô. The battle was savage, one of the nastiest fights of the war, worse than D-Day itself. Gains were measured in yards. At every farmhouse the enemy had to be flushed out like protesting birds. In the Bocage country around St. Lô, American tanks and infantry became snarled among the hedgerows—hundreds of thick dirt-banks, with thorn-bushes growing on top, which lined the roads and lanes of Normandy. The hedgerows, forming a natural defense, forced the heavy tanks to operate only on the roads. Not until the tanks were outfitted with new cutting devices could advances be made through the sticky hedgerow country.

With St. Lô won, General Bradley planned a massive attack launched along the St. Lô-Periers road, west of St. Lô, to be preceded, as was the earlier British attack at Caen, by waves of big bombers laying a lethal carpet in front of the infantry and tanks. Launched on July 26 by Hodges' First Army, the attack turned quickly into a breakthrough operation. Bradley quickly committed the new Third Army under General Patton to drive past

Avranches at the base of the Cotentin peninsula and break into open country.

Now the gateway to the south and east was open. American forces might break out of Normandy, seal off the enemy in Brittany, and streak eastward and northeastward across the waist of France. Turning one corps into Brittany, Patton sent the bulk of his tanks eastward in company with the armor of Hodges' First Army.

As the rampaging tanks poured through Avranches the Battle of Normandy merged into the Battle of France. Racing through the fields at a daily 40-mile clip, the American tank columns headed south and stormed into Rennes, the capital of Brittany. Three columns then wheeled westward and cut a wide corridor to the coast. St. Malo on the north coast surrendered on August 17, 1944, but the garrisons at Brest, Lorient, and St. Nazaire to the west and southwest fought on. Except for Brest, they were left, bottled up and ignored, as the tide of battle turned east.

For a normal military mind the situation obviously called for a prompt German withdrawal from Normandy. But the stubborn, pig-headed Hitler instead ordered four *Panzer* divisions of the German Seventh Army to counterattack westward. He would move westward through Mortain to Avranches, thereby cutting the U.S. corridor in two and breaking through to the sea. Always the sea, the ephemeral sea, the Hitler-designated burial-place for Allied power.

On August 7, 1944, the Germans launched their major counterattack in the direction of Avranches. They fought furiously, with a desperation whip-lashed by Hitler. They succeeded in penetrating the American lines for a few miles. And they kept it up for five days.

But around the German salient a four-pronged trap was being forged. The main body of the U.S. First Army took the brunt of the German thrust at Mortain while a portion of this same army joined with part of Patton's Third to swing north and hit the enemy salient on its left flank in the direction of Argentan. At the same time the British Second Army held firm on the west while the Canadian First Army moved southeast from Caen toward Falaise to strike at the German right flank. This Falaise-Argentan pocket was a beautiful pincers movement, classic in its simplicity, annihilating in its power. The bulk of two German field armies (the Fifth Panzer and the Seventh) was trapped.

From August 16–21, 1944, the encircling Allies relentlessly sewed up the pocket. The Germans were being strangled. Thousands of them were killed or wounded, 50,000 were captured, including what was left of the proud Seventh Army. The remainder, heavily battered from the air, staggered in disorder toward the Seine.

The Battle of Normandy was over. It was a resounding Allied victory.

THE "HONOR" SUICIDE OF FIELD MARSHAL ROMMEL

By the middle of July 1944 the Allied armies were on the verge of breaking through to Paris. The position of the Germans was critical: Their supply lines and reinforcements were breaking down under steady air bombardment. Meanwhile, the Allies were landing new forces daily and bringing masses of war matériel ashore.

On the morning of July 17, 1944, Field Marshall Erwin Rommel set out in an open staff-car for the front to do what he could to restore order among his exhausted and demoralized troops and to encourage them for another stand. After visiting forward headquarters, he entered his car for the return trip. On the road between Livarot and Vimoutiers, Allied fighter craft discovered the unaccompanied car. Three of them swooped low and strafed it before it could reach the concealment of a grove of poplars.

The pilots had no idea of their prize. The driver was killed and Rommel suffered critical injuries, his skull, cheekbones, and temples fractured and his left eye badly damaged. More dead than alive, he was removed to a *Luftwaffe* hospital, where he did not regain consciousness until July 24.

In the spring of 1944 Hitler had transferred Rommel to Europe to help prepare the defense for the expected Allied invasion of France. By this time Rommel had come to the conclusion that the leader he once venerated as the unifier of the nation and as the "liberator from Versailles" was a clay-footed idol. A man of fundamentally decent instincts, Rommel had had enough of this foul-minded and foul-mouthed adventurer who was blackening the name of Germany.

After a bitter examination of his conscience (he, too, had taken the oath of loyalty to Hitler), Rommel decided to throw in his lot with the group of generals, headed by Colonel General Ludwig Beck, who were conspiring to overthrow Hitler. But the *Fuehrer* was spared by the failure of the bomb plot of July 20, which took place while Rommel lay unconscious from his wounds. Ironically, Rommel never knew that the conspirators had selected him to be the new chief of state after Hitler's death.

To maintain their power, dictators must keep a wary eye on their immediate henchmen. As early as 1527, Niccolò Machiavelli in his *Principe* warned that it was a matter of self-preservation for the Prince to "secure himself against his brilliant and victorious general, do away with him, or strip him of his renown." The cunning Hitler sensed this without the benefit of higher learning. He was careful to stir up rivalries among Goering, Goebbels, Himmler, and others in his entourage, and to make certain that no single one would attain too much popularity. Rommel the incomparable field general, the idol of Germany's fighting men, the great Rommel was a most inconvenient asset. There must be no national hero besides Hitler in the Nazi hierarchy. Moreover, in Hitler's eyes Rommel was responsible for the disaster of the Normandy breakthrough.

On July 21, 1944, one day after the bomb plot misfired, one of the conspirators implicated Rommel. It was an incredible piece of bad luck for Rommel. General Karl Heinrich von Stuelpnagel attempted to kill himself, but upon regaining consciousness after an operation cried out the name "Rommel!" This was enough for Hitler, who now found the perfect excuse for ridding himself of a potential rival.

Rommel, recovering from his wounds, characteristically refused to hold his tongue. "Hitler," he said, "that pathological liar, has now gone completely mad. He is venting his sadism on the conspirators of July 20 and this won't be the end of it." And again to his astonished doctor: "I fear that this madman will sacrifice the last German before he meets his own end." It was strongly probable that Rommel knew at this time that he was the next to be sacrificed.

On October 14, 1944, General Wilhelm Burgdorf and Lieutenant General Ernst Maisel, loyal toadies of the *Fuehrer*, came to visit Rommel, who had been removed to his home near Ulm to recuperate from his injuries. The envoys brusquely told him that the testimony of the conspirators had implicated him in the plot against Hitler. But there was an "honorable" way out for a German officer thus accused. He would have the choice of taking poison or appearing before the People's Court to defend himself. He could see that the house and surrounding grounds were guarded by S.S. men with machine guns.

In 15 minutes Rommel was dead.

An autopsy was forbidden. The body was delivered to Frau Rommel, who was informed that her husband had suffered an embolism. The German press announced that Field Marshal Rommel had died from the effects of "the automobile accident." There were long eulogies paying tribute to a great son of the Fatherland. Hitler ordered a state funeral, held four days later in the city hall at Ulm. His face ashen, Field Marshal Gerd von Rundstedt, representing Hitler, read the funeral oration. It included a sentence that might have come straight from the Oracle at Delphi: "His heart belonged to the *Fuehrer!*"

OPERATION ANVIL-DRAGOON

While the Germans caught in the Falaise pocket were being crushed, another Allied encirclement on a greater circumference was being shaped.

Operation Anvil, later renamed Dragoon, the invasion of France from the south, was designed to ensnare the reeling Germans in another greater trap. The Allies planned to strike at the weak German Nineteenth Army,

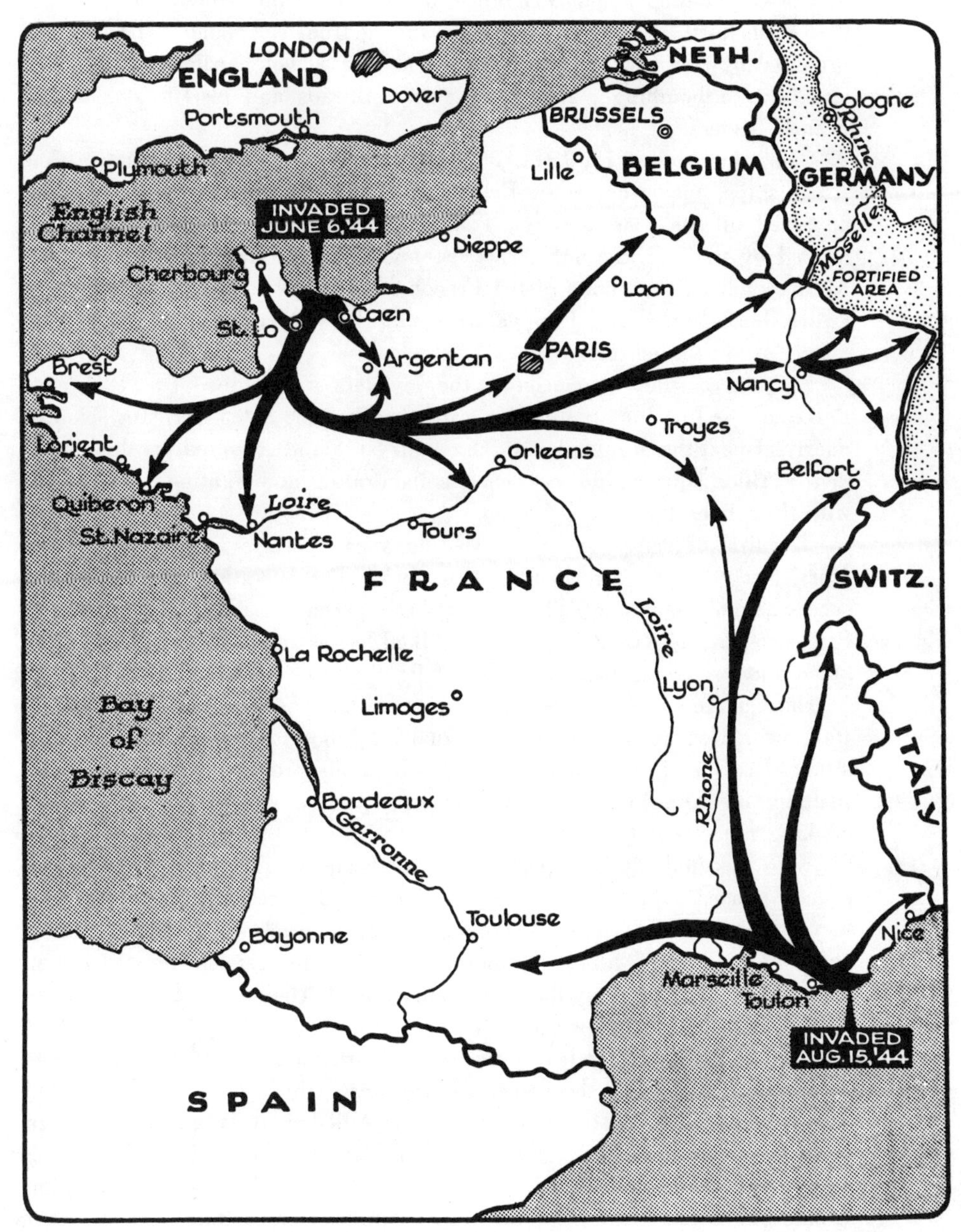

THE BATTLE OF FRANCE

which was holding a hundred miles of the coast from Toulon to Nice, and then push north to join the forces advancing from Normandy. The way was prepared by two weeks of sustained air and naval bombardment. From Italy and Corsica bombing planes hammered railheads and installations on the French Riviera.

Then, on August 15, 1944, in ideal weather, a huge fleet of more than 1,500 ships, including seven British and two American aircraft carriers, appeared off the coast between Toulon and Cannes. The attack was spearheaded by the U.S. Seventh Army, commanded now by Lieutenant General Alexander M. Patch, units of the French First Army under General Jean de Lattre de Tassigny, and U.S. paratroopers. These were veteran troops with much battle experience.

As soon as they were ashore, the invaders were joined by the French Forces of the Interior, spoiling for a fight against the hated Germans. Though poorly armed, the *Maquis* knew the countryside and rendered invaluable aid to the Allies, hunting down French collaborators and fighting side by side with their liberators.

The first objectives were the Mediterranean ports of Nice, Toulon, and Marseilles. All were taken within two weeks. The operation was a complete success. Commented one Allied officer: "Compared to Salerno, the landing in Provence was just guerrilla warfare." Allied losses were 1,500, including both killed and wounded, after two days of fighting.

Once again the Germans, who had expected another leapfrog attack in Italy near Genoa, were caught off-guard by both the time and place of attack. Even if Hitler had been able to hold his ground in Normandy and Brittany, his forces in France would eventually have been exposed to a strong flanking movement from the south.

With the vital southern ports and beachheads secure, the Americans and French pushed rapidly northward through the Durance Valley. In ten days they were surging through Avignon, and soon reached the Rhône Valley above Montélimar, a hundred miles from the Mediterranean. Small German forces which tried to delay them were annihilated. The onrushing Allied army headed straight north toward Lyons and Dijon.

Farther to the east other units moved northward along the main route to Grenoble. Here, too, the resistance was weak; thousands of prisoners fell into the hands of the fast-moving army. This Allied right flank passed through Besançon on September 7, 1944, and four days later the left flank pushing north from Lyons was at Dijon. Both flanks, then wheeled east, swinging around the Swiss border to link up at Épinal with Patton's Third Army tumbling down from the north.

All the Allied armies now formed a continuous front from Switzerland to the sea.

THE LIBERATION OF PARIS

What to do about Paris?

The Allied High Command had taken great pains to avoid direct bombing of the French capital, concentrating instead on railway bottlenecks outside the city rather than the terminals inside it. "At the moment," said Eisenhower, "we were anxious to save every ounce of fuel and ammunition for combat operations, in order to carry our lines forward the maximum distance, and I was hopeful of deferring actual capture of the city, unless I received assurance of starvation or distress among its citizens."

Eisenhower's hand was forced by what happened inside the city itself. During the first three critical weeks of August 1944 the Germans stationed in Paris began to stampede out of the city. Many got away to ford the bridgeless rivers or to be caught on roads by Allied air power. The Fighting French forces inside Paris decided to wait no longer. On August 19, 1944, more than 20,000 members of the F.F.I. (French Forces of the Interior) revolted against the rear-guard German garrison. Eisenhower then moved rapidly to their support.

Again came thc nutcracker assault. American Sherman tanks, driving forward at full speed, swept toward Paris in two arcs, one racing through Chartres and Orléans to the south and another appearing simultaneously north of the Seine. The tanks suddenly halted outside the city. For the honor of first entry General Bradley selected Brigadier General Jacques Philippe LeClerc's French Second Armored Division, which three years before, in the latter phase of the African campaign, had made an amazing march across the Sahara Desert to join up with the British Eighth Army. Some further American assistance was required before order was restored in Paris.

At 2 P.M. on August 25, 1944, General LeClerc, speaking in a baggage room at the Gare Montparnasse, announced the surrender of the German garrison of 10,000.

The next day General de Gaulle walked stiffly along the boulevards amidst an ecstatic populace. "I went on foot," de Gaulle reported. "This was not the day for passing in review with arms glittering and trumpets sounding. . . . Since each of all these here had chosen Charles de Gaulle in his heart as the refuge against his agony and the symbol of his hopes, we must permit the man to be seen, familiar and fraternal, in order that at this sight the national unity should shine forth."

After four years of captivity Paris was at last free, the first capital of the Allies to be reconquered from the Germans. The delirious celebration lasted for three days. The climax came when General Eisenhower reviewed French and American troops marching past the Arc de Triomphe and down the Champs Élysées.

But this was only a temporary phase for the battle-hardened Allied troops. The motorized stampede quickly moved across the Seine and headed toward Germany in pursuit of the enemy.

ROLLING THUNDER TOWARD GERMANY

The second battle of France was a costly one for Adolf Hitler. Since the Normandy invasion his armies had suffered 500,000 casualties, including 200,000 penned and by-passed in ports along the coast. Approximately twenty infantry and five *Panzer* divisions were totally destroyed, 12 more infantry and six *Panzer* divisions were seriously mauled. The *Fuehrer's* defeated legions, now under command of Field Marshal Walther Model, were streaming eastward to the shelter of the Siegfried Line, the last defensive barrier of the Third Reich.

For the Allies the picture was considerably brighter. By September 5, 1944, D-Day plus 90, they had put more than 2,000,000 troops and 3,500,000 tons of supplies ashore. From the Normandy beachheads across France the famed Red Ball Express, motorized caravans, carried huge supplies of fuel and ammunition to the onrushing troops. There were heavy casualties—224,000 killed, wounded, and captured, but there was consolation for the victors in the knowledge that the enemy was at last being strangled.

After the liberation of Paris, four great spearheads of Allied armor, in a *Blitzkrieg* unmatched by the 1940 German version in the first Battle of France, raced along a dozen different routes through eastern France and Belgium at a rate of from 20 to 50 miles a day.

In the extreme north, on the Allied left flank, the Canadian First Army on August 22, 1944, trapped the Germans in a pocket below Le Havre and Rouen, sealed off the German garrison at Dieppe, and pushed across the Belgian frontier.

Just below the Canadians, Montgomery's Second Army moved northeast across the Seine between Rouen and Paris, advancing 60 miles in two days, and entered Amiens on August 31, 1944. The commander of the German Seventh Army was captured at breakfast. Crossing the Somme, the British took Arras and drove on to Lille just off the Belgian border.

Simultaneously, Hodges' U.S. First Army, in the center of the Allied lines, advanced quickly across the Seine, pushed eastward across the Marne and Aisne, and took Laon. Storming Sedan, it reached the Belgian border on August 31, 1944. In the process the First Army cut off five retreating German divisions and took 22,000 prisoners. Smashing into Belgium, it took Liége on September 2, Brussels on September 3, and Antwerp on September 4, three key Belgian cities in three days.

On the extreme southern flank of the Allied front, Patton's Third Army maintained a similar rapid pace. Passing south of Paris, his armored spearheads reached the Marne on August 27, 1944, drove through Château-Thierry of World War I fame, and overran Reims and Châlons. There was no stopping Patton. On he went through the Argonne Forest, through Verdun, all the way to the Moselle from Nancy to Metz.

Behind these surging armies some 20,000 bypassed Germans tried to move from the Bay of Biscay area all the way across northern France through Allied lines back to Germany. This desperate maneuver collapsed quickly. All the Germans were captured.

On September 16, 1944, Patch's Seventh Army, driving up from the south after Operation Anvil-Dragoon, joined the U.S. Third at Dijon. It was a further entrapment for the bewildered enemy.

Meanwhile, Allied power was turned on the French and Belgian Channel ports. The Canadians bore the brunt of this heavy fighting, capturing Dieppe (September 1, 1944), Ostend (September 8), Boulogne (September 18), and Calais (September 30).

The French Atlantic ports of Bordeaux, St. Nazaire, and Lorient had been stubbornly defended by German troops left behind and supplied by plane and submarine. The Allied High Command, certain that these ports were doomed to ultimate capture, decided to risk no lives in investing them, and bypassed the areas. But on September 18 the U.S. Ninth Army captured Brest in the extreme northwest, with 36,000 prisoners, but so badly damaged was the port that it could not be used by Allied supply ships.

In the middle of September 1944 the Allies decided on a spectacular gamble to help bring the war to a conclusion. Why a bloody assault on the Siegfried Line, defended by an army as large as that of the Allies? Why not outflank the line? This could be done at Cleve, its northern hinge, just as the Germans had swung around the Maginot Line in 1940. Assigned to this task were the glider troops and paratroopers of the First Allied Airborne Army, commanded by Lieutenant General Lewis H. Brereton, and consisting of the British First and the U.S. 82nd and 101st Airborne Divisions.

The plan—Operation Market-Garden—was simple. The Americans would take Eindhoven and Nijmegen and the key bridges across the Maas and Waal Rivers. The British would land farther north at Arnhem. Then the British Second Army, under Lieutenant General Sir Miles C. Dempsey, would drive up from the south, effect a juncture, and help open the way into Germany.

September 17, 1944. The airborne units (20,000 men, in 1,500 transports and 425 gliders) flew from bases in England and dropped on Holland. In a few days it became the biggest airborne operation of all time. The Americans landed around Eindhoven, seized the main communications centers, and joined up with elements of the British Second Army which had come across the Dutch border.

The Americans also landed at Nijmegen, where the Waal, wide and swift, was spanned by a huge steel and concrete bridge. When the Germans staunchly defended the south end of the bridge, U.S. paratroopers in a hastily improvised operation made a heroic assault crossing of the Waal in frail little canvas assault boats and came upon the big bridge from the north. Even as the paratroopers reached the north end, British tanks at last broke through on the south. For the Germans, who had delayed blowing the bridge in hope of using it for launching counterattacks at Nijmegen, it was too late.

So far so good. But at Arnhem on the Lower Rhine, ten miles to the north, the whole operation became a nightmare. Here 8,000 Red Devils of the British First Airborne Division, in bright red berets, had the most difficult assignment of all. They would have to wait longest for the ground forces to reach them.

The Germans reacted violently, slashing at Dempsey's Second Army with such fury that he was able to put only two regiments through to the Lower Rhine.

An eyewitness told the tragic story:

> It lasted for nine days and nights, and all the time the Red Devils were being cut up into smaller groups, in packed patches of screeching shells, fire-spouting tanks, strafing planes, sleepless nights, foodless days. The food allotment was cut to one-sixth. Ammunition was rationed. The men had almost nothing left with which to fight. Finally, they were shooting their pistols at German tanks.

After a heroic resistance in their isolated pocket, the bedraggled remnants of the Red Devils, about 2,000 men, were evacuated to the British lines.

It was a disaster—the airdrop did not go as well as expected, communications broke down, air support was lacking in the foggy weather, and worst of all, the complete Allied battle plan had been captured by the Germans after the first landings.

The reaction was great disappointment in the Allied nations, which had optimistically expected an easy way to Berlin. It was clear that the headlong Allied drive had finally overreached itself and that the fluid front had now hardened. It was necessary to halt, rest, reinforce, regroup. This meant still another winter of hard fighting for the Allied armies drawn up on the German frontier on a line stretching from the mouth of the Maas River in the Netherlands to Switzerland. One of the first orders of business was to clear stubborn Germans from the banks of the Schelde Estuary along the 60 miles from Antwerp to the sea.

CHAPTER 21

Closing the Trap on Hitler

> ***Proclamation to the German People: "We come as conquerors but not as oppressors. . . . We shall overthrow the Nazi rule, dissolve the Nazi party and abolish the cruel, oppressive, and discriminatory laws and institutions which the party has created. We shall eradicate that German militarism which has so often disrupted the peace of the world."***
>
> **—General Dwight D. Eisenhower, September 28, 1944**

FINAL OFFENSIVE IN ITALY

The fighting in Italy in the winter of 1943–1944 had been as fierce as on any front in the global war. The Allies were slowly pushing ahead but it was hard going. Allied units had been contained at Anzio and the concentrated assault on Cassino had failed.

The Allied High Command, regrouping its forces, transferred the U.S. Fifth Army to the west coast along the Tyrrhenian Sea, reinforced the Anzio beachhead, and moved the British Eighth Army in to replace the Fifth Army around Cassino. The plan was to build up terrific power for an assault on Rome.

In preparation, Allied air power began Operation Strangle, designed to block the three major rail lines and the roads coming south from North Italy. Swooping down in strong formations, Allied airmen systematically destroyed railroad stations, bridges, and aqueducts. In the one month of April 1944 they flew 21,000 sorties. To avoid this hail of fire the Germans were forced to send their supplies across sea routes guarded by the British fleet. Hitler then found himself between the rock of Scylla and the whirlpool of Charybdis.

To meet the expected offensive Field Marshal Albert Kesselring had two strongly fortified mountain barriers: the Gustav Line centered at Cassino and spread along the Garigliano and Rapido Rivers, and the Adolf Hitler Line behind it, running in a triangle from Pontecorvo to Aquino to Piedemonte. In early May 1944 he ordered the flooding of the Pontine Marshes which lay between the Cassino and Anzio fronts.

On May 11, 1944, both the Fifth and Eighth Armies moved in unison. In the course of the next day the Garigliano and Rapido Rivers were crossed and advances of several miles made. In a week of savage fighting the Allies broke the Gustav Line. Polish troops pushed in behind Monte Cassino and joined British forces to encircle and capture both town and monastery; the British took the town and the Poles the monastery. The triumphant Poles, themselves Catholics, raised their standard on Monte Cassino. The Allies took 1,500 prisoners.

While the Eighth Army pushed northward through the Hitler Line toward Rome, simultaneously the Fifth Army slugged its way north on the Via Appia to relieve Anzio.

May 23, 1944, was a memorable day. British and American forces, with tremendous air support, launched an offensive from the Anzio beachhead, the veteran troops there bursting out of its perimeter. The French, fighting with Clark's Fifth Army, broke through the German lines west of the Liri Valley, thus enabling the Americans, British, and Canadians to advance.

The punishment went on without pause. The next day fighter-bombers attacked German road convoys, destroying or damaging more than 600 motor vehicles. A thousand American field guns directed a deadly fire on Cisterna, where the Germans had concentrated the bulk of their strength. The latter counterattacked a dozen times with tank formations but they were repelled each time. On May 25 another 1,171 German vehicles were destroyed or damaged on the roads.

Once again the Germans had to retire northward. There were two strong points covering their escape, Velletri and Valmontone, about 20 miles southeast of Rome. Fighting doggedly up and down extinct volcanoes, the Americans captured both cities. Though the Germans had not been cut off completely, they had left the roads to Rome open.

On June 4, 1944, at 7:30 P.M., just nine months after touching the toe of Italy, the 88th Division of the U.S. Fifth Army under Lieutenant General Mark W. Clark marched into the Piazza Venezia, heart of the Eternal City. Allied tankmen were greeted with cheers, flowers, fruit, Chianti, and kisses, from a grateful people who had feared the leveling of the city. Earlier in the day it had been announced from Hitler's headquarters that German troops had been ordered to withdraw northwest of Rome, and Kesselring had sent proposals via the Vatican for making Rome an open city.

"The first Axis capital is in our hands," commented President Roosevelt. "One up and two to go!"

Kesselring, fighting a skillful rear-guard action, withdrew his troops to positions along the Gothic Line, a natural defensive barrier running from Pisa across Italy to Rimini on the heights above the Arno River, some 150 miles north of Rome. Without pausing to celebrate their victory at Rome, the Allies, in vigorous pursuit, crossed the Tiber and pressed northward over roads strewn with mines and demolitions.

On June 17, 1944, the Fifth Army, which had pushed forward at the rate of seven miles a day, entered Leghorn. It found the docks demolished and the harbor clogged with a dozen wrecks. Here again, as at Naples, American engineers promptly restored the port for use as a supply base.

While the Fifth Army was moving up the Tyrrhenian coast, Polish troops on the Adriatic side straightened out the Allied lines by seizing Ancona, while the British Eighth Army in the center, fighting against fanatical resistance, moved to Perugia (June 20, 1944).

British patrols probing through Tuscany reached the outskirts of Florence on August 4, 1944, and found the beautiful Italian city badly mangled. Here, as at Naples, the retreating Germans had committed much senseless destruction, wrecking every bridge across the Arno except the Ponte Vecchio.

On January 6, 1945, President Roosevelt reported to Congress: "Over very difficult terrain and through adverse weather conditions, our Fifth Army and the British Eighth Army . . . have, in the past year, pushed north through bloody Cassino and the Anzio beachhead and through Italy until now they occupy heights overlooking the valley of the Po."

But it was not yet over. On April 9, 1945, General Clark's Fifth Army jumped off on Operation Grapefruit. Three days later the Allies threw their weight into a final offensive from positions in the Apennines. After a week of heavy fighting, they broke into the Po Valley and entered Bologna from the west and south.

In the final weeks the British Eighth Army swept along the northeast Adriatic coastal plain, liberating Padua, Venice, and Mestre. At the same time the American Fifth Army drove into the foothills of the Alps along the Brenner route, and raced up the valley of the Po, reaching Milan on April 29, 1945. Meanwhile, the Eighth Army was advancing on Trieste and making contact with the Yugoslav Partisans at Monfalcone, north of Trieste. On May 1 German headquarters in Italy agreed to unconditional surrender.

From Salerno to the Po Valley it had been a long and bloody battle straight up the Italian boot. The main struggle against Hitler was being fought out on the Eastern and Western fronts, but Italy had been more than a sideshow. Fourteen divisions of Germany's best fighting troops had been tied

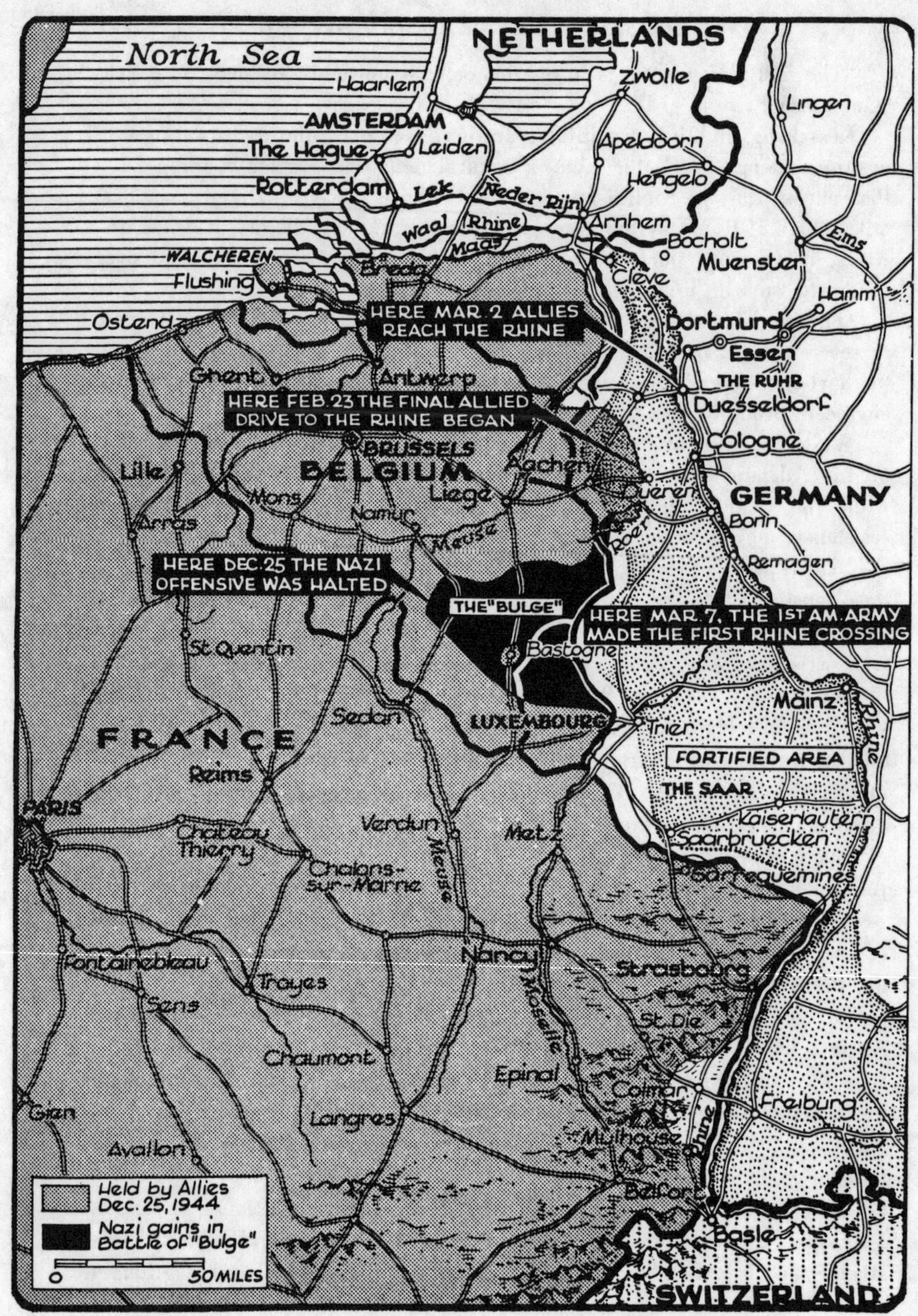

BATTLE OF THE RHINE

down in the Italian campaign—an important factor in the final collapse of Hitler's drive for world power.

COUNTEROFFENSIVE AND BULGE

Adolf Hitler's "thousand-year" Third Reich, shrinking day by day, was bleeding from every vein. On every front—west, south, and east—Allied power was surging toward Germany itself. The German army was being broken into pieces. The Western Allies were poised on the Siegfried Line ready to drive into the German homeland. In the south their armies in Italy were rumbling northward. And in the East, Soviet troops were already on German soil in East Prussia and were heading toward Germany via Warsaw and Budapest.

Germany was being crushed in a tightening chain of disasters. But there was still a residue of deadliness in the wolf's fangs.

In the greatest of secrecy, Hitler prepared his last gamble, bearing the code name of Operation Herbstnebel ("Autumn Fog"). He would dispatch all available men and war matériel to the West Wall and strike in the Ardennes, that favorite hunting ground of German strategists. Here in the Monschau-Echternach sector the Allied forces were thin enough to permit a breakthrough. He would surprise the Allies, who did not expect an attack anywhere, by hitting them in bad weather when their planes were grounded. Then, after the breakthrough, his troops would become mobile again in open country, seize the bridgeheads over the Meuse between Namur and Liége, bypass Brussels, and drive irresistibly on to Antwerp. This would change the entire complexion of the war. Success, Hitler said, was a "guaranteed certainty."

Planning began in September 1944 after three months in which Anglo-American forces had fought their way from the Normandy beaches to a foothold in Germany itself. On December 11 and 12, 1944, Hitler called a meeting at his Eagle's Nest in Bavaria of all commanders who were to take part in the counteroffensive. On one side of the room were Germany's most experienced generals, professional soldiers who understood all the ramifications of war. Facing them was the Supreme Amateur, the Teutonic Napoleon who regarded his experts as ignorant puppets.

But gone was the self-confident, arrogant *Fuehrer* of the early victorious days, who needed only to consult his astrologer before hurling his troops into battle. The assassination attempt of July 20, 1944, had left visible marks. One of his officers described him as "a stooped figure with a pale and puffy face, hunched in his chair, his hands trembling, his left arm subject to a violent twitching which he did his best to conceal, a sick man apparently borne down by the burden of his responsibility. When he walked he dragged one leg behind him."

Hitler spoke for an hour and a half in a low and hesitant voice. He was setting up "fresh, completely battleworthy formations for the offensive." The prospects were entirely favorable. Every officer present was expected to advance regardless of what might happen on his flanks. He must be ready, if need be, to die.

Hitler's plan was to deliver his strongest blow in the center and in the north while a less powerful force established a blocking line through northern Luxembourg and southeastern Belgium to protect the main thrusts. The final plan called for a surprise attack by 20 divisions (later increased to 25) of the Fifth and Sixth *Panzer* Armies and the Seventh Army, largely infantry. Field Marshal Gerd von Rundstedt would lead his divisions, ten of them armored, across the Ardennes battlefield he knew so well from 1940. "I am determined," Hitler said, "to carry out this operation despite all risks. Even if the impending Allied attacks on either side of Metz and toward the Ruhr should result in great loss of territory and of fortified positions, I am, nevertheless, determined to go ahead with this attack."

Von Rundstedt had little faith in the operation and advised Hitler against it. But the *Fuehrer* had spoken. On December 15, 1944, von Rundstedt issued an Order of the Day: "Soldiers of the West Front, your great hour has struck. Everything is at stake!"

Only Pearl Harbor could compare with the surprise dawn attack on December 16, 1944, when a quarter of a million of Germany's best troops struck in the Ardennes. First the Germans opened a shattering artillery attack against the Americans (mainly the V and VIII Corps of Bradley's 12th Army Group) along a 70-mile front in the Ardennes between Monschau and Echternach. Two of the American divisions consisted of green troops, while two others were composed of tired remnants of the recent fighting in the Huertgen Forest.

Hitler ordered that every plane left in the *Luftwaffe* be placed at Rundstedt's disposal. "Goering," he told one of his generals, "has reported that he has 3,000 planes available for the operation. You know Goering's reports. Discount one thousand, and that still leaves a thousand for you and a thousand for Sepp Dietrich."

Commando Otto Skorzeny, the S.S. colonel who had freed Mussolini on the Gran Sasso, was in charge of Operation *Greif*. The idea of *Greif* was to penetrate the American lines with German troops disguised at G.I.'s. They would attempt to capture the Meuse bridges before they could be blown up. For weeks beforehand Skorzeny ran a "school for Americans," teaching his men that Americans smoke dry and Germans don't (the latter wet the lip), that when Americans light a match they scratch it inward, not outward. Very important, the phony Americans had to know all about baseball leagues and Betty Grable.

Operation *Greif* was a failure, although the commandos did manage to sneak through a half-dozen jeeps. The plot was foiled when a German officer, bearing plans for the operation, was taken prisoner by the Americans. The Americans soon supplemented passwords with quizzes. General Bradley himself was tested by being asked to name the capital of Illinois and Betty Grable's latest husband. Delighted American troops reported that he flunked the last question. A sentry allowed him to pass after smilingly supplying the answer: "It's Harry James, sir."

Despite bad weather and poor road conditions, von Rundstedt's offensive quickly gathered momentum in the center, pushing ahead a dozen miles the first day. Again it was *Blitzkrieg*, recalling the early days of the war. British and American infantry, seeking desperately to stem the assault, placed trees on the roads to block the German advance. But the Nazi avalanche flowed over and around them. Fog, snow, and freezing temperatures added to the confusion. On occasion there was no such thing as a front or rear in this tactical chaos. Nevertheless, a great gash, 45 miles long and 65 miles deep, was being cut into the Allied lines. Von Rundstedt was on the verge of a breakthrough.

But there was unexpected trouble for the Germans in the center. Here the town of Bastogne, key to the southern Ardennes, commanded a network of roads spreading out like the spokes of a wheel. Bastogne in Allied hands would be an ideal jumping-off point to imperil the entire German operation. Here von Rundstedt's forces collided head-on with contingents of the 10th Armored Division and its big Sherman tanks. The American mechanical monsters crashed through the cobblestoned streets of Bastogne without pausing and turned east to meet three German spearheads. There were tank duels on the roads, in the fields and forests around the town. For 36 hours the 10th Armored and other units traded lives for time.

Balked in his attempt to take Bastogne by direct assault, von Rundstedt sent powerful columns of his élite troops to the north and south of the town to envelop it in a pincers movement. The issue was still in doubt.

The devastating surprise of the attack was due more to German efficiency than to American negligence. Bad flying weather had restricted Allied air reconnaissance. But once Hitler's intentions became clear, Eisenhower acted with speed and decision. On December 19, 1944, three days after the Germans had begun their Ardennes offensive, the Supreme Commander named Field Marshal Bernard L. Montgomery as commander of all Allied forces north of the Ardennes salient (including the U.S. First and Ninth Armies), and Lieutenant General Omar N. Bradley in command of all forces to the south.

"Brad," Eisenhower told Bradley, "you've always wanted a German counterattack—now you've got it."

Eisenhower then sent Lieutenant General George S. Patton, Jr., with his battering ram of tanks and infantry to the southern bulge of the German salient and ordered him to drive through Luxemburg and Arlon to relieve Bastogne. He had already dispatched the 101st Airborne Division, which had been resting behind the lines, to reinforce the 10th Armored Division at Bastogne.

From here on the battle for Bastogne was furious and deadly. From positions almost completely surrounding the town, the Germans slammed artillery shells onto the Americans with terrible precision. The Americans fought courageously in cold and snow, paying a toll of blood for every hill and roadway. They had to hold or the entire Ardennes would be open to the enemy.

On December 21, 1944, two officers of the *Panzer* Demonstration Division were sent into Bastogne under a flag of truce to demand surrender. They bore a message stating that the Americans were in a hopeless position, they were caught in a trap, they would be chewed to pieces. An immediate answer was requested.

General Anthony McAuliffe gave a one-word reply: "Nuts!"

The one-syllable reply was handed to one of the German officers by a Colonel Joseph H. Harper. The Germans, a major and a captain, were baffled by the word "Nuts" and asked for an explanation. Colonel Harper said: "If you don't understand what 'Nuts' means, in plain English it is the same as 'Go to Hell!' And I tell you something else—if you continue to attack, we will kill every goddam German who tries to break into this city."

The two Germans clicked their heels and saluted. "We will kill many Americans," said the captain. "This is war."

"On your way, bud," growled Colonel Harper.

German military historians recorded the response in sober terms: "Our demand for surrender was refused."

Today, in the square of Bastogne, there is a sign which reads: "This way to the Nuts Museum"—pointing to the building where mementos of the siege are enshrined.

Instead of strangling Bastogne, von Rundstedt found both sides of his bulge squeezed by powerful American divisions. As the weather cleared, more than 5,000 Allied aircraft laid bomb carpets on the roads and railways behind the front and throttled the German supply system. The Germans were also pounded by artillery shells with the deadly new proximity fuses.

Hitler, nevertheless, threw division after division into the battle. Again his replacements were low in quality, mostly older men or ill-trained youngsters. Von Rundstedt realized on Christmas Day that he had lost the battle, but Hitler insisted upon further extension of the salient.

By the middle of January 1945 the Ardennes salient was practically reduced. When word came that the Russians had started a gigantic offensive from the Baranov bridgehead, Hitler at last ordered a massive withdrawal of troops and equipment from the Bastogne area and transferred them eastward with all possible speed. By the end of the month all the ground the Germans had gained in the Ardennes offensive was lost.

This was the last desperate convulsion of the *Wehrmacht* in the west. It had only delayed the end of the war. It cost the Germans 120,000 killed, wounded, prisoners, and missing, at least 500 tanks, and 1,600 planes. And all the Battle of the Bulge had done for the Germans was to halt the Anglo-American advance for a month. No one profited from it with the exception of the Russians, for Hitler had gambled away his reserves that he needed for a last-ditch defense in the east. Worst of all was the catastrophic effect on what was left of German morale. It was clear now that the Allied threat to the Saar, the Palatinate, and the Ruhr could no longer be staved off.

The Americans lost 76,890 killed, wounded, or missing. It was a bitter price, but the Americans had demonstrated their moral and material superiority over Hitler's warriors. Through guts and blood the U.S. units had burned their way into history.

"The Battle of the Bulge," said Winston Churchill, "was the greatest American battle of the war."

AERIAL DAMNATION FOR A DAMNED NATION

"If a single bomb drops on Berlin you can call me Meyer!"

Thus, in special German slang, Field Marshal Hermann Goering, chief of the German *Luftwaffe*, boasted in the early days of the war to the Germans and the world at large about his overwhelming air power. The Fatherland would be protected and there would be no annihilation of German cities such as that visited upon Warsaw, Rotterdam, Coventry, and other cities.

But before the war was over, many a Berliner, his bitter humor intact, was asking, "Where's Meyer?"

For the Germans it was a persistent, galling question. What had happened to the *Luftwaffe*? What, indeed?

Apparently Goering's air force had been designed and built originally for a short offensive war. It would be used as a spearhead for *Blitzkrieg* and as a weapon to terrorize the enemy. But the Germans were left far behind in the battle of plane production. In order to achieve mass output, Hitler froze his plane types at the very beginning of the war. He had two superb fighting planes—the *Focke-Wulf* and the *Messerschmitt*. The rest were medium short-range bombers with limited bomb load and defensive armament, the *Heinkels*, *Dorniers*, and *Junkers*. There were no effective long-range heavy bombers to match the British Lancasters and the American Flying Fortresses. Moreover, the Battle of Britain demonstrated that, though the *Luftwaffe* seemed unbeatable, it was not organized for strategic tasks. That was a fundamenal, crippling error.

On the night of May 20, 1942, came a shock that sent a tremor of fear throughout the Third Reich. More than a thousand planes of the Royal Air Force Bomber Command dropped 2,000 tons of bombs during a 90-minute attack on Cologne. Three days later a similar assault was made on Essen, site of the Krupp munitions works.

This was a message even Hitler understood. Unlike the *Luftwaffe* attacks on London, the R.A.F. struck in sudden mass attacks. The British bombers were carefully timed to appear from different directions over the target almost simultaneously; meanwhile, using deft feinting tactics, British fighter pilots drew off squadrons of enemy planes to other points.

The air-power events of 1942 were dwarfed by what followed in 1943. By this time the British had produced bombers that would carry eight-ton "block-busters" instead of the earlier two-ton loads. More, Allied striking power was supplemented by the U.S. Eighth Air Force now based in Britain. The Americans, unlike the British, who concentrated on saturation attacks at night, preferred daylight bombing on specific targets. The Flying Fortresses, with strong defensive armor and the precision Norden bombsight, pushed through screens of enemy flak and struck at ball-bearing and synthetic-rubber factories, research stations, steel plants, electric-power installations, railroads, dams, and dikes, and later at the V-1 and V-2 launching sites.

There were revolutionary improvements in techniques. The development of radar allowed Allied planes to strike in all kinds of weather and hit their targets despite darkness and foul weather. The conquest of North Africa was followed by a system of shuttle bombing between England and North Africa, which reduced aircraft losses. The run was shortened as the Allies advanced in Italy. A projected shuttle-run at this time between Italy and the Soviet Union foundered on the rock of Russian suspicions.

Beginning in January 1943, as Operation Overlord was being prepared, the combined Allied air forces based on England began round-the-clock bombing of Germany for days in succession. Good weather meant terror to the Germans. The principal target was the vital industrial area of the Ruhr Valley, such cities as Essen, Düsseldorf, Solingen, Dortmund, Duisburg, and Mühlheim. In May 1943 the Eder and Moehne dams were wrecked, causing floods which immobilized many industrial plants. Scores of attacks were made on Cologne, with its submarine equipment plants; the city was reduced to rubble, but the great Gothic cathedral was spared.

The raids were not restricted to the Ruhr area alone. Throughout Hitler's Fortress Europe, from Norway in the north to Italy in the south, the Allied bombers flew on their errands of death and annihilation. They preferred such targets as: the vital Schweinfurt ball-bearing plants; the submarine bases at St. Nazaire and Lorient; the huge Ploesti oil refineries in Rumania; the Diesel works at Nuremberg; the Skoda arms plants in Czechoslovakia; the Zeiss optical-instruments factory at Jena; and the locomotive plants at Kassel.

German war production was heavily damaged by these raids, but by no means crippled. The war plants recovered quickly, and some of them even increased their output despite repeated raids. Efforts were made to continue war production in underground plants.

The attack on German industry was coupled with raids on such arteries of communication as rail junctions, canals, and bridgeheads. In the single month of May 1944 more than 900 locomotives and 16,000 freight cars were destroyed in Western Europe by Allied bombers.

The British kept careful records of their air operations. The summary of air operations for several months gives an indication of the size and scope of the raids:

> August 1944: During August R.A.F. Bomber Command is out on 30 days and 26 nights, flying 10,000 daylight sorties to drop 40,000 tons of bombs, and dropping 25,000 tons of bombs at night. Operations in 4 categories (a) strategic bombing of Germany (including targets assisting Russian armies); (b) German oil production and storage; (c) direct support of armies in France; (4) attacks on V-weapon launching and storage sites. . . .
>
> September 1944: R.A.F. Bomber Command operates every day and 24 nights, dropping 52,400 tons of bombs, 37,400 tons by day, 15,000 by night; 21,000 tons are dropped on Germany and some German towns previously bombed strategically are now targets as supply and communications centers for German armies. . . .
>
> October 1944: R.A.F. Bomber Command drops 50,000 tons of bombs on Germany during month, and 10,000 tons on Occupied Territory; major attacks are made on 15 German towns. . . .

The effects of the bombing on German industry and transportation were evaluated in the United States Strategic Bombing Survey:

> Prior to the summer of 1943, air raids had no appreciable effect either on German munitions production or on the national output in general. . . . The effects . . . became more noticeable from the summer of 1943 onward. . . . For the first four months of 1944 the A.A.F., capable for the first time of carrying out repeated attacks deep into Germany, concentrated its strength on aircraft and ball-bearing targets. During the attacks beginning in February, about 90 per cent of German fighter production was attacked and 70 per cent destroyed. . . .
>
> The attack on transportation beginning in September 1944, was the most important single cause of Germany's ultimate collapse. Between August and December freight car loadings fell by approximately 50 per cent. . . . From

> December 1944 onward, all sectors of the German economy were in rapid decline. "The German economy," [Albert] Speer wrote in his report of March 15, 1945, "is heading for an inevitable collapse within four to eight weeks." The German armies [were] completely bereft of ammunition and motive power.

The Germans had started the bombing of cities, despite "open city" declarations. The Allies had no compunctions about replying in kind. Hitler was repaid a thousandfold for his attacks on Rotterdam and Coventry. On July 24, 1943, and for a period of six days thereafter, Hamburg, Germany's greatest seaport, was hammered by 8,000 tons of explosives in the greatest air attack before Hiroshima. Thousands were killed, the city three-quarters destroyed.

One after another the great cities of Germany—Frankfurt, Hanover, Munich, Stuttgart, Nuremberg, Berlin—at least 50 of them—were from 30 to 80 per cent destroyed. Nearly 6,500 acres, or ten square miles, in the heart of Berlin were reduced to rubble, as compared with the 600 acres of London obliterated earlier by the *Luftwaffe*.

It was a methodical campaign of destruction, a terrible and convincing response to Hitler's contention that all was fair in war. More than 300,000 Germans fell victim to the giant air raids, 780,000 were wounded, and nearly 8,000,000 rendered homeless. It was necessary to assign a million workers to the tasks of clearance and repair and to ease the traffic jams on battered roads, railroads, and canals.

The effect on German morale was catastrophic. To embittered Germans, Goebbels's propaganda slogan, "For this we are indebted to the *Fuehrer*," took on new meaning. The little propaganda chief at first tried to bolster public morale with fanciful tales of equally devastating bombings in New York, but later had to admit the extent of the damage in Germany. Hatred and a spirit of vindictiveness, said that expert, would arouse the German people to greater effort.

What was left of the *Luftwaffe* struck back fiercely but without success. The climax of the air war came in February 1944 when the German air force made a last-ditch effort to drive the Allies from the skies. The battle raged for a week over Regensburg and Merseburg and other industrial cities. From this time on Goering's *Luftwaffe*, hopelessly outnumbered, became progressively weaker.

The destruction was not cheap for the Allies. The British lost a total of 22,000 planes and 79,281 airmen, the Americans 18,000 planes and 79,625 airmen. The raid on Schweinfurt alone, which cut in half German production of ball bearings, cost 60 planes and 593 men.

"Air power," said General Eisenhower, "depleted the usefulness of anything it attacked, and, in large concentrations, carried the process of depletion to near perfection." "This mighty weapon," commented General Montgomery, "enabled us first to win a great victory quickly, and secondly, to win that victory with fewer casualties than would otherwise have been the case."

The enemy agreed. After the war Field Marshal von Rundstedt admitted that Allied air power was decisive among the causes for Germany's military collapse. German troop movements, he said, were hampered by the Allies' tremendous air superiority; the air offensive crippled the production of German oil plants and smashed the Rumanian oil fields; incessant bombing hopelessly snarled German rail communications and immobilized Germany's industrial centers. It was a reluctant but accurate tribute.

THE YALTA CONFERENCE

By early 1945 there had been great and magnificent Allied victories—the successful invasion of Normandy, the fall of Paris, Brussels, and Rome, and the surge of the Anglo-American armies to the Rhine. The war in Europe was now nearing its end. The defeat of Japan would mean the termination of the global conflict.

In this favorable situation the Big Three—President Roosevelt, Prime Minister Churchill, and Generalissimo Stalin—met from February 4–12, 1945, at Yalta, in the newly liberated Russian Black Sea province of Crimea. The purpose was to lay the groundwork for a postwar settlement.

On the surface there was an atmosphere of great cordiality, of absolute certainty that the first great victory of the peace had been won. "The Russians had proved," wrote Robert E. Sherwood, "that they could be reasonable and farseeing and there wasn't any doubt in the minds of the President or any of us that we could live with them and get along with them peacefully for as far into the future as any of us could imagine."

This mood of exaltation was revealed in a series of toasts at a dinner given by Stalin on February 8, 1945. Stalin proposed a toast to Churchill, "the bravest governmental figure in the world." It was due in large measure to Mr. Churchill's courage and staunchness that England, standing alone, had divided the might of Germany at a time when the remainder of the world was falling flat on its face before Hitler. There were few examples in history, Stalin concluded, when the courage of one man had been so important to the future history of the world.

In his reply Churchill toasted Marshal Stalin as "the mighty leader of a mighty country, which had taken the full shock of the German war machine, had broken its back, and had driven the tyrants from her soil." He was certain that in peace no less than in war Stalin would continue to lead his people from success to success.

Stalin then rose and proposed the health of the President of the United States. Even though his country was not directly imperiled in the war, President Roosevelt had been the "chief forger of instruments which had led to the mobilization of the world against Hitler." Lend-Lease, Stalin continued, was one of the President's most remarkable and vital achievements in the creation of the anti-Hitler combination.

Roosevelt, responding to the toast, said that the atmosphere at this dinner was that of a family, and these were the words he liked to use in describing the relations that existed between the three countries. The objective at Yalta was "to give every man, woman, and child on this earth the possibility of security and well-being."

Sweetness, light, friendliness, mutual back-slapping—all probably reflecting the potency of Russian vodka more than it did the actual situation. There had been many signs during the war that all was not well among the "friendly nations" and the "happy family" combined against the Axis. The Western leaders were hopeful that something resembling the liberal Europe of the 1920's would arise from the too-copious ashes. But they had not reckoned with the inflexible will of Stalin. To the Russian dictator the Western democracies in 1945—even as in 1939—represented a threat to the Soviet Union second only to that of Fascism. As Lenin's disciple, Stalin was looking forward to the burial of the capitalistic world. Moreover, to Stalin the security of his country meant regaining the position of influence in Eastern Europe, in the Near East, and in the Far East that Russia had lost in her era of weakness at the opening of the twentieth century. There were vacuums to be filled, and Stalin meant to extend his political influence in many areas, especially since there was not likely to be any serious opposition.

Thus, at Yalta, there was a head-on clash between the Western statesmen dedicated to the ideals of the Atlantic Charter, and the Soviet dictator firmly convinced that the Soviet way of life would not be secure as long as any major area of the world remained under an alien form of government.

Nevertheless, crucial decisions were made at Yalta:

Future World Organization: It was agreed that a future world organization would be formed to maintain the peace of the world and that a conference be called at San Francisco on April 25, 1945, to prepare a charter based on the proposals made at Dumbarton Oaks.

The Occupation and Control of Germany: There would be common policies and plans for enforcing the terms to be imposed on Nazi Germany. There would be three separate zones of occupation. Coördinated administration and control would be provided through a central Control Commission. France would be invited to take over a zone of occupation and to participate as a fourth member of the Control Commission. But Stalin made it clear that he expected the Fourth Zone to be created out of territories assigned to Great Britain and the United States.

There was a strong statement on the future treatment of Germany:

> It is our inflexible purpose to destroy German militarism and Nazism and to ensure that Germany will never again be able to disturb the peace of the world. We are determined to disarm and disband all German armed forces; break up for all time the German General Staff that has repeatedly contrived the resurgence of German militarism; remove or destroy all German military equipment; eliminate or control all German industry that could be used for military production; bring all war criminals to just and swift punishment and exact reparation in kind for the destruction wrought by the Germans; wipe out the Nazi Party, Nazi laws, organizations, and institutions, remove all Nazi and militarist influences from public office and from the cultural and economic life of the German people; and take in harmony such other measures in Germany as may be necessary to the future peace and safety of the world. It is not our purpose to destroy the people of Germany, but only when Nazism and militarism have been extirpated will there be hope for a decent life for Germans, and a place for them in the comity of nations.

Agreement Concerning the Far East: The terms on which Russia would enter the war against Japan were made in secret and without the knowledge of Chiang Kai-shek, who was directly concerned. The Big Three agreed that within two or three months after the surrender of Germany and the end of the war in Europe, the Soviet Union would enter the war against Japan.

But the Russians imposed heavy conditions. The Chinese province of Outer Mongolia, which had had a separate existence as the Mongolian People's Republic since the 1920's, would be granted permanent autonomy. The former rights of Russia "violated by the treacherous attack of Japan in 1904" would be restored, viz.:

> a. The southern part of Sakhalin as well as all the islands adjacent to it shall be returned to the Soviet Union.
> b. The commercial port of Dairen shall be internationalized, the preëminent interests of the Soviet Union in this port being safeguarded and the lease of Port Arthur as a naval base of the U.S.S.R. restored.
> c. The Chinese Eastern Railroad and the South Manchurian Railroad which provides an outlet to Dairen shall be jointly operated by the establishment of a joint Soviet-Chinese Company, it being understood that the preëminent interests of the Soviet Union shall be safeguarded and that China shall retain full sovereignty in Manchuria.

Further, the Kurile Islands were to be handed over to the Soviet Union. It was understood that the agreements concerning Outer Mongolia and the ports and railroads mentioned would require the concurrence of Chiang Kai-shek. President Roosevelt was to take measures to obtain this concurrence.

To make doubly sure of these terms:

> . . . the Heads of the Three Great Powers have agreed that these claims of the Soviet Union shall be unquestionably fulfilled after Japan has been defeated. [And, finally,] for its part the Soviet Union expresses its readiness to conclude with the National Government of China a pact of friendship and alliance between the U.S.S.R. and China in order to render assistance to China with its armed forces for the purpose of liberating China from the Japanese yoke.

Postwar Organization of Eastern Europe: As the war neared its end, Russia had already made important political gains in Eastern Europe. The Allies operated on the principle that until the war was over each great power would have the right to supervise the political life in those areas over which its armies had passed in subjugating the Axis. For the Soviet Union this meant all Eastern European territory north of Greece. Finland, Bulgaria, Hungary, and Rumania had already signed armistice terms which gave the U.S.S.R. virtual politico-economic control of those nations. In Greece, Yugoslavia, and Albania, Communist guerrillas, encouraged by the Soviet Union, were in revolt against the governments-in-exile. The Czechoslovak government-in-exile had concluded a 20-year treaty of alliance with the Soviet Union in 1943. The Polish government-in-exile, however, which had broken relations with Soviet Russia, still held out. In general, Stalin had an iron grip on Eastern Europe.

The Big Three at Yalta agreed that the eastern frontier of Poland should follow the Curzon Line (originally drawn up by the Supreme Allied Command in December 1919) with digressions, in some regions, of five to eight kilometers in favor of Poland. At the same time they recognized that Poland must receive substantial accession of territory in the north and west, meaning eastern Germany. Stalin agreed that in both Poland and Yugoslavia the Communist regimes established under Soviet supervision would be broadened by including representatives from the governments-in-exile.

> This Polish Provisional Government of National Unity shall be pledged to the holding of free and unfettered elections as soon as possible on the basis of universal suffrage and secret ballot. In these elections all democratic and anti-Nazi parties shall have the right to take part and to put forward candidates.

Declaration of Liberated Europe: The Big Three agreed that the establishment of order in Europe and the rebuilding of national economic life must be achieved by processes that would enable the liberated peoples to destroy the last vestiges of Nazism and Fascism and to create democratic institutions of their own. A statement of critical importance was included at this point:

> To foster the conditions in which the liberated peoples may exercise these rights, the three governments will jointly assist the people in any European liberated state or former Axis satellite state in Europe where in their judgment conditions require (*a*) to establish conditions of internal peace; (*b*) to carry out emergency measures for the relief of distressed peoples; (*c*) to form interim governmental authorities broadly representative of all democratic elements in the population and pledged to the earliest possible establishment through free elections of governments responsive to the will of the people; and (*d*) to facilitate where necessary the holding of such elections.

This was the famed Yalta Agreement, destined to be blackened by the smoke of controversy. But at the time it was received with acclaim. As Robert E. Sherwood tells us:

> The mood of the American delegates, including Roosevelt and Hopkins, could be described as one of supreme exultation as they left Yalta. They were confident that their British colleagues agreed with them that this had been the most encouraging conference of all, and the immediate response of the principal spokesmen for British and American public opinion added immeasurably to their sense of satisfaction with the job that had been done.

Correspondent Raymond Gram Swing was even more emphatic: "No more appropriate news could be conceived to celebrate the birthday of Abraham Lincoln." The Philadelphia *Record* described the conference as "the greatest United Nations victory of the war." The *New York Herald Tribune* commented that the conference "has produced another great proof of Allied unity, strength, and power of decision."

After the war, however, there was a rising crescendo of criticism of Yalta as "another Munich" and "Stalin's greatest victory." Attacks came from all sides:

Charge (1): At Yalta, President Roosevelt had been physically and mentally unfit to make decisions of vital political importance. He was clinging to power with hands that were too weak to use it effectively, with the result that Stalin outwitted him completely. "Among the symptoms of the President's bad health," wrote William Henry Chamberlin, "were liability to severe debilitating colds, extreme haggardness of appearance, occasional blackouts of memory, and loss of capacity for mental concentration."

Charge (2): The Yalta Agreement with respect to Poland was a shameful capitulation to Stalin, the deathblow to Poland's hopes for independence and a democratic form of government. It was directly against the spirit of the Atlantic Charter, which aimed to restore sovereignty to countries deprived of it by the war. Not only that, but the high-sounding generalizations of the "Declaration on Liberated Europe" had lost all significance. Even worse, the treatment of Poland broke the back of opposition to Communist rule in every country that had been overrun or was about to be overrun by the Soviet Union.

Charge (3): According to Patrick J. Hurley, the American ambassador to China at the time of Yalta, the Far Eastern decisions were "immoral and cowardly" and played a major role in the final victory of the Chinese Communists over Chiang Kai-shek. "American diplomats," he wrote, "surrendered the territorial integrity and the political independence of China, surrendered the principles of the Atlantic Charter, and wrote the blueprint for the Communist conquest of China in secret agreement at Yalta." Like the agreement on Poland, it was a deal to the detriment of a weaker nation and without its consent.

Charge (4): President Roosevelt was overeager in his desire to obtain Stalin's aid in the war against Japan. Both General MacArthur and Admiral Nimitz, the two commanders directly concerned, were said to have told the President at Pearl Harbor in July 1944 that "Japan could be forced to accept our terms of surrender by the use of sea and air powers without the invasion of the Japanese homeland." The Soviet intervention was of no military benefit to the United States, since it took place only a few days before Japan surrendered.

Charge (5): Former Ambassador William C. Bullitt judged that "no more unnecessary, disgraceful, and potentially disastrous document has ever been signed by a President of the United States." A British historian, Chester Wilmot, concluded: "The real issue for the world and for the future is not what Stalin would or could have taken, but what he was given the right to take. This agreement provided Stalin with a moral cloak for his aggressive designs." And G. F. Hudson placed the blame squarely upon President Roosevelt: "The main source of the tragedy of Yalta was an obsession in Roosevelt's mind with the idea of Big Three unity, combined with an increasing disregard of the rights of weaker nations. . . . In this trend of his thinking there was probably a subtle intoxication of personal power, for the international stage enabled him to gratify the latent appetite for autocracy which he could never indulge in the domestic politics of America."

In these attacks the critics held that many of the ills with which the world was afflicted in the postwar years were due to the various "surrenders" to the Russians made by Roosevelt and Churchill at Yalta.

But others hotly defended the Yalta agreement as the best that could be obtained under the circumstances, and declared that far from being a "surrender" it was just the opposite. They replied to the arguments, one by one:

Reply (1): The complete records of the Conference, said the defenders, by no means substantiate the theory that Roosevelt was taken in because he was a "dying man." In the words of Robert E. Sherwood: "Roosevelt appears to have been in full possession of all his faculties. Only at the end of seven days of long meetings, covering a wide range of tremendous subjects, did he make a concession which, in my belief, he would not have made if he had not been tired out and anxious to end the negotiations relative to Russia's entry into the war with Japan."

Reply (2): On the issue of Poland, the defenders pointed out that the Soviet Union already exercised a tremendous influence in Eastern Europe, and the fact that any agreement at all was reached on Poland constituted a victory. James F. Byrnes, a member of the American delegation at Yalta and soon to become Secretary of State, made a vital comment: "It was not a question of what we would *let* the Russians do, but what we could *get* the Russians to do." This view was also expressed by Charles E. Bohlen, interpreter and adviser to Roosevelt at the Conference: "I have never been able to see afterward that you could have done much more that would have been of benefit to Poland or the Polish people." Furthermore, it was said, Stalin at Yalta agreed on free elections with secret ballot in Poland and elsewhere. If he had honorably carried out that part of the agreement, there would have been no difficulties later.

Reply (3): On the Far Eastern decisions, many agreed that it was a grievous error to promise the Soviet Union rights that belonged to the Nationalist government of China. But other defenders insisted that nothing done at Yalta contributed to Chiang Kai-shek's loss of power in China. The inability of the Chinese Nationalist government to maintain its control over China was due to the fact that Stalin did not honor the Sino-Soviet agreements. How could one foresee Stalin's lack of honesty?

Reply (4): To the charge that Soviet intervention against Japan was of no military benefit, the defenders explained that the perfection of the atomic bomb was still a remote possibility. Further, the Allies had not forgotten the setback in the Battle of the Bulge, nor had they yet crossed the Rhine. It was impossible to know how long the European war would last and how great the casualties would be. The American Chiefs of Staff had warned Roosevelt that without the assistance of Russia the United States might lose a million men in the effort to conquer Japan in its home islands.

Reply (5): The defenders insisted that Yalta was successful as a prelude to the United Nations. Furthermore, the primary objective of Roosevelt and Churchill was to maintain Russia as an effective fighting ally, and in this they had succeeded. W. Averell Harriman, American ambassador to Russia, who was present at the talks, summarized the accomplishments: "The one great thing accomplished by our constant efforts during and since the war to reach a settlement with the Soviet Union is that we have firmly established our moral position before the world. Had these efforts not been made, many people of the free world would still be wondering whether we and not the Kremlin were to blame for the tensions that have developed. The fact that the Soviet Union did not live up to its undertakings made clear the duplicity and the aggressive designs of the Kremlin. This fact has provided the rallying point for the free world in their collective effort to build their defenses and to unite against aggression."

And, finally, the defenders, while they agreed that it was an error to keep part of the agreement secret, maintained that nothing else could be done in view of Stalin's intransigence and the necessity for coming to terms with him. This was due in large part to fear in the matter of security. At Yalta, Stalin informed Roosevelt that he would start the movement of 25 Russian divisions across Siberia to the Far East but that the operation must be conducted in the utmost secrecy. Hence, it would be dangerous to inform the world of Russian intentions in the war against Japan. Roosevelt agreed to hold this portion of the agreement secret, but made it plain that after the Russian movement of troops had been completed, presumably within three or four months, he would send a representative to Chungking to inform Chiang Kai-shek. That hope, unfortunately, was not realized, since President Roosevelt died on April 12, 1945.

Thus the argument rages around one of the most controversial events of the twentieth century. On the one side Yalta is violently denounced as a shameless sellout responsible for many of the world's future ills. On the other, it is claimed that the Western Allies conceded nothing to Stalin that he did not already have or could not have taken; moreover, hindsight is the easiest of all intellectual exercises.

The Great Debate continues—on Yalta, as well as on Munich and Pearl Harbor.

THE BATTLE OF GERMANY

Adolf Hitler made two final radio speeches to the German people at the beginning and end of January 1945. Between those two speeches were bracketed gigantic military actions from both east and west which culminated in the defeat of the Third Reich.

In his New Year's address, Hitler warned that defeatists would be destroyed in the merciless struggle for existence. "The end of the war will not come before 1946 unless by a German victory, because Germany will never capitulate." And again came the now stale tirades: "We know the democratic statesmen, the Bolsheviks and Jews want to bring Germany to slavery, despoil her youth, and let millions starve. Because we know the aims of our enemies and we know the fate that awaits us if we lose this war, we are fighting for our Fatherland, for survival of the German people, for our culture, and for our prosperity."

In his second address (January 20, 1945), designed to commemorate the start of the thirteenth year of his rule, Hitler called upon an unusual source—for him—for help: "Almighty God will not abandon the man who throughout life wanted nothing but to preserve his people from a fate they did not deserve." Then from pious humility to threats: "I expect every German to do his duty to the last. I expect from all women and girls that they will support this war with utmost fanaticism. Whoever stabs us in the back will die an ignominious death."

Between these two messages the Nazi cause went from critical to hopeless.

Allied and Soviet armies, 10,000,000 strong, moved against the German troops from both east and west. They began a series of mighty offensives that literally pulverized the Third Reich. The *Fuehrer* was being beaten with two of his own strategies—lightning warfare and divide-encircle-annihilate. Fortress Germany shrank even more rapidly than Fortress Europe.

In one of the greatest military comebacks in history the Russians had marched more than a thousand miles westward from Stalingrad. By January 1945 they had three gigantic spearheads slashing onto German soil and headed for Berlin. The Red armies were moving into Czechoslovakia, cutting off East Prussia, and trampling the war industries of Silesia. By February 1945 they were sweeping from East Prussia to the lower Vistula, and from the upper Vistula to the Oder. By March 1945 Marshal Georgi Zhukov had taken Königsberg on his right wing and Breslau on his left, thereby securing his flanks for the final drive on Berlin. General Hasso von Manteuffel wrote later:

> On January 12-13 [1945], the Russians opened their great offensive from the Baranov Bridgehead. Its effects were felt on the Western Front at once. The transfer of forces eastward now took place with all speed. . . . The effect that this massive withdrawal of troops and equipment had upon our chronic and critical fuel shortage can well be imagined. . . . The exhausted condition of our troops had been underestimated at Supreme Headquarters. . . . Replacements received in January were inadequate both in quality and quantity. . . . The armament industry in Germany was crumbling beneath the growing weight of the Allied bombing raids. The soldiers on the Western Front lost their faith in ultimate victory.

It was a correct appraisal. There was no letup day or night for the Germans. As in the final months of World War I, they once again threw striplings in their teens, older men, and the physically deficient into the battle lines. Refugees streaming west from East Prussia clogged the roads. In Berlin, where the people had little or nothing to eat, there was increased rioting.

The situation in the West was equally gloomy for the Germans. Deployed along Germany's western frontier in a series of concentrated strong points were huge Allied armies poised for invasion. They were like a long, running fuse which, when touched off, would send a series of explosive offensives hurtling across German soil.

"*Fest steht und treu,*" ran the German song, "*die Wacht am Rhein.*" True to legend, the mighty western moat of Germany would be held and the invaders driven back. But once again German hopes were to be exploded by Allied speed and skill.

The Allied Supreme Command planned three coördinated campaigns to reach the Rhine. In the north the Canadian First, the British Second, and the U.S. Ninth Armies, grouped under the command of Field Marshal Bernard L. Montgomery, were primed for two operations. In Operation Veritable, the Canadian First and the British Second, astride the lower Rhine in Holland, were to strike southeastward between the Maas and Rhine Rivers, to the general line of Xanten-Geldern.

Directly below them the U.S. Ninth Army, in Operation Grenade, was to hit northeast toward the Rhine with its right flank on the line Jülich-Neuss. The two forces—British-Canadian and American—were to squeeze the Germans between them in the triangle formed by the Maas and the Rhine and clear the west bank of the Rhine facing the Ruhr.

In the center, the U.S. Twelfth Army Group, consisting of the First and Third Armies, both under General Omar N. Bradley, was assigned to Operation Lumberjack. It was to move north of the Moselle between Cologne, Bonn, and Coblenz, and clear that area.

In the south, the Sixth Army Group, made up of the U.S. Seventh and French First Armies, under Lieutenant General Jacob L. Devers, was assigned to Operation Undertone. It would converge south of the Moselle, close in on the Rhine south of Mainz down toward Freiburg, and join the southern flank of the U.S. Third Army south of Coblenz.

Together, these offensives would clear the entire west bank of the Rhine. The details were carried out so beautifully that a mere recital of the plan almost tells what did actually happen. With the defeat of their Ardennes offensive, the Germans were no longer able to forestall an Allied breakthrough to the Rhine.

In early February 1945 the weather was still with the Germans. The thaw had melted the thick snows, turning rivers into torrents and fields into lakes. Nevertheless, on February 8, 1945, the Canadian First and the British Second Armies at the northern extremity of the Allied lines jumped off on Operation Veritable. Following very strong air preparation, the offensive was launched southeast of Nijmegen. It turned out to be one of the bloodiest battles of the war. Nasty weather prevented a swift armored punch—the attacks for a time became bogged down in a quagmire of flooded and muddy ground. But the Germans were steadily pushed back. By February 21, 1945, the Canadians and British were at the Rhine. The Germans blew up the bridges and retreated across the river.

At this time, in the latter weeks of February 1945, the Allies mobilized all their strength in the air—the U.S. Twelfth and Fifteenth Air Forces in Italy, the U.S. Eighth and Ninth Air Forces on the Western front, and the full strength of the Royal Air Force—for an all-out assault on German communications. On two days, February 22 and 23, 1945, more than 16,000 sorties were flown and 20,000 tons of bombs dropped. The shattered *Luftwaffe* could not stop it. All Germany was open to massive and appalling devastation.

Meanwhile, the U.S. Ninth Army, on the southern wing of the north flank, was poised on the Roer River, where the Germans clung desperately to the two dams that controlled the waters of the river. To meet the American attack, the Germans, on February 7, 1945, blew up the floodgates of the Schwammanuel dam, preventing the use of assault floating bridges on the Roer and flooding large areas in and near Düren and Jülich. Soon the Roer was flooded four feet higher than its normal level. The Americans waited two weeks until the water fell and then crossed the Roer in assault boats. By March 13, all the northern length of the west bank of the Rhine was in Allied hands.

It was the same story in the center. Here Germany's river barriers also began to collapse. The U.S. First and Third Armies in Operation Lumberjack stormed ahead in simultaneous strikes. The U.S. First Army took Cologne on March 7, 1945, after a severe bombardment by planes and artillery. The Germans retreated across the Hohenzollern bridge spanning the Rhine, and then blew it up.

At the same time, the U.S. Third Army reached the Rhine near Coblenz. General Patton's 4th Armored Division raced 65 miles in 58 hours. The U.S. First Army now turned south to join up with the Third Army.

THE BRIDGE AT REMAGEN

On March 7, 1945, came one of those incredible strokes of fortune, one of the luckiest breaks in military annals.

Neither the Allied nor the German High Commands expected an easy crossing of the treacherous waters of the Rhine. No one had successfully crossed that river in war since Napoleon in 1805. The Rhine barrier was strongest at its center, at which steep mountains rise from the east bank of the river and from which the Germans could mount a murderous defense. Nevertheless, Eisenhower had primed all his units to seize any chance to cross the river.

On that fateful day Sergeant Alexander A. Drabik, a butcher from Holland, Ohio, serving in the U.S. 9th Armored Division, led his platoon through a metal screen of enemy fire to his objective, the town of Remagen, between Bonn and Coblenz. He and his men were ordered to take and hold defensive positions while the troops to the north would mass their power for an assault crossing of the river.

One after another the bridges up and down the Rhine had been demolished by the retreating Germans. Captain Willi Bratge, a German officer, was ordered to blow up the Ludendorff bridge across the Rhine at Remagen at precisely 4 P.M. At 3:30 P.M. a preliminary charge went off, blowing a crater in the western flooring of the span. But the charge was weak and the bridge remained intact.

At exactly 3:50 P.M. Drabik and his platoon reached the western end of the bridge. Without pausing they started in a catlike line through a hail of bullets to cross over. Just then the second preliminary explosion, which came as the Americans were surging across, knocked out one of the principal supports. But, strangely, the main charge of 500 pounds of T.N.T. failed to go off. (Later it was believed that an accidental hit from an American tank had broken the wrist-thick cable connected to the exploding charge.)

The 34-year-old sergeant told the story: "We ran down the middle of the bridge, shouting as we went. I didn't stop because I knew if we kept moving they couldn't hit me. My men were in squad column and not one of them was hit. We took cover in some bomb craters. Then we just sat and waited for the others to come. That's the way it was."

That's the way it was, indeed! By 4 P.M. more than a hundred men were across the span. American combat engineers sped to the bridge. Working quickly and efficiently, they restored the heavy planking and supporting beams to enable trucks, tanks, and trains to cross. Within 24 hours, more than 8,000 troops were across the Rhine. Simultaneously, two more temporary bridges were constructed near by, a pontoon bridge in 29½ hours and a floating Treadway bridge in 39½ hours.

The Germans struck back furiously. The *Luftwaffe* sent 21 of its new jet dive bombers to attack all three spans. All but five of the planes crashed or were shot down. Eleven V-2 rockets exploded harmlessly near the three bridges.

The daring Remagen feat came nine years to the day after German troops had moved into the demilitarized Rhineland zone created by the Treaty of Versailles. It was one of those rare and fleeting opportunities which occur occasionally in combat and which, if grasped, has incalculable results. Germany was opened as if by a surgeon's scalpel.

"This was one of my happy moments of the war," said General Eisenhower. "This was completely unforeseen. We were across the Rhine, on a permanent bridge; the traditional defensive barrier to the heart of Germany was pierced."

"While the bridge lasted," commented Lieutenant General Walter Bedell Smith, "it was worth its weight in gold."

To General George C. Marshall, Remagen was a windfall that had been hoped for but not expected. "The prompt seizure and exploit of the crossing demonstrated American initiative and adaptability at its best, from the daring action of the platoon leader to the Army commander who quickly redirected all his moving columns in a demonstration of brilliant staff management.... The bridgehead proved a serious threat to the heart of Germany . . . a springboard for the final offensive to come."

The German military, caught off balance, was appalled by the Remagen disaster. Hitler later admitted that the Normandy beachhead and the Remagen bridgehead had sealed the fate of Germany. The four officers considered most responsible for the fiasco were brought before a drumhead court-martial and shot. The German Captain Bratke to whom the faulty demolition wires were attributed, accidently survived because he was captured by the Americans.

Hitler, in his now daily bout of fury, removed Field Marshal Gerd von Rundstedt, commander in chief of the German Armies in the West, and ordered Field Marshal Albert Kesselring from Italy to replace him.

After the war Hermann Goering said: "The capture of the Remagen bridge made a long Rhine defense impossible and upset our entire defense scheme along the river. We had to rush reserves to the Remagen bridgehead, as a result of which the Rhine was badly protected between Mainz and Mannheim."

Ten days after the capture of the Remagen bridge, its center span, repeatedly attacked by German planes and by long-range artillery shells, collapsed. Twenty-seven American engineers died, 63 were wounded in the wreckage. But the Americans already had several divisions across the bridge, and in another two weeks the bridgehead was expanded to a depth of eight miles and a length of 25 miles.

Then came another sensational move which left the incredulous Germans popeyed with awe. In a matter of days American engineers, 75,000 of them, built 62 bridges, including 46 pontoon, 11 fixed highway, and 5 railway bridges, across the river. The new floating Treadways, easy to install, were capable of sustaining heavy military loads. One of these spans, 330 yards long, was set up in the record time of 10 hours and 11 minutes.

Using the Remagen bridgehead as a fulcrum, seven armies, interspersed from north to south along the entire length of the river, surged simultaneously across the river. The troops went over in every conceivable way—on Treadway spans, Bailey bridges, pontoons. The Navy joined in the act, supplying land craft, Sea Mules, and DUKW's for this coördinated onslaught. It also supplied some American seamen with ammunition for tall stories about naval combat experience in the midst of the European continent.

By March 25, 1945, all seven armies were across the Rhine with the greatest concentration of tanks ever assembled, ready to join the airborne troops already dropped behind the German lines. To meet them the Germans had some 70 understrength and demoralized divisions.

SPRINGING THE RUHR TRAP

After clearing the Saar and Palatinate and crossing the Rhine barrier, the Allies turned to the encirclement and reduction of the Ruhr. Here was the industrial heart of Germany—the huge blast furnaces of the Krupp works in Essen, the Thyssen factories at Mühlheim, and a host of lesser but key industrial cities—Dortmund, Duisburg, Wuppertal, Ruhrort, Hagen, Solingen, Wesel, Hamm, and Lippstadt. Without steel and guns from the Ruhr, Hitler's legions would be paralyzed.

The air bombardment to isolate the Ruhr from the rest of Germany had already begun. During the third week of March 1945 at least 42,000 sorties were flown over the area, hitting the 18 major railroad bridges and viaducts, reducing many of the mighty blast furnaces to ruins, and cratering every airfield.

Hitler again elected to stand and fight. He ordered that the Ruhr be made into another "fortress." Again came the *Fuehrer*'s automatic reaction—whenever his troops were being soundly thrashed, he immediately chose to name them a fortress, as if word-magic could change the nature of things. To defend the Ruhr he sent into action all the elderly men he could find and the ulcer brigades of the physically unfit.

Again the Allied strategy was the classic double envelopment, this time executed in brilliant fashion. On March 24, 1945, Lieutenant General William H. Simpson's U.S. Ninth Army struck in an arc on the northern rim of the Ruhr above Essen and Dortmund and headed for Lippstadt. The Germans resisted savagely. Simultaneously, Lieutenant General Courtney H. Hodges' U.S. First Army, advancing from the Remagen area, swung around the eastern flank of the Ruhr.

On March 3, 1945, Eisenhower issued another proclamation to the German troops and people urging the former to surrender and the latter to begin planting crops. Their situation, he pointed out, was hopeless, and further resistance would only add to their misery. "My purpose," Eisenhower wrote later, "was to bring the whole bloody business to an end. But the hold of Hitler and his associates was still so strong and was so effectively applied elsewhere, through the medium of the *Gestapo* and S.S., that the nation continued to fight."

The next day, April 1, 1945, the two great wings of the U.S. Ninth and First Armies effected a juncture at Lippstadt, near Paderborn, thus enveloping the Ruhr. Field Marshal Walter Model's troops were now trapped inside a circle some 80 miles in diameter. During the next two weeks, from April 2–18, the great industrial area of the Ruhr was split into two parts and its defenders were systematically annihilated. More than 400,000 Germans fell into Allied hands.

On April 21, 1945, in a wood near Duisburg, Model, depressed by his inability to carry out the *Fuehrer*'s orders, committed suicide. It was a prologue for the coming *Götterdämmerung*, the twilight of the gods.

INTO THE *HERZLAND*

It was senseless to prolong the struggle. The Allied armies were racing at will through the collapsing Third Reich, cracked and buckled at the seams. Twenty-one German divisions had been cut to ribbons. But from Hitler came an order to his surrounded troops in the Ruhr to attack the Allies in the rear!

While the Ruhr trap was being sprung, Lieutenant General Jacob L. Devers' Sixth Army Group, at the southern flank, pushed eastward into Germany. The U.S. Seventh Army captured Mannheim on March 29, 1945, continued on to Würzburg and Schweinfurt, encircled and took Nuremberg, shrine of Nazism (April 20), and captured Munich (April 30). The French First Army swung south to storm Karlsruhe (April 9), Stuttgart (April 21), and the next day reached the Swiss border. Soon the French troops captured Friedrichshafen and crossed the Austrian border (April 30).

In the center, too, Bradley's Twelfth Army Group drove eastward. After encircling the Ruhr, the U.S. Ninth and First Armies turned east, taking Kassel (April 4) and Hanover (April 10). By April 15, the U.S. First Army was at the Mulde River south of Dessau and within another week captured Halle and Leipzig. The 2nd Armored Division of the Ninth Army shot forward 50 miles in a single day's thrust, and by April 15 had a bridgehead over the Elbe near Magdeburg.

Among the fastest of all was Patton's Third Army. Moving with lightning speed over Hitler's superhighways, his tanks crossed the Salle River near Jena while other units headed south, capturing Bayreuth and closing in on Chemnitz, advanced to the Harz mountains, and reached the Czechoslovakian frontier (April 23).

One after another, German towns and cities toppled under the impact of Patton's drive. The teamwork was remarkable: The fast-moving tanks and infantry depended on the engineers to clear mine fields and road blocks ahead of them; the artillery kept the way open with a blanket of protective fire; the ordnance units replaced or repaired the hard-driving tanks; the signal-

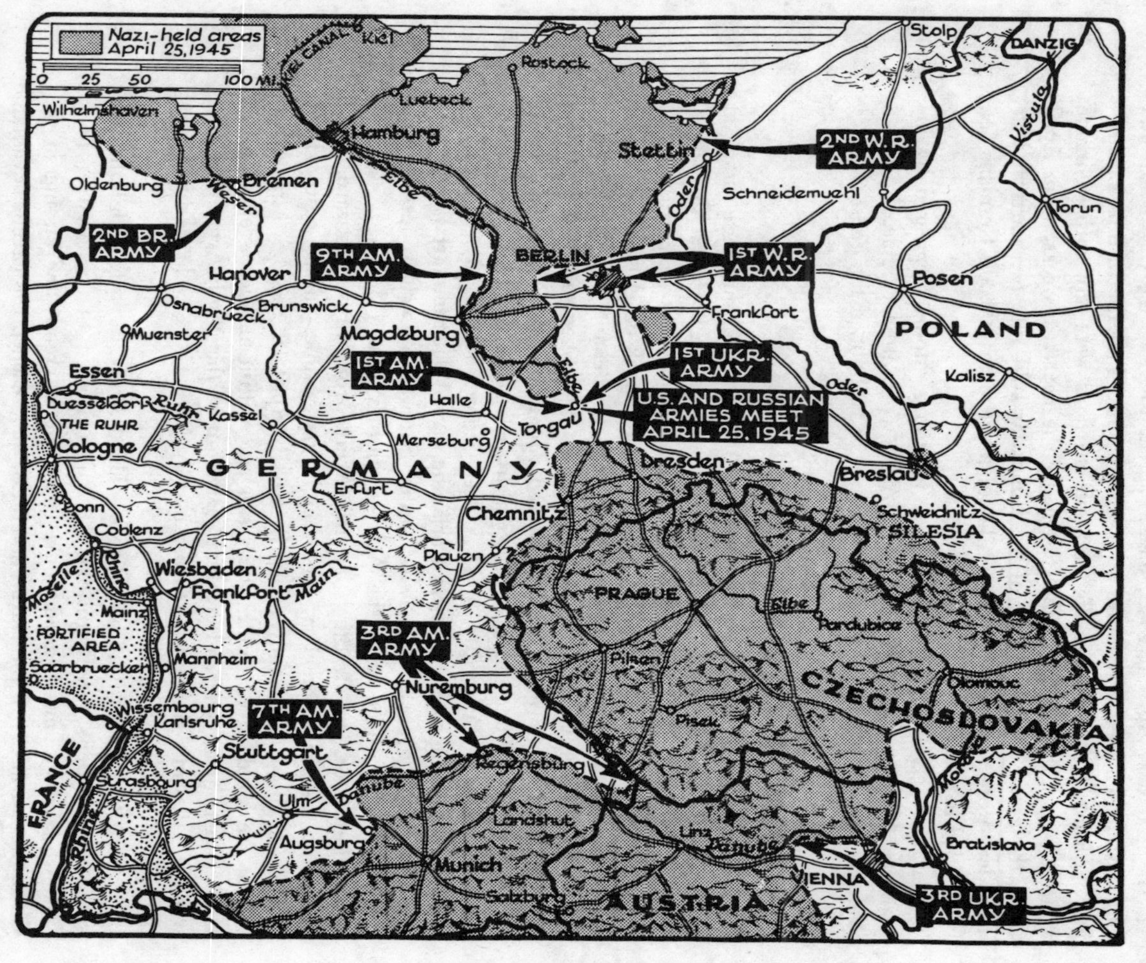

GERMANY'S COLLAPSE

men maintained the lines of communication; the air arm worked in close coördination with the ground troops. Despite rigid training and long combat experience, German troops could not withstand Patton's steel spearhead.

In the north Montgomery's Twenty-first Army Group stormed into Holland and the German coastal area. The Canadian First Army swung in a wide arc into Holland, taking Ijsselmeer near Amsterdam (April 18, 1945). The British Second Army reached Bremen on April 8, only to meet fierce German resistance. One part of the army turned north toward Denmark, while another occupied Lübeck (May 2), a day before the Germans began negotiations for surrender.

All along the great front the Allied armies now began to halt roughly along the line agreed upon with the Russians at Yalta. German troops were surrendering so fast that they overflowed the prison cages. Tens of thousands stampeded to surrender to the Western Allies instead of the dreaded Russians. Some, preferring death to captivity, ended their lives with poison, a rope, or a gun.

By accident Patton's troops discovered a Nazi hoard in the lower levels of a salt mine. This treasure trove, worth about $250,000,000, included gold bars, minted gold, silver and gold plate looted from private homes throughout Europe, and precious oil paintings. Here was eloquent testimony to the porcine nature of Nazi barbarism.

THE ROAD TO WARSAW

The year 1944 had been a busy one for the ceremonial cannon of Moscow. The year of Allied invasion in the West, it also saw breathtaking Russian gains on the Eastern front. In Churchill's words the Russians "were tearing the guts out of the German army."

Blow after blow descended upon the *Wehrmacht*, in the north, in the center, and in the south, as the Red steam roller ground westward far beyond the Soviet frontier of 1939. Hitler was in desperate straits. By this time Russian manpower was overwhelming—some 5,000,000 men in 300 divisions were in the field against 2,000,000 German and Axis troops in 200 divisions.

The Germans were hit by a series of ten blows:

Blow No. 1, Leningrad: In the Leningrad and Novgorod sector in the north the Germans had set up "permanent defenses," including pillboxes, booby traps, and mine fields. Hitler's order was to stand fast, especially since retreat would have meant the isolation of his Finnish ally. In January 1944 the Russians struck at Hitler's 30 divisions with a tremendous artillery barrage, smashing the German defense to smithereens and rattling the *Fuehrer*'s teeth. By the end of the month the Reds were headed for the Baltic.

Blow No. 2, Western Ukraine: In the Western Ukraine, southeast of Kiev, between the upper Dnieper bend and the Bug, the Germans held a front of some 50 miles. In early February 1944, Russian tankmen attacked in this area, pushing ahead in a series of sweeping arcs which they called "Soviet rat traps." The Germans were pushed all the way back to the Dniester River, from which they had started in 1940.

In a thousand days Hitler's legions had made the round trip all the way to Stalingrad and the Volga and back to their starting point.

Blow No. 3, The Crimea: To keep the enemy off balance, the Russians shifted from one front to another. In April and May 1944 came a gigantic offensive in the south. Sevastopol, the largest Black Sea port and Russia's Gibraltar, was still in German hands, though defended mostly by Rumanians. On May 9 an irresistible Red force stormed the city, threw out the enemy, and overran the entire Crimean peninsula within a few days. All South Russia was now redeemed.

Blow No. 4, Finland: In June 1944 the weight of the assault was shifted once more to the far north. The old Mannerheim Line was breached and the Russians stormed into Viipuri on June 30. The Finns were thoroughly beaten this time.

Blow No. 5, White Russia: Directly to the west of Smolensk the Germans had established what they called the Fatherland Line, running southward on the central front from Vitebsk to Orsha to Mogilev to Bobruisk. Here, in June and July 1944 the Russians struck a solar-plexus blow, the impact of which carried them westward within a week across the Beresina toward the Minsk area. Within a short time they were at the Niemen River in both Poland and Lithuania and were threatening the borders of East Prussia.

Blow No. 6, Poland: In July and August 1944 the Russians captured Lwów in Galicia and sent one spearhead at ancient Kraków while another crossed the Vistula and headed for the outskirts of Warsaw. At the same time, other Red forces reached the Carpathians in the south.

Blow No. 7, Rumania and Bulgaria: In August 1944 the Russians crossed the Dniester and opened a terrific offensive against Hitler's ally, Rumania. In a major battle near Kishinev, the Germans lost 12 divisions, the Rumanians virtually their entire army. With her armed forces out of commission, Rumania hastened to quit the war, signed an armistice ceding Bessarabia and Bukovina to the U.S.S.R., and agreed to pay some $300,000,000 in reparations within six years.

The elimination of Rumania opened the way into Bulgaria, which had never been a full-fledged belligerent and which had not even declared war on the Soviet Union. In August 1944, Bulgarian plenipotentiaries secretly met Allied agents in Cairo, and early the next month Bulgaria installed a pro-Allied cabinet. As Soviet forces poured into the country, Bulgaria declared war on Germany (October 8) and hastened to sign an armistice at Moscow on October 28.

Blow No. 8, The Baltic: To clear the northern flank for a drive on Warsaw and Berlin, the Russians swept through the Finnish and Baltic areas. In September 1944 the defeated Finns signed an armistice, by which their boundaries were set much the same as at the end of the Russo-Finnish War of 1940, except that the U.S.S.R. got the Petsamo district. The Germans in the Baltic states were trapped and destroyed, Tartu in Estonia fell (August 25), Tallinn in Estonia (September 22), and Riga in Latvia (October 10).

Blow No. 9, Hungary and Yugoslavia: Next to feel the weight of the Russian bear was Hungary, Hitler's last ally in Europe. In October 1944 Admiral Nicholas Horthy, Hungary's regent, denounced the Germans for violating Hungarian sovereignty and hinted that he would sue for an armistice with the Russians. He was promptly deposed in favor of a pro-Fascist regime. But in November and December the invading Russians were greeted wildly as liberators from Hitlerism. The Hungarians signed an armistice on January 20, 1945.

Meanwhile, Yugoslav Partisans were gnawing away at the German lines in a furious guerrilla campaign. Tito's tough army pushed north to join the Russian columns coming in from the east. On October 20, 1944, Belgrade, the capital of Yugoslavia, and Dubrovnik were liberated by the Russians and Yugoslavs.

Blow No. 10, Poland: The Russian onslaught against the citadel of Warsaw carried through the last half of the year 1944. At the end of July, Marshal Konstantin Rokossovsky, commanding one of the Russian central armies, approached Warsaw, aiming to cross the Vistula and seize the Polish capital before his Western Allies might get across the Rhine. Meantime, inside Warsaw, the Polish General Tadeusz Bor-Komorowski, the famed General Bor, commander in chief of the underground Polish Home Army, responding to urging from the Moscow radio, began to fight in the open. The Poles quickly captured several districts of the city. But Rokossovsky suddenly brought his forces to a halt outside Warsaw, whereupon the Germans inside the capital turned viciously on the patriots.

It was a fantastically brutal massacre: The Germans, using heavy artillery and tanks, annihilated a quarter of a million Poles and destroyed great areas of Warsaw. For 60 days the Partisans held out, fighting desperately in the streets, cellars, and sewers, only to be obliterated by the infuriated Germans.

Many believed that this tragic Warsaw episode was deliberately instigated by the Russians. It was said that the Russian High Command delayed the Soviet entry into Warsaw until the large Polish underground, loyal to the exiled Polish regime in London, had been destroyed. Moreover, it was charged that the Soviet High Command had refused the Western Allies the use of airfields behind Russian lines for an air shuttle-service to help the Partisans.

The Russians countered by accusing the Polish underground of acting too soon, which might have allowed large amounts of supplies to fall into German hands.

Timing their move to coincide with the Allied counterattacks in the West, the Germans during January 1945 counterattacked at Warsaw and Budapest, almost destroying both cities. But Russian armies under Zkuhov, Rokossovsky, and Konev absorbed the impact and struck back with irresistible force on a line running all the way from East Prussia in the north down through Warsaw and Budapest. As in the West, the Germans clung desperately to the seaports, but Memel fell on January 27, 1945. Lithuania was now completely freed of Germans.

By early February 1945 the Russians were at Frankfort-on-Oder. At this point they decided not to strike directly at Berlin. They had left behind many pockets of German resistance in their rapid advance across Poland, and they wanted no Stalingrad-in-reverse. Instead, they began a gigantic encircling movement headed toward Königsberg in the north and Vienna in the south.

Budapest fell (February 13), Königsberg (April 9), and Vienna (April 13, 1945). The way to Berlin was open.

AMERICANS AND RUSSIANS MEET AT TORGAU, APRIL 25, 1945

Fortress Germany was now caught in a giant nutcracker from both east and west.

American and Russian forces met on April 25, 1945, at Torgau on the Elbe, about 75 miles south of Berlin. Patrols of the 69th Division of the U.S. Fifth Corps greeted elements of the Russian 58th Guards Division commanded by Marshal Ivan Konev.

The next day, while columns of dejected German troops marched westward to escape Russian vengeance, Americans and Russians staged a riotous celebration. "It was like the finale of a circus," said one eyewitness. The men saluted one another regardless of rank, drank toasts in liberated German champagne and cognac, whooped, yelled, slapped backs.

"Today," said a Russian major in a formal speech of welcome, "is the happiest day in all our lives. The most difficult for us were those days when the Germans were at Stalingrad. Now we meet one another and this is the end of our enemy. Long live your great leader! Long live our great leader!" Then came hours of singing, eating, drinking, and dancing.

Moscow hailed the Torgau meeting with 24 salvos from 324 guns. Happy crowds celebrated in Times Square in New York.

The end was near. The two great Allied armies, West and East, now faced one another across several hundred miles of the Elbe and Mulde Rivers. But there was no letup.

The situation on May 6, 1945, immediately preceding the German surrender, as shown on a military map in *The New York Times*: British troops entering Copenhagen. In the Netherlands clashes between Nazis and patriots reported. Soviet forces capture the islands of Usedom and Wollin and the port of Swinemünde. German forces west of Berlin are being reduced by the Russians. Russians also attacking south of Moravska Ostrava, and east of Bruenn are pinching off the end of the Czechoslovak pocket. The American Third Army cutting into the Czechoslovak pocket, taking Lohm and St. Brunst, and are driving five miles across the border east of Regen. Patton has taken Linz and pushes on to Ried. In western Austria and southwestern Germany, the U.S. Seventh and the French First Armies are accepting the surrender of German Army Group G.

On April 16, 1945, preceding the Allied and Russian juncture, Hitler had issued a General Order dividing Germany into two defense areas. He would remain in Berlin and command the North Defense Area. Heinrich Himmler, S.S. chief and minister of the interior, would take charge of the South Defense Area, the "National Redoubt" in the Bavarian uplands, a mountainous district where a last-ditch stand would be made.

But the phony quality of Nazism persisted even in its last days. The National Redoubt turned out to be another gigantic hoax. Far from battling to the death, Himmler tried to save his own hide by seeking peace negotiations with the Allies.

CHAPTER 22

Finis Germaniae: *Victory in the West*

The lesson taught by the 1914-1918 war was repeated a quarter of a century later: Germany is not in a position to fight and win a war on more than one front. Today, God be praised, we have learned more than that. We have understood profounder truths. The German people is now sincerely anxious for a deep and final reconciliation with its former enemies. We have one fundamentally held belief, which is that we must never cross swords with our neighbors again.

—Lieutenant General Siegfried Westphal, chief of staff to Commander in Chief West (1944-1945), 1956

HITLER'S *INFERNO*

Buchenwald. Bergen-Belsen. Dachau. Lublin-Maidanek. Auschwitz. Gotha. Erla. Nordhausen. Ohrdruff. Luckenwalde. Ganow. Oberusel. These were some of the worst Nazi concentration camps—names written in blood on the darkest pages of the chronicles of civilization.

Rumors of unspeakable horrors in Nazi death camps had leaked out of Germany before the end of the war. But few people believed them. Many remembered the exaggerated Allied propaganda of World War I—the bizarre tales of Germans cutting off the arms and legs of victims and boiling infants in hot oil to make grease for the Kaiser's war machine. They would not be fooled again.

And then came the ghastly, scarcely believable facts of Nazi bestiality to send waves of indignation throughout the world. This time it was no war propaganda, but diabolical atrocity irrefutably substantiated by camera and pen. Gradually, it dawned upon an appalled humanity that Hitler and the Nazis had deliberately begun and systematically carried out a vast program of biological warfare against civilians and prisoners of war, the most terrible human slaughter in history. It was incredible but incontrovertible. The idea was to weaken the so-called "inferior" and "culture-destroying" peoples of Europe as catalogued by Hitler—Jews, Poles, Czechs, Frenchmen, and Russians—so that the way would be eased for domination by the "pure-blooded Aryan-Nordic stock."

More than 10,000,000 human beings were killed in Nazi extermination factories to achieve this end. The Jews of Europe bore the brunt of a merciless campaign. Of the 9,600,000 Jews living in Nazi-controlled Europe, at least 5,700,000 disappeared, most of them put to death in gas chambers. There was ghastly variety in method—gassing, shooting, hanging, starvation, branding with hot irons, disemboweling, burying alive, injections of poison, "experimental" surgery, freezing in water.

The whole story was revealed as the Allied armies, plunging swiftly into the interior of Germany, liberated one death camp after another. Battle-hardened veterans, inured to the sight and smell of death, were sickened by what they saw in these pestholes. They could scarcely believe their eyes. But there was the evidence—rows of incinerators, gas chambers camouflaged as shower rooms, thousands of bodies piled up like logs, others cast into pits and trenches. And staggering out to meet them were the walking skeletons—human beings whose bodies were stripped of flesh, their eyes staring in disbelief, their voices hollow, their minds crippled by starvation and disease. Strong men wept in the presence of this miserable army of unfortunates.

General Eisenhower, who saw his first horror-camp near the town of Gotha, recorded that he had "never at any other time experienced an equal sense of shock." He visited every corner of the camp so that he could testify at first hand "in case there ever grew up at home the belief or assumption that 'the stories of Nazi brutality were just propaganda.' " That evening he sent messages to both Washington and London, urging the two governments to assign instantly to Germany a group of newspaper editors and legislators to see the indisputable evidence. He wanted no room for "cynical doubt."

The enormity of the crimes was later attested in the Nuremberg indictments:

Item: There were mass shootings to the accompaniment of music played by interned prisoners.

Item: Concentration-camp officials and guards bleached human skulls for souvenirs and used the skin of prisoners to make lampshades, handbags, and gloves.

Item: Prisoners still alive were thrown indiscriminately into carts loaded with the dead and taken to the crematory.

Item: Bodies of the dead were sent to barbers, who removed the hair, and to the dentists, who extracted gold from the teeth before cremation.

Item: Prisoners who refused to talk were placed in heated asbestos-lined cells until they were cooked beyond endurance.

Not even children were exempted from the German hell. From the Nuremberg indictment:

> Along with adults the Nazi conspirators mercilessly destroyed even children. They killed them with their parents in groups and alone. They killed them in children's homes and hospitals, burying the living in the graves, throwing them into flames, stabbing them with bayonets, poisoning them, conducting experiments upon them, extracting their blood for the use of the German army, throwing them into prison and *Gestapo* torture chambers and concentration camps where the children died from hunger, torture, and epidemic disease.

The sadism plunged to its nadir in medical experiments. Vivisection was practiced with prisoners as guinea pigs. New toxins and antitoxins were tried out on them. Two hundred German physicians participated in such experiments as amputating shoulders and arms in transplanting attempts; injecting gasoline in order to produce a rapid death; prolonged human exposure in freezing water to test reactions; placing persons in decompression chambers at simulated altitudes of 70,000 feet; sealing glass, soiled rags, and dirt into wounds to approximate and study battlefield conditions. Those prisoners who volunteered for experimentation were guaranteed better living quarters and rations. All this was done in the name of science under the New Order.

One of the worst death factories was at Buchenwald, four miles outside Weimar, celebrated as the home of German culture and famous for its rich literary associations—Goethe, Schiller, Wieland, and others. On April 10, 1945, Buchenwald was liberated by troops of the American 80th Division. The Americans found an institution apparently built for permanency. There was a Little Camp for the reception of prisoners, the regular barracks, a hospital, a medical experimentation building, a body-disposal plant, and an armament factory. The latter building, used for the manufacture of machine guns, small arms, and ammunition, was in operation 24 hours a day with two 12-hour shifts of prisoners.

A Congressional investigating committee reported on conditions at Buchenwald:

> In the Little Camp, where prisoners slept 16 to a shelf, an infraction of discipline—particularly an attempt to escape—not infrequently resulted in all 16 being condemned. Such persons were immediately marched on foot to

a small door in the fence of the back yard at a point immediately adjacent to the incinerator building. . . .

The condemned prisoners, on being hurried and pushed through the door in the fence, inevitably fell into a shaft and crashed 13 feet down to the cement floor. This . . . was the strangling room. As they hit the floor they were garroted with a short double-end noose by S.S. guards and hung on hooks along the side walls, about 6½ feet above the floor, the row of hooks being 45 or 50 in number.

Edward R. Murrow, of the Columbia Broadcasting System, saw it:

There surged around me an evil-smelling crowd; men and boys reached out to touch me. They were in rags and remnants of uniforms. Death had already marked many of them. . . .

When I entered one of the barracks, men crowded around, tried to lift me to their shoulders. They were too weak. Most of them could not get out of bed. I was told that this building had once stabled 80 horses. There were 1,200 men in it, five to a bunk. The stink was beyond all description. . . .

I pray you to believe what I have said about Buchenwald. I reported what I saw and heard, but only part of it. For most of it, I have no words.

Dead men are plentiful in war, but the living dead—more than 20,000 of them in one camp . . . and the country around was pleasing to the eye, and the Germans were well-fed and well-dressed. . . .

Six days after the camp was liberated, some 1,200 of the "well-fed and well-dressed" German civilians from the neighboring city of Weimar were taken on a forced tour of Buchenwald to see for themselves that the horror and indecency were not figments of Allied imagination. They saw it all—gallows, torture rooms, dissection rooms, crematoria. There were collections of human skin "parchment," human skeletons packed into three-tiered bunks, the aged and dying. And around them thousands of liberated slaves stared at them silently.

Their reaction, according to Gene Currivan of *The New York Times*:

The German people saw all this today, and they wept. Those who didn't weep were ashamed. They said they didn't know about it. . . .

Some Germans were skeptical at first, as if this show had been staged for their benefit, but they were soon convinced. . . . Men turned white and women turned away. It was too much for them.

These persons, who had been fed on Nazi propaganda since 1933, were beginning to see the light. They were seeing with their own eyes what no quantity of American propaganda could convince them of. Here was what their own government had perpetrated.

An English historian, Patrick Gordon-Walker, recounted the nightmare of Belsen:

I went to Belsen. It was a vast area surrounded by barbed wire. . . . Outside the camp, which is amidst bushes, pines, and heather, all fairly recently

> planted, were great notices in red letters: *Danger—Typhus*. . . .
>
> Next day some men of the Yeomanry arrived. The people crowded around them, kissing their hands and feet—and dying from weakness. Corpses in every state of decay were lying around, piled up on top of each other in heaps. . . .
>
> About 35,000 corpses were reckoned, more actually than the living. Of the living there were about 30,000. . .
>
> The S.S. men were driven and pushed along and made to ride on top of the loaded corpses and then shove them into their great mass open graves. They were so tired that they fell exhausted among the corpses. Jeering crowds collected around them, and they had to be kept under strong guard. . . .
>
> The next morning I left this hellhole, the camp. As I left, I had myself deloused. . . . This is what you are fighting. None of this is propaganda. This is the plain and simple truth.

Perhaps the worst atrocity-center of all was Dachau, near Munich, where 32,000 were liberated on April 29, 1945. Here the method of execution was diabolical. Victims were provided with a towel and a piece of soap with orders to enter the *Brausebad*, the shower bath. They were lined up outside, marched into a room, ordered to undress. They expected water to flow from the shower heads in the ceilings. But, instead, gas descended upon them. As fast as they were killed, their bodies were removed through a back exit to the adjoining crematory, where five furnaces, each holding several bodies, worked around the clock. It was a model of Nazi efficiency!

For this grisly business of wholesale slaughter a Polish scholar and attorney, Dr. Raphael Lemkin, invented a new word "genocide," derived from the Greek word *genos* (tribe, race) and the Latin *cida* (kill or exterminate). Professor Lemkin called attention to Hitler's statement in *Mein Kampf* —"the greatest of spirits can be liquidated if its bearer is beaten with a rubber truncheon."

For mass murder and pillage, for multiple crimes and atrocities, the Nazi leaders had to answer before the postwar tribunal at Nuremberg. Along with them were tried a number of underlings ("We are not responsible; we did only what we were ordered to do") including the brutal-faced Josef Kramer, the Beast of Belsen, and the glacial Ilse Koch, notorious as the Bitch of Buchenwald.

THE DEATH OF F.D.R.

Franklin Delano Roosevelt, 32nd President of the United States, pivotal leader of the Allied cause and architect of victory, did not live to see the day of final triumph. For months the 63-year-old President had been in declining health. Visitors to the White House noted his pallor and there was much public speculation that he was either in serious physical condition or was about to undergo an operation.

In the third month of his fourth term as President, Roosevelt had gone to his second home, the Little White House on top of Pine Mountain, in Warm Springs, Georgia, for a badly needed rest. Shortly after noon on April 12, 1945, the President sat quietly before the fireplace of his cottage while an artist near by sketched his portrait.

Suddenly he spoke: "I have a terrific headache." Those were his last words. In a few minutes he lost consciousness and died two hours later from the effects of a massive cerebral hemorrhage.

The news of the President's death soon was spread by flashes and bulletins to every corner of the world. Millions of people were plunged into grief by the tidings. At first they refused to believe it, but then had to accept it. Everywhere there were the choked whispers: "Roosevelt is dead! Roosevelt is dead!" Men and women gave way to frank, unashamed tears.

"It finally crushed him," said Robert E. Sherwood. "He couldn't stand up under it any longer." The "it" was the awful responsibility that had been piling up for so many years.

A simple Italian undertaker on Mulberry Street in New York City: "It is too bad—too bad this great man could not have carried his burden just a little while longer, to enjoy the peace he had won for us." A sorrowful Negro standing outside a Lenox Avenue store: "Don't worry. He was a great man with great ideas, and he didn't let any grass grow under his feet. His plans are made and somebody's gonna carry them out." Thousands reacted in precisely the same way: "I never set eyes on him—but I knew him, I knew him."

The New York Philharmonic Symphony Society immediately canceled its concert at Carnegie Hall. The only other time in its 103–year history that this had been done was in April 1865, when Lincoln was assassinated.

Expressions of sympathy came from the great as well as the humble. To Prime Minister Churchill it was "the loss of the British nation and of the cause of freedom in every land." Pope Pius XII received the news with visible sorrow. Generalissimo Chiang Kai-shek, stunned, could touch no food and went into sorrowful meditation.

F.D.R. had captured the hearts of the American people. They knew the warmth of his nature. They had come to know him almost as a member of the family through his fireside chats on the radio. They had been fascinated by his cheerful personality and unfailing courage, his power "to soar above circumstances which would have held other men earth-bound." They knew of his battle against polio. Instead of giving way to despair, he had fought the cruel disease until he was able to move with the help of steel braces and canes, though he was in constant pain.

Roosevelt's tradition-shattering career spanned the critical years from 1933 to 1945, during which he became the first American President to be elected to a third term and then to a fourth. During the peace years he labored mightily to lift the nation out of a crushing financial depression. "The only thing we have to fear," he said, "is fear itself." Gently but firmly he led Americans from bewilderment "to face evil and rise up and destroy it." He was responsible for the prodigious war-production program and to a great extent for the planning of the victory over the Axis.

There were, of course, strongly dissenting opinions. Some regarded Roosevelt as a dangerous demagogue with pretensions toward dictatorship. Many of the wealthy whose fortunes he had saved by prompt action in 1933 turned on him as a "traitor to his class." They resented this blue-blooded aristocrat who showed too great an interest in the ill-clothed, ill-housed, ill-fed. Few American Presidents, with the possible exceptions of Washington and Lincoln, were subjected to more frequent and violent abuse. He was, indeed, not without faults. He could be stubborn and he could be vindictive; he was human.

But most people were inclined to agree with the verdict of Winston Churchill: "I conceived an admiration for him as a statesman, a man of affairs, and a war leader. I felt the utmost confidence in his upright, inspiring character and outlook, and a personal regard—affection I must say—for him beyond my power to express today. . . . It is indeed a loss, a bitter loss to humanity, that those heartbeats are stilled forever."

The press announcement was unique and a real tribute:

ARMY-NAVY
CASUALTY LIST

Washington, April 13—Following are the latest casualties in the military services, including next-of-kin.

Army-Navy Dead

ROOSEVELT, Franklin D., Commander in Chief, wife, Mrs. Anna Eleanor Roosevelt, the White House.

F.D.R. would have liked that final notice.

One of the largest crowds in Washington's history witnessed the funeral procession down Pennsylvania Avenue. On a black army caisson the body was borne past the silent multitude, many weeping. It was placed in the East Room of the White House. To one side stood a vacant wheel chair, symbol of the illness that had struck down the President in the prime of life.

Religious services for the dead President were held throughout the world.

A mass held at Notre Dame Cathedral in Paris was attended by General de Gaulle. The Paris Jewish colony held memorial services at the Grand Synagogue, where many of the congregation wept over the great American who had rescued them from Hitler's gas chambers.

The nation was fortunate in its new President, Harry S. Truman, former Missouri county judge, U.S. Senator, and Vice-President. To him fell the task of liquidating the war and charting the peace. A modest man, Truman told the press: "I don't know if any of you fellows ever had a load of hay or a bull fall on him, but last night the whole weight of the moon and stars fell on me. I feel a tremendous responsibility. Please pray for me!"

In a brief 20-minute speech President Truman outlined his course of action. The Axis could expect no more favorable terms than "unconditional surrender" as proclaimed by President Roosevelt at Casablanca in 1943. War criminals would be punished. Allied military action would continue under the same admirals and generals chosen by Roosevelt. A world organization to prevent future wars must become an accomplished fact. The great nations of the world must demonstrate that they would "serve" and not "dominate" in the scheme of things.

ODIOUS END OF THE SAWDUST CAESAR

Benito Mussolini, egotistic demagogue, was the first of the totalitarian dictators to grasp power and the first to lose it. The way in which he died, in the words of Milton Bracker, correspondent for *The New York Times*, was "a finish to tyranny as horrible as any ever visited upon a tyrant."

April 25, 1945. The Allied armies were converging on Milan. Together with his young mistress, Clara Petacci, and a dozen last-ditch followers, Mussolini headed in a caravan northward in an attempt to escape to Switzerland. With him he took a hoard of gold.

The *Duce* was still under the protection of the Germans. He was only a shadow of the confident dictator who had entered the war lusting after empire and exhorting the Italians to "Believe, Obey, Fight!" Gone was the blustering, arrogant master of invective who had swayed multitudes of screaming Fascists with his hypnotic eloquence. Now despised by his own people, chattering with fear, he was like an animal caught in a trap. The man whom Churchill had called "a jackal and tattered lackey" had come to the end of the road.

Mussolini's nemesis was a Lieutenant Colonel Valerio, a Communist and former metal worker, who led an expedition "to apply on the spot the decree of the North Italian Committee of National Liberation against those responsible for the catastrophe into which Italy had been led." By accident Valerio and his Partisans on April 28 found Mussolini and his mistress in a farmhouse near the town of Giulano di Mezzegere on Lake Como. Petacci, in a ruffled white blouse, was lying on the bed. Mussolini strode around the room, wearing a brown mackintosh, a cap of the Republican Guard, and a pair of black boots.

Mussolini expressed his resentment at being disturbed.

Valerio said calmly: "I have come to free you."

The two prisoners were pushed outside the room. It suddenly dawned upon Mussolini that these were not friends. Then came one of the most unique offers of a bribe in the history of crime: "Let me go," the *Duce* beseeched his captors. "I shall give you an empire!"

Valerio said nothing. The prisoners were pushed into an automobile. On the pretext that he had heard a noise, Valerio stopped the car and stepped out.

"Get out quickly, both of you. Stand at the corner of that wall."

Petacci screamed hysterically, "You can't do that!"

Valerio pumped bullets into Mussolini and his mistress. "I execute the will of the Italian people," he said.

The bodies, plus those of a dozen other Fascists, were brought to Milan for public display in the Piazza Loretto, the huge open square where 15 Italian patriots had been executed by the Fascists a year before. There, bloody and mudstained, the bodies of Mussolini and the others were dumped like carrion, beaten, kicked, trampled, spat upon.

A mob surged around the grisly spot. A hysterical woman emptied a pistol into the *Duce's* body. "Five shots!" she screamed. "Five shots for my five murdered sons!"

Eyewitness Milton Bracker wrote:

> At 9:30 A.M. today, Mussolini's body lay on the rim of the mass of corpses, while all around surged a growing mob wild with the desire to have a last look at the man who once was a Socialist editor in this same city. The throng pushed and yelled. Partisans strove to keep them back, but largely in vain. Even a series of shots in the air did not dissuade them.
>
> Mussolini had changed in death, but not enough to be anyone else. His closely shaved head and his bullneck were unmistakable. His body seemed small and a little shrunken. . . .
>
> As if he were not dead or dishonored enough, at least two young men in the crowd broke through and aimed kicks at his skull. One glanced off. But the other landed full on his right jaw, and there was a hideous crunch that wholly disfigured the once-proud face. . . .
>
> His yellowing face [was] propped up with a rifle butt to turn it into the sun for the only two Allied cameramen on the scene. When the butt was removed the face flopped back over to the left. . . .

The degradation did not end at this point. The bodies were strung with wire by the feet from an exposed steel girder of a former gasoline station a few yards from the original dumping point. Signs bearing their names were posted above them. Later the bodies were cut down, removed to a morgue, and placed in rude coffins. The top half of Mussolini's coffin was open, revealing his battered head and chest. Those who saw the body described it as strangely small, like a horrible wax doll.

Meanwhile, a cardinal of the Roman Catholic Church, appalled by the actions of people gone wild, appealed for a halt. The bodies were taken to a potter's field, where they were buried in secret lest there be demonstrations. But the mob quickly found the unmarked grave, hurled stones at it, and spat upon it.

Thus was reviled the memory of the dictator, who, like the mythological frog, had attempted to huff and puff himself and his Fascism to world grandeur, only to explode. For nearly a quarter of a century the Italian people had acquiesced in the whims of this sawdust Caesar who was obviously operating in the wrong century. Mussolini had obliterated their freedom and given them in return inedible slogans, the *ersatz* (substitute) glory of triumphal arches, the odor of beastliness, and, finally, the odium of defeat.

BERLIN IN AGONY

Hitler had intended to make Berlin, the huge, sprawling metropolis on the Spree, capital of his Nazi world-empire. The city still had political and psychological significance as the symbol of what remained of German power.

The approaches to Berlin from the east were protected by a dense system of trenches. In the city itself pillboxes, mines, and booby traps were placed at strategic points. The streets were barricaded. Everywhere on the walls Goebbels's appeals were scrawled in white paint.

"Every German will defend his capital!"

"We shall halt the red hordes at the walls of our own Berlin!"

"Victory or Siberia!"

"*Wir kapitulieren nie!*" ("We shall never surrender!")

But already Berlin was in its death throes, pounded to pieces by American and British air power and by Russian artillery. Unopposed, British Lancasters and American Liberators and Flying Fortresses bombed the city. Between raids by the giant planes, fast medium bombers called Mosquitoes droned over the city to keep the people underground. Most of the famous landmarks—the Opera House, the Chancellery, the Air Ministry—were ruined, crumbled to dust.

The Russians worked their way into the city from the east, northeast, and southeast. Adding to the destruction, the Red artillery lobbed shell after shell into the heart of the metropolis. Flames poured from broken gas mains, lighting up the blackened shells of the buildings.

Terrorized, Berliners waited for the end. Caught between the air raids and the Russian artillery, they cringed in cellars and subways. Desperate housewives stole food from the stores.

Dr. Joseph Goebbels came to the microphone for the last time and appealed to Berliners to "fight to the death." Boys in their teens and men in their sixties and seventies were hurriedly rounded up for a final stand.

At the end of April 1945, Soviet troops broke through the suburbs and headed toward Unter den Linden in the center of the city. Heavy Russian tanks and rocket-firing trucks lumbered through the rubble-filled streets and over the barricades. From hiding places last-ditch German suicide squads dashed at the tanks and hurled bottles filled with gasoline into the tank treads. They fought with tommy guns, rifles, and pistols, ranging from rooftops to corridors, slit trenches, cellars, tunnels, fuel bins, and subways.

But the Russian tidal wave swept irresistibly on through sector after sector, block after block. Here it was—Stalingrad in reverse!

On April 23, 1945, the First White Russian Army broke through the northern and eastern defences of Berlin and reached the air-raid shelters. Two days later two Soviet forces merged in the center of the city, and occupied the government offices.

On May 2, 1945, Berlin formally surrendered to the First White Russian and the First Ukrainian Armies. It was a terrible spectacle at the end. The great city was reduced to a hollow shell. Giant rubble heaps made the streets impassable. For mile after mile grotesque skeletons of buildings swayed on their foundations. It was as if a gigantic scourge of nature had leveled the metropolis. The air was foul with the stench of dead people in the ruins and dead beasts in the streets. For the living there was nothing more than the slow-motion, visceral, unthinking life of animal existence.

Hindsight strategists criticized General Eisenhower. Why had he permitted the Russians to take Berlin? British observers, particularly, accused the Supreme Commander of making a "stupid error" in not turning his armies north against Berlin after the successful thrust across the Rhine. They resented as "American jingoism" the charge that the "British Empire wanted troops in Berlin before the Russians got there." Further, they charged, Berlin would have more quickly surrendered to the Western Allies than to the dreaded Reds. Had the Americans and British taken the German capital, they said, many of the subsequent difficulties with the Russians would have been avoided.

The issue had both political and military facets. Allied political agreements had already divided Germany into occupation zones, the north-south line allotted to the British and Americans running from Lübeck southward to Eisenach and the Austrian border. This decision excluded Berlin. President

Roosevelt was criticized for the "incredible blunder" of leaving the decisions for the closing weeks of the war to General Eisenhower.

Eisenhower reported to the Combined Chiefs of Staff: "Berlin, I am now certain, no longer represented a military objective of major importance. . . . Military factors, when the enemy was on the brink of final defeat, were more important in my eyes than the political considerations involved in the Allied capture of the capital."

Further, in his *Crusade in Europe*, Eisenhower pointed out that when the Americans stood on the Rhine in the last week of March 1945, they were 300 miles from Berlin, the Russians only 30 miles. If he attempted a power-crossing of the Elbe to invest Berlin, the Russians would be around the city long before he could get there. It was more desirable, he concluded, to thrust rapidly across Germany, make a junction with the Reds, and divide the country.

In the first week of April 1945 Eisenhower was still doubtful about a near-final defeat, and believed that the war might well last through the summer. It looked as if the Germans intended to withdraw into their National Redoubt in southern Bavaria, western Austria, and northern Italy, where they would attempt to hold out indefinitely. American Intelligence had also reported on the organization of an underground secret army of Werewolves, consisting of boys and girls as well as adults, who hoped to carry on. They would terrify the countryside and make the occupation so difficult that the conquerors would be glad to get out. The way to stop all this, in Eisenhower's estimation, was to forget about Berlin and overrun the entire country.

As it turned out, it was not necessary to penetrate and destroy the National Redoubt. The Werewolves dwindled to nothing. The swiftness of the American armored columns, which moved into Bohemia and down to the Brenner Pass, foiled the fanatical plan for a guerrilla war. German troops surrendered *en masse*, competing for the privilege of giving themselves up to any opponent other than the Russians.

But criticism persisted. A British writer, H. V. O'Neill ("Strategicus"), concluded that "Mr. Roosevelt, with only a week or two to live, was responsible for an almost incredible political directive and Eisenhower was left to rationalize it in military terms. We should have preferred this great man to turn the last page of his life with a decision that better became him, and the causes for which he stood."

The critics howled, but the important fact was that Hitler's lunatic structure was falling stone by stone in total *Zusammenbruch* (collapse). The amazing story of the final days of the Third Reich was revealed by an American archivist, Dr. Gerhard Weinberg, who was microfilming 11,000,000 pages of Nazi party and military records captured by American forces. Surprisingly, the record shows not traditional German efficiency but unbelievable bureaucratic waste and futility in Hitler's Third Reich. One document showed that "In April of 1945, with Allied tanks clanking past the shattered windows of party headquarters, the *Fuehrer's* faithful were working out paper-clip requirements for the third quarter of 1945."

The Germany of traditional thoroughness had fallen into authoritarian anarchy. In Dr. Weinberg's opinion: "Happy was the *Pilzfachberater*, the adviser for mushroom affairs. He knew that he had to be a citizen of undoubted expertness on mushrooms, and that his duty was to advise the district chief of the party, the *Kreisleiter*, on all matters pertaining to mushrooms. The vast majority of officers were not so fortunately situated in having their qualities and duties precisely prescribed."

GÖTTERDÄMMERUNG— THE LAST DAYS OF ADOLF HITLER

The wild fanaticism of the last days was revealed by the incident of the *Leibstandarte Adolf Hitler*. This unit, most faithful of the Nazi faithful, was fighting on the upper Danube, where it had been ordered by the *Fuehrer* to attack against impossible odds. The weather turned foul, but the troops, regarding Hitler's command as sacred, nevertheless went ahead, straight into a disastrous defeat, indeed a massacre.

The news sent Hitler into paroxysms of rage. As a dishonoring punishment, he issued an order requiring all survivors of the L.A.H. to remove their armbands. Equally angered, the shock troops tore off their decorations and sent them to Hitler in a tin chamber pot. Along with it went the severed arm, complete with armband, of one of their dead comrades. Such was the crazy-quilt pattern of the Third Reich in its dying days.

In the ten days preceding Hitler's fifty-sixth birthday, April 20, 1945, disaster followed disaster. The Ardennes counteroffensive, the dying gasp of Germany's armies in the West, had failed to stem the rising Allied tide, now across the Rhine. The massed Nazi divisions in the East did not have the strength to halt the oncoming Russians. The Third Reich was almost bisected: There was only a small corridor dividing the Americans, already across the Elbe, from the Russians who had crossed the Oder and Neisse and were hammering at the gates of Berlin. In the north the British were surging on Bremen and Hamburg. Eisenhower, Montgomery, and Zhukov were chopping the Third Reich to bits.

One by one, the chief Nazis, aware that the end was near and almost petrified with fear of the Russians, left Berlin to seek sanctuary elsewhere. But what about Adolf Hitler? Would he, as the legendary Frederick Barbarossa, retire to some mountain cave from which he would some day lead the German people to victory against their enemies?

The unpredictable *Fuehrer*, spurning all pleas to retire to the Bavarian redoubt, decided to remain in Berlin. There, surrounded by his camarilla of toadies, quack doctors, and astrologers, he would meet death in a thunderous Wagnerian finale.

The Reich Chancellery, vast monument to Hitler's ego, a mausoleum with tasteless slabs of marble, tremendous doors, and gaudy candelabra, had already been bombed and blackened by Allied air power and Russian artillery. Deep below it an elaborate maze of bunkers had been constructed during the war. In Hitler's quarters, consisting of 18 small and uncomfortable rooms, came the last act of the cheap drama that was Hitlerism. It took place, said the British historian H. R. Trevor-Roper, in "a cloud-cuckoo land."

Here Hitler, among his last-ditch followers, continued to play the role of war lord. He called daily conferences, studied the giant war maps, issued attack orders to already banished army units, and called on his defunct air force to belabor the enemy. He would collapse with rage at each evidence of treason and on occasion would shriek that there was nothing left but to die.

At first he clung to the hope that some miracle would raise the siege of Berlin. "He persisted in behaving," wrote Arthur Bryant, "as though he was at the head of a vast army, spoke of skeleton formations of disorganized survivors as though they were army corps in full strength, and stormed at his marshals. . . . He cared nothing for peace; he was only concerned with recovering his former empire." The hope soon vanished into nothingness.

It was a weird and fantastic scene. One day Hitler would rise to heights of euphoria and the next day descend to abject despair. It was not a pretty sight—the final agony of what Churchill called "this evil man, this monstrous abortion of hatred and conceit."

The war had taken a heavy toll of Hitler's health. As early as 1942, Goebbels had broadcast a pathetic story of the "lined and haggard *Fuehrer*, with the face of an Atlas, bearing the whole world on his shoulders." The next year Goebbels wrote in his diary: "The *Fuehrer* seems to have aged 15 years during the three-and-a-half years of war."

By April 1945, with his world crashing around him, Hitler was a shadow of his former self. So pale were his face and hands that he seemed to have no circulation; his extremities trembled; his left leg dragged on the ground; he was bent and stooped. Either he had developed a progressive case of Parkinson's disease, or, as now seems more likely, his physical alterations were due to rising hysteria. Shunning air, exercise, and food, hardly able to sleep more than three hours a night, he remained in the dark, insanitary bunker and complained of continual headaches and stomach cramps. The *Attentat* of July 20 had left him bruised physically and damaged psychically. In November 1944 an operation had been performed on his ear to relieve the pressure caused by concussion.

Hitler was being poisoned slowly by the ministrations of Dr. Theodor Morell, his personal physician from 1939 to 1945. A former ship's doctor, Morell had set up a practice catering to ladies of easy virtue in Berlin, and later had become a successful manufacturer of vitamin chocolates, stimulants, aphrodisiacs, and an insecticide which he called "Russian lice powder." He claimed to be the true discoverer of penicillin, the secret of which, he charged, had been stolen from him by the British Secret Service. This pretentious quack had Hitler's confidence. By his own admission he used 28 different mixtures of drugs, in addition to morphia and hypnotics, on his neurasthenic patient. During the last two years of his life, Hitler received daily injections of Morell's concoctions and throughout the day munched a supply of varicolored pills.

Though Hitler suffered from no organic disease, he became a physical wreck. In the words of Trevor-Roper: "Ceaseless work, the loss of all freedom, the frustration of all his hopes, Morell's drugs, and perhaps more than all these, the violence of his temperament when bitterness and disappointment had multiplied around him, had reduced that once powerful conqueror to a trembling spectre."

Hitler not only recalled the old treacheries, but he found new ones. "Everyone has deceived me," he wailed. "No one has told the truth!"

He still tried to show the old defiance to his enemies: "We shall never capitulate—never. We may be destroyed, but if we are, we shall drag a world with us—a world in flames." To Albert Speer, his minister of armaments, he said: "If the war is to be lost, the nation will also perish. . . . There will be no need any longer for even a most primitive existence. On the contrary, it is better to destroy even that, and to destroy it ourselves. The nation has proven itself weak, and the future belongs to the stronger eastern nations. Besides, those who remain after the battle are of little value; for the good have fallen."

On April 12, 1945 came the news of Roosevelt's death. Goebbels was in absolute ecstasy. Was this not the work of Hitler's lucky star? Here was a parallel to that Historical Necessity, that miracle that had brought death to Frederick the Great's enemy, the Tsarina Elizabeth, in 1762 just at the moment when the Prussian king's fortunes were at their lowest ebb. Goebbels hastened to telephone Hitler: "My *Fuehrer*, I congratulate you! Roosevelt is dead! It is written in the stars that the second half of April will be a turning point for us. This is Friday, April the 13th. . . . It is the turning point!"

Three days later Hitler issued an Order of the Day: "At the moment when fate has removed the greatest war criminal of all times from this earth, the war will take a decisive turn."

On April 19, 1945, the eve of Hitler's birthday, Goebbels broadcast a speech admonishing the Germans never to forget their Leader. "We are witnessing the last acts of a tremendous tragedy. The decision is very near. Let us stake our hopes on our lucky star."

Hitler still showed some confidence during the round of birthday celebrations: "We are now starting a battle as fanatical as that we had to fight in our ascent to power years ago." The next day the *Fuehrer* ordered still another "final attack."

Hitler's final conference with his war leaders came on April 22, 1945. He went into a tantrum, shouting that he had been deserted, harried by failure, corruption, lies, treason. He denounced the army and its leaders. The entire *Luftwaffe* should be hanged! Everything was finished. The Third Reich was a failure. He had nothing left to do but to take his life. He would under no circumstances go south. He would remain in Berlin and die.

The next day came a telegram from Goering:

> My *Fuehrer*: In view of your decision to remain at your post in the fortress of Berlin, do you agree that I take over, immediately, the total leadership of the Reich, with full freedom of action at home and abroad, as your deputy, in accordance with your decree of 29 June 1941? If no reply is received by ten o'clock tonight, I shall take it for granted that you have lost your freedom of action, shall consider the conditions of your decree as fulfilled, and shall act for the best interests of our country and our people. You know what I feel for you in this gravest hour of my life. Words fail me. May God protect you, and speed you quickly here despite all. Your loyal
>
> HERMANN GOERING

From Hitler came an explosion of helpless wrath, one of his last fierce blazes of fury. This foul traitor, this damnable drug addict, this *Schweinehund*—pig-dog! It was *Dolchstoss* again, stab-in-the-back! The *Fuehrer* replied by wire. Goering was guilty of high treason to the *Fuehrer* and to National Socialism. The penalty was death. But, in view of Goering's earlier services to the Party, he would be excused from the extreme penalty. But he must resign all his offices at once.

There was no end to the treachery. Heinrich Himmler, head of the S.S. and the *Gestapo*, suddenly decided that he would do something on his own to extricate Germany from her predicament. Without Hitler's knowledge he began surrender negotiations with the Western Allies through an intermediary, the Swedish Count Folke Bernadotte. The Allies coldly rejected the overtures. Radio reports of Himmler's attempt penetrated into the Berlin bunkers. Hitler went into another convulsion of rage. "Nothing now remains!" he screamed. "Nothing is spared me! No loyalty is kept, no honor observed! There is no bitterness, no betrayal that has not yet been heaped upon me."

Outside, the Russians were closing in on the Chancellery. Artillery shells were bursting in the yard.

On April 29, 1945, convinced that the end was near, Hitler dictated two documents: his personal will and his political testament.

In his private will Hitler bequeathed all he possessed to the Party. "Should this no longer exist, to the State; should the State also be destroyed, no further decision of mine is necessary." He left his art collection to his home town of Linz. He named as his executor—"my most faithful Party comrade, Martin Bormann." "I myself and my wife—in order to escape the disgrace of deposition or capitulation—choose death."

Hitler could not resist one final political harangue, a two-part political testament. For three decades, he said, he had been moved solely by love and loyalty to his people in making "the most difficult decisions that ever confronted mortal man." It was untrue that he wanted war in 1939. "It was desired and instigated exclusively by those international statesmen who were either of Jewish descent or worked for Jewish interests." He could not forsake Berlin. "I die with a happy heart, aware of the immeasurable deeds and achievements of our soldiers at the front, our women at home, the achievements of our farmers and workers and the work, unique in history, of our youth who bear my name."

In the second part of his political testament, Hitler expelled Goering and Himmler from the party and deprived them of all rights. As his political heir he named not one of his Nazi thugs but a stiff-necked Prussian admiral, Karl Doenitz, who was to become President of the Reich and Supreme Commander of the Armed Forces for 20 days. He went on to request Bormann, Goebbels, and the others who were willing to perish with him to set the interests of the nation above their own feelings and escape to help build the National Socialist state. And finally, Hitler reverted to his *bête noire*, the eternal object of his hatred: "Above all, I charge the leaders of the nation and those under them to scrupulous observance of the laws of race and to merciless opposition to the universal poisoner of all peoples, international Jewry."

Goebbels, who was a witness to both documents, characteristically had to get into the final act. "For the first time in my life I must categorically refuse to obey an order of the *Fuehrer*. . . . Otherwise—quite apart from the fact that feelings of humanity and loyalty forbid us to abandon the *Fuehrer* in his hour of greatest need—I should appear for the rest of my life as a dishonorable traitor and common scoundrel. . . . At the side of the *Fuehrer* [I shall] end a life which will have no further value to me if I cannot spend it in the service of the *Fuehrer*."

In his last hours Hitler took a step he had avoided throughout his adult years. He had feared women ostensibly because they might interfere with his political aspirations. But Eva Braun, his secret friend of a dozen years, was different. An attractive woman, unobtrusive, anxious to please, undemanding, she supplied the harried *Fuehrer* with the domesticity which his petty bourgeois soul craved. Their relationship was kept secret; only a handful of Hitler's immediate circle knew of his affection for "E.B."

On April 15, 1945, Eva Braun appeared at Hitler's bunker in Berlin. The *Fuehrer* tried in vain to send her away. He was deeply touched. Since he now had nothing to lose, he would grant her that respectable status she had long desired and he would allow her to share with him a ritual death.

On April 29, in that subterranean madhouse to the cacophonous music of shells and bombs, Hitler took Eva Braun as his lawfully wedded wife. In brief formalities both participants declared that they were of Aryan descent and free of any hereditary disease. There were congratulations from several generals and secretaries. The couple withdrew into their private apartment for a wedding breakfast. Hitler then left to work on his will.

April 30. After luncheon Hitler had his favorite Alsatian dog, Blondi, destroyed. Then, his face pale, his limbs trembling, he walked silently through the bunker passageways, shaking hands with all those who remained. He finally retired to his own suite. At 3:15 P.M. a single shot was heard. Hitler was found lying on a sofa soaked with blood. He had shot himself through the mouth. Beside him lay Eva Braun, who had taken poison.

Thus death came in ignominy to this hate-ridden monster who had created nothing and who had solved nothing, but who had destroyed more than any other man in history. The bodies were burned in the courtyard. No traces were ever found.

Almost immediately came the legends. Hitler was still alive. The bunker suicides were an elaborate hoax. Hitler had escaped by submarine, by plane. He was in Argentina, on a Pacific island, at the North Pole. The evidence points the other way: Hitler died in Berlin.

Hitler went to his death certain that history would judge him glorious for all his actions except his failure to punish the traitors who caused him to lose the war. "One day," he said at the height of his lunacy, "ceremonies of thanksgiving will be sung to Fascism and National Socialism." Of his berserk Nazi state little is left except the memory of ritualistic pageants in which millions of hypnotized Germans massed to seek tribal fraternity with their *Fuehrer*. More than 30,000,000 human beings were sacrificed to the pretensions of this abominable tyrant. Compared to him, Genghis Khan, the Mongol conqueror, was a mild and benevolent statesman.

After waiting a "decent interval" in tribute to his master, Goebbels poisoned his six little children, unwilling to allow them life in a world that was not National Socialist. Then he and his wife committed suicide. Their bodies, not completely destroyed by burning gasoline, were recovered by the Russians. Bormann escaped alive, but was never heard of again. Meanwhile, General Robert von Greim, who had been appointed commander in chief of the *Luftwaffe* to supplant the "traitor" Goering, left Berlin on the last plane for Doenitz's headquarters with instructions for a last-ditch defense.

May 1, 1945. The Hamburg radio reported that "our *Fuehrer*, Adolf Hitler, fighting to the last breath against Bolshevism, fell for Germany this afternoon in his operational headquarters in the Reich Chancellery."

Admiral Doenitz then spoke: "German men and women, soldiers of the armed forces: Our *Fuehrer*, Adolf Hitler, has fallen. The German people bow in the deepest sorrow and respect. . . . The *Fuehrer* has appointed me as his successor. Fully conscious of the responsibility, I take over the leadership of the German people at this fateful hour." Then came the playing of Wagner's *Götterdämmerung*, the Twilight of the Gods. Lord Haw Haw, renegade Englishman, repeated the ritual in English.

That same day Doenitz issued an Order of the Day:

> German Armed Forces, my comrades:
>
> The *Fuehrer* has fallen. Faithful to his great ideal to save the nations of Europe from Bolshevism, he has given his life and has met a hero's death. In him one of the greatest heroes of German history has appeared. With proud respect and grief we lower our standards.
>
> The *Fuehrer* has designated me to be the head of the State and Supreme Commander. . . . I am resolved to continue the struggle against the Bolsheviks. . . . Against the British and Americans I am bound to continue to fight as far and as long as they impede me in the struggle against Bolshevism. . . . For every single one of you the oath to the *Fuehrer* is transferred straight to my person as the *Fuehrer's* appointed successor.
>
> German soldiers! Do your duty! The existence of our people is at stake.

Doenitz was whistling in the dark of defeat. He set up a new government with Count Lutz Schwerin von Krosigk, formerly finance minister, as the new foreign minister. He ignored Ribbentrop altogether. He appointed Admiral Hans Georg von Friedeburg as commander in chief of the German navy.

On May 2, 1945, Doenitz moved his headquarters from Plön to Flensburg, ancient town in Schleswig, and sent Admiral Friedeburg to Field Marshal Bernard L. Montgomery with a proposal to capitulate in the West but to continue fighting in the East.

Montgomery brusquely rejected the offer and demanded unconditional surrender on all fronts.

THE GERMAN UNCONDITIONAL SURRENDER, MAY 7, 1945

The terms of the surrender ending World War II in Europe were signed by German envoys starting at 2:41 A.M. on May 7, 1945. This was the last dramatic event in the long reign of gunpowder.

The scene was in a dismal brick schoolhouse, the *Collège Modèrne et Technicale* at Reims, which for some months had been General Eisenhower's Supreme Headquarters. The walls of the small room were covered with maps in red and green, battle orders, charts of communications systems and supply networks, casualty lists. At one end was a long, rickety wooden table painted black.

At one side of the table sat three German emissaries, their uniforms immaculate, their faces blank—Admiral Hans Georg von Friedeburg, commander in chief of the German navy; Field Marshal Alfred Gustav Jodl, chief of the German General Staff; and the latter's aide, Major General Wilhelm Oxenius. Admiral Friedeburg seemed relaxed, but his calmness was deceptive. Jodl's face was like a death mask: Hitler's strategic adviser and close friend, he was fated for death on the scaffold.

Opposite them were Allied officers of equivalent rank, all silent but tense: British Lieutenant General Sir Frederick Morgan, staff deputy; General François Sevez of France; Admiral Sir H. M. Burrough, commander of the Allied Naval Expeditionary Force; Lieutenant General Walter Bedell Smith, chief of staff to Eisenhower, Lieutenant General Ivan Chermiaev and General Ivan Suslaparov of the Soviet Union; and General Carl A. Spaatz, commander of the U.S. Strategic Air Forces.

The Supreme Commander, General Dwight D. Eisenhower, and his deputy, Air Chief Marshal Sir Arthur Tedder, were conspicuously absent. Both remained in another office.

The room buzzed with a swarm of photographers who fought for advantageous positions. All seemed fascinated by General Suslaparov's interpreter, a bullnecked Russian with completely bald head "and a glittering eye which he fixed on the Germans like the very eye of doom."

The four instruments of surrender—one each for the United States, Great Britain, France, and Russia—were signed quickly, within four minutes. The terms were simple and explicit: "We, the undersigned, acting by authority of the German High Command, hereby surrender unconditionally to the Supreme Commander, Allied Expeditionary Force, and simultaneously to the Soviet High Command, all forces on land, sea, and in the air who are at this date under German control." No obligations were placed on the victors, nor were there any loopholes. A lesson had been learned from the experience of World War I, after which the Germans claimed that they had never been beaten on the battlefield.

Jodl, his bald pate shining under the naked light bulbs, asked Smith's permission to speak. Smith nodded. Jodl got up stiffly and with eyes staring straight ahead spoke in a strangled voice, almost a sob: "With this signature, the German people and armed forces are, for better or worse, delivered into the victor's hands. In this war, which has lasted more than five years, both have achieved and suffered more than perhaps any other people in the world. In this hour, I can only express the hope that the victor will treat generously with them."

From the Allied representatives there was only stony silence. Most of them had just seen the abysmal horrors of the Nazi death camps, and they were in no mood to reply to this plea for mercy. Some undoubtedly recalled Churchill's dictum that the Germans are either at your throats or groveling at your feet.

The Germans were then led down a hall to General Eisenhower's office. His blue eyes hard, his voice cold, Eisenhower, in a clipped, incisive tone, asked through an interpreter if Jodl thoroughly understood all the provisions of the document he had just signed. Jodl answered, "*Ja*."

Eisenhower then said: "You will, officially and personally, be held responsible if the terms of this surrender are violated, including its provisions for German commanders to appear in Berlin at the moment set by the Russian High Command to accomplish formal surrender to that government. That is all." Jodl saluted, and together with his dejected companions left the building.

That same day, Count Lutz Schwerin von Krosigk, former Rhodes scholar and never active in Nazi affairs, who had been appointed foreign minister by Grand Admiral Karl Doenitz to succeed Joachim von Ribbentrop, issued a formal announcement from the new German seat of government, Flensburg, near the Danish border: "The High Command of the armed forces today at the order of Grand Admiral Doenitz declared the unconditional surrender of all fighting German troops."

Under the terms of the surrender at Reims the heads of the German armed services were required to appear in Berlin to sign a ratification in the Russian headquarters. The second ceremony was designed to symbolize the unity of the Western Allies and the Soviet Union, as well as to give notice to the Germans and the whole world that the surrender was made to all, not merely to the Western Allies.

Accordingly, a half-hour before midnight on May 8, 1945, the Instrument of Unconditional Surrender was ratified in Berlin. It was accepted and signed by Field Marshal Wilhelm Keitel for the German army, Admiral Hans Georg von Friedeburg for the German navy, and Colonel General Hans von Stumpf for the *Luftwaffe*. Marshal Georgi Zhukov signed for the Soviet Union, General Carl A. Spaatz for the United States, and Lieutenant General Jean de Lattre de Tassigny for France. Air Chief Marshal Sir Arthur Tedder, as General Eisenhower's deputy, also signed the final articles of capitulation.

Keitel, arrogant and angered, signed the articles of surrender, then suddenly complained that he had not read the document. He insisted that he must have an additional 24 hours to inform his troops that they were required not only to surrender but to give up their guns. Through an interpreter he asked Zhukov for a 24-hour reprieve. Zhukov, his face expressionless, stared straight ahead and gave no answer. Keitel slammed his portfolio shut, saluted, and left the room.

For the first time in modern history, the entire armed forces of a nation, officers and enlisted men alike, became prisoners of war.

The Russians made an elaborate documentary film for home consumption portraying highlights of the ceremony at Zhukov's headquarters. Eisenhower, who some months later saw the film in Moscow, noted that it included no mention of the earlier surrender at Reims.

The circumstances of the surrender touched off a violent journalistic controversy. Sixteen reporters, who had been chosen to witness the signing at Reims, were pledged on their honor not to communicate the fact of its existence or its results until the story was cleared for release by the public relations director of SHAEF (Supreme Headquarters, Allied Expeditionary Force). The idea was to withhold the news of the first signing until the ratification could be accomplished in Berlin the next day, so that the news could be synchronized in Washington, London, and Moscow.

After the signing at Reims, Edward Kennedy, an Associated Press correspondent, managed to get to a telephone and put in a call to London. Within minutes the flash set off a wild victory celebration in the Allied world. Kennedy took a merciless tongue-lashing from outraged fellow reporters, who accused him of "the most disgraceful, deliberate, and unethical double cross in the history of journalism." Others praised him for scoring one of the greatest journalistic beats in history.

Kennedy defended himself: "My only pledge was not to break the story until after the surrender was signed. There was no security involved. I was simply doing my job and I was not interested in whether or not I had a beat." The Associated Press did not support him, and he was discredited as a war correspondent, but his credentials were restored by General Eisenhower who saw in the outcome "no real harm, except to other publications."

A similar incident had occurred at the end of World War I when Roy W. Howard of the United Press reported the Armistice four days before it happened. The two cases were almost an exact parallel, with the exception that Howard's report was wrong and Kennedy's right.

At long last Hitler's brutal military machine lay crushed and smoldering. This was complete, ultimate defeat, the most devastating inflicted upon a nation in modern times.

Many and diverse were the contributory factors: the unconquerable and resolute resistance of the British when they stood alone in 1940; the overwhelming impact of American industrial power; the clearing of the sea lanes so that American resources could be hurled in full strength at the enemy; the achievements of Allied scientists in the battle of the laboratories; the spiraling resistance movements in the occupied countries; the cumulative effects of Allied air power which drove the *Luftwaffe* from the skies and steadily drained Germany of the means and will to resist; the effectiveness of Allied leaders who worked together in unity to achieve a common end; the skill, courage, and ingenuity of the Allied armies which on a hundred battlefields from North Africa to and beyond the Rhine bested Hitler's robots in their own type of mobile warfare.

Added to these sledgehammer blows were the blunders—German blunders. Hitler's cardinal military mistake was overconfidence. The provincial-minded little Austrian underestimated the strength and staying powers of his opponents. He miscalculated on Allied production capacity, on Allied will to strike back, on Allied leadership. He misunderstood the significance of Allied air power and was unprepared for the mammoth blows inflicted on his factories, cities, and communications.

The Nazi *Fuehrer*, intoxicated by his early victories, failed to adopt any clear-cut, consistent strategy. He had no idea of how to exploit his great conquests. His policy of holding everywhere at all costs was militarily grotesque and naïve. Despite his gaudy boastfulness, he drew back from the one venture—the invasion of Britain—that might have brought the war to a victorious end for Germany. And there were other costly blunders, especially his failure to evacuate the Russian trap in time and his bullheaded "hold-the-ports" strategy in the West.

Even more significant was the fact that Nazi Germany, despite its boasted efficiency, never really mobilized for total war. Hitler failed to expand his steel and oil capacities. He wasted money on useless displays of Nazi triumphs. He used his manpower ineffectively. He refused to organize women adequately for the war effort. Instead of taxing and thereby curtailing civilian consumption, this neophyte economist turned to deficit financing. Worst of all, his entire strategy was based on a series of brief and swift campaigns, with little attention to preparing and centralizing procurement for a long effort. The governing of the Nazi state turned out to be merely regimented inefficiency.

The German moral collapse was crippling to Hitler's cause. Neither Hitler, his generals, the armed forces, nor the German people were aware of what was happening to them. The strength of an outraged humanity was raised against the bestial Nazi regime, with its utter and wanton disregard of civilized behavior, its unparalleled brutality, its shocking atrocities, its stupid ruthlessness. It was this misunderstanding of human decency that lay at the base of Hitler's incompetence and bungling and that led straight to his destruction. The peoples of the Allied countries had no intention of living out their lives in a Nazi world. They rose in mighty wrath and struck it down.

Once again it was the tragedy of German history. Herbert Butterfield, professor of modern history at the University of Cambridge, declares that it was the fault and tragedy of the Germans that they repeatedly gambled everything on a policy which would have had brilliant results but which did not quite anticipate God, fortune, and caprice, and therefore led to unspeakable tragedy.

Shortly after World War I a German author wrote these words: "There may hardly be a people who learn more about history than the Germans, but there is also hardly a people who apply the lessons of history worse."

The author's name—Adolf Hitler. The book—*Mein Kampf.*

V-E DAY, MAY 8, 1945

After five years, eight months, and seven days of conflict the European phase of World War II had come to an end. On V-E Day, May 8, 1945, hysterical celebrations erupted all over the world as relieved millions flocked to the streets and shouted "It's all over! It's all over!" Overjoyed people sang and screamed, hugged and kissed strangers, joined impromptu parades. Everywhere it was the same—in Times Square, Piccadilly Circus, the Place de la Concorde, the Nevsky Prospekt, Coventry, Kiev, Indianapolis, Rotterdam—gaiety, laughter, clamor, the blare of horns. The Nazi madman and his rowdies had been struck down. Now for the Japs—and the blessings of peace!

General Eisenhower issued a Victory Order of the Day:

> It is my special privilege, in the name of all the nations represented in the theatre of war, to commend each of you for the valiant performance of duty. . . . Your accomplishments at sea, in the air, on the ground, and in the field of supply have put 5,000,000 of the enemy permanently out of the war. You have taken in stride military tasks so difficult as to be classed by many doubters as impossible. You have confused, defeated, and destroyed your savagely fighting foe. . . .
>
> The route you have traveled through hundreds of miles is marked by the graves of former comrades. Each of the fallen died as a member of the team to which you belong, bound together by a common love of liberty and a refusal to submit to enslavement. Our common problems of the immediate and distant future can be best solved in the same conceptions of coöperation and devotion to the cause of human freedom as have made this Expeditionary Force such a mighty engine of righteous destruction.
>
> Let us have no part in the profitless quarrels in which other men will inevitably engage as to what country, what service, won the European war. Every man, every woman, of every nation here represented has served according to his or her ability, and the efforts of each have contributed to the outcome. This we shall remember—and in doing so we shall be revering each honored grave, and be sending comfort to the loved ones of comrades who could not live to see this day.

President Truman spoke to the American people in a radio address:

> This is a solemn but a glorious hour. . . . I only wish that Franklin D. Roosevelt had lived to witness this day.
>
> For this victory we join in offering our thanks to the Providence which has guided and sustained us through the dark days of adversity.
>
> Our rejoicing is sobered and subdued by a supreme consciousness of the terrible price we have paid to rid the world of Hitler and his evil band. . . .
>
> We must work to finish the war. Our victory is but half-won. The West is free, but the East is still in bondage to the treacherous tyranny of the Japanese. When the last Japanese division has surrendered unconditionally, then only will our fighting job be done.
>
> We must work to bind up the wounds of a suffering world—to build an abiding peace, a peace rooted in justice and in law. We can build such a peace only by hard, toilsome, painstaking work—by understanding and working with our Allies in peace as we have in war.

At one minute past midnight on May 9, 1945, the guns fell silent. As the roar of victory reverberated throughout the Allied world, there was only the dead silence of the tomb in Berlin, Frankfurt, Hamburg, and Berchtesgaden.

COYOTE ROUNDUP

One by one the élite of Hitler's Third Reich were rounded up and herded into prisons. Some preferred death to capture. Admiral Hans Georg von Friedeburg, whom Doenitz had sent to Montgomery in an unsuccessful surrender mission, slipped quietly into a bathroom and bit into a vial of cyanide of potassium. Some, belatedly, cast scorn on the dead *Fuehrer*. Colonel General Nikolaus, commander of the German forces in Norway, commented: "Germany has fought the most insane war in history."

It was a tremendous bag of prisoners. It included Grand Admiral Karl Doenitz, Hitler's designated successor, and a platoon of field marshals—Wilhelm Keitel, most faithful lackey among the army brass; Ewald von Kleist, who was active in the 1940 conquest of France; Albert Kesselring, last commander in the West; Ferdinand von Schoerner, assigned to the Russian front; Siegmund Wilhelm List; and others. There was S.S. General Karl Oberg, the "Butcher of Paris." And there were leading Nazi politicians—Dr. Robert Ley, chief of the German Labor Front; Julius Streicher, notorious Jew-baiter; Hans Frank, governor of Poland; Alfred Rosenberg, philosopher of Nazism; Franz von Papen, conspiratorial "devil in top hat"; and a host of lesser fry. Into jail with them went William Joyce, the Lord Haw Haw of the Nazi radio, and other miscellaneous turncoats.

Goering surrendered on May 8, 1945, near the town of Kitzbühel, in Austria. The first Nazi bigwig to fall into American hands, the *Luftwaffe* chief immediately demanded food and deference, and equally as loudly denounced Hitler as "a narrow-minded ignoramus" and Ribbentrop as "an unmitigated scoundrel." The *Fuehrer*, he complained in an effort to find sympathy, had condemned him to die because he had sought to take over the reins and surrender to the Allies. He was clapped into prison to await the judgment of Nuremberg.

On May 20, 1945, the most sinister Nazi of all fell into Allied hands. Heinrich Himmler, looking for all the world like a benevolent schoolmaster, was one of the most vicious mass murderers of all time. Head of the *Gestapo*, destroyer of Lidice, exterminator of Jews, Himmler had feathered his nest with a million dollars (discovered by Allied troops in a barn near Berchtesgaden). With his mustache shaved off, a black patch over his right eye, dressed in civilian clothes, he was picked up by British troops as he tried to cross a bridge at Bremervoerde, near Hamburg. To his captors he presented forged identity papers bearing the name of one Nitzinger, a discharged member of the German security police.

When an examining doctor ordered Himmler to open his mouth, the *Gestapo* chief bit into a small blue vial containing poison. In a few minutes he was dead. It was the one objectively decent act in the life of a mass murderer.

The body was dumped into a grave in a patch of pines. The only words spoken at this impromptu funeral service came from a British Tommy: "Let the worm go to the worms!"

POTSDAM—THE FINAL WARTIME CONFERENCE

From July 17–August 2, 1945, the Potsdam Conference, officially called the Berlin Conference, met in the Cecilienhof in Potsdam, former home of German emperors. The United States was represented by President Harry S. Truman and Secretary of State James F. Byrnes; Great Britain by Prime Minister Winston Churchill and Foreign Secretary Anthony Eden; and the Soviet Union by Joseph Stalin and Foreign Minister Vyacheslav Molotov.

The parley was interrupted briefly on July 26, 1945, to allow Churchill to return to England to face the final results of the general election of July 5. The Socialists won by two to one in an amazing landslide, surprising Churchill as much as it did the rest of the world. The British sent their new Prime Minister, Clement R. Attlee, who had served in the War Cabinet, to Potsdam to replace Churchill.

The Potsdam conferees immediately put into force the previous agreement made at Yalta. Germany was split into four administrative zones—the Americans in the south, the French in the southeast, the British in the northwest, and the Russians in the east and center. But it was expressly stipulated that, during the occupation, Germany would be treated as a single unit. This was a historically unique attempt by four powers of varying political philosophies to rule in their own manner a strongly integrated nation.

A 6,000-word communiqué issued on August 1, 1945, dealt with the denazification, demilitarization, and decentralization of defeated Germany.

> It is not the intention of the Allies to destroy or enslave the German people. It is the intention of the Allies that the German people be given the opportunity to prepare for the eventual reconstruction of their life on a democratic and peaceful basis. If their own efforts are steadily directed to this end, it will be possible for them in due course to take their place among the free and peaceful peoples of the world.

The three powers then set down the terms for conquered Germany. First, there would be complete disarmament and demilitarization of Germany and the elimination or control of all German industry that could be used for military production. All German land, naval, and air forces, as well as all clubs and associations that were designed to keep alive the military tradition in Germany, "shall be completely and finally abolished in such a manner as permanently to prevent the revival or reorganization of German militarism and Nazism." Further, all arms, ammunition, and implements of war and all specialized facilities for their production would be held at the disposal of the Allies or destroyed. The maintenance and production of all aircraft and all arms, ammunition, and implements of war were to be prevented.

It was essential, agreed the conferees, to convince the German people that they had suffered a total military defeat and that they could not escape responsibility for what they had brought upon themselves, "since their own ruthless warfare and the fanatical Nazi resistance have destroyed the German economy and made chaos and suffering inevitable." For this purpose it was decided to destroy the National Socialist Party and its affiliated and supervised organizations, to dissolve all Nazi institutions, and to prevent their revival in any form. German political life would be reconstructed on a democratic basis and prepared for eventual peaceful coöperation in international life. All Nazi laws which established discrimination on grounds of race, creed, or political opinion were abolished.

And what about the plethora of war criminals? The men at Potsdam decreed that "those who have participated in planning or carrying out Nazi enterprises involving or resulting in atrocities or war crimes shall be arrested and brought to judgment." This included Nazi leaders, influential Nazi supporters, and high officials of Nazi organizations. Thus, unobtrusively but with deadly finality, the stage was set for the drama of Nuremberg.

To make possible the progress of democracy in Germany and to eliminate Nazi and militarist doctrines from German life, it was agreed that the German educational system would be reorganized and controlled. The judicial system was to be recast in accordance with the principles of democracy, of justice under law, and of equal rights for all citizens without distinction of race, nationality, or religion. The administration of affairs in Germany was to be directed toward the decentralization of the political structure and the development of local responsibility.

In the new Germany there would be freedom of speech, press, and religion, "subject to the necessity for maintaining military security." Similarly, the formation of free trade unions was permitted.

The economic clauses of the declaration were designed to prevent the development of a war potential by Germany in the future. "In order to eliminate Germany's war potential, the production of arms, ammunition, and implements of war as well as all types of aircraft and seagoing ships, shall be prohibited and prevented. Production of metals, chemicals, machinery, and other items that are directly necessary to a war economy shall be rigidly controlled and restricted to Germany's approved postwar peacetime needs." Germany's economy would be decentralized to eliminate the previous excessive concentration of economic power in cartels, syndicates, trusts, and other monopolistic arrangements. There would be Allied controls to carry out programs of industrial disarmament, to assure the costs of occupation, to insure a balanced economy between the four occupation zones, to handle all international financial transactions, and to control all German public or private scientific bodies connected with economic activities.

Germany would have to pay reparations "to compensate to the greatest possible extent for the loss and suffering she has caused to the United Nations and for which the German people cannot escape responsibility." To the Soviet Union went the lion's share of reparations, on the ground that she had suffered the greatest economic losses.

First of all, the U.S.S.R. was permitted to meet its reparations claims by removing from its zone in Germany industrial equipment and other assets. In addition to the reparations taken from its own occupation zone, the Soviet Union was to receive in addition from the Western zones 25 per cent of metallurgical, chemical, and machine-manufacturing industries unnecessary for the German peace economy. For 15 per cent of this equipment the Soviet Union was to pay "an equivalent value of food, coal, potash, zinc, timber, clay products, petroleum products, and such other commodities as may be agreed upon." The other 10 per cent of this equipment was to be transferred to the Soviet Government on reparations account "without payment or exchange of any kind in return." The Soviet Union was also given complete control over German assets in the Eastern zone of Germany, as well as German foreign assets in Bulgaria, Finland, Rumania, and eastern Austria. The U.S.S.R. undertook to settle the reparations claims of Poland from its own share of reparations.

The reparations claims of the United States, the United Kingdom, and other countries entitled to reparations would be met from the Western zones and from appropriate German external assets.

Several more concessions were made to the Russians. It was agreed that the Soviet Union was to be allotted "tentatively" the northern portion of East Prussia, including the great port of Königsberg. Further, as a concession to Russian feelings, Poland was to be given the remainder of East Prussia, including the port of Danzig as well as the district of East Germany running to the Oder and Neisse Rivers and to the Czech frontier, pending the final peace conference. It was decreed that there would be an "orderly transfer" of the German population driven out by the Poles (the same formula to be applied to Germans leaving Hungary and Czechoslovakia).

These decisions cost Germany a quarter of the territory she had held in 1937 and made it certain that the population of Rump Germany—what became the new West Germany—would rise materially because of an influx of refugees from the East.

The Conference also agreed in principle upon arrangements for the use and disposal of the surrendered German fleet and merchant ships. It was decided that the three Powers would appoint experts to work out together detailed plans to give effect to the agreed principles.

Finally, it was agreed that preparations should be made to draw up peace treaties with Italy and the Axis satellites. For this purpose parleys of foreign ministers of the Big Five nations were to meet later at London and Moscow to settle specific issues until the United Nations was able to take over further consideration of postwar problems.

The communiqué of August 1, 1945, was designed to give the impression of Allied unity after the defeat of Nazi Germany. Little publicity was given at the time to strong disagreements between the Soviet Union and the Anglo-American Allies. But already there were signs of that hardheaded Russian intransigence that was to lead to the cold war.

The acute Polish question was not solved at Potsdam, nor was there any real agreement on the future status of Eastern Europe and the Balkans. There were battles over the formation of the Polish Provisional Government of National Unity. Although the communiqué also gave the impression of unity on German reparations, there were struggles behind the scenes on the extent of Soviet demands.

The war with Japan was still on. Truman informed Stalin at Potsdam that the United States possessed a new secret weapon of extraordinary power, but the Soviet dictator showed little interest. He still vacillated on the question of an immediate Soviet declaration of war on Japan.

On July 26, 1945, Truman, Attlee, and Chiang Kai-shek issued an ultimatum to Japan warning her that the alternative to instant and unconditional surrender was "complete and utter destruction." The war lords of Japan paid no attention until atomic bombs dropped on Hiroshima and Nagasaki made it plain that there was immeasurable force behind the ultimatum.

CHAPTER 23

Cracking the Inner Defenses of Japan

> ***The summer grasses!***
> ***All that is left of the***
> ***warrior's dream.***
> **—Basho (1644-1694)**

OPERATION FORAGER: THE MARIANAS

The great counteroffensive against Japan was rolling.

By early summer, 1944, in a little over 12 months, American forces in the Southwest Pacific, with the assistance of Australian units, had pushed more than a thousand miles closer to Tokyo, and had cut off 135,000 troops beyond hope of rescue. American task forces keyed for battle, and with a striking power considerably stronger than that of the enemy, were ranging far and wide over the vast Western Pacific.

The Japanese, appalled by the cracking of their defense perimeter, sent out a fleet to meet the American warships.

June 19, 1944, was a bright, warm day, with unlimited ceiling and visibility, with few clouds to give cover to aviators waiting for unwary prey. In the clear atmosphere, long white vapor trails flew back from the wing tips of aircraft. On this perfect day for air combat there took place the greatest carrier battle of the war, what American pilots thenceforth called the Great Marianas Turkey Shoot. The forces engaged were nearly four times those employed at Midway. For more than eight hours, from mid-morning to darkness, there was continued and desperate battle in the air over and around Guam. When it was all over, the outcome was so decisive that Japan could never again rise in force to challenge U.S. air power.

On the first Japanese raid 16 Zeke fighters, 45 Zekes carrying bombs, and

8 torpedo-bearing Jills were launched from carriers at 8:30 A.M. The formation was quickly picked up by radar, whereupon Vice-Admiral Marc A. Mitscher ordered Task Force 58 to launch every available fighter for interception. U.S. Hellcats took to the air.

The Japanese apparently had no set defense plan. Their bombers scattered at once, thereby leaving themselves vulnerable, and the fighters, instead of covering the bombers, went into individual fancy, acrobatic rolls to escape the Hellcats. Some 42 of the 69 Japanese planes on that opening raid failed to return.

So it went all through that mad day. On Raid II there were 128 Japanese planes, 47 on Raid III, and 82 on Raid IV. The Japanese were going to keep up the battle every hour on the hour. The resulting battle royal was a fierce melee in which flashing aircraft went into zooms and sideslips, skids, barrel rolls, wingovers. Pilots of both sides maneuvered at top speed to get on the tail of enemy planes and then fire effective bursts. Aircraft went into spirals from which they never recovered; others took a burst of fire and exploded in mid-air; still others went into perpendicular dives and splashed flaming into the ocean. The Americans, more skillful and better trained, had the best of it by far.

As darkness fell over Guam, Japanese aircraft disappeared from the air. The Great Marianas Turkey Shoot was over. Casualty figures were one-sided. The Americans lost only 23 of their 300 Hellcats. The Japanese had used 373 planes of varying types, of which only 130 returned from combat. More, they lost at least 50 Guam-based planes, while others went down in sunken carriers or were lost in crashes. The total loss on that day for Nippon was 315 planes and her best pilots. The heart was blasted out of Japanese air power.

The Japanese carrier force, stripped of its planes, was chased halfway to the Philippines. American pilots, closing in, dealt heavy punishment. They sank one carrier and two oilers. American submarines sank two more carriers. Enemy cruisers and destroyers were damaged.

This was the Battle of the Philippine Sea. As at Coral Sea and as at Midway, the opposing warships did not exchange a shot. The battle was fought entirely by aircraft. A crushing defeat for Japan, it assured success of American occupation and conquest of the Marianas.

The first objective of Operation Forager in the Marianas was Saipan. This 12-mile-long island, with its curving mountainous spine, was a key target in the group, 3,800 miles west of Pearl Harbor, 1,585 miles south of Tokyo, and 100 miles north of bypassed Guam, still in enemy hands. Dug in on Saipan behind a honeycomb of pillboxes and caves were 30,000 crack Japanese troops.

The initial attacks on Saipan came on June 15–19, 1944. Resistance was as fierce as any during the war, more deadly than at Tarawa, more protracted than at Kwajalein. For three weeks the Japanese fought desperately until they were gradually forced back into a small pocket in the north. Then, again, there were the usual counterattacks, *Banzai* charges, suicides.

On the night of July 6–7, 1944, came the biggest *Banzai* attack of the war. The mass suicide was ordered by Lieutenant General Yoshitsugu Saito, military commander on Saipan, and Vice Admiral Chuichi Nagumo, who had been demoted from his fast carrier command to a small area fleet with headquarters on Saipan. The plan was simple—every remaining Japanese on Saipan was to kill at least 10 Americans before taking his own life. The target was to be the U.S. 27th Division.

On that memorable day, more than 3,000 Japanese swarmed into a 300-yard gap between two battalions of the 27th Division. Some were armed with guns, others only with bayonets; some had no weapons at all. But all screamed "*Banzai!*" Overrunning command posts, they inflicted heavy casualties. It was a wild, desperate attack, but from the Western viewpoint pointless and even stupid. Eventually, all the attackers were killed.

Meanwhile, the two Japanese commanders, realizing that their position was hopeless, prepared to take their own lives. General Saito issued a final message to his troops, stating that he would die with them "to exalt true Japanese manhood." Then he sat down in his headquarters cave on a rock facing Tokyo, cried "*Tenno Haika! Banzai!*" ("Hurrah for the Emperor!") and carefully opened an artery with his sword. He then nodded to his adjutant, who promptly shot him in the head. Most of his staff joined their ancestors in similar fashion. In another cave Admiral Nagumo killed himself with a pistol shot. Thus the arrogant commander of the Pearl Harbor Striking Force came to his end on a little out-of-the-way island far from the plaudits of the Tokyo mobs.

After the capture of Saipan came another grisly episode—the suicide of hundreds of Japanese civilians at the northern cliffs. Refusing to believe the surrender leaflets guaranteeing honorable treatment, they took their own lives in a macabre display of hysteria. Parents dashed their babies to death on the rocks and then, one after another, screaming wildly, jumped off the cliffs. American troops, open-mouthed with amazement, watched as Japanese civilians grimly went about the task of cutting each others' throats. Some deliberately drowned themselves, a few blotted out their own lives with hand grenades. Others holed up in the caves and ravines, from which they were blasted out by searing flame-throwers.

When the battle was over, 23,811 Japanese lay dead on Saipan. Surprisingly, nearly two thousand were taken prisoner, the biggest bag to date in the war. American losses, too, were heavy, including 3,426 killed and missing in action and 13,099 wounded.

Saipan was a shocking blow to the Japanese war lords. Premier Hideki Tojo, distressed, resigned with his entire cabinet on July 18, 1944, the day that the loss of Saipan was publicly announced. General Kuniaki Koiso formed a new cabinet, and promised a more vigorous and ruthless prosecution of the war. But to those who understood Japanese ways the change of ministry actually meant an admission of defeat and a desire for peace. But no one in Japan would accept the responsibility of proposing peace. The result was that the Pacific war dragged on for another twelve months.

The relentless Americans pressed on in the Marianas. On July 23, 1944, they won the smaller island of Tinian, in what Lieutenant General Holland M. Smith described as "the perfect amphibious operation in the Pacific War." A new entry on the bloody score card read: "Killed: 5,745 Japanese; 195 Americans."

After 17 days of air and naval bombardment, American landing forces on July 20, 1944, went ashore on Guam, which the Japanese had seized the day after Pearl Harbor. "This campaign," wrote Rear Admiral W. L. Ainsworth in his action report, "was brilliantly conceived, splendidly planned, and precisely executed." It took three weeks of fighting, but the island came back into American hands. Ledger: "Killed, 10,693 Japanese; 1,290 Americans."

Thus Operation Forager was completed in exactly two months. It took the greatest carrier action of the war and three land campaigns. By the middle of August the Philippine Sea and the air over it, as well as the three islands of Saipan, Tinian, and Guam, were under American control.

The Japanese inner defense perimeter was now broken. The Tojo government was no longer in power. The end was in sight.

TARGET: THE PHILIPPINES

The capture of Saipan, Tinian, and Guam gave the Americans control of the Marianas bastion. The precious Marianas airfields could be used not only to strike at the Philippines but also to wreak havoc on the home islands of Japan.

The Mikado's fleet, unmercifully drubbed, had crawled back to Okinawa—a lacerated dragon with its tail beneath its legs. From there it had wearily steamed home to its base in Japan's Inland Sea. But it could not stay there. It had to recuperate and gather strength for its next vital mission—Operation *Shō-Go*—defense of the Philippines.

While Admiral Chester W. Nimitz's amphibious forces were taking one island after another in the Central Pacific, pressure was maintained on the enemy in the southwest. In the spring of 1944 giant Japanese armies were neutralized and isolated on Bougainville in the northern Solomons and on New Ireland and New Britain between the Solomons and New Guinea.

On the northern New Guinea coast another Japanese army of 60,000 was held between Madang and the Moluccas. From late April to early August, 1944, General Douglas MacArthur's American and Australian forces pushed their way 800 miles up the coastline in a series of brilliant combined operations. They sliced the Japanese into manageable segments, surrounded them, and wiped them. out. They took few prisoners.

On November 24, 1944, from speedily constructed airfields in Saipan, Tinian, and Guam, as well as from bases in China, the huge new American Superfortresses commenced round-trip missions to batter the tinderbox cities of Japan. The B-29's, now in mass production, were twice as large as the older B-17's (Flying Fortresses); they had a wing span of half a New York City block, a speed of 300 miles an hour, and a bomb load of 10 tons. Their prime targets were the Yawata steel works and the naval base at Sasebo, as well as varied industrial areas. The air offensive mounted day by day.

At the same time American submarines methodically whittled down the enemy's merchant shipping. By the summer of 1944 they had sunk nearly 700 Japanese merchant ships, damaged more than 100 more. Japanese garrisons scattered throughout the Pacific were isolated from the homeland.

The over-all U.S. strategy was working to perfection. The Gilberts, the Marshalls, the Marianas were conquered. MacArthur was storming up the New Guinea coastline. Truk and Rabaul, major Japanese strongholds, were immobilized and bypassed. Enemy supply lines were weakened. The Nipponese fleet was cut down to approved size. The way was open to direct assault on the Philippines. The only remaining strong barrier was the enemy garrison in the Palaus, directly east of the Philippines. This had to be eliminated to secure MacArthur's right flank for his dash to the Philippines.

On September 15, 1944, came the initial landings on Peleliu Island, preceded by bombing and bombardment by the U.S. Navy. Entrenched in pillboxes and caves around Bloody Nose Ridge, the Japanese resisted ferociously. After a month of brutal fighting, Peleliu Island was in American hands. Nearly 12,000 Japanese died in the futile defense.

Japan was fast losing the war, but her propagandists remained wildly optimistic. In an action off Formosa only two American cruisers, the *Canberra* and the *Houston*, were damaged, and fewer than 100 American planes lost. But a few days later a Japanese plane appeared over the captured island and dropped leaflets bearing this wild claim:

FOR RECKLESS YANKEE DOODLE

> Do you know about the naval battle by the American 58th [sic] Fleet at the sea near Taiwan [Formosa] and the Philippine? Japanese powerful Air Force had sunk their 19 aeroplane carriers, 4 battleships, 10 several cruisers and destroyers, along with sending 1,261 ship aeroplanes into the sea. . . .

Then came pre-invasion air strikes up and down the Philippines. American airmen hit from Mindanao in the south to Luzon in the north, smashing the enemy in the air and on the ground, leaving in flaming wreckage nearly 3,000 Japanese planes, scattered over the islands. Planes from Admiral Marc A. Mitscher's Task Force 58 struck powerfully at Japanese feeder-airfields as far north as Formosa, sank any enemy ships they could find, and forced others out of the theatre of operations.

A mood of dismay infiltrated Tokyo. To relieve the gloom, Japanese newspapers on October 18, 1944, repeated the highly emotional account of a phony naval engagement off Formosa in which Task Force 58 had been "annihilated." It was nothing new. For years Japanese newsmen had been eloquently sinking one unit after another of the American fleet in a sea of printer's ink.

On October 21, 1944, the Americans, bypassing the great island of Mindanao in the south, stormed ashore on Leyte Island in the heart of the central Philippines. This was invasion in force: 600 warships, 250,000 men, the U.S. Seventh and Third fleets, the U.S. Sixth Army. Once again the Americans had demonstrated the effectiveness of leapfrogging tactics.

From one of the ships "annihilated" by Japanese newsmen, General MacArthur stepped ashore, just two and a half years after he had left Corregidor. Colonel Carlos Romulo, the Filipino leader, later gave this version: "There was the tall MacArthur, with the water reaching up to his knees, and behind him there was little Romulo, trying to keep his head above water."

"People of the Philippines!" said MacArthur. "I have returned. By the grace of Almighty God our forces stand again on Philippine soil—soil consecrated in the blood of our two peoples. . . . Rally to me. Let the indomitable spirit of Bataan and Corregidor lead us on."

General MacArthur credited his accomplishment to the Deity, but later in the classrooms at Annapolis it was attributed in large part, not without justification, to the United States Navy.

Within four days the two American beachheads were joined and the troops surged inland. At first it seemed that the campaign might be an easy one. But for the Japanese it was do or die. American control of the Philippines would cut off Japanese communications with Indo-China, Malaya, and the Netherlands East Indies, and without oil from the Indies, Japan would be finished. The Imperial Navy could still hit at the Americans from Singapore, through the South China Sea, or across the Sulu Sea through the San Bernardino Strait north of Leyte.

The American challenge could not be ignored. This was the showdown.

LEYTE: "THE BATTLE OF BULL'S RUN"

"Douglas, where do we go from here?" asked President Roosevelt.

"Leyte, Mr. President, and then Luzon," replied General MacArthur.

That brief exchange on board the cruiser *Baltimore* at Pearl Harbor in July 1944 generated the campaign for the recapture of the Philippines.

The name "Leyte" was destined for glory in the annals of American naval warfare. During the last week of October 1944 came the Battle for Leyte Gulf, the greatest sea engagement ever fought. Engaged were 166 American and approximately 70 Japanese warships, 1,280 American and 716 Japanese warplanes.

The American landings on Leyte had already begun. To counter this move the Japanese activated Operation *Ta*, their sea-reinforcement program, pouring troops and supplies into the island through its back door at Ormoc. Their *Kamikazes*, suicide planes, were striking at American shipping in the Gulf. They would commit their navy in a last-ditch operation for victory.

Japanese planning visualized a simultaneous triple-threat. Most of what was left of the Imperial Navy was split into three groups. The southern force would enter Surigao Strait between Mindanao and Leyte. The main striking force in the center, commanded by Vice Admiral Takeo Kurita, would steam into the San Bernardino Strait north of Leyte between Samar and Luzon. These two fleets would rendezvous at Leyte Gulf, annihilate the enemy craft there, and isolate the Americans already ashore. To a third task force under Vice Admiral Jisaburo Ozawa was assigned the mission of playing sacrificial decoy to lure the U.S. Third Fleet north. It could expect a mauling, but it would draw enemy power away from the two main fleets and so permit a knockout blow. Besides, was it not good to die for the Emperor?

The Americans had long awaited this engagement. In the Leyte area they had the Seventh Fleet under Vice-Admiral Thomas C. Kinkaid and the Third Fleet under Admiral William F. ("Bull") Halsey, Jr., in direct support. The mission was to defend the five-day-old Leyte beachhead, come to grips with the invading fleets, annihilate them, and thereby open the back door to Tokyo.

There were three separate but simultaneous actions in the Battle for Leyte Gulf, each with its own special tone.

The southern Japanese task force, under Vice Admiral S. Nishimura, was divided into two sections. The first sailed serenely at night to Leyte through Surigao Strait. Waiting for it was a heavy battle line of the U.S. Seventh Fleet under the tactical command of Rear Admiral Jesse B. Oldendorf. The American force was deployed so that the enemy had to pass through a screen of PT boats, then destroyers, and finally heavy cruisers and battleships at the northern end of the strait.

It was a slaughter. Before the break of dawn Nishimura had lost both his battleships, three of his four destroyers, and his own life. That same day the only Japanese cruiser in Nishimura's task force was sent to the bottom by American planes.

Oldendorf had realized the dream of all naval officers—the classic maneuver of crossing the enemy's *T.* He destroyed virtually the entire southern enemy task force; only one single destroyer survived. "My theory," commented Oldendorf later, "was that of the old-time gambler. *Never give a sucker a chance.* If my opponent is foolish enough to come at me with an inferior force, I'm certainly not going to give him an even break."

The second Japanese section in southern waters turned tail and fled. The only damage sustained by the Americans in the Battle of Surigao Strait was by gunfire on the destroyer *Albert W. Grant.* One more victory was chalked up in the wardrooms of the Pacific Fleet.

The Japanese central force under Admiral Kurita moved on Leyte from the west. Detected by two U.S. submarines, Kurita quickly lost two heavy cruisers and later a battleship to American air attack. But he surged on through Mindoro Strait with a still powerful force of five battleships, six heavy and two light cruisers, and a dozen destroyers. He could expect no help from Nishimura, whose task force in the south had been pounded to bits.

But fortune was with Kurita. The decoy maneuver in the north was working beautifully. Halsey, receiving word that the enemy fleet to the north included carriers, hastily swung around and headed in its direction. Behind him he left nothing to protect the exposed beachhead. Not even a patrolling destroyer.

Off Samar, Rear Admiral C. A. F. Sprague was cruelly trapped with a small escort of six baby flattops, three destroyers, and four escort destroyers. The warriors of this puny fleet found themselves staring up at Kurita's big guns. "It was like a puppy being smacked by a truck," said one officer. Sprague's little carriers were so lightly armored that enemy shells punctured them without exploding. But they went to the attack.

"In no engagement in its entire history," wrote Samuel Eliot Morison, "has the United States Navy shown more gallantry, guts, and gumption."

Sprague's planes sank an enemy heavy cruiser and a destroyer. But in the surface engagement that followed, Kurita's big guns wrought havoc on the underdog U.S. fleet. They sank the carrier *Gambier Bay*, the destroyers *Johnston* and *Hoel*, and the destroyer escort *Roberts*, while damaging four other escort carriers. *Kamikaze* pilots accounted for the escort carrier *Saint Lô.*

Admiral "Bull" Halsey had reacted precisely like his nickname when his search-planes discovered Ozawa's northern force. He sailed northward to Cape Engaño straight into a naval controversy of the first magnitude. His action is still being refought from Annapolis to San Diego.

But before he could deal the *coup de grâce* to the Japanese northern fleet, Halsey had to turn south in response to urgent calls from Kinkaid. When he arrived at the central theatre, the bulk of the enemy fleet there had vanished. There was some consolation for the frustrated admiral; he did not come away from Cape Engaño empty-handed. His airmen sank four of Ozawa's carriers, a light cruiser, and two destroyers.

Many of the Japanese ships escaped destruction, but Nippon lost 4 carriers (1 large and 3 light carriers), 3 battleships, 10 cruisers, 12 destroyers, and 4 submarines. The United States lost a light carrier, the *Princeton*, 2 escort carriers, the *St. Lô* and *Gambier Bay*, and several destroyers and smaller ships.

The box score showed a resounding American victory. Actually, it was far less a battle than a four-day miniature war fought in three dimensions—a complicated epic of belching naval fire, smoke-screening, torpedo attacks, zigzagging warships, bombing, and strafing, with the Americans meting out the heavier damage.

The fortunes of war shifted decisively at Leyte. Whatever chance Japan might have had of winning the war in the Pacific was irretrievably lost. From this time on the Imperial Navy never dared to halt an American landing operation, except at Okinawa where it committed and straightway lost the giant new battleship *Yamato*.

At Leyte the Japanese missed the boat when, after drawing Halsey northward to strike at the diversionary force, leaving the San Bernardino Strait open for the main Japanese force, they suddenly abandoned the mission with victory in sight. Had they kept on, they could have entered Leyte Gulf and destroyed a million tons of American shipping. "It proved once more," said Major General George C. Kenney, "that the Jap had no business starting a war with the United States in the first place. He just wasn't good enough to play in the big leagues."

The great naval battle left the Japanese in a critical position in the Philippines. General MacArthur now had a land wedge firmly planted in the vulnerable flank of the enemy. With their naval power weakened, the Japanese could no longer provide reinforcements or supplies for their tens of thousands of picked troops scattered in isolated pockets over the Philippines. "Most of them," said General Marshall, "might as well have been on the other side of the world as far as the enemy's ability to shift them to meet American thrusts was concerned." To these lost troops came a peremptory order from the Emperor: "Enemy ground forces will be destroyed."

Tokyo's *Shō* plan at Leyte Gulf had ended as a fiasco, but it was an incomplete victory for the United States—despite the lopsided box score. The Japanese fleets avoided complete annihilation: Kurita was able to escape with four capital ships, Ozawa with 10 of his original vessels.

The Battle for Leyte Gulf, probably the last great fleet-battle in history, quickly found its way into classrooms and armchairs to join the Jellicoe-Beatty controversy after Jutland in World War I and other naval controversies on what should have been done. Both Admirals Kinkaid and Halsey charged that the other could have and should have covered San Bernardino Strait.

Kinkaid's arguments were:

1. Halsey relied too heavily on the exaggerated claims of his pilots.

2. Halsey made a critical error of judgment when he dashed 300 miles to the north with all six of his battleships, leaving behind too weak a force to insure the destruction of Kurita's fleet. Then, just as he was on the verge of accounting for all of Ozawa's force, he compounded the error by turning about and speeding south.

3. Kinkaid's own Seventh Fleet, with its old and slow battleships and weak in firepower, was designed only to provide support for the landing and not for major combat.

4. Halsey took all six of his battleships north, when only two were needed. He should have left four at San Bernardino Strait and thereby have prevented Kurita from passing through. When Halsey dashed south, once again he took all six battleships with him, this time depriving Vice-Admiral Marc A. Mitscher, commanding a task group, of the two battleships he desperately needed.

5. In sum, according to Kinkaid, Halsey did exactly what the enemy wanted him to do. In a polite way, Kinkaid was accusing Halsey of being a prime sucker for a Japanese feint.

Halsey entered a vigorous dissent:

1. His decision to go north was not based solely on pilots' reports, he said. It was a calculated risk, amply justified. He was playing the game on Saturday, not "Monday-morning quarterbacking."

2. Halsey felt that Kinkaid's Seventh Fleet could and would take care of Kurita's "battered forces." "I knew what I was doing at all times, and deliberately took the risks, in order to get rid of the Jap carriers."

3. Halsey agreed that he had made a mistake in "bowing to pressure and turning south." "I consider this the gravest error I committed during the Battle of Leyte Gulf."

4. The trouble was in divided command and unsatisfactory communications. "Had either Admiral Kinkaid or I been put in supreme command, the battle would have been fought quite differently." And further, "There is only one word to describe the communications on the American side during the battle, and that word is rotten."

5. Halsey was not convinced that Ozawa's force in the north was intended solely as a lure. "The Japs had continually lied during the war, even to each other. Why believe them implicitly as soon as the war ends?"

In his autobiography, *Admiral Halsey's Story* (1947), Halsey stated that, given the same circumstances and the same information as he had then, he would make the same decision. He had reason to believe that the enemy forces in the central and southern sectors were being handled effectively by Kinkaid. The Northern Force was "fresh and undamaged." Having chosen his antagonist, it remained only to select the best way to meet him. Halsey noted three alternatives:

1. *He could guard San Bernardino with his whole fleet and wait for the Northern Force to strike him.* Rejected. This would give the Japanese use of their airfields on Luzon as well as their carriers.

2. *He could guard San Bernardino with Task Force 34 while he struck the Northern Force with his carriers.* Rejected. The fleet had to be kept intact for most striking and defensive power.

3. *He could leave San Bernardino unguarded and strike the Northern Force with his whole fleet.* Accepted. This would preserve the integrity of his fleet, it left the initiative with him, and it promised the greatest possibility of surprise.

Halsey headed for the enemy, 300 miles to the north. While he was closing in and attacking, he received a series of dispatches from Kinkaid, each calling in increasing urgency for help.

Finally, Halsey continued, he was goaded into fury by a message supposedly from Commander in Chief of the Pacific Fleet Chester W. Nimitz:

> FROM: CINCPAC
> TO: COM THIRD FLEET
> THE WHOLE WORLD WANTS TO KNOW WHERE
> IS TASK FORCE 34 (Halsey's version)

Halsey recorded that he was stunned as if he had been struck in the face. He was so angry he could not talk, utterly unable to believe that Admiral Nimitz had sent him such an insult. The message was, in fact, an error. To increase the difficulty of breaking codes, most naval dispatches were padded with gibberish, easily discovered and deleted by decoding officers. Somehow, somewhere along the line, the decoders had regarded the passage as plausible and left it in.

Halsey, in a rage, ordered his forces split. "At that moment the Northern Force, with its two remaining carriers crippled and dead in the water, was exactly 42 miles from the muzzles of my 15-inch guns." Halsey stated that he had turned his back on the opportunity he had dreamed of since his days as a midshipman.

Finally, Halsey pointed to what he had done to the enemy in the north: sunk: 4 carriers, 1 light cruiser, 2 destroyers; damaged: 2 battleships, 2 light cruisers, 4 destroyers.

And there the matter rests, with plenty of fuel for a thousand hot-stove arguments as the greatest naval battle in history is refought by professional and amateur experts. The furore is inconsequential. The Battle for Leyte Gulf, despite Halsey's dash for the north, was as decisive as Salamis, where the Greek navies defeated Xerxes' fleet in 480 B.C.

A Japanese admiral, too, became enmeshed in postwar controversy concerning his behavior at Leyte. On October 25, 1944, the second day of the battle, Vice-Admiral Kiyohide Shima steamed north toward Surigao Strait with two heavy cruisers, a light cruiser, and four destroyers to join the main Japanese attack-force converging on Leyte Gulf. Seeing gun flares on the horizon, Shima decided to disobey orders and stay away. His entire contribution to the battle, as Samuel Eliot Morison observed, was to ram his battleship into a crippled heavy cruiser of another Japanese force, after firing 16 torpedoes at two islands he mistook for American ships.

For years Admiral Shima, criticized and ridiculed as "the buffoon of the Japanese tragedy," maintained a dignified silence. Finally, in January 1959, in response to a California schoolboy who had written to him for information for his history-class term paper, Shima explained that he headed for the fringes of the vast Leyte engagement after other Japanese naval forces were already there. The necessity for radio silence meant that he could not coördinate his strategy or tactics with theirs. Hampered by bad luck, disorganized communications, and evidence that the bulk of the Japanese fleets was being annihilated, all he could do was withdraw.

"It was quite clear," Shima wrote, "that we should fall into a ready trap. I considered all possibilities. Then I came to my decision that it would be better to . . . wait a chance to know how everything went."

It was a wise judgment. Historian Morison concluded that "the most intelligent act of any Japanese commander in the entire battle was Admiral Shima's retirement."

RECONQUEST OF THE PHILIPPINES

By the end of October 1944 the Japanese had been driven from southern and northeastern Leyte. But, reinforced via the port of Ormoc with new divisions under command of General Tomoyuki Yamashita, they dug in to hold the rest of the island.

The sanguinary struggle for the next two months recapitulated on a giant scale the earlier ground-battles on Pacific islands. The Japanese defended every inch, the Americans pushed inexorably forward with tanks, artillery, flame throwers, bazookas, and hand grenades.

On the night of December 6–7, 1944, while seeking to bring reinforcements to Leyte, six Japanese warships loaded with troops and supplies were sunk by American warships. A week later, three more transports were trapped northwest of Leyte and sunk. American troops captured key Ormoc on December 16, 1944. By the end of the month organized enemy resistance ceased, although isolated units still held out.

The plight of the Japanese on Leyte was hopeless. Gone were the days of heady triumph. With their supply lines from the homeland cut, trapped in the midst of a hostile population, harried unmercifully by a persistent foe, the Nipponese troops were paying a ghastly toll.

Men of the U.S. 32nd Division found this letter written by an unknown Japanese soldier on December 21, 1944:

> I am exhausted. We have no food. The enemy are now within 500 meters from us. Mother, my dear wife and son, I am writing this letter to you by dim candlelight. Our end is near. What will be the future of Japan if this island shall fall into enemy hands? Our air force has not arrived. General Yamashita has not arrived. Hundreds of pale soldiers of Japan are awaiting our glorious end and nothing else. This is a repetition of what occurred in the Solomons, New Georgia, and other islands. How well are the people of Japan prepared to fight the decisive battle with the will to win?

The Japanese on Leyte lost 56,263 killed and 389 prisoners. American casualties were 2,888 killed, 8,422 wounded, and 161 missing.

While the battle raged on Leyte, General MacArthur, bypassing Mindanao, Negros and Panay, sent an assault force to the southwestern coast of Mindoro. Landing on December 15, 1944, the Americans pushed ahead against light resistance, captured an airstrip, repaired it, and put it to use for the invasion of Luzon. Manila was only 155 miles away.

In early January 1945 a U.S. assault force, the U.S. Sixth Army under Lieutenant General Walter Krueger, gathered east of Leyte, slipped through Surigao Strait over the sunken wrecks of Japanese warships, and passed into the Mindanao and Sulu Seas. The target was Luzon, the northernmost island of the Philippines, seat of the capital Manila, and scene of Bataan and Corregidor. The invaders used the same route that the Japanese had taken in 1941–1942, the Lingayen Gulf, the point of greatest vulnerability.

On January 9, 1945, after three days of concentrated sea and air barrage, the American force stormed ashore at Lingayen. The first beach casualty was an embarrassed American soldier who was butted by an angry carabao, infuriated at having its siesta disturbed. By nightfall 68,000 troops were on land carving out a 15-mile beachhead, 6,000 yards deep.

Newspaper headlines in Tokyo screamed that the invading Americans had been driven off with heavy casualties. Exactly the opposite was true. The 175,000 remaining Japanese troops were destined to defeat.

The campaign on Luzon was orthodox, but it was one of the most vicious of all in the Pacific theatre. Plastered from the air, smashed on the ground, harassed by guerrillas, the Japanese decided not to defend the central plain, but instead retreated to the mountains to the north and east.

The opening drive took the Americans across the Agno River, up and down low hills, and out onto the great plain leading to Manila, 110 miles to the southeast. Here the open terrain and the fine roads could be used to good advantage for the final drive to the capital.

Almost immediately the invaders discovered ghastly evidence of Japanese brutality. From the liberated prisons of the Philippines emerged a stream of haggard and hungry military and civilian captives. It was a nauseating spectacle. American Rangers and Filipino scouts, infuriated by scenes at the liberated prisons, moved inside the Japanese lines on January 30, 1945, to free 500 emaciated prisoners from the Cabanatuan prison camp, and killed an equal number of the enemy in the process. American airborne and infantry troops, aided by Filipino guerrillas, freed several thousand prisoners on February 23, 1945, from the hell-camp at Los Baños, south of Manila, after disposing of several hundred Japanese guards. The responsible Japanese officers were later to pay for these atrocities with their lives.

In early 1945 the Americans made new landings in the west and south of Luzon. All columns now converged on Manila. Twenty-six days after the initial landings on Luzon, three years and six weeks after the American-Filipino forces had abandoned the capital, the Americans were back in Manila.

The city was wrecked. The business district was a fiery hell; the water mains were empty; the fire department was helpless in the rubble-strewn streets. The entire city was seared, gutted, smashed, empty. In the ruins, behind barricaded doors and from rooftops, the remaining Japanese fought with the courage of trapped animals.

American parachutists dropped on the rock fortress of Corregidor, where Lieutenant General Jonathan M. Wainwright had made his last desperate stand in 1942. The Japanese defenders retired to the American-built tunnels. After a week of furious fighting, the Americans heard a series of terrific explosions. The enemy had destroyed the entire system and themselves along with it. The remaining caves were sealed off by the attackers. On February 22, 1945, the Japanese garrison on Corregidor was officially listed as "practically destroyed."

Two weeks later, General MacArthur was at Corregidor. "Hoist the colors," he told his troops, "and let no enemy ever haul them down."

Die-hard Japanese fanatics retired to the malaria-infested reaches of the Sierra Madre Mountains to the east. They posed no problem for the victors.

Mindanao, the second largest island of the Philippines, was invaded on March 10, 1945. Again the Japanese tried piecemeal commitment, only to be hunted down and destroyed. Davao, the capital city, was stormed and occupied on May 4. By early July all the enemy forces on the island were split up and isolated.

On July 5, 1945, MacArthur announced that all the Philippine Islands were liberated and that the campaign could be regarded as ended. Twenty-three Japanese divisions, he estimated, had been almost annihilated by 17

American divisions and the Filipino guerrillas. The Japanese Imperial Army had lost more than 400,000 of its best troops in the Philippines.

This strategic land mass in the Western Pacific was now in American hands and ready for use as a staging area for final moves against the enemy.

OPERATIONS IN BURMA

In 1942 the Japanese had overrun Burma and seized the road in the north over which supplies rolled into China. Their strategy envisioned a drive all the way through India. This grandiose plan might have worked but for unexpected resistance.

To the Allied Chiefs of Staff the China-Burma-India theatre, the C.B.I., was for the time being the least important of the Pacific areas of war. It was nearly two years after the fall of Burma before the Allies could undertake a major offensive there. It was difficult to send reinforcements and supplies to the area; in addition, ground operations were limited from May to October by the monsoon season. The Allies had to be content with halfway, improvised measures to contain the enemy until a full-scale assault could be launched.

First, the doorway to India had to be closed. There were serious problems inside India. Field Marshal Sir Archibald Wavell, viceroy of India, disturbed by evidences of rebellion, threw Mahatma Gandhi, Jawaharlal Nehru, and other members of the Indian National Congress into prison as a safety measure. He then reorganized the Anglo-Indian forces.

In March 1943, Brigadier General Orde C. Wingate, who had won a reputation as a roving soldier in Palestine and Ethiopia, and who had organized British troops and Indian raw recruits into tough, resilient units, began guerrila war behind the Japanese lines in Burma. His "long-range penetration groups," called Chindits (a mispronunciation of the Burmese *Chinthé*, lion), supplied entirely by air, struck at Japanese communications on the upper Irrawaddy River. They destroyed bridges and supply dumps and in general harried the enemy.

Wingate's Raiders were aided later by a similarly trained American group. Under command of Brigadier General Frank D. Merrill, some 3,000 officers and men volunteered to form the 5307th Composite Unit (Provisional) to fight far behind the Japanese lines in Burma. A conglomeration of tough jungle fighters, Merrill's Marauders (sometimes called the Galahad force) had a specific mission: While Stilwell's Chinese troops held the Japanese in position in the hill country to the north and west of Myitkyina, the Marauders sliced around the enemy's flanks and set up road blocks in the rear. They fought a succession of small but savage actions. Their daily fare turned out to be ambushes and forced marches. Even more dangerous than Japanese bullets were the typhus, malaria, and dysentery.

Throughout the year 1943 the guerrillas led by Wingate and Merrill ranged far and wide behind the enemy lines. It was small-scale but effective fighting, which kept the Japanese off balance and prevented them from moving into India. Operating in units of a thousand men and supplied by air, they crossed mountain ranges, pushed through the deep valleys, and avoided being caught in force by the enemy. They severed enemy communications lines running north and south in the valleys of the Irrawaddy, Chindwin, and Salween rivers, as well as the north-south railway from Myitkyina to Mandalay. Most important of all, the guerrillas proved that in modern war a small army could be maintained in the field exclusively by air. The early success of these operations in disorganizing the enemy rear convinced the Allied leaders at the Quebec Conference that this was the way to carry on war in Burma.

Wingate was not destined to see the results of his work: On March 24, 1944, he was killed at 41 in a plane crash in Burma. In a stirring obituary, Winston Churchill hailed Wingate as "a man of genius who might well have become also a man of destiny."

The problem of supplying China, whose long coastline was under Japanese control, was a thorny one. For the time being war matériel was sent by air over the "Hump," a range of 17,000-foot mountains between Allied bases in Northeast India and Kunming. To remedy this deficiency General Joseph W. Stilwell's engineers began to build the Ledo Road running from India into North Burma to link up ultimately with the Burma Road to China.

Stilwell's Ledo Road, ridiculed by many as a harebrained scheme, turned out to be one of the most extraordinary achievements of the war. It was built while the conflict for Burma raged in all its fury. The thousand and one supplies needed for the vast undertaking had to be transported hundreds of miles over a rickety, narrow-gauge railway to Ledo at the northeast corner of India before even a foot of the road could be built. Then, under American engineers, an army of human ants literally scratched the road out of the jungles and mountains. The Chinese coolies worked as had their ancestors 2,000 years ago when they built the Great Wall of China. They chipped away by hand at the earth and hauled the dirt in their own baskets. With infinite patience they battled huge precipices, landslides, dust, rain, and the deadly ubiquitous mosquitoes. Inch by inch, foot by foot, mile by mile, they carved out this new Chinese lifeline over the jagged mountain ranges.

The work began in December 1942 at the rate of three quarters of a mile a day. By May 1943 only 47 miles had been built, with 431 miles to go. In the next three months only 10 miles were added. Then came the crippling monsoons, leaving rivers of mud, which had to be removed before work could be resumed. The backbreaking work went on despite staggering odds.

On January 7, 1945, after two years and 23 days, the amazing 478-mile Ledo Road, a masterpiece of engineering, a monument to human ingenuity, was completed. Most of it ran in dizzy semicircles, a zigzagging, corkscrew road over enormous mountains and deep canyons. In early February 1945, after a 28-day trip, the first convoy completed the journey. By this time the airlift over the Hump was delivering 45,000 tons a month to embattled China.

Added to the problems of logistics, terrain, and weather in the Burmese campaign were complications of command. The British Lord Louis Mountbatten, commander in chief of the Southeast Asia Allied Forces, was more concerned about the immediate conquest of central and southern Burma. Rangoon, Mandalay, and eventually Singapore attracted him more than the remote upper valleys of Burma and the route to China. At first he was adamantly opposed to Stilwell's pet Ledo Road project. Build an impossible road over impassable mountains? Fantastic nonsense! There was serious friction between Mountbatten and Stilwell, his deputy commander. But Mountbatten finally gave in to his hard-bitten deputy and threw his support into the Ledo project.

The key objective now of the Allied forces in Burma was Myitkyina, the northern terminus of the Ledo Road. In early 1944, before the monsoon season, Stilwell led his Chinese troops on Myitkyina from northeast and southeast. Assisted by troops under Merrill, Stilwell's forces pushed up the Hukwang Valley, penetrating the jungle a mile a day for 40 days. The aim was to cover the construction of the Ledo Road.

On February 4, 1944, in the Araken region of the Burma-India frontier, to the south of Stilwell, the Japanese launched a tactical offensive of their own. The idea was to cut off the Sino-American-British forces in northern Burma, isolate them, starve them out, and then drive on into Bengal and toward Calcutta. But the Japanese had not counted on Allied air superiority. Down from the skies to the trapped troops rained food and munitions, everything from guns to beer. The Japanese were caught with rations for only 10 days. Allied counterattacks sent them reeling back east, leaving thousands of dead in the Burmese jungles. The Allies finally captured Myitkyina, the key terminus, on August 3, 1944.

Still farther to the south the Japanese tried again, this time hurling 80,000 shock troops at Imphal. They inflicted heavy losses. But the Allies surging down from the north hit them head-on, killed 50,000, and dispersed the rest.

The triumph was a brilliant but costly one. The British Fourteenth Army, which bore the brunt of the fighting in Burma, suffered more than 40,000 casualties in the first half of 1944. There were no fewer than 237,000 cases of sickness in the abominable climate.

What came after was anticlimax. The Ledo Road was opened to traffic.

In the first half of 1945 all Burma was liberated. The Japanese were driven from storied Mandalay and Rangoon and sent into headlong retreat toward the border of Thailand. After three years of inconclusive jungle fighting, the Japanese had now been driven from all Burma, an area larger than France.

To the Allies it was a victory not only over fanatical enemy resistance but over rugged terrain, miserable weather, malaria, jaundice, dysentery, searing dust, choking jungle. This was a major triumph against fantastically heavy odds.

THE LONG ROAD IN CHINA

The only Far Eastern theatre of war in which the Japanese continued to make headway was China. Defensively, they wanted to protect their own shipping as well as the *Nansei Shotos* from American bombers. Offensively, they aimed to cut the coastal plain of East China from Chungking and use it as an inland supply route to their bases in Indo-China, Malaya, and Burma.

As early as 1938 the Nationalist government (*Kuomintang*) under Chiang Kai-shek had withdrawn into Chungking in Szechwan province. Its war effort was hampered by a host of problems—graft, indolence, corruption, procrastination. In a dizzy inflationary spiral, prices rose some 500 per cent between 1937 and 1944. After the Japanese occupation of Indo-China and Burma in 1940–1941, Chinese contact with the outer world was virtually severed, except for smuggling operations and supplies brought from India by American airmen over the Hump in the southern Himalayas.

There was plenty of manpower in China. But the Chinese peasant-soldier, with his threadbare uniform, his straw shoes, and his ration of rice, was no match for the trained and equipped Japanese shock trooper. In courage, yes, but his ancient rifle was of little use against Japanese machine guns.

Worst of all was the interminable strife between the Nationalist government and the Chinese Communists. It was war within war. From 1937 to 1941, the two parties, united in their hatred of Tokyo, fought together against the invaders.

But in January 1941, unable to take any longer what they regarded as treason and sabotage, the Nationalists strongly attacked 5,000 Communists, who were withdrawing across the Yangtze, and virtually annihilated them. From that moment on the war in China turned into a grueling, wasteful triangular struggle between Nationalists, Communists, and Japanese. The Chinese Communists, 80,000,000 in number, were concentrated in the northwest provinces with their capital at Yenan, with their own currency and taxes. They would fight the Japanese in their own way.

The situation was made to order for the Japanese. In the spring of 1944 they launched a major offensive to obtain control of the remaining railway line running south from Hankow to Canton. At the same time they sent powerful spearheads against Hunan, Kwangsi, Kwantung, and Kiangsi provinces to hit the forward bases of the U.S. Fourteenth Air Force.

A half million Chinese troops melted away before these attacks. The Americans were forced to evacuate their forward air bases. The Japanese sealed off one coastal port after another between Canton and Shanghai. Within six months they cut China almost in half, dominating a land route all the way from Korea to Malaya. It looked like disaster for the Allies.

General Joseph W. Stilwell, Chiang Kai-shek's stubborn chief of staff and adviser, urgently recommended that his touchy chief stop using his troops to ride herd on the Communists and instead unite with them in a single striking force. Chiang indignantly refused. Stilwell then proposed that he himself be placed in direct command of the Nationalist forces. But neither Chiang nor the provincial generals would accept "domination" from a foreigner. The matter was complicated by Stilwell's openly expressed dislike for his chief.

The battle between Vinegar Joe and the Reluctant Dragon finally ended with Stilwell's recall, at Chiang's own request, in October 1944. Major General Albert C. Wedemeyer, Stilwell's successor, had a profound and sympathetic admiration for the sorely tried Chinese leader. He did his best to bring strength to Chiang's floundering army and troubled government. But he had little success.

Though painfully hurt by their losses in 1944, the Chinese Nationalists, trained, led, and goaded by American advisers, finally mounted an offensive in the spring and summer of 1945. By this time the Japanese were so weakened that they had to relinquish even their conquests in China. The Allies slowly won back the chain of airfields in the coastal cities. When the Japanese corridor to Malaya was narrowed to the danger point, the Nipponese were forced to withdraw to avoid capture.

China remained a sideshow to the main Pacific conflict. As Japan gradually sank to her knees, Nationalists and Communists continued their protracted military and political struggles. Each side wanted to seize as many advantages as possible from the coming peace.

After the war came bitter criticisms of Allied war policies in China. Some observers denounced Washington's withholding of essential support from Chiang Kai-shek at a critical time, to which they attributed Communism's present triumph in the Far East.

CHAPTER **24**

Victory in the East

> ***"My God!"***
>
> **—Crew members on board the *Enola Gay* over Hiroshima, August 6, 1945**

> ***Be like pine trees,***
> ***Which do not change color***
> ***Although they bear the weight***
> ***Of continuously falling snow.***
>
> **—Emperor Hirohito, 1946**

JAPAN *IN EXTREMIS*

Splashed over the front pages of Tokyo's newspapers were stories of heroism, glory, victory. But the man on the street knew that something was desperately wrong. If the war were being won, why all the horror and destruction? Why the chaos and confusion? The flying white devils were reducing Nippon's flimsy cities to ashes. Millions of people were fleeing to the countryside. Schools were closing. The transportation system was breaking down under the weight of the mass exodus. Most depressing of all, the farmers were hoarding rice and the city folk faced starvation.

The truth was that Japan by early 1945 was no longer capable of sustaining the war effort. The Allied blockade had choked off supplies of oil, coal, iron, bauxite, all absolute essentials for Nippon's tight economy. Little was left of the Imperial transportation network that had sprawled all over the Pacific. Japan-bound convoys had disappeared from the South China Sea.

Singapore, the old terminal of the great trunk line from Indonesia to Tokyo, was no longer anything more than a useless stump.

True, the military force of 6,000,000 men was almost intact, most of them stationed in the home islands. But all over the Pacific, bypassed Imperial troops waited glumly for evacuation—100,000 in the Solomons and New Guinea, 83,000 in the Carolines (50,000 at Truk alone), 30,000 in the Palaus, 15,000 in the Marshalls, 10,000 on Marcus and Wake Islands, 4,000 on Ocean and Nauru Islands, an unknown number in the Netherlands East Indies. All these eagerly scanned the horizons for sight of rescue fleets which never appeared.

It was almost all over, on the sea and in the air. Smashed on history's trash heap were 12 battleships, 19 aircraft carriers, 34 cruisers, 125 submarines of the Imperial Navy. There was no more protection from the naval arm. The sacred home islands for the first time were wide open to invasion.

Equally disastrous was the fate of Japan's prewar merchant fleet. Sinkings and damage by air attack and submarine attrition had reduced it from 10,000,000 to a mere 1,000,000 tons. From the Malay barrier to the home islands the ocean bottom was a junkyard heaped with wrecked Nipponese vessels.

The damage was described by Admiral Kichisaburo, who had made a survey of Japanese losses since the time of Pearl Harbor: "Submarines initially did great damage to our shipping and later, combined with air attack, made our shipping very scarce. Our supply lines were cut and we could not support these supply lines. Our experts knew that it was necessary to have 3,000,000 tons of shipping just for civilians living in Japan."

Hardest to take was the stepped-up air war. From their new bases the Americans coördinated Superfortress raids with fighter-plane attacks. By 1945 nearly 100,000 tons of bombs had been dropped on Japanese airfields, industrial targets, naval installations, cities, towns, and villages. Nearly half of Yokohama was obliterated in a single hour. Tokyo was almost scorched to the earth.

From Major General George C. Kenney, commander of the U.S. Far East Air Force, came a deadly challenge: Surrender, or he would strike Japan with 5,000 planes a day and transform it into a nation of nomads.

But still the war lords harangued and temporized. Their miscalculation had been great. They had grabbed too much too soon and they had found that guarding a 4,000-mile perimeter was beyond their capacity. But once more they voted to continue the suicidal resistance. "One hundred million die together!" Thousands of Japanese, Americans, and British were to lose their lives in the subsequent months because the war lords wanted to save face.

As early as 1943, a peace movement had been supported by such senior

Japanese statesmen as Prince Fumimaro Konoye, Reijiro Wakasuki, Baron Kiichiro Hiranuma, and Admiral Keisuke Okada. In February 1945 the Emperor, seriously concerned about the way the war was going, held several individual conferences with former prime ministers, his senior statesmen. Prince Konoye, who had resigned on October 16, 1941, after placing the responsibility for the decision to make war squarely on Hideki Tojo, chief spokesman of the army, made a frank statement in his audience with the Emperor.

"Sad though it is," said Konoye, "I believe that Japan has already lost the war. . . . I believe that it has at length become clear that the Manchurian Incident, the China Incident, and the Great East Asia War were all perpetrated by the national renovation faction of the militarists as part of a purposeful plan. . . . In my desire to achieve national unity I failed to perceive the real purpose hidden behind the contentions of the extremists. Since there is absolutely no excuse for my lack of foresight, I can only say that I feel gravely responsible for my failure in this respect. . . ."

The Imperial Navy was gone, the war machine out of fuel, the nation bankrupt, but still the war lords counseled no capitulation. Again came the interminable debates, explanations to save face, arguments about national polity, calls for suicidal defense, prophecies of miracles.

Japan was on the verge of total collapse. But the war went on.

ISLAND IN CONVULSION: THE ASHES OF IWO JIMA

Iwo Jima was just an ugly little island, eight miles square, on the doorstep of Japan. It had no vegetation. Its beaches were covered with soft and treacherous volcanic ash. The north end was a jungle of rocks, boulders, chasms, a maze of volcanic crevices, lava ledges, and steaming sulphur pits. At the southern end rose the slopes of Mount Suribachi, a rocky, extinct volcano, to which the Americans had given the grimly prophetic name, Hot Rocks.

But this miserable excrescence of volcanic rock was for both Japan and the United States one of the most important strategic points in the entire Far East. Just 750 miles from Tokyo, Iwo Jima was the indispensable island both for defensive and offensive operations.

Iwo Jima was the seat of Japan's "seeing eye" to warn Tokyo of the approach of bombers. With meticulous attention to detail, the Japanese transformed it into a rugged fortress, a kind of miniature Maginot Line in depth. They combined the volcanic ash with cement to make a concrete of high quality, and used this mixture to reinforce walls to a thickness of eight feet. They covered the entire island with interlocking underground strongholds, built thousands of blockhouses and pillboxes with steel-reinforced concrete, and fortified the caves, all cleverly camouflaged. They set up artillery and machine-gun nests to command every inch of the island. They sowed the beaches and the interior with heavy land mines. They had three airfields from which their fighter craft could rise to attack enemy aircraft coming from the Marianas. And to defend this island the Japanese sent the cream of their troops, some 23,000 men under the command of Lieutenant General Tadamichi Kuribayashi.

For the Americans this tiny speck of earth was equally desirable. The American bases in the Marianas Islands—Saipan, Tinian, and Guam—were 1,300 miles from Tokyo. A round trip by the huge B-29's took some 16 hours, leaving only a tiny fuel margin. In rough weather the giant planes were often doomed to crash landings in the Pacific. Iwo Jima, therefore, in American hands would be invaluable. One of the last outposts in the series of island-hops from New Guinea to Japan, it would be a perfect refueling depot for returning B-29's, a haven for crippled aircraft, and a base for fighter planes to accompany the bombers.

While General MacArthur was pushing ahead in the Philippines and the British Lieutenant General Sir William J. Slim was driving the Japanese out of Burma, the United States concentrated its naval, air, and land power on Iwo Jima. First the island was softened up by 74 consecutive days of pounding from the air and sea. By February 1, 1945, every available American plane in the Pacific was assigned to the Iwo mission. Two weeks later a task force consisting of six battleships and a screen of cruisers and destroyers slowly circled the island and plastered it with tons of huge shells.

Meanwhile, the Japanese defenders, secure in their blockhouses and caves, moved up more artillery to cover the beaches.

At dawn on February 19, 1945, a huge fleet of American transports joined the bombarding warships. Packed aboard these vessels were 30,000 Marines under the command of Major General Harry Schmidt. It was an extraordinary spectacle. The invading fleet formed a huge semicircle some seven miles out, while inside the arc amphibious landing craft churned the sea into foaming patterns. The Marines scrambled down shipside landing-nets into the landing craft. The small boats moved out to floating flags, around which they circled, waiting the signal to move ashore. On signal each unit moved behind its leader which, when close to land, turned parallel to the beach. When the whole line was parallel, the boats turned individually and made a dash for the shore, by this time smoldering under the terrific barrage.

The invaders, including veterans of every Marine landing since Guadalcanal, stepped into one of the bloodiest operations in their history. Not only did they find themselves up to their ankles in the loose volcanic ash, but they also became the targets for an enveloping fire that seemed to come from nowhere. Automatic weapons spat from narrow apertures only a few inches above ground level. The Marines had to pay in blood for every yard of progress. Nevertheless, within hours they carved out on the southeast coast a beachhead about 4,500 yards long and 500 yards deep.

The next stage was to advance up the rocky hillsides to the plateau. For 48 hours the assault troops had no sleep as they fought doggedly in drenching rain. At least 3,650 Marines were killed or wounded in the first two days of the battle. But at the end of three days the Americans controlled one-third of the blazing island.

Now the Marines commenced an enveloping drive against the second airfield, known as Motoyama No. 2. There was no cover on the approaches. Flame throwers and demolition experts were sent ahead to spearhead the assault.

A Marine correspondent described the hellish scene:

> The Japs were hard to kill. Cube-shaped concrete blockhouses had to be blasted again and again before the men inside were silenced. Often the stunned and wounded Japs continued to struggle among the ruins, still trying to fire back. A sergeant fired 21 shots at a semiconcealed Jap before the latter was killed. Another Marine assaulting a pillbox found a seriously wounded Jap trying to get a heavy machine gun into action. He emptied his clip at him but the Jap kept reaching. Finally, out of ammunition, the Marine used his knife to kill him.

In this ghastly slugging match the Marines took more than three days to cover 700 yards up sloping ground through the flaming defenses to the southern tip of the airstrip. With flame throwers and bazookas, with grenades and pistols, they pushed through the mouth of the Japanese fortifications. In an area only 1,000 yards long and 200 yards deep they smashed some 800 enemy pillboxes, one by one. At the crest of the slope bayonet-wielding Marines fell on the Japanese. American casualties were now more than 5,000.

Morrie Landberg, Associated Press correspondent, reported by radio:

> The whole of the small, gourd-shaped island is a battle zone, in the gray mist of day and through the chill blackness of the night. The front line may be the northern edge of the southern airfield captured by the Marines. It may be at the foot of Suribachi Yama under assault by other leathernecks. Or it may be just anywhere on the bomb- and shell-torn beachhead.

At the end of the fourth day the Marines had pushed their way to the base of Mount Suribachi. This was the key defensive position, from which the Japanese rained a torrent of shells on the beaches already littered with wrecked boats, tanks, and equipment. The congestion on the beaches was so great that almost every Japanese shell found a target.

There were now three divisions of Marines on the small island, so many of them that they found it difficult to avoid stepping upon one another. The

5th Division fought its way to the western shore, cutting the island in half, while the 4th Division in the north pushed westward. Then both divisions turned north to drive up the island.

Simultaneously, a tremendous barrage was loosed on Mount Suribachi from warships offshore and from bomber and rocket planes. The bombardment was not too effective; the Japanese defenses here had been planned for just such an emergency. The Marines of the 28th Regiment pushed their way straight up the extinct volcano, sidestepping the numerous Japanese mines, systematically blowing up the dugouts, foxholes, pillboxes, and caves.

On the morning of February 23, 1945, a patrol pushed over the brow of the topmost ridge and within minutes swung a flag-bearing pole into position. By a rare stroke of fortune this instant was caught forever by an Associated Press photographer, Joe Rosenthal. His shot became the most talked-about picture of World War II. For Rosenthal it won international praise and a Pulitzer prize. It was reprinted millions of times on posters for war-bond campaigns, in newspapers, magazines, books, eventually on a commemorative postage stamp. It became the new "Spirit of '45." After the war, for the first time in the history of civil or military art, a photograph was turned into a bronze statue group.

Mount Suribachi was captured. But it took a full 26 days. Not until March 15, 1945, was the American flag raised over all Iwo Jima. It was a costly triumph. The 3rd, 4th, and 5th Marine Divisions suffered 20,196 casualties, including 4,189 killed.

Appraising the action, Lieutenant General Holland M. Smith, commander of the Marine forces in the Pacific, commented: "The fighting was the toughest the Marines ran across in 168 years."

From Admiral Chester W. Nimitz came a message of congratulations to the Marines:

> In capturing Iwo, which is as important as it was tough, you have overcome the most difficult defenses that skill and ingenuity could construct on a small island that Nature herself had already made strong for military defense. Your victory, which was assured almost from the first landing, will brighten the pages of American history. Today, your fellow countrymen humbly and proudly sing your praise.

For the Japanese it was a heartbreaking catastrophe. To them, Iwo Jima was a part of the Tokyo prefecture, a piece of the homeland. Their troops on the island fought almost to the last man. More than 21,000 were killed and many others wounded. Just over 200 were taken prisoner.

A few weeks later, on the near-by island of Ie Shima, the American people sustained a sad loss when a shy, gnomelike little war correspondent was killed by a Japanese machine-gun bullet. Ernie Pyle hated the dirty business of war, but he felt his place to be with the men at the front. His dispatches were filled with homey details about acts of kindness and unselfishness, the loneliness of men bored to distraction behind the lines, the raw courage of boys who in battle became men. He told of the tired, dirty soldiers who did not want to die, of heroism and cowardice, of flowers and graves. "I believe that I have a new patience with humanity that I've never had before. . . . I don't see how any survivor of war can ever be cruel to anything, ever again."

The fighting men loved the bald little reporter from Indiana, who pictured so well their worm's-eye view of the war. Disconsolate, they placed this inscription on a simple monument at the place where he was killed:

At This Spot
The
77th Infantry Division
Lost a Buddy
Ernie Pyle
18 April 1945

OPERATION SUICIDE—THE *KAMIKAZES*

For the first time in history a nation at war used suicide as an official military weapon and called upon its warriors to go into combat with the prospect of certain death. But even this was too late to save Japan.

On the eve of Okinawa, Japanese Premier Kuniaki Koiso, appalled by the prospect of defeat, issued a solemn warning: "One hundred million countrymen! The enemy now stands at our front gate. It is the gravest moment in our country's history."

The Koiso cabinet resigned on April 5, 1945, just as Moscow denounced its 10-year nonaggression pact with Japan. Koiso's panicky successors decided on a desperate gamble. They would commit the remnants of the Imperial fleet in an all-out attack to shatter the American invasion at Okinawa. There was immediate action. A task force, including Japan's last battleship *Yamato* and a screen of cruisers and destroyers, left home waters and headed for Okinawa. It never reached its objective.

Intelligence reports of the Japanese move brought great joy to the U.S. Pacific Command. At long last that moment for which the U.S. Navy had worked and prayed!

Task Force 58 caught the Japanese fleet about 50 miles southwest of Kyushu in the East China Sea. Four hundred carrier-based fighters and bombers swooped down on the enemy. They sank the *Yamato*, two light cruisers, and three destroyers, and they left three more destroyers aflame. This was the last gasp of the navy that Tokyo had believed to be invincible.

Five months earlier, in October 1944, American sailors taking part in the raging sea battles off the Philippines reported that Japanese pilots were attempting to crash-dive their planes on American warships. Were these last split-second decisions? No one knew then. But when many warships, including the U.S. cruiser *Nashville*, received direct hits from diving planes, it became clear that the enemy had started a controlled suicide offensive.

Publication of Japanese records after the war revealed that at the great Battle for Leyte Gulf, Vice-Admiral Takijiiro Onishi, commander of the Japanese air forces in the Philippines, ordered a temporary measure to deal with a critical situation. He would be making his last mass attack on the enemy. Since his naval air arm could no longer provide adequate air cover, he concluded that it was necessary to immobilize the American carriers before they could launch their planes.

How to do this? Onishi would send out his pilots on bomb-laden Zero fighters to crash on enemy carrier decks. True, there was only a slight possibility that the big enemy battlewagons would be sunk this way, but they could be forced out of action during the decisive period when the Imperial Navy was making its final bid to destroy the enemy fleet. Onishi's pilots failed in this major task. The Americans were able to launch a horde of planes that wrought tremendous damage on the unprotected Nipponese capital ships.

After the Battle for Leyte Gulf, Onishi decided to carry on with the suicide tactics. Japan was now too weak in the air for conventional attacks on the enemy. He gathered his remaining pilots and told them: "The salvation of our country can come only from spirited young men such as you." He outlined his theory of a glorious death for Emperor and homeland and then presented his listeners with a launching poem:

In blossom today, then scattered:
Life is so like a delicate flower.
How can one expect the fragrance
To last forever?

Note that this was not particularly and peculiarly different from that legendary U.S. sergeant, who, going over the top in World War I, shouted to his men: "Come on, you bastards! Do you want to live forever?"

The difference was that the Americans, unlike Onishi's hot pilots, had a chance for life. But the Japanese airmen reacted with enthusiasm. From that moment was born the *Kamikaze Tokubetsu Kogekitai* (*Kamikaze* Special Attack Squad). It had all the volunteers it needed.

Behind it was a curious combination of Japanese theology and psychology baffling to Americans. The *Samurai*, or military code, refused to recognize even the possibility of defeat. From his early days in both family and school the Japanese child was taught that the only alternative to victory was death and that surrender was so disgraceful as to be unthinkable. Similarly, Japanese troops on the verge of defeat were expected to fall on the enemy, no matter what the odds.

Kamikaze tactics, born of desperation in the last stage of the war, were in effect a streamlined, air-minded improvement on the *Banzai* charge. They suggested the ritual Japanese obedience to superiors, veneration of the Emperor, loyalty to family and country, and belief in life of the spirit after death.

A favorite legend told the story of a *Kamikaze* (Divine Wind, Divine Tempest, Divine Typhoon), a providential typhoon sent by the Sun Goddess to wreck the huge fleet of the Mongol conqueror Kublai Khan in 1281. Now similar man-made strikes would be made to destroy the invaders from far-off America and keep the shores of the homeland inviolable. This was the secret weapon to snatch victory from the jaws of defeat.

There were two types of *Kamikazes.* The more refined was a piloted Japanese version of the German V-1 rocket. One model, the *Maraudi* glide bomb, a piloted 2,640-pound warhead, was launched from a conventional bomber, and guided at 600 miles per hour to its target by a single suicide pilot. The *Oka* (Cherry Blossom) model, dubbed *Baka* (stupid) by the Americans, was first used on March 21, 1945, off Japan's western shore and again at Okinawa. But there were too few of these piloted glide bombs to swing the tide of battle. Of some 800 constructed, only 50 were launched, and only three hit the target.

The second and more numerous type of *Kamikaze* was a plane of minimum construction, in design five years behind the current aircraft, without armor, but holding in its nose a supply of T.N.T., from 250 to 550 pounds, set to go off on contact.

Most of the pilots were youngsters who had only the minimal training necessary for their last assignment. Added to these were the few hard-bitten veterans—what was left of the Japanese air force. Before locking themselves in their cockpits to take off on their last journey on earth, the pilots held formalized parties in their ready rooms at which they were given ceremonial belts inscribed with the code of *Bushido.* They drank final toasts to the Emperor, to the life of the Japanese Empire, and to a glorious death. It would be bitter-sweet to die for the homeland, to conform to the code of their ancestors in this last noble act, to break the spirit of those weak Americans who considered human life so precious that they outfitted their planes with outlandish defensive devices. Nippon would smash the enemy with this ultimate weapon.

Some broke spontaneously into the strains of the *Kamikaze Song of the Warrior*:

In serving on the seas, be a corpse
saturated with water.

In serving on land, be a corpse covered
with weeds.
In serving the sky, be a corpse that
challenges the clouds.
Let us all die close by the side of
our sovereign.

Then the pilots composed their last letters home:

"We shall plunge into the enemy ships cherishing the conviction that Japan has been and will be a place where only lovely homes, brave women, and beautiful friendships are allowed to exist."

"May our death be as sudden and clean as the shattering of crystal . . . like cherry blossoms in the spring let us fall clean and radiant."

Reserve Ensign Susumu Kaijitsu: "My activities are quite ordinary. My greatest concern is not about death, but rather of how I can be sure to sink an enemy carrier. . . . Please watch for the results of my meager effort. If they prove good, think kindly of me, and consider it my good fortune. . . . Most important of all, do not weep for me."

Spaced out for miles off the shores of Okinawa was a huge armada of 1,500 Allied vessels, chiefly American, sitting ducks for the suicide squadrons. Most inviting targets of all were the aircraft carriers with their flat tops and enormous supplies of inflammable gasoline. Almost as vulnerable were the thin-skinned destroyers.

It was the most eerily gallant spectacle of the war. Like a swarm of angry wasps the *Kamikazes* descended on the fleet below, most aiming for the prized carriers. They came by the hundreds first during daylight, later at night, each pilot waiting for the opportune moment to sacrifice his life in a flaming dive.

"Babe Ruth, go to hell!" These were the last words of many a *Kamikaze* pilot, screaming what he considered to be the supreme insult.

From the American warships flowed a steady stream of antiaircraft shells in this most fantastic of all shooting galleries. Off in the distance were the fighting *Kamikazes*—planes ordered to draw off American sucker pilots and engage them while their comrades headed for the fleet. From carriers leaped fighters to destroy the attackers before they could make their final dives.

The suicide pilots failed to sink any capital ships during the 82 days and nights of the assault. But they did come close to eliminating one of the great American warships, the giant carrier *Enterprise*. Variously called "The Big E," "The Lucky E," "The Old Lady," and "The Galloping Ghost of the Oahu Coast," the *Enterprise* had seen action in every major sea battle since the beginning of the war. She had destroyed more than 70 enemy warships and had shot down nearly a thousand planes. Six times the ghost carrier had been reported sunk, but despite the fanciful stories of Japanese newsmen she had remained very much alive.

On May 14, 1945, planes from the *Enterprise* took off on a mission to strike at airfields in southern Japan. The next morning two dozen *Kamikazes* came roaring out of the southwest and headed for the carrier. One after another they were shot down or missed the target as they crashed into the sea.

One pilot, however, in a single-engined Zeke fighter loaded with a 600-pound bomb, craftily played hide-and-seek with the enemy below. Weaving in and out of a low cloud, he bided his time and then suddenly came hurtling down toward the island of the *Enterprise*. The plane, upside down, smashed into the center of the carrier, penetrating three decks. Fourteen American seamen were killed. The explosion blew a 30-ton elevator high into the air. Quick work by the damage-control crew saved the life of the venerable warship.

Statistically, the *Kamikazes* took a heavy toll: 34 American ships sunk and 288 damaged, including 36 carriers, 15 battleships, and 87 destroyers. During the Luzon operations, almost 2,000 U.S. and Australian navymen were killed by the suicide pilots. During the Philippines campaign, one in four *Kamikazes* damaged a target. At the height of the battle for the home islands the *Kamikazes* caused so much damage that shipyards in California were filled with warships sent home for repairs, while others had to be sent clear to the East Coast. A United States Strategic Bombing Survey concluded that the *Kamikazes* had wrought such damage that if the attacks had been sustained "in greater power and concentration they might have been able to cause us to withdraw or revise our strategic plans."

For their Divine Wind vengeance the Japanese paid with losses variously estimated at from 1,228 to 4,000 planes and pilots. But despite patriotism or stupidity, fanaticism or infantilism, Japan was doomed.

INCREDIBLE OKINAWA

Okinawa was the next objective in the final series of island hops.

The Japanese expected it. The Tokyo radio talked about it for days. When the invasion came, a broadcast solemnly informed the people that "It is a matter of a short time before the rise or fall of our people will be decided."

The main island in the southern part of the Ryukyu Archipelago, about 362 miles southwest of the major home island of Kyushu, Okinawa was regarded as an integral part of Japan. Commodore Matthew Calbraith Perry had visited it in 1853 when it was called Great Lew Chew. Strategically, it was of the utmost importance. There was plenty of room here for staging troops as well as airfield sites equipped to handle 5,000 planes.

Not only was Okinawa half again as close to Japan as Iwo Jima, but also it dominated the East China Sea and the Chinese coast from Foochow to Korea. It sat astride Japan's sea lanes to the supply-rich East Indies, already endangered by American occupation of the Philippines. From Okinawa, B-29's could range over the Yellow Sea and Straits of Shimonoseki and return with fuel to spare.

Okinawa was built by nature for rugged defense. Sixty-seven miles long and from three to 20 miles wide, its terrain was cut up in a maze of ridges, cliffs, and limestone and coral caves. On it the Japanese constructed ingenious fortifications, interlocking and intercommunicating tunnels, concrete blockhouses, pillboxes, and caves. Thus elaborately entrenched, they were certain to resist stubbornly and for a long time. They defended the malaria-ridden island with a garrison of 70,000 troops, later to be augmented with additional manpower, and 500 artillery guns. They were under no illusions—they had to make a stand here or lose the war. Okinawa was so important to the Japanese that their garrison there would fight to the death to defend it.

The Allies planned the invasion with minute care. Because of the large size of the island, the landing operations did not have to be limited to one or two heavily defended beaches as at Iwo Jima. But past experience made it certain that the defenders would resist fiercely.

On March 22, 1945, and continuing for ten days, Admiral Raymond A. Spruance's Fifth Fleet maintained a terrific bombardment of Okinawa and the Ryukyus, while B-29's now stationed at Iwo Jima attacked enemy bases on Kyushu. During the last four days before the landings, the Americans were joined by elements of the British fleet, which struck at the Sakishimas, the southernmost group of the Ryukyus. Under cover of this naval hail of fire a preliminary landing was made on Kerama Retto, west of Okinawa, by the 77th Division of the Tenth Army, under the command of Lieutenant General Simon Bolivar Buckner III. Within a few days these troops had their big guns trained on Okinawa.

Offshore waited the greatest invasion fleet ever to operate in the Pacific—1,300 warships of all kinds and sizes, and 100,000 soldiers and Marines aboard them. This was the armada attacked by Japan's *Kamikazes*.

Then came the big moment. On Easter morning, April 1, 1945, after the Japanese were thrown into confusion by a series of realistic feints against the southern tip and the east coast of Okinawa, the U.S. Tenth Army's 3rd Amphibious Corps and 24th Corps landed on the west coast. It turned out to be a repeat version of the storming of Iwo Jima. The attackers braced for an immediate vicious defense.

Then, in one of the strangest surprises in a war filled with surprises, the Japanese ashore offered little resistance. It looked easy. The troops swarmed ashore and quickly made the landing beaches secure in the face of only sporadic artillery, mortar, and machine-gun fire. Then came the mass of supplies in a seemingly endless stream.

The invaders pushed up the slopes into the interior, driving rapidly from the coral beachheads over the high terraces. The Marines headed toward the mountainous terrain to the north against only light resistance, while the Army infantry moved across the narrow island in the direction of Nakagusuku Bay on the east coast. By the second day the attackers penetrated three miles inland along an eight-mile front and captured two important airfields. By the end of the week the island was cut into two, and the central third was firmly in American hands. To the north the Marines advanced five miles. The Army's 24th Corps headed south.

Here, in the southern part of the island, the Japanese elected to make their stand. At a little "Siegfried Line" they massed the core of their army, protected by blockhouses, pillboxes, and machine-gun nests. The 85 square miles bristled like a porcupine.

At the end of the third week the Marines cleared the northern tip of the island. The Americans now held four-fifths of Okinawa, almost as a gift. Reinforcements were brought in for an all-out assault on the Japanese bastion in the south. The 7th, 27th, and 96th Divisions were augmented by two Marine divisions and the 77th Infantry Division, brought over from Kerama Retto. Veterans of Tarawa and Saipan were ready for battle.

The big push came on April 19, 1945, after a 13-day stalemate, as three American divisions stormed the enemy defenses in the south. The attack was preceded by a capital-gun bombardment from field artillery, battleships, and cruisers, while a huge umbrella of carrier planes shielded the ground forces.

During the opening days of the invasion, the Japanese had played possum, but now they began two months of most furious fighting. They fought from caves, pillboxes, even burial vaults. They had to be cleaned out from fortified ridge to ridge by flame throwers and demolition experts. Gains were reckoned in yards.

It was mid-May before the Marines broke into the suburbs of Naha, the western pivot of the Japanese position, and into Shuri, equally important strategically. The fighting was most intense around Sugar Loaf Hill, near Naha, and Conical Hill, dominating Shuri, both of which changed hands again and again. On May 21, 1945, the Marines finally took Sugar Loaf Hill, and about the same time the 96th Division captured Conical Hill. On May 30 the First Marines captured Shuri. A fortnight later Naha and its airfield were taken. The Japanese defenders were now reduced to 15,000 fanatical troops holding out in the hills and caves.

On June 11, 1945, General Buckner urged the Japanese to surrender. The offer was ignored. The fighting went on with the defenders cut into shallow pockets of resistance. Out went orders to "cut them to pieces."

On June 18, 1945, on the eve of victory, General Buckner, a hearty, white-haired, 58-year-old Kentuckian, was sitting on a coral rock at the front lines watching the Marines in action. He was struck and killed by a shellburst. "The general was smiling when he was hit," reported an aide, "and the smile remained on his face even in death. He didn't know what hit him." Buckner eventually was succeeded by the celebrated General Joseph W. Stilwell, hero of the campaign on the Asiatic mainland.

Four days later, on the morning of June 22, 1945, Lieutenant General Mitsuru Ushijima, commander of the Japanese forces on Okinawa, and Lieutenant General Isama Cho, dressed themselves in full field uniforms with their medals and insignia of rank pinned on their tunics. At 3:40 A.M. the two generals, accompanied by some aides and staff members, went to a narrow ledge before their cave headquarters. Assistants placed a heavy comforter on the rough shelf and laid a white sheet over it as a symbol of death. Ushijima knelt on the sheet. Cho knelt to his left. According to the *Samurai* code, it was customary in committing *Hara-kiri* to face toward the Japanese Imperial Palace, but the two commanders had to face west to the Pacific because of the narrowness of the ledge. Then came *Seppuku*, honorable suicide. The generals ripped open their bowels, whereupon a lieutenant struck off their heads with a sword. American troops were in foxholes just a hundred yards away.

Simultaneously, came a grotesque series of suicides. Many Japanese leaped to their deaths from the cliffs. One Marine lieutenant told an extraordinary story to the Associated Press. Together with four other Marines he was chasing the enemy when they came to a clearing and found themselves surrounded by 350 Japanese holding swords, guns, and grenades. The lieutenant, with rare presence of mind, smiled and offered them cigarettes. Several dropped their weapons and reached for the cigarettes. The officers, all accompanied by women, refused the gift. One drove his sword through his woman companion, handed his sword and a wrist watch to the astonished lieutenant, stepped back, and blew off his own head with a grenade. The infection spread rapidly, until the killing of the women and the suicides mounted to the rate of one a minute. For two hours the transfixed Americans watched the slaughter. Just as their cigarettes ran out, reinforcements appeared, whereupon the rest of the enemy surrendered.

The behavior of trapped Japanese troops was inexplicably bizarre. Naked men would dash out of their caves, throw dirt in the faces of the Americans, then race back behind the rocks and either slit their throats or blow themselves up with grenades. One crazed soldier fired at a Marine, missed, and became so infuriated with himself that he screamed and threw his rifle away in disgust. Others sought death in frenzied *Banzai* charges. Many a flabbergasted Marine stared open-mouthed in amazement.

Japanese casualties at bloody Okinawa amounted to 109,629 killed, 7,871 taken prisoner. There was despair in Tokyo. The loss of Iwo Jima had been bad enough, but that island was only a pinpoint in the ocean and it had only three airfields. Okinawa was something else again. The enemy was on the doorstep and the chances were that he would not remove his shoes.

For the Americans, Okinawa was the costliest of all Pacific conquests—12,520 killed and missing, 36,631 wounded. This was almost twice the casualty rate of Iwo Jima. But in terms of strategy the victory was worth the cost.

In the words of Admiral Chester W. Nimitz: "Establishment of our forces on Okinawa has practically cut off all Japanese positions to the southward as far as sea communications are concerned. It has made the Japanese situation in China, Burma, and the Dutch East Indies untenable and has forced withdrawals which are now being exploited by our forces in China."

Okinawa was set up as the final base for Operations Olympic and Coronet, the invasion of the Japanese home islands. The contemplated date was November 1945.

This potentially bloody dual project never took place. There was something considerably more final in the air.

HOLOCAUSTAL INCANDESCENCE: HIROSHIMA AND NAGASAKI

24 July 1945

TO: General Carl Spaatz
Commanding General
United States Strategic Air Forces

1. The 509 Composite Group, 20th Air Force will deliver its first special bomb as soon as weather will permit visual bombing after about 3 August 1945 on one of the targets: Hiroshima, Kokura, Niigata, and Nagasaki. To carry military and civilian scientific personnel from the War Department to observe and record the effects of the explosion of the bomb, additional aircraft will accompany the airplane carrying the bomb. The observing planes will stay several miles distant from the point of impact of the bomb.

2. Additional bombs will be delivered on the above targets as soon as made ready by the project staff. . . .

/s/ Thos. T. Handy
General, GSC
Acting Chief of Staff

With this military order, one of the most fateful in mankind's long history, the wheels were set in motion for a highly secret and daring enterprise. The incredible blasts of atomic bombs on Hiroshima and Nagasaki knocked Japan out of the conflict. So great was the shock among all humanity that even the end of the global war became secondary news.

Behind the atomic bomb was an extraordinary story of how scientists wrested from Nature the secrets of dynamic energy. Toward the end of the nineteenth century there arose a doubt about the indivisibility of the atom (the word *atom* is derived from the Greek *atomos*, meaning "indivisible"). The reason for this doubt was an observation made by a French physicist, Antoine Henri Becquerel, who had noted that a piece of uranium kept in a desk caused the blackening of some photographic plates near by. This peculiar property of uranium to emit radiation was called radioactivity.

Soon two new elements, polonium and, somewhat later, radium were discovered by Pierre and Marie Curie. Radium when kept enclosed produced a gas which appeared to be helium. It began to be obvious that heavy atoms did not stay unchanged, but rather broke apart.

To buttress the experimental evidence, Max Planck's quantum theory (1900) and Albert Einstein's special theory of relativity (1905) provided formulae to determine the amount of energy released by the atom. The French mathematician, Jules Henri Poincaré, suggested to the then-unknown young physicist Einstein that the speed of light should be accepted as the "limiting value" in the study of mass and energy. Einstein accepted the advice, and out of it came his famous formula $E = mc^2$, E being energy, m being the mass in grams, and c being the velocity of light in centimeters per second.

Physicists throughout the world now bent their energies to the task of splitting the atom and turning loose the energy within its core, which they believed to be staggering. Niels Bohr of Denmark, with his publications on the structure of the atom, laid the foundation for everything that was to follow. Lord Ernest Rutherford of England, using radium, found three different kinds of rays, *alpha, beta,* and *gamma,* which shot out from the radium very much as if fired out of a gun barrel. The critical year was 1932, when two associates of Lord Rutherford, C. D. Cockcroft and E. T. S. Walton, built an "atom smasher" in the physics laboratory at Cambridge University, England, in which they accomplished the transformation of lithium and hydrogen into helium and in the process confirmed Einstein's equation.

The same year, 1932, saw a series of remarkable discoveries. Sir James Chadwick, realizing that some of the experiments on the atom had produced results that could not be explained only with protons and electrons, discovered the electrically neutral particle in the atom which he called the *neutron.* During the same year, Professor Harold C. Urey, then of Columbia University, isolated one of those isotopes (radioactive versions of common and harmless elements), that had long been talked about as a theoretical necessity in splitting the atom. It was in 1932, too, that J. Fréderic Joliot and his wife Irène Curie (daughter of Pierre and Marie Curie) produced radioactivity artificially.

Two years later, in 1934, Professor Enrico Fermi, then at the University of Rome, began bombarding uranium with neutrons. Subsequently, Fermi escaped from Fascist Italy and came to the United States. His experiments paid off in the fall of 1938 when a team of scientists at the Kaiser Wilhelm Institute in Berlin, composed of Dr. Otto Hahn, Dr. Fritz Strassmann, and Dr. Lise Meitner, split the uranium atom, publishing the statement that neutron bombardment of uranium caused the formation of barium. Meanwhile, Dr. Meitner, being Jewish, had to leave Nazi Germany and went to Denmark to work with Niels Bohr. Both Meitner and Bohr came to the United States.

A fantastic truth began to dawn on the scientists—uranium–235 would split when hit with a neutron and the fission of one such atom would release several free neutrons which would set off a chain reaction.

The international race to produce an atomic bomb was on. On August 2, 1939, Einstein sent a historic letter to President Franklin D. Roosevelt:

> In the course of the last four months it has been made probable through the work of Joliot in France, as well as [Enrico] Fermi and [Leo] Szilard in America, that it may become possible to set up a nuclear chain reaction in a large mass of uranium, by which vast amounts of power and large quantities of new radium-like elements would be generated. Now it appears this could be achieved in the immediate future.
>
> This new phenomenon would also lead to the construction of bombs, and it is conceivable, though much less certain—that extremely powerful bombs of a new type may thus be constructed. A single bomb of this type, carried by boat and exploded in a port, might very well destroy the whole port, together with some of the surrounding territory. . . .

Spurred on by Einstein, Roosevelt, without consulting Congress because of the necessity for secrecy, set in motion a giant project that ultimately expended $2,500,000,000. The war itself stimulated the battle of the laboratories. In 1940, although the United States was not at war and Britain was, Roosevelt and Churchill agreed to pool the resources of both their countries to find the secrets of the atom and to yoke its energies to military use. British scientists had already played a major role in the spectacular discovery of radar and in the stages leading toward the atomic bomb, but England was constantly exposed to bombing and the possibility of invasion, while the United States, far from the range of enemy aircraft, had the enormous industrial and economic resources required for the tremendous experiment.

There was real reason to fear that the Germans might win the battle to produce the bomb. In 1942 it was learned that German scientists were hard at work on the project, which they hoped to add to V-1 and V-2 flying bombs to bring destruction to the Allies. A vital factor in the eventual outcome of the race was a daring raid by British and Norwegian commandos on German heavy-water (*deuterium*) installations in Norway during the winter of 1942–

1943. At a heavy cost of life the raiders destroyed the Nazi source of heavy water, an important element in one of the processes used to produce the atomic bomb.

The original undertaking in the United States was placed in the hands of Dr. Vannevar Bush, Chief of the Office of Scientific Research and Development. President Roosevelt named a policy committee composed of Vice-President Henry A. Wallace, Secretary of War Henry L. Stimson, Chief of Staff General George C. Marshall, and Dr. James B. Conant, President of Harvard University. At the suggestion of this group a committee of scientists was set up, including Dr. J. Robert Oppenheimer, Dr. Arthur H. Compton, Dr. Ernest O. Lawrence, and the Italian-born Dr. Enrico Fermi. In 1942 the task of creating the bomb was entrusted to a special unit of the Army Corps of Engineers, headed by Major General Leslie R. Groves. Thus was born the famed Manhattan Project.

On December 2, 1942, the first controlled chain reaction in history was produced on the campus of the University of Chicago. Meanwhile, two gigantic plants were constructed for the task of producing the bomb, one at Oak Ridge, Tennessee, and the other at the Hanford Engineer Works at the government-built town of Richland, in an isolated area 15 miles northwest of Pasco, Washington. Both these plants were government owned and operated. At Los Alamos, on an isolated high mesa near Santa Fe, New Mexico, a special laboratory was set up under the direction of Professor Oppenheimer to deal with technical problems concerned with the production of the bomb.

It was a tremendous undertaking, without parallel in history. Some 125,000 workers were needed to construct the huge plants and at least 65,000 to operate them. The work was so completely compartmentalized that no one worker was given any more information than was absolutely necessary for his particular job. It was the best-kept secret of the war. Only a very few Americans knew the nature of the project. The secrecy was so great that even the highest-ranking officials in Washington, including Harry S. Truman, later to be President, did not have the slightest idea of what was going on.

When the first bomb was dropped on Japan, the workers at Oak Ridge were as astonished as the rest of the world. One enterprising Oak Ridge newsdealer sold 1,600 copies of a local newspaper at a dollar each in 35 minutes to the amazed men who had worked to produce the bomb.

July 16, 1945. A great cloud of cosmic fire and smoke, the atomic-age version of the old Arabian story about a poor fisherman and a jinni imprisoned in a bottle, rose more than eight miles to the stratosphere over the New Mexico desert near Alamogordo. In this secret test a steel tower holding the test model was vaporized when the bomb exploded. The hard, solid desert was depressed to a depth of 25 feet, forming a huge saucer-shaped crater. Windows rattled 250 miles away. People hundreds of miles from the spot of the explosion were mystified when a brilliant light flamed over the entire landscape.

The spectacle was described by Brigadier General Thomas F. Farrell, deputy to the general in charge of the bomb project:

> The effects could well be called unprecedented, magnificent, beautiful, stupendous, and terrifying. No man-made phenomenon of such tremendous power had ever occurred before. The lighting effects beggared description. The whole country was lighted by a searching light with [an] intensity many times that of the midday sun. It was golden, purple, violet, gray, and blue. It lighted every peak, crevasse, and ridge of the near-by mountain range with a clarity and beauty that cannot be described.
>
> Thirty seconds after the explosion, came, first, the air blast, pressing hard against the people and things, . . . followed almost immediately by the strong, sustained, awesome roar which warned of doomsday and made us feel that we puny things were blasphemous to dare tamper with the forces heretofore reserved to the Almighty.

At long last the secret weapon to put a quick end to World War II had been found. Man, pygmy though he was, had invaded the sacred precincts of the cosmos.

The weapon was perfected too late to be used on the European theatre of war. "If we had had the atomic bomb in Europe," said General Carl A. Spaatz, "it would have shortened the war six to eight months."

But what about Japan? Plans had already been laid for amphibious landings in the fall of 1945 in Kyushu, southernmost of the Japanese home islands. But, in view of fanatical Japanese resistance in the past, it was believed that it would take until the fall of 1946 before Japan could be defeated by conventional military action. General Marshall estimated that it would cost at least half a million American lives to force a Japanese surrender.

True enough, Japan was being plastered unmercifully by conventional means. Swarms of American long-distance bombers and fighters were assaulting the home islands daily almost without opposition. The two most frequently bombed cities. were Nagoya, aircraft-manufacturing center, and Tokyo, military and political fulcrum. Nagoya was blasted almost beyond recognition. Attempts were made to disperse Nagoya's machine and assembly lines, but the B-29's relentlessly tracked down each move and smashed the new sites as soon as they were in working order.

Similar devastating attacks were made on other cities. By the end of July 1945 nearly a hundred Nipponese cities and towns were burned, seared, and charred. Only four major cities remained undamaged: Kyoto, Sapporo, Hiroshima, and Nagasaki.

Many Japanese wondered why.

Secretary of War Henry L. Stimson, the man directly responsible to President Truman for the entire atomic bomb program, believed that, despite the tremendous damage caused by conventional weapons, the United States must use every possible means of shocking Japan into surrender. The atomic bomb would do it, he reasoned. Admittedly, thousands of civilians would be killed in the explosion, but in the long run many more American as well as Japanese lives would be saved by using the weapon. Moreover, the blast would give the hard-headed Japanese a method of face-saving that would lead directly to peace.

Stimson's arguments carried weight.

Saving a half-million American lives was the determining factor in the decision to use the atomic bomb. The committee of scientists who developed the bomb recommended that it be used immediately against the enemy on a target that would show its devastating power. The scientists rejected the idea that a specific warning be given by demonstrating the effectiveness of the bomb on an uninhabited island. "We can propose no technical demonstration likely to bring an end to the war; we see no acceptable alternative to direct military use."

The final decision of when and where to use the bomb was left to President Truman.

> Let there be no mistake about it, [he wrote later] I regarded the bomb as a military weapon and never had any doubt that it should be used. The top military advisers to the President recommended its use, and when I talked to Churchill he unhesitatingly told me that he favored the use of the atomic bomb if it might aid to end the war.

The American top command decided that the bomb should be dropped as close as possible to a war-production center of major military importance. General Henry H. Arnold, of the Air Force, suggested that Kyoto be the target because it was a center of military activity, but this plan was dropped when Secretary Stimson pointed out that the city was a Japanese cultural and religious shrine. The targets were listed in this order: Hiroshima, Kokura, Niigata, and Nagasaki.

On July 24, 1945, at the Potsdam Conference, President Truman mentioned to Stalin that the Americans had a powerful new weapon from which the Japanese could expect "a rain of ruin from the air, the like of which has never been seen on this earth." The Russian dictator revealed no special interest. He simply said that he was glad to hear the news and hoped that the Americans "would make good use of it against Japan." It is possible that Stalin already knew basic details of the atomic bomb through the work of the American Communist agents Julius and Ethel Rosenberg, later to be executed for espionage activities.

An ultimatum to Japan issued at Potsdam on July 26, 1945, by the United States, Great Britain, and China received no formal reply, but on July 28

Radio Tokyo announced that the Japanese would fight on. The decision was then made to drop the bomb on or about August 3 unless the Japanese surrendered before that day.

A specialized unit of seven B-29 Superfortresses, known as the 509th Composite Group, with pilots and crews ready, waited at Tinian in the Marianas for the order to strike. The plane selected to carry the lethal cargo was assigned to Colonel Paul W. Tibbets, Jr., who as a major had been sent to England to join the newly formed Eighth Air Force. In this capacity he had piloted the first B-17 to cross the English Channel on a bombing mission over German-occupied France. flown nine missions over Germany, and led the first formation to bomb North Africa. The B-29 he piloted over Hiroshima was named *Enola Gay*.

Only three men aboard the *Enola Gay* were fully aware of the nature of the mission—Tibbets, Navy Captain William S. Parsons of Santa Fe, New Mexico, an ordnance expert. and Major Thomas W. Ferebee of Mocksville, N. C., the bombardier. The rest of the crew knew little beyond the fact that they were on a highly secret, vital mission.

Everything seemed to be normal in Hiroshima, a city of 343,000, on that Monday morning, August 6, 1945. Then came an air-raid warning as two B-29's flew over the city. As was customary, the people hurrying to work rushed for the safety of shelters. They emerged when the all-clear sounded. Then a lone Superfortress appeared over the city. This time there was no alert, no rush for the shelters. After all, it was just one plane.

From the bomb bay of the *Enola Gay* a large black object hurtled toward the earth.

Suddenly a piercing, blinding light, as bright as the sun, burst over the city. There was an instant of deadly silence. Then an earth-shaking shock thundered violently down over the center of the city, crumbling everything in its range to rubble and dust.

Pilot Tibbets described the time immediately after the impact:

> After we dropped the bomb we did a roundhouse turn to get out of the shock wave.
>
> When the shock wave hit us the plane was in a bank. The plane snapped like a tin roof, but there was more noise than shock. . . .
>
> Twice we made our S-shaped maneuvers taking pictures with our two cameras, one in the nose and one in the tail. We were never closer than a mile from the cloud, but we were close enough to watch it boil. It turned many different colors—orange and blue and gray. It was like looking over a tar barrel boiling. There was lots of black smoke and dust and rubble that gave the appearance of boiling. We couldn't see the city at all through the thick layer of dust nor could we see the fires beneath. A circle of dust outlined the area of destruction.

In a few moments most of Hiroshima was smashed flat, all living things in its center burned beyond recognition.

Navy Captain Parsons:

> It was 0915 when we dropped our bomb and we turned the plane broadside to get the best view. Then we made as much distance from the ball of fire as we could.
>
> We were at least ten miles away and there was a visual impact even though every man wore colored glasses for protection. We had braced ourselves when the bomb was gone for the shock and Tibbets said "close flak" and it was just like that—a close burst of antiaircraft fire.
>
> The crew said "My God" and couldn't believe what had happened.
>
> A mountain of smoke was going up in a mushroom with the stem coming down. At the top was white smoke but up to 1,000 feet from the ground there was swirling, boiling dust. Soon afterward small fires sprang up on the edge of town, but the town was entirely obscured. We stayed around two or three minutes and by that time the smoke had risen to 40,000 feet. As we watched the top of the white cloud broke off and another soon formed.

This one bomb, holding in its vitals a destructive force of 20,000 tons of T.N.T., descended five miles by parachute, exploded before it landed, and left no crater.

The violent blast following the flash crushed trees and telephone poles as if they were toothpicks, ripped sheets of metal from buildings, squashed buildings, and lifted streetcars from their tracks. When the great rolling cloud of dust and smoke, spiraling upward to form a long-necked mushroom, lifted, some 60 per cent of Hiroshima had vanished—about $4\frac{1}{10}$ square miles of a city of $6\frac{9}{10}$ square miles. Hiroshima had become a trash heap. Five major industrial targets were obliterated. Thousands never knew what hit them. At least 78,000 were killed outright, more than 10,000 were never found, and 37,000 were injured, without counting those who later developed serious disease from exposure to the deadly gamma rays.

Large drops of water the size of marbles began to fall—drops of condensed moisture spilling from the tower of dust, heat, and fission fragments. Streets were littered with fire-blackened parts of shattered houses. Sheets of flame whipped through the city. Panicky people fled in every direction. The eyebrows of many were burned off and skin hung loosely from their faces and hands. Others, in uncontrollable pain, held their arms forward as if they were carrying something. Some vomited as they staggered along. Throughout the area of impact there was a strong odor of ionization, an electric smell given off by the bomb's fission.

The novelist-journalist, John Hersey, who later investigated the situation at Hiroshima, revealed what had happened in a sensational 30,000-word story, to which the *New Yorker* magazine devoted its entire issue of August 31, 1946. He reported the experiences of six survivors at the moment when the bomb exploded. The Reverend Mr. Kiyoshi Tanimoto, a Methodist pastor, although two miles from the center of the explosion, was surrounded by collapsing homes. Mrs. Hatsuyo Nakamura, widow of a tailor, 1,350 yards from the center of the blast, "seemed to fly into the next room over the raised sleeping platform, pursued by parts of the house." Miss Toshi Sasaki, a clerk in a tinworks plant 1,600 yards away, was crushed when her room suddenly collapsed, and her left leg was pinned down by a falling bookcase. "There, in the tin factory, in the first moment of the atomic age, a human being was crushed by books." On the front porch of his private hospital, Dr. Masakayu Fujii was caught by two long timbers forming a V across his chest, "like a morsel suspended between two huge chopsticks." Father Wilhelm Kleinsorge, a Jesuit priest, stunned by the blast, found himself wandering around in his mission's vegetable garden in his underwear, while his housekeeper, near by, cried in Japanese, "Our Lord Jesus Christ, have pity on us!" Dr. Terufumi Sasaki, the only surgeon in the Red Cross hospital to escape injury, kept himself occupied by treating maimed and dying citizens, an invasion "that was to make Dr. Sasaki forget his private nightmare for a long, long time."

That same day President Truman was on the cruiser *Augusta* on the fourth day of his journey home from Potsdam. He was handed an urgent message:

> To the President
> from the Secretary of War
>
> Big bomb dropped on Hiroshima August 5 at 7:15 p.m. Washington time. First reports indicate complete success which was even more conspicuous than earlier test.

In a few minutes there came a second message:

> Following info regarding Manhattan received. Hiroshima bombed visually with only one tenth cover at 052315A. There was no fighter opposition and no flak. Parsons reports 15 minutes after drop as follows: "Results clear cut successful in all respects. Visible effects greater than in any test. Conditions normal in airplane following delivery."

The President, accompanied by Secretary of State James F. Byrnes, went to the *Augusta*'s wardroom, where the ship's officers were at lunch.

In a voice tense with excitement, he said:

> Keep your seats, gentlemen. I have an announcement to make to you. We have just dropped a bomb on Japan which has more power than 20,000 tons of T.N.T. It was an overwhelming success.

Then the President repeated the news to crew members in various parts of the ship. To the correspondents aboard he issued a statement, which read in part:

> The greatest marvel is not the size of the enterprise, its secrecy, nor its cost, but the achievement of scientific brains in putting together infinitely

complex pieces of knowledge held by many men in different fields of science into a workable plan. . . . It is doubtful if such another combination could be got together in the world. What has been done is the greatest achievement of organized science in history. It was done under high pressure and without failure.

We are now prepared to obliterate more rapidly and completely every productive enterprise the Japanese have above ground in any city. We shall destroy their docks, their factories, and their communications. Let there be no mistake; we shall completely destroy Japan's power to make war.

From Winston Churchill came a statement saying that it was "by God's mercy" that American and British, instead of German, scientists had discovered the secret of atomic power.

The stunned Japanese press denounced the attack as "inhuman," "barbaric," "bestial." "This diabolical weapon brands the United States for ages to come as a destroyer of justice and of mankind." Radio Tokyo reported:

The impact of the bomb is so terrific that practically all living things, human and animals, literally were seared to death by the tremendous heat and pressure engendered by the blast. All the dead and injured were burned beyond recognition. With houses and buildings crushed, including emergency medical facilities, authorities are having their hands full in giving every available relief possible under the circumstances. The effect of the bomb is widespread. Those outdoors burned to death, while those indoors were killed by the indescribable pressure and heat.

The Japanese High Command ignored an ultimatum to surrender. Three days after Hiroshima a second atomic bomb, improved so far that the first was already obsolete, was dropped on Japan with even more devastating results.

This time the target was the Kyushu Island city and railroad terminal of Nagasaki. Though its population of 250,000 was smaller than that of Hiroshima, Nagasaki was a major supply port for Japanese military and naval operations throughout the Pacific and an important shipbuilding and repair center for both warships and merchantmen. Its combined area was nearly double that of Hiroshima.

An eyewitness, William L. Laurence of *The New York Times*, who accompanied the mission, told how a giant ball of fire rose from Nagasaki as though from the bowels of the earth, belching forth enormous white rings. "The entity assumed the form of a giant square totem pole, with its base about three miles long, tapering off to about a mile at the top. Its bottom was brown, its center was amber, its top white. But it was a living totem pole, carved with many grotesque masks grimacing at the earth."

In Nagasaki itself all was chaos. Not even the range of protecting canyons and hills surrounding the city could save it from the destructive blast of atomic energy. The bomb hit between Japan's largest torpedo factories and a huge steel mill, reducing these modern steel buildings to a mass of twisted girders. In the municipal area, three miles long and two miles wide, there was nothing left except debris. Tens of thousands died in the searing white blast.

This was the convincer—for even the most obtuse of Tokyo's war lords. It was clear now that nothing, not even a million fanatical *Kamikazes*, could counter this "divine wind" from the laboratories of America. More of this, and Japan would be wiped from the face of the earth.

There were many in the Allied countries who were overjoyed by the almost certain end of the war. But there were also many others who were appalled and saddened by the use of this superhuman fireball of destruction.

THE JAPANESE SURRENDER

It was Sunday, September 2, 1945, exactly three years, eight months, and 25 days since the attack on Pearl Harbor. While a stream of giant Allied transport planes poured airborne troops onto the Japanese airfields and while seaborne troops moved ashore, the formal ceremony of surrender took place aboard the United States battleship *Missouri* in Tokyo Bay. The stage was set for an impressive ritual.

The 45,000-ton *Missouri*, U.S. Pacific Fleet flagship, which only a few weeks earlier had been blasting the Japanese mainland with her 16-inch guns, was now anchored peacefully within sight of Fujiyama. Her bow was directed toward the heart of Japan, her great rifles pointed skyward to allow room for the ceremony. From her foremast flew the same flag that had waved over the Capitol in Washington on December 7, 1941—the date that had lived in infamy. Also flying was the historic flag of Commodore Perry, which, with its 31 stars, had been the first American flag to be used on Japanese soil some 92 years before. Surrounding the *Missouri* was a gigantic array of American and British fighting strength.

Nine members of the Japanese delegation, three in formal clothes and top hats, and six in uniform, were piped aboard. All their faces showed strong muscular tension. Led by Foreign Minister Mamoru Shigemitsu, limping on his artificial leg, they were escorted to a table on the galley deck on which were two copies of the surrender documents, one bound in gold and the other in black. Every inch of available deck space was taken by Allied fighting men.

With the Japanese delegation standing before him, General Douglas MacArthur faced the microphones and began to speak:

> We are gathered here, representatives of the major warring powers, to conclude a solemn agreement whereby peace may be restored. The issues, involving divergent ideals and ideologies, have been determined on the battlefields of the world and hence are not for our discussion or debate. Nor is it for us here to meet, representing as we do a majority of the peoples of the earth, in a spirit of distrust, malice or hatred. But rather it is for us,

both victors and vanquished, to rise to that higher dignity which alone benefits the sacred purposes we are about to serve, committing all of our peoples unreservedly to faithful compliance with the undertakings they are here formally to assume.

It is my earnest hope and indeed the hope of all mankind that from this solemn occasion a better world shall emerge out of the blood and carnage of the past—a world founded upon faith and understanding—a world dedicated to the dignity of man and the fulfillment of his most cherished wish—for freedom, tolerance and justice.

The terms and conditions upon which the surrender of the Japanese Imperial Forces is here to be given and accepted are contained in the instrument of surrender now before you.

As Supreme Commander of the Allied Powers, I announce it my firm purpose, in the tradition of the countries I represent, to proceed in the discharge of my responsibilities with justice and tolerance, while taking all necessary dispositions to insure that the terms of surrender are fully, promptly and faithfully complied with.

I now invite the representatives of the Emperor of Japan and the Japanese Government and the Japanese Imperial General Headquarters to sign the instrument of surrender at the places indicated.

Shigemitsu stepped forward, took off his silk top hat, pulled off his long yellow gloves, checked two watches, took out his pen, and then signed the two copies, writing his name in English on one of them. Next, General Yoshijiro Umezu, representing the General Staff, nervously and quickly signed for the Japanese army and all the Japanese armed forces as personal representative of the Emperor of Japan.

General MacArthur then asked two of his colleagues to step forward and accompany him while he signed. They were Lieutenant General Jonathan M. Wainwright, commander of Bataan and Corregidor, and Lieutenant General Arthur Percival, the British commander at Singapore, both of whom had been rescued only a few days earlier from Japanese prisoner-of-war camps. The two generals, gaunt but smiling, saluted. General MacArthur used five pens in signing the documents, handing the first two silver-plated pens to the two commanders who had been forced to surrender Corregidor and Singapore.

Then came a series of additional signatures: Admiral Chester W. Nimitz for the United States; the youngish General Hsu Yung Chang for the Chinese Republic; Sir Bruce Fraser for Great Britain; and Lieutenant General K. Derevyanko, flanked by an honor guard of three Russians—one navy, one air force, one army—for the Soviet Union. There was a momentary hitch when Sir Thomas Blamey, the Australian representative, signed the Japanese document first by error.

As further signatures were affixed to the documents by representatives of the Allied nations, the sun, which had been behind the clouds during the early part of the ceremony, broke through and bathed the scene in brilliant light.

General MacArthur: "Let us pray for peace . . . and that God will preserve it always. These proceedings are closed."

Thus came to an end the long, tragic trail from Bataan and Corregidor through New Guinea, the Marianas, and the Philippines to Japan. The guns at last were silent.

After the ceremony a great flight of 436 Superfortresses sped over Tokyo in a demonstration of American air power for the Japanese people. Simultaneously, a 42-ship convoy steamed into Tokyo Bay and by nightfall landed some 13,000 troops to augment the first 20,000 already ashore.

From the White House, President Harry S. Truman informed the American people by radio about the unconditional surrender. He proclaimed Sunday, September 2, 1945, to be V-J Day, the day of the formal surrender of Japan.

Two days later Emperor Hirohito, after worship at *Shinto* shrines in the imperial palace grounds, instructed his people to "win the confidence of the world" by obeying the nation's commitments (he pointedly avoided the use of the word "surrender"). He issued an order to all Japanese field commanders "forthwith to cease hostilities, to lay down their arms."

On September 8, 1945, an American flag was raised over Tokyo. It was that same flag that had flown over the dome of the Capitol at Washington on the day of Pearl Harbor, over Casablanca, Rome, and Berlin, and at the foremast of the *Missouri* on V-J Day.

This was total, devastating defeat, the first in Japanese history, the end of the Japanese dream to control half or all the world. In the first six months after Pearl Harbor the Nipponese military hierarchy as well as the people, both conditioned by centuries of myth and tradition, believed themselves to be unconquerable and invincible. But in a little over a year the balance, both quantitatively and qualitatively, had shifted to the Allies. By 1945 the homeland was being bombed unmercifully and Japan was on the verge of complete collapse when she surrendered.

Why did the Japanese fail? One of the main reasons was that their strategists never understood the meaning of total war nor how to wage it. Modern war is a coöperative effort in which every element of a nation's life is brought into play. The Japanese made the mistake of challenging a country whose productive capacity was ten times their own. Their leaders, uninspired, unrealistic, failed to understand that the strategic and tactical methods of the past were obsolete in twentieth-century war. Lacking the scientific knowledge to meet the Americans on equal terms, the Japanese did not realize that a perfect imitation of last year's weapons was just not enough. Weak in imagination, creativity, and originality, they were never able to match such new weapons as proximity fuses, radar, aerial mines, ground-to-air rockets, the whole galaxy of new weapons thrown at them by the Allies.

Above all, the Japanese underestimated the role of air power. At the end of the war about half the Japanese fighter planes were essentially the same Zero that had been used in China years beforehand. The planners in Tokyo labored under the fantastic idea that this plane would win the war. The Zero was in truth a beautiful, fast-climbing, maneuverable weapon of attack, but it was quickly outmoded in the crucible of combat experience. Further, the Japanese were never successful in developing mass-bombing techniques nor were they ever able to maintain a sustained heavy air offensive. They were out-planned, out-guessed, out-fought.

Similarly, the Japanese foot-soldier, nourished on the principle of attack, found it difficult to function in a situation that called for initiative and resourcefulness. True, he had courage—tested on a hundred battlefields—but he had little training in the intelligent use of courage. The American soldier, caught in a defensive trap, made it his business to fight his way out and remain alive; the Japanese soldier, once on the defensive, poured out his strength in frustrated, suicidal, useless *Banzai* charges. From his limited point of view it was a glamorous death bringing glory and honor to his family and to himself, but it was poor soldiering.

Added to these factors was the brilliant success of American strategy in the Pacific War. The plan was simple: Chop off the tentacles of the Japanese octopus, one by one, and advance air power to the point where its full fury could be unleashed on the four home islands. Japan's far-flung empire was useless to her unless she could keep it supplied and could import the raw materials to keep her factories humming. The American response was to destroy enemy shipping and smash the Japanese industrial potential.

The teamwork of American ground, sea, and air forces was phenomenally successful. U.S. submarines gradually whittled down the Japanese merchant fleet; American air and naval power in combination reduced the enemy's navy to impotence; American ground forces met and conquered the Japanese on scores of islands; American air power made a heap of scarred ruins of Japan's war industry and burned down her cities. The Nipponese wilted and broke under the impact of this concentrated power.

Part VII

EPILOGUE

CHAPTER 25

Aftermath

Give me ten years and you will not be able to recognize Germany.

—Adolf Hitler, 1933

I see the world gradually becoming a wilderness, I hear the ever-approaching thunder, which will destroy us, too. I can feel the suffering of millions, and yet, if I look up into the heavens, I think that . . . this cruelty, too, will end.

—Anne Frank (died at Bergen-Belsen)

THE LEDGER OF DEATH AND DESTRUCTION

Two thousand, one hundred and ninety-one—*repeat,* 2,191—days of conquest, slaughter, misery, famine, and death.

The most devastating conflict in man's bloody history had finally come to an end. The war had been fought by the greatest number of men, 70,000,000 in all, with the greatest number of machines, over the greatest spaces ever recorded.

The peoples of the United Nations, suddenly released from the agony of suspense and terror, hailed the victory that they thought might never come. In the Axis countries the people wept for their lost sons and vanished dreams.

The skeptics played the sour note. The war, they said, had been an unnecessary tragedy. It had settled nothing. Men had died in vain. But others saw the achievement of a not ignoble end: The triumvirate of Hitler-Mussolini-Tojo, striking with weapons of hatred, cynicism, terror, and butchery, had come within inches of destroying the code of Western civilization and introducing a world of slavery. That challenge had been thwarted.

The cost in human lives was astronomical. At least 17,000,000 men were killed on the battlefields, one out of every 22 Russians, of 25 Germans, of 46 Japanese, of 150 Italians, of 150 Englishmen, of 200 Frenchmen, of 500 Americans. More than 18,000,000 civilians died in one way or another. The casualties were twice those of World War I. And the lists would have been immeasurably higher had not one out of every two wounded soldiers been saved by new sulfa drugs and by blood plasma transfusions.

Equally depressing were the material losses. The direct cost in military expenditures was a trillion dollars; property damage was at least twice that figure. Throughout Europe the land was laid waste as if by a gigantic scythe. From the Seine to the Volga, from the Oder to the Tiber, Europe was crisscrossed by trails of destruction. Great cities were smashed to rubble; square miles of factories were obliterated; transportation was in chaos. In the countryside large tracts of farmland were taken out of production for years by the scorched-earth policy of one side or another; productivity of the soil was reduced by inadequate fertilization; flocks and herds were decimated. The whole structure of European society seemed to be shattered.

It would take decades to make up the huge deficits of food, clothing, and housing. Most European and Asiatic countries were crippled by economic dislocations and their people were haunted by the specter of inflation. Vast populations were on the move. Prisoners of war streamed back to their homelands. Millions of refugees wandered—or were shunted—from one land to another in search of safety and security.

Human misery, distress, agony of spirit cannot be measured in quantitative terms. The moral fabric of mankind had been damaged almost beyond repair. The years of hatred, emotional torment, and starvation had left a mark that even time could not erase.

The German people paid heavily for the attempt to dominate Europe. Some 20,000,000 of them went to Hitler's war; 3,250,000 died in battle, 3,350,000 died from other causes, 7,250,000 were wounded, and 1,300,000 were missing. Added to this melancholy list was the appalling physical destruction. It is estimated conservatively that their adventure in Hitlerism cost the Germans at least $272,000,000,000.

World War I had ended with German troops everywhere on enemy soil and their homeland virtually untouched. But in 1945 Hitler's Third Reich was overrun by Allied troops and devastated almost beyond recognition. Of Germany's 20,000,000 buildings, some 7,000,000 were either completely destroyed or damaged. More than 2,000 bridges were ruined; 3,000 miles of railroad track were smashed into grotesque metal puzzles. The streets of virtually all the major cities were blocked by giant heaps of rubble. Berlin was a ghost city, its public and private buildings in ruins, its transportation facilities and public utilities wrecked. Hovering over the capital was the stench of death. Dazed survivors trudged among the ruins searching for families and friends or competing with the rats for food.

More than anything else the Germans had wanted victory in World War II. What they got was utter defeat, almost as complete as that of ancient Carthage. Psychologically unprepared for the catastrophe, inured by tradition to obedience and discipline, they now floundered as helplessly as fish out of water. There had been in Germany no organized resistance to the bestial Nazi dictatorship (postwar publicists manufactured a whole series of anti-Hitler movements). Relief from the Nazi strait jacket came from the outside.

For Japan the taste of defeat was equally bitter. Of her 9,700,000 men under arms, 1,270,000 were killed in battle, 620,000 died otherwise, 140,000 were wounded, and 85,000 were missing. Her navy was totally annihilated, her merchant marine 95 per cent destroyed. Gone were both the great empire and the dreams of expansion. From one end of the islands to the other, Japanese cities were reduced to ruins.

The Japanese had cause to "remember Pearl Harbor" in a different sense. The militarists of Tokyo had assumed that one great and sudden blow would leave the Americans confused, irresolute, and divided. They could have made no greater mistake. Pearl Harbor was instead a huge galvanic shock that made the American people united, determined, and invincible. Japan paid heavily for that error.

Brutal marks were left on Italy, the third major Axis power. Of her 3,100,000 men under arms, there were 144,496 battle deaths, 66,716 wounded, and 135,070 missing. Some 208 Italian warships were destroyed, and 49 more surrendered. Italy lost 90 per cent of her merchant marine. The total military cost for Italy was enormous, as a result of which the public debt was increased sixfold and the lira lost 90 per cent of its purchasing power. This is what the Italians had to pay for 23 years of paper-and-tinsel Fascist glory! Instead of a world-blinding new Roman Empire, they got the bitter taste of defeat, frustration, misery. Vanished were Mussolini's vaunted bayonets, gone was the flamboyant *Duce* himself. Postwar Italy was a vast poorhouse, filled with breaking hearts and apathetic minds, with hunger in the streets and ruin in the marketplaces. From north to south along the entire Italian boot almost every railway station lay wrecked by Allied bombers. An already impoverished people, faced with starvation, scrounged through the countryside searching for food. For many the black market meant the difference between life and death.

The United Nations, too, suffered heavily. Even triumphant Britain was gravely weakened in the conflict. Britain had mobilized 5,896,000 men, of whom 357,116 died, 369,267 were wounded, and 46,079 were missing. Her great merchant marine, despite the surge of wartime construction, declined from 23,000,000 to 16,000,000 tons. There was serious destruction in the home island. A half-million homes were smashed to ruins, another 4,000,000 were damaged. The national debt spiraled from $40,000,000,000 to more than $100,000,000,000, while the foreign debt increased more than sixfold from $2,000,000,000 to $13,000,000,000. Britain's vast overseas investments, which had long enabled her to maintain a favorable balance of trade, disappeared into thin air. Britain was now eclipsed in power and prestige by her mighty American partner.

The British contribution to victory was a magnificent one. With extraordinary single-mindedness they had stood alone against the Axis in the early days of the war, and then had carried through to the end. "There'll Always Be an England!" ran the popular ditty. And many recalled the words of Shakespeare:

This England never did, nor never shall,
Lie at the proud feet of a conqueror.

The impact of World War II on France was not as catastrophic as that of World War I, but it was nevertheless severe. Of her armed forces there were 201,568 killed, 261,577 other deaths, 400,000 wounded, and 140,000 missing. Thirty thousand Frenchmen died before firing squads, 188,000 other civilians lost their lives, 150,000 were deported, and 38,000 prisoners of war died in captivity.

French human losses were matched by property damage. A half-million homes were totally destroyed, another million and a half seriously damaged. The country was covered with wrecked bridges, smashed factories, and demolished farms. Only 3,000 of 17,000 locomotives were left at the end of the war; 10 per cent of all railway tracks were destroyed. More than a half of the French merchant marine was gone, nearly three-quarters of the port facilities. The countryside was strewn with thousands of land mines left behind by the retreating Germans.

The unexpected defeat by Germany and five years under the conqueror's heel had dealt French morale a vicious blow. Something had vanished from the traditionally self-confident French character. Even the will-to-life seemed to have been affected. The French government, concerned by the stagnant birth rate, hastened to supply testosterone—male hormones—to the emaciated prisoners returned from captivity or to any others who requested it.

The Soviet Union suffered worst of all—6,115,000 military deaths from all causes, 14,012,000 wounded. In the defense of Stalingrad alone the Russians lost more than did the Americans in all their World War II campaigns. More than 10,000,000 Russian civilians were killed, and at least 25,000,000 were left homeless. Marshal Stalin was reported to have said that for the

Allied victory the Russians gave blood, the British contributed time, and the American supplied goods. Distorted as this conclusion was, it still emphasized the tremendous human sacrifice necessary for the Russians to expel the German invaders.

Almost as tragic was the trail of destruction left by Nazi hordes on Russian soil. More than 800,000 square miles of western Russia were laid bare. Towns, villages, factories, railroads were wiped from the face of the earth. The destruction was almost incredible: 13,000 bridges, 4,100 railroad stations, 482,000 freight cars, 15,800 locomotives. It was truly a Nazi scourge.

Russian losses in life and property, as enormous as they were, were counterbalanced in part by important gains. The U.S.S.R. emerged from the war with a gain of 262,533 square miles of territory and 22,162,000 more people. In Eastern Europe, where she had been sealed off by buffer states after World War I, the Soviet Union set up a series of satellite states dominated from Moscow—Poland, East Germany, Lithuania, Latvia, Estonia, Rumania, Bulgaria, Czechoslovakia, and Albania, an area totaling 433,504 square miles with a population of 90,874,358. For the first time in nearly a century, since the humiliating Crimean War, the Russians had finally won a great and decisive victory. The U.S.S.R. now surged to the topmost level among the world powers. The United States and the Soviet Union became the new titans of world society.

For the United States, too, the cost of victory was high. World War II was the most costly in lives of all American conflicts since the Revolution of 1775–1783. Of the total of 16,112,566 Americans serving in all branches of the armed forces, there were 1,078,674 casualties, including 293,986 battle deaths, 113,842 other deaths, and 670,846 wounded. Americans killed from December 7, 1941, onward were greater than the combined losses of both the Union and Confederate forces in the Civil War. In 1943 the American casualty rate was about 5,000 a month; in the early months of 1944, as the tempo of fighting increased in the Mediterranean area, it went to 13,700 a month; after the Normandy invasion it leaped to 59,000 and then to 81,000 a month by December 1944. American dead were buried from Bastogne to Iwo Jima.

"It is impossible," said General George C. Marshall, "for the Nation to compensate for the services of a fighting man. There is no pay scale that is high enough to buy the services of a single soldier during even a few minutes of the agony of combat, the physical miseries of the campaign, or of the extreme personal inconvenience of leaving his home to go out to the most unpleasant and dangerous spots on earth to serve his Nation."

Military and civilian property losses for the United States amounted to at least $350,000,000,000. But there was some comfort in the fact that the United States had contributed its fair share to the destruction of the Axis tyranny.

It was a costly but necessary sacrifice upon the altar of freedom. It boiled down to a simple matter—Americans had no intention of living as slaves of Hitler, Mussolini, or Tojo.

GENERAL MARSHALL REPORTS

The deeds of battlefield commanders like Eisenhower, MacArthur, Montgomery, and Rommel exploded in headlines throughout the world. But behind them, chained to desks, were the great strategists, leaders trained to large-scale thinking, wise in the ways of managing a technocratic war. Among these great men was General George C. Marshall, Chief of Staff of the United States Army, and one of the American representatives on the Combined Chiefs of Staff.

In his final report to the Secretary of War, General Marshall gave a comprehensive review of the war. "For the first time since assuming office six years ago," he wrote, "it is possible for me to report that the security of the United States of America is entirely in our own hands." In order to establish for the historical record where and how Germany and Japan failed, General Marshall requested General Eisenhower to have his Intelligence officers promptly interrogate the ranking members of the German High Command who were now prisoners of war.

The results of these interviews are of remarkable interest. Here is a précis of the sections of the Marshall Report on what the interrogations of the captured Germans disclosed:

Hitler intended to create a Greater Reich which would dominate Europe. But no evidence has yet been found to show that the German High Command had any over-all strategic plan to achieve Hitler's goal. The High Command approved Hitler's policies in principle, but his impetuous strategy outran German military capabilities and ultimately led to Germany's defeat.

During the early campaigns in Poland, Norway, France, and the Low Countries serious divisions developed between Hitler and the General Staff on details of execution of strategic plans. In each case the General Staff favored an orthodox offensive, Hitler an unorthodox attack with objectives deep in enemy territory. In each case Hitler won out, and his prestige rose to a point where he was no longer challenged. There was no General Staff objection when he made the fatal decision to attack Soviet Russia.

Italy's entry into the war, contrary to her agreement with Germany, was undesired by Germany because it put an added burden on German war potential. Mussolini's unilateral action in attacking Greece and Egypt forced Hitler into the Balkan and African campaigns. This resulted in overextension of the German armies which became one of the principal factors in Germany's defeat.

Nor was there any evidence of close strategic coördination between Germany and Japan. It appeared that Tokyo acted unilaterally and not in accordance with an over-all unified strategic plan.

"Here were three criminal nations," General Marshall reported, "eager for loot and seeking greedily to advance their own self-interest by war, yet unable to agree on a strategic over-all plan for accomplishing a common objective."

The steps in the German defeat, as described by captured members of the High Command, were indicated in the Marshall Report:

1. *Failure to Invade England.* Hitler's first military setback occurred when, after the collapse of France, England did not capitulate. The German High Command did not believe that England would continue to fight, hence it was unprepared for an invasion of England. Field Marshal Wilhelm Keitel stated that the risk was thought to be the British fleet. The German army was ready, the navy dubious, the air force limited by weather. Meanwhile, the *Luftwaffe* suffered irreparable losses in the Battle of Britain from which it never recovered.

2. *The Campaign of 1941 in the Soviet Union.* In the autumn of 1941 the Germans stood exhausted but apparently victorious before Moscow. But a sudden change in weather brought disaster. It was the turning point of the war.

3. *Stalingrad.* Despite the reverse at Moscow in 1941 Germany might have avoided defeat if it had not been for the campaign of 1942 which culminated in the disaster at Stalingrad. Responsible were the magnificent Russian defense of that city and the fact that in the northern foothills of the Caucasus there was a breakdown of German transport which stalled German armor for three critical weeks in the summer of 1942. The Germans failed completely to estimate properly the reserve of Russian industrial and productive power east of the Urals.

4. *The Invasion of North Africa.* Allied landings in North Africa came as a surprise to the German High Command. Allied security and deception measures for the landing operations were highly effective. The Germans made no advance preparations to repel such an Allied invasion of North Africa; hence all subsequent efforts to counter the Allies suffered from hasty improvisation. Since evacuation was impossible, the Germans had only the choice of resisting or surrendering.

5. *The Invasion of France.* All German headquarters expected the Allied invasion of France. Both the general direction and the strength of the initial assault in Normandy were correctly estimated. But the Germans were not sure exactly where the Allies would strike and considered Brittany as more probable because of the three major U-boat bases located there.

Prior to the invasion, divergences of opinion developed between Field Marshal Gerd von Rundstedt, Commander in Chief West, and Field Marshal

Erwin Rommel, commander of the threatened Army Group. Rundstedt wanted to hold his armored reserve in a group around Paris and in eastern France; Rommel to push them forward to the coast. Rommel won out.

Soon after the Allied capture of Cherbourg, dissension again broke out in the High Command. Von Kluge and Rommel wanted to evacuate all southwestern France and withdraw from Normandy before disintegration began. Hitler refused and ordered von Rundstedt to continue the Battle of Normandy to its final denouement.

6. *The Ardennes Counteroffensive.* The German offensive in December 1944 was Hitler's personal conception. The objective of the attack was Antwerp. Hitler hoped that overcast weather would neutralize Allied air superiority and that a rapid breakthrough could be achieved. Other German officers pronounced the operation reckless in the extreme, because it irreparably damaged Germany's strategic reserves, at a moment when every available reserve was needed to repulse the expected Soviet attack in the East.

7. *The Crossing of the Rhine.* Even after the Ardennes failure, the Germans believed that the Rhine line could be held. The loss of the Remagen bridge, however, exploded this hope. The entire Rhine defensive line had to be weakened in the attempt to contain the bridgehead. The disorderly German retreat in the Saar and Palatinate made easy the eastward Allied drive toward Hamburg, Leipzig, and Munich.

Meanwhile, the Eastern partner of the Axis, Japan, was working in even greater discord. The Axis really existed only on paper. Eager to capitalize on the preoccupation of the Western Allies in Europe, Japan was so greedy for her own immediate conquests that she laid her strategy, not to help Hitler defeat Great Britain and Soviet Russia, but to accumulate her own profit. Had the way been open Germany and Japan would undoubtedly have joined in Central Asia. But to Tokyo this objective was secondary to looting the Far East while there was no real force to stop her.

Japan's strategy initially failed when she missed the opportunity of landing troops on Hawaii, capturing Oahu and the important bases there, and denying the United States a necessary focal point from which to launch operations in the Western Pacific.

In General Marshall's opinion, there could be no doubt that the greed and mistakes of the war-making nations as well as the heroic stands of the British and Soviet peoples saved the United States a war on her own soil. The crises at Stalingrad and El Alamein had come and passed before the United States could take part in the fighting in a determining manner. Had the Germans won at these two points—as well they might have if Germans, Japanese, and Italians had better coördinated their plans, resources, and successive operations, then the United States would be standing in the Western Hemisphere, confronted by enemies who had control of a greater part of the world.

SEQUEL IN IGNOMINY: RETRIBUTION FOR RENEGADES

Postwar France was in moral chaos.

Five years of Nazi occupation, years of ceaseless propaganda, treachery, and terror, had left deep psychological scars on the French people. The heroes of the Resistance discovered that those same qualities that had once aroused the admiration of their fellow citizens were now regarded as antisocial and disruptive of law and order. It was not easy to cast aside the patterns learned during the occupation period—black markets, petty thievery, false identity cards, counterfeit ration coupons, lying, deceit, betrayal. But on one thing the French were adamant—there must be *revanche* for the renegades who, under the Nazi heel, had disgraced the good name of France.

In the first intoxication of victory the French public took things into its own hands, seeking out and killing known collaborators. Women who had fraternized with the Germans were shorn of their hair, forced to march through the streets while carrying placards identifying their misdeeds, and spat upon by enraged Frenchmen. There was a countrywide demand that the Vichy officials still at work be deprived of their jobs. The courts began to grind out convictions of some 100,000 collaborationists. In July and August 1945 more than 500 traitors were sentenced to death.

What to do with the aged Marshal Henri Pétain, nearly 90, was an agonizing problem. Not only had the World War I hero of Verdun accepted the German armistice terms on June 22, 1940, but he had also become the first chief of the puppet Vichy government, in which capacity he had danced like an aged prima donna to Nazi demands. Some Frenchmen attributed Pétain's defection to senility. But he was convicted of treason and sentenced to death. General Charles de Gaulle, provisional president, unwilling to allow his old chief to die a traitor's death, commuted the penalty to life imprisonment.

There was mercy for Pétain, but none for the real master of Vichy France—Pierre Laval. The name of Laval, long despised, was now anathema to the furious French public. Stocky, swarthy, beetle-browed, the 61-year-old chief of the collaborationists had had a checkered career distinguished by deceit, underhandedness, and trickery. "What can you expect?" asked a political enemy. "The name of Laval can be spelled backward as well as forward!"

A former delivery-wagon driver, Laval had pushed his way to financial success as a newspaper publisher. In World War I he posed as a pacifist, but there was reason to believe that even at that time he had helped the Germans by subtle defeatist propaganda. An effective orator and a rugged politician, he quickly worked his way to the top political level, becoming premier in 1931 and again in 1935. His ever-present trade mark—a white tie—became a symbol for the world's cartoonists.

An early admirer of Mussolini, Laval was the co-author of the notorious Hoare-Laval Agreement of December 1935, which invited Italy to cease its war against Ethiopia in return for annexation of the extensive territory she had conquered and a large measure of authority over the rest of that kingdom. The disclosure of this unscrupulous "plan for peace" aroused a storm of public indignation in both England and France.

After France had been defeated by Germany in 1940, Marshal Pétain, the new Chief of the French State, designated Laval as his first assistant and successor. In December 1940 Pétain dismissed his aide upon hearing rumors that Laval, with Nazi help, intended to execute a *coup d'état* on December 15 during ceremonies connected with removal of the remains of Napoleon's son, the Duke of Reichstadt, from Vienna to Paris. Laval was placed in confinement, but was given his freedom when the Germans demanded his release.

On August 27, 1941, a youngster, Paul Colette, in protest against the rumor that Laval intended to raise a volunteer French army for German use against Russia, attempted to assassinate the collaborationist. The young Frenchman was arrested with a smoking pistol in his hand. Laval, seriously wounded, recovered rapidly.

In April 1942 the Germans, aware of Laval's usefulness, prevailed upon the old marshal to bring him back into power. This time Laval became Chief of the Government, leaving Pétain with the empty title of Chief of the State. Now in effective control of the internal and foreign policy, Laval emerged as the virtual dictator of Vichy France. He worked closely with the Germans, helping the dreaded *Gestapo* to ferret out resistance groups and sending suspects to German concentration camps. In October 1942 he announced plans to draft French factory workers between 18 and 50 to be shipped to Germany; in exchange, the Nazis would return one French prisoner of war for each three skilled French workers received. Such was the nature of Nazi mathematics.

Before the scheme could be put into effect, Hitler occupied all France following the landing of Allied forces in French North Africa in November 1942. In 1943 Laval announced to all the world that "German victory will save civilization." For plenty of good reasons the man with the white tie was passionately hated by French patriots.

Laval was brought to trial before a jury in Paris. He proved an obstreperous witness. He shouted denunciations at his accusers, who in turned cursed him openly in court. The trial lasted four days, but during the last two days the accused boycotted the courtroom, remained in his cell, and entered no defense. In just one hour the jury returned a verdict of death.

Early on the morning of October 15, 1945, the date fixed for his execution, Laval made an unsuccessful attempt to take his own life by poison in his prison cell at Fresnes. Later, under similar circumstances, Hermann Goering, the No. 2 Nazi, was to succeed in cheating the executioner. Doctors restored Laval to sufficient life to be led to the prison courtyard. After he declined a proffered blindfold, his last request was that he be allowed to give the firing order to the execution squad. It was refused.

His last words: "It is not the fault of the soldiers. They know not what they do. *Vive la France!*"

The riflemen fired. Laval, still alive, sank to his knees. An officer hurried up, placed his pistol to Laval's ear, and pulled the trigger. The body was cast unceremoniously into a hearse and borne to Thais cemetery, where it was thrown into the ground and covered. A newsman took note of another grave near by marked: "Here lies an unknown collaborator."

Nine days later, at dawn on October 24, 1945, in the execution square of the ancient Akershus Fortress in Oslo, Vidkun Quisling paid his penalty to Norwegian justice. For five years after the conquest of Norway, this pompous weakling had been Hitler's satrap. His attempts to convince his countrymen that their destiny lay with the Germans had fallen flat. Unreconciled Norwegians carried on a steady campaign of strikes and sabotage. The Quisling regime could exist only on a prop of Nazi bayonets.

In greatest secrecy Quisling was hurried through a drizzling rain to the execution spot. To the end he maintained that he was a patriot misunderstood by his fellow countrymen. A firing squad of 10 Norwegian military police, all of whom had once been forced to leave the country, ended the life of this miserable puppet.

Elsewhere it was the same stern story.

On December 12, 1945, a special Dutch court in The Hague decreed death for Anton Adrian Mussert, leader of the Nazi party in The Netherlands. Mussert had worked hand-in-hand with the German invaders.

The British, too, had their share of renegades. On September 17, 1945, William Joyce, known as Lord Haw Haw, who had broadcast insulting and ridiculing speeches to England from Germany, was brought to trial for high treason. He sought in vain to evade the penalty of British law by claiming American citizenship. Convicted, he turned to the House of Lords, the English court of last resort, but his appeal was denied. He was executed later.

On December 19, 1945, John Amery, 33-year-old son of L. S. Amery, former secretary of state for India, was found guilty of treason and was hanged at Wandsworth Prison. Young Amery had broadcast over the Nazi radio the startling world-wide news beat that the *Wehrmacht* was defending European civilization.

Outstanding among American collaborators was Ezra Pound, Idaho-born poet, editor, and literary critic, the most famous of the American expatriate writers of the post-World War I period and leader of the disillusioned "Lost Generation." Fascinated by the grandiloquent trappings of Fascist Italy and perhaps nursing an old Semitophobia dating from his Idaho childhood, Pound, during World War II, broadcast pro-Axis propaganda lauding the dictators and violently denouncing Jews and democracy. In 1945 he was charged with treason, flown on a military transport from Rome to Washington, and handed over to the Department of Justice. On December 21, 1945, a board of four psychiatrists pronounced the eccentric poet insane and found that he was mentally unfit to stand trial. He was committed to St. Elizabeth's Hospital in Washington, where he remained for 13 years.

Pound was finally released in the early summer of 1958 as still mentally deranged but harmless. The now 73-year-old poet, still bitter and unreconciled, went to Italy, where he greeted his friends with the Fascist salute, again damned the Jews as destroyers of civilization and as the cause of his own troubles, and announced that he was happy to quit America, "that huge insane asylum."

THE NUREMBERG TRIALS: JUSTICE OR *REVANCHE*?

The triumphant Allies came out of the war flushed with victory but divided upon many policies except one—the Axis war criminals were to be punished.

This time the mass murder, the multiple crimes, the atrocities against millions of persons and dozens of nations had been so flagrant and so terrible that any evasion of punishment could not be tolerated. In an agreement dated August 8, 1945, among the United States, Great Britain, and the Soviet Union, it was decided to bring the Nazi leaders to trial. The decision was subsequently indorsed by 19 member states of the United Nations.

Four judges were selected for this International Military Tribunal. British Lord Justice Geoffrey Lawrence was named the presiding judge. The United States was represented by Francis Biddle, former United States Attorney General, France by Henri Donnedieu de Vabres, and the Soviet Union by Major General Johann T. Nokitchenko. At the prosecutor's table sat Justice Robert H. Jackson of the United States Supreme Court, Sir David Maxwell-Fyfe heading the British delegation, Charles Dubost for France, and Colonel Yuri Pokrovsky for the Soviet Union.

On October 18, 1945, the four prosecutors filed a 24,000-word indictment against six German organizations and 24 of Hitler's Nazi hierarchy and German military and naval leaders. The indicted organizations were:

1. The German General Staff and the High Command of the German armed forces.

2. The Reich Cabinet, including the secret Cabinet Council, members of the Defense Council, state ministers, ministers without portfolio, and governmental department heads.

3. The Nazi party leadership, "the central core of the conspiracy," including all party officers, *Gauleiter*, and the like.

4. The S.S. (*Schutz-Staffeln*), or Élite Guard, originally set up as a personal bodyguard for Hitler and other Nazi leaders, which later developed into a repressive police force and German army auxiliary.

5. The S.A. (*Sturm-Abteilung*), the Nazi storm-trooper organization, consisting of the mass of Hitler's early followers.

6. The *Gestapo*, or secret police, accused of the most horrible kinds of torture.

Indictments were drawn up against 24 individuals:

Hermann Wilhelm Goering, No. 2 Nazi, commander of the *Luftwaffe* through the war, creator of the first concentration camps, one of the prime Nazi leaders.

Joachim von Ribbentrop, Nazi foreign minister, former ambassador to England, the motivating agent behind the Hitler-Stalin pact of 1939, instigator of anti-Jewish measures.

Alfred Rosenberg, close friend of Hitler, philosophical leader of National Socialist ideology, director of "spiritual training of the Nazi party."

Wilhelm Frick, Thuringian civil servant, early Nazi leader in the *Reichstag*, later Nazi "protector" for Bohemia and Moravia.

Julius Streicher, foul-mouthed bigot and Nazi editor of the notorious pornographic *Der Stürmer*, whose vulgar anti-Semitism strongly influenced the coarser Germans. "The Jew is the devil in human form." Franconian *Gauleiter*.

Walther Funk, former minister of economics, *Reichsbank* president, active go-between for the Nazis and big business.

Rudolf Hess, deputy to the *Fuehrer*, No. 3 Nazi, moderator and adjuster in intraparty squabbles and conflicts.

Hans Frank, Bavarian lawyer responsible for harmonizing National Socialism with law. "Hitler is the greatest lawgiver in history." "Law is the will of the *Fuehrer*." Nazi governor general of Poland.

Konstantin von Neurath, former Nazi foreign minister, later protector of Bohemia and Moravia.

Franz von Papen, debonair political adventurer in both world wars, behind-the-scenes schemer, Nazi diplomat, wartime ambassador to Turkey.

Ernst Kaltenbrunner, chief of the Nazi security police, bearer of directives from Hitler and Himmler for extermination of the Jews, S.S. general, member of the *Reichstag*, state secretary for security in Austria, police leader of Vienna.

Hjalmar Horace Greeley Schacht, financial wizard, former Nazi economics minister, *Reichsbank* president, technical expert behind the huge Nazi rearmament program.

Fritz Sauckel, S.S. and S.A. general.

Baldur von Schirach, head of the Nazi youth movement. "I read Henry Ford's book *The International Jew* . . . and I became anti-Semitic."

Artur von Seyss-Inquart, Nazi chancellor of Austria, later commissar for The Netherlands.

Albert Speer, technical genius responsible for building the Nazi war machine.

Hans Fritzsche, leading Nazi editor and propagandist.

General Wilhelm Keitel, field marshal, chief of the German High Command.

General Alfred Jodl, chief of staff of the German army.

Admiral Erich Raeder, grand admiral and former navy chief.

Admiral Karl Doenitz, grand admiral and commander in chief of the German navy.

Robert Ley, chief of the Nazi Labor Front.

Gustav Krupp von Bohlen und Halbach, German industrialist and head of the famous Krupp steel and arms works.

Martin Bormann, chief of the S.A., head of the *Volksturm* (People's Army), instigator of the mass killings of German clergymen.

Twenty-one of the 24 defendants indicted were given 30 days to prepare their defense. Martin Bormann, who either died in the ruins of Berlin or made his escape, was tried *in absentia*. Robert Ley, apparently overwhelmed by a sense of guilt, committed suicide before the trials began. And Gustav Krupp von Bohlen und Halbach, who was not a member of the Nazi Party, was declared too ill to be tried.

Of the defendants, the two generals, Keitel and Jodl, and the two admirals, Doenitz and Raeder, in addition to Krupp, were not listed as Nazi party members. The names of these four top military and naval leaders were included in the indictment at the insistence of Justice Jackson of the United States. Representatives of Britain, France, and Russia opposed the move on the ground that these men were merely soldiers who were carrying out orders from a superior, Adolf Hitler, who had committed suicide. The American position was that these officers could have "stopped what became a norm fostered or condoned by headquarters," and, therefore, headquarters, in the person of the commander, was directly responsible. The indictments of the military and naval leaders were retained.

All the defendants were indicted on four counts: conspiracy to commit crimes against peace; crimes against peace; war crimes; and crimes against humanity.

The wording was coldly legal: "The defendants, with divers other persons, are guilty of a common plan or conspiracy for the accomplishment of crimes against peace; of a conspiracy to commit crimes against humanity in the course of preparation for war and in the course of the prosecution of the war; and of a conspiracy to commit war crimes not only against the armed forces of their enemies but also against nonbelligerent populations."

The list of crimes: Murder, deportation to slave labor, ill-treatment of prisoners, piracy on the high seas, the taking and killing of hostages, plunder of public and private property, wanton destruction of cities, towns, and villages, and devastation not justified by military necessity.

Recorded were violations of The Hague regulations of 1907, the laws and customs of war, the general principles of criminal law, and the internal penal codes of individual countries.

It was a fantastic story of conspiracy, aggression, and brutality unparalleled in history—the killing of more than 10,000,000 European civilians and captured war prisoners; the slaughter of 5,700,000 Jews; systematic gassings, beatings, starvation, torture, medical experiments; plundering conquered countries of millions of tons of raw materials, industrial equipment, and agricultural produce; war prisoners buried alive, thrown into flames, stabbed with bayonets; carting off to slave labor of millions of citizens from the occupied countries.

A typical paragraph from the indictment: "In the Ganow camp 200,000 peaceful citizens were exterminated. The most refined methods of cruelty were employed in this extermination, such as disemboweling and freezing of human beings in tubs of water; mass shootings took place to the accompaniment of the music of an orchestra recruited from the persons interned."

To bolster its case the prosecution brought to Nuremberg a huge variety of documents. The U.S. Army alone shipped some 20 carloads of material which it had captured from the Germans in the last days of the war. From these, plus additional material supplied by the British, French, and Russians, about 3,000 documents were finally selected to be placed in evidence.

The Nuremberg tribunal sat continuously from November 20, 1945, to October 1, 1946. Throughout this long period the presiding justice exhibited a model judicial temper and procedural ability. The transcript of the proceedings fills some 42 bulky printed volumes.

The stage at Nuremberg was ghastly, repellent. The entire world was shocked by this parade of human vice and folly. Twenty-one broken-down men, most with gray faces and puffy eyes, stultified, seemingly dead, sat in two banks in the courtroom. No trace remained of their one-time power and glory. Gone now were the arrogance of command, the domineering tone of the lunatic Nazi milieu, the medals and fine clothing. Day after day these sagging little men heard the loathsome details of crimes beyond normal human imagination.

Rebecca West, the distinguished British journalist, described it:

> All the time they make quite unidiosyncratic gestures, expressive of innocence and outraged common sense, and in the intervals they stand up and chat among themselves, forming little protesting groups which, painted in a mural, could be recognized as the men who would have saved the world if it had let them. But all this they do more weakly every day. They are visibly receding from the field of existence. . . . They are praying with their sharpest nerves, "Let this trial never finish, let it go on forever and ever, without end."

There were occasional flurries in the days of dull boredom. Kaltenbrunner collapsed with a cranial hemorrhage and was absent from the prisoners' dock for some time. Hess, who spent most of his time in the dock reading romantic novels and giggling, suddenly confessed that he had simulated a loss of memory. When a shrunken human head and lampshades made of human skin were submitted as evidence, the unnerved defendants slumped sluggishly in the dock. When motion pictures were introduced as evidence, Schacht, who considered himself personally abused by the proceedings, deliberately turned his back on the screen. A newsman present described him as giving the impression of "a corpse frozen by *rigor mortis*."

On and on it went, an apparently endless parade of death-camp horrors, a crushing weight of evidence in the prisoners' own words. Goering recoiled on seeing the motion pictures. "It is true," he admitted, "that I started the concentration camps. But all I wanted to do was to re-educate political prisoners. From 1934 on, it was Himmler who ran the camps. I had no idea that such terrible things took place." Surely no trial such as this had ever been held anywhere in the world.

The tribunal started its summation of war crimes with this general introduction:

> The evidence relating to war crimes has been overwhelming in its volume and its detail. It is impossible for this judgment adequately to review it, or to record the mass of documentary and oral evidence that has been presented. The truth remains that war crimes were committed on a vast scale, never before seen in the history of war. They were perpetrated in all the countries occupied by Germany, and on the high seas, and were attended by every conceivable circumstance of cruelty and horror. There can be no doubt that the majority of them arose from the Nazi conception of "total war," with which the aggressive wars were waged. For in this conception of "total war" the moral ideas underlying the conventions which seek to make war more humane are no longer regarded as having force or validity. Everything is made subordinate to the overmastering dictates of war. Rules, regulations, assurances and treaties all alike are of no moment; and, so, freed from the restraining influence of international law, the aggressive war is conducted by the Nazi leaders in the most barbaric way. Accordingly, war crimes were committed when and wherever the *Fuehrer* and his close associates thought them to be advantageous. They were for the most part the result of cold and criminal calculation.

"Tod durch den Strang!"—"Death by the rope!"

On the afternoon of October 1, 1946, came these fatal words through the headphones to 11 of the defendants—to Goering (age 52), von Ribbentrop (53), Kaltenbrunner (43), Rosenberg (53), Frank (46), Streicher (61), Frick (69), Sauckel (48), von Seyss-Inquart (54), Keitel (63), and Jodl (56). Bormann, *in absentia*, was also sentenced to death.

Three others were found guilty and sent to prison for life—Hess (52), Funk (56), and Raeder (70).

Four were condemned to various terms of imprisonment—Doenitz (55) to ten years, von Schirach (39) to twenty years, von Neurath (72) to fifteen years, and Speer (40) to twenty years.

Fritzsche (46), von Papen (66), and Schacht (69) were acquitted. From the beginning of the trial Schacht had been certain that he would be found not guilty. The tribunal agreed that, although he was the central figure in Germany's rearmament program, rearmament in itself was no crime. Furthermore, the judgment gave credit to Schacht for participating in the plot to assassinate Hitler. The Russians denounced the Schacht verdict on the ground that he had actively assisted Hitler in the seizure of power, that he had closely collaborated with him for more than a decade, and that he had prepared Germany's economy for waging aggressive war. But the economic wizard of the Third Reich went free.

In conformance with the spirit of the entire trial, the judgments were precise and meticulous. Here are several brief excerpts:

> GOERING: From the moment he joined the party in 1922 and took command of the street fighting organization, the S.A., Goering was the adviser, the active agent of Hitler and one of the prime leaders of the Nazi movement. As Hitler's political deputy he was largely instrumental in bringing the National Socialists to power in 1933, and was charged with consolidating this power and expanding German might. He developed the *Gestapo* and created the first concentration camps, relinquishing them to Himmler in 1934; conducted the Roehm purge in that year and engineered the sordid proceedings which resulted in the removal of von Blomberg and von Fritsch from the Army. . . .
>
> Goering commanded the *Luftwaffe* in the attack on Poland and throughout the aggressive wars which followed. . . . The record is filled with Goering's admission of his complicity in the use of slave labor. . . .
>
> There is nothing to be said in mitigation. . . . His guilt is unique in its enormity. The record discloses no excuse for this man.
>
> VERDICT: GUILTY on all four counts.
>
> SENTENCE: Death by hanging.
>
> RIBBENTROP: Ribbentrop was not present at the Hossbach Conference held on November 5, 1937, but on January 2, 1938, while ambassador to England, he sent a memorandum to Hitler indicating his opinion that a change in the *status quo* in the East in the German sense could only be carried out by

force and suggesting methods to prevent England and France from intervening in a European war fought to bring about such a change. . . .

He played an important part in Hitler's "final solution" of the Jewish question. In September 1942 he ordered the German diplomatic representatives accredited to various satellites to hasten deportation of the Jews to the East. . . . It was because Hitler's policy and plans coincided with his own ideas that Ribbentrop served him so willingly to the end.

VERDICT: GUILTY on all four counts.

SENTENCE: Death by hanging.

ROSENBERG: Rosenberg was recognized as the Party's ideologist. He developed and spread Nazi doctrines in the publications *Völkischer Beobachter* and *N.S. Monatshefte*, which he edited, and in the numerous books he wrote. . . .

VERDICT: GUILTY on all four counts.

SENTENCE: Death by hanging.

HESS: . . . As deputy to the *Fuehrer*, Hess was the top man in the Nazi party with responsibility for handling all Party matters and authority to make decisions in Hitler's name on all questions of Party leadership. . . . Hess was an informed and willing participant in German aggression against Austria, Czechoslovakia, and Poland. . . .

With him on his flight to England, Hess carried certain peace proposals which he alleged Hitler was prepared to accept. It is significant to note that this flight took place only ten days after the date on which Hitler fixed the time for attacking the Soviet Union. . . .

VERDICT: GUILTY on counts 1 and 2.

SENTENCE: Life imprisonment.

Verdicts of guilty were also handed down on the leadership corps of the Nazi Party, on the S.S., the S.A., and the *Gestapo*.

Early on the morning of October 16, 1946, an hour before he was scheduled to lead his condemned colleagues to the scaffold, Hermann Goering, mocking to the end, chewed a capsule containing cyanide of potassium. Ribbentrop was the first of the remaining ten to be hanged, one by one, in the grimy, barnlike interior of a small gymnasium inside one of the prison yards of the Nuremberg city jail. The executions took just an hour and a half. In this sordid scene one after another of the monstrous leaders fell to his death.

Kingsbury Smith, European general manager of the International News Service, was chosen by lot to represent the combined American press at the proceedings. An excerpt from his report tells the macabre story of Julius Streicher's execution:

As in the case of all the condemned, a warning knock by a guard outside preceded Streicher's entry through a door in the middle of the hall.

An American lieutenant colonel sent to fetch the condemned from the death row of the cell block to the near-by prison wing entered first. He was followed by Streicher, who was stopped immediately inside the door by two

American sergeants. They closed in on each side of him and held his arms while another sergeant removed the manacles from his hands and replaced them with a leather cord. . . .

This ugly, dwarfish little man, wearing a threadbare suit and a well-worn bluish shirt buttoned to the neck but without a tie, glanced at the three wooden scaffolds rising up menacingly in front of him.

Two of these were used alterna ely to execute the condemned men while the third was kept in reserve.

After a quick glance at the gε ,s, Streicher glanced around the room, his eyes resting momentarily up,n the small group of American, British, French, and Russian officers on hand to witness the executions.

By this time Streicher's hands were tied securely behind his back. Two guards, one to each arm, directed him to No. 1 gallows on the left entrance. He walked steadily the six feet to the first wooden step, but his face was twitching nervously. As the guards stopped him at the bottom of the steps for official identification requests, he uttered his piercing scream:

"*Heil Hitler!*". . .

As its echo died away, another American colonel standing by the steps said sharply:

"Ask the man his name."

In response to the interpreter's query Streicher shouted:

"You know my name well."

The interpreter repeated his request, and the condemned man yelled:

"Julius Streicher!"

As he mounted the platform Streicher cried out:

"Now it goes to God!"

After getting up the 13 steps to the eight-foot-high and eight-foot-square black-painted wooden platform, Streicher was pushed two steps to the mortal spot beneath the hangman's rope.

This was suspended from an iron ring attached to a crossbeam which rested on two posts. The rope was being held back against a wooden rail by the American Army sergeant hangman.

Streicher was swung around to face toward the front.

He glanced again at the Allied officers and eight Allied correspondents representing the world's press who were lined up against a wall behind small tables directly facing the gallows.

With burning hatred in his eyes, Streicher looked down upon the witnesses and then screamed:

"*Purim Fest*, 1946!" [Purim is a Jewish holiday, celebrated in the spring, commemorating the hanging of Haman, Biblical oppressor of the Jews.]

The American officer standing at the scaffold said:

"Ask the man if he has any last words."

When the interpreter had translated, Streicher shouted:

"The Bolsheviks will hang you one day."

As the black hood was being adjusted about his head, Streicher was heard saying:

"Adele, my dear wife."

At that moment the trap was sprung with a loud bang. With the rope snapped taut and the body swinging wildly, a groan could be heard distinctly within the dark interior of the scaffold.

Kingsbury Smith later reported that while Streicher was audibly strangling, the hangman disappeared into the dark interior of the scaffold. Streicher's groans immediately ceased. "After it was over," Smith wrote, "I was not in a mood to ask what he did, but I assumed that he grabbed the swinging body and pulled down on it."

The next day, October 17, 1946, *The New York Times* commented editorially that the condemned men of Nuremberg had performed in death at least one service—their hanging was a "grim warning to all who would emulate them in the future that mankind has entered a new world of international morality and that in the end the angered forces of humanity must triumph over those who would outrage it."

In December 1945 the Allied Control Council established military tribunals in each zone to try lesser men and organizations. The United States tribunal conducted 12 trials between April 1947 and April 1949, trying I. G. Farben and Krupp officials, medical men, governmental ministers, and heads of the concentration camps. Of some 185 indicted, more than half received prison terms, and 24 were sentenced to hang. Among those condemned to die were Josef Kramer, the notorious Beast of Belsen, and the blonde Irma Grese, the "queen" of the same slaughter camp.

The legality of the Nuremberg and post-Nuremberg proceedings troubled many jurists and others. Were there not *ex post facto* implications to such trials? Was the Nuremberg tribunal a true court of law since there was no world state in existence? Were not the judgments merely political acts of victors against the vanquished? Some dissenters argued that at least one power represented in the tribunal should have been sitting in the defendants' box and accused of conspiracy, aggression, and crimes against humanity.

Others defended the trials as juridically competent. Although special courts, they said, had been set up in the past to judge political crimes by extraordinary authority, no such court had ever obtained such universal recognition as that at Nuremberg. With all its flaws and inconsistencies, they argued, with all the cynical doubt justified by the presence of Soviet judges, the Nuremberg trial "will remain one of the truly great and constructive acts in the era following World War II." Further, they said, one fact stands out in this melancholy episode—for the first time in recorded history, humanity not only spoke out but acted against evil men who plotted war and aggression.

In its summing up and judgment the Nuremberg tribunal itself met the *ex post facto* argument with these words:

> It was urged on behalf of the defendants that a fundamental principle of all law—international and domestic—is that there can be no punishment of crime without a pre-existing law. *Nullum crimen sine lege, nulla poena sine lege.* It was submitted that *ex post facto* punishment is abhorrent to the law of all civilized nations, that no sovereign power had made aggressive war

a crime at the time the alleged criminal acts were committed, that no statute had defined aggressive war, that no penalty had been fixed for its commission and no court had been created to try and punish offenders.

In the first place, it is to be observed that the maxim *nullum crimen sine lege* is not a limitation of sovereignty, but is in general a principle of justice. To assert that it is unjust to punish those who in defiance of treaties and assurances have attacked neighbouring states without warning is obviously untrue, for in such circumstances the attacker must know that he is doing wrong, and so far from it being unjust to punish him, it would be unjust if his wrong were allowed to go unpunished. Occupying the position they did in the government of Germany, the defendants, or at least some of them, must have known of the treaties signed by Germany outlawing recourse to war for the settlement of international disputes; they must have known that they were acting in defiance of all international law when in complete deliberation they carried out their designs of invasion and aggression. On this view of the case alone, it would appear that the maxim has no application to the present facts.

This view is strongly reinforced by a consideration of the state of international law in 1939, so far as aggressive war is concerned. The General Treaty for the Renunciation of War of August 27, 1928, more generally known as the Pact of Paris or the Kellogg-Briand Pact, was binding on 63 nations, including Germany, Italy and Japan at the outbreak of war in 1939.

The question is, what was the legal effect of this pact? The nations who signed the pact or adhered to it unconditionally condemned recourse to war for the future as an instrument of policy, and expressly renounced it. After the signing of the pact any nation resorting to war as an instrument of national policy breaks the pact. In the opinion of the Tribunal the solemn renunciation of war as an instrument of national policy necessarily involves the proposition that such a war is illegal in international law; and that those who plan and wage such a war, with its inevitable and terrible consequences, are committing a crime in so doing. War for the solution of international controversies undertaken as an instrument of national policy certainly includes a war of aggression, and such a war is therefore outlawed by the pact.

Execution did not undo the evil wrought by the craven men of Nuremberg, nor could it bring back to life a single one of the millions they had slaughtered. The appalling record remains to haunt the civilized world.

JAPAN: THE FINAL RECKONING

Japan, too, witnessed a Far Eastern version of the Nuremberg trials. The oligarchs who masterminded the Nipponese drive for world power, the insatiable war lords, leaders of the great business dynasties of the Zaibatsu—the Mitsui, Mitsubishi, Sumitomo, and Yasuda—and a host of less-known Japanese were rounded up and placed on trial for conspiracy, war crimes, and crimes against humanity.

On November 19, 1945, General Douglas MacArthur ordered the arrest of 11 Japanese war leaders to stand trial not only for acts committed during the war but going all the way back to the rape of Nanking, the Mukden incident, and the bombing of the U.S. gunboat *Panay*. Included among them were Baron General Sadao Araki, the notorious militarist who was regarded as the brains behind Tojo; Yoshihisa Kuzuu, leader of the Black Dragon terrorists; Marquis Koichi Kido, the Emperor's right-hand man during the war; two former premiers, Baron Kiichiro Hiranuma and Koki Jirota; the 71-year-old Prince Morimasa Nashimoto; and several industrialists, bankers, and newspaper executives.

Two of those wanted for trial committed suicide—Baron General Shigeru Honjo, an army leader, and Prince Fumimaro Konoye, thrice premier of Japan. Before his death Konoye intimated that Emperor Hirohito had attended key meetings of military planners for the war in the Pacific and had known of the intentions of his cabinet ministers. But since American occupation policy had decreed that the Emperor was to be retained in his office as a means of winning Japanese public support, Hirohito was never brought to trial.

The case of General Hideki Tojo, 61-year-old Razor Brain, the top Nipponese warmonger, aroused global attention. Just as Hitler and Goebbels had committed suicide in a frenzy of Wagnerian self-immolation, so did Tojo attempt to kill himself. He intended to perform the act of *Hara-kiri*, but, as he explained later, he had no suitable aide present to cut off his head after the ceremonial disembowelment.

On the afternoon of September 11, 1945, a party of American officers and war correspondents came to the home of the former premier to arrest him. Tojo opened a large sliding window of his house, peered at the Americans, and said, "I am Tojo." As the visiting party headed for the front door, they heard a shot. Breaking through several doors, they found Tojo on the floor of his study, his chest covered with blood. He had shot himself with a .32-caliber automatic pistol, aiming the bullet at his chest. He explained that he did not wish to disfigure his face because he wanted no doubts about his fate. He was wearing full uniform with six rows of ribbons on his tunic. A hastily summoned doctor refused to treat the wounded premier, who was now in a state of shock. He was given American blood plasma and was brought to a hospital in Yokohama, where American doctors pulled him through.

While convalescing, Tojo informed a Japanese reporter: "I am sorry for the peoples of Greater East Asia. I will shoulder the whole responsibility. I hope they will not go amiss in dealing with the situation. The war of Greater East Asia was a just war. With all our strength gone, we finally fell. I do not want to stand before the victor to be tried as the vanquished. This is my own case. I wanted to kill myself at one stroke. I first thought of using my sword to kill myself, but instead I used the revolver for fear I might fail and survive."

To his captors Tojo said: "You are the victors and you are now able to name who was responsible for the war. But historians 500 or 1,000 years from now may judge differently."

On October 7, 1945, Tojo was moved to the desolate Omoro prison camp to await trial.

In Manila, on October 29, 1945, began the trial of General Tomoyuki Yamashita, the Tiger of the Philippines. A parade of witnesses offered damaging testimony: Yamashita had angrily refused to revoke an order "to kill all Filipinos and destroy all their cities"; his men had indulged in berserk orgies of slaughter, torture, and rape; they had poured gasoline on the heads of women and set them afire; they had shut up prisoners in walled yards, set the entrances afire, and thrown grenades at the helpless captives; they had blindfolded prisoners and shoved them alive into pits into which they threw hand grenades; they had bayoneted two captive American airmen, saturated them with gasoline, and cremated them alive; they had burned down entire villages.

Yamashita protested heatedly that he was under orders from his superior, Field Marshal Count Juichi Terauchi, the Supreme Japanese Commander in the Southwest Pacific. He never knew of any atrocities. He never ordered any. "This is the first time I have heard about these matters," Yamashita complained. "When and if such acts were committed by my subordinates it was in complete disagreement with my own ideas. I never ordered such actions at all."

It was less than a successful defense. On December 7, 1945, the anniversary of Pearl Harbor, Yamashita was convicted of condoning atrocities and sentenced to death by hanging.

On December 22, 1948, Tojo and six of his colleagues, their appeals denied, mounted the 13 steps to the gallows in Tokyo's quiet Sugamo prison and were hanged. Japan's wartime dictator, who had led his people along the road to disaster, left a poem:

It is good-by.
Over the mountains I go today
To the bosom of Buddha.
So, happy am I.

In accordance with Japanese funerary customs, as final mementos for his wife Tojo sent such personal articles as a lock of hair, a fingernail clipping, his glasses, and his false teeth. The reaction of the Japanese to the executions was *Kinodoku, kinodoku* (Pity, pity).

FIVE PEACE TREATIES

In 1919, after World War I, the delegates of the victor powers hastened to the peace-conference table at Versailles in a climate of hatred and vengeance. It turned out to be a riot in a parrot house. And it resulted in unstable compromises and the seeds of future conflict. This time, all agreed, it was going to be different. Agreements would be worked out among the great powers slowly, carefully, deliberately.

But it soon became clear that the Allied coalition had been held together during the war years only by immediate and common dangers. The harmony vanished once the Axis capitulated. Russian intransigence made it a nasty business from the very beginning. The Russians had been dealt terrible blows in the conflict—their manpower had been decimated and their towns and cities devastated. But the Western Allies, too, had suffered at the hands of the Nazi maniac. The victory over Germany had been a joint undertaking, and that over Japan had been primarily an American effort. Now the Russians acted as if they alone had been responsible for both victories.

The Western leaders, recognizing the extent of Russian suffering, were willing to work in the spirit of compromise and even offer liberal concessions. In the Soviet code of political ethics this was weakness. At the conference tables the Russians were cold, hard, unyielding, unrelenting, demanding ever more and more, using every weapon from sarcasm to vituperation to threats.

Gone was the community of effort, the urge to compromise for the common good, even a minimum regard for the essentials of fair bargaining. To the monolithic minds of the Kremlin, negotiation meant 100 per cent their way, thence to the next subject. For example, despite previous agreements, the Russians started with the assumption that they were in Central and Eastern Europe to stay. Let's go on from there!

At Potsdam, in July 1945, the Council of Foreign Ministers, representing the four major victorious powers, was established to draft peace treaties with Italy and the smaller states of Eastern Europe. The council held its first meeting in London (September 1945). The Russian delegate, Vyacheslav Molotov, promptly hurled a bombshell by demanding Soviet trusteeship over the former Italian colony of Libya. Obviously, the problem of reaching a settlement with the suspicion-drenched Soviet leaders would be as difficult as winning the war.

The foreign ministers met again at Moscow in December 1945. This time agreement was attained, but only on procedural matters. Allied occupation troops would be removed from the defeated countries after the necessary treaties were made. But the Russians insisted that their troops remain in Rumania and Hungary to guard lines of communication as long as they occupied Austria. The strategy was obvious even to the most obtuse: The

Kremlin delayed the negotiation of an Austrian peace treaty year after year, thus preserving the fiction of a legal occupation of Rumania and Hungary.

Next, the foreign ministers went to Paris, where they held two meetings from April to July 1946. They prepared drafts of five treaties and called a conference of all United Nations members who had fought the Axis.

Delegates of the Big Four, who dominated the conference, and the Little Seventeen, who could only recommend, assembled in the French Senate Chamber on July 29, 1946. For 11 weeks it dragged on, the delegates wrangling in stormy, disorganized debate. The Soviet delegates introduced endless arguments on procedural problems and used the podium mostly for propaganda purposes. Plenipotentiaries of the Western Allies became more and more disgusted with the time-wasting performance. "The real peace we now need," commented one observer, "is between the East and the West."

In November 1946 the Council of Foreign Ministers met again, this time in New York. Here the first five treaties, with Italy, Rumania, Bulgaria, Hungary, and Finland, were finally ironed out. The signing by 21 members of the United Nations and the five defeated countries took place on February 10, 1947, in the Salle de l'Horloge of the Quai d'Orsay, the great hall in the French Foreign Office in Paris. The table used in the ceremony was that upon which the wounded Robespierre had lain before he was guillotined.

All five defeated countries, except Bulgaria, were saddled with territorial losses. Each was to pay reparations calculated on the basis of the United States dollar at its gold parity on July 1, 1946, $35 for one ounce of gold. Each was to be demilitarized. All were required to restore the legal and property rights of the victor states, and to guarantee "the enjoyment of human rights and the fundamental freedoms" to all their citizens including minorities.

The first treaty signed was with Italy. She was shorn of her African empire, losing all rights to Libya, Eritrea, Italian Somaliland, and Ethiopia, an area of more than a million square miles, as well as all her special interests in China. In Europe she ceded to France the Alpine districts of the Little St. Bernard Pass, the Mont Cenis Plateau, and the areas of Mount Thabor, Chaberton, Briga, and Tenda. To Greece went the Dodecanese Islands, Rhodes, and Castellorizo, and to the new republic of Albania the island of Saseno. Yugoslavia was awarded two-thirds of eastern Venezia and some Adriatic islands, but Trieste, which Yugoslavia also wanted, was made a free territory. The South Tyrol was to remain Italian, but with equal rights and part autonomy for the German-speaking portion of the population.

The reparations bill for Italy was $360,000,000, to be paid in kind over a period of seven years: $125,000,000 to Yugoslavia, $105,000,000 to Greece, $100,000,000 to the Soviet Union, $25,000,000 to Ethiopia, and $5,000,000 to Albania. In addition, Italy had to pay up to two-thirds of the value of Allied property damaged in Italy during the war. The Italian army was limited to 250,000, the navy to 25,000, and the air force to 25,000 men. Fortifications along the French and Yugoslav borders and on the islands of Sardinia and Sicily were to be destroyed.

The treaty with Rumania confirmed the earlier cession of Bessarabia and northern Bukovina to the Soviet Union, and of the southern Dobruja to Bulgaria. Rumania was to regain the Transylvanian territory which Hitler had forced her to give Hungary in 1940. She was required to pay $300,000,-000 in reparations to the Soviet Union. The Rumanian army was limited to 120,000, the navy to 5,000, and the air force to 8,000 men.

Bulgaria, alone among the five, lost no territory. She was given the southern Dobruja previously assigned to Rumania. Her reparations bill was $70,-000,000, of which $45,000,000 was to go to Greece and $25,000,000 to Yugoslavia, to be paid over eight years. The Bulgarian army was limited to 55,000, the navy to 3,500, and the air force to 5,200 men.

Hungary was ordered to return to Rumania that part of Transylvania given her by Hitler in 1940, and to relinquish to Czechoslovakia the towns in Slovakia she had been given in 1938. The reparations settlement included $200,000,000 to the Soviet Union, $50,000,000 to Yugoslavia, and $50,000,-000 to Czechoslovakia. The Hungarian army was limited to 65,000 and the air force to 5,200 men.

The treaty with Finland confirmed for the most part the gains of the Soviet Union by the Treaty of Moscow in 1940 and the armistice of September 1944. The Soviet Union assumed control of the Karelian Isthmus and the ice-free port of Petsamo; in addition, she was granted a 50-year lease to establish a naval base on Porkkala-Udd, west of Helsinki. The Finns were ordered to pay to the Soviet Union $300,000,000 in reparations in commodities over eight years. Their army was reduced to 34,400, the navy to 4,500, and the air force to 3,000 men.

Thus, 21 months after V-E Day, formal peace was made with five of the defeated nations. Four of the five states, only Finland abstaining, launched immediate protests.

Italians reacted with an emotional outburst, demonstrating in the streets, shouting imprecations before Allied legations, and tearing an American flag to bits. Where was the reward for the Italian resistance movement in the closing months of the war? Why the eternal prejudice against Italy? Newspapers appeared with heavy black borders, flags were flown at half-mast, windows were draped with black crepe. As a further protest a ten-minute silence was observed at the moment when the treaty was signed. Italian-Americans joined in denouncing the treaty.

All this availed nothing. Someone, preferably Italians, had to pay for Mussolini's grandiose mistakes. Too many of them had supported Mussolini and his brutalities against his Yugoslav, Arab, and Ethiopian subjects in the years of his triumphs.

STALEMATE IN TWO GERMANIES

Peace had been concluded with the smaller defeated countries. But what about Germany, the key nation of Central Europe? Here was the real stumbling block.

No progress was made on a German treaty at the early meetings of the foreign ministers. Again there came the interminable wrangling, the poker-faced squabbling. When the foreign ministers met in Moscow in March 1947, Molotov suddenly claimed that the Soviet Union had been pledged $10,000,-000,000 in reparations from Germany in a secret protocol of the Yalta Conference. He demanded that this sum be paid in full from current German production. Since the United States and Britain were then financing their two zones in West Germany, this would in effect mean that American and British funds would be transferred ultimately through West Germany to the Soviet Union. "Reparations from current production," commented Secretary of State George C. Marshall, "that is, exports of day-to-day German production with no return, could be made only if the countries at present supplying Germany, notably the United States, foot the bill. We put in and the Russians take out."

Despite toasts and honeyed concluding speeches, little was accomplished at Moscow. The Western Allies and the Soviet Union were farther apart than ever. There were no agreements on the amount of reparations, the problem of economic unification of the occupied zones in Germany, the matter of Germany's final eastern frontier, or the future of the Ruhr and the Saar.

Another effort was made in London in November 1947. It was stalemate again, after two years. It was the same dreary performance by four men on a merry-go-round. Still another effort in December 1947 evoked similar depressing results. The Russians used the conference to denounce the Western powers, blandly accusing them of the sins the Soviet Union had already committed. "I reluctantly conclude," reported Secretary of State Marshall, "that no useful purpose would be served by debates on other points in our agenda." He suggested adjournment. No date or place was set for another session on Germany.

Agreement on Germany vanished under the pressures of the ensuing cold war.

THE AUSTRIAN SETTLEMENT

Immediately after the war Austria was divided into four occupation zones. Vienna, like Berlin, was also split into four sectors, the occupying powers—

the United States, the Soviet Union, Britain, and France—exercising control through the Allied Council for Austria.

In their zone of Austria the Soviet authorities promptly requisitioned factories, farm equipment, livestock, even food and clothing. By unilateral action they seized former German assets in Austria, such as oil refineries and river transport, insisting that German property even in Austria was subject to reparations.

Meanwhile, all was complicated by endless arguments and hardheaded refusals to come to terms. In successive conferences the Foreign Ministers' Council failed to draft an Austrian peace treaty, agreeing only on the decision to leave the southern Tyrol in Italian possession.

The state treaty with Austria finally came ten years after the end of the war. On May 5, 1955, the four occupying powers signed an agreement giving Austria her independence. The Soviet terms were harsh. As price for its consent, the Kremlin demanded 10,000,000 tons of oil over a 10-year period and $150,000,000 worth of goods over a six-year period.

Austria had at last won liberation from her liberators.

THE PEACE TREATY WITH JAPAN

> In order to secure our country's safety and speed up the end of the war, the Soviet Union went to war against the Japanese. On September 2, 1945, under the crushing blows of the Soviet Army, Japan admitted its defeat and laid down arms.

Thus the explanation from a Russian textbook at the third-grade level. In the negotiations for peace with Japan, Russian statesmen acted precisely as if this passage were the Leninist gospel truth. Little wonder then that the peace with Japan was delayed for seven years. The Russian objected both to procedures and policy. The United States wanted a conference of all 11 members of the Far Eastern Commission, with decisions made by a two-thirds majority, and no veto right. The Russians insisted on a settlement by the Big Four—the United States, Great Britain, the Soviet Union, and China—with each holding the right of veto. The Americans, by now thoroughly familiar with Soviet techniques, declined to take the bait. They decided at long length to go ahead on their own, without Soviet "coöperation."

After a year of preparation, a draft treaty was finished and 50 nations were invited to San Francisco, not to negotiate but to sign the Japanese peace treaty. The Soviet Union and its satellites, Poland and Czechoslovakia, refused to sign. Nationalist China and India signed separate treaties formally opening relations with Japan.

The treaty, which became effective April 28, 1952, ended the state of war with Japan and recognized her full sovereignty. Provision was made for prompt withdrawal of occupation troops. Japan was limited in territory to her four home islands, but the treaty did not recognize Soviet seizure of the Kurile Islands and southern Sakhalin. Japan agreed to renounce all rights in China. No restrictions were placed on her political institutions or economy, but Japan accepted the obligation of the United Nations Charter "to refrain in its international relations from the threat or use of force." Reparations were to be arranged individually with the separate victor powers. Tokyo agreed to accept the judgments of the Allied war crimes trials.

At the same time the United States and Japan signed a security pact by which the former would maintain armed forces in Japan to discourage armed attack from either Red China or the U.S.S.R. The pact was to end whenever the two nations agreed that international peace and security could be maintained in the islands.

Premier Shigeru Yoshida formally expressed his thanks to the Allies for "a magnanimous peace unparalleled in history," which enabled the Japanese now to follow the broad highway of peace and democracy. President Harry S. Truman commented that "Japanese sincerity and earnestness have won the respect of the world." The Kremlin dissented.

Meanwhile, the entire structure of Japanese society was being revolutionized under the MacArthur regime. Hirohito retained his position as titular head of a people who were being democratized overnight. The power of the militarists was shattered, the great estates broken up, peasant proprietorship established, Shintoism discouraged, and education reformed along democratic lines.

"The Japan of today," said Yoshida, "is no longer the Japan of yesterday. We will not fail your expectations of us as a new nation, dedicated to peace, democracy, and freedom."

POST-MORTEMS, APOLOGIAS, AND BRICKBATS

The guns were scarcely quiet before there came the flood of adulatory, self-congratulatory, or critical books by or about the leaders of World War II.

The tenor was uneven, ranging from the smoothness of Winston Churchill and the modesty of Dwight D. Eisenhower to the pomposity of Montgomery of Alamein, oracle of martial infallibility. The great and near-great were attacked for deplorable strategy and faulty judgment in narratives ranging from hard skepticism to picayune criticism. All the Monday-morning quarterbacks knew exactly what strategy and tactics would have worked on the preceding Saturday.

From defeated Germany came a stream of apologetic memoirs. Almost without exception these books presented the thesis that the authors were "good Germans" who had been caught in political paralysis and who did not seek to leave the danger scene but instead sought to stick it out and fight for a just peace.

In his *Moskau, Tokio, Berlin* (1949), diplomat Herbert von Dirksen admitted: "That it was honorable not to serve the Hitler regime altogether was a thought that escaped me at that time." The foreign service officer, Erich Kordt, in his *Nicht aus den Akten* (*Not From the Documents*), gave a remarkable eyewitness picture of the unstable members of Hitler's immediate entourage as well as the fantastic story of Nazi malice in Hitlerland. In his *Memoirs* (1951), Baron Ernst von Weiszäcker, holder of numerous posts under the Nazis, revealed that it became crystal clear to him that Hitler and his insufferably fawning yes-man, Joachim von Ribbentrop, were determined to make war in 1939. In his book *Hitler's Interpreter* (1951), Paul Schmidt described his leader as an absent-minded brooder, pale from sleeplessness, who, almost without warning, would suddenly fly into a rage. "Hitler had an extraordinary capacity for self-deception."

Similarly, Hitler's generals, among others Hasso von Manteuffel, Guenther Blumentritt, Fritz Bayerlein, Werner Kreipe, and Kurt Zeitzler, denounced the *Fuehrer* as an incompetent military bungler. They outdid one another in heaping scorn on the man already dead in the ruins of Berlin. It was always the same theme: The professionals were infallible masters of the military art, but they were crushed because of Hitler's stupid intervention in matters about which he knew nothing. They were helpless against Hitler's criminal sense of intuition. But instead of rejecting a role in Hitler's crimes, almost all followed devious paths and held onto their jobs.

The victorious Allies, too, had their spate of *ex post facto* books. Typical was *Wedemeyer Reports* (1958) by General Albert C. Wedemeyer, who, in October 1944, was sent to replace General Stilwell as U.S. commander in the China theatre of war. Wedemeyer excoriated both Roosevelt and Churchill. Because of their support for Stalin, he charged, and their demand for the obliteration of Germany, they were responsible for "snatching defeat from the jaws of victory." Further, he said, they were jointly guilty of allowing the Russians to penetrate deep into Central Europe.

Roosevelt, said Wedemeyer, was possessed of a "fevered imagination" and a "cynical disregard for the will of the people." "Roosevelt maneuvered us into the war by his patently unneutral actions against Germany and the final ultimatum to Japan." The American President's 1941 warning of Hitler's intentions against the American continent, in Wedemeyer's opinion, was "fear strategy and a fraud." Moreover, Roosevelt's demand for Germany's unconditional surrender stiffened German resistance and united all elements behind Hitler, thus prolonging the war. "After slaying one dragon we found ourselves confronted with a bigger and more dangerous one."

Equally harsh was Wedemeyer's denunciation of Churchill—a "pseudo-strategist," guilty of "folly with a senseless lust for blood." He charged that the cost of Churchill's Mediterranean strategy, the thrust at the soft underbelly, was an extra year of war, as well as the loss of a large part of the Continent.

Wedemeyer's assaults were by no means unique. As early as 1948, with the publication of Charles A. Beard's *President Roosevelt and the Coming of the War* there began a new campaign of revisionism. Roosevelt, it was charged, was the real instigator of the war with Japan. The revisionists accused the American President of intending to enter the conflict from its very beginning and declared that he coldly and calculatingly set about the double task of instigating the Japanese to attack the United States while he subtly prepared American public opinion for war. Pearl Harbor, by this reasoning, became the fruit of Rooseveltian machinations.

Defenders of Roosevelt, among them Robert E. Sherwood, Harry S. Truman, and James F. Byrnes, dismissed these charges as fantastic nonsense.

That all was not sweetness and light at the Allied high military level was revealed in the blazing memoirs (1958) of Field Marshal Viscount Montgomery of Alamein. The testy Briton challenged the reputations of top Allied commanders and triggered new battles over the battlefields of Western Europe.

Montgomery praised Eisenhower as a human being and warm friend ("the wonderful humanity of the man . . . such an awfully decent chap . . . a remarkable and lovable man"). Then he proceeded to condemn the Supreme Commander as a hesitant, indecisive, and changeable military leader, who displayed a lack of grip and operational direction, whose philosophy of war was expensive in lives, and whose broad-front strategy unnecessarily prolonged the war into 1945.

"Control was lacking," Montgomery wrote. "Our operations had, in fact, become ragged and disjointed and we now had got ourselves into a real mess." Further: "Ike and I were poles apart when it came to the conduct of war. My military doctrine was based on unbalancing the enemy while keeping well-balanced myself. I planned always to make the enemy commit his reserves on a wide front in order to plug holes in his defenses; having forced him to do this, I then committed my own reserves in a narrow front in a hard blow. . . . Eisenhower's creed appeared to me to be that . . . everybody must attack all the time."

Thus, in Montgomery's opinion, Eisenhower was not a great soldier. The Briton quoted Lieutenant General Walter Bedell Smith's description of Eisenhower as rather like "a football coach . . . up and down the line all the time, encouraging everyone to get on with the game."

Essentially the differences revolved around two issues. One was the command structure: Montgomery had wanted a single ground commander—himself. The other was Eisenhower's broad-front strategy, proposing a double thrust sending the British to the Ruhr and the Americans to the Saar, as opposed to Montgomery's one massive spearhead, a "single punch" into Germany.

The end of the war, said Montgomery, was within reach after the fall of Paris. "But what was now needed were quick decisions and above all a plan. . . . I had a plan ready." It called for a swift thrust by a striking force of 40 divisions, under his command, directly across the Low Countries from the coastal areas to the Ruhr and Berlin. Montgomery went to General George C. Marshall, head of the Combined Chiefs of Staff, with his complaints about Eisenhower as well as two of his subordinate generals, Bradley and Patton. "Marshall listened, but said little. It was clear that he entirely disagreed."

Support for Montgomery's thesis came from inside defeated Germany when General Guenther Blumentritt, chief of staff of the Western German armies, commented: "I am absolutely convinced that the war would have been over by Christmas, 1944, that there would have been a saving of Allied lives, and that the Western Allies would have been in Berlin before the Russians had Montgomery's plan been carried out."

These were grave charges. Eisenhower deeply resented the accusation that his strategy had cost lives. None the less, he refused to indulge in bitter excoriations—he was not that kind of man. Upon publication of Montgomery's memoirs, President Eisenhower told a press conference: "We won the war in 11 months from the day we landed, and I heard no single prediction that, at that time, before we made that election, when the war would be over, in less than two years. As a matter of fact, Winston Churchill told me that if we were as far as Paris and captured Paris by Christmas time, he would remark that that was the greatest military operation of all time. I think I have been criticized by everybody who can write a book, and I will be in the future."

Eisenhower had already commented in his *Crusade in Europe* (1948) about his differences with Montgomery, both in the matters of command and strategy.

> [On command:] [In August 1944] Montgomery suddenly proposed to me that he should retain tactical coördinating control of all ground forces throughout the campaign. . . . The proposition was fantastic. . . . The only effect of such a scheme would have been to place Montgomery in a position to draw at will, in support of his own ideas, upon the strength of the entire command.
>
> [On strategy:] I knew that any pencillike thrust into the heart of Germany such as he proposed would meet nothing but certain destruction. . . . I would not consider it. . . . General Montgomery was acquainted only with the situation in his own sector. . . . He did not understand the impossible situation that would have developed along the rest of our great front when he, having outrun the possibility of maintenance, was forced to stop or withdraw.

Anglo-American friction came partly from the American belief that the British were not sufficiently aggressive. "I repeatedly urged Montgomery," Eisenhower wrote, "to speed up and intensify his efforts to the limit."

Lieutenant General Omar N. Bradley, commenting in his memoirs on problems of closing the Argentan-Falaise trap, lent support to the criticism:

> [The plan was that] while U.S. Forces drove up from the south, Montgomery would drive from the north through Falaise to cut off the enemy. . . . As we waited patiently for Monty at Argentan, the enemy reinforced the [*Falaise*] gap. . . . But instead of redoubling his push to close that leak, Monty shifted his main effort against the pocket farther west. . . . If Monty's tactics mystified me, they dismayed Eisenhower even more.

Lieutenant General George S. Patton, Jr., even more shocked, looked on helplessly as the enemy fled the trap. When stopped by Bradley at Argentan, Patton raged: "Let me go to Falaise and we'll drive the British back into the sea for another Dunkirk."

Such were the brotherly battles among the top Allied brass.

Montgomery was infuriated when he learned that Eisenhower had complained to Churchill that the British should be more on the offensive and intimated that the British were leaving most of the fighting to the Americans. "Just when final victory was in sight," Montgomery wrote, "whispers went round the British forces that the Supreme Commander had complained that we were not doing our fair share of the fighting. I do not think that great and good man, now one of my greatest friends, had any idea of the trouble he was starting. From that time onwards there were always 'feelings' between the British and American forces."

This post-mortem battle centered mostly around the personality of Montgomery. Behind the sleek, almost ecclesiastical exterior of the victor of El Alamein was an extraordinary ego, a sublime self-confidence, a pomposity of herculean proportions. Even Churchill judged Montgomery to be "indomitable in defeat, invincible in retreat, insufferable in victory."

What was behind it all? In all probability Montgomery was annoyed by the necessity of remaining a deputy to a Supreme Commander whom he regarded as inferior to himself in both ability and experience. This was too much for his sensitive stomach. Yet, it seems clear that had he been allowed to drive his "single punch" into the heart of the Reich, he would have gotten a far worse bloody nose than he got at Arnhem.

In November 1959 Montgomery was joined in the postwar pattern of dressing down General Eisenhower by Field Marshal Viscount Alanbrooke, chief of the British Imperial General Staff during most of World War II. In Arthur Bryant's *Triumph in the West* (1959), the second volume based on Lord Alanbrooke's diaries, Alanbrooke (formerly Alan Brooke) described his old comrade as "a charming personality. . . . But no real commander." In the Alanbrooke version, at the time when the Battle of the Bulge was impending, there was "a very unsatisfactory state of affairs in France with no one running the land battle. Eisenhower, though supposed to be doing so, is on the golf links at Reims—entirely detached and taking practically no part in running the war." Alanbrooke again emphasized the theme that weak American leadership prolonged the conflict: "The main impression I gathered was that Eisenhower was no real director of thought, plans, energy, or direction. Just a coordinator, a good mixer, a champion of inter-allied cooperation."

Eisenhower maintained a dignified silence, but James Hagerty, his press secretary, denied the golf-playing charge. In the midst of the roar of outrage came this retort from a careful reader: that at the very time the Battle of the Bulge was about to begin, it was not Eisenhower but Montgomery who was playing golf. On page 307 of his memoirs Montgomery said: "On the morning of the 16th December [*1944*] . . . I decided to . . . play a few holes of golf. . . . But our game was soon interrupted by a message to say that the Germans had launched a heavy attack that morning."

Alanbrooke soon withdrew his statement about Eisenhower's golf, intimating that it was a figure of speech, so to speak. But the charge was resented by those sensitive to the fact that, as President, Eisenhower was widely accused by his political opponents of spending too much time on the golf course.

It was all a storm in a golf-cup, but it left a residue of bad feeling. General Carl Spaatz, wartime chief of the U.S. strategic bomber fleet, pointed out that how the Allies managed to win World War II handicapped as they were by American generals, is a mystery. "Is it possible," he asked, "that the war was won by a succession of strategic or tactical blunders by Churchill, Marshall, and Eisenhower, and could have been lost by the more brilliant plans now being exposed by Montgomery and Alanbrooke?"

One observer asked a final question: "Why don't old soldiers fade away, instead of sniping at their former comrades-in-arms?"

RETROSPECT AND PROSPECT

At the opening of the twentieth century it seemed that a decent world society was in the process of formation. Phenomenal were the strides in science, industry, and communications. There was hope in the minds of men of good will that at long last human beings would finally reject the cult of force as inappropriate to civilized society.

Henry Adams had predicted that in 1938 (exactly a century from his own birth) the world might start being civilized. Others, too, believed that war, relic of barbarism, would be placed where it belonged—in the category of cannibalism.

Yet, twice within the first half of the twentieth century great wars brought ruin and disorder. In 1914 the squabbles of nationalism, clashing imperialistic ambitions, trade rivalries, and militarism set the world aflame. Germany was thwarted in this, her first attempt, to find "a place in the sun." The tragic results of the war included vast human and material losses, the disruption of the world economy, and a residue of irreconcilable hatreds. Economic collapse was followed by challenge from totalitarian movements—Communism in Soviet Russia, Fascism in Italy, and National Socialism in Germany. Bitter was the struggle for the continued existence of democratic ideas and institutions.

Out of Conflagration I came a new Europe of accentuated nationalities. Individual national states relied more and more upon their own power and on the power of military alliances. Rivalries between nations became more and more pronounced.

In 1939 Hitler's insane ambition for global power was the immediate cause that plunged the world into another war to the death. Many of the same general causes that had motivated World War I acted to generate the new conflict.

Hitler and the Axis were smashed down.

But the uneasy peace brought new problems. This time the human and material losses were inestimably greater than in the preceding war. Again there was a residue of staggering tasks for victors and vanquished alike. Swords had to be beaten into plowshares; cities rebuilt; trade and communication restored; hunger, misery, and disease overcome. Income from exports had declined to a minimum and investments had been used to pay for critical war materials. At the close of the war gold and dollar reserves of most nations were at the vanishing point. And most difficult of all was the psychological problem of dealing with weariness, inertia, and cynicism.

The sovereignty of the national state was reëstablished. The atomistic force of nationalism, far from being weakened by the conflict, became stronger and stronger, spreading to Africa, the Near East, and the Far East. There was an increase in xenophobia, hatred of foreigners, fear of the stranger.

The basic phenomenon was not new. In one of his *Dialogues*, Plato tells the story of a visitor to Athens from one of the Greek settlements in Magna Graecia, who complained about the Hellenic disposition to divide all the world's inhabitants into two species—Greeks and barbarians. The disgusted foreigner added a touch of sarcasm: "Some wise and understanding creature, such as a crane is reputed to be, might in imitation of you make a similar division, and set up cranes against all other animals, to their own special glorification, at the same time jumbling together all the others, including man, under the appellation of brutes."

This same kind of arbitrary, unrealistic, and irrational classification was applied to the body of humanity by integral nationalists. The phenomenon is understandable—man has a natural attachment for his home, which he wants to protect against all dangers. He gravitates toward the nation—the extension of the family and the crowd—because it seems to promise self-preservation and safety.

But therein was—and is—the trap. Exploding nationalism—and more war.

And the future?

As always, there are two diametrically opposed views. One sees a hopeless drift into chaos, the other stands firmly on the platform of human progress.

From the pessimists comes the warning that a technological monster has been created that may eventually destroy all mankind. Watch the signs. In 1945 the bomb dropped on Hiroshima contained the equivalent of 20,000 tons of T.N.T. In 1948 an improved bomb had the equivalent of 120,000 tons of T.N.T., to be followed in 1952 by another with the equivalent of 3,000,000 tons of T.N.T., blowing a mile-wide hole in the ocean. In 1954 a bomb containing the equivalent of 20,000,000 tons of T.N.T. was tested. Natives in the Marshall Islands who had been evacuated several hundred miles from the center of the explosion, and Japanese fishermen, far away, were affected by radioactive ash, or fallout.

This, say the pessimists, is the wave of the future. Some madman or group of monsters may well touch off the explosion that will bring an end to life on this planet.

In contrast to the prophets of doom, others say that after World War II mankind showed a tremendous recuperative power. There has been a rapid growth in economic productivity, in birth rate, and in technology. The optimists point to the first steps from national to world sovereignty as expressed in the League of Nations and the United Nations. There is hope, they say, that the old notion of integral nationalism will give way to cultural nationalism. Then there will be more emphasis upon tolerance and understanding of other peoples, and all peoples will eventually see the necessity for submerging localized selfish feelings in the interest of a common humanity.

"Large parts of mankind," says Hans Kohn, "seem impatient today with the hard discipline of individual thinking, and full of desire to march in masses, to feel the comradeship of masses, to overcome the loneliness and fear in the growing complexity of the human situation. . . . Twentieth-century man has become less confident than his nineteenth-century ancestor was. He has witnessed the dark powers of history in his own experience. Things which seemed to belong to the past have reappeared: fanatical faith, infallible leaders, slavery and massacres, the uprooting of whole populations, ruthlessness and barbarism. But against all the expectations of totalitarians, by the middle of the twentieth century, Western civilization has proved its power of resistance against fanatic ideologies."

For those who believe in human progress there is the hope that, despite the fears and insecurity of the present, there may be a better future. It is possible, they say, that a new era of civilization may somehow open out beyond the stage of xenophobic nationalism. The intense faith of man in liberty can survive the unpleasant troubles of the present.

In the words of Winston Churchill: "It may well be that the lively sense of universal brotherhood and of bright hopes of the future may stir in humanity those qualities which will enable it to survive the dread agencies which have fallen into its as yet untutored hands."

APPENDICES

APPENDIX A

Recommended Reading

Alsop, J. and Kintner, R., *American White Paper* (1940).
Arnold, H. H., *Global Mission* (1949).
Baldwin, H. W., *Great Mistakes of the War* (1950).
Bekker, C. D., *Defeat at Sea: The Struggle and Eventual Destruction of the German Navy, 1939–1945* (1955).
Bolitho, H., *Combat Report: The Story of a Fighter Pilot* (1943).
Bor-Komorowski, T., *The Secret Army* (1951).
Bradley, O. N., *A Soldier's Story* (1951).
Brereton Diaries: The War in the Air in the Pacific, Middle East, and Europe, 3 Oct. 1941–8 May, 1945 (1946).
Bryan, J., *Aircraft Carrier* (1954).
Bullock, A. C. L., *Hitler: A Study in Tyranny* (1952).
Busch, H., *U-Boats at War* (1955).
Butcher, H. C., *My Three Years with Eisenhower, 1942–1945* (1946).
Byrnes, J. F., *Speaking Frankly* (1947).
Cant, G., *The Great Pacific Victory: From the Solomons to Tokyo* (1946).
Churchill, W., *History of the Second World War* (6 vols., 1948–1953).
Clark, M. W., *Calculated Risk* (1951).
Clay, L. D., *Decision in Germany* (1950).
Clostermann, P., *The Big Show* (1951).
Collected Wartime Messages of Generalissimo Chiang Kai-shek (2 vols., 1946).
Congdon, D., ed., *Combat: European Theatre* (1958).
—*Combat: Pacific Theatre* (1958).
Craven, W. F. and Cate, J. L., eds., *The Army Air Forces in World War II* (9 vols., 1948–1949).
Davies, J. E., *Mission to Moscow* (1941).
Davis, F. and Lindley, E. K., *How War Came* (1942).
Deane, J. R., *The Strange Alliance: The Story of Our Efforts at Wartime Coöperation with Russia* (1947).
De Weerd, H. A., *Great Soldiers of World War II* (1944).
Divine, A. D., *Dunkirk* (1945).
Doenitz, K., *Memoirs: Ten Years and Twenty Days* (1959).
Eisenhower, D. D., *Crusade in Europe* (1948).
Fitzgibbon, C., *Officers' Plot to Kill Hitler* (1956).
Fleming, P., *Operation Sea Lion* (1957).
Frank, W. and Rogge, B., *The German Raider* Atlantis (1956).

Freiden, S. and Richardson, W., eds., *The Fatal Decisions* (1956).
Fuller, J. F. C., *The Second World War, 1939–1945: A Strategical and Tactical History* (1949).
Galland, A., *The First and the Last: The Rise and Fall of the German Fighter Forces, 1938–1945* (1954).
Gantenbein, J. W., ed., *Documentary Background of World War II, 1931–1941* (1948).
Gibson, H. A., ed., *The Ciano Diaries, 1939–1943* (1946).
Gilbert, F., *Hitler Directs the War: The Secret Records of His Daily Military Conferences* (1950).
Gilbert, G. M., *Nuremberg Diary* (1947).
Grew, J. C., *Turbulent Era* (2 vols., 1952).
Guderian, H., *Panzer Leader* (1952).
Gunther, J., *D-Day* (1944).
Hall, W. P., *Iron Out of Calvary* (1946).
Halsey, W. F., *Admiral Halsey's Story* (1947).
Hambro, C. J., *I Saw It Happen in Norway* (1940).
Hassel, U. von, *Von Hassel Diaries, 1938–1944* (1947).
Hayes, C. J. H., *Wartime Mission to Spain, 1942–1945* (1945).
Henderson, H., *Failure of a Mission* (1940).
Hersey, J., *Men on Bataan* (1943).
Hinsley, F. H., *Hitler's Strategy* (1951).
Ickes, H. L., *The Secret Diary of Harold L. Ickes* (3 vols., 1953–1954).
Kato, M., *The Lost War* (1946).
Kenney, G. C., *General Kenney Reports* (1949).
Kimmel, H. E., *Admiral Kimmel's Story* (1955).
King, E. J., *The U.S. Navy at War, 1941–1945* (1946).
Kohn, H., *Revolution and Dictatorships: Essays in Contemporary History* (1939).
Langer, W. L., *Our Vichy Gamble* (1947).
Langsam, W., *Historic Documents of World War II* (1958).
Lawson, T. W., *Thirty Seconds over Tokyo* (1943).
Lee, A., *The German Air Force* (1946).
Lemkin, R., *Axis Rule over Occupied Europe* (1944).
Liddel Hart, B. H., *The Rommel Papers* (1953).
Lochner, L., ed., *The Goebbels Diaries, 1942–1943* (1948).
Manstein, E., *Lost Victories* (1958).
Maurois, A., *Why France Fell* (1941).
McInnis, E., *The War* (6 vols., 1940–1946).
Memoirs of Cordell Hull (2 vols., 1948).
Mendelssohn, P. de, *Design for Aggression: The Inside Story of Hitler's War Plans* (1946).
Miller, F. T., *Eisenhower, Man and Soldier* (1944).
Millis, W., *This is Pearl! The United States and Japan* (1947).
—*Why Europe Fights* (1940).
Montgomery, B. L., *El Alamein to the River Sangro* (1949).
—*Memoirs* (1958).
—*Normandy to the Baltic* (1948).
Morison, S. E., *History of U.S. Naval Operations in World War II* (14 vols., 1947–1960).
—*Strategy and Compromise* (1958).

Nazi Conspiracy and Aggression, Official Records of the International Military Tribunal at Nuremberg (8 vols., 1946).
Puleston, W. D., *The Influence of Sea Power in World War II* (1947).
Riess, C., *Total Espionage* (1941).
Romulo, C. P., *I Saw the Fall of the Philippines* (1942).
Ryan, C., *The Longest Day: June 6, 1944* (1959).
Schaeffer, H., *U-Boat 977* (1952).
Sherwood, R. E., *Roosevelt and Hopkins* (1948).
Shirer, W. L., *Berlin Diary, 1934–1941* (1942).
Singer, K. D., *Spies and Traitors of World War II* (1945).
Smith, H. K., *The Last Train from Berlin* (1942).
Speidel, H., *Invasion 1944* (1949).
Stettinius, E. R., Jr., *Lend-Lease: Weapon for Victory* (1944).
Stilwell, J. W., *The Stilwell Papers*, ed. by T. H. White (1948).
Stimson, H. L., *On Active Service in Peace and War, 1940–1945* (1948).
Straubel, J. H., ed., *Air Force Diary* (1947).
Sykes, C., *Orde Wingate* (1959).
Toland, J., *Battle: The Story of the Bulge* (1959).
Tolischus, O. D., *Tokyo Record* (1943).
Tregaskis, R., *Guadalcanal Story* (1943).
Trevor-Roper, H. R., *The Last Days of Hitler* (1947).
Truman, H. S., *Years of Decision* (1955).
U.S. Congress, *Hearings Before Joint Committee to Investigate the Pearl Harbor Attack* (38 Parts, 1946).
U.S. Strategic Bombing Survey (1946 ff.).
Wainwright, J. M., *General Wainwright's Story* (1946).
Wedemeyer, A. C., *Wedemeyer Reports* (1958).
Welles, S., *The Time for Decision* (1944).
Werth, A., *Moscow War Diary* (1942).
—*The Year of Stalingrad* (1947).
Wheeler-Bennett, J. W., *Munich: Prologue to Tragedy* (1948).
—*The Nemesis of Power* (1952).
White, W. L., *They Were Expendable* (1942).
Wilmot, C., *The Struggle for Europe* (1952).
Wolff, L., *Low Level Mission* (1957).
Young, D., *Rommel* (1951).

N.B. Attention is also directed to the excellent publications of the Office Chief of Military History, Department of the Army, of which the following have been especially useful:

Cannon, M. H., *Leyte: The Return to the Philippines* (1954).
Cline, R. S., *Washington Command Post* (1951).
Harrison, G. A., *Cross-Channel Attack* (1951).
MacDonald, C. B., and Mathews, S. T., *Three Battles: Arnaville, Altuzzo, and Schmidt* (1952).
Miller, J., Jr., *Guadalcanal: The First Offensive* (1949).
Morton, L., *The Fall of the Philippines* (1953).

APPENDIX B

Headline History of World War II

1939

Sept. 1	Germany invades Poland. Ultimatum from Britain and France.
Sept. 3	Britain and France declare war.
Sept. 17	Soviet troops enter Eastern Poland.
Sept. 27	Warsaw surrenders.
Sept. 28	Poland partitioned by Germany and Russia.
Nov. 30	U.S.S.R. invades Finland.
Dec. 17	*Graf Spee* is scuttled at Montevideo.

1940

March 12	Peace signed in Moscow between U.S.S.R. and Finland.
April 9	Nazis invade Denmark and Norway.
May 10	Nazis invade Netherlands, Belgium, and Luxemburg. Chamberlain resigns as British Prime Minister. Churchill takes office.
May 12	Germans cross French frontier.
May 15	Dutch army capitulates.
May 16	French line broken at Sedan.
May 28	King Leopold of Belgium capitulates.
May 26–June 4	Dunkirk evacuation.
June 10	Italy declares war on Britain and France. Italy invades France.
June 14	Germans enter undefended Paris.
June 15–16	Russians occupy Lithuania, Latvia, and Estonia.
June 22	France and Germany sign armistice at Compiègne.
June 27	Rumania cedes Bessarabia and Northern Bukovina to Soviet Russia.
July 3	British attack French capital ships at Oran.

July 10	Beginning of Battle of Britain.
Sept. 3	U.S.—Great Britain destroyer-base exchange. Abdication of King Carol of Rumania.
Sept. 7	Opening of London *Blitz.*
Sept. 16	Selective Service Act in U.S.
Sept. 27	German-Italian-Japanese Tripartite Pact, 10-year agreement, signed in Berlin (Pact of Berlin).
Oct. 28	Italy invades Greece.
Nov. 11–12	Royal Air Force attacks Taranto.
Nov. 14–16	Germans raid Coventry.
Nov. 20–25	Hungary, Rumania, Slovakia join Tripartite Pact.

1941

Jan. 6	President Roosevelt's speech on the Four Freedoms.
Jan. 10	Lend-Lease Bill introduced into Congress. Soviet-German trade pact.
March 1	Bulgaria joins Tripartite Pact.
March 11	Lend-Lease Bill signed by President.
March 27	Revolution in Yugoslavia.
March 28	Battle of Cape Matapan.
March 30	German counteroffensive in North Africa.
April 6	Germans invade Greece and Yugoslavia.
April 11	Russo-Japanese Neutrality Treaty.
May 2–31	Revolution in Iraq suppressed by British.
May 10–11	Rudolf Hess flies to Scotland.
May 20	Germans invade Crete.
May 27	German battleship *Bismarck* sunk.
June 1	British withdraw from Crete.
June 8	Allies enter Syria.
June 14	Roosevelt freezes Axis funds in U.S.
June 18	Germany and Turkey sign treaty of friendship.
June 22	Hitler attacks Soviet Union.
July 12	British-Soviet mutual aid pact.
Aug. 14	Atlantic Charter. Roosevelt and Churchill meet at sea and agree on war aims.
Aug. 25	British and Russian troops enter Iran.
Sept. 19	Germans occupy Kiev.
Oct. 11	General Hideki Tojo becomes Premier of Japan.

Nov. 18	Eighth Army's desert offensive in Libya.
Nov. 26	Strong U.S. note to Japan.
Nov. 28	Russians retake Rostov.
Dec. 1	Russians counterattack at Tula.
Dec. 7	Japan attacks Pearl Harbor. Pacific Fleet crippled. Japan declares war on Britain and U.S.
Dec. 8	Japanese landings in Thailand and Malaya. Great Britain and U.S. declare war on Japan.
Dec. 9	H.M.S. *Prince of Wales* and H.M.S. *Repulse* sunk by Japanese air attacks off Malayan coast.
Dec. 10–11	Germany and Italy declare war on U.S. U.S. declares war on both those countries.
Dec. 13	Hungary and Bulgaria declare war on U.S.
Dec. 22	Japanese begin major attack on Philippines. First Washington Conference. Churchill in Washington.
Dec. 25	Hong Kong surrenders.

1942

Jan. 1	Twenty-six nations sign United Nations Declaration.
Jan. 10–11	Japanese invade Netherlands East Indies.
Jan. 21	German counteroffensive in North Africa.
Feb. 12	*Scharnhorst*, *Gneisenau*, and *Prinz Eugen* escape from Brest.
Feb. 15	British surrender Singapore.
March 7	Evacuation of Rangoon.
March 17	MacArthur arrives in Australia.
April 9	U.S. forces on Bataan surrender.
April 18	Tokyo bombed by U.S. Army planes.
May 4–9	Battle of the Coral Sea.
May 26	German counteroffensive in North Africa. Twenty-year Anglo-Soviet Treaty signed in London.
May 30–31	First R.A.F. 1,000-bomber raid on Cologne.
June 4	Battle of Midway Island.
June 21	Germans take Tobruk.
June 25–27	Second Washington Conference between Roosevelt and Churchill.
Aug. 7	U.S. Marines land on Guadalcanal.
Aug. 12	First Moscow Conference.
Aug. 19	Raid on Dieppe.
Oct. 23	Montgomery strikes at El Alamein.

Nov. 7–8	U.S. and Britain land great army in North Africa.
Nov. 11	German troops enter unoccupied France.
Nov. 19–22	Stalingrad counteroffensive.
Dec. 24	Admiral Darlan, Chief of State in North Africa, assassinated.

1943

Jan. 14–24	Casablanca Conference.
Jan. 23	Eighth Army enters Tripoli.
Feb. 2	German forces surrender at Stalingrad. Turning point of war in Russia.
March 2	Battle of the Bismarck Sea.
May 11–27	Third Washington Conference between Roosevelt and Churchill.
May 12	Organized Axis resistance in Tunisia ends.
May 15	Third International (Comintern) dissolved in Moscow. (Announced May 22.)
May 18	United Nations Food Conference at Hot Springs, Virginia.
May 20	Victory parade in Tunis.
July 9–10	Allied invasion of Sicily.
July 19	Bombing of Rome.
July 25	Mussolini replaced by Badoglio as Italian Premier.
Aug. 17–24	First Quebec Conference.
Aug. 28	Death of King Boris III of Bulgaria. Succeeded by son, 6-year-old Simeon II.
Sept. 3	Allied invasion of Southern Italy.
Sept. 8	Italy surrenders.
Sept. 9	Allied landing at Salerno.
Sept. 10	Germans occupy Rome.
Oct. 13	Italy declares war on Germany.
Oct. 18–Nov. 1	Moscow Conference of foreign secretaries (Hull, Eden, Molotov).
Nov. 6	Recapture of Kiev by Russians.
Nov. 9	Establishment of the United Nations Relief and Rehabilitation Administration (U.N.R.R.A.)
Nov. 22–26	First Cairo Conference (Roosevelt, Churchill, Chiang Kai-shek).
Nov. 28–Dec. 1	Teheran Conference (Roosevelt, Churchill, Stalin).
Dec. 4–6	Second Cairo Conference (Roosevelt, Churchill, Inönü).

Dec. 12	Czecho-Soviet Alliance for mutual assistance.
Dec. 26	Nazi battleship *Scharnhorst* sunk off North Cape.

1944

Jan. 22	Allied troops land at Anzio behind German lines.
March 8	Finns reject Soviet armistice terms.
March 19	German troops cross Hungarian frontier.
April 10	Russians recapture Odessa.
May 23	Allied offensive from Anzio beachhead.
June 4	Rome captured by Anglo-American troops.
June 6	D-Day. Allied invasion of Normandy.
June 13–14	First flying bombs land in England.
June 15	First Superfortress raid on Japan.
July 1–15	International Monetary Conference at Bretton Woods.
July 3	Russians recapture Minsk.
July 20	Hitler wounded in bomb plot.
July 27	U.S. troops break through, west of St. Lô.
Aug. 11	U.S. forces complete conquest of Guam.
Aug. 15	Allied forces land on south coast of France.
Aug. 21–Sept. 29	Dumbarton Oaks Conference, Washington, D.C.
Aug. 23	Rumania accepts Russian armistice terms.
Aug. 25	Paris liberated.
Sept. 3	British liberate Brussels.
Sept. 4	End of Finnish-Russian fighting.
Sept. 5	The Soviet Union declares war on Bulgaria.
Sept. 8	First V-2 lands on London.
Sept. 9	Bulgarian armistice.
Sept. 10	Second Quebec Conference (Churchill and Roosevelt). Finnish armistice signed.
Sept. 17	Allied airborne army lands in Holland.
Oct. 9	Third Moscow Conference (Churchill, Eden, Stalin).
Oct. 14	Allies occupy Athens.
Oct. 20	Belgrade liberated by Russians and Yugoslavs. American troops invade Philippines.
Oct. 21–22	Battle of Leyte Gulf.
Nov. 12	*Tirpitz* sunk in Tromsö Fiord by R.A.F.
Dec. 16	Germans launch counteroffensive. Battle of the Bulge.

1945

Jan. 9	U.S. forces land on Luzon in Philippines.
Jan. 11	Russians capture Warsaw.
Jan. 20	Provisional Government of Hungary signs armistice.
Jan. 27	Memel liberated.
Jan. 31	Churchill and Roosevelt meet at Malta.
Feb. 3	U.S. troops enter Manila.
Feb. 4–12	Yalta Conference (Roosevelt, Churchill, Stalin).
Feb. 19	U.S. Marines land on Iwo Jima.
March 4	Finland declares war on Germany as from September 15, 1944.
March 7	U.S. First Army crosses Rhine on bridge at Remagen.
April 1	U.S. invasion of Okinawa.
April 12	Death of President Roosevelt. Truman becomes President.
April 13	Vienna liberated by Soviet army.
April 25	United Nations parley opens at San Francisco. Russian and U.S. forces meet at Torgau on the Elbe.
April 28	Mussolini executed by Partisans.
April 30	Hitler commits suicide in bunker at Reich Chancellery in Berlin. 33,000 inmates of Dachau concentration camp freed by U.S. forces. Soviet flag raised over *Reichstag* in Berlin.
May 1	Grand Admiral Doenitz takes command in Germany.
May 2	Fall of Berlin to Russians. German armies in Italy make complete surrender.
May 3	Rangoon captured.
May 7	Germany surrenders unconditionally to Western Allies and Russia.
May 8	V-E Day.
June 26	World Security Charter signed at San Francisco.
July 17–Aug. 2	Potsdam Conference (Truman, Stalin, Churchill and later Attlee).
Aug. 6	First atomic bomb dropped on Hiroshima.
Aug. 8	U.S.S.R. declares war on Japan.
Aug. 9	Second atomic bomb dropped on Nagasaki.
Aug. 14	Japanese unconditional surrender.
Sept. 2	Japanese sign surrender terms on U.S.S. *Missouri* in Tokyo Bay.

APPENDIX C

Selected List of World War II Military Code Names

ANVIL — Allied invasion of southern France begun on August 15, 1944. The code name was changed to Dragoon.

APOSTLE 1 — Allied plan to return to Norway following the liberation of France. The operation took place on May 10, 1945.

AVALANCHE — The Allied amphibious attack on Salerno initiated on September 9, 1943.

BARBAROSSA — The German code name for the invasion of Soviet Russia on June 22, 1941.

BOLERO — The task of transferring U.S. forces from the United States to England.

CORKSCREW — Allied occupation of Pantelleria, Italy, which took place on June 11, 1943.

CORONET — The operation planned against Honshu, the mainland of Japan. The two atomic bombs exploded over Hiroshima and Nagasaki brought cancellation of this operation.

CROSSBOW — The Allied air onslaught on German V-bomb rocket sites.

DYNAMO — British evacuation of Dunkirk from May 26 to June 4, 1940.

FANFARE — A generic term used to denote all Allied operations in the Mediterranean.

FELIX — Intended German operation across Spain to capture Gibraltar.

FLINTLOCK — Allied attack on the Marshall Islands in early 1944.

FORAGER	Allied operations in the Marianas in mid-June 1944.
FORMER NAVAL PERSON	Prime Minister Winston Churchill.
FRANTIC	Allied air shuttle between Berlin and Russia.
GALVANIC	Allied assault to win back the Gilbert Islands in November 1943.
GOOSEBERRY	One of the artificial breakwaters constructed and established off the coast of France by the Allies in conjunction with Operation Overlord.
GRAPEFRUIT	Offensive in North Italy by the U.S. Fifth Army in early April 1945.
GREIF	A German operation which employed special troops dressed in American uniforms to capture the bridges on the Meuse during the Battle of Ardennes in December 1944.
GRENADE	Operation by U.S. Ninth Army driving toward the Rhine, February 23, 1945.
GYMNAST	President Roosevelt's suggested American attack against northwest Africa outside the Mediterranean. Later revised to include the British and American assault within the Mediterranean.
HERBSTNEBEL	Code name for Hitler's counteroffensive in the Ardennes in December 1944.
HUSKY	The Allied invasion of Sicily, which began on July 9–10, 1943.
JUBILEE	The Allied raid on Dieppe, France, on August 19, 1942.
LUMBERJACK	The Allied attack north of the Moselle between Coblenz, Bonn, and Cologne in late February 1945.
MARKET	The Allied operation to seize the bridges at Nijmegen and Arnhem on September 17, 1944. The code name GARDEN was used to describe the land operation in conjunction with MARKET.
MULBERRY	The main artificial harbor set up outside France for Operation Overlord.
OVERLORD	The Allied invasion of the Normandy coastline which began on June 6, 1944.
PLUNDER	The Allied plan to cross the Rhine north of the Ruhr on March 23, 1945.

ROUNDUP	Original operation planned against France. Replaced by Overlord.
SEA LION	Hitler's projected invasion of England in 1940. Plan abandoned.
SHINGLE	Allied operation in early 1944 to outflank the Gustav Line in Italy.
SHŌ-GO	Japanese plan to defend the Philippines in 1944.
SLEDGEHAMMER	Alternate, limited Allied operation to invade the Continent and to be used if, by September 1942, Russia were on the verge of collapse.
SOAPSUDS	The Allied air bombing of the Ploesti oil fields in Rumania on August 1, 1943.
STRANGLE	Allied air attack to seal off Germans in North Italy in the spring of 1944.
SUPERCHARGE	General Montgomery's plan to annihilate the German combat forces in North Africa at El Alamein, October 1942.
TA	Japanese reinforcement program for the Philippines in late 1944.
TORCH	The Allied landings on the coasts of North Africa which began on November 8, 1942.
UNDERTONE	U.S. and French operation south of the Moselle on March 15, 1945.
VERITABLE	Canadian and British operation between the Rhine and the Meuse on February 8, 1945.
WHITE	Hitler's offensive against Poland in September 1939.
YELLOW	Hitler's offensive action against the northern flank of the Western front crossing the area of Luxemburg, Belgium and Holland. "Case Yellow" was prepared as early as October 1939 but was executed in May 1940.

APPENDIX D

Glossary of Major Conferences of World War II

Place	*Date*	*Code Name*	*Main Participants*	*Major Decisions*
ARGENTIA BAY	Aug. 14, 1941	....	Roosevelt, Churchill	Agreement on war aims. Atlantic Charter.
WASHINGTON (First)	Dec. 22, 1941–Jan. 1, 1942	ARCADIA	Roosevelt, Churchill	Anglo-U.S. War Council places first priority on Atlantic theatre of war. 26 nations sign United Nations Declaration.
WASHINGTON (Second)	June 25–27, 1942	....	Roosevelt, Churchill	Subjects discussed: war production; shipping; aid for China; diversion of German strength from Eastern Front; North African invasion.
CASABLANCA	Jan. 14–23, 1943	SYMBOL	Roosevelt, Churchill	Plans for invasion of Sicily. Decision for cross-Channel invasion in 1944. Stepped-up Battle of the Atlantic. "Unconditional surrender" declaration by Roosevelt.
WASHINGTON (Third)	May 11–27, 1943	TRIDENT	Roosevelt, Churchill	Plans for further pressure in Italy. Increased air attack on Germany. Stepped-up war in the Pacific. Invasion of France.
QUEBEC (First)	Aug. 17–24, 1943	QUADRANT	Roosevelt, Churchill	"Final" decision to invade France. Reorganization of Southeast Asia command.

Place	*Date*	*Code Name*	*Main Participants*	*Major Decisions*
MOSCOW	Oct. 18–Nov. 1, 1943	....	Foreign ministers Hull, Eden, Molotov	Declaration with China on postwar security and coöperation. Establishment of European Advisory Council. Advisory Council for Italy. Democratic regime for Austria. Punishment of war criminals.
CAIRO	Nov. 22–26, 1943	SEXTANT	Roosevelt, Churchill, Chiang Kai-shek	Agreement on military operations against the Japanese in China. Manchuria promised to China. Free Korea.
TEHERAN	Nov. 28–Dec. 1, 1943	EUREKA	Roosevelt, Churchill, Stalin	Agreement on date of invasion of Western Europe. Declaration on Iran. Aid for Tito and Jugoslav Partisans.
BRETTON WOODS	July 1–15, 1944	....	Representatives of 44 nations	Agreement on International Monetary Fund. Establishment of International Bank for Reconstruction and Development.
DUMBARTON OAKS	Aug. 21–Sept. 29, 1944	....	Representatives of U.S., U.K., and U.S.S R.	Agreement on an international organization.
QUEBEC (Second)	Sept 10, 1944	OCTAGON	Roosevelt, Churchill	Plans for completion of European war. Plans for Pacific war.

Place	*Date*	*Code Name*	*Main Participants*	*Major Decisions*
YALTA	Feb. 4–12, 1945	ARGONAUT	Roosevelt, Churchill, Stalin	Plans dealing with defeat of Germany. Declaration of policy for liberated Europe. Recommendations on establishment of new Polish Provisional Government. Formation of new Yugoslav Government. Permanent machinery for consultation of foreign ministers. Decision to call Conference of United Nations at San Francisco on April 25 to prepare United Nations Charter. Kurile Islands and South Sakhalin to be handed over to the Soviet Union for aid in war against Japan (secret agreement).
SAN FRANCISCO	April 25–June 26, 1945	....	Representatives of 50 nations	World Security Charter signed. Approval of Statute of International Justice. Establishment of Preparatory Commission of United Nations Organization.
POTSDAM	July 17–Aug. 2, 1945	TERMINAL	Truman, Churchill, Attlee, Stalin	Potsdam Declaration. Agreement on Council of Ministers. Agreement on political and economic principles to govern treatment of Germany during control period. Agreement on reparations. Statement on Poland. Statement on peace with the satellites.

Index